Lancashire

A Green Audit

A First State of the Environment Report

Front Cover: Shows Lancashire, and its surrounding region, as seen by Landsat satellite from a height of 700 kilometres (435 miles) on 14 May 1988. Image processing and enhancement by Hunting Technical Services Ltd., Hemel Hempstead, Hertfordshire HP2 7SR. A similar image has been used to compile the land cover information contained in Chapter 8 of this Report.

Preface

I am delighted to introduce this first ever Green Audit of Lancashire.

Lancashire County Council has shown the important role local government can play in spearheading environmental initiatives by providing this Audit as part of its action plan to improve the County's environment. The Audit is the most comprehensive analysis of the environment of an area yet produced in this country.

The County Council has placed environmental concerns as one of its top priorities and the Audit marks a major step forward in the drive to clean up our local environment. It contains a wealth of information which all involved can now draw upon, to set priorities and to target action. The Audit has been produced by the County Council's new Environment Unit with assistance from the County's innovative Environment Forum, which brings together a wide range of statutory and voluntary organisations for the first time.

Lancashire pioneered the Industrial Revolution and helped to generate the wealth and living improvements that came with it. But the process bequeathed a legacy of poor conditions. Most of the serious dereliction has now been removed, but our water quality still suffers from old, worn-out water supply and sewage disposal systems. A continuing reliance on carbon-based fuels to heat and light our homes, schools and work-places means that the County's air is still not as clean as it could be. And, of course, we now realise that this is helping to warm the climate and threatens our coastline as sea levels seem set to rise. Problems of more recent origin include the consequences of the growth in road traffic, the loss of rare wildlife habitats, dealing with growing amounts of waste and litter and a deterioration in the quality of our towns and countryside.

These – and many other matters – are addressed in this Audit. For the first time, the people of Lancashire, and those with statutory responsibilities can assess the County's environment in a comprehensive way. Important though this understanding is for its own sake, it is only a start. It is the first step in accelerating the campaign to improve our quality of life. The Audit, and the issues it raises, set an agenda for this campaign, and the County Council is committed to working with its partners on the Lancashire Environment Forum and with the public to turn this into an Action Plan.

Co-operation is in everybody's interest, because no individual or organisation can do all that is needed in this field on their own. Pooling ideas, effort and resources can also bring forward action that might otherwise have to wait. The value of the joint approach is demonstrated already by the Audit itself, because the information it contains has been co-ordinated by the County Council's Environment Unit from contributions from a wide range of bodies and people. There are too many to thank by name. I would like to express the gratitude of the County Council to all who have helped in the production of the report.

Having led the way with so many things in the past, Lancashire is now pioneering action on the environment. This Green Audit is a landmark in that process. It will help us to reverse past mistakes and improve the quality of the surroundings that we pass on to those who follow us.

County Councillor Mrs. L.J. Ellman.
Leader of Lancashire County Council.

Contents

List of Figures

List of Tables

Glossary, Abbreviations, Symbols and Conversions

Glossary

Access Areas: Areas of privately owned Open Country to which the public are allowed access by virtue of ''access agreements or orders''.

Acid Rain: Precipitation which is acidified by airborne pollutants.

Algae: A group of simple lower plants.

Algal Bloom: A population explosion of free floating algae.

Alluvial Gley: Soils developed in loamy or clayey alluvium.

Alpha Particle: A particle produced by radioactive decay, with little penetrative power, but damaging when in contact with living tissue.

Ambient: Surrounding.

Anaerobic: Absence of oxygen.

Anoxic: Oxygen depleted.

Aquifer: A water bearing stratum or bed of permeable rock, sand or gravel.

Areas of Outstanding Natural Beauty: Areas of national landscape importance designated under the National Parks and Access to the Countryside Act 1949.

Attenuated: Weakened.

Becquerel: The standard unit measuring radioactivity, equalling one nuclear disintegration per second.

Benthic: Organisms living close to the sea or lake bottom.

Best Practicable Means: The best possible level of control attainable within technological and economic capabilities.

Beta Particle: A particle produced by radioactive decay, which has moderate penetrative power and can damage living tissue.

Biochemical Oxygen Demand: The amount of oxygen used for biochemical oxidation under fixed conditions. Used to measure organic pollution of water.

Biodegradable Waste: Waste which is broken down by micro-organisms.

Bioengineering: The employment of biochemical processes.

Biofuels: Readily renewable organic fuel sources such as wood.

Biota: The flora and fauna of an area.

Biotic: The living or biological components of an environment.

Brown Earths: Non-cultivated loamy soils with non-calcareous sub-soil without sufficient clay enrichment.

By-way: A highway over which the public have right of way for vehicular and all other kinds of traffic, used mainly as a footpath or bridleway.

Carbon dioxide: A 'greenhouse' gas released during the burning of fossil and biomass fuels.

Carboniferous: Geological period.

Carbon Monoxide: A colourless odourless gas produced by the incomplete combustion of carbon.

Carboxyhaemoglobin: Compound formed between carbon monoxide and blood haemoglobin reducing the bloods ability to transport oxygen.

Catalyst: A substance causing or assisting a chemical reaction without taking part in it.

Catalytic Converter: Device fitted to the exhaust of petrol vehicles to reduce the emission of gaseous pollutants.

Catchment: The area from which a major river system or lake collects its water.

Chemical Energy: Energy trapped in high energy bonds between and within atoms.

Chemical Oxygen Demand: The weight of oxygen taken up by the organic matter in a water sample. Used to assess the strength of sewage or trade waste.

Chlorofluorocarbons: Compounds of carbon, fluorine, chlorine and hydrogen, widely used in aerosols and regrigerants. A 'greenhouse' gas.

Climax: A community of organisms that is balanced with environmental conditions, forming the final stage of natural succession.

Clinical Waste: Waste arising from medical, nursing, dental, veterinary, pharmaceutical or similar practice, and all human and animal tissue, blood, swabs, dressings, drugs, syringes and needles, including those arising in the home.

Co-disposal: The disposal of difficult waste with household or similar waste.

Combined Heat and Power: The use of cooling water from power plants to provide water and space heating in nearby buildings.

Commercial Waste: Waste arising from trade, business, sport, recreation and entertainment premises, excluding Household, Industrial and Mine and Quarry Waste.

Conservation Area: Area designated by a local authority for preservation and enhancement due to historic or architectural quality.

Construction and Demolition Waste: Masonry and rubble wastes.

Containment Site: Landfill where leachate is contained within the site to allow biodegradation and attenuation.

Decibel: Sound intensity unit.

de Facto: Existing in fact, whether legally recognised or not.

Demersal: Organisms living in the lowest part of a sea or lake.

Demographic:	Appertaining to a population/population statistics.
Dinantian:	Geological series within the Carboniferous.
Directive:	An instruction based on agreements among ministers within the European Economic Community, issued to member Governments to enforce.
Disperse and Attenuate:	Landfill sites which allow the migration of leachate, to allow the reduction and conversion of polluting species to take place in the surrounding strata.
Distributor Roads:	Act as distributors of traffic within towns and to rural settlements.
Dose Equivalent:	Absorbed dose of radiation weighted for harmfulness.
Drift Geology:	Superficial deposits caused by wind, ice or water.
Earthy Peat:	Organic drained soils, well aerated and structured with few or no recognisable plant remains.
Ecosystem:	A community of interdependent organisms together with the environment they inhabit.
Effluent:	Waste fluid produced by agricultural, industrial or human processes.
Effluvia:	Gaseous waste.
Entomophilous:	Pollinated by insects.
Environment:	The physical, chemical and biotic conditions surrounding a living organism.
Environmentally Sensitive Areas:	Scheme promoted in Britain to secure habitat conservation within the farming landscape.
Epidemiology:	The study of epidemics and patterns of disease incidence.
Eutrophication:	The natural enrichment of water with organic nutrients.
Faecal Coliforms:	Bacterial indicators of faecal pollution. Typically *E. coli*.
Fault:	A fracture surface within a rock mass.
Fauna:	The animals of a particular region.
Fissile:	Isotopes of elements capable of undergoing nuclear fission, capable of being split.
Flashpoint:	Combustion threshold.
Flora:	The plants of particular regions.
Fly Ash:	Fine particles of ash from fuel combustion.
Flytipping:	Illegal deposit of waste.
Gamma Ray:	A discrete quantity of electromagnetic energy without mass or charge.
Geothermal:	Heat and power generated from the internal heat of the earth.
Global Warming:	The warming of the lower atmosphere through the build-up of insulatory 'greenhouse' gases.
Green Belts:	Areas of land, largely rural in character, and adjacent to urban areas, where strict planning controls apply.
Greenhouse Effect:	The warming of the earth through the build-up of greenhouse gases, causing worldwide changes in climate and sea levels.
Groundwater:	Water that occupies pores and crevices in rock and soil, below the surface.
Habitat:	Dwelling place of a species or community, providing a particular set of environmental conditions.
Half-life:	The time taken for the activity of a radionuclide to lose half its value by decay.
Holocene:	Geological series within the Quaternary.
Household Waste Disposal Centre:	Site for the disposal of household waste not normally handled by the District Council collection service.
Hydrocarbons:	Organic compounds containing only carbon and hydrogen.
Hydrology:	Study of water on and below the surface.
Hydrometric Area:	Catchment areas of convenient size defined by the NRA and the Water Companies.
Hypereutrophication:	Accelerated enrichment with nutrients.
Impermeable:	Structures having the capacity to prevent fluid movement.
Inert Waste:	Waste that will not physically or chemically react or undergo biodegradation.
Intertidal Zone:	Area between the mean high water spring tide and the mean low water spring tide.
Ionising Radiation:	Radiation that causes changes in the structure of atoms it passes through, causing changes in the structure of material, including living tissue.
Joule:	SI unit of energy.
Kettlehole:	A depression in glacial drift.
Kilowatt hour:	Board of Trade unit of work.
Kinetic:	The energy of motion.
Landfill:	The deposit of waste onto or into land.
Landfill Gas:	By-product of the anaerobic digestion of putrescible matter. Predominantly methane and carbon dioxide.
Landsat:	Series of satellites orbiting the earth monitoring land cover.
Leachate:	Liquid that seeps through a landfill becoming contaminated by substances with the deposited waste.
Leaching:	The removal of soluble constituents by percolating water.
Lek:	Traditional breeding ground for the grouse.

Lepidoptera:	Butterflies and moths.
Limestone Pavement:	An area of limestone that has been exposed by glacial activity and shaped by weathering.
Littoral Zone:	The inter-tidal zone.
Local Nature Reserve:	Nature reserve designated by a local Planning Authority together with the Nature Conservancy Council.
Local Roads:	Provide access to adjoining land or development and link small rural communities.
Maximum Admissible Concentration:	The highest concentrations of parameters allowable in drinking water defined by EC Directive.
Mesotrophic:	Moderately rich in plant nutrients.
Methane:	The simplest hydrocarbon, formed during anaerobic decomposition. A 'greenhouse' gas.
Microbe:	Minute organisms.
Micro-organism:	Any living organism too small to be seen with the naked eye.
Monoculture:	The cultivation of a crop of the same type in successive years to the exclusion of all other crop types.
Namurian:	Geological series within the Carboniferous.
National Nature Reserves:	Reserves declared and managed by the Nature Conservancy Council under the National Parks and Access to the Countryside Act 1949.
National Vegetation Classification:	System of classifying the vegetation communities of habitats on the basis of plants that commonly occur together.
Nephrops:	Type of shellfish.
Nitrogen Oxides:	A range of compounds formed by the oxidation of atmospheric nitrogen including nitrogen dioxide and nitrous oxide.
Noise and Number Index:	A measurement of the disturbance caused by aircraft noise.
Nutrient:	An environmental substance necessary for the growth and development of plants and animals.
Organic:	Derived from living organisms.
Oxidation:	The combination of oxygen with a substance or the removal of hydrogen.
Ozone:	A blue pungent greenhouse gas, which is an irritant to eyes, nose and throat. It contributes to photochemical smogs.
Ozone Layer:	Atmospheric layer where ozone concentration is higher than elsewhere.
Pathogen:	An organism that causes a communicable disease.
Pelagic:	Organisms that inhabit the open water of a sea or lake.
Perceived Noise Level:	An index designed to account for the noisiness or annoyance of jet aircraft.
Permian:	Geological period.
pH:	The measure of acidity or alkalinity.
Phase 1 Habitat Survey:	A field-by-field survey to map the extent and distribution of wildlife habitats.
Photochemical Smog:	A light haze caused by the action of sunlight on hydrocarbon and nitrogen oxide pollution.
Photosynthesis:	Process by which green plants use the sun's energy to create carbohydrates from atmospheric carbon dioxide and water.
Photovoltaic:	The use of photoelectric cells to generate electricity from sunlight.
Physiography:	Science of the earth's surface.
Phytoplankton:	Microscopically small plants, including algae.
Pixel:	Small area for which reflected radiation is measured in the production of a satellite image.
Pleistocene:	Geological series within the Quaternary.
Polychlorinated biphenyls:	A group of closely related chlorinated hydrocarbon compounds.
Prescribed Concentrations or Values:	Term used by the 1989 Water Supply Regulations which defines the maximum concentration or value permitted for parameters in drinking water.
Primary Routes:	National network of high quality roads.
Primary Treatment:	Process for removing floating and suspended solids from waste water.
Protozoa:	Unicellular animals.
Public Bridleway:	Highway over which the public have right-of-way on foot, cycle and on horseback.
Public Footpath:	Highway over which the public have right-of-way on foot only.
Quaternary:	Geological period.
Queens:	Type of shellfish.
Radiation:	The emission of any energy particles or rays from an energy source.
Radiation Fog:	Fog caused by the cooling of the land surface at night.
Radioactive Waste:	Material contaminated by the production, storage or use of radioactive material.
Radioactivity:	Property exhibited by unstable isotopes of elements that decay emitting radiation.
Radionuclide:	An unstable nuclide that undergoes spontaneous radioactive decay emitting ionising radiation.
Radon:	A naturally occurring inert radioactive gas.

Radon Daughters:	The decay products of Radon.
Ramsar Sites:	Sites designated under the Ramsar Convention for the protection of wetlands of international importance.
Raptors:	Birds of prey that hunt by day.
Raw Peat:	Undrained organic soil, remaining wet to within 20cm of the surface since their formation.
Riparian:	Land bordering sea-shore, lake or river.
Scenic Quality Survey:	A visual appraisal of the landscape where aspects are given a numeric value.
Screenlines:	Monitoring points.
Secondary Treatment:	Process to remove dissolved organic matter from waste water.
Sewage Sludge:	Sludge resulting from the treatment of raw sewage.
SI:	Système International d'Unités, an internationally agreed system of units.
Sievert:	The SI unit of radiation dose equivalent.
Silviculture:	The care and cultivation of trees.
Sinks:	In air pollution, a place or mechanism associated with the removal of air pollutants from the atmosphere.
Site of Biological Importance:	Non-statutory site considered by the LTNC to be of significant nature conservation value.
Site of Special Scientific Interest:	Area of land considered by NCC to be of special scientific interest by reason of its flora, fauna, geological or physiographical features.
Slurry:	Muddy liquid mixture containing farm animal excreta.
Solid Geology:	Geology laid down before the superficial drift deposit.
Special Protection Areas:	Areas designated for the protection and conservation of nationally important wild birds.
Special Waste:	Wastes which are sufficiently hazardous to present a threat to human life or have a flashpoint of 20°C or less.
Stagnogley:	A topsoil, occurring widely in lowland Britain on tills and soft rocks.
Stagnohumic Gley:	A peaty topsoil found mainly in upland areas.
Stagnopodzol:	Mainly upland soil with a peaty topsoil and/or periodically wet, faintly mottled subsurface horizon overlying an iron-rich layer.
Sulphur Dioxide:	A product of the combustion of a wide range of fuels. Used as an indicator for atmospheric pollution levels.
Therm:	Unit of heat.
Topography:	Detailed description of the natural and artificial land surface.
Transfer Station:	Premises used for the temporary storage of waste.
Triassic:	Geological period.
Trunk Road:	Main roads forming primary routes.
Virus:	Simple, microscopic organisms able to cause diseases.
Watt:	SI unit of power.
Westphalian:	Geological series within the Carboniferous.
Wind Rose:	Diagram summarising the frequency, strengths and directions of winds.

Abbreviations

AA 1863	Alkali Act 1863
ACE	Association for the Conservation of Energy
ADAS	Agricultural Development and Advisory Service
AGR	Advanced Gas-cooled Reactor
ALARA	As Low As Reasonably Achievable
AOE	Action on the Environment Report
AONB	Area of Outstanding Natural Beauty
AW	Ancient Woodland
AWRA 1906	Alkali etc. Works Regulation Act 1906
BAe	British Aerospace
BATNEEC	Best Available Technology Not Entailing Excessive Cost
BCC	British Coal Corporation
BETA	Building Efficiency Awards
BNFL	British Nuclear Fuels Limited
BOD	Biochemical Oxygen Demand
BPM	Best Practicable Means
BR	British Rail
BRECSU	Building Research Energy Conservation Support Unit
BSE	Bovine Spongiform Encephalopathy
BSI	British Standards Institution
BTCV	British Trust for Conservation Volunteers
BWB	British Waterways Board
CA 1968	Countryside Act 1968
CAA 1956 and 1968	Clean Air Act 1956 and 1968
CoCo	Countryside Commission
CEC	Commission of Economic Communities
CFC	Chlorofluorocarbons
CH_4	Methane
CHP	Combined Heat and Power
CIS	Community Insulation Scheme
CMA	Countryside Management Area
CNL	Corrected Noise Level
CO	Carbon Monoxide
CO_2	Carbon Dioxide
COPA 1974	Control of Pollution Act 1974
COSHH	Control of Substances Hazardous to Health Regulations 1988
CPRE	Council for the Protection of Rural England
CRA 1965	Commons Registration Act 1965
CREATE	Centre for Research, Education and Training in Energy
CSPA 1989	The Control of Smoke Pollution Act 1989
DC	District Council
DEn	Department of Energy
DHSS	Department of Health and Social Security
DOE	Department of the Environment
DTI	Department of Trade and Industry
DTp	Department of Transport
EC	European Community
ECMT	European Conference of Ministers of Transport
EEC	European Economic Community
EERU	Environmental Epidemiology Research Unit
EHO	Environmental Health Officer
EIA	Environmental Impact Assessment
EMU	Energy Management Unit
EPA 1990	Environmental Protection Act 1990
ESA	Environmentally Sensitive Areas
et al.	And Others
ETSU	Energy Technology Support Unit
FGD	Flue Gas Desulphurisation
FOE	Friends of the Earth
FWAG	Farming and Wildlife Advisory Group
GDO	General Development Order
GEM	Gas Energy Management
GIA	General Improvement Area
GMT	Greenwich Mean Time
GWT	Groundwork Trust
HA 1980	Highways Act 1980

HAA	Housing Action Area
HC	Hydrocarbons
HEP	Hydro Electric Power
HEX	Uranium Hexafluoride
HGV	Heavy Goods Vehicle
HIS	Home Insulation Scheme
HMIP	Her Majesty's Inspectorate of Pollution
HMSO	Her Majesty's Stationery Office
HSE	Health and Safety Executive
HSWA 1974	Health and Safety at Work Act 1974
HWDC	Household Waste Disposal Centres
IAEA	International Atomic Energy Authority
IAP	Inner Area Partnership
ICAO	International Civil Aviation Organisation
ICRP	International Commission on Radiological Protection
IMO	International Marine Organisation
IPC	Integrated Pollution Control
IPCC	Intergovernmental Panel on Cimate Change
LARRMACC	Local Authorities Radiation and Radioactivity Monitoring Advice and Collection Centre
LAWDC	Local Authority Waste Disposal Company
LCC	Lancashire County Council
LNR	Local Nature Reserve
LTNC	Lancashire Trust for Nature Conservation
LUAU	Lancaster University Archaeological Unit
LUEAU	Liverpool University Environmental Advisory Unit
MAFF	Ministry of Agriculture, Fisheries and Food
MAPAC	Manchester Air Pollution Advisory Council
MNR	Marine Nature Reserve
NAWPU	National Association of Water Power Users
NAZ	Noise Abatement Zone
NCC	Nature Conservancy Council
NCR	Nature Conservation Review
nd	no data available
NEA	Neighbourhood Energy Action
NIA 1965	Nuclear Installations Act 1965
NII	Nuclear Installations Inspectorate
NK	Not Known
NNI	Noise and Number Index
NNR	National Nature Reserve
NO_2	Nitrogen Dioxide
N_2O	Nitrous Oxide
NO_x	Oxides of Nitrogen
NPACA 1949	National Parks and Access to the Countryside Act 1949
NPFA	National Playing Field Association
NRA	National Rivers Authority
NRPB	National Radiological Protection Board
NSCA	National Society for Clean Air
NSNR	Non Statutory Nature Reserve
NT	National Trust
NVC	National Vegetation Classification
NWC	National Water Classification
NWCSR	The North West Council for Sport and Recreation
NWNWSFC	North West and North Wales Sea Fisheries Committee
NWW	North West Water plc
NWWDO	North West Waste Disposal Officers
O_3	Ozone
OECD	Organisation for Economic Co-operation and Development
O/H	Overhead
ONR	Other Nature Reserves
OPCS	Office of Population Censuses and Surveys
OPTA	Ormskirk to Preston Travellers Association
Pb	Lead
PBA 1954	Protection of Birds Act 1954
PCB	Polychlorinated biphenyls
PEP	Power for Efficiency and Productivity
pers. comm.	personal communication
PFA	Pulverised Fuel Ash

plc	public limited company
PNdB	Perceived Noise Levels in Decibels
PORG	Photochemical Oxidants Review Group
PSV	Public Service Vehicle
RADMIL	Radioactive Monitoring in Lancashire
RAF	Royal Air Force
RCEP	Royal Commission of Environmental Pollution
RIMNET	Radioactive Incident Monitoring Network
RSA 1960	Radioactive Substances Act 1960
RTA 1972	Road Traffic Act 1972
SBI	Site of Biological Interest
SCOSPA	Standing Conference of South Pennine Authorities
SI	Système International d'Unités
SO₂	Sulphur Dioxide
SOE	State of the Environment Report
SPA	Special Protection Area
SSSI	Site of Special Scientific Interest
STELLA	Support the East Lancashire Line Association
TGB	Tidy Britain Group
TBI	Trent Biotic Index
TCPA	Town and Country Planning Association
TCPA 1971	Town and Country Planning Act 1971
TM	Thematic Mapping
TPO	Tree Preservation Order
TPP	Transport Policies and Programme
TRRL	Transport and Road Research Laboratory
TSG	Transport Supplimentary Grant
TUL	Tidy up Lancashire
UK	United Kingdom
UKAEA	United Kingdom Atomic Energy Authority
UNEP	United Nations Environment Programme
WACH	Winter of Action on Cold Homes
WCA 1981	Wildlife and Countryside Act 1981
WDA	Waste Disposal Authority
WHO	World Health Organisation
WRA	Waste Regulation Authority
WT	Woodland Trust
WWT	Wildfowl and Wetlands Trust

Symbols and Conversions

km = kilometre

m = metre

cm = centimetre

mm = millimetre

um = micrometre

km^2 = square kilometre

m^2 = square metre

ha = hectare

l = litre

ml = millilitre

kg = kilogram

g = gram

mg = milligram

ug = microgram

t = tonne

mg/l = milligram per litre

ug/l = microgram per litre

ug/m^3 = microgram per cubic metre

ng/l = nanogram per litre

ml/day = millilitres per day

w = watt

kw = kilowatt

MW = megawatt

GW = gigawatt

TW = terawatt

mg/therm = milligram per therm

Bq = becquerel

Bq/m^3 = becquerel per cubic metre

TBq = terabecquerel

GBq = gigabecquerel

MBq = megabecquerel

Sv = sievert

mSv = millisievert

dB = decibel

dB_A = 'A' weighted decibel

$dB_A L_{10}$ = 'A' weighted decibel exceeded for 10% of the time

L_{Aeq} = equivalent continuous sound level

L_{10}(18 hour) = The average L_{10} reading between 06.00 and 24.00 hours

$unit^{-1}$ = per unit

$unit^{-2}$ = per unit squared

$unit^{-3}$ = per unit cubed

< = less than

> = greater than

T = tera = 10^{12} = 1,000,000,000,000

G = giga = 10^{9} = 1,000,000,000

M = mega = 10^{6} = 1,000,000

k = kilo = 10^{3} = 1,000

c = centi = 10^{-2} = 0.01

m = milli = 10^{-3} = 0.001

u = micro = 10^{-6} = 0.000001

n = nano = 10^{-9} = 0.000000001

Conversions

Metric *Imperial*

Length

1 millimeter (mm)	=	0.0394 in.
1 metre (m) = 100cm	=	1.0936 yd.
1 kilometre (km) = 1000m	=	0.6214 mile

Area

1 sq. metre (m^2)	=	1.1960 sq. yd.
1 hectare (ha) = 10,000m^2	=	2.4711 acres
1 sq. kilometre (km^2) = 100 ha.	=	0.3861 sq. mile

Volume

1 cu. metre (m^3)	=	1.3080 yd^3
1 millilitre (ml)	=	0.0352 fl. oz.
1 litre (l)	=	1.76 pint

Mass

1 milligram (mg)	=	0.0154 grain
1 gram (g) = 1000mg	=	0.0353 oz.
1 kilogram (kg) = 1000g	=	2.2046 lbs.
1 tonne (t) = 1000kg	=	0.9842 ton

Chapter One
Introduction

Purpose of the Initiative

1.1   Concern for the environment is now at the top of everybody's agenda. We have realised that unless we act urgently, we risk inflicting life-threatening damage upon our planet. The seriousness of the situation is emphasised by the fact that world governments have started meeting regularly to address some of the issues that confront us.

1.2   And there are many issues involved, including global warming, holes in the ozone layer, population growth, acid rain and vanishing tropical forests. More locally, publicity is given to the state of bathing beaches, litter, traffic congestion, loss of wildlife, air quality and development in the countryside. It is not surprising that concern and awareness are rising sharply. At the same time, however, the enormity, complexity and number of the world's environmental problems seem daunting and confusing.

1.3   Relating many of these problems to ourselves, and to our immediate surroundings here in Lancashire, is not easy. Yet we need to be able to do this, because the condition of the environment in which we spend our daily lives is clearly of the greatest significance to each of us. Knowing more about that condition is not just of value for its own sake. We need such information so that we can begin to understand what is right and wrong with our local environment, and why. It is also essential to the process of deciding what needs to be done to put things right. Fortunately, many of the solutions to what might seem to be difficult and widespread problems actually lie in our own hands. What we do as individuals, families, organisations and local communities, has a cumulative influence. It follows that if we have the will and the means, then environmental impacts can be modified for the common good. But first, we need to find out what the current situation is.

1.4   This explains why the County Council, in conjunction with its many partners, decided to research and publish this Green Audit (Lancashire County Council, 1989). The overall purpose of the initiative is to provide the people of Lancashire, and all interested parties, with the first ever comprehensive picture of their own environment. It is hoped that this increased knowledge and awareness will then be used to stimulate and assist all concerned to put in hand the action needed to sustain and improve the quality of Lancashire's environment.

1.5   The Green Audit deals with environmental conditions within the administrative County of Lancashire. Figure 1 (inside front cover) shows Lancashire's principal geographical features. The County is located in the North West of England Region of the United Kingdom, (UK). Its 306,951 ha cover some 42% of the Region but just under 1.5% of the area of the UK. In comparison with other Shire Counties, Lancashire is 21st (out of 47) in order of size but 4th largest in population (1,390,800 persons) and 9th in population density (at 453 persons per km^2). The County is divided into 14 administrative District Councils, listed, with their areas, in Table 1. In most cases, information in the Report is presented by District area and their boundaries appear on all maps.

1.6   By assessing the present state of health of the principal components of the County's environment, this Audit makes an important contribution to a wider environmental programme. The nature of the assessment itself is best described as a State of the Environment report. The data it contains provides a basis for identifying the key environmental problems and opportunities facing Lancashire today. These are to be addressed further in an Action on the Environment report which will be published during 1991. This will recommend what needs to be done to deal with the issues raised in this report.

1.7   The County Council's approach is strongly endorsed by the recent Government White Paper on the environment (Department of the Environment, 1990). This expresses support for the preparation of environmental Audits by local authorities. Equally encouraging is the commitment in the White Paper that in two years' time the Government will commence publication of statistical reports on the state of the national environment. If comprehensive enough, (and the list of draft subject matter contained in the White Paper suggests that this may be so), these national statements will provide the essential overall framework within which local Audits like Lancashire's can be placed.

1.8   The rest of this Chapter describes what the State of the Environment report deals with, outlines its format, and explains how it fits into the County Council's wider initiative.

Table 1   Administrative Areas in Lancashire. 1990

District	Area (ha)	% of County Covered
Lancaster	57,671	19
Wyre	28,332	10
Ribble Valley	58,478	19
Blackpool	3,498	1
Fylde	16,501	5
Preston	14,239	5
South Ribble	11,307	4
West Lancashire	33,770	11
Chorley	20,292	7
Blackburn	13,723	4
Hyndburn	7,302	2
Burnley	11,077	4
Pendle	16,950	5
Rossendale	13,811	4
LANCASHIRE	306,951	100

Source: Lancashire County Council

The State of the Environment Report Explained

Objectives

1.9 Building upon the broad purposes just defined, the report has six objectives. These are:

* to provide a comprehensive statement and analysis of the present condition of Lancashire's environment by collecting and presenting together available data for all environmental components and comparing these with accepted indicators, standards and targets;

* to establish a base-line of information against which future changes and developments in the condition of Lancashire's environment can be monitored regularly and which will form an extensive data-base that will be continuously kept up-to-date;

* to identify short-falls and inadequacies in available information, so that these can be addressed and remedied;

* to furnish data that are essential to the task of deciding the action required for sustaining and improving the health and condition of Lancashire's environment;

* to help the County and District Councils to further develop the process of ensuring that their services are delivered in an environmentally-friendly manner and to help others to achieve similar improvements in their own operations;

* to act as a focus for enlisting the support and co-operation of the people of Lancashire and all agencies, whether local, regional or national, in caring for and safeguarding the County's environment.

1.10 The present report, in itself, fulfils the first objective. Equally, it provides the information that will help the County Council, and its partners, to achieve each of the other objectives over the months and years ahead. Two dominant themes underpin this approach. Firstly, valuable though it is in its own right, the Audit is not a once-and-for-all survey. It represents the initial stage in a long-term, and continuous, commitment towards cleaning up the environment of Lancashire and keeping it clean.

1.11 Secondly, though this initiative has been launched, and is co-ordinated, by the County Council, it is not just a County Council exercise. Many organisations and individuals are actively involved and make an invaluable contribution to Lancashire's environment. District Councils play a particularly important part in terms of local action and monitoring, whilst a host of public, private and voluntary bodies exercise responsibilities within their own spheres of influence. Partnership and co-operation are fundamental to achieving the wide-ranging action and benefits implicit in the approach, and the objectives reflect this in a number of ways. The County Council will work hard, on many fronts, to secure effective joint-working with all organisations that have a part to play in Lancashire's environment. They will also ensure that the people of the County are fully involved in the initiative and are properly informed of its progress, on a regular basis.

1.12 A final point needs to be made about the specific rôle of the County Council. As one of Lancashire's largest organisations, providing and consuming a wide range of services, the Council's actions have major implications for both the local and the wider environment. However, the present report cannot, and does not, deal with all of these implications. A parallel exercise is taking place to ensure that the County Council 'puts its own house in order' in so far as the environmental impact of its overall operations are concerned (see below).

Scope

1.13 How safe is the air we breathe? Is the water we drink and swim in clean? What damage do land-uses like farming and industry cause? And are we in danger of disappearing under a blanket of tarmac and choking on a cloud of pollution from the growing number of cars and lorries? These are only a few of the many issues that the Green Audit seeks to address. Given the wide-ranging nature of such matters, and the many factors that are shaping and influencing Lancashire's environment, the Audit must have a broad base. It begins, therefore, by reviewing the major building-blocks which make up the underlying environmental structure of the County: geology, topography, soils, climate and vegetation being the principal of these. This is followed by a more detailed analysis of the specific topics which indicate the overall state of health of Lancashire's environment.

1.14 A separate Chapter is devoted to each of these topics:

* AIR – which assesses the nature and incidence of atmospheric pollutants and their effects;
* WATER – which describes the extent and quality of our rivers, reservoirs and coastal waters, and the condition of drinking water;
* WASTE – which gives information about the waste and litter that we generate and how it is dealt with;
* NOISE – which investigates noise sources and the problems associated with them;
* ENERGY – which analyses the amount of energy we use and the sources and impacts of it;
* LAND AND AGRICULTURE – which details our pattern of land-use and the impact of agriculture as the dominant of these uses;
* WILDLIFE – which outlines the extent and distribution of plant and animal resources;
* LANDSCAPE AND TOWNSCAPE – which explores the quality of the appearance of rural and urban areas;
* OPEN SPACE – which looks at the amount of land and facilities available for leisure and recreation;
* TRANSPORT – which presents the position on traffic levels, the use of our transport system and its consequences;
* ISSUES – which highlights the issues that will need to be addressed in the future.

Nature of the Data

1.15   A number of points need to be clarified about the data included in the Audit. Firstly, the Report is based upon existing, readily available, information. Very little original research has been conducted to fill gaps in current knowledge. Significant short-falls inevitably exist in some areas, whilst in others, data are inadequate to allow firm conclusions to be drawn. In these situations, the Audit notes and highlights them as issues for further consideration. Where good quality data are available, these are presented, wherever possible, by District Council area. In some cases, though, it has been necessary to use material relating to the County as a whole, or to the North West Region. Sometimes National statistics are relied upon and for certain circumstances, this is not only necessary but desirable. Finally, though the Audit is based principally on data for conditions originating within Lancashire, the County is subject to many environmental influences arising beyond its boundary. Where such information exists, it has also been incorporated.

1.16   To help with the collection and analysis of some of the data in this report, the County Council enlisted the services of specialists in two local Universities. Scientists from the Liverpool University Environmental Advisory Unit were responsible for collecting the material contained in the Chapters on Air, Water, Noise and Energy. Salford University Geography Department analysed a satellite image of the County using remote sensing techniques, and collected data on farming, to form the basis of the Land and Agriculture Chapter.

1.17   A principal function of this first Green Audit is to provide a 'snap-shot' of the environmental health of Lancashire existing at the end of 1990. It provides a factual base-line against which future change can be assessed. Ideally, its data should all relate to 1990 but this, of course, is not possible. Inevitably, some information is not as up-to-date as this. The Audit is based, therefore, on the most recent material available. As this report will form the first part of a County-wide environmental data-base, which will be regularly improved and updated, it will be possible to base subsequent versions of the Audit on more recent, and more relevant information.

1.18   Another longer-term benefit that will stem from the data-base, will be the opportunity to identify and analyse trends in environmental conditions. This will enable a much better picture to be obtained of how situations are improving or deteriorating. For the present report, the inclusion of data on trends is, of course, limited by the availability of what exists already. All data are being placed in a computerised Geographical Information System which will make data-base renewal and analysis much easier.

1.19   One final point needs to be made about data availability and use. Some environmental information is subject to restriction and cannot be published. This applies particularly to material relating to industrial processes, where commercial interests have to be protected. A similar difficulty arises with information held privately by landowners, or concerning activities related to the exercise of private rights. No confidential, or restricted, data has been used knowingly in this report. The material that has been collected, analysed and presented is that which is publicly available from registers, published sources or agencies who have been prepared to release it in the knowledge of what it will be used for.

Format of the Report

1.20   Each topic Chapter is laid out to a standard format, comprising four sections:

* INTRODUCTION – which sets the scene, describes the scope of the material covered and explains why it is important to the County's environment;
* LEGISLATION – which summarises the principal Directives, Statutes, Regulations and other legal requirements applying to each topic. European legislation is usually dealt with first, followed by United Kingdom law;
* ORGANISATIONS – which describes the more important authorities and agencies responsible either for the operations that have an impact on Lancashire's environment, or for regulating and monitoring them;
* INFORMATION – which outlines the data for each topic and, where relevant and possible, sets these against any standards or limits which apply. For other environmental conditions or indicators, quantitative data are given as often as possible. In some situations, qualitative description is more appropriate. In all cases where adequate data exist, the environmental impacts of particular pollutants or conditions are described.

1.21   A variety of devices have been adopted, to assist readers to find their way around the Audit and to aid understanding. Maximum use has been made of Figures (maps, diagrams, graphs and charts) and Tables. To the lay person, some of the material contained in the report might seem complicated and 'scientific'. Jargon has been kept to a minimum, but technical terms cannot be avoided altogether and a Glossary of these is found at the beginning of the report, together with a list of the most frequently used abbreviations. Environmental data and standards are expressed in a wide variety of forms, measurements and conventions and those used most commonly in the report are also listed earlier. The origin of data is indicated in two ways. References to publications from which information has been extracted are to be found at the end of the Chapter to which they relate, whilst all Figures and Tables are specifically sourced. Finally, detailed explanations or amplifications that would otherwise disrupt the flow of the text, are relegated either to footnotes (at the bottom of the page to which they relate) or Appendices (at the rear of the report).

1.22   A major purpose of this Green Audit is to give Lancastrians, for the first time, a comprehensive understanding of the quality of the environment where they live. To help to pin-point this more precisely, a clear-film overlay is located inside the back cover of the report. The overlay shows, and names, the County's principal towns and also gives Ordnance Survey grid-lines at 5 km intervals. It fits exactly over all full-page maps, provided the referencing points are lined up with the guide-marks on every map. Once the overlay is in place, readers should be able to see how the area where they live relates to the environmental conditions shown on the map. Anyone familiar with Ordnance Survey maps will be able to mark their home grid-reference co-ordinates on to the overlay to aid understanding even further.

The County Council's Wider Environmental Initiative

1.23 It has been mentioned that the Audit is part of a wider County Council programme. This pro-gramme has to be seen in the context of the wide range of work that other agencies are carrying out. District Councils all have their own programmes which parallel, add to and complement what the County Council can do. Industry, voluntary groups and many others are actively engaged. Thus, the County Council's initiative forms a part of a much wider, comprehensive range of environmental action. The County programme is based on six elements which together focus attention upon key problems and opportunities and seek to accelerate the pace of improvement:

* The present report and the Action on the Environment report;

* Existing Policies and Action;

* Policy and Practice Review (or Internal Audit);

* Campaigning on Issues;

* Environmental Epidemiology Research Unit (EERU);

* Lancashire Environment Forum.

1.24 The first of these has been explained. A brief outline of the others shows how each fits into the overall context of the wider initiative.

Existing Policies and Action

1.25 Much of what the County Council does has a deliberately beneficial impact upon the environ-ment. Examples include the protection and improvement policies contained in formal planning statements like the County Structure Plan. Informal strategies like those for Countryside Recreation, for Landscape and Wildlife and the Statement of Intent for the Forest of Bowland Area of Outstanding Natural Beauty, also play their part. Policies on waste treatment, and recycling, public transport and traffic management, looking after the County's buildings, and rural estate, are other cases in point.

1.26 By implementing such policies and strategies, the County Council makes a very direct contribution to the environment. Environmental programmes channel expenditure and action, in a variety of ways. Reclamation of derelict land, wildlife con-servation, tree planting and woodland manage-ment, improving listed buildings and townscape, recreational facilities, and improvements to local amenities all feature prominently. This reflects a

clear commitment to increasing the County Council's involvement in direct action to improve the environment; a commitment that will continue into the future.

Internal Audit

1.27 The County Council's impact upon the environment is not confined to such direct action. The purchase and use of materials and equipment, energy consumption, operation and maintenance of an extensive vehicle fleet, design and upkeep of a huge number of buildings and the use of paper are examples of other activities which have widespread environmental implications. As well as reviewing the state of the environment outside of County Hall, the County Council recognise that they must investigate and address the implications of their 'internal operations'.

1.28 As a parallel, and closely-linked exercise, therefore, the County Council has initiated a thorough review of its existing policies and prac-tices. This 'Internal Audit' covers every Depart-ment and all functions and will work towards the overall goal of reducing (and, wherever possible, eliminating) damage to the environment by chang-ing bad policy and practice. The principal objectives of this Internal Audit are:

* to reduce air, land and water pollution asso-ciated with County Council activity;

* to discourage waste and encourage the conser-vation and recycling of resources;

* to ensure that people have access to a built and natural environment which is safe, diverse and pleasant;

* to promote understanding of the environment by the public and staff alike.

* to promote the conservation and sustainable use of natural resources.

Campaigning on Issues

1.29 The County Council's approach is based on partnership and co-operation. Agreement and joint action are by far the best ways to achieve environ-mental protection. Every effort is, and will be, made, at all times, to secure effective collaboration. In some situations, though, agreement or com-promise are not possible and where this has been the case in the past, and the issues involved were considered to be of the utmost importance, the County Council has taken a firm stand. An example of this was opposition to the proposal to dispose of raw sewage by long sea outfall into the coastal waters off Fleetwood. Here, the County Council believed that the scheme would have been detrimental to the marine environment and to public health. Now that the original scheme has been abandoned, the County Council is co-operating fully in the production of a new, environ-mentally acceptable, alternative.

1.30 This Audit and the Action Report, and all other aspects of the Council's environmental initiative, will raise many new issues. In dealing with these, the County Council will follow its well-established policy, and seek solutions based on co-operation. With goodwill on all sides, this should be possible in every case. Should this not prove so, however, the County Council will lobby and campaign, where this is necessary, to prevent avoidable damage to the environment of Lancashire and to the health and well-being of its residents.

Environmental Epidemiology Research Unit

1.31 Environmental epidemiology is the study of patterns of disease occurrence and of their possible environmental causes. In order to investigate such issues in Lancashire, the County Council has funded the establishment of a specialist unit (EERU) in Lancaster University for an initial 5 year period. EERU is headed by a full-time epidemiologist, supported by specialist medical geographers on the University staff. The Unit conducts research into a programme of topics set by the County Council, and reviewed annually. The current programme consists of investigations into the possible incidence of:

* links between sewage disposal to the sea and bacterial and viral related illnesses in coastal and inland areas;

* disease associated with the levels of aluminium contained in drinking water;

* adverse effects on health and development associated with the levels of lead in drinking water;

* an assessment of the health of the population in the vicinity of Heysham Power Station to provide a base-line for evaluating future change.

1.32 The results of these studies will indicate the action required to deal with any public health problems identified. Information will also be provided for the Green Audit data-base, and for future versions of this report. Conversely, the Audit may highlight issues that can be investigated by EERU in its future programme.

Lancashire Environment Forum

1.33 To provide a focus for discussing Lancashire's environmental opportunities and problems, and to stimulate wider co-operation in tackling them, the County Council has invited a range of organisations to form a county-wide Environment Forum. Membership currently stands at 64 organisations, drawn from the following five sectors:

* Central Government and Regional Agencies;

* Industry;

* Local Government in Lancashire;

* Interest Groups;

* Academic Establishments.

A full list of Forum members and its terms of reference appear in Appendix A.

1.34 Meetings commenced in December 1989, and the Forum has assisted at all stages in the task of preparing the present report. Now that it has been published, the Forum's rôle will diversify and it is hoped that it will become a major force in improving and safeguarding the County's environment.

What Happens Next?

1.35 Publication of the Audit is a major step forward in the effort to protect Lancashire's environment. Never before has such a wide body of data about the state of the County's environment been brought together in one place. Particularly significant, is the fact that this information has been made available to the public. For the first time, Lancastrians can see for themselves how the environments of their County, and their own locality, are faring.

1.36 Having produced this analysis, the County Council will take the following steps, in accordance with the objectives stated earlier. Firstly, the key findings will be explored and developed further into an agenda for action. An initial version of this will appear shortly and it will form the basis for consultation to determine an agreed programme. The views of the public, the Forum and other official and voluntary organisations, will be sought and it is hoped that this will generate proposals that command a wide measure of support and commitment.

1.37 As a preliminary stage in this consultative process, the County Council will be interested to receive comments on the present report. A brief questionnaire will be found at the rear of the report, asking for views on the content and conclusions of the Green Audit. Please return the form. It will help the County Council, and their partners on the Environment Forum, to find out what the people of Lancashire think about the state of their environment and will assist in identifying those aspects which require priority action.

References

Department of the Environment (1990). This Common Inheritance. Britain's Environmental Strategy. Cm. 1200. HMSO.

Lancashire County Council (1989). Minutes of the County Council. (9.3.89)

Chapter Two

The Structure of Lancashire's Environment

Introduction

2.1 This Chapter outlines the main structural components of Lancashire's environment. It forms an essential introduction to the information on specific conditions, which follows. By describing the building blocks that have created our present environment, and which will continue to shape its future, the Chapter lays the foundation for the whole of the Green Audit report.

2.2 Lancashire's underlying environmental structure has evolved over a long period as a result of the inter-actions between a number of processes. Geology, topography, soils, climate and vegetation have been the main contributors and their rôle is summarised. Appearing very recently upon the stage created by these processes, the human population has accelerated and diversified environmental change to a tremendous degree. Indeed, the state of the environment described in the rest of this report is largely the result of human activity and its impact upon the County's physical framework. Hence, the Chapter concludes with an overview of the population history of Lancashire and of current levels and trends.

2.3 Occurrences like flooding, changing climate, soil erosion or vegetation loss, (often due to human causes), are sharp reminders of how ultimately dependent we are upon our basic physical environment. The inter-relationships between physical and human factors are crucial to any understanding of how our environment functions and changes. These connections are many, varied and highly complicated. A method commonly used to make it easier to see how the components of an environment relate to, and affect, each other, is to think of each component as being part of a total system. The Chapter begins by applying this concept to the environment of Lancashire in the form of a simple model.

Lancashire as an Environmental System

2.4 The Oxford English dictionary defines the word 'environment' as 'the conditions or influences under which any person or thing lives or develops'. A more acceptable definition is one which acknowledges the nature of the processes that are causing the influences. For the purpose of this report, therefore, the environment is taken to be 'the physical, chemical and biotic conditions surrounding and influencing living organisms in Lancashire'.

2.5 At the root of this meaning lies the principle that the environment is an integrated whole, made-up of many inter-related parts. The inter-relationships are critical. They are the driving-forces of change in the environment and are responsible for its highly sensitive and dynamic nature. Polluting air, for example, can have direct and readily apparent consequences for many other parts of the environment. Sulphur dioxide emissions from power generation can acidify water resources, defoliate vegetation, erode buildings, and, in conjunction with other air pollutants, damage human health. These effects can occur many miles from the source of the emission itself. Levels of emissions, and their impact, can be measured and quantified, but it is equally possible for damage to occur indirectly, or in less obvious ways, and for monitoring to be extremely difficult. Impacts can be beneficial, or neutral, as well as harmful, and can change over time and when subjected to other influences. Even action taken with the best of environmental intentions, can have unforeseen results.

2.6 So it is essential that any analysis of the state of Lancashire's environment takes as much account as it can of the dynamic links between each of the components of the environment under review. The best way to present, and understand, this idea, is to think of the County's environment as a functioning system. Given the adopted definition of 'environment', applying the concept of the 'ecosystem' – well-known to biologists and ecologists – is particularly helpful. An ecosystem is a community of living organisms, interacting with their environment. The principle of the ecosystem provides a unifying theme for considering Lancashire's overall environmental condition.

2.7 The idea can be presented in the form of the model shown in Figure 2. Lancashire is represented at the heart of the model by the County rose. The fact that the County is not a closed system, but exchanges inputs and outputs with many external and far larger systems, is symbolised by the image of the Earth in the background. At the core of the Lancashire system, (beneath the rose), lies the County's underlying environmental structure. Here are the fundamental physical and human components which feature in the remainder of this Chapter – geology, soils, topography and population. Around the outside of this central structure, are the principal 'sub-systems' which make-up the remaining key elements of the County's environment. The current condition of each of these sub-systems is described in separate Chapters in the report. On the model, the arrows linking each part of the system together are a critical feature. They signify the way in which each part of the environment has an influence upon, and is in turn influenced by, every other part.

Geology

2.8 Geology is one of the basic components of the environment. When acted upon by physical processes and climate, rocks determine an area's soils and topography. They are part of the series of relationships that influence vegetation, wildlife and human activity. Agriculture, mining, industry and settlement pattern are, for instance, all particularly dependent upon geology (Chapters 8, 9 and 10).

2.9 Lancashire's geological history has followed a complex sequence of events, including periods when the present County was covered by deep and shallow seas, swamps, ice sheets, lakes and deserts. This has created a distinctive and diverse range of rocks. Those laid down before the superficial (or 'Drift') deposits of more recent times are known as

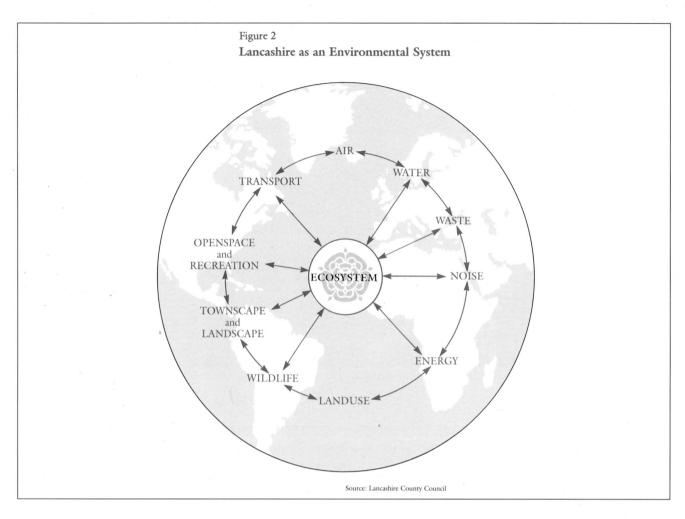

Figure 2
Lancashire as an Environmental System

AIR

WATER

TRANSPORT

WASTE

OPENSPACE
and
RECREATION

ECOSYSTEM

NOISE

TOWNSCAPE
and
LANDSCAPE

WILDLIFE

ENERGY

LANDUSE

Source: Lancashire County Council

'Solid' geology. Drift geology, which masks much of this solid geology, is made up of deposits left by retreating glaciers over ten thousand years ago, or formed from more recent windblown sand, peat and river sediments; a process which continues today.

Solid Geology

2.10 Solid formations were laid down in Lancashire in three main periods; the oldest being the Carboniferous, followed by the Permian and the Triassic. Their distribution is shown on Figure 3 whilst the geological timescale involved is shown in Table 2.

2.11 Carboniferous deposits are the most resistant and form higher ground in areas like the Pennines, the Forests of Bowland, Trawden and Rossendale and Arnside-Silverdale. The period is divided into three series – the Dinantian, the Namurian and the Westphalian – each having different associated rock types.

2.12 The oldest Dinantian rocks are the basal conglomerates found only in the extreme north-east of the County. These underlie Carboniferous 'Great Scar' limestone which was deposited in shallow seas, covering the far north of the County. At the same time, to the south, in the Bowland and Ribble Valley areas, interbedded limestones, sandstones, calcareous shales and reef limestones formed in layers. Today, the latter form isolated hills or knolls particularly around Clitheroe. Dinantian rocks occur around the Forests of Pendle and Bowland

and Morecambe Bay, forming scenically beautiful high ground, economically valuable for building stone. Great Scar limestone is especially important in cement manufacture.

2.13 Namurian millstone grits were laid down in the Ribble Valley and in a slowly subsiding delta to the north. This created different rock types in the north (alternating limestones, sandstones and shales) and the south (massive sandstone beds with alternating beds of gritstones, shales and coals). Namurian rocks outcrop today in the north and south east, forming the high ground of the Rossendale Moors and the Lancaster Fells. Extraction in Ribble Valley, Chorley, West Lancashire, and Rossendale has long supplied the construction industry, whilst upland millstone grits form water-gathering grounds, especially in Rossendale and the West Pennine Moors.

2.14 Westphalian Coal Measures were deposited in swamps and shallow lakes as interbedded sandstones, shales, mudstones, coals and fireclays. They occur mainly in the south and east of the County, outcropping between Chorley and Skelmersdale and along the Darwen and Calder Valleys and were formerly of great economic importance. Industrial towns like Blackburn, Accrington and Colne developed on and around them, and many old mine workings exist as reminders of a once-extensive coal industry. Mining today is limited to a few small-scale private operations in East Lancashire. Sandstones and mudstones are still extracted for building stone and brick manufacture.

Figure 3
Lancashire - Solid Geology.

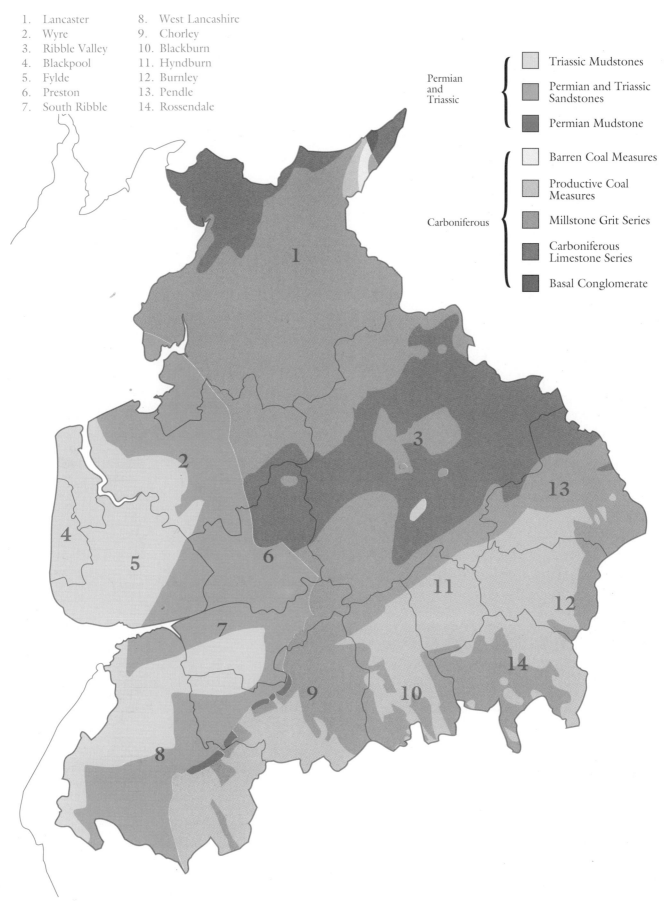

1. Lancaster
2. Wyre
3. Ribble Valley
4. Blackpool
5. Fylde
6. Preston
7. South Ribble
8. West Lancashire
9. Chorley
10. Blackburn
11. Hyndburn
12. Burnley
13. Pendle
14. Rossendale

Permian and Triassic
{
Triassic Mudstones

Permian and Triassic Sandstones

Permian Mudstone
}

Carboniferous
{
Barren Coal Measures

Productive Coal Measures

Millstone Grit Series

Carboniferous Limestone Series

Basal Conglomerate
}

Table 2	Geological Timescale and Major Rock Types Present in Lancashire		
Millions of Years before Present	Period	Series or Epoch	Major Rock Types Present in Lancashire
0.01 2	Quaternary	Recent or Holocene Pleistocene Pliocene	Peat, Sand and Silts Clay and Sand
65	Tertiary		
135	Cretaceous	Not Present	—
190	Jurassic		
225	Triassic		Mudstones
270	Permian		Sandstones
345	Carboniferous	Stephanian Westphalian Namurian Dinantian	— Coal Measures Millstone Grit Carboniferous Limestone

Source: Anderton, et al. (1979)

2.15 The Permian and Triassic are often considered as one period, (the Permo-Trias), because their rocks are very similar. These were laid down in shallow seas as sandstones and calcareous mudstones (or marls). They are found mainly in the west, with an isolated sandstone pocket in the extreme north east, and form an important resource for the chemical and building industries.

2.16 The oldest rocks of this period are the marine-based marls occurring on the north west edge of the Westphalian coal measures. Sandstones were deposited throughout the Permo-Trias and are often referred to as the Bunter and Keuper sandstones. The youngest Permo-Trias are the Keuper marls, forming silty red clays. These were deposited in a shallow sea that went through phases of evaporation. This created rock salt deposits, which have provided a raw material for the chemical industry. Salt is extracted at Preesall near Fleetwood.

Drift Geology

2.17 The drift geology of Lancashire (Figure 4) is made up of deposits from the Pleistocene and Holocene (or Recent) periods. Such deposits overlay most of Lancashire's solid geology, and consist largely of unconsolidated clays, sands and gravels left by the Ice Age. Pleistocene deposits (the Pennine, Lakeland and Northern Drifts on Figure 4) are generally referred to as boulder clays. Pennine Drift occurs in a broad band through the middle of Lancashire, from north to south, whilst Lakeland Drift is deposited in a narrow strip around Morecambe Bay. Northern Drift covers much of the Fylde and South West Lancashire and fringes the Forest of Bowland.

2.18 Holocene deposits are mainly unconsolidated sands and silt, often laid down as a consequence of changing sea levels. Downholland silt was deposited when sea levels rose along the Fylde coast, the Ribble estuary and the River Douglas.

Shirdley Hill sand appeared at approximately the same time, but as sandy beaches and dunes in South West Lancashire. It forms coarse grained, thin and sporadic beds.

2.19 Blown sand appears in pockets along the Blackpool coastline as a fine grained, calcareous sand. Both lowland and upland peats are present in Lancashire, due to the impact on trees and vegetation of climate change, fluctuating sea-levels (in the lowlands) and early human activity (in the uplands). Hill peat covers large areas in the north and east of the County, whilst lowland peat is present mainly in the south and central west.

2.20 Some deposits are important economically. Shirdley Hill sands, with their consistent grain size, are much-sought for the manufacture of glass and fine concrete. Coarser grained sands and gravels are used generally in the construction industry, whilst alluvium, silts and peats have created some of the highest quality agricultural land in the County – particularly in West Lancashire (see Chapter 8).

Topography

2.21 Topography influences the County's environment in a number of ways. Climate is greatly affected, because an increase in height raises rainfall and lowers temperatures. Lancashire's fells and moors face the prevailing south-westerly winds which also increases rainfall. Inter-relationships between geology, climate and topography have helped to fashion the County's soils, providing the basic parent material and the drainage and erosion processes essential to their development. These factors have combined in turn to influence vegetation and wildlife (Chapter 9), whilst human activity – particularly settlement, land-use and communications – has also been controlled by topography (Chapters 8, 10 and 12).

2.22 Lancashire is a county of great scenic diversity, ranging from coastal lowlands in the west to hills and uplands in the east. Figure 5 shows the progressive increase in height, from sea level to over 600 m, in a relatively short distance. The County's major physical sub-divisions are also indicated on Figure 5.

The Lancashire Plain

2.23 The lowlands of the Lancashire Plain spread inland as far as the 120 m contour. Permo-Trias sandstones and marls make up the majority of the floor of the Plain, rising only infrequently above the thick covering of drift. Drainage and soil characteristics, therefore, have had a greater influence in shaping lowland landscape than solid geology and have created a gently rolling relief, with small, isolated hills. The highest of these are the Carboniferous outcrops forming Parbold Hill (157 m) and Ashurst's Beacon (168 m).

2.24 With its undulating surface of irregular mounds and ridges separated by flat-floored depressions, the Plain is naturally badly drained due to its covering of boulder clay. However, much of the present landscape is an artificial one of neatly-ordered fields, with carefully maintained ditches and drains constructed over the last two hundred

Figure 4
Lancashire - Drift Geology.

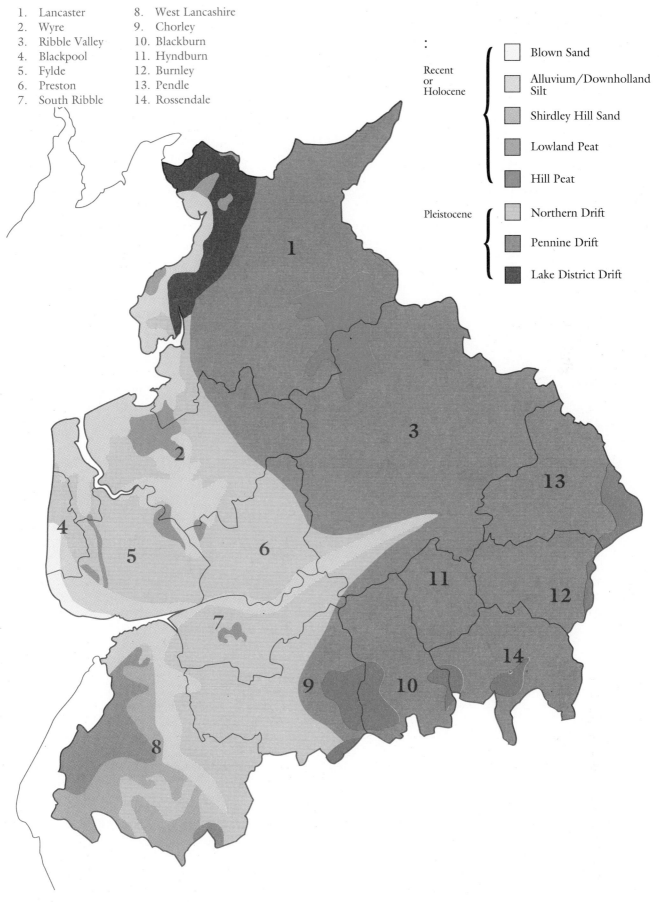

1. Lancaster
2. Wyre
3. Ribble Valley
4. Blackpool
5. Fylde
6. Preston
7. South Ribble
8. West Lancashire
9. Chorley
10. Blackburn
11. Hyndburn
12. Burnley
13. Pendle
14. Rossendale

Recent or Holocene
- Blown Sand
- Alluvium/Downholland Silt
- Shirdley Hill Sand
- Lowland Peat
- Hill Peat

Pleistocene
- Northern Drift
- Pennine Drift
- Lake District Drift

Source: Hall and Folland (1970) and Trueman (1971)

years. The former landscape can be seen in relict areas like Winmarleigh Moss, near Cockerham.

2.25 A higher, more irregular landscape is apparent around Chorley and Leyland where glacier melt-water channels have cut into the drift and solid rock. Here, too, a low level cliff line was eroded by the rise and fall in sea level after the last Ice Age. Most of this has now been removed but sections can still be seen at Hesketh Bank near Preston and Hill House in West Lancashire.

2.26 Fringing the western limit of the Plain, are marine deposits of silt, sand and shingle beaches, dunes and salt marshes. They produce the traditional, open, low-lying landscape of the Lancashire coast, which is so important for tourism and as wildlife habitat. Much of the coast is now fronted by defences to prevent incursions by the sea. These are a reminder of our long history of advancing and receding sea levels and of the need to pay careful heed to the potential consequences of global warming, and predicted sea-level rises (Chapter 3).

Hills and Uplands

2.27 Lancashire's uplands start abruptly east of the 120 m contour line, corresponding closely with the faulted boundary between Permo-Triassic and Carboniferous rocks. Development of the canal, motorway and railway north of Preston has kept very closely to this marked physical boundary.

2.28 The Forests of Bowland, Rossendale and Trawden, the West Pennine Moors and Lancaster Fells, form the County's highest ground. Here, weakly folded sandstones and gritstones have led to bleak open moorland landscapes with gently rounded summits, ranging between 400 m and 600 m. These include the County's tallest vantage points and its most prominent landscape features – Winter Hill (456 m), Boulsworth Hill (517 m), Pendle Hill (557 m), Ward's Stone (561 m) and Leck

Fell, (at 627 m, the highest point in Lancashire). Shale bands within the gritstones have worn down to form lower areas, creating a landscape of undulating ground broken by low scarps and deeply cut valleys. Fast-running streams within these valleys provided the power for early industrial development. Above the scarps and valleys, the grits form gentle slopes and broad, stepped, plateaux which remain waterlogged for long periods. This has resulted in the development of blanket peat, eroded in some places to form broad gullies.

2.29 Along the western Pennine margins, through Ribble Valley, a subdued shale and limestone relief is found with outcrops of reef-knoll limestone producing rounded hills, contrasting with the higher limestone plateaux of the Bowland Fells to the north. Around Morecambe Bay, in Arnside-Silverdale, the massive limestone has been cracked and faulted to create a highly distinctive landscape of upthrown blocks, pavements and grassy hollows.

River Valleys

2.30 Figure 5 shows the principal river valleys of Lancashire. These form major landscape features in their own right and have acted as corridors for human settlement and movement since earliest times. From north to south, the main valley systems are those based on the rivers Lune, Wyre, Ribble, (with its tributaries the Hodder, Calder, Darwen and Douglas), and the Irwell (which drains to the Mersey). These rivers form the basis of the County's drainage and effluent disposal system and serve as a recreational resource and wildlife habitat; aspects dealt with more fully in Chapters 4, 9 and 11.

Soils

2.31 The wide range of parent materials and soil-forming conditions mentioned above have furnished Lancashire with a complex mosaic of soils. Fine and medium-textured types predominate, derived principally from the Pleistocene drift. Soil is crucial to economic activity – especially agriculture – and, as a key determinant of vegetation, is of great significance to the County's landscape and wildlife.

2.32 Soils are classified according to the national system of the Soil Survey of England and Wales (Avery, 1980). Figure 6 shows the eight dominant soil groups which occur in Lancashire, whilst Table 3 gives their extent.

2.33 Dominant soil groups are sub-divided further into soil series, some 33 of which occur in Lancashire. These are highly fragmented and have been excluded from Figure 6[1]. However the major series are described briefly below[2].

Table 3 Extent of Dominant Soil Groups in Lancashire		
Soil Group	Area (ha)	% of County Covered
Alluvial Gley	15,284	5
Earthy Peat	9,368	3
Brown Earth	23,382	8
Gleypodzol	13,970	5
Stagnopodzol	5,300	2
Stagnogley	150,969	49
Stagnohumic Gley	62,590	20
Raw Peat	15,613	5
Unclassified	10,475	3
LANCASHIRE	306,951	100

Source: Soil Survey and Land Research Centre (1983).

---

(1) The 'Soils of Northern England' map, published by the Soil Survey at 1:250,000 scale, gives this more detailed information.
(2) All soil series reviews are from Ragg *et al.* (1984), and (for stagnogley soils) Hall and Folland (1970).

Figure 5
Lancashire - Topography.

1. Lancaster
2. Wyre
3. Ribble Valley
4. Blackpool
5. Fylde
6. Preston
7. South Ribble
8. West Lancashire
9. Chorley
10. Blackburn
11. Hyndburn
12. Burnley
13. Pendle
14. Rossendale

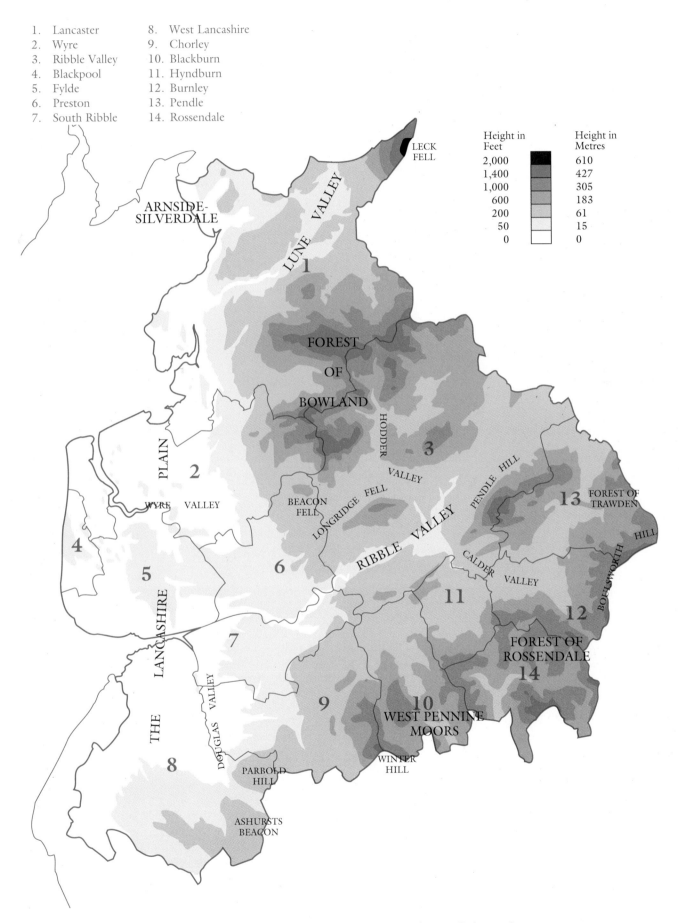

Height in Feet	Height in Metres
2,000	610
1,400	427
1,000	305
600	183
200	61
50	15
0	0

LECK FELL

ARNSIDE-SILVERDALE

LUNE VALLEY

FOREST OF BOWLAND

PLAIN

WYRE VALLEY

HODDER VALLEY

BEACON FELL

LONGRIDGE FELL

RIBBLE VALLEY

PENDLE HILL

FOREST OF TRAWDEN

BOULSWORTH HILL

CALDER VALLEY

FOREST OF ROSSENDALE

THE LANCASHIRE

DOUGLAS VALLEY

WEST PENNINE MOORS

WINTER HILL

PARBOLD HILL

ASHURSTS BEACON

Source: Ordnance Survey

Alluvial Gley

2.34   The Enbourne series are fine loamy soils in non-calcareous flood-plains affected by seasonal flooding and fluctuating ground-water levels. They are found in the Lune, Wyre, Douglas, Lostock, Yarrow and Darwen Valleys. Climate, soil-wetness and, in places, the narrowness of the flood-plain make the series unsuitable for sustained arable cropping. However, these crops are grown widely on alluvium in the Douglas Valley where drainage has been installed and maintained. The Rockcliffe series occurs on reclaimed stoneless marine alluvium at the southern edge of Morecambe Bay and in the Ribble estuary. With effective drainage, it produces some of the best soils in Lancashire, being particularly suitable for brassicas. The Down-holland 2 series is clayey, non-calcareous and typical of alluvial gley soils. It is found along the Lancashire Plain from the river Alt, (near Formby), to north of Carnforth, being particularly extensive between Preesall and Heysham where it is known locally as skirt soil. Where drained, Downholland soils can be very fertile and are suited to arable cropping. However, grassland predominates where pumped drainage has not been installed, (for example around Heysham, Thurnham and south of Pilling).

Earthy Peat

2.35   The Turbary Moor series is the main constituent of this group. It is found in lowland raised peat bogs, modified by drainage, peat cutting and reclamation. Recent expansion of the peat industry has reduced the extent of this old, 'cut-over' land, often exposing underlying fen peat or mineral alluvium substrate. Turbary soils are very easy to cultivate and have a long landwork period. Intensive arable use though, has been a major cause of the loss of much of this rare, natural peat habitat. The Altcar series is also extensive on the Plain around Altcar and Banks, and between Southport and Scarisbrick. It flanks the river Douglas near Rufford and the river Wyre and its tributaries on the Fylde. Where drained, it is easy to cultivate and can again be worked well into the autumn. As with the Turbary Moor series, peat extraction, drainage and cultivation have gradually lowered the land surface, creating a characteristic landscape where roads and settlements stand above the surrounding farm-land.

Brown Earth

2.36   Brown earths are dominated by the Flint series. They provide good mixed-farming land, though arable crops are rare in the Fylde and the series here is particularly suited to grassland farming. The Rivington series is another typical brown earth, being coarse and well drained. It is widespread on the Pennine slopes and foothills, from Longridge Fell to the south. It also occurs in the Wyre Valley and north of Skelmersdale, where Carboniferous sandstones protrude through the drift. On the Pennine slopes and foothills, it is mostly put to grass for sheep and beef cattle rearing, though dairying is localised. Upper slopes, above 225 m, are not used as intensively and have become dominated by matt-grass and wavy hair-grass. Soils

here tend to become acidic and require frequent liming to prevent reversion to moorland.

Gleypodzol

2.37   The majority of this group occurs on the Lancashire Plain between the Mersey and the Ribble as the Sollom series. This comprises deep, sandy or loamy/clay soils, often having impeded drainage. Around Ormskirk, the series is found on broad expanses of flat land over the Shirdley Hill Sand. Its soils are intensively farmed; cereals, root crops and brassicas being the main crops.

Stagnopodzol

2.38   The Belmont series is the main stagnopodzol, occurring in the Forest of Bowland, Pendle Hill, West Pennine Moors and Rossendale. It is coarse, loamy, and very acid with a wet peaty surface horizon and thin ironpan. Where unimproved, it is only marginally suitable for grazing but where sufficiently limed and fertilised, grass will yield well. The semi-natural moorland vegetation provides only poor grazing, but better grazing is possible where matt-grass and purple-moorgrass are dominant. Forestry is possible following deep ploughing.

Stagnogley

2.39   The Stagnogley group covers over half of the County, with the Salop series being its most extensive constituent. It is based on medium to fine-textured, slightly calcareous till and occupies flat or gently sloping ground below 800 m. Poor drainage caused by negligible run-off and slow percolation is the chief limiting factor on farming. Marling was widespread in Lancashire before the development of the lime and fertiliser industries, and many fields on the Salop series, (notably in the Fylde and South Lancashire), contain disused, often flooded, marl-pits. The Brickfield 2 and 3 series are also widespread. They cover an almost continuous tract along the Pennine Fringe, taking in the lower footslopes of the Forests of Bowland, Pendle, Trawden and Rossendale and the trough between Blackburn and Colne. Formed on Pennine Drift as medium to fine-textured 'till and head' derived from Carboniferous parent material, Brickfields have impermeable subsoils and are poorly drained. Much of the series is devoted to permanent grassland. Being strongly leached, regular liming is required particularly on the footslopes of Rossendale, where atmospheric pollution has accelerated calcium loss.

Stagnohumic Gley

2.40   The Wilcocks series is an extensive stagnohumic gley with an acid organic surface layer, with underlying clayey loam or sandy, clay loam. In North Lancashire, it is found normally above 200 m, where the climate favours the development of peaty topsoils. Climate is also the overriding influence on use of the Wilcocks series. Relatively low temperatures, high rainfall and low soil moisture, combined with slowly permeable subsoils, cause inherent wetness and the accumulation of organic matter at the surface.

Figure 6
Lancashire - Soils.

1. Lancaster
2. Wyre
3. Ribble Valley
4. Blackpool
5. Fylde
6. Preston
7. South Ribble

8. West Lancashire
9. Chorley
10. Blackburn
11. Hyndburn
12. Burnley
13. Pendle
14. Rossendale

Dominant Soil

- Alluvial Gley Soils
- Earthy Peat Soils
- Brown Earths and Soils
- Gley Podzols
- Stagnopodzols
- Stagnogley Soils
- Stagnohumic Gley Soils
- Raw Peat Soils
- Unsurveyed

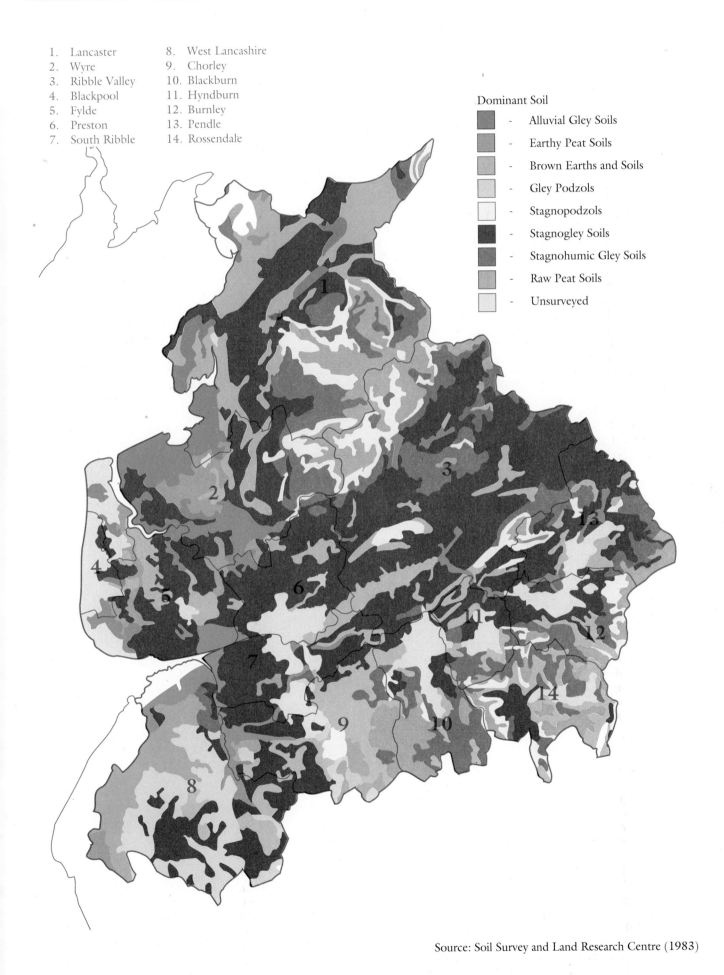

Source: Soil Survey and Land Research Centre (1983)

Raw Peat

2.41 The Winter Hill series is Lancashire's major raw peat soil, being found on hillsides, ridges and plateaux above 190 m. It develops here because the climate is cold, wet and exposed, inhibiting the organisms which decompose plant remains and incorporate them into mineral soil. Flat, or gently sloping ground, leads to peat infilling of hollows and a smooth undulating land surface. Winter Hill soils provide poor grazing at best. Tussock-forming cotton-grass dominates the most characteristic plant community, with purple-moor grass and deer-grass common locally. In the wettest places, cotton-grass and sphagnum moss predominate, the former often colonising bare peat deposited by streams issuing from gullies. Because of its limited value for agriculture and forestry, other land-uses like grouse management, military training, water gathering, recreation and nature conservation receive priority.

Climate

2.42 Climate is another of the major forces driving Lancashire's environmental system. It helps to shape landscape and the distribution of plants, animals and people, and influences the way land is used. The first part of this section, summarises the climate experienced at specific locations in the County. This is followed by information on trends, leading to a brief discussion on historic climate change within Lancashire. The implications of global climate change are dealt with in Chapter 3.

Figure 7
Meteorological Office Stations in Lancashire.

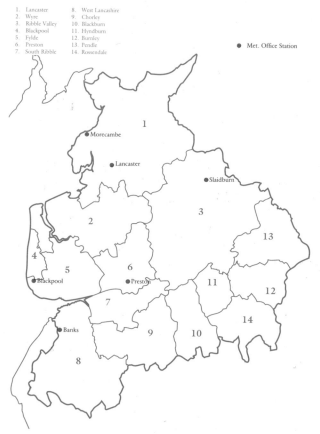

Source: Met. Office (pers. comm.)

2.43 The locations of six Meteorological Office stations for which Lancashire data are available are shown Figure 7. Data covering several climatic elements for these stations are presented in Figures 9 to 14[1]. The stations concerned are:

* Morecambe – station no. 7239;

* Lancaster (Hazelrigg) – station no. 7236;

* Slaidburn – station no. 4002;

* Preston (Moor Park) – station no. 7245;

* Blackpool (Squires Gate) – station no. 7213;

* Banks (near Southport) – station no. 7223.

Rainfall

2.44 The close relationship between topography and rainfall can be seen by comparing Figures 5 and 8. Rainfall contours shown on the latter are based on averages for the period 1941 to 1970. They closely follow the relief contours, particularly in East Lancashire. Average annual rainfall at Slaidburn (on land above 200 m) is 1,500 mm contrasting with 860 mm at Blackpool (10 m above sea level).

2.45 The monthly distribution of rainfall for six County locations is given in Figure 9. This shows that February and April are the driest months, and November and December are the wettest. Average monthly totals of less than 50 mm are exceptionally rare, occuring only twice, (both in April), at Lancaster and Blackpool. Both Blackpool and Banks show the lowest average monthly annual rainfalls. Despite this, Banks holds the record for the maximum fall in 24 hours, (91.4 mm occurring on 25 September 1968), and the wettest month (again September 1968). The driest month was February 1986 at Blackpool with only 0.7 mm precipitation.

Temperature

2.46 Like rainfall, temperature is closely related to altitude, falling roughly by 1°C for every 150 m increase in height. Coastal areas of Lancashire experience typical west coast temperatures with an annual mean of about 9.5°C, whilst inland hills experience much colder conditions, with an annual mean of 8°C (at Slaidburn). Figure 10 details average monthly temperatures for six locations. Examination shows a lower range between average maxima and minima in coastal locations compared to inland areas. There are more pronounced extremes of temperature, and an increase in the number of days with ground frost, as distance increases from the coast. Incidence of ground frost rises from an average of about 70 days a year in coastal areas to about 140 days a year in the uplands. Extremes of over 32°C are very rare. The hottest day on record was 3 July 1976, when a temperature of 33.7°C was recorded at Blackpool. This was almost reached again during the hot spell at the end of July, 1990. The lowest temperature was minus 16.1°C recorded at Banks on 16 February 1969.

---

(1) Average monthly amounts shown on these Figures are calculated from data covering the period January 1959 to December 1988, except for Lancaster, for which data cover the period January 1977 to December 1988. Data are unavailable for wind speed at Morecambe and for sunshine at Preston.

Sunshine

2.47 Average monthly sunshine for five locations is presented in Figure 11. The number of days with sunshine decreases gradually with increasing distance from the coast. Until the Clean Air Acts, were implemented, (see Chapter 3), smoke pollution meant that sunshine levels in some towns was up to 15% lower than it was in the surrounding countryside. Sunniest months are May and June, with Blackpool being the sunniest location. July 1975 was the sunniest month on record with Blackpool receiving 306.3 hours. The dullest month was December 1971 with just 11 hours sunshine at Slaidburn. Morecambe holds the record for the sunniest day, with 16.6 hours on 22 June 1977.

Fog

2.48 The number of days with fog,[1] varies considerably between the six locations (see Figure 12), and also between years. On the coast, sea and radiation fog both contribute significantly to the total. Improved pollution conditions (see Chapter 3) have helped to reduce the incidence of fog. Nelson, for example, once had over 100 days a year with fog. These prolonged fogs, (worsened by atmospheric pollution), decreased sunshine, lowered daytime temperatures, and badly affected public health. The higher frequency of fog at Banks today is due to sea fog, however, not atmospheric pollution.

---

(1) When the range of vision is less than 1,100 yards at 0900 hours GMT.

Figure 8
Lancashire – Average Annual Rainfall. 1941-1970

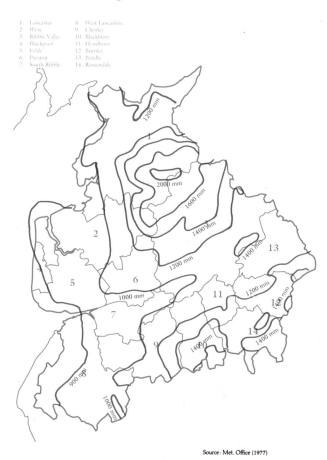

Source: Met. Office (1977)

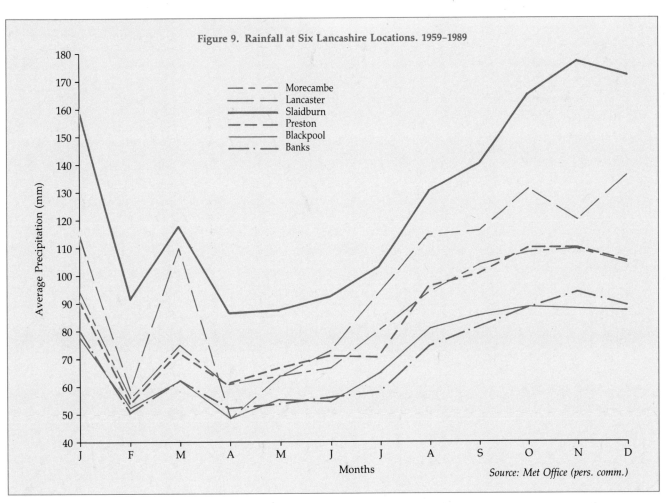

Figure 9. Rainfall at Six Lancashire Locations. 1959–1989

Source: Met Office (pers. comm.)

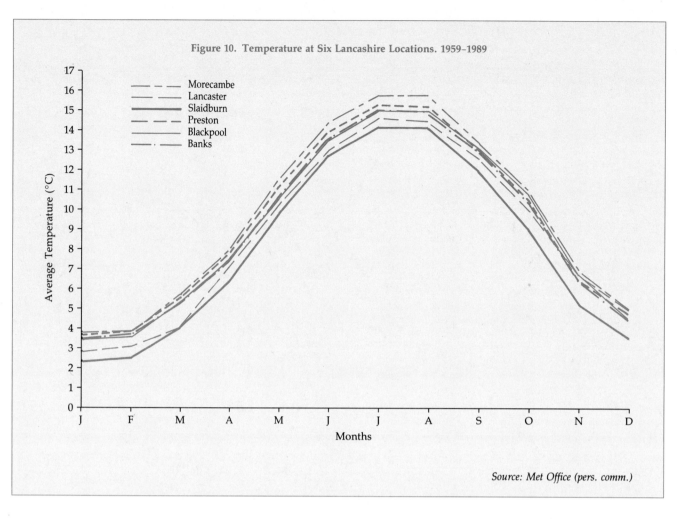

Figure 10. Temperature at Six Lancashire Locations. 1959–1989

Morecambe
Lancaster
Slaidburn
Preston
Blackpool
Banks

Average Temperature (°C)

Months

Source: Met Office (pers. comm.)

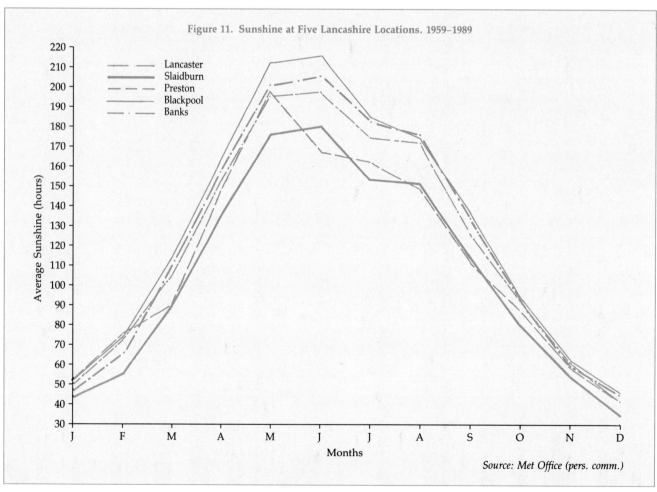

Figure 11. Sunshine at Five Lancashire Locations. 1959–1989

Lancaster
Slaidburn
Preston
Blackpool
Banks

Average Sunshine (hours)

Months

Source: Met Office (pers. comm.)

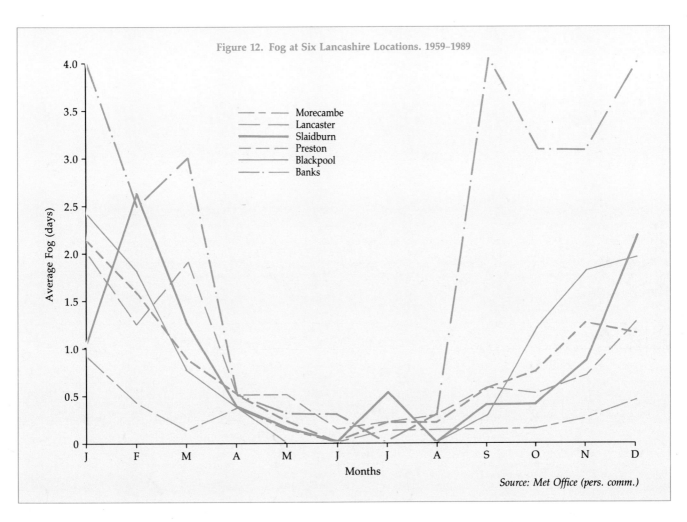

Figure 12. Fog at Six Lancashire Locations. 1959–1989

Source: Met Office (pers. comm.)

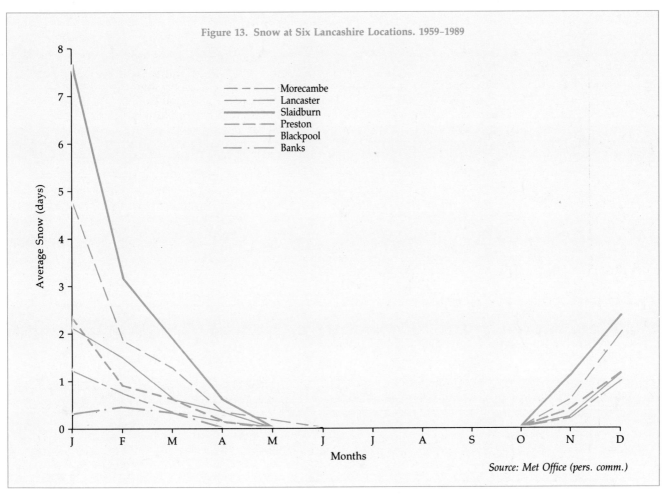

Figure 13. Snow at Six Lancashire Locations. 1959–1989

Source: Met Office (pers. comm.)

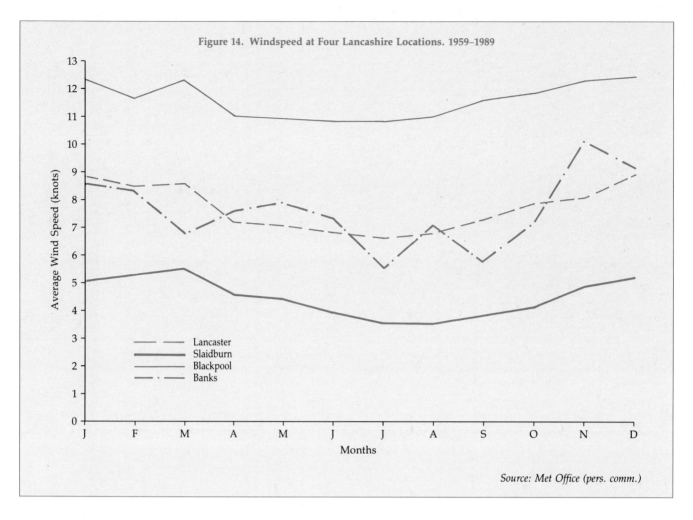

Figure 14. Windspeed at Four Lancashire Locations. 1959–1989

Source: Met Office (pers. comm.)

Snow

2.49 The number of days with snow[1] varies greatly from year to year and between locations. In coastal Districts, some years may be completely free from snow, while elsewhere (as in 1947), snow may occur on up to 40 days. On average, (as shown on Figure 13) snow falls between 1 and 6 days per year on the Coastal Plain and between 7 and 10 days further inland. Slaidburn can experience up to 16 days snow per year, however, whilst on the very highest ground, up to 30 days a year is common (Manley, 1940, 1947).

Wind

2.50 Figure 14 shows that Lancashire's lightest winds occur between May and August, whilst the strongest blow in January and February. Blackpool is easily the windiest location, whilst Slaidburn has the least variation in wind speed. The highest daily average wind speed was 39.7 knots recorded at Blackpool on 1 November 1965. This location also experienced the highest gust (76 knots), on 1 December 1966.

2.51 Wind direction is just as important as wind speed, having a pronounced effect on such diverse aspects as vegetation, physical erosion processes and coastal defence. Combined data on speed and direction is usually presented in the form of a 'wind rose'. For Lancashire, such roses are available for

three coastal locations – Heysham (Low), Blackpool (Squires Gate) and Aughton (see Figure 15).[2]

2.52 Examination of the hourly mean wind data for all months in Figure 15, shows that the percentage frequency is slightly higher from the western quadrants than from the south-eastern. At Heysham and Blackpool winds are predominantly westerly between June and August. However, south-easterly winds become increasingly significant (especially at Blackpool), between December and February. Consideration of the Aughton situation shows that westerly and north-westerly winds are most significant between March and August, whilst south-easterly winds become more so between September and February.

Climate Trends

2.53 Data covering a longer timescale are essential to any examination of climate trends and for identifying any real changes. For Lancashire, there is some material on both long-term rainfall and temperature trends.

2.54 Rainfall data are available for Preston for the past 140 years, and are shown in Figure 16. An accepted form of presenting rainfall figures is by

---

(1) Defined as a day when 50% of the ground is covered snow.

(2) On Wind Roses a number of bars radiate from the centre of the compass, one for each wind direction. The lengths of these bars are proportional to the frequency of wind occurrence. They are subdivided to represent the contributions from different wind-strength bands.

Figure 15
Wind Roses for Three Lancashire Locations.

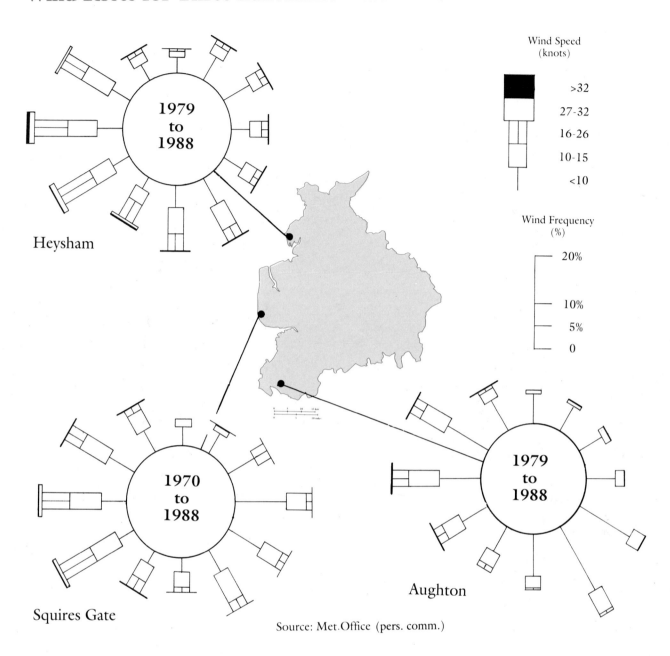

Wind Speed
(knots)

>32
27-32
16-26
10-15
<10

Wind Frequency
(%)

20%
10%
5%
0

Heysham

1979
to
1988

1970
to
1988

Squires Gate

1979
to
1988

Aughton

Source: Met.Office (pers. comm.)

way of 'running ten year means'[1]. This allows real and sustained trends to show through and reduces the statistical effect of 'one-off' unusually, dry, or wet, years. Figure 16 shows a striking minima in the graph around the turn of the present century. The reason for this is unknown. But, the overall trend over the whole period is upwards; and, in fact, present average annual rainfall is about 250 mm higher than it was around the middle of the nineteenth century (bearing in mind that what appears on the left of the graph may be the later part of an earlier minimum).

(1) The first ten years of the database (1849–1858) are averaged. A single year is then added and a new ten year average calculated, (i.e. for 1850–1859). This process is repeated, dropping a year from the start of the period and adding one at the end, until the process reaches the average annual rainfall for 1980–1989.

2.55 This additional rainfall corresponds to just under an extra inch of rain every month. The effect of the below-average rainfall in 1989 causes the graph to turn downwards for the first time since the mid 1970s. Points added in future years will show if this is the beginning of a new down-ward trend or is merely a 'hiccup' in the upward trend.

2.56 Whilst Figure 16 shows that Preston is now wetter than it used to be, records also confirm that there has been a marked increase in Lancashire's mean temperature over the last 210 years. Data adapted from Manley (1946) are presented in Figure 17. He used a hybrid of sources and adjusted each source to represent a 'typical' station on the Lancashire Plain at an altitude of 15m. Though Manley's data set is not continuous for any specific location, it is accepted that his adjustments are

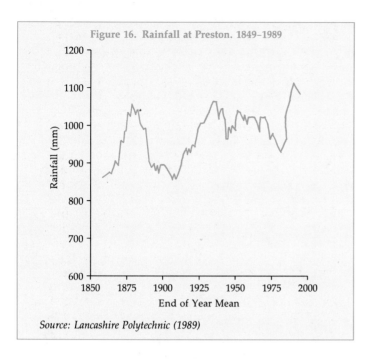

Figure 16. Rainfall at Preston. 1849–1989

Source: Lancashire Polytechnic (1989)

sound (Meteorological Office, and Climatic Research Unit, University of East Anglia, pers. comms.).

2.57 From the curve of 10-year running means shown on Figure 17, it can be seen that mean Lancashire temperatures have risen by 0.5°C since 1750. The curve of cumulative residuals shows that this is real change. (Cumulative residuals are calculated by subtracting the 210 year average from each of the annual totals in sequence.) Figure 17 shows that there have been three distinct temperature régimes over the last two centuries:

* a 'cold' period with a mean of 8.7°C from 1750 to 1816;

* a slightly warmer period with a mean of 8.8°C from 1817 to 1891;

* an even warmer period with a mean of 9.2°C since 1892.

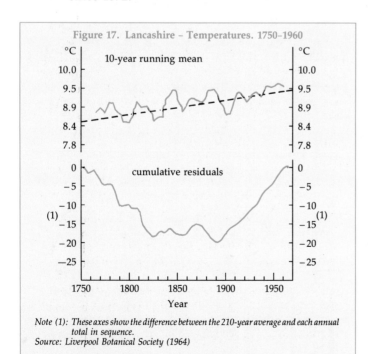

Figure 17. Lancashire – Temperatures. 1750–1960

Note (1): These axes show the difference between the 210-year average and each annual total in sequence.
Source: Liverpool Botanical Society (1964)

Manley found that the main changes stem from a rise in winter temperatures, whereas summer temperatures have remained almost constant throughout the 210 years. The most marked change has been a rise of 1.7°C in January temperatures since 1820. Other trends include increases of 0.5°C in February temperatures, 0.8°C in those for November and a 1.1°C rise for December over the last 150 years.

Vegetation

2.58 Vegetation is a basic component of all landscape and provides the habitat for most of our wildlife. It plays a key rôle in forming and controlling our climate and is vital to the human economy. Without human influence, however, the vegetation cover of Lancashire would be quite different. The natural 'climax' vegetation of most of the County, resulting from the interplay of climate, soils and topography, would be a general canopy of broadleaved woodland. Exceptions would occur on the highest ground, along parts of the coast and in lowland moss areas. The fact that broadleaved woodlands now cover only 3.3% of the County is testimony to the lengthy and persistent activity of generations of Lancastrians.

2.59 Pollen records confirm that 5,000 years ago the greater part of Lancashire was covered by broadleaved forest. The climate of the time encouraged the growth of species like oak, alder and hazel. Encroachment of the sea then covered the lowest lying forests with marine deposits. When the sea retreated, it left behind the freshwater fens and bogs which developed into today's lowland peat areas. The uplands were also subject to change. From 3,000 BC, Neolithic people began to make significant clearings in woodland cover. The onset of a warmer climate signalled wider upland colonisation by Bronze Age settlers, who accelerated this clearance. This, coupled with a deteriorating wetter climate, saw the continued development of moorland and peat bog. Lancashire's uplands have never regained their woodland.

2.60 Further depletion of lowland woodlands occurred in the Anglo-Saxon period when the heavy clays on which the forests grew were cultivated widely for the first time. The process was continued by the incursion of Norse peoples, especially on the mossland fringes of the Lancashire Plain. Deforestation has carried on throughout the present millenium, parallelled by the spread and intensification of agricultural activity, settlement growth, expansions to the communication pattern and industrial development. The rate of change has increased dramatically since the Industrial Revolution and though natural forces have also played an important part, it has been the human hand which has largely shaped the vegetation pattern that we have today. The current composition of Lancashire's vegetation cover is detailed in Chapter 9.

Population

2.61 Human activity is the most significant force for environmental change, globally and locally.

Since first appearing on the planet 400,000 years ago, the human race has been altering the physical and natural components of the system. In Lancashire, the process began with the first pre-historic hunters in the County in 10,000 BC, though by far the greatest change in population and population impact has come about since the eighteenth century.

Population Development

2.62 Lancashire was thinly settled in pre-historic times, and the people of the day lacked the technology to alter radically a basically inhospitable environment. However, they did begin the process of changing the natural vegetation cover. Roman occupation (AD 43–fifth century AD) brought only a few military settlements because the County was unattractive for commercial exploitation. The native British or Celtic inhabitants of the area remained scattered in small settlements during this period.

2.63 During the early medieval period (fifth century–AD 1066), the County was still thinly peopled with few settlements above the 150 m contour and, as far as we know, none at all above 250 m. However, numerous scattered settlements, surrounded by closely and regularly cultivated fields, appeared in the lower, drier lands of the central Fylde, in the foothills and valleys around Morecambe Bay and along the Ribble Valley. Norse settlers (from AD 910) generally stayed in the coastal areas and on the edge of the mossland, which earlier Anglian invaders (from AD 570) had left alone.

2.64 Medieval Lancashire (1066–1540) saw agricultural development and growing individual wealth leading to the establishment of markets and fairs. Some new market centres of this period (for example, Preston and Burnley), were to become important towns of the modern period. Others, like Croston, are still villages. Other main towns of today – Blackburn, Chorley, Clitheroe, Lancaster, Leyland and Ormskirk – were also reasonable-sized settlements by this time.

2.65 Textile industries existed at Colne and Burnley towards the end of the thirteenth century and shallow surface workings of coal were being made at Colne and Trawden. However, until well into the seventeenth century, Lancashire's wealth lay in its agriculture. Sheep provided the raw material for the emerging textile industry and in the agriculturally poor moorland areas the population turned to spinning and weaving. Although other industrial activity developed in the seventeenth century (e.g. small-scale coal and metal working), the County's wealth was still thinly spread.

2.66 It is estimated that in 1690 the population of Lancashire was 196,100. However, the number living in towns of any size greater than a village cannot have exceeded 30,000. At the very most, about 15% of the County's population were townspeople (compared with today, when 75% are urban dwellers).

2.67 The eighteenth century brought momentous changes stemming from the Industrial Revolution. The population of the County increased threefold between 1690 and 1801 to 672,700 people. (Compared to a two-fold increase for England and Wales over the same period.) The overriding influence on growth was economic development – without which this great and growing population could not have been sustained.

2.68 The Industrial Revolution created an urbanised, mechanised society. By 1750, the English cotton industry was mainly concentrated in Lancashire, with yarn being spun on domestic spinning wheels in houses scattered throughout the countryside. However, the first machine spinners were set up in factories or cotton 'mills', and came to represent a new way of industrial life. With the factories, came the building of nearby cottages, generally piecemeal, producing strings of settlements along the valley bottoms of Rossendale and elsewhere. Lancashire towns of the nineteenth century expanded rapidly. Buildings and people were concentrated in small areas, providing inadequate drainage and sewerage which led to social and sanitary ills.

2.69 By 1851, two-thirds of the County's population lived in towns as people continued to move in from the Lancashire countryside. They left the land for a variety of reasons: poverty, poor housing, winter unemployment (common in arable areas), the need to find jobs for children, and agricultural depression being the major ones. Lancashire villages, in fact, only began to decline in total population in the middle of the nineteenth century.

2.70 Between World War I and the present day, the County suffered two serious economic blows: the decline of cotton and coalmining, its principal industries. This has been reflected in a rate of population increase well below the national average – largely because young people have been leaving the older textile towns and (until very recently) the promoters of new industries have been unwilling to establish in these areas. Spinning towns like Preston, Chorley and Blackburn grew in population by less than 7% in the first half of the present century. The position is now more bouyant, with empty cotton mills often taken over by light industry undertaking a variety of activities and the establishment of new industrial estates. Engineering and metal working are by far the largest employers followed by chemicals, clothing, food and paper. The new towns of Skelmersdale and Central Lancashire have also helped to arrest population decline in the County.

Current Population and Trends

2.71 The population of Lancashire at mid-year 1989 was 1,390,800 (Office of Population Censuses and Surveys, 1990). The breakdown by District is shown in Table 4. The most populated Districts are Blackburn, Blackpool, Lancaster, Preston, Wyre and West Lancashire. However, it can be seen that in terms of density (Figure 18) population is concentrated into the main urban areas of Lancaster, Morecambe, Blackpool, Preston, Blackburn and Burnley.

Figure 18
Lancashire - Population Density by Wards. 1989

1. Lancaster
2. Wyre
3. Ribble Valley
4. Blackpool
5. Fylde
6. Preston
7. South Ribble
8. West Lancashire
9. Chorley
10. Blackburn
11. Hyndburn
12. Burnley
13. Pendle
14. Rossendale

Persons per hectare

40 - 105

5 - 40

0 - 5

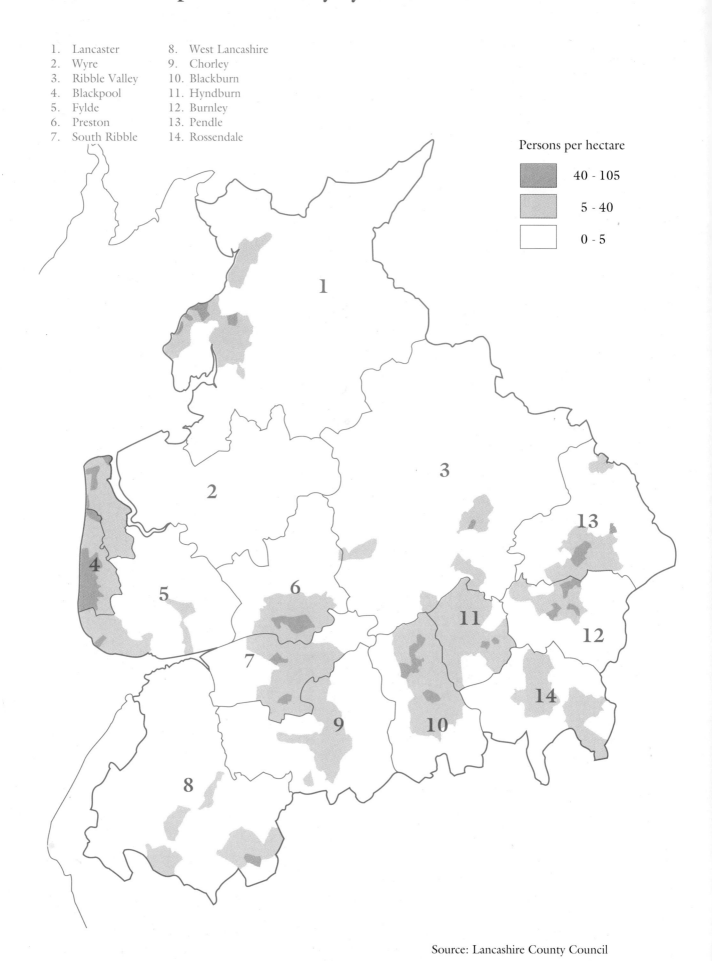

Source: Lancashire County Council

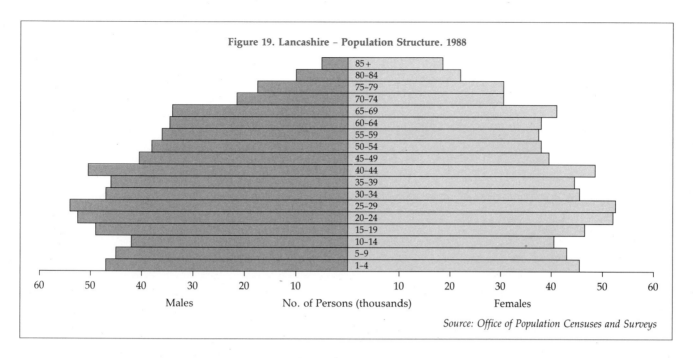

Figure 19. Lancashire – Population Structure. 1988

	85+
	80–84
	75–79
	70–74
	65–69
	60–64
	55–59
	50–54
	45–49
	40–44
	35–39
	30–34
	25–29
	20–24
	15–19
	10–14
	5–9
	1–4

60   50   40   30   20   10   10   20   30   40   50   60

Males   No. of Persons (thousands)   Females

Source: Office of Population Censuses and Surveys

2.72 Population structure is shown in Figure 19. One characteristic is that Lancashire has a higher proportion of population of pensionable age than the national average and a higher proportion of people aged 75 and over (Lancashire County Council, 1988). High numbers occur in coastal retirement areas and nearby rural localities; the Fylde, Morecambe, Heysham, Hest Bank, Bolton-le-Sands, Silverdale and parts of West Lancashire. In wards here, between 25% and 40% of the population can be over retirement age (Lancashire County Council, 1984). A further consequence is that the County has a death rate of 13.2 deaths per 1,000 resident population (Office of Population Censuses and Surveys, 1990) which is higher than the national average and exceeded by only five other counties. (Lancashire County Council,1988).

2.73 Having experienced population increase during most of this century, (although at a rate below the national average), the 1980s witnessed a decline. Between 1981 and 1986 population dropped by 0.4% against a national rise of 1% (Lancashire County Council, 1987).

2.74 Apart from the effect of births and deaths, there is a significant volume of migration between Lancashire and the rest of the UK. These migrations vary between age groups. Lancashire has attracted population from the northern regions but lost a greater number of mainly younger people to the south. The outflow from Lancashire to the south shows a greater bias to younger age groups (16–24 and 25–44 year olds) (Lancashire County Council, 1989).

2.75 Within the County, the recent trend is for population to be lost from older industrial Districts like Burnley, Blackburn and Pendle and for rural and resort villages and towns in Fylde, Wyre and Lancaster to be gaining (Lancashire County Council, 1987). There is also considerable growth within the central Lancashire Districts of Preston, South Ribble and Chorley, partly as a result of the activities of the former Central Lancashire New

Town Development Corporation. This is in line with a national trend for population gain in rural areas and population loss from urban areas; a reversal of the trend from 1750 to the early part of the present century.

2.76 Thus, the most significant impact of the population of the environment in Lancashire has come about since the eighteenth century. Lancashire's population helped to bring about the world's industrialistation but at a cost to the environment of the County and beyond. A legacy

Table 4 Lancashire. Population by District. 1989

District	Population	% of County Total
Lancaster	130,800	9
Wyre	103,700	7
Ribble Valley	52,400	4
Blackpool	143,100	10
Fylde	73,200	5
Preston	128,400	9
South Ribble	101,600	7
West Lancashire	104,500	8
Chorley	96,700	7
Blackburn	135,700	10
Hyndburn	79,200	6
Burnley	90,900	7
Pendle	85,100	6
Rossendale	65,400	5
LANCASHIRE	1,390,800	100

Source: Office of Population Censuses and Surveys (1990).

Note: Figures do not add up due to rounding by OPCS. The rounded total of 1,390,800 is used throughout this report.

of poor housing and pollution has had an effect upon both public health and the image of the County. Upgrading the physical environment and tackling pollution problems in recent years has helped create a better, healthier environment for the County's population and presented a better image to the outside world. However, pressures associated with human activity remain the principal factors influencing Lancashire's environmental system and present the greatest challenge that we face.

References

Anderton, R. *et al.* (1979). A Dynamic Stratigraphy of the British Isles. Allen & Unwin.

Avery, B.W. (1980). Soil Classification for England and Wales (Higher Categories). Soil Survey Technical Monograph No. 14. Harpenden.

Edwards, W. & Trotter, F.M. (1954). The Pennines and Adjacent Areas. HMSO

Hall, B.R. & Folland, C.J. (1967). Soils of the SW Lancashire Coastal Plain. Memoirs of the Soil Survey of Great Britain. Harpenden.

Hall, B.R. & Folland, C.J. (1970). Soils of Lancashire. Harpenden.

Lancashire County Council (1984). Census Atlas of Lancashire. LCC.

Lancashire County Council (1987). Monitor No. 43. LCC.

Lancashire County Council (1988). Monitor No. 47. LCC.

Lancashire County Council (1989). Monitor No. 49. LCC.

Lancashire Polytechnic (1989). Annual Report of the Director of the Observatories. Lancashire Polytechnic.

Liverpool Botanical Society (1964). Travis's Flora of South Lancashire. Liverpool Botanical Society.

Manley, G. (1940). Snowfall in Britain. Meteorology Magazine, 75: 41–48.

Manley, G. (1946). The Climate of Lancashire. Memoirs and Proceedings of the Manchester Literary and Philosophical Society, 87: 73–95.

Manley, G. (1947). Snowfall in the British Isles. Meteorology Magazine, 76: 1–8.

Marshall, J.D. (1974). Lancashire. David & Charles.

Meteorological Office (1977). Average Annual Rainfall. International Standard Period Map 1941–1970 Map. Meteorological Office.

Office of Population Censuses and Surveys (1990). OPCS Monitor. HMSO.

Ordnance Survey (various dates). Landranger Maps 97, 98, 102, 103, 108, 109. O.S.

Soil Survey and Land Research Centre (1983). Soils of Northern England. Sheet 1. Northern England. Soil Survey of England and Wales.

Ragg, J.M. *et al.* (1984). Soils and their use in Midland and Western England. Soil Survey of England and Wales Bulletin No. 12. Harpenden.

Trueman, A.E. (1971). Geology and Scenery in England and Wales. Pelican.

Chapter Three
Air

Introduction

3.1 Air is a fundamental component of our environmental system. Its quality is of primary importance for human health. It is also vital for maintaining healthy crops and livestock and sustaining all wildlife. Atmospheric pollution is, therefore, of great concern on global, national and local scales.

3.2 Human activities are responsible for virtually all emissions of atmospheric pollutants in the UK, particularly through fuel combustion and industrial processes. Recent years have brought major changes in the extent and distribution of air pollution. Traditional domestic and industrial pollutants, like smoke and sulphur dioxide, have decreased and this has eliminated the recurrence of dangerous smogs. However, the dramatic increase in road traffic has increased vehicular pollutants, like the oxides of carbon and nitrogen, hydrocarbons and ozone. Issues of major international concern about the environment have also arisen, focussing attention on the problems of global warming, acid rain and the deterioration of the ozone layer.

3.3 The degree of air pollution is determined by the processes of emission, transport and deposition. All can vary considerably. The composition, concentration and rate of emission of pollutant discharges determine the amount entering the environment at any one time. The location of emission sources, the mode of emissions, the nature of the pollutants and weather conditions determine the extent to which pollutants are transported, deposited, or concentrated in the lower atmosphere. Thus, air quality is continually variable and pollution loads in particular areas are often concentrated into short periods of time dependent on weather conditions. Assessment of air quality over periods of a year or longer must, therefore, acknowledge the day to day variation in air quality which can occur.

3.4 This Chapter assesses the quality of Lancashire's atmosphere and examines the factors influencing it. It describes the major air pollutants in the County, their sources, the areas of concern and the measures which have been implemented to control emissions. Initially, the legislative controls over atmospheric pollution, and the appropriate bodies involved, are outlined.

Legislation

3.5 Controls over visible air pollution have largely developed out of the Clean Air Acts of 1956 and 1968 (CAA 1956, CAA 1968) which were enacted to deal with gross pollution in towns. These have been significantly supplemented by the Control of Pollution Act 1974 (COPA 1974), and various other legislative measures. Major new controls have been introduced by the closely-linked Environmental Protection Act (EPA, 1990). A number of legal measures have been adopted by the Europoean Commission and the UK Government to reduce air pollution. Because of the inter-connected nature of this legislation, this section deals with the statutory position on a type, or source, of pollutant basis, rather than following the procedure adopted in other chapters.

Particulate Emissions

3.6 District Councils are responsible for the control of emissions of smoke, grit, dust and fumes under the CAA 1956 and 1968. Certain forms of air pollution have been declared statutory nuisances, including industrial releases of smoke, dust, effluvia and spent steam which are likely to be prejudicial to health. The emission of 'dark' smoke from a chimney, boiler or industrial plant is generally also an offence. Certain smoke emissions from chimneys are, however, permissible for specified periods under the special case exemptions of the CAA 1956, the Dark Smoke (Permitted Periods) Regulations 1958 and the Clean Air (Emission of Dark Smoke) Exemption Regulations 1969.

3.7 Further controls are afforded under the CAA 1956 by the use of Smoke Control Orders for the designation of Smoke Control Areas. These are delineated by District Councils and both the emission of smoke and the sale of unauthorised fuels are offences within them. Irrespective of the existence of a Smoke Control Order, CAA 1956 requires that all new furnaces, (except small domestic), must be capable of operating continuously without emitting smoke. However, unless constrained by an Order, they need not be so operated provided they do not breach the Dark Smoke Regulations. The CAAs have been particularly successful in reducing air pollution from domestic sources.

3.8 Furnaces are potential sources of grit, dust, fume and smoke nuisance. The CAAs 1956 and 1968 define a range of controls applicable to their emission from large furnaces. These include specifications for arrestment plant and the burning of specific types of fuel. The CAA 1968 made it possible to impose quantitative limits upon emissions and the Secretary of State has done this in the Clean Air (Emission of Grit and Dust from Furnaces) Regulations 1971 (in force since 1978). The control of fumes has not yet been made subject to any similar regulations, other than those fumes emitted from scheduled processes, as controlled by Her Majesty's Inspectorate of Pollution (HMIP) (see below).

3.9 Another aspect of air pollution control covered in the CAA 1968, concerns the height of chimneys above a certain minimum size. Under the Building Regulations 1985, District Councils are required to assess the suitability of planned chimney heights for industrial premises. Heights must be sufficient to prevent emissions of smoke, dust, grit or gases becoming prejudicial to health or a nuisance. The chimneys of industrial furnaces and boilers require separate approval outside the specification guidelines presented in the Building Regulations 1985.

3.10 Recent additions have been made to the controls over smoke pollution. The Control of Smoke Pollution Act 1989 (CSPA 1989) extends the statutory nuisance coverage of the CAA 1956 to include smoke emitted from a private residence outside a Smoke Control Area. This only constitutes a statutory nuisance if it is prejudicial to health or a nuisance under the Public Health Act 1936. It also tightened controls over the emission of 'dark' smoke to be emitted from trade or industrial premises. A District Council now only has to substantiate that the conditions of burning certain materials would have led to the dark smoke emission rather than actually prove that this had taken place by monitoring at the time of emission. This goes some way to preventing the uncontrolled burning of smoke-emitting substances at night.

3.11 Standards for suspended particulates (smoke), within the European Community (EC) area, are given in a Directive on air quality (80/779/EEC). This prescribes guide and limit values for concentrations of smoke in air which now apply in the UK.

Noxious Pollutants

3.12 A wide range of industrial premises which have emissions to the atmosphere are controlled by HMIP. This body is primarily concerned with the control of noxious or offensive emissions of gases and fumes. Its powers are granted by the Alkali Act 1863, (AA 1863) the Alkali, etc. Works Regulation Act 1906, (AWRA 1906), the CAA 1968 and the Health and Safety at Work etc. Act 1974 (HSWA 1974). Powers of jurisdiction are restricted to a list of scheduled processes, which must be registered with HMIP. Registrable works are listed in the Health and Safety (Emissions into the Atmosphere) Regulations 1983, as amended in 1989. The latter bring the list of scheduled works more closely in line with the European Directive (84/360/EEC) on combating Atmospheric Pollution from Industrial Plant. The Control of Industrial Air Pollution (Registration of Works) Regulation 1989, prescribes the information which must be contained in applications to HMIP for the registration of works.

3.13 Atmospheric discharges from works where scheduled processes are undertaken are controlled either through fixed statutory limits on emissions or the use of 'best practicable means' (BPM) to minimise emissions. The latter is the more widely used. Generally, HMIP seeks to enforce compliance with statutory requirements by co-operation. Where this fails, the following measures are available:

* a letter of infraction, which states why a Company is in breach of its legal responsibilities. If the Company fails to comply with recommendations in the infraction letter, prosecution can ensue;

* an Improvement Notice may be issued where contravention of a statutory provision has been established. A right of appeal to tribunal exists;

* a Prohibition Notice may be served where HMIP are of the opinion that members of the public are at risk of serious personal injury. This requires immediate cessation of the operations causing the risk. HMIP may also control emissions of grit, dust and smoke from works undertaking a Scheduled process.

Vehicular Emissions

3.14 Pollution from road vehicles is controlled through regulations on fuel composition made under the COPA 1974 and regulations on vehicle construction and operation pursuant to the Road Traffic Act 1972 (RTA 1972). There are also numerous EC Directives concerning vehicular emissions.

3.15 EC Directive (70/220/EEC) sets limits for carbon monoxide (CO) and hydrocarbon (HC) emissions in petrol engine exhausts and has been amended several times. Other Directives have established limits on concentrations of CO, HC and nitrogen oxides (NO_x) in both petrol and diesel engined vehicles (88/76/EEC, 88/436/EEC, 89/458/EEC, 88/77/EEC). The sulphur and lead contents of fuel have been addressed in other Directives (75/716/EEC, 78/611/EEC). In the UK, the composition of motor fuel is governed by the Motor Fuel (Lead Content of Petrol) Regulations 1981 (amended in 1985) and the Motor Fuel (Sulphur Content of Gas Oil) Regulations 1976. These regulations have been used to implement the EC Directives.

3.16 The Motor Vehicles (Construction and Use) Regulations 1986 are concerned with emission standards and require all vehicles to be constructed so that no visible vapour or avoidable smoke is emitted. Amendments to several motor vehicle regulations in 1988, ensured that all new vehicles in the UK can run on unleaded petrol. As from October 1991, the MOT test will include an examination of gas emissions. In 1992, EC requirements will make the fitting of catalytic converters – which prevent most emissions from cars – compulsory to all new vehicles.

Other Pollutants

3.17 Action over the emission of odours can be taken under the nuisance provisions contained in Part III of the Public Health Act 1936. If odour problems are a recurring nuisance from a particular site, District Councils can serve a prohibition notice under the Public Health (Recurring Nuisances) Act 1969.

3.18 The EC has introduced air quality standards for sulphur dioxide (SO_2) and suspended particulates (smoke), nitrogen dioxide (NO_2) and lead through a series of Directives (80/779/EEC, 85/203/EEC, 82/884/EEC). These set guide and/or limit concentrations for each pollutant which have been implemented in the UK through the Air Quality Standards Regulations 1989.

3.19 Additional control is afforded through the limits on the sulphur content of fuel oils used in non-scheduled processes. The Oil Fuel (Sulphur Content of Gas Oil) Regulations Act 1976 specifies a maximum limit of 0.5% sulphur in gas oil used in any furnace or engine in Great Britain.

3.20 EC Directive (87/217/EEC) laid down standards for emissions of asbestos from asbestos works, and these have been implemented in the UK through the Control of Asbestos in the Air Regulations 1989.

Air Pollution Control

3.21 Powers of control are afforded by five means,

comprising:

* Common Law proceedings brought mainly by individuals;

* controlling new developments through the planning system and building regulations;

* local authority powers;

* HMIP controls over emissions from more complex industrial plant;

* police, through enforcement of the RTA 1972.

3.22 Individuals rarely use their powers in Common Law to bring private or public nuisance actions. This is mainly because of the costs and the difficulty of providing scientific evidence to substantiate a case.

3.23 Under the Town and Country Planning Act 1971, (TCPA 1971) and the Local Government, Planning and Land Act 1980, planning authorities may prevent unacceptable pollution from a development by refusing planning permission. Recognition that registered works may have an environmental impact is enshrined also in the Town and Country Planning Act (Use Classes) Orders, which require that all such works have a Special Industrial Use classification. Major developments involving significant environmental impact may also be subject to special impact assessment under the Town and Country Planning (Assessment of Environmental Effects) Regulations 1988. Land-use planning policies in Development Plans can also be used to secure longer-term improvements. Building regulations covering appliances used for heating and cooking state that appliances should be designed to burn only fuel gas, coke or anthracite. There are also regulations to cover flue design to prevent discharges prejudicial to health or causing a nuisance.

3.24 The COPA 1974 empowers District Councils to assess the scale of an air pollution problem by obtaining information about emissions. This can be done by issuing notices to an occupier of premises to obtain information concerning estimates of discharges. Otherwise, the Council may measure and record emissions on the premises providing it has issued a notice as to the nature of the monitoring to be carried out. An occupier of any premises (other than a private dwelling) may also be required to undertake monitoring on behalf of the Council. Information is usually sought directly from the polluter through less formal means.

3.25 Responsibility for enforcing statutory controls (other than those involving scheduled processes) lies with District Councils. In practice relatively few prosecutions are brought except in severe cases where there is an immediate threat to the public. Usually pollutant emissions are reduced by discussion with owners to persuade them to undertake remedial works or alter operating practices. This is partly because if the offender can show that BPM have been applied to prevent or reduce emissions, the Courts cannot impose disciplinary measures.

3.26 HMIP controls emissions from registered premises where scheduled processes take place.

The enforcement of the use of BPM has been the most widely used form of control. BPM are established by working groups which define what can reasonably be achieved on economic grounds using currently available technology and good working practices. They also include consideration of the benefits of pollution control measures upon the surrounding land use and local communities. However, the use of BPM will be superseded by new procedures contained in the EPA 1990 (see below).

Radioactivity

3.27 The bulk of legislation concerning the use of radioactive substances and the operation and construction of nuclear installations is provided by the Radioactive Substances Act 1960 (RSA 1960) and the Nuclear Installations Act 1965 (NIA 1965).

Nuclear Installations

3.28 For the purpose of legislation, nuclear installations are those which carry out one or more of the following:

* the use or production of atomic energy;

* operation of processes capable of emitting ionising radiation;

* storage, processing or disposal of nuclear fuel or other radioactive matter in bulk which has been produced or irradiated in the course of production of nuclear fuel.

3.29 The TCPA 1971 and the NIA 1965 control the siting of nuclear power stations. If a local planning authority objects to the siting, a public inquiry must be held. However, if the Secretary of State authorises the building of the plant he may, and normally does, direct that planning permission should be given.

3.30 Under the NIA 1965 the installation or operation of nuclear plant requires a nuclear site licence issued by the Health and Safety Executive (HSE). Operating without a licence or operating in breach of licence conditions are criminal offences. Previously, any person other than the United Kingdom Atomic Energy Authority (UKAEA) wishing to operate a site for the production of plutonium or uranium for irradiated matter (or uranium enrichment) required a written permit from the Secretary of State for Energy. From October 1990, the UKAEA will require a site licence for these processes.

3.31 The HSE attaches two schedules to the site licence. One describes the site being licensed and the other imposes conditions for monitoring site personnel and rules concerning the design, construction, maintenance and operation of plant on site. The Nuclear Installations Inspectorate (NII) makes a detailed assessment of each licensed site, to ensure that it complies with the safety principles established by them. They also monitor plant construction and ensure that it is inspected regularly once operational. The Inspectorate may shut down a plant if flaws are revealed. As installations reach the end of their design life, the NII carry out a long term safety review of the plant. From September 1990, British Nuclear Fuels were granted a new Model Site Licence. In common with all UK nuclear establishments, this licence has three schedules. The first describes the site, the second lists the conditions pertaining and the third formalises any arrangements transferred from previous licences.

3.32 As part of the licence conditions, an emergency plan must be provided which states first-aid practices, emergency services and monitoring procedures which will be used in the event of an incident. Emissions of ionising radiation, or of dangerous or toxic substances which cause death to persons inside or outside the plant, must be reported. The NIA 1965 requires that the report should be made by the quickest means available. Notifications are made to the NII in accordance with the Nuclear Installations (Dangerous Occurrences) Regulations 1965, the Nuclear Site Licences, the Ionising Radiations Regulations 1985 and, in certain circumstances, by specification from the Secretary of State for Energy.

Storage and Use of Radioactive Substances

3.33 The storage and use of radioactive substances is controlled by the RSA 1960. All premises which use significant amounts of radioactive substances must be registered with the Secretary of State for the Environment. An application for registration must include details of the premises, the substances used, the quantities involved and the way in which they are used. Accumulations or deposits of radioactive material are also covered by the Act. Persons wishing to accumulate or dispose of radioactive material require authorisation from the Secretary of State. The Ministry of Agriculture, Fisheries and Food (MAFF) also plays an important rôle in determining disposal and discharge limits. No authorisation for accumulations is required by the UKAEA, site licensees or government departments. Disposal on, or from, the premises of the UKAEA or a site licensee must be authorised by both the Secretary of State and MAFF.

Transport of Radioactive Substances

3.34 Transport of radioactive materials by road is covered by the Radioactive Substances (Carriage by Road) (Great Britain) Regulations 1974. Supplementary measures are contained in the Regulations for the Safe Transport of Radioactive Materials 1973, issued by the International Atomic Energy Authority (IAEA). There are no statutory controls for transport by rail. Control is exercised by British Railways Board Regulations and packaging standards must comply with IAEA regulations and methods laid down in British Standard 3895 (Part I, 1965). Fissile radioactive material may only be carried with the approval of the Department of the Environment and packaging for such material must be approved by the Secretary of State for the Environment. Sea carriage is controlled under the Merchant Shipping (Dangerous Goods) Rules.

Public Controls

3.35 An individual member of the public cannot easily exercise any rights with respect to the location or operation of nuclear installations. A large responsibility to protect the public interest rests with the NII and the HSE. In recent years, the nuclear industry has formed Local Liaison Committees to communicate with the local population. Site operation methods are discussed, together with the nature and toxicity of effluent discharges. Such committees exist at both of Lancashire's nuclear installations – Heysham and Springfields.

Proposed Changes in Air Pollution Control

3.36 The EPA 1990 introduces important new measures. Part I of the Act contains a new strategy for pollution control based on a more comprehensive and integrated approach and a better use of resources. Integrated Pollution Control (IPC) seeks to address the waste products of an industrial complex or process as a whole. Previously, air pollution control was applied entirely separately from liquid and solid waste discharges control. This was clearly inadequate, when the emission of waste to one medium nearly always has implications for other parts of the environment. For example, if emissions to the atmosphere are reduced then this will normally result in waste being diverted to another environmental medium.

3.37 Potentially more serious emissions from scheduled processes (listed under a new 'Schedule A'), and of listed noxious, or offensive, substances remain under the control of HMIP. The number of Schedule A processes in the UK will be reduced from 58 to approximately 32, grouped under six main headings, and subject to IPC measures. IPC is likely to apply to some 5,000 industrial operations nationwide. All new and substantially altered processes prescribed for IPC will require HMIP authorisation from January 1991. Existing operations will be reviewed and brought into line by April 1995, giving operators three to eight years to improve plant and operation processes.

3.38 Changes are also introduced to the controls afforded by application of BPM. Measures to alleviate aerial emissions will now be determined by the 'best available technology not entailing excessive cost' (BATNEEC). BATNEEC will be established in the same way as BPM were formerly determined.

3.39 District Councils will have powers of jurisdiction over a further group of processes (Schedule B) which will cover 25,000 operations in the UK from April 1991. This will extend the powers of control of local authorities over emissions of smoke, dust, grit, fume and odour.

3.40 Important new legislation also applies to the control of atmospheric emissions from incinerators. All chemical and toxic waste incinerators, and those with a capacity to burn at least one tonne of waste per hour, are under the jurisdiction of HMIP. New controls were included in the 1989 amendment of the Health and Safety (Emissions into the Atmosphere) Regulations 1983, made under the provisions of the HSWA 1974. They came into force in March 1989. There are also new EC directives for the operation and emission limits of municipal waste incinerators. Hospital waste incinerators

(Previously exempt from legislation) have been brought into line with other incinerators by the EPA 1990.

3.41 The EPA 1990 extends controls on the use of radioactive substances by giving the Secretary of State for the Environment powers to appoint inspectors to assist him in duties relating to the RSA 1960. A Chief Inspector will be appointed for England and Wales with a separate Inspector for Scotland. A scheme of fees and charges for authorisations and registrations under the Act will help pay for the administrative work involved.

3.42 The powers of Chief Inspectors will be the same as those currently held under the Act by the Secretary of State. Thus they may serve notices if any person fails, (or is likely to fail), to comply with the conditions of an authorisation or registration. A notice will include the Chief Inspector's opinion on the matter, the reasons for failure of compliance and remedial steps required within a given period.

3.43 A notice may be served for any activity involving the use, transport, disposal or accumulation of radioactive material if the activity poses an imminent risk to the environment or human health. This may be done regardless of whether the activity accords with registration or authorisation guidelines.

3.44 One of the most important amendments concerns the removal of exemptions currently afforded to the UKAEA in respect of authorisations and registrations under the RSA 1960. This amendment brings the UKAEA into line with other users of radioactive substances.

Public Information

3.45 The EPA requires HMIP and District Councils to maintain public registers containing particulars of:

* applications for authorisations made to, and granted by, the authorities (and the conditions attached to authorisations);

* revocations of authorisations;

* Variation notices, enforcement notices and prohibition notices issued;

* directions given under Part I of the EPA by the Secretary of State;

* appeals under Section 14 of the EPA;

* convictions for any offence under Section 20 of the EPA;

* information obtained or received in pursuance of the conditions of authorisations.

The register maintained by District Councils must also contain prescribed particulars of HMIP registered works within the Council's area. No information will be included which, in the opinion of the Secretary of State, will prejudice commercial interests. In effect, it appears that the public will have only limited increased access to information above that which is available now. The major improvement will be that data will be gathered together in one place.

Organisations

International

3.46 Global pollution-related problems, linked to the greenhouse effect and ozone depletion, present the world community with its greatest environmental challenges. International action and co-operation is essential if the challenges are to be met, and the United Nations Organisation and its agencies like the United Nations Environment Programme (UNEP), are playing an increasingly important part. UNEP has been addressing the issue of global warming via its Intergovernmental Panel on Climate Change (see below), whilst collaboration between individual governments is increasing. The Montreal Protocol on reducing CFC emissions, signed in 1987, is a good example of the latter.

European

3.47 The EC has taken a leading rôle in environmental protection measures, principally through the Directives referred to above. Current policy is directed at ensuring international agreement on the control of long-range transboundary pollutants. Movements of polluted air masses across Europe and the UK can cause pollution problems at distance from the source and the EC is seeking to obtain international co-operation to lessen the incidence of such problems by reducing source emissions throughout Europe.

Central Government

3.48 The Government is required to implement EC Directives by drafting leglislation to supplement existing statutory controls. The DOE is responsible for all matters connected with the environment, including air pollution. In co-operation with the Department of Trade and Industry (DTI), it is responsible for establishing national monitoring programmes of atmospheric pollutants. These programmes are co-ordinated through the DTI's Warren Spring Laboratory, which is the major source of information regarding the distribution of atmospheric pollution in the UK.

3.49 The Department of Transport (DTp) is responsible for enforcing controls on vehicle manufacture and emissions. The police also have duties with respect to ensuring that vehicles causing an obvious pollution problem are prevented from using the roads.

3.50 The Government is also responsible for controls over the use of radioactive substances and for enforcing legislation. MAFF plays a role in the assessment of applications for authorisation under the RSA 1960. MAFF also undertakes a comprehensive monitoring programme and identifies the 'critical groups' in relation to radioactive discharges (see below).

3.51 HMIP has the primary responsiblity for controlling noxious industrial emissions. They have powers to inspect registered works and are responsible for introducing and enforcing the new IPC measures contained in the EPA 1990.

Table 5 EC Directives on Emissions of Smoke, Lead, Sulphur Dioxide and Nitrogen Dioxide

Substance	Directive	Guide values[1]	Limit values[1]
Nitrogen Dioxide	(85/203/EEC)	50% of the values should not exceed 50 ug/m^3 (measured as the mean of hourly concentrations in any one year) and 98% should not exceed 135 ug/m^3.	98% of the mean hourly concentration should not exceed 200 ug/m^3.
Sulphur Dioxide	(80/799/EEC)	The annual mean of daily concentrations should not exceed 40–60 ug/m^3 and the daily mean value should not exceed 100–150 ug/m^3.	The annual median of daily values should not exceed 120 ug/m^3 if smoke is less than 34 ug/m^3 and 80 ug/m^3 if smoke is greater than or equal to 34 ug/m^3. The median of daily winter values (Oct–March) should not exceed 180 ug/m^3 if smoke is less than 51 ug/m^3 or 130 ug/m^3 if smoke is greater than or equal to 51 ug/m^3. 98% of daily values should not exceed 350 ug/m^3 if smoke is less than 128 ug/m^3 and 250 ug/m^3 if smoke is greater than or equal to 128 ug/m^3.
Smoke[2]	(80/779/EEC)	The annual mean of daily values should not exceed 34–51 ug/m^3 and the mean value over any one day should not exceed 85–128 ug/m^3.	The annual median of daily values should not exceed 68 ug/m^3 and the median of daily winter values should not exceed 111 ug/m^3. 90% of daily values should not exceed 213 ug/m^3.
Lead	(82/884/EEC)	—	Annual mean concentrations of lead in air should not exceed 2 ug/m^3.

Source: Warren Spring Laboratory

Note: [1]*Guide values are not mandatory and Member States are advised to meet them. Limit values are mandatory and must be met or the Member State is in breach of the Directive.*
[2]*Limit and guide values given for smoke are for the BSI method as used in the UK, whereas those given in the EC Directive are for the OECD method. The relationship between the two methods is given as: OECD = BSI divided by 0.85.*

3.52 The HSE are responsible for regulating the nuclear industry, by issuing site licences and attaching initial conditions prior to construction. The NII assess plant safety and emergency procedures as well as conducting routine inspections of equipment.

3.53 The National Radiological Protection Board (NRPB) work closely with the nuclear industry using current research on the toxicological effects of radiation to devise guidelines for permissible and acceptable levels of exposure of workers and members of the public.

Local Government

3.54 District Council Environmental Health Departments are the main regulatory bodies for local air pollution control. They are also the main point of contact for the public on pollution matters. Districts are responsible for enforcing controls over all emissions (except those covered by HMIP), including most smoke, grit, dust, fume and odour emissions. Local authority powers have been extended under the EPA1990, because the number of processes controlled by HMIP has been reduced so that they can concentrate on IPC. Thus, a greater load is being placed on the Environmental Health Officers.

Other Organisations

3.55 Environmental pressure groups such as Greenpeace and Friends of the Earth campaign, comment and draw attention to air pollution issues, globally, nationally and locally. The National Society for Clean Air (NSCA) is one of the most authoritative organisations concerned with atmospheric pollution in the UK. They publish information and reports on environmental, and especially atmospheric, issues and have an annual conference which deals with a current matter of particular concern. Local Authorities are important sponsors of NSCA.

Air Quality in Lancashire

Introduction

3.56 This section deals with the incidence and environmental impact of the major pollutants affecting Lancashire's atmosphere. A variety of sources have been used, though the amount and quality of data varies from pollutant to pollutant. Information for smoke and sulphur dioxide (SO_2) and radiation is reasonably extensive, whilst that for ozone, nitrogen oxides, carbon oxides, grit, dust and fumes is patchy at best. In a number of cases, Lancashire-specific data is non-existent and UK material has been relied upon.

3.57 Each pollutant is considered in turn, and available data are presented for smoke and SO_2, nitrogen oxides, grit, dust and fumes, noxious and offensive emissions, odour, lead, ozone and air-related radiation. Because of the significance of their contribution to air quality, vehicle exhaust emissions, acid rain and the phenomenon of global warming are dealt with separately. Because these conditions are fed by many of the same gases, there is some limited, but unavoidable, repetition.

Smoke and SO$_2$

3.58 Smoke is made up of suspended particulate matter or liquids of varying composition, depending upon the source. It is most often produced by incomplete combustion of fossil fuels. Larger particles are not generally a problem to human health since they are trapped by nasal hair and mucous. High concentrations of smaller particles (less than 3 um), however, in low to medium doses can disturb respiratory tissues. In extreme circumstances, the lungs can be coated with particles, causing asphyxiation.

3.59 SO$_2$ is a colourless gas produced largely through burning fossil fuels. In some instances it can be an irritant to eyes and mucous membranes but these effects are generally transient. However, consequences can be serious in people whose cardio-respiratory systems are impaired.

3.60 Since the establishment of the DTI National Air Pollution Survey (NAPS) in 1961/62, a considerable amount of information has become available on the distribution of concentrations of smoke and SO$_2$. Each District Council was requested to establish and maintain monitoring points approved by the DTI's Warren Spring Laboratory. Since 1982, NAPS has been reorganised because urban smoke and SO$_2$ levels have fallen. The revision was planned in part to fulfil Britain's responsibilities under the EC Directive 80/779/EEC, which set health protection standards for levels of smoke and SO$_2$. Table 5 explains the prescribed values. Initially, NAPS was concerned with urban concentrations but in 1987 it was extended to include 35 rural areas. This was due to the increased interest in the transport of airborne pollutants from other regions.

3.61 Responsibility for compliance with the EC Directive lies with the Government, who in turn base their decision on NAPS findings. This measures daily average levels of smoke and SO$_2$. Results are sent monthly to Warren Spring Laboratory where they are analysed in accordance with Directive requirements. Information is passed back to the DOE in respect of sites close to breaching limit values. The DOE advises District Councils to implement smoke control programmes where the Directive levels could be breached.

3.62 There were 13 locations in Lancashire for monitoring smoke and SO$_2$ in 1979/80. These were:

* Lancaster: Caton;
* Blackpool: Blackpool;
* Fylde: Lytham St. Annes (smoke only);
* South Ribble: Leyland;
* Chorley: Chorley;
* Blackburn: Blackburn;
* Hyndburn: Accrington;
* Pendle: Barnoldswick;
* Rossendale: Bacup, Haslingden, Helmshore, Rawtenstall, Whitworth.

3.63 Today, rationalisation of NAPS in the light of air quality improvements since the 1960s, means that monitoring has been reduced to the five sites shown on Figure 20 (Chorley, Bacup, Rawtenstall, Accrington and Blackpool). Figures 21 to 25 show smoke and SO$_2$ levels recorded at the five sites

Figure 20
Air Monitoring Sites in Lancashire.

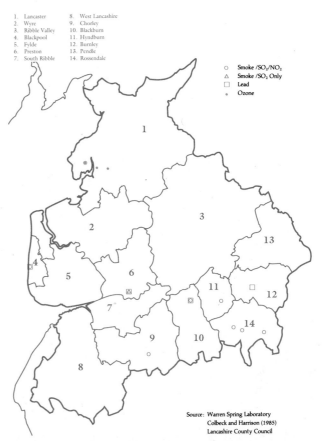

Source: Warren Spring Laboratory
Colbeck and Harrison (1985)
Lancashire County Council

between 1979 and 1988, set against the corresponding EC guide and limit values. In general, they show a gradual decrease in concentrations over the period. The exception is Accrington, where SO$_2$ levels have risen sharply since 1985 and by 1988 were not far short of the EC guide limit. The reason for this is unknown. All other cases now give concentrations which are below EC guide levels, with SO$_2$ concentrations averaging 20–25 ug/m^3 above smoke concentrations. This is a significant change from 9 years ago when all but Blackpool gave results above the EC guide level for SO$_2$ and the EC guide level for smoke was exceeded in Chorley.

3.64 Chorley, Bacup, Rawtenstall and Accrington all have considerably higher values for SO$_2$ than Blackpool. This is because they are located in the more industrial parts of Lancashire and in areas more likely to receive polluted air masses entering the County. A local authority survey (for 1988/89) carried out in four schools in Preston revealed smoke and SO$_2$ concentrations well below EC limit levels and in all cases within or below EC guide levels.

3.65 Smoke Control Orders declared under the CAA 1956 and 1968 are in force in eleven Lancashire Districts. These are summarised in Table 6. The extent of Smoke Control Areas covered by these Orders is shown in Figure 26. This shows the predominance of smoke control in urban and eastern areas of the County. Seven Districts have completed their Smoke Control programmes. The use of such Orders has been the major contributor to the decline in smoke and SO$_2$ concentrations in the County.

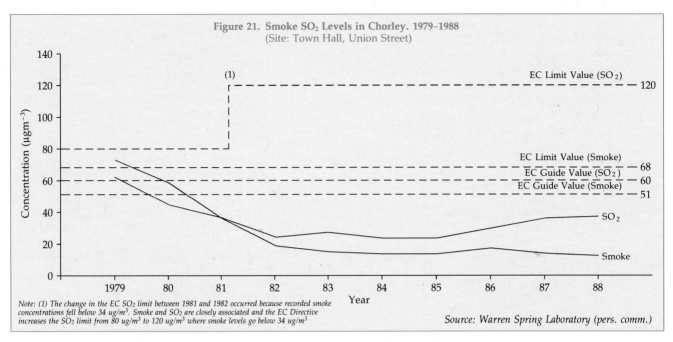

Figure 21. Smoke SO₂ Levels in Chorley. 1979–1988
(Site: Town Hall, Union Street)

Note: (1) The change in the EC SO₂ limit between 1981 and 1982 occurred because recorded smoke concentrations fell below 34 ug/m³. Smoke and SO₂ are closely associated and the EC Directive increases the SO₂ limit from 80 ug/m³ to 120 ug/m³ where smoke levels go below 34 ug/m³

Source: Warren Spring Laboratory (pers. comm.)

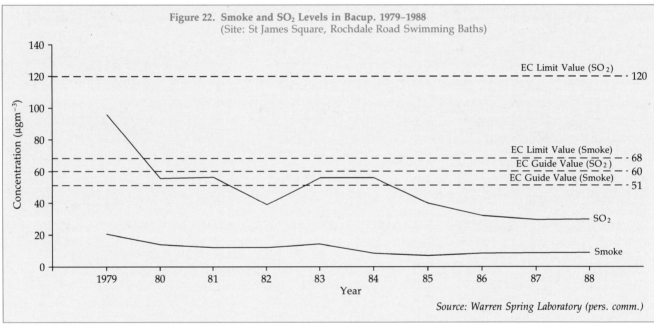

Figure 22. Smoke and SO₂ Levels in Bacup. 1979–1988
(Site: St James Square, Rochdale Road Swimming Baths)

Source: Warren Spring Laboratory (pers. comm.)

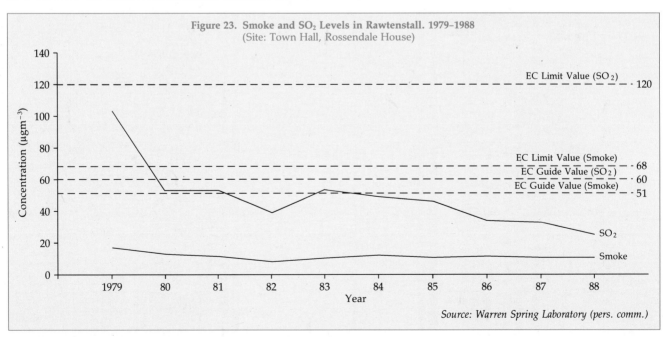

Figure 23. Smoke and SO₂ Levels in Rawtenstall. 1979–1988
(Site: Town Hall, Rossendale House)

Source: Warren Spring Laboratory (pers. comm.)

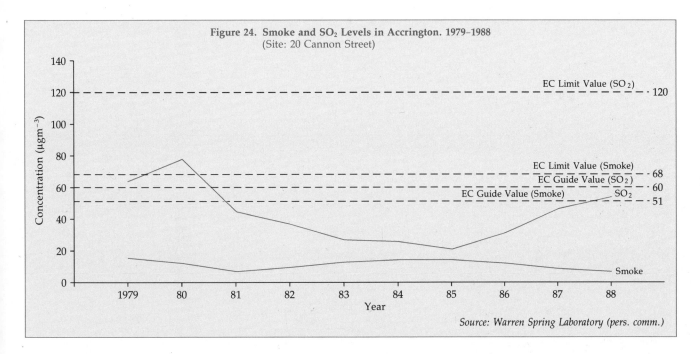

Figure 24. Smoke and SO₂ Levels in Accrington. 1979–1988
(Site: 20 Cannon Street)

Source: Warren Spring Laboratory (pers. comm.)

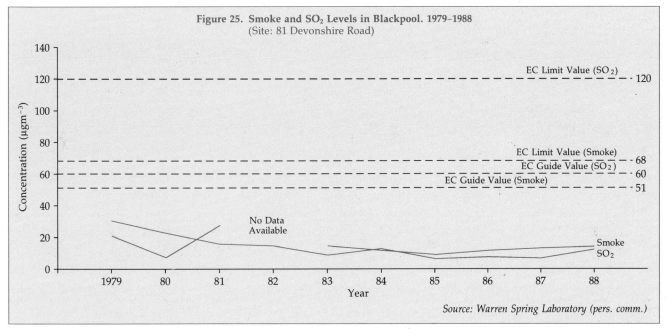

Figure 25. Smoke and SO₂ Levels in Blackpool. 1979–1988
(Site: 81 Devonshire Road)

Source: Warren Spring Laboratory (pers. comm.)

3.66 Emissions of dark or black smoke, or any emission of smoke in a Smoke Control Area, are offences under the CAAs 1956 and 1968 and render the polluters liable to prosecution by the District Council. Contraventions of the CAAs are recorded by Environmental Health Departments and incidence varies from year to year throughout the County. The number of smoke-related contraventions in Lancashire are given in Figure 27. These are usually remedied informally by District Council Environmental Health Officers without resorting to prosecution.

3.67 An independent study carried out in 1977 in association with Lancaster University (Harrison and McCartney, 1980) addressed airborne pollution, including SO₂, within the more rural parts of North West England. Part of the study was carried out in the centre of the Heysham Peninsula in Lancaster District. The site was chosen because there appeared to be only a limited source of locally

derived air pollutants in the area. The results revealed that concentrations of pollutants measured at the site were probably associated with regional transport into the area. In particular, SO₂ blown into the area was greater than that from local sources, even under the most unfavourable conditions for pollution dispersal. This would suggest that the more rural parts of Lancashire may be subject to levels of airborne pollutants approaching those found in our towns.

3.68 Lancashire's own smoke and SO₂ emissions obviously contribute to local levels in our own lower atmosphere. However, there is a substantial, albeit discontinuous, supply from other parts of the UK and Europe, brought in by slow-moving air waves under favourable meteorological conditions. Whatever controls of smoke and SO₂ emissions exist within Lancashire, co-operation on a national and international level is thus essential if overall levels of these pollutants are to be reduced.

Figure 26
Smoke Control Orders in Lancashire. 1989

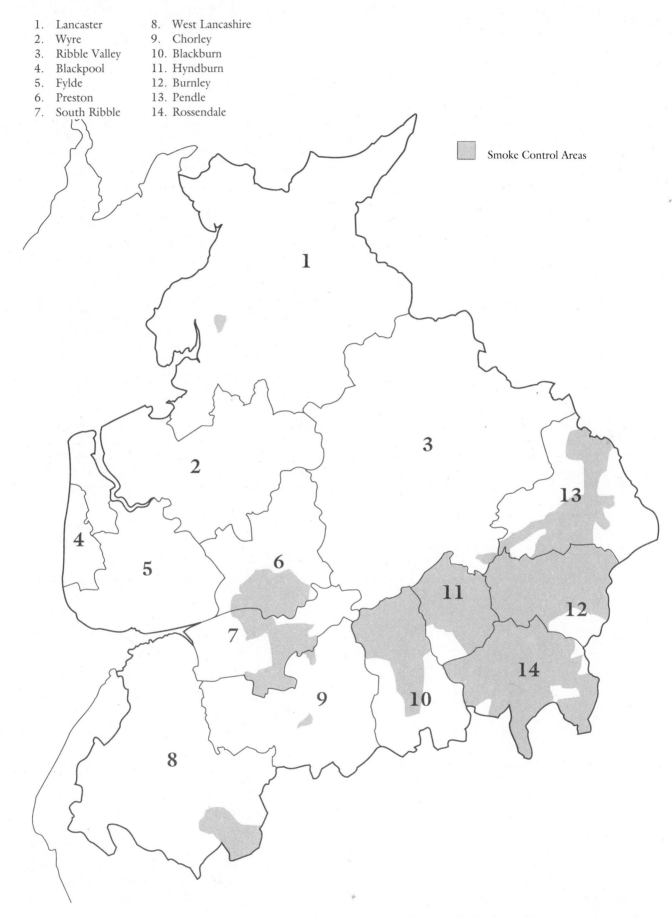

1. Lancaster
2. Wyre
3. Ribble Valley
4. Blackpool
5. Fylde
6. Preston
7. South Ribble
8. West Lancashire
9. Chorley
10. Blackburn
11. Hyndburn
12. Burnley
13. Pendle
14. Rossendale

Smoke Control Areas

Source: District Councils

Table 6 Smoke Control Orders in Lancashire. 1989

District	Number of Smoke Control Orders	Number of Premises Covered
Lancaster	8	9,478
Wyre	–	–
Ribble Valley	2	848
Blackpool	–	–
Fylde	–	–
Preston	54	34,000
South Ribble	22	21,647
West Lancashire	8	14,236
Chorley	3	1,301
Blackburn	42	51,345
Hyndburn	40	37,976
Burnley	24	42,050
Pendle	38	29,500
Rossendale	18	23,609
LANCASHIRE	259	265,990

Source: District Councils

Nitrogen Oxides

3.69 Nitrogen oxides (NO_x) are formed during combustion processes when nitrogen, in either the fuel or in the air, combines with oxygen. Effects of NO_x on health are varied and include respiratory problems. They can also adversely affect plant growth. Nitrogen oxides contribute to both global warming and acid rain (see below). The main oxide contributing to acid rain is nitrogen dioxide (NO_2).

3.70 A national monitoring survey, co-ordinated by Warren Spring Laboratory, was set up by the

DOE in 1986 using 363 (mainly) urban sites (also including SO_2 monitoring). Concentrations of NO_2 across the UK are shown in Figure 28. Most sites at risk of exceeding the EC Directive limits are located in London, though the eastern parts of Lancashire fall within the next most serious band.

3.71 The results of the survey generally reveal highest NO_2 concentrations near busy roads and in urban areas. The extent of the monitoring does not, however, show the potential for long-distance movement of NO_2 within air masses to rural areas; a phenomenon experienced in Lancashire (Harrison and McCartney, 1980).

3.72 NO_2 monitoring is an ongoing programme and, despite a recent reduction in the number of monitoring sites, information on levels of NO_2 in the UK will continue to be available. The original monitoring survey contained eight monitoring sites within Lancashire. These are shown on Figure 20 and listed in Table 7 with their monthly observed concentrations. The EC guide and limit values correspond to $135 \, ug/m^3$ and $200 \, ug/m^3$ respectively and all Lancashire sites had concentrations below the EC guide level. If future National plans to reduce emissions of NO_2 succeed, it is unlikely that Lancashire will experience any increases in NO_2 concentrations.

3.73 Additional data on NO_2 for two Lancashire Districts is provided by the Manchester Air Pollution Advisory Council (MAPAC). MAPAC is a consortium of 17 local authorities, including Rossendale and West Lancashire District Councils. A recent survey conducted by MAPAC, monitored levels at 6 sites in these Districts. Results are presented in Table 8. They show NO_2 concentrations below EC guide values, and reinforce the results given in Table 7.

Grit, Dust and Fumes

3.74 These pollutants are derived from sources like furnaces, construction sites, and quarries. Grit, dust and fumes from industrial plants undertaking

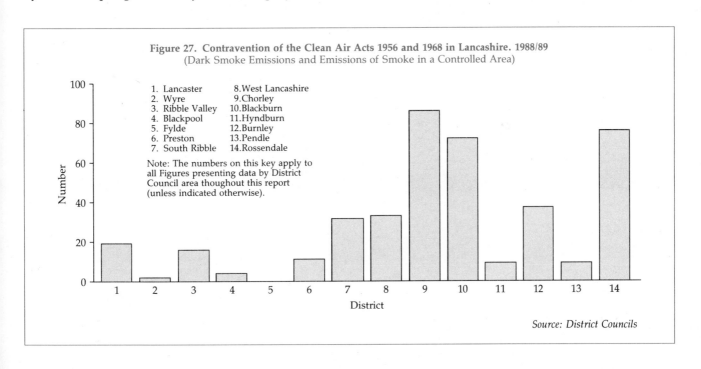

Figure 27. Contravention of the Clean Air Acts 1956 and 1968 in Lancashire. 1988/89
(Dark Smoke Emissions and Emissions of Smoke in a Controlled Area)

1. Lancaster
2. Wyre
3. Ribble Valley
4. Blackpool
5. Fylde
6. Preston
7. South Ribble
8. West Lancashire
9. Chorley
10. Blackburn
11. Hyndburn
12. Burnley
13. Pendle
14. Rossendale

Note: The numbers on this key apply to all Figures presenting data by District Council area thoughout this report (unless indicated otherwise).

Source: District Councils

Figure 28
Mean NO$_2$ Concentration within the Lower
Atmosphere in the UK. 1987

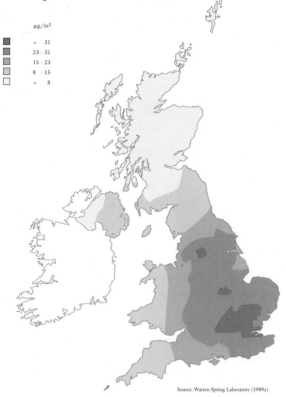

μg/m^3

■ > 31
▨ 23 - 31
▨ 15 - 23
▨ 8 - 15
□ < 8

Source: Warren Spring Laboratory (1989a)

3.75 There are no emission data available for sites in Lancashire. The number of furnaces in the County is also difficult to determine, partly because there is no clear definition of what constitutes a furnace, but also because not all District Councils keep comprehensive lists. All new furnaces, (except for small domestic types), must be notified to District Councils under CAA 1956. However, they are only required to approve certain larger installations, or those where the installer seeks prior approval. Effectively, therefore, local authorities control only a minority of furnaces.

Table 8 Mean NO$_2$ Concentrations in Rossendale and West Lancashire Districts. 1988–1989

District	Location	Mean Concentration (ug/m^3)
Rossendale	Back Street	105
,,	Haslingden Town Hall	88
,,	Bacup Grammar School	73
,,	Bacup Baths	74
,,	Whitworth Council Offices	77
West Lancashire	Burscough St., Ormskirk	120

Source: Manchester Air Pollution Advisory Council (1989)

Notes: EC guide value = 135 ug/m^3
EC limit value = 200 ug/m^3

scheduled processes are under HMIP control, but other sources are the responsibility of District Councils. These pollutants are defined according to particle size:

* Grit – particles exceeding 76 um in diameter, (Clean Air Act, 1971);

* Dust – small, solid particles between 1 um and 75 um diameter, British Standard BS 3405);

* Fumes – any airborne solid matter smaller than dust, (CAA 1968).

3.76 In urban areas, furnace-related dust, grit and fume emissions arise primarily from industrial plants, hospitals, crematoria and, to a lesser extent, from public and domestic properties. Hospital incinerators and crematoria are major potential sources. There are currently 29 hospital incinerators in Lancashire and eight crematoria, these being shown in Figure 29. Only South Ribble and Pendle Districts have neither type of furnace. A 1988 County Council Survey of NHS and private hospital incinerators found that of the 31 then

Table 7 NO$_2$ Concentrations at Sites in Lancashire, July–December 1986

Site	July	August	September	October	November	December	Mean
Accrington	50.5	73.4	73.4	ND	87.2	82.6	73.4
Bacup	59.7	68.8	68.8	87.2	91.8	87.2	77.1
Blackburn (1)	64.2	59.7	91.8	114.7	87.2	110.1	87.6
Blackburn (2)	34.4	59.7	73.4	87.2	91.8	82.6	71.6
Blackpool	55.1	64.2	105.5	101.0	25.7	68.8	70.2
Chorley	59.9	101.0	16.1	123.9	123.9	101.0	87.2
Haslingden	59.7	68.8	73.4	96.4	101.0	87.2	80.8
Rawtenstall	82.6	91.8	119.3	119.3	101.0	59.7	95.4

Source: Warren Spring Laboratory (1989b)

Notes: ND – no data available
All measurements in ug/m^3
EC guide value = 135 ug/m^3
EC limit value = 200 ug/m^3

operating, 19 had a variable performance, 10 performed badly and only 2 were performing well. Since the Survey, two incinerators have closed and several others have been modified or refitted.

3.77 Lancashire also experiences dust and grit emissions from construction sites and quarries. Quarrying of limestone, sandstone and millstone grit causes dust and grit problems in Lancaster, Ribble Valley, Rossendale and Chorley. Industrial premises such as cement works are also major dust and grit sources in the County.

Noxious Emissions

3.78 Under the new system introduced by the EPA 1990, HMIP will be responsible for all emissions from registered works, (i.e. those which have been identified as requiring IPC). HMIP will control all emissions from these works to air, water or land on the basis of the BATNEEC principle.

3.79 Lancashire has 55 registered works at present (prior to any incorporation of the new style authorisations) which are relatively evenly distributed between Districts. These are listed in Appendix B, whilst the distributions of registered works and processes are illustrated in Figures 30 and 31 respectively. The list of scheduled processes in Lancashire, and the nature of their emissions, are given in Appendix C. Blackpool is the only District which has no registered premises. The range of works include chemical production plants (acid production in particular), toxic waste incinerators, metal works and tar works. It should be noted that each works may have a varying number of scheduled processes. In terms of the potential polluting impact of a works it is usually the number of individual processes which is of particular importance. Thus, while Wyre Borough Council has only three works, there are a total of 17 registered processes operating at these premises.

3.80 There were no infractions, improvement or prohibition notices issued for Lancashire premises during 1988/89 (Her Majesty's Inspectorate of Pollution, 1990). However, a number of complaints were dealt with during the year. These included:

* a spillage of ethyl acetate and leakages of hydrogen chloride, phosgene and monochlorobenzene, plus odour problems at ICI Petrochemicals and Polymers Ltd., Thornton Cleveleys;

* odours associated with the bisulphate and sulphide processes at William Blythes and Co. Ltd., Hapton;

* a chlorine gas leak leading to the evacuation of local residents arising from Westbond Chemicals, Oakenclough near Garstang (Her Majesty's Inspectorate of Pollution, 1990).

3.81 The new regulations will also increase the workload of District Council Environmental Health Departments, because they are now responsible for a wider range of processes and premises which cause atmospheric emissions. In general, these 'Schedule B' processes are those which give rise to emissions of smoke, grit, dust, fume or odour. Such works will be registered with, and authorised, by District Councils. The number of Schedule B processes has yet to be determined for four Lancashire Districts. Those Districts where numbers have been determined are shown in Figure 32.

Odour

3.82 It is usual to describe odour by the nature of the process causing it. Most arise from industrial or agricultural operations and processes. Process odours, especially where animal or vegetable matter is heated, are often complex mixtures of many substances.

3.83 In recent years, 'odour strength measurements' have been used to gauge the effect of specific sources and to study their distribution in the community. The place of odour emission can then be investigated to determine which operations contribute to the total odour emission rate. Abatement equipment can be used to remove or dilute the offending odour.

3.84 In Lancashire, public complaints have related to both agricultural and industrial sources. A list of such sources is found in Table 9 whilst the numbers of complaints by District Council in 1988/89 are given in Figure 33. The total for the County in that year was 765.

3.85 Industrial plants dealing with organic chemicals or processing animal by-products cause particular problems in some parts of the County. Indeed, the number of odour complaints in connection with industrial premises almost doubled between 1988/89 and 1989/90, despite the number of premises remaining constant. One of the most intractable problems concerns the rubber chemicals plant operated by ICI Chemicals and Polymers Ltd. on behalf of Vulnax International Ltd., at Thornton Cleveleys (Her Majesty's Inspectorate of Pollution, 1990). Its source is a particular mercaptan compound which has an odour threshold of only 4 parts per billion.

3.86 Further advances in the control of odours will depend on improved technology and the effectiveness of BATNEEC, but a more thorough and detailed approach to monitoring and recording odour complaints would undoubtedly assist. The effectiveness of applying enforcement action has also been demonstrated in Burnley. In 1986/87, there were 391 complaints from two industrial premises in the town, indicating a major odour problem. The following year revealed an improved situation with only 38 complaints from four industrial premises, following a prosecution for breaching the odour control legislation brought by the Borough Council.

Lead

3.87 Almost all lead (Pb) in air, soil, water and the built environment arises from human activities, although there is a natural, low-level release through weathering at the earth's surface. Mining, smelting and oil refining have been largely responsible for increased concentrations, particularly in air. Increases in environmental lead levels began in the Industrial Revolution, but totals have accelerated in the last fifty years. Lead is a cumulative

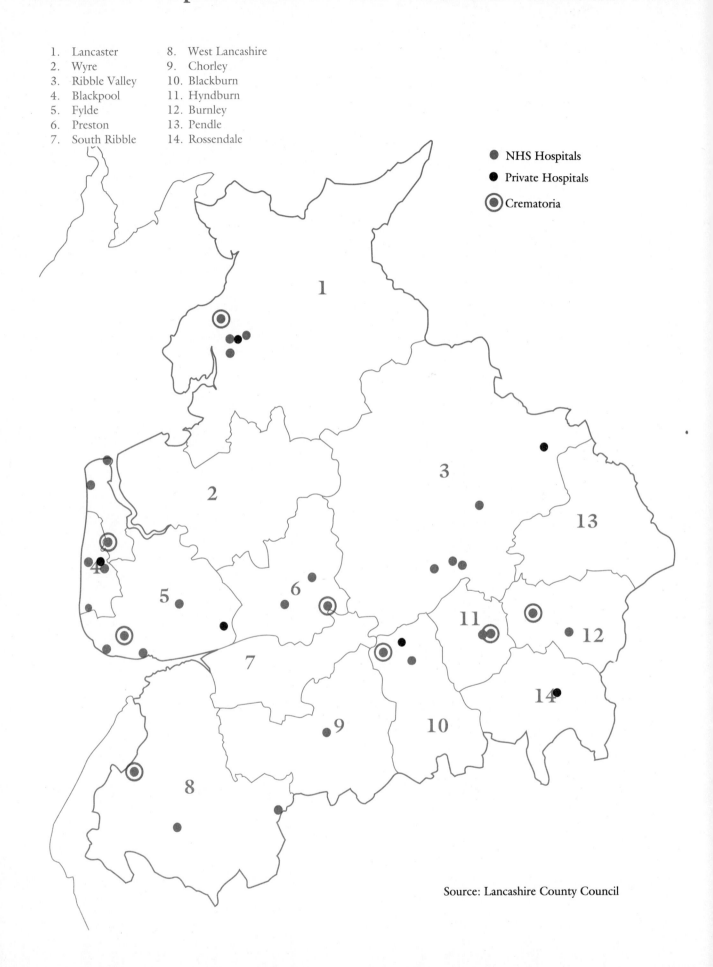

Figure 29

Location of Hospital Incinerators and Crematoria in Lancashire . 1990

1. Lancaster
2. Wyre
3. Ribble Valley
4. Blackpool
5. Fylde
6. Preston
7. South Ribble

8. West Lancashire
9. Chorley
10. Blackburn
11. Hyndburn
12. Burnley
13. Pendle
14. Rossendale

● NHS Hospitals

● Private Hospitals

◉ Crematoria

Source: Lancashire County Council

Figure 30
Location of Works Registered with HMIP in Lancashire. 1990

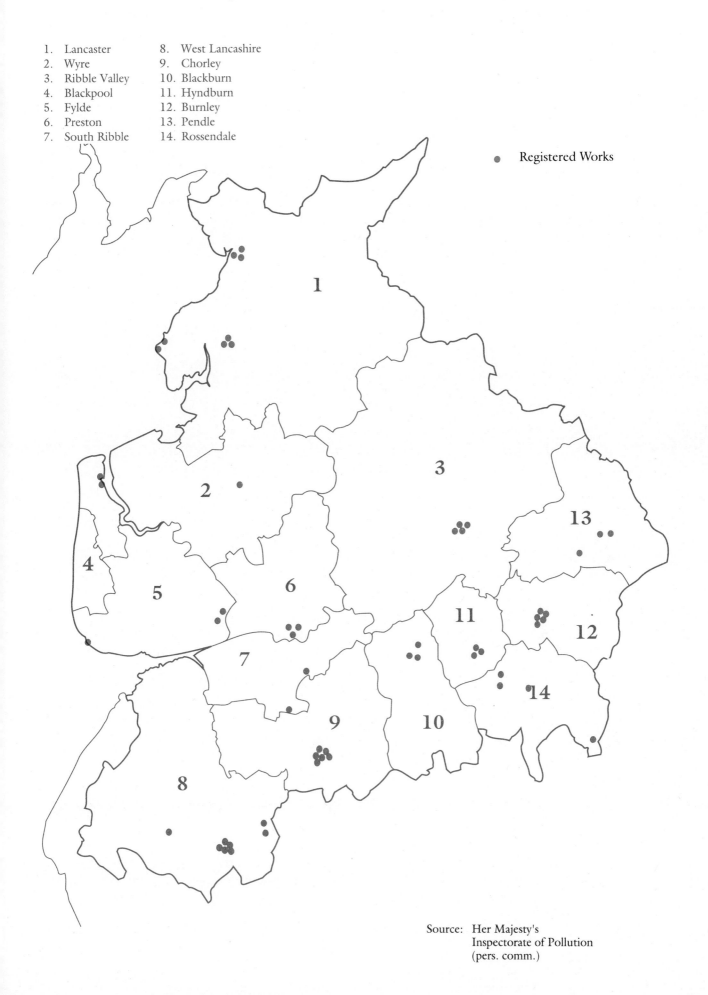

1. Lancaster
2. Wyre
3. Ribble Valley
4. Blackpool
5. Fylde
6. Preston
7. South Ribble
8. West Lancashire
9. Chorley
10. Blackburn
11. Hyndburn
12. Burnley
13. Pendle
14. Rossendale

● Registered Works

Source: Her Majesty's
Inspectorate of Pollution
(pers. comm.)

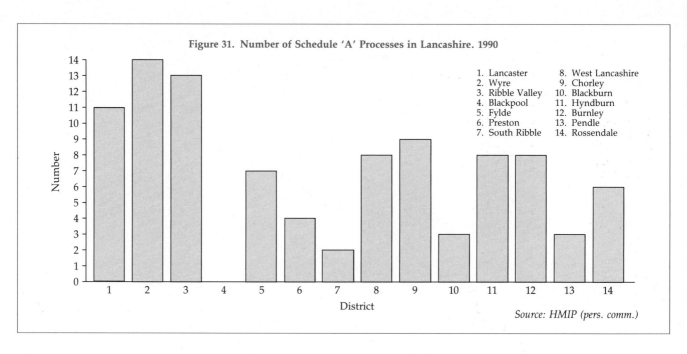

Figure 31. Number of Schedule 'A' Processes in Lancashire. 1990

1. Lancaster
2. Wyre
3. Ribble Valley
4. Blackpool
5. Fylde
6. Preston
7. South Ribble
8. West Lancashire
9. Chorley
10. Blackburn
11. Hyndburn
12. Burnley
13. Pendle
14. Rossendale

Source: HMIP (pers. comm.)

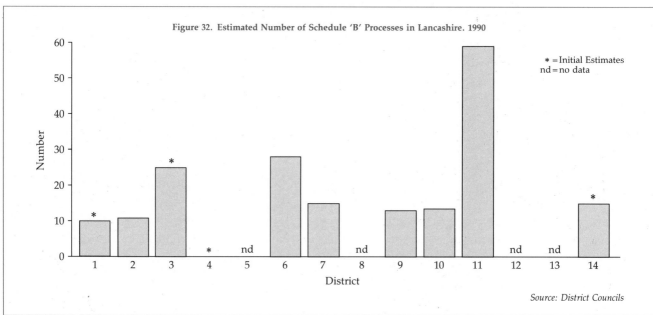

Figure 32. Estimated Number of Schedule 'B' Processes in Lancashire. 1990

* = Initial Estimates
nd = no data

Source: District Councils

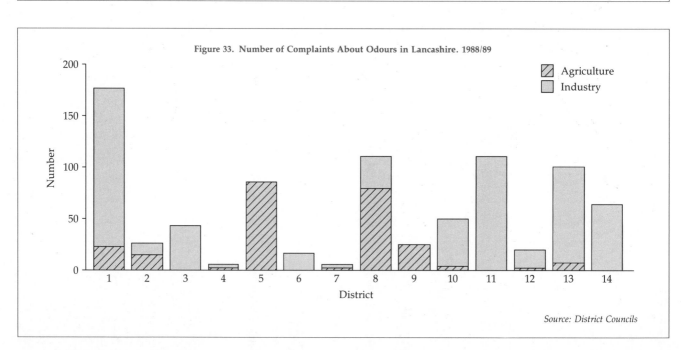

Figure 33. Number of Complaints About Odours in Lancashire. 1988/89

Agriculture
Industry

Source: District Councils

Table 9	Sources of Odour Complaints in Lancashire	
Agricultural Sources	**Industrial Sources**	
Slurry/manure spreading	Textile printing/dyeing/finishing	
Livestock buildings	Vehicle spraying booths	
Slurry/manure storage	Manufacturing joiners – lacquer spray plant	
Silage dumps	Wallpaper manufacture	
Animal feed processing	Vinyl wallcovering manufacture	
Mushroom farm	Car insulation manufacture (Phenol resins)	
Maggot farm	Fibre glass manufacture	
Mink farm	Pet food manufacture	
	Fish food manufacture	
	Cold blast cupola furnace (fume)	
	Animal by-products	
	Vinyl coating	
	Carpet making	
	Solvent recovery	
	Plastic manufacture	
	Adhesives and tape manufacture	
	Asphalt and tape manufacture	
	Asphalt depot	
	Metal castings	
	Shoe factory	
	Chemical works	
	Fish meal works	
	Plastic recycling	
	Paper making	

Source: District Councils

poison and can impair brain functions, especially in children.

3.88   Once released into the environment, lead can be trapped within 'sinks' such as soil and water bodies. From these and other sources, some lead can find its way into the food chain, domestic water supplies and the air. About 28% of lead assimilated by the body comes from the air. Inhaled lead is derived from petrol combustion (about 80% according to National Society for Clean Air, 1990) , industrial emissions (about 10%), tobacco smoke and resuspended dust. Ingested lead is derived from food and drink, water, dust and soil, paints, domestic utensils, toys, cosmetics and other miscellaneous sources.

3.89   The EC Directive 82/884/EEC requires that the annual mean concentration of lead in air does not exceed 2.0 ug/m^3. It is estimated that the concentration of lead in air in rural areas is usually below 0.15 ug/m^3 and most urban areas will have levels below 1.0 ug/m^3. In 1980, a report by a DHSS working party, ('Lead and Health'), revealed that airborne lead was only a minor contributor to body lead levels. Nevertheless, it recommended action to keep the annual concentrations of lead in air below 2.0 ug/m^3.

3.90   Studies on the health effects of lead on urban populations have shown that blood lead levels for UK cities are generally 20–30 ug Pb/100 ml blood, with an average of 23 ug Pb/100 ml blood. The EC recommended limit is 35 ug Pb/100 ml of blood and the revised UK threshold is 25 ug Pb/100 ml blood.

3.91   There have been a number of studies of lead in Lancashire's environment, carried out jointly between 1983 and 1989 by the County and District Councils. The use of similar sampling and analysis techniques allows data for 1983 to 1989 to be compared:

*   in 1983/84 four monitoring points were established close to schools in Blackpool and Preston (mean lead in air concentrations ranged from 0.18 to 0.33 ug/m^3);

*   in 1984/5, monitoring points were set up around four Lancashire factories (including a battery works, mixed industrial complex and fragmentation plant) (mean lead in air concentrations ranged from 0.22 to 0.42 ug/m^3);

*   also in 1984/5 two monitoring points were maintained in housing areas in Preston and Burnley (mean lead in air concentrations of 0.34 and 0.22 ug/m^3 were found);

*   in 1986/87 two monitoring points in Pendle, remote from industrial influence, recorded mean lead in air levels of 0.14 and 0.15 ug/m^3;

*   in 1987/88 five monitoring points in South Ribble produced mean lead in air levels of between 0.06 and 0.23 ug/m^3;

*   in 1988/89 four monitoring points in West Lancashire showed mean lead in air levels ranging from 0.07 to 0.23 ug/m^3;

*   a study currently underway in Hyndburn is showing a similar pattern of data to that found elsewhere in Lancashire.

3.92   These limited airborne measurement data show that lead in air levels in Lancashire are below the current EC Directive annual mean target. Figure 20 locates the monitoring sites referred to.

3.93   Lead is also found in roadside and household dust contaminated from sources such as petrol combustion, industry and flaking paintwork. There are no statutory standards or national guidelines for lead in dust levels, as the relationship between this and body uptake is not fully understood. Dust lead levels may, however, affect children more than adults, and those in more socially deprived situations may be particularly at risk.

3.94   The Royal Commission on Environmental Pollution (1984) gives 'typical' lead in urban street dust concentrations in the range 500–5,000 mg/kg. Guidelines for interpretation of lead in dust levels have been the subject of much debate and notable recommendations have included the concepts that

Table 10 Lead in Dust in Lancashire. 1983–84

	Playgrounds	Pavements	Overall
Number of samples	286	241	527
Mean lead level (mg/kg)	750	1,000	850

Source: Lancashire County Council

levels above 1,000 mg/kg are 'undesirable' and levels above 5,000 mg/kg may warrant 'action'.

3.95   In 1983/84, playground and pavement dust was sampled from 27 schools throughout Lancashire. The results of that exercise are shown in Table 10.

3.96   In 1985/86, 432 samples of dust from around several industrial sources were analysed. Overall, 35% of individual measurements were above 1,000 mg/kg whilst 4% exceeded 5,000 mg/kg. Also in 1985/86, dust was sampled from inside and outside houses in Preston and Burnley. 113 'internal' dust samples showed a mean level of 800 mg/kg and 112 'external' dust samples showed a mean level of 2,200 mg/kg.

3.97   The airborne lead level data for sites not influenced by specific sources show levels generally below the EC target. However, the data for Lancashire are generally not extensive and there is a need for more widespread and continued monitoring to complete and maintain the required database. Furthermore, the lead in dust data are inherently difficult to interpret and the sporadic nature of monitoring adds to that difficulty. There is some indication of a need for further study of industrial sources of lead.

Ozone

3.98   Ozone is a compound formed naturally in the lower atmosphere from a chain reaction between nitrogen oxides, hydrocarbons and oxygen in the presence of sunlight. As the most common photochemical oxidant, it is a good indicator of photochemical pollution. High, and more significant, concentrations can, however, be formed in a similar manner within polluted air as a result of the presence of nitrogen dioxide. A third, but less commonly occurring, source of ozone is the downward intrusion of upper atmospheric air associated with vigorous air mass movement.

3.99   High ozone concentrations are often associated with anticyclonic weather conditions. These trap photochemical pollutants within a temperature inversion and the accompanying high insulation and temperatures favour ozone formation. Such conditions occur more commonly in the summer, explaining seasonal variations of summer high and winter low ozone concentrations.

3.100   The critical level for ground ozone has been defined as the concentration in air which, if exceeded, has direct adverse effects on plants, ecosystems or materials. In humans, ozone may cause runny eyes and some breathing difficulties, especially in asthmatics, but probably no serious debilitation. The critical level for one hour's exposure to ozone is 200 ug/m^3 and 120 ug/m^3 for eight hours exposure (WHO).

3.101   The sources of ozone-forming pollutants are both long-range (Continental), middle-distant (UK/urban) and local. Monitoring carried out at various rural sites in North West England during May and June 1978 attributed elevated levels to both long and middle distance transport. Concentrations of 100–160 ug/m^3 are attributed to long range transport of ozone from Europe, whilst middle distance sources within Britain contributed an additional 40–100 ug/m^3 (Harrison and Holman, 1979). Background ozone concentrations were found to be in the range of 40–100 ug/m^3 (Harrison and Holman, 1979).

3.102   Between 1977 and 1983, three rural sites near Lancaster (Heysham, Hazelrigg and Stodday) were chosen for monitoring ground ozone concentrations (Colbeck and Harrison, 1984) (see Figure 20). The results are shown in Table 11. They indicate levels generally below the WHO recommended level of 200 ug/m^3. However, this limit was exceeded on 27 days out of the 1,755 days monitored (or 1.5%). Overall levels were, though, sufficiently high to cause damage to agricultural crops, (adverse effects on plants have been observed at levels as low as 120 ug/m^3). These Lancaster concentrations were mainly due to incoming air masses transporting photochemical pollutants from distant and middle range. This situation still exists and Lancashire can be seen primarily as a net importer of photochemical pollutants. However, no more recent Lancashire-specific data exists.

3.103   Over recent years there has been increasing interest in the concentrations and distribution of photochemical pollutants in Britain, and in particular in the significance of ozone in crop and forest

Table 11 Number of Days per Year Exceeding Indicated Levels for Peak Hourly Ozone Concentrations, Lancaster Area. 1977–1983

Year	Site	No. of Days Monitored	No. of Days When 3 Specified Levels Were Exceeded			Maximum Level Recorded (ug/m^3)
			120	160	200[1]	
1977	Heysham	239	24	6	2	220
1978	Heysham	341	32	16	8	240
1979	Heysham	230	14	6	3	244
1981	Hazelrigg	221	13	6	0	198
1982	Hazelrigg/Stodday	359	58	21	8	266
1983	Stodday	365	57	18	6	312

Source: Colbeck and Harrison (1984)

Note: [1]*The World Health Organisation (WHO) recommended maximum level is 200 ug/m^3.*

damage. During 1983 and 1984, the Royal Commission of Environmental Pollution and the House of Commons Select Committee on the Environment (1984) concluded that available data on ozone and NO_x were limited and incomplete, which, in turn, led to uncertainty as to the likely range and seriousness of resulting effects on the environment.

3.104 In response, the Government, via the Warren Spring Laboratory, has developed a new systematic network for monitoring ozone and oxides of nitrogen throughout Britain. The DOE also set up the Photochemical Oxidants Review Group (PORG) which is responsible for assessing photochemical oxidants in Britain (Photochemical Oxidants Review Group, 1987).

3.105 Seventeen national monitoring sites have been established, though none are in Lancashire. The nearest is at Ladybower Reservoir in the Peak National Park. The national network now provides, for the first time, a generalised coverage of the UK ozone measurements.

3.106 It can be concluded that localised problems of ground ozone concentrations, and their associated pollutants, have been replaced by the issue of long distance transport of pollutants. This has resulted in environmental problems in areas remote from pollution sources. The limited evidence available points to Lancashire being affected in this way. The complete absence of ozone monitoring in the County makes it impossible to draw any detailed conclusions as to present conditions. There is a total lack of urban data, which is of even more concern.

Vehicular Emissions

3.107 Gases emitted from vehicles are increasingly important contributors to total air pollutant loadings. The principal pollutants from vehicles are carbon monoxide (CO), hydrocarbons (HC) and various particulates, NO_x, SO_2 and lead. Vehicles also emit large quantites of the main greenhouse gas, carbon dioxide (CO_2). Exhaust gases are the main source of pollutants, but approximately a third of the HC emitted comes from fuel evaporated from petrol tanks and carburettors, and leakage from crank cases.

3.108 Diesel engines emit less CO and HC but more SO_2 and particulates than petrol engines (Table 12). The quantity of pollutants emitted from both types of engine varies considerably with engine workload and is much greater when the engine is idling (Table 13). In large towns, vehicle emissions are the most important source of the atmospheric pollutants identified above (Harrison, 1990). Under bright sunlight and relatively still air conditions, NO_x and HC products combine to form smog. This can cause respiratory difficulties and harms vegetation. In Lancashire, though, the prevailing climatic conditions are unlikely to result in smog formation, except in the height of summer.

3.109 No specific data exists on any of these vehicle-related pollutants for Lancashire, though estimates are presented below.

Table 12 A Comparison of Diesel and Petrol Exhaust Emissions

	Carbon monoxide (%)	Hydrocarbons (ppm)	Nitric oxide (ppm)	Sulphur dioxide (ppm)	Particulates (g/m³)
Diesel engine	0.1	300	4,000	200	0.5
Petrol engine	10.0	1,000	4,000	60	0.01

Source: Harrison (1990)

Table 13 Composition of Exhaust Gases Against Engine Workload

Pollutant	Idling	Accelerating	Cruising	Deceleration
Petrol engines:				
Carbon monoxide	690,000	29,000	27,000	39,000
Hydrocarbons	5,300	1,600	1,000	10,000
Nitrogen oxides	30	1,020	650	20
Aldehydes	30	20	10	290
Diesel engines:				
Carbon monoxide	Trace	1,000	Trace	Trace
Hydrocarbons	400	200	100	300
Nitrogen oxides	60	350	240	30
Aldehydes	10	20	10	30

Source: Watkins (1972)

Note: Readings given in parts/million by volume.

Carbon Monoxide

3.110 CO is produced from incomplete combustion in the engine and is released from the exhaust. It has an affinity towards haemoglobin in the blood and is absorbed in very low concentrations in preference to oxygen. This makes it relatively toxic and human uptake is increased by heavy work and physical activity. Over-exposure to CO affects the mental ability of children and often causes headaches and nausea in adults.

3.111 Town centres in the UK have ambient levels between 12–23 ug/m³, but residential areas have a typical value of less than 2.5 ug/m³ with even lower background levels. 58 ug/m³ is considered as a sub-lethal threshold. CO dissipates quickly in the atmosphere and is generally only likely to be a hazard in confined spaces such as tunnels. People most likely to be at risk are policemen, traffic wardens, construction workers and people who cycle regularly through congested traffic.

Carbon Dioxide

3.112 Over 16% of the UK emissions of this principal greenhouse gas come from motor vehicle exhausts. (National Society for Clean Air, 1990). No Lancashire data exists.

Hydrocarbons

3.113　HC are released to the air from incomplete burning of fuel. Sixty-five percent of total HC emitted from traffic are released through the exhaust, 20% are released from crank case gases, and 15% come from evaporation of fuel in the fuel tank and carburettor. Benzene and other hydrocarbons are toxic. They have an unpleasant smell and help in the formation of photochemical smogs.

Nitrogen Oxides

3.114　These are formed by the combination of atmospheric oxygen and nitrogen gas generated during combustion. The gases are emitted through the exhaust and are toxic and acidic in their own right as well as helping in the formation of photochemical smogs and acid rain. Lean burn engines, in which the air/petrol ratio is greater than the normal 14.7:1, produce less NO_x, carbon monoxide and hydrocarbons.

3.115　NO_x emitted from vehicles has virtually no short term health effects since oxidation in the atmosphere is a slow process. EC directives consider NO_x as a transborder secondary pollutant and set limits at $200 \, ug/m^3$ with a guide level at $135 \, ug/m^3$. The guide level has only been exceeded once in the whole of the UK due to excessive traffic. The effects of NO_x on the environment usually impact on a wide scale, rather than locally.

Sulphur Dioxide and Smoke

3.116　SO_2 is derived from trace amounts of sulphur in fuel, which is present even after refining. SO_2 emitted from the exhaust is acidic and moderately toxic, but does not usually occur in toxic or sub-lethal concentrations. Smoke is one pollutant, which, though not particularly harmful, has visible effects. It arises mainly from diesel engines pulling heavy loads, notably buses and lorries. Smoke is generally undesirable and absorbs NO_x and SO_2, thus preventing their dispersal. Gradual reductions from coal fires, power stations and other sources throughout the UK mean that vehicular emissions are an increasingly significant source of smoke and SO_2.

Lead

3.117　Organo-lead compounds are additives to petrol used as anti-knock agents, to save raising the octane level of fuel. During combustion, organo-lead compounds breakdown and lead is released via the exhaust. After release, 25–50% of the lead emitted becomes airborne as an aerosol of lead halides and oxides.

3.118　Of all vehicle pollutants, lead has the greatest impact on the local environment. Marked increases in traffic levels bring about significant increases in lead concentrations in roadside soils and air. However, traffic flow and lead levels do not always correspond closely because of the effects of windspeed and temperatures. Pollutants from traffic are rapidly dispersed in well ventilated areas.

For instance, lead levels generally return to rural background levels at 600 m from the edge of motorways.

3.119　Concentrations in cities vary between $2-4 \, ug/m^3$ of air. This is generally 20 times greater than levels in rural areas, whilst a normal town has a mid-summer average of $1 \, ug/m^3$. The highest concentrations of lead in air are found at the kerbside of busy junctions, especially during times of low windspeed and atmospheric stability. The ambient levels of lead in air at night are generally considered to be 60% of daytime levels when there is greater traffic.

3.120　Lead emissions from vehicles have been reduced over the last decade, both as a result in the reduction of lead added to fuel and the conversion of vehicles to run on unleaded petrol. The maximum permissible lead content of fuel is 0.15 g/litre. In 1986, an estimated 2,900 tonnes of lead were emitted from petrol engined vehicles in the UK. Assuming that most of these were cars, the amount of lead emitted from Lancashire vehicles in that year was in the region of 76 tonnes. Since 1986, a substantial number of vehicles have been converted to run on lead free petrol and lead emitted annually now is probably 10–20% lower than the level in for 1986.

3.121　National data indicate that air concentrations of lead have fallen in parallel with reductions in lead content of fuel. However, blood levels of lead (which are a good indicator of recent exposure to lead) were only slightly lower following vehicle emission reductions. Also, levels in groups at high risk of exposure to airborne lead were only marginally higher than low risk groups. This indicates the importance of other sources of lead including intake from diet, drinking water and beverages.

Vehicle Emissions in Lancashire

3.122　Recent data indicate that 2.6% of vehicles in the UK are licensed in Lancashire (Department of Transport, 1989). This corresponds to a total of 604,000 vehicles of which 495,000 (81%) are cars. The following calculations of the pollutant loading emitted by vehicles are based on the following assumptions:

* all cars are petrol fuelled;
* all other vehicles are diesel fuelled;
* the average mileage of a car is 13,000 miles per annum;
* the average of the other vehicles is 50,000 miles per annum.

3.123　The average output of pollutants per car over a year has been estimated at:

* 35.5 kg HC;
* 22.7 kg NO_x;
* 489 kg CO.

(McCarthy and Rowan, 1989)

Assuming that Lancashire's 495,000 cars emit the same quantity of pollutants, the annual pollutant loading from cars registered in the County would be:

* 17,572 tonnes HC;
* 11,236 tonnes NO$_x$;
* 237,600 tonnes CO.

3.124   The vehicles other than cars are assumed to be diesel fuelled, giving 109,000 for Lancashire. The amount of pollutants emitted annually from these diesel engined vehicles is estimated to be:

* 1,308 tonnes HC;
* 5,505 tonnes CO;
* 4,905 tonnes NO$_x$;
* 1,254 tonnes Particulates.

3.125   This gives total annual vehicular emissions from all Lancashire vehicles of:

* 18,880 tonnes HC;
* 16,141 tonnes NO$_x$;
* 243,105 tonnes CO.

3.126   When set against total UK vehicle pollutant emissions, (Holman, Fergusson and Robertson, 1990) Lancashire's contribution is 3% of HC, 1% of the NO$_x$ and 5% of the CO.

Acid Rain

3.127   Acid deposition, otherwise known as acid rain, is a major concern in many parts of Europe and North America because of its long term effects on freshwater, groundwater, soils, forests, crops and buildings. It occurs either in the form of dry deposition, whereby gas and particles from the lower atmosphere are deposited directly onto buildings and vegetation (particularly common in low lying areas of the UK) or as acidified rain, (more common in upland areas).

3.128   The airborne pollutants which cause the phenomenon are SO$_2$ and NO$_x$. Power stations and industrial processes contribute by far the greatest proportions of SO$_2$. In urban areas, however, ground level concentrations depend more on domestic and commercial/public sources. Vehicular emissions and power station emissions in the UK contribute equally (40%) to the supply of nitrogen oxides in the atmosphere, but in urban areas the dominant source is motor vehicles.

3.129   Rainwater is naturally slightly acidic due to the presence of carbonic acid formed when atmospheric carbon dioxide dissolves in the water droplets. The pH can fall as low as pH 5 in some mountainous areas. Man-made pollutants can increase acidity (i.e.decrease pH) by several orders of magnitude. The oxides of sulphur and nitrogen dissolve in the rainwater to form dilute acids (sulphuric and nitric acid respectively). Hydrochloric acid may also occur in areas where power stations burn coal that is rich in chlorine.

3.130   During 1987, the Warren Spring Laboratory set up a programme to monitor rainfall acidity at 59 UK sites on a weekly basis. None of these sites were in Lancashire (although Rossendale Borough Council will commence their own programme shortly). Monitoring continued in 1988 and 1989, but at fewer sites. The data collected were used to compile contour maps of UK rainfall acidity. Figure 34 shows that in 1988, rainfall acidity in Lancashire

Figure 34
Acidity of Rain in the UK. 1988

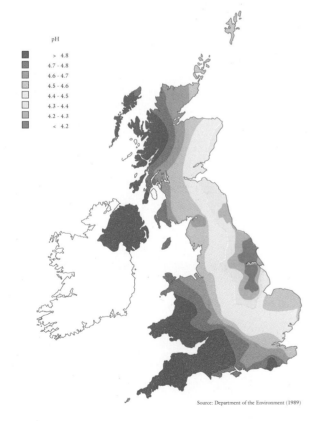

pH

> 4.8
4.7 - 4.8
4.6 - 4.7
4.5 - 4.6
4.4 - 4.5
4.3 - 4.4
4.2 - 4.3
< 4.2

Source: Department of the Environment (1989)

Figure 35
Wet Deposited Acidity in the UK. 1988

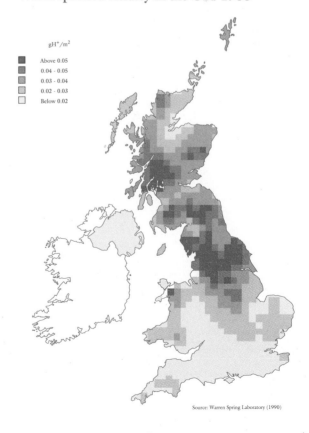

gH$^+$/m^2

Above 0.05
0.04 - 0.05
0.03 - 0.04
0.02 - 0.03
Below 0.02

Source: Warren Spring Laboratory (1990)

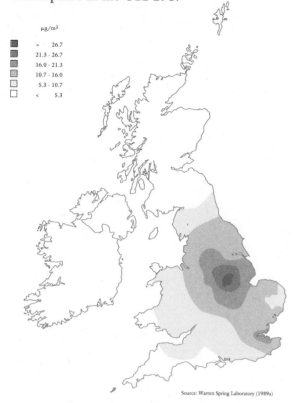

Figure 36

Annual Mean SO$_2$ Concentration in the Lower Atmosphere in the UK. 1987

μg/m³

■	> 26.7
■	21.3 - 26.7
■	16.0 - 21.3
▨	10.7 - 16.0
□	5.3 - 10.7
□	< 5.3

Source: Warren Spring Laboratory (1989a)

was average for the UK, lying between pH values 4.4 to 4.6. Levels were highest in Yorkshire and Humberside. Contour lines tend to run north to south and it is interesting to note that the acidity of precipitation east of the Scottish Highlands is similar to that of south east England, indicating the importance of long range transportation of pollution in determining precipitation quality. In some cases, acid rain occurs hundreds of kilometres away from the source of acidic pollutants.

3.131   Total acid load determines the potential stress on the environment at any particular place. This is a function of the amount of rain falling on an area as well as its acidity (see Figure 35). In this case the most affected places will be in the mountainous parts of Scotland, around Loch Lomond, parts of North Wales, Cumbria and the Pennines. The levels of total acidic load within these areas are comparable to the acid rain damaged regions of Southern Norway.

3.132   Lancashire is most prone to acid damage of crops/vegetation and buildings in the east of the County, near the Pennines, with the effect decreasing sharply towards the coast. The type of acid rain damage that Lancashire is likely to experience consists mainly of an accelerated acidification of soils and freshwaters, with subsequent changes in their biology. Agricultural crops are more likely to be directly damaged as a result of increased levels of atmospheric pollutants in the lower atmosphere than by acid rain.

3.133   Emissions of SO$_2$ and NO$_x$, the two main contributors to acid rain, are monitored across the UK and detailed readings for Lancashire have been given earlier. Monitoring of SO$_2$ has been conducted on a national scale since the early 1960s, with 287 sites being monitored continuously between 1978 and 1989. Concentrations of SO$_2$ in the lower atmosphere during 1987 are shown in Figure 36 which illustrates Lancashire's position in the national context. Areas where limit values were exceeded fell from 11 in 1983/84 to 3 in 1988/89, none of which was in Lancashire. Urban concentrations of SO$_2$ have fallen by 48% since 1978, mainly because of the reductions in emissions from domestic and industrial premises. Concentrations of SO$_2$ in Lancashire have reflected this pattern due to similar changes in domestic and industrial fuel consumption.

3.134   Power stations, industry and motor vehicles are the major man-made sources of NO$_x$ in the atmosphere. Because they are emitted at ground level, vehicle pollutants make a considerably larger impact on local air conditions and do not vary much throughout the year. However, other NO$_x$ sources such as power stations and domestic and commercial heating exhibit greater seasonality, with increased emissions during the winter months. It is from these latter sources that Lancashire is a 'net importer' of NO$_x$ from other parts of the UK, including that which arrives in the form of acid rain. National concentrations of NO$_2$, are given in Figure 28.

Global Warming and Sea Levels

3.135   The Earth's temperature is, in part, controlled by atomspheric gases, the most significant of which are CO$_2$, water vapour and (to a lesser extent) methane (CH$_4$), N$_2$0 and ozone (see Figure 37). These allow the sun's short-wave energy to penetrate to the earth, but prevent the long-wave energy, radiated back from the earth, returning to space. The effect of trapping this energy, (most of which is heat), is similar to that of a greenhouse; hence the phrase 'greenhouse' effect.

Figure 37.   Relative Contributions of Greenhouse Gases to Global Warming in the 1980s.

- Surface Ozone (12%)
- Nitrous Oxide (6%)
- CFC (14%)
- Carbon Dioxide (50%)
- Methane (18%)

Source: Association for the Conservation of Energy (1989)

3.136 Greenhouse gases are naturally occurring and contribute 34°C to the average surface temperature of the earth. Recently, however, concern has been growing that man-made pollution and the gases derived from some of man's activities are accelerating the greenhouse effect. So far, about 30 gases produced by human activities have been implicated. The main ones are CO_2 (due primarily to fossil fuel burning and deforestation); CH_4 (primarily from biological sources and landfill sites); Chlorofluorocarbons or CFCs (used as refrigerants and in some aerosol sprays); N_2O, (due to the breakdown of fertilisers and, to a lesser degree, from combustion processes) and ozone.

quantified and emissions from landfill sites, coal mining and leakages are only estimates.

3.139 Figure 40 shows UK methane emissions from 1960–1987. Their general trend is downwards. Historical changes in methane emissions include an increase from landfill, gas leakages and vehicles, a decrease from coal sources, and a near stable situation from cattle. The current contribution of these sources to UK methane emissions is shown in Figure 41.

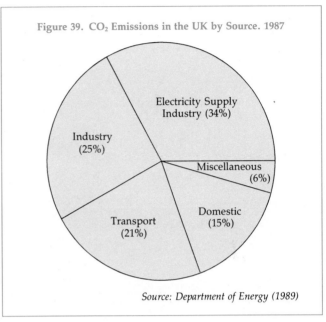

Figure 39. CO_2 Emissions in the UK by Source. 1987

Source: Department of Energy (1989)

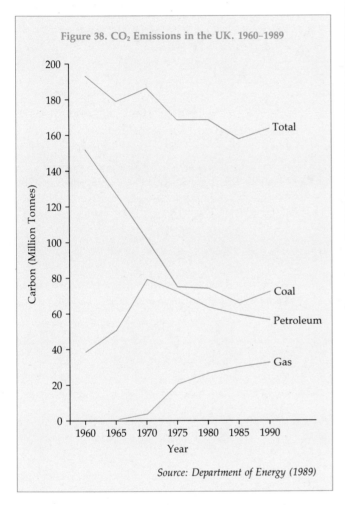

Figure 38. CO_2 Emissions in the UK. 1960–1989

Source: Department of Energy (1989)

3.137 UK emissions of CO_2 have reflected the variations in the volume, type and pattern of fuel use over the years (Figure 38). Overall, they have declined from the 1960s (except for peaks in 1973 and 1979) to a point where they are now generally 15% lower. This reflects the change from use of coal to natural gas. The relative contributions to total UK CO_2 emissions is shown in Figure 39.

3.138 Methane is about 27 times more potent a greenhouse gas than CO_2 and is produced when organic carbon compounds break down in waterlogged soils (for example in peat mosses) and as a result of digestion by ruminants such as cattle. Biomass burning, fossil fuel extraction, processing and combustion, and landfill gas-leaks are also significant sources. Emission data on methane are incomplete, whilst biological sources are not easily

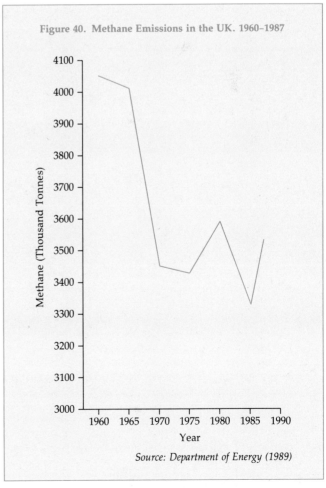

Figure 40. Methane Emissions in the UK. 1960–1987

Source: Department of Energy (1989)

3.140 CFCs contribute both to the reduction in the ozone layer and to the greenhouse effect. In the latter context, they are approximately 10,000 times more effective at trapping heat than CO_2. An international agreement (the Montreal protocol) which came into force in 1989 requires industrialised nations to reduce their consumption of CFCs by 50% by 1999. Evidence suggests, however, that an immediate 85% reduction is necessary simply to stabilise current atmospheric concentrations of chlorine which contribute to the ozone damaging process.

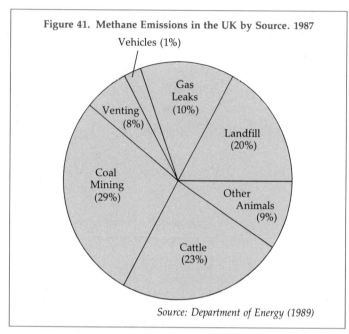

Figure 41. Methane Emissions in the UK by Source. 1987

Vehicles (1%)

Gas Leaks (10%)

Venting (8%)

Landfill (20%)

Coal Mining (29%)

Other Animals (9%)

Cattle (23%)

Source: Department of Energy (1989)

3.141 N_2O, is released into the atmosphere as a result of the application of fertilisers and the burning of fossil fuel and biomass (wood, organic refuse). Atmospheric concentrations in the UK have risen from around 550 ug/m^3 (by volume) in the nineteenth century to more than 590 ug/m^3 today. This gas remains in the atmosphere for 170 years and atmospheric concentrations have been rising at approximately 0.4% per year over the past decade. As in the case of the other greenhouse gases, it is clear that a reduction in the overall output of N_2O is needed in order to resume normal background levels. There will, however, be a time lag of at least 170 years involved in this process.

The Intergovernmental Panel on Climate Change

3.142 The United Nations Intergovernmental Panel on Climate Change (IPCC) was set up in November 1988 by UNEP and the World Meteorological Organisation to review the scientific evidence for global warming and to recommend action to deal with the phenomenon. The first IPCC report appeared in the Summer of 1990 and is the most authoritative evaluation of global warming and the greenhouse effect to date.

3.143 The IPCC Science Working Group report confirms that there is a natural greenhouse effect that keeps the Earth warmer than it would otherwise be. Indeed, without this, life on the planet would be impossible. However, gas emissions from human activities are substantially increasing natural atmospheric concentrations of greenhouse gases. These increases will enhance the greenhouse effect, resulting in additional warming of the Earth's surface.

3.144 The IPCC report further concludes that:

* some gases are potentially more effective than others at changing climate, and their effectiveness can be estimated. CO_2 has been responsible for more than half of the enhanced greenhouse effect in the past, and is likely to remain so;

* atmospheric conditions of the 'long-lived' gases CO_2, NO_x and CFCs adjust only slowly to changes in emissions. If emissions continue at the present rate, increased concentrations will persist for decades or centuries. The longer that emissions continue to increase at present rates, the greater the reductions required for concentrations to stabilise;

* the 'long-lived' gases require immediate reductions in emissions from human activity even to stabilise todays levels; methane, for example will require a 15% to 20% reduction.

3.145 The IPCC presents four scenarios (A to D) based on progressively increased levels of controls.

* Scenario A, the 'Business as Usual' case, in which current trends of coal, oil and gas consumption continue, predicts an average world-wide temperature increase of 0.3°C per decade;

* Scenario B, assumes that measures to control fossil fuel burning are imposed, that there is a switch from coal to natural gas, that energy efficiency is improved and that there is a halt to deforestation. The predicted rate of increase is 0.2°C per decade in this case;

* Scenario C, assumes a shift towards renewable energy sources such as wind, sun and tidal in the second half of the next century. This predicts a rate of increase of just above 0.1°C per decade;

* Scenario D, assumes that a shift to renewable energy sources and nuclear power between the year 2000 and 2050 stabilises CO_2 emissions in the developed world, leading to a stabilisation of atmospheric greenhouse gases. The predicted rate of increase of temperature is about 0.1°C per decade.

3.146 Global warming brings with it the prospect of world-wide sea-level rise. Under the IPCC 'Business as Usual' scenario, a 'best estimate' of average global mean sea level rise of about 6 cm per decade is predicted over the next century. This will be mainly due to thermal expansion of the oceans and the melting of some low-level land ice and could lead to a rise of 18 cm in global average sea level by 2030, 44 cm by 2070 and 66 cm by 2100.

3.147 All predictions are subject to uncertainty, with regard to timing, magnitude and regional patterns of climate change. The complexities of the clouds, oceans and polar ice sheets means that unforseen elements cannot be ruled out. Nevertheless, it is a recorded fact that global average surface air temperatures have increased by between 0.3°C and 0.6°C over the last 100 years, with the five warmest years on record occurring in the 1980s. Over the same period, the IPCC reports that global sea level has risen by between 10 cm and 20 cm. These changes are broadly consistent with predictions of climate models, but are also within the range of natural climate variability.

3.148   Thus, though the IPCC report has provided scientific evidence that global warming is occurring, uncertainty remains as to the exact predicted consequences of this warming. The storms and long dry spells experienced in Lancashire of late may be no more than a minor aberration, but the risk of ignoring the warnings could be severe. With a low-lying coastal plain, and a largely 'soft' coastline, Lancashire looks set to be affected by whatever changes occur.

Radiation

3.149   Radiation refers either to the process of emitting energy, (as waves or charged particles) or to the actual energy emitted. It originates from the continuous decay of unstable nuclides, which are described as radioactive. The radiation emitted is called 'ionising' radiation because it causes changes (ionisation) in the matter with which it collides. The strength of the ionisation depends on the nature of the particle or wave.

3.150   The least penetrating but strongest ionising form of radiation are alpha particles which are positively charged and cannot penetrate a sheet of paper. Negatively charged beta particles have greater penetration but are still easily stopped. Gamma rays, which are waves and not charged particles, however, are very penetrative and require lead shielding to stop them. Because it penetrates furthest into the body, gamma radiation is the most damaging of external sources. However, alpha rays are the most damaging of internal sources (e.g. from food) and gamma the least harmful. All these forms of radiation are derived from both natural materials and artificial sources.

3.151   Exposure to radiation occurs continuously at very low levels from a number of sources of which the natural gas radon constitutes almost half the average effective human dose equivalent of 2.5 mSv per year (Figure 42). In all, natural sources constitute 87% of the dose in the UK, whilst, of the artificial sources, radioactive discharges from nuclear installations, hospitals and universities contribute the least (i.e. <0.1%). The dose from medical sources is mostly due to diagnostic X-rays.

3.152   Human tissues are susceptible to attack by radiation and the ionising capabilities of radionuclides can cause tissue burn or alter the functioning of cells, leading to cancers. The extent of damage to the body is dependent on the dose received. Damage is also dependent on the energy of the radiation and on the particular chemical emitting it. The time taken for a radioactive chemical to decay, (measured by its half-life), is also relevant. Iodine 131, for example, has a half-life of 8 days, whilst plutonium 239 has one of 22,000 years.

3.153   Another form of radiation is electromagnetic radiation, which is non-ionising. This takes the form of electromagnetic waves, usually emitted from electrical sources such as overhead power lines and the electricity systems within buildings. The precise nature of the effects of non-ionising radiation on human health is a subject of debate, though it is accepted that some people suffer headaches as a result of exposure to it. Links to more serious ailments are suspected, but not proven.

3.154   This section concentrates on sources of ionising radiation in Lancashire and the possible effects of radioactive emissions.

Monitoring

3.155   Most holders of authorisations for radioactive substances are required to conduct monitoring and sampling and communicate the results to the relevant Ministries. Independent monitoring is also undertaken by the DOE and MAFF to measure levels of radioactivity in air, waters, sediments, soils, foodstuffs and natural organisms.

3.156   Following the Chernobyl accident in 1986, it was recognised that a monitoring network was required to enable airborne gamma radioactive contamination to be monitored. As a result, the Radioactive Incident Monitoring Network (RIMNET) was established, which consists of 85 permanent monitoring stations, of which two, (at Manchester and Carlisle), are located in the North West. RIMNET has been set up to deal primarily with effects on the UK of incidents which occur overseas.

3.157   The rôle of local government in radiation incidents includes the dissemination of Government information to the public. Local authorities can be called upon to monitor animals and foodstuffs with a view to prohibiting their sale if significantly contaminated. They can also be asked for supplementary data to substantiate Government monitoring. This requires the use of accredited sampling and analytical procedures. A co-ordinated programme of monitoring and collation of data from local government is to commence shortly, under the auspices of the Local Authorities Radiation and Radioactivity Monitoring Advice and Collation Centre (LARRMACC), a non government organisation. At present, annual monitoring reports are produced by the Institute of Environmental Health Officers.

3.158   Extensive monitoring of radioactivity in the environment and in foodstuffs is undertaken already by all Lancashire District Councils and the County Council. This is co-ordinated under the RADMIL (Radioactivity Monitoring in Lancashire) project, established to provide independent assessment of radiation exposure and a vehicle for improved reassurance of the Lancashire community. Monitoring reports containing a compendium of data are published annually and there have been five since RADMIL was established in 1985. The approach is one of the best examples of co-operation in environmental monitoring in the County.

Radon

3.159   Radon is an inert, radioactive gas caused by the decay of natural uranium in rocks in the earth's crust. The quantity of uranium present depends on rock type, but tends to be greatest in igneous rocks (and granite in particular). Radon emitted from near surface soils and bedrock can migrate into buildings. Where a building is poorly ventilated, the gas can accumulate and increase in concentration. Radon is virtually insoluble in water and can therefore be released when ejected under pressure from a spraying device such as a shower head. It decays to form radioactive decay products (radon 'daughters') which may be inhaled and can irradiate lung tissue leading to cancer.

3.160   The NRPB conducted a nationwide survey in 1987 to determine the levels present in typical households. NRPB fixed the action level for radon at 200 Bq/m^3. They concluded from the 67 homes for which measurements were made in Lancashire that levels in the County were likely to be very low.

Further joint monitoring has been undertaken since by RADMIL.

3.161   The RADMIL survey is ongoing but two of its three stages are complete. The results of the first survey of 391 homes were reassessed due to changes in the action levels for radon. However, certain areas including central, north and north eastern Lancashire appeared to have higher radon levels than elsewhere in the County. These areas were targeted for further sampling in the second stage.

3.162   The results from both stages show that radon concentrations in dwellings are predominantly low and range between 4 and 214 Bq/m^3, with a mean of 20 Bq/m^3. Complete results are presented in Table 14. Houses with radon levels above RADMIL's 'Further Investigation Level' of 75 Bq/m^3 are being monitored over a longer period. A total of 17 residences are involved. Clearly, the vast majority of residences fall below the NRPB action level of 200 Bq/m^3 and it is not expected that Lancashire will be designated an 'affected area' i.e. an area in which 1%, or more, of housing is at or above the action level.

Nuclear Installations

3.163   There are two nuclear installations in Lancashire. These are the British Nuclear Fuels Ltd., Springfields plant, near Preston, and the nuclear power station at Heysham, near Morecambe, operated by Nuclear Electric.

3.164   The BNFL Springfields plant manufactures two uranium products. Imported uranium ore concentrate is converted either to uranium metal fuel for use in Magnox reactors or to uranium hexaflouride (HEX) which is exported. Enriched HEX is also treated to provide oxide fuel for Advanced Gas Cooled Reactors (AGRs). Useful by-products of processing are magnesium flouride slag and hydrogen flouride which are sold to the chemical industry. The UKAEA also has research laboratories on the site.

Table 14   Radon Monitoring in Lancashire. 1987–1990

	First survey	Second survey	Combined results
Number of houses monitored	391	283	674
Range of Radon levels (Becquerels/m^3)	4–151	5–214	4–214
Mean Radon level (Becquerels/m^3)	17	27	20
Number of radon measurements above 75 Becquerels/m^3	6	11	17

Source: RADMIL (1990)

Note: NRPB action level is 200 Bq/m^3

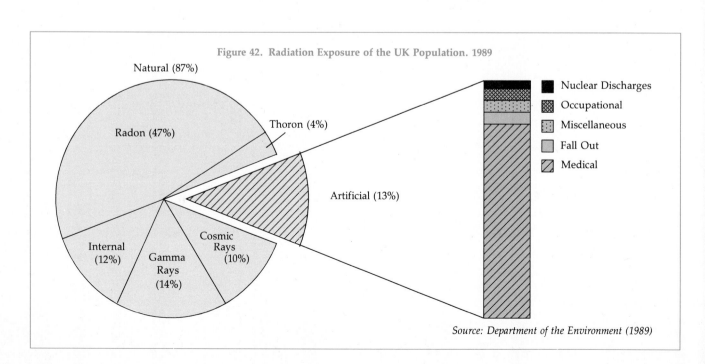

Figure 42.   Radiation Exposure of the UK Population. 1989

Natural (87%)
Radon (47%)
Thoron (4%)
Internal (12%)
Gamma Rays (14%)
Cosmic Rays (10%)
Artificial (13%)

Nuclear Discharges
Occupational
Miscellaneous
Fall Out
Medical

Source: Department of the Environment (1989)

3.165 Discharges to the environment are either liquid, solid or gaseous and are monitored to ensure that they fall within specified limits. Liquid and solid discharges are discussed in Chapters 4 and 5.

3.166 Discharges to air are made via a number of stacks, ten of which have been identified by HMIP as being of significance. All stack emissions are filtered prior to discharge to remove radioactive dust or fume. Over the period 1984–1988, the annual discharge of alpha activity was 0.001 TBq. This consisted mainly of alpha uranium activity together with some beta activity from uranium daughters. Discharge levels are described as being small and their environmental significance would appear to be negligible. This conclusion is based upon routine monitoring of environmental media including bovine faeces and milk, soils and air close to the works.

3.167 Heysham Power Station consists of two Advanced Gas Cooled Reactors (AGRs) referred to as Heysham 1 and Heysham 2. These came into operation in 1983 and 1988 respectively. Atmospheric discharges of radioactive material are consistently well below authorised limits according to data supplied by Nuclear Electric (see Tables 15 and 16).

Other Premises Using Radioactive Materials

3.168 In addition to Heysham and Springfields, a further 23 premises in the County are authorised to use radioactive substances (Table 17). Most are either medical or commercial/industrial premises. Four educational establishments also use radioactive materials for experimental research purposes. There are no radioactive substances users in Fylde, Hyndburn, Pendle, Rossendale or South Ribble Districts, whereas Lancaster has the highest concentration, with nine of the 23 premises.

Chernobyl

3.169 The RADMIL programme was established in time to monitor the effects of the Chernobyl accident in April 1986. A series of reports was published detailing the impact of fall-out and these concluded that while the principal components of the fallout, (caesium and iodine), were detectable, their impact upon meat and milk was minimal.

3.170 RADMIL's earliest reports on the impact of Chernobyl, identified downward trends in radiation levels and contamination in the months following the accident. The most recent report confirms earlier findings and RADMIL's assessment of the consequence of Chernobyl pollution on Lancashire's environment remains unchanged.

Table 15 Particulate and Gaseous Discharges from Heysham Nuclear Power Station 1. 1989

Month	Particulate Discharges Alpha (MBq)	Particulate Discharges Beta (MBq)	Discharges of I-131[1] (MBq)	Discharges of S-35[2] (GBq)	Discharges of Ar-41[3] (TBq)
January	<0.17	<4.1	<100	5.98	1.6
February	<0.17	<4.0	<100	0.94	0.1
March	<0.17	<4.0	<100	1.14	0.2
April	<0.17	<4.0	<100	1.02	0.6
May	<0.17	<4.0	<100	1.17	0.6
June	<0.17	<4.2	<100	1.51	0.8
July	<0.17	<4.0	<100	1.19	0.8
August	<0.18	<4.0	<101	0.95	0.6
September	<0.17	<4.0	<100	<0.93	0.6
October	<0.17	<4.0	<101	2.29	0.6
November	<0.17	<4.0	<101	1.40	0.9
December	<0.17	<4.0	<101	1.40	0.5
TOTAL	<2.05	<48.3	<1,204	19.9	7.6
ANNUAL AUTHORISATION	–	–	500,000	7,500	750

Source: Nuclear Electric (1990)

Notes: [1]I-131 is an isotope of Iodine.
[2]S-35 is an isotope of Sulphur.
[3]Ar-41 is an isotope of Argon.

Table 16 Particulate and Gaseous Discharges from Heysham Nuclear Power Station 2. 1989

Month	Particulate Discharges Alpha (MBq)	Particulate Discharges Beta (MBq)	Discharges of I-131[1] (MBq)	Discharges of S-35[2] (GBq)	Discharges of Ar-41[3] (TBq)	Discharges of H-3[4] (GBq)	Discharges of C-14[5] (GBq)
January	<0.10	<2.54	20.0	3.31	2.21	244.5	26.82
February	<0.11	<2.83	20.0	3.89	0.97	230.2	24.09
March	<0.13	<3.51	20.0	2.73	6.48	127.3	24.89
April	<0.13	<3.42	20.0	3.94	0.90	76.5	38.01
May	<0.18	<4.42	20.0	5.65	0.80	210.5	50.51
June	<0.19	<3.90	20.0	6.44	1.84	482.5	91.43
July	<0.25	<13.98	40.0	7.76	2.97	622.1	151.26
August	<0.27	<6.91	30.0	1.88	0.60	120.4	15.35
September	<0.24	<6.46	30.0	0.60	0.14	307.2	16.72
October	<0.39	<31.80	30.0	0.97	0.04	87.0	69.47
November	<0.26	<6.83	30.0	1.00	0.40	16.7	6.14
December	<0.52	<8.94	30.0	1.35	0.67	122.3	13.23
TOTAL	<2.76	<95.55	<290.0	39.52	18.0	2647.0	527.9
ANNUAL AUTHORISATION	—	6,000	5,000	1,800	300	36,000	4,000

Source: Nuclear Electric (1990)

Notes: [1]I-131 is an isotope of Iodine.
[2]S-35 is an isotope of Sulphur.
[3]Ar-41 is an isotope of Argon.
[4]H-3 is an isotope of Hydrogen (known as Tritium).
[5]C-14 is an isotope of Carbon.

Table 17 Number of Premises in Lancashire with Authorisations for the Accumulation, Storage and Disposal of Radioactive Substances. 1990

Type of Premises	Non discharging	Gas discharging only	Gas and Liquid	Total
Medical	7	1	0	8
Education	1	1	2	4
Commercial/ industrial	2	2	4	8
Other	3	0	0	3
LANCASHIRE	13	4	6	23

Source: HMIP (pers. comm.)

References

Association for the Conservation of Energy (1989). Solutions to Global Warming; Some Questions and Answers. ACE.

Butler J.D. (1974). Air Pollution Chemistry. Academic Press.

Chartered Institute of Public Finance and Accountancy (1989). Environmental Health Statistics, 1987/88 Actuals. Statistical Information Service. CIPFA.

Colbeck I. and Harrison R.M. (1984). The frequency and causes of elevated concentrations of ozone at ground level at rural sites in North-West England. Atmospheric Environment 19 (10) p.1577–1587.

Department of the Environment (1989). Digest of Environmental Protection and Water Statistics. Government Statistical Service. HMSO.

Department of Energy (1989). An Evaluation of Energy Related Greenhouse Gas Emission and Measures to Ameliorate Them. Energy Paper No. 58. UK Country Study for the Intergovernmental Panel on Climate Change. HMSO.

Department of Transport (1989). Transport Statistics in Great Britain. HMSO.

Harrison R.M. and Holman C.D. (1979). The contribution of middle and long range transport of tropospheric photochemical ozone to pollution at a rural site in North West England. Atmospheric Environment, 13, p.1535–1545.

Harrison R.M. and McCartney H.A. (1980). Ambient air quality at a coastal site in rural North-West England. Atmospheric Environment, 14: p.233–244.

Harrison R.M. (Ed.) (1990). Pollution Causes Effects and Control, 2nd edition. Royal Society of Chemistry.

Her Majesty's Inspectorate of Pollution (1990). District B Annual Report for 1988/89. DOE.

Holman, C., Fergusson, M. and Robertson, T. (1990). The Route Ahead: Vehicle Pollution, Causes, Effects, Answers. Worldwide Fund for Nature, UK.

House of Commons Select Committee on the Environment (1984). Fourth Report from the Environment Committee (Session 1983-4) – Acid Rain. HMSO.

McCarthy M. and Rowan D. (1989). There is more than lead in exhaust fumes. The Times.

Manchester Air Pollution Advisory Council (1989). Monitoring Report 1989 – Nitrogen Oxides. MAPAC

National Society for Clean Air (1990). 1990 Pollution Handbook. NSCA.

Nuclear Electric (1990). Report on Radioactive Discharges and Environmental Monitoring at Nuclear Sites during 1989. Nuclear Electric.

Photochemical Oxidants Review Group (1987). Ozone in the United Kingdom: An Interim Report from the UK Photochemical Oxidants Review Group. DOE.

RADMIL (1990). Second Report on a Survey of Exposure to Radon Daughters in Lancashire Homes. RADMIL.

Royal Commission on Environmental Pollution (1984). 10th Report. Tackling Pollution – Experiences and Prospects. HMSO.

Warren Spring Laboratory (1988). Ozone Monitoring in the UK: A Review of 1987/88 Data from Monitoring Sites Operated by Warren Spring Laboratory. Warren Spring Laboratory.

Warren Spring Laboratory (1989a). A Preliminary Assessment of the Air Pollution Climate of the UK. Warren Spring Laboratory.

Warren Spring Laboratory (1989b). Results of a National Survey of Ambient Nitrogen Dioxide Levels in Urban Areas of the United Kingdom. Warren Spring Laboratory.

Warren Spring Laboratory (1989c). Acid Rain in the United Kingdom: Spatial Distributions in 1987. Warren Spring Laboratory.

Warren Spring Laboratory (1990). United Kingdom Acid Rain Monitoring. Warren Spring Laboratory.

Watkins L.H. (1972). Urban transport and environmental pollution. Transport and Road Research Laboratory, Department of the Environment. TRRL Report LR455.

Chapter Four
Water

Introduction

4.1 Water is an essential human resource. We rely on it for every process from domestic consumption and recreation to power generation, industrial processes, agriculture and for waste disposal. We are not alone in our need. All living things depend to varying degrees on the availability of adequate, clean water. Effective use and conservation of the resource, therefore, are essential to all life.

4.2 Average domestic water consumption has increased over the last few decades in the North West to about 150 litres per person per day (North West Water, pers. comm.). Water to meet this demand is abstracted from surface waters such as rivers and reservoirs, and from groundwaters. The water supplied must be high quality and free from harmful elements. It therefore requires treatment to ensure its quality and must then be efficiently distributed. Thus the supply of water has become a major industry.

4.3 The quality of surface waters has, in the past, been determined largely by the natural characteristics of catchments and regional meteorological conditions. Catchment geology and vegetation cover both influence the quality of water from each catchment. Human activities now also affect water quality. Watercourses have been used traditionally for the disposal of domestic and industrial wastes. Activities like farming can, and do, alter the quality of surface water entering watercourses and groundwater. Thus, agriculture and industry, and an increasing population concentrated into large settlements, have combined, over many years, to exercise an overwhelming influence on the quality of water.

4.4 These alterations of natural waters, through the addition of unnatural substances, or an excess of naturally occurring substances, are termed 'pollution'. The environmental consequences of water pollution vary according to the nature and concentrations of the pollutants. Gross pollution can lead to the loss of most plant and animal life and can limit the use of the resource by humans.

4.5 In addition to their impact on inland surface waters, human activities influence water in coastal areas. This can reduce the recreational potential of beaches, affect coastal fisheries and damage wildlife interest.

4.6 This Chapter considers both fresh and coastal water resources in Lancashire, presenting available information about their chemical and biological quality and the factors that influence that quality. It also outlines the ways in which water is used, particularly with regard to drinking water supply and public health.

Legislation

European Measures

4.7 The EC has introduced a range of important water pollution Directives concerning the discharge of dangerous substances and quality objectives for specific uses. Directive 76/464/EEC provides a system of authorisations for the discharge of dangerous substances into the water environment. An annex to the Directive lists the substances involved.

4.8 List I, (the 'Black List'), identifies 129 substances thought to be so toxic, persistent or bio-accumulative in the environment that steps should be taken to eliminate contamination by them. It includes organohalogens, organophosphorous, cadmium and mercury and their compounds. Various 'Daughter' Directives set emission limits, and quality objectives for List I substances like mercury, cadmium, hexachloro-cyclohexane, DDT, pentachlorophenol, carbon tetrachloride, aldrin, eldrin, dieldrin, isodrin, hexachlorobenzene and hexachlorabutadiene. The UK Government has included 23 of these Black List substances on a 'Red List', and all processes producing them in the UK have been brought under the control of measures in the Environmental Protection Act (EPA) 1990.

4.9 List II, (the 'Grey List'), covers substances considered by Directive 76/464/EEC to be less harmful when discharged to water. Metals like zinc, nickel, chromium, lead, arsenic, copper, various biocides and substances such as cyanide and ammonia, are included. The Directive requires member States to create pollution reduction programmes and to provide environmental quality objectives for List II substances. DOE Circular 7/89 gives guidance on the implementation of these.

4.10 A suite of extremely important Directives have been adopted regarding surface waters used for drinking, recreation and harvesting freshwater fish and shellfish. Directive 75/440/EEC laid down basic quality guidelines for the abstraction of drinking water, whilst Directive 79/869/EEC addressed the methods and frequency of measurement needed to achieve Directive 75/440/EEC. Drinking water quality is further addressed by Directive 80/778/EEC, which sets quality standards for some 60 substances, as well as sampling frequencies. Guide Levels (GL), Maximum Admissible Concentrations (MAC's) and Minimum Required Concentrations (MRC's) are laid down in respect of certain parameters.

4.11 Bathing waters are defined as fresh or sea waters (other than swimming pools) where bathing is 'traditionally practised by a large number of bathers'. Bacteriological and chemical quality standards have been established for these waters in Directive 76/160/EEC. Quality requirements for waters intended to support shellfish and freshwater fish have been laid down in Directives 79/923/EEC and 78/659/EEC respectively.

United Kingdom

4.12 The Water Act (WA) 1989 forms the basis of all water related legislation in the UK. Its major innovation was to separate the regulating functions of the water industry from the supply functions. The Act is divided into six parts, but Parts I, II and III have a direct bearing on water quality and water resource management. Part I established the National Rivers Authority (NRA), as the principal regulating body with responsibilities for water pollution control, resource management, flood defence and fisheries. Part II created private water companies to supply drinking water and sewage services. Part III contains various detailed, related measures.

4.13 A major aim of the NRA is to achieve a continuing improvement in the quality of rivers, estuaries and coastal waters, through the control of water pollution. To fulfil this, the NRA is required to monitor regularly all surface, ground, estuarine and bathing waters, and to licence and monitor discharges to these from sewage, industrial and agricultural sources. The NRA is also required to investigate reported pollution incidents and to instigate any action arising. The WA 1989 also gave the NRA responsibility for controlling water abstraction, for the overall conservation and redistribution of water resources, and for general flood defence (except for coastal protection on local authority land). As part of the WA 1989, the NRA are charged with maintaining and developing salmon, trout, freshwater and eel fisheries. These responsibilities relate to all freshwater bodies, plus territorial waters extending three nautical miles from the coast.

4.14 Under Section 52 of the WA 1989, private water undertakers are obliged to supply only water which is 'wholesome at the time of supply' to any premises for domestic purposes. Section 54 makes it an offence to supply water which is unfit for human consumption, (except in exceptional circumstances). The Water Supply (Water Quality) Regulations (1989), made under the WA 1989, concern the quality of water supplied for drinking, washing and cooking and the publication of information about water quality. Part II of the Regulations prescribes standards of wholesomeness in respect of water supplied by water companies and other private suppliers. They stipulate that water is wholesome if it contains concentrations, (or values), in respect of various properties, elements, organisms and substances which do not contravene prescribed maximum, or minimum, concentrations or values (PCVs).

4.15 Part III of these Regulations enables the Secretary of State, (or, in the case of private water suppliers, the Secretary of State or the appropriate local authority), to relax the requirements of Part II. Parts IV and V provide for the monitoring of water supplies by reference to analysis of samples taken from consumers' taps, whilst Part VI regulates the substances, processes and products that water undertakers may apply to drinking water. Part VII relates to the provision of information by water companies and Part VIII imposes requirements on local authorities in relation to the quality of water supplied by companies.

4.16 Sections 67 to 74 of the WA 1989 oblige every water company, as sewage undertaker, to provide and maintain a system of public sewers and sewage disposal. They must also accommodate the discharge of trade effluent into public sewers, and its disposal. The Trade Effluents (Prescribed Substances and Processes) Regulations 1989 describe two categories of trade effluent. The first are effluents containing 'red list' concentrations exceeding those that would be present regardless of the activities within the industrial premises from which the effluent is discharged. The second are effluents from processes involving chlorinated organic chemicals, paper pulp manufacture, asbestos, cement, paper and board manufacture.

4.17 A primary function of the NRA is to maintain and enhance the quality of 'controlled waters' (i.e. inland, coastal, ground and territorial waters). Sections 103 to 124 of the WA 1989 specify how this is to be done and various Regulations and Orders have been implemented under them. The Controlled Waters (Lakes and Ponds) Order (1989) brings reservoirs not discharging into a watercourse within the definition of 'controlled waters', other than those containing water which has been treated prior to entering supply. The Surface Waters (Classification) Regulations 1989 prescribe the system for classifying the quality of inland waters according to their suitability for abstraction by water undertakers for supply (after treatment) as drinking water. This is achieved by setting mandatory requirements for a number of parameters.

4.18 Sections 107 to 116 of the WA 1989 have a direct bearing on the release of polluting matter into controlled waters. Polluting controlled waters is an offence, as is discharging effluent in breach of a prohibition. Under the Control of Pollution (Consents for Discharges) (Secretary of State Functions) Regulations 1989 an application for a consent to discharge has to be made to the NRA. District Councils are consulted on most of these. If consent is granted, the NRA may impose conditions. Where an application is refused, revoked or varied, the applicant has a right to appeal to the Secretary of State. The Control of Pollution (Discharges by the National Rivers Authority) Regulations 1989 requires that discharges by the NRA are determined by the Secretary of State.

4.19 Section 112 of the WA 1989 provides powers for the establishment of nitrate sensitive areas in England and Wales, in which controls can be introduced over agricultural activity in order to reduce the amount of nitrate leaching from agricultural land into water sources.

4.20 Section 117 of the WA 1989 has been implemented through the Control of Pollution (Registers) Regulations. This requires the NRA to maintain public registers, containing details of applications for discharge consents, consents issued with their conditions, certificates of exemption, results of analysis of water and effluent samples taken by the NRA and information on samples taken by others.

4.21 Under Section 123 of the WA 1989, the Secretary of State has issued the Control of Pollution (Radioactive Waste) Regulations 1989 which brings radioactive waste within the scope of the Water Act, including offences of polluting controlled waters, requirements to take precautions against pollution and the public availability of information on registers.

Organisations

Central Government

4.22 The Government, through the DOE, is responsible for interpreting and applying EC Directives and for the enactment of all legislation. This involves the establishment and authorisation of regulatory bodies and the imposition of duties and responsibilities on the water supply and sewerage companies. Parliament also establishes Select Committees, and Royal Commissions, to examine particular issues. Examples include the House of Lords Select Committee Report on Nitrates in Water (1989), The House of Commons Environment Committee Report on Bathing Waters (1990) and the Royal Commission on Environmental Pollution. The other Government department with responsibility related to water, is MAFF. This has an important rôle in controlling commercial fisheries and pollution inputs to offshore waters.

4.23 Since its establishment on the 1 September 1989, the NRA is the primary national organisation for control of water resources. As the watchdog body for all water users, it is responsible for: issuing all abstraction licences and discharge consents; responding to pollution incidents; setting water quality objectives and maintaining quality; controlling fisheries; ensuring conservation of aquatic wildlife; flood defence schemes and groundwater quality.

4.24 The NRA is split into 10 regions, and Lancashire falls under the authority of the North West Region. The regional headquarters are in Warrington but there is an office at Bamber Bridge, near Preston. Regional boundaries are shown in Figure 43. The NRA hold water quality information for the region, much of which is available to the public as the Water Register. This also contains data on discharges and information on their quality. The material in this Chapter leans heavily on the records maintained by the NRA.

4.25 The Drinking Water Inspectorate is a new body, established by the WA 1989. It is responsible to the Secretary of State for the Environment for ensuring the quality of the mains water supplied by North West Water and for enforcing the Water Supply (Water Quality) Regulations 1989. The Director General of Water Services has responsibility for ensuring the effective operation of the water supply and sewerage companies. His remit is to oversee their development, ensure the correct functioning of their services and to monitor their charges.

Water Supply and Sewerage Company

4.26 North West Water (NWW) is the company responsible for supplying drinking water to virtually all Lancashire (except for one small area of Pendle supplied by Yorkshire Water, and those served by private supplies). NWW is responsible for treating and disposing of sewage from the whole of Lancashire, except where private treatment facilities are installed. Under the WA 1989, NWW are required 'to develop and maintain an efficient and economical system of water supply' ensuring that wholesome water is supplied, that water mains and other pipes are maintained and improved. They must also maintain and improve a public sewer system, make provision for emptying sewers and for effectively dealing with the contents of those sewers.

4.27 NWW monitors mains water quality throughout its region, and makes information available on a public register. Their sampling data are supplied to both the Drinking Water Inspectorate and District Councils. All aspects of NWW activity, other than drinking water quality, are under the regulatory control of the North West NRA.

Local Government

4.28 District Council Environmental Health Departments are entitled to receive drinking water quality information from NWW under the Drinking Water Regulations. They also respond to consumer complaints about drinking water quality. The District Councils are responsible for monitoring private water supplies and ensuring that they comply with the Water Supply (Water Quality) Regulations 1989. Some Districts also do their own river quality monitoring e.g.Preston and Pendle.

4.29 The County Council has no direct regulatory rôle in water-related issues. However, the Council can, and does, carry out analytical investigations of water pollution, using the County Analyst, and has lobbied and increased public awareness about certain issues. The most notable example of this has been the County Council's involvement in campaigning to achieve the best solution for the Fylde Coastal Waters Improvement Scheme.

Other Organisations

4.30 There are many organisations involved in lobbying about aquatic issues and in practical conservations schemes. These include Friends of the Earth (FOE) through their Water, Waste and Toxics Campaign, Greenpeace, and the Marine Conservation Society. Government research and educational establishments also conduct studies on many aspects of the aquatic environment. The Irish Sea Study Group (ISSG) was established in 1985 following two seminars organised by the Royal Society of Arts, in which concern was expressed about the 'health' of the Irish Sea. The Group reported in October 1990 to a Conference in the Isle of Man on the current condition of the Irish Sea, under four main headings: nature conservation, waste inputs and pollution, the exploitation of living marine resources and planning and development on the coastline around the Sea.

Water Quality in Lancashire

Water Quality Monitoring

4.31 Of all environmental conditions, most data exist for the quality of the County's water. An extensive monitoring system has existed for a number of years, generating statistics on a range of aspects. These underpin what follows in this Chapter, and it is appropriate first to explain the monitoring system from which they stem. Reflecting the broad structure of the Chapter as a whole, this section

Figure 43
North West Water and National Rivers Authority Administrative Boundaries. 1990

1. Lancaster
2. Wyre
3. Ribble Valley
4. Blackpool
5. Fylde
6. Preston
7. South Ribble
8. West Lancashire
9. Chorley
10. Blackburn
11. Hyndburn
12. Burnley
13. Pendle
14. Rossendale

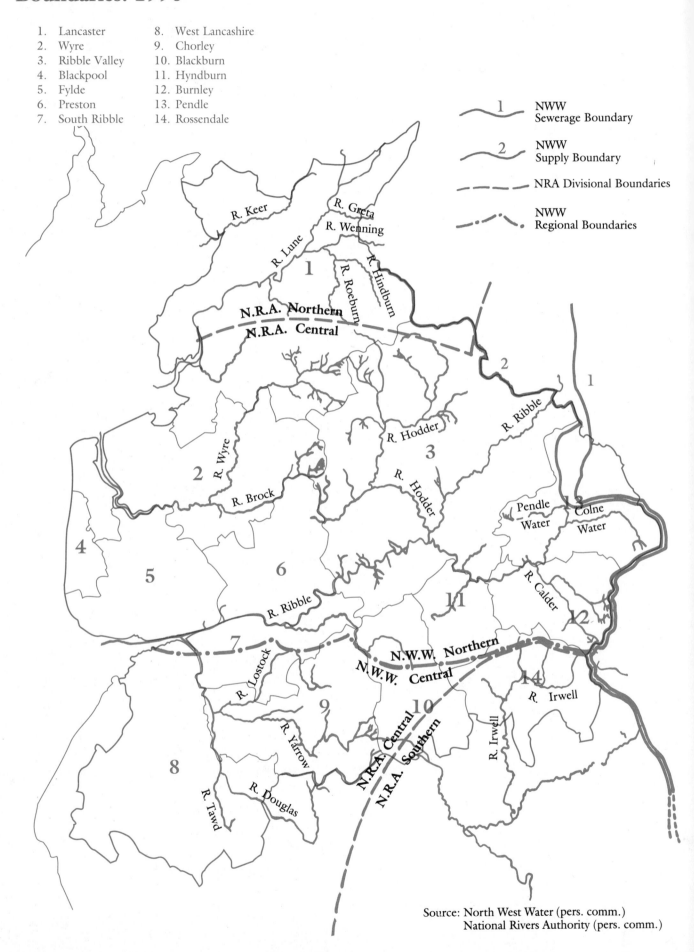

Source: North West Water (pers. comm.)
National Rivers Authority (pers. comm.)

Figure 44

Rivers, Tributaries and Primary Flow Gauging Stations in Lancashire. 1990

1. Lancaster
2. Wyre
3. Ribble Valley
4. Blackpool
5. Fylde
6. Preston
7. South Ribble
8. West Lancashire
9. Chorley
10. Blackburn
11. Hyndburn
12. Burnley
13. Pendle
14. Rossendale

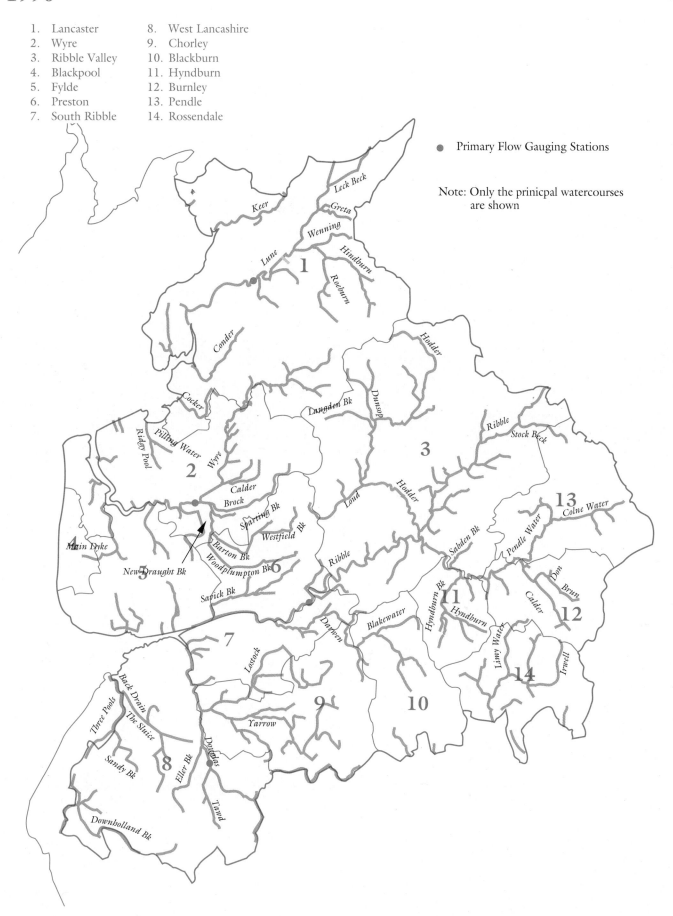

● Primary Flow Gauging Stations

Note: Only the prinicpal watercourses are shown

Source: National Rivers Authority (pers. comm.)

describes the monitoring arrangements for inland surface waters, followed by groundwaters, coastal and Irish Sea waters, discharges to these waters and, finally, drinking water.

Inland Surface Waters

4.32   All the statutory monitoring requirements for inland surface waters are now the responsibility of the NRA. They conduct both chemical and biological monitoring of water quality.

4.33   The NRA has to ensure that water resources do not become depleted through overuse, and that rivers meet their prescribed flow conditions. Consequently, they monitor river flows, reservoir levels and rainfall. Through consultation and negotiation with NWW, the major water abstractor in the County, the NRA must ensure that the County's water supplies are managed responsibly.

4.34   River flows are monitored either by flow gauges, intermittently, or continuously at four automatically operated primary river gauging stations. These are located on the four major rivers, Lune, Wyre, Ribble and Douglas (Figure 44), and enable the NRA to assess the water resource status of the major catchments in the County.

4.35   The routine monitoring programme of the NRA is used for river classification purposes. Data are required annually for internal reporting, and, for the DOE's National River Quality Survey, every five years. Sampling is also conducted to determine compliance with long-term water quality objectives, to monitor the effects of continuous discharges and for capital planning requirements. The number of sampling points on any river varies with the nature of the catchment and the activities within it. For example, many points are retained in agricultural catchments because water quality is more variable than in locations receiving continuous effluent discharges (National Rivers Authority, 1989).

4.36   The NRA has two complementary routine monitoring programmes on Lancashire rivers and streams. These consist of over 200 chemical sampling points and about 150 biological sampling points. Basic chemical monitoring includes the following physical and chemical parameters: temperature; dissolved oxygen (% saturation); dissolved oxygen (concentration); pH; conductivity; chloride; alkalinity/acidity; ammoniacal nitrogen; nitrite nitrogen; nitrate nitrogen; ortho-phosphate; chemical oxygen demand (COD); biochemical oxygen demand (BOD); suspended solids; ash. Other determinands are specified where local needs are indicated for fisheries or pollution control. These may include aluminium, fluoride, colour, turbidity or, occasionally, trace metals like iron, manganese, cadmium, chromium, copper, nickel, zinc, lead, mercury and arsenic.

4.37   Biological monitoring includes a summary of all invertebrate species present in samples and the calculation of appropriate 'biotic indices'. The NRA (NW) use three indices, the Biological Monitoring Working Party (BMWP) score, the Trent Biotic Index (TBI) and the Community Description Class (CDC), as complementary and integrated indicators of water quality.

Table 18   Key River Monitoring Points in Lancashire. 1990

River	Location	Monitoring Requirement					Number of samples per year
		1	2	3	4	5	
Keer	A6 Road Bridge				★		3
Lune	A65 Kirkby Lonsdale		★		★		12
Lune	Denny Bridge	★	★	★	★	★	12
Greta	R. Lune confluence				★		3
Wenning	R. Lune confluence				★		3
Conder	Old Galgate Bridge				★		3
Wyre	Gubborford Bridge				★		12
Wyre	St. Michaels	★	★	★	★	★	12
Brock	R. Wyre confluence				★		3
Ribble	Mitton Bridge	★	★		★		52
Ribble	Samlesbury	★	★	★	★	★	52
Hodder	Lower Hodder Bridge				★		12
Calder	Whalley	★	★				52
Darwen	A6 Blue Bridge	★	★	★			26
Douglas	Wanes Blades Bridge	★	★	★			26
Yarrow	Croston		★				26
TOTAL		7	9	5	12	3	

Source: NRA (pers. comm.).

Notes: 1 – Harmonised Monitoring Network Site
2 – NRA Key Point
3 – National Network (EC Dangerous Substances Directive)
4 – EC Freshwater Fisheries Directive
5 – EC Decision on Exchange of Information

4.38   Routine chemical monitoring is undertaken throughout the year, though sampling frequency varies from point to point. All sites are sampled at least three times a year and the majority are sampled either four or six times. Biological sampling is usually conducted twice a year at all sites. A greater sampling frequency is not necessary because biotic indices are much longer term indicators of water quality than a single water sample taken at one point in time for chemical analysis.

4.39   The DOE have specified sampling frequency and determinand requirements for a series of key sites throughout the UK. These sites form the 'Harmonised Monitoring Network' (HMN), data from which must be reported quarterly. The HMN provides a means for assessing national water quality on a more regular basis than the five year river classification scheme. There are seven HMN sites in Lancashire (see Table 18). These are monitored chemically for all routine parameters and other determinands, including trace metals. In addition, NRA (NW) have selected 'key' sampling points on river catchments to measure 'total pollution loads'. All HMN sites are included as key points and there are two additional sites (Table 18).

4.40 Two EC Directives require specific water quality monitoring; the Dangerous Substances Directive (76/464/EEC) and the Freshwater Fish Directive (78/659/EEC). In response to the former, five National Network Sites have been established in Lancashire. European Black and Grey List substances are monitored at these sites. The Freshwater Fish Directive requires that designated fishery waters are regularly monitored. There are eleven sites in Lancashire, plus one on the border with Cumbria. These sites are included in the routine monitoring programme, which satisfies the Directive requirements. The EC Decision on the Exchange of Information also requires some water quality monitoring, and three of the HMN sites are used, with the addition of bacteriological sampling, to satisfy its requirements. These locations are given in Table 18.

4.41 Some surface water monitoring is conducted by other organisations. NWW monitors the quality of water supply reservoirs for operational purposes. Water is assessed prior to entering treatment plants, to determine the degree of treatment required and to ensure that it remains of sufficiently high quality to be used for drinking purposes.

4.42 Some Districts Councils also monitor. Pendle Borough Council have instigated the Pendle Rivers Monitoring Programme (Pendle Pollution Control, 1990), in response to a serious pollution incident in the District. Preston Council has monitored bacteriological concentrations in the Ribble and Preston Dock for a number of years, due to local concern about the impact of sewage effluent. Samples are analysed by the Public Health Laboratory to detect *E. coli*, total coliforms, salmonella and campylobacter (see below).

4.43 Some educational establishments also conduct local monitoring as part of research and teaching programmes. The Lancashire College of Agriculture holds information about the River Brock at Myerscough whilst Liverpool University have sample records from many years for the Leeds and Liverpool Canal.

Groundwaters

4.44 The NRA has a responsibility for groundwater protection and, in that capacity, conducts groundwater monitoring. A network of 200 observation boreholes exists in the County, most of which have been sampled over the past five years. Monitoring of groundwater associated with waste disposal sites is also carried out, and records can be viewed by the public. NWW, as a major abstractor, also monitors abstracted water prior to its use for operational purposes.

Coastal Waters

4.45 The NRA is responsible for coastal waters for three nautical miles offshore. Monitoring of coastal waters is, however, limited and seems to have declined in recent years. The North Western and North Wales Sea Fisheries Committee used to conduct an offshore water quality survey, but this was terminated in 1986. Monitoring is now largely restricted to bathing waters designated under EC Directive (76/160/EEC), with some MAFF monitoring of offshore waters and also of radioactivity in coastal waters.

4.46 Bathing water monitoring is carried out by the NRA and, although the Directive specifies various physico-chemical parameters, it is usually restricted to microbiological quality. An Annex to the Directive lays down minimum sampling frequencies, (for several parameters, this is fortnightly during the bathing season) and specifies where, and how, samples are to be taken. Several sites in each designated bathing water used to be sampled, but, since 1988, only one site from each designated water has been used to assess bathing water quality.

4.47 Supplementary sampling is undertaken by some local authorities in order to compile a more accurate picture of bathing water quality. Blackpool and Lancaster Councils both conduct their own bathing water quality monitoring.

4.48 Responsibility for pollution in offshore waters lies with MAFF, who are the licensing authority for sludge and spoil dumping. They undertake some monitoring in offshore waters, but this is usually restricted to areas close to sludge dumping grounds. In the case of Lancashire, the largest of these lies in Liverpool Bay, though there are dredged spoil dumping sites in Morecambe Bay.

4.49 Radioactivity in coastal waters is also monitored by MAFF, through their Fisheries Laboratory in Lowestoft. The Lancashire coast is monitored, principally to determine the impact of Sellafield discharges, but also to detect any influence from Heysham and Springfields. MAFF monitor radioactivity both in the water and in sediments, fish and shellfish. RADMIL also monitors sediments, fish, shellfish and intertidal areas.

Discharges

4.50 Monitoring of most discharges to surface waters is the responsibility of the NRA, who also issue discharge consents. They have to ensure that consented limits for discharges are not breached. Consequently, all discharges, and the levels of the consented determinands, are measured several times a year. Sample data are placed on the Water Register, which is available for public consultation. Exceptions to the above, are the new procedures contained in the EPA 1990, which establish HMIP as the regulating and licencing body for the discharge of red list substances to the water system.

4.51 Monitoring of sewage discharges by NRA is largely determined by the nature of the discharge. Sewage treatment works are classified into three bands dependent on the volume of sewage treated, and hence the population served. The band then determines sampling frequency and the maximum number of failures permitted before a breach of consent conditions occurs. The three bands are given in Table 19. In Band A, for example, a breach only occurs if there are more than three failures of the same determinand in any one year. A total of more than three failures, but for different determinands, would not constitute a breach of consent.

Table 19	Classification of Sewage Treatment Works.		
Band	Volume of Sewage (Ml/day)	Number of Samples per Year	Maximum Permitted Failures per Determinand
A	>2.0	26	3
B	0.5–1.99	13	2
C	<0.49	6	1

Source: NRA (pers. comm.)

4.52 A similar procedure is adopted by the NRA for monitoring industrial and farm discharges. Sampling frequency is determined by the nature of the individual discharge. Large discharges, or those which have consistently poor quality, are monitored more frequently than minor ones. As with sewage discharges, only a persistent failure of the same determinand will constitute a breach of consent. All discharges must, however, be monitored every year and sample data is available to the public on the Water Register.

Drinking Water

4.53 NWW has a statutory duty to monitor drinking water quality, and does this at consumers' taps in each of its 'compliance' water supply zones (WSZ). The frequency of monitoring varies according to the particular determinand, the potential risk to human health, the volume of water distributed and the population supplied.

4.54 There are three grades of sampling frequency – reduced, standard and increased. The normal rate is the standard frequency, but, if particular problems are experienced within a WSZ sampling frequency will be increased. On the other hand, if no problems are encountered in a WSZ for three years, the sampling frequency may be changed from the standard to reduced. A zone sampled at increased frequency can revert to the standard rate once it is certain that the problem has been solved. Similarly, a reduced sampling frequency can revert to standard if problems arise. This system provides a flexible response and concentrates resources on WSZ where problems arise.

4.55 NWW samples at random addresses in each WSZ. These data are recorded on a register which is updated continuously and made available to the public. Public register information is also supplied to District Councils on a monthly basis.

4.56 NWW drinking water sample data must also be supplied to the Drinking Water Inspectorate, who are the regulatory body for drinking water supply. NWW also monitors water quality in their service reservoirs and at the inflow and outflow of water treatment works. This information is used to assess the operating efficiency and effectiveness of treatment works.

4.57 District Councils have statutory duties to ensure the quality of private water supplies and monitor these accordingly. They also take a close

interest in mains drinking water quality and will sample in response to public complaints. In addition to receiving NWW results, some authorities undertake their own drinking water monitoring programme. Eight Lancashire Districts either currently undertake, or will shortly be starting, mains water monitoring programmes. These are Lancaster, Blackpool, Preston, West Lancashire, South Ribble, Blackburn, Burnley and Rossendale. These programmes concentrate on bacteriological sampling, but chemical sampling is increasing.

Quality of Rivers and Streams

Introduction

4.58 Lancashire has a wealth of flowing waters, ranging from innumerable small upland streams to large lowland rivers and their estuaries. They vary considerably in volume, quality and biological value. The relief of Lancashire dictates that its rivers flow principally from east to west, draining off the eastern Pennine uplands to the Irish Sea. NWW estimates that Lancashire has some 1,032 km of non-tidal, flowing water (North West Water, 1988), but this excludes many small streams and brooks running off the fells.

4.59 The DOE, through the former National Water Council (NWC), has defined hydrometric areas as a basis for examining river systems. A hydrometric area comprises the whole basin, or catchment, drained by any river system. Each hydrometric area is numbered, and split into sub-catchments, which are also numbered. Every river location in England and Wales can thus be classified by a precise national hydrological reference (NHR) number. Because it is defined by river catchment boundaries, the hydrometric system does not usually match County or District boundaries.

4.60 Analysis of rivers by hydrometric areas is the best method of assessing river systems because the physical and chemical characteristics of any particular river are largely defined by the nature of its catchment. The river system is also clearly defined by the extent of its catchment and can be considered as a complete whole. These areas have thus been used as the basis for establishing the regional and divisional boundaries of the former water authorities, the new water companies and NRA regions (see Figure 43).

4.61 Lancashire is covered by five hydrometric areas, none of which are wholly within the County. These are:

* NHR 73. Morecambe Bay, (River Keer in the Carnforth/Silverdale area);
* NHR 72. Rivers Lune and Wyre;
* NHR 71. River Ribble;
* NHR 70. River Douglas;
* NHR 69. River Mersey, (River Irwell in the Rossendale area).

Large areas of 70, 71 and 72 but only small areas of 69 and 73, lie within the County.

NWC River Classification

4.62 The standard assessment of river water quality in the UK is the classification scheme devised by the NWC, used by the DOE to conduct a national survey of river water quality every five years. There are two parts to the classification; the first dealing with rivers, lakes and canals and the second with estuaries. For rivers, five classes are used, based on various criteria including dissolved oxygen concentration, biochemical oxygen demand (BOD) and ammonia levels in water samples. The classes are:

* Class 1a. (GOOD) Water of high quality, suitable for potable supply abstractions, game or other high class fisheries, high amenity value;

* Class 1b. (GOOD) Water of less high quality than Class 1a but usable for basically the same purposes;

* Class 2. (FAIR) Waters suitable for potable supply after advanced treatment, supporting reasonably good coarse fisheries, moderate amenity value;

* Class 3. (POOR) Waters which are polluted to an extent that fish are absent or only sporadically present, may be used for low grade industrial abstraction purposes, considerable potential for further use if cleaned up;

* Class 4. (BAD) Waters which are grossly polluted and are likely to cause nuisance.

4.63 The lengths of NWC river classes in Lancashire in 1988 are given in Table 20, whilst Figure 45 shows the quality of Lancashire's rivers from the 1989 survey. River water quality throughout the County is now generally high, with nearly half of all rivers classified as Good. Most of this category lies in the north of the County. There is, however, cause for concern over the quarter classified as Poor or Bad, which are concentrated in South and East Lancashire. Paragraphs 4.74 to 4.127 inclusive compare quality changes in individual rivers between the 1985 National River Survey (Department of the Environment, 1985) and the position recorded in the NRA's monitoring results for 1989 (NRA pers. comm.).

4.64 EC Directive 78/659/EEC requires member States to designate fresh waters needing protection, or improvement, to support fish life. Two categories are involved; those suitable for salmon and trout (salmonids) and those for coarse fish (cyprinids). An Annex to the Directive sets fourteen physical and chemical parameters, against which are listed Imperative (I) and Guide (G) values for salmonid and cyprinid waters. A pollution reduction programme has been established to ensure that designated waters (designated in July 1980) conform to standards. Figure 46 shows salmonid and cyprinid waters in Lancashire. There are 314.2 km of the former and 25.8 km of the latter.

General Assessment of Lancashire River Quality

4.65 Detailed information on the quality of the County's rivers is presented for each hydrometric area in the sub-sections which follow. For ease of presentation, the data on the Lune and the Wyre sub-catchments are separated. The main rivers and tributaries, shown in Figure 44, are:

Table 20	NWC Classification of Lancashire's Rivers. 1988		
Class	Quality Description	1988 Surveyed Length (km)	%
1 (a + b)	Good	476	46
2	Fair	268	26
3	Poor	232	23
4	Bad	56	5
LANCASHIRE		1,032	100

Source: North West Water (1988)

* River Keer;

* River Lune,
  – Main channel
  – River Greta
  – River Wenning
  – River Hindburn
  – River Roeburn
  – Rivers Conder and Cocker
  – Lune estuary (Pilling Water);

* River Wyre,
  – Main channel
  – River Calder
  – River Brock and New Draught
  – Wyre estuary (Main Dyke);

* River Ribble,
  – Main channel
  – River Hodder
  – River Calder
  – Rivers Brun and Don
  – Colne Water
  – Pendle Water
  – Hyndburn Brook
  – River Darwen;

* River Douglas,
  – Main channel
  – River Tawd
  – River Lostock
  – River Yarrow
  – Ribble estuary (Three Pools and The Sluice);

* River Irwell,
  – Main channel
  – Limy Water.

4.66 The assessment of river quality uses information from the 1985 National River Survey, the NRA 1989 NWC survey and summary sample statistics from the period 1980–1990, supplied by the NRA. These show the extent of organic pollution and trace metal contamination in Lancashire's rivers. Complementary data, derived from samples of the invertebrate fauna, are also used to give an indication of water quality.

4.67 Chemical water quality information described, is based on the guidelines and standards in the Freshwater Fish Directive (78/659/EEC), with additional material about the substances listed in the Dangerous Substances Directive (76/464/EEC).

Table 21 Water Quality Standards for Support of Freshwater Fisheries.

Determinand	Standard For Protection of Salmonids	Standard For Protection of Cyprinids	Guide/ Limit Value	Variation with Hardness
Dissolved Arsenic	50 ug/l	50 ug/l	★	No
Total Cadmium	5 ug/l	5 ug/l	★	No
Dissolved Chromium	5-50 ug/l	150-250 ug/l	★	Yes
Dissolved Copper	1-28 ug/l	1-28 ug/l	★	Yes
Dissolved Lead	4-20 ug/l	50-250 ug/l	★	Yes
Total Mercury	1 ug/l	1 ug/l	★	No
Dissolved Nickel	50-200 ug/l	50-200 ug/l	★	Yes
Total Zinc	30-500 ug/l	300-2000 ug/l	★	Yes
Dissolved Phosphate as P	65 ug/l	131 ug/l	G	No
Dissolved Ammonia as N	0.78 mg/l	0.78 mg/l	L	No
Free NH_3 as N	20.6 ug/l	20.6 ug/l	L	No
Nitrite as N	3 ug/l	9 ug/l	G	No
BOD	3 mg/l	6 mg/l	G	No
Chlorine as Cl_2	6.8 ug/l	6.8 ug/l	L	No
Dissolved O_2 (50% of values)	>9 mg/l	>8 mg/l	L	No
(100% of values)	>7 mg/l	>5 mg/l	L	No
pH	6-9	6-9	L	Yes
Temperature	21.5	28	L	No
Suspended solids	25 mg/l	25 mg/l	G	No

Source: Gardiner and Mance (1984)

*Note: * WRC recommended standards*

The standards required to support both salmonid and cyprinid fisheries have been included and relevant parameters and standards are given in Table 21. Some trace metal standards vary according to water hardness, as shown by Table 22.

4.68 Water quality data from 131 sample points throughout the County was obtained from the NRA. Concentrations of trace metals had been measured at 37 of these sites. Mean concentrations of the parameters listed in Table 21 at each site were compared with the appropriate standard. The numbers of sites in each main hydrometric area where standards were exceeded are given in Table 23. The results show that there are few problems with metal contamination in the County's rivers. Most of those that do occur are in the Ribble catchment.

4.69 The main water quality problems in the County are:

* organic pollution, illustrated by exceedance of standards for BOD, suspended solids and ammonia;

* nutrient enrichment, (eutrophication), illustrated by the exceedance of nitrite and dissolved phosphate standards.

There is a consistent failure of the nitrite standard throughout the County. Only seven sites actually meet the standard. However, this is mainly because the EC guide level is set very low, and not because there are problems with high nitrite levels.

4.70 Invertebrate sample data were also obtained from the NRA for 89 sites. Data for the most recent ten samples from each site has been examined and the median value taken. Aquatic invertebrates are very good indicators of water quality, since they respond to changes in water quality characteristics over a period. This contrasts with the more limited assessment obtained from water samples, which indicate quality at a single point in time.

4.71 Assessment of water quality using invertebrates is based on the premise that clean waters, generally, support diverse invertebrate communities and that particular groups (such as stoneflies, mayflies and caddis flies) are always associated with unpolluted conditions. Poor quality waters have sparse invertebrate communities, which include mainly detritus feeders and species tolerant of lower oxygen concentrations (such as hog louse, blood worms and leeches).

4.72 Numerous water quality classification schemes, based on invertebrate sampling, have been developed. The scheme used in this Chapter and perhaps, the one most commonly used, is the Trent Biotic Index (TBI). The TBI is based on community diversity and the occurrence of certain indicator invertebrate groups. Water quality improves from class 1 (lifeless) to class 15 (excellent). Class 10 is regarded as being of 'good' quality.

Table 22 WRC Recommended Standards for Trace Substances: Variation with Water Hardness.

Determinand ug/l	Hardness (mg/l CaCO₃) >50	50-100	100-150	150-200	200-250	>250
Salmonids:						
Chromium	5	10	20	50	50	50
Copper	1	6	10	10	10	28
Lead	4	10	10	20	20	20
Nickel	50	100	150	150	200	200
Zinc	10	50	75	75	125	125
Cyprinids:						
Chromium	150	175	200	200	250	250
Copper	1	6	10	10	10	28
Lead	50	125	125	250	250	250
Nickel	50	100	150	150	200	200
Zinc	75	175	250	250	250	500

Source: Gardiner and Mance (1984)

Note: All values refer to dissolved concentrations, relative to annual average, except for zinc, which refer to total concentrations, (dissolved plus particulate).

Figure 45

NWC Classification of Lancashire's Rivers, Tributaries and Estuaries. 1989

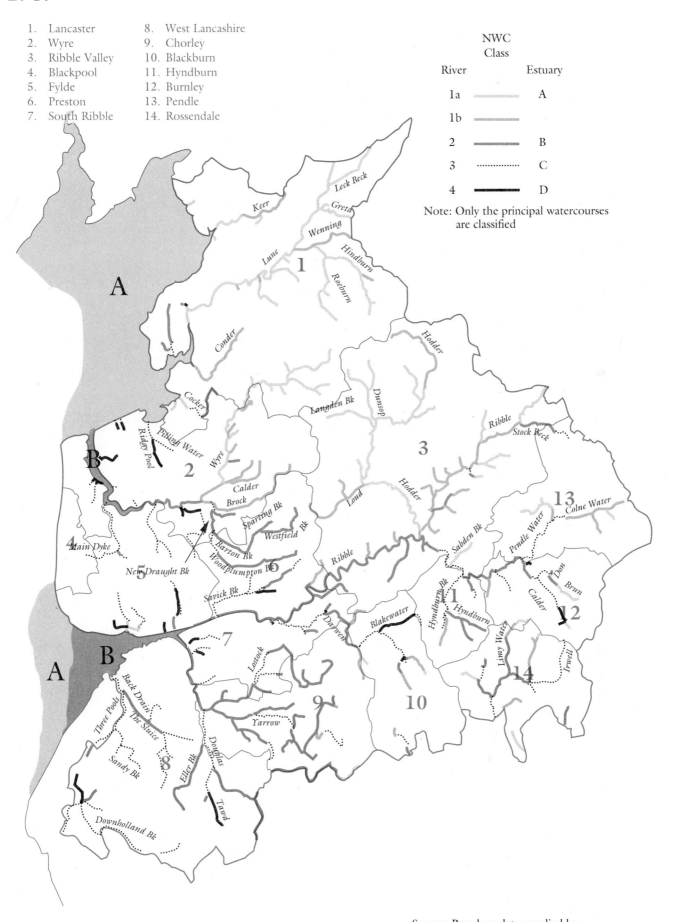

1. Lancaster
2. Wyre
3. Ribble Valley
4. Blackpool
5. Fylde
6. Preston
7. South Ribble

8. West Lancashire
9. Chorley
10. Blackburn
11. Hyndburn
12. Burnley
13. Pendle
14. Rossendale

NWC Class

River		Estuary
1a		A
1b		
2		B
3		C
4		D

Note: Only the principal watercourses are classified

Source: Based on data supplied by the National Rivers Authority

Figure 46
EC Designated Salmonid and Cyprinid Waters in Lancashire. 1990

1. Lancaster
2. Wyre
3. Ribble Valley
4. Blackpool
5. Fylde
6. Preston
7. South Ribble
8. West Lancashire
9. Chorley
10. Blackburn
11. Hyndburn
12. Burnley
13. Pendle
14. Rossendale

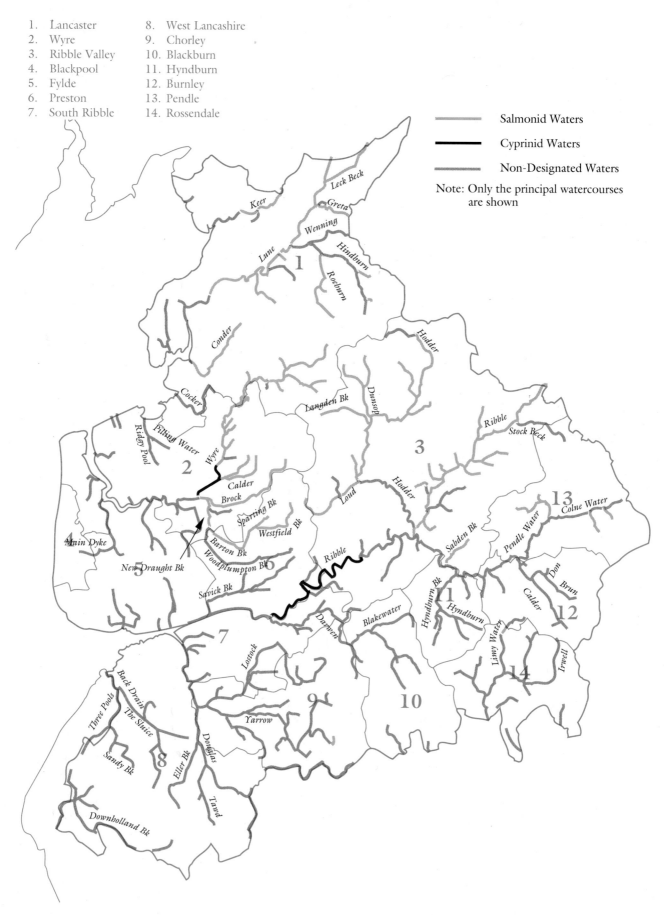

Salmonid Waters

Cyprinid Waters

Non-Designated Waters

Note: Only the principal watercourses are shown

Source: National Rivers Authority (pers. comm.)

4.73 The median value of TBI for the most recent ten samples from each site has usually been used, though occasionally, the most recent six samples are used. TBI scores complement both the NWC and chemical water quality data, and confirm the observation that river quality in Lancashire is much better in the north of the County than in the south and east. This reflects the historical pattern of settlement, land use and industrial development.

River Keer

4.74 The River Keer is a small river rising in the hills above Carnforth, flowing through the town and into Morecambe Bay. It is tidal below Carnforth. It is approximately 9 km long above its tidal limit and has a normal mean daily flow of approximately 20 million litres per day (Ml/day) in its middle reaches and 70 Ml/day near Carnforth. Its entire length was classified as class 1a in 1985 but the inland stretches were classified 1b in 1989. Water quality data obtained from the NRA for two sites on the river confirm this classification, although the minimum recorded oxygen concentration at one of the sites was below the EC standard for salmonid waters. The average concentration is, however, well above the recommended 50% limit. The Keer supports a salmonid fishery and 7.7 km of the river is a designated EC salmonid water. A small tributary of the Keer (1 km) is likewise designated.

River Lune and Tributaries

4.75 The River Lune (main channel) rises in the northern Pennines in Cumbria, above Tebay. It enters Lancashire south of Kirkby Lonsdale, some 37 km downstream of its source and flows southwest to Lancaster and out to the Irish Sea at the southern end of Morecambe Bay. It is tidal below Skerton Weir in Lancaster.

4.76 The non-tidal length of the Lune in Lancashire is approximately 25 km, with an annual mean daily flow of 3,259 Ml/day at the Caton primary river gauging station (Figure 44). Flow measurements between 1979 and 1989 are shown in Figures 47 to 49. Total annual flows, and annual mean daily flows, show the variation in flow from year to year. The monthly mean daily flows show the great variation in flow between summer and winter; with the maximum flow in December and the minimum in May.

4.77 The entire length of the Lune was classified 1a in 1985 and 1989. Analysis of water quality statistics from 1980–1990 confirm that the Lune is an unpolluted, high quality river. In common with all Lancashire's rivers, the nitrite standards are exceeded but apart from one other parameter at one site (the salmonid standard for lead is exceeded at Kirkby Lonsdale) the Lune meets all the standards for a salmonid water. BOD, which can be used as a measure of organic pollution, is consistently low in the Lune (see Figure 50). The high quality of the River Lune is further confirmed by its high TBI scores (also Figure 50). These show that it has a diverse invertebrate fauna containing many clean water species.

Table 23 Exceedances of Water Quality Standards in Lancashire by Catchment

Determinand	Keer S	Keer C	Lune S	Lune C	Wyre S	Wyre C	Ribble S	Ribble C	Douglas S	Douglas C	Irwell S	Irwell C
Arsenic	0	0	0	0	0	0	1	4	0	0	0	0
Cadmium	0	0	0	0	0	0	0	4	0	0	0	0
Chromium	0	0	0	0	0	0	0	0	0	0	0	0
Copper	0	0	0	0	0	0	—	7	—	2	0	0
Lead	0	0	0	0	0	0	6	0	2	0	0	0
Mercury	0	0	0	0	0	0	0	0	0	0	0	0
Nickel	0	0	0	0	0	0	0	0	0	0	0	0
Zinc	0	0	0	—	1	5	5	0	0	0	0	0
Phosphate	1	0	—	7	1	16	10	31	5	16	3	1
Ammonia as N	0	0	—	6	—	6	—	13	—	12	0	0
Nitrite as N	—	3	—	17	—	26	—	52	—	21	—	5
BOD	0	0	2	2	7	2	23	7	10	9	4	0
Chlorine as Cl$_2$	0	0	0	0	0	0	0	0	0	0	0	0
Oxygen	2	0	—	5	7	9	10	23	3	14	0	0
pH	0	0	0	0	0	0	0	0	0	0	0	0
Temperature	0	0	2	0	0	0	0	0	0	0	0	0
Suspended solids	0	0	—	2	—	8	—	17	—	12	—	1
Total number of samples	3		22		26		52		21		7	
Samples with metal data	0		4		5		23		5		0	

Source: Liverpool University EAU (derived from water quality data provided by NRA).

Notes: S – samples exceeding standard for the protection of salmonid fish only.
C – samples exceeding the standards for protection of both salmonid fish and cyprinid fish.

4.78 The whole of the Lune main channel is an EC designated salmonid water, and there is a total length of 76.1 km of designated salmonid waters within its catchment in Lancashire. It is one of the most important salmon runs in the north-west, as illustrated by the high catches recorded on the river.

4.79 The River Greta rises in the Pennines above Ingleton and flows west to join the Lune. It enters Lancashire west of Burton in Lonsdale, approximately 11 km from its source, and flows a further 4 km to its confluence with the Lune. It has a mean flow of 167 Ml/day prior to its confluence with the Lune. The Greta was wholly class 1a in 1985 and 1989 and, apart from nitrite, it meets all the standards for salmonid waters. The 11.8 km stretch from Ingleton to the Lune is a designated salmonid water.

4.80 The River Wenning rises in the Pennines near Austwick and flows westwards, entering Lancashire below Low Bentham where it serves as the County boundary for 1.5 km, before flowing on through Wennington and into the Lune. The Wenning is 28 km long, of which 8 km lies in Lancashire. Prior to its confluence with the Lune, the

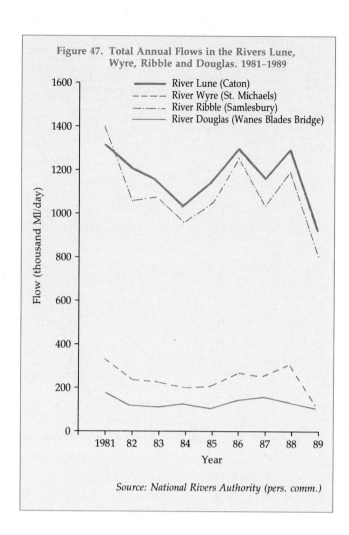

Figure 47. Total Annual Flows in the Rivers Lune, Wyre, Ribble and Douglas. 1981–1989

Source: National Rivers Authority (pers. comm.)

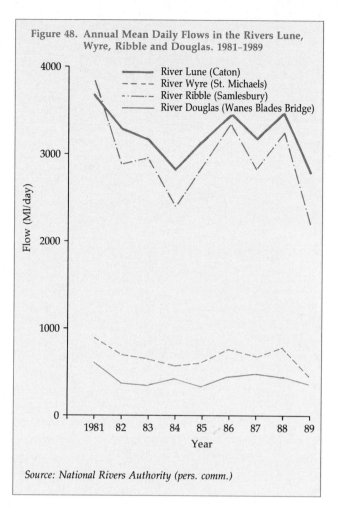

Figure 48. Annual Mean Daily Flows in the Rivers Lune, Wyre, Ribble and Douglas. 1981–1989

Source: National Rivers Authority (pers. comm.)

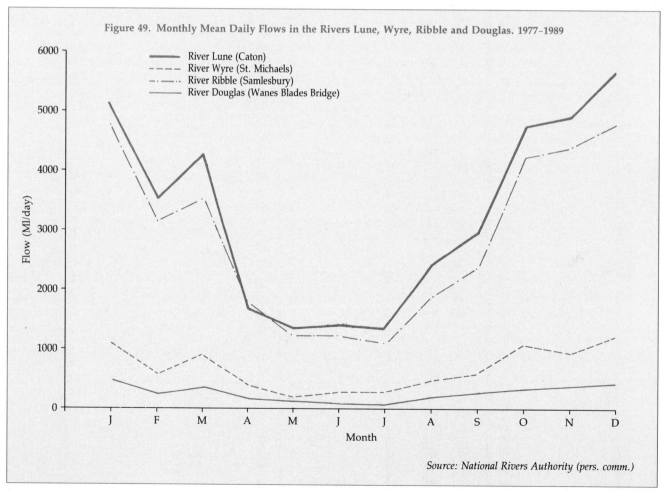

Figure 49. Monthly Mean Daily Flows in the Rivers Lune, Wyre, Ribble and Douglas. 1977–1989

Source: National Rivers Authority (pers. comm.)

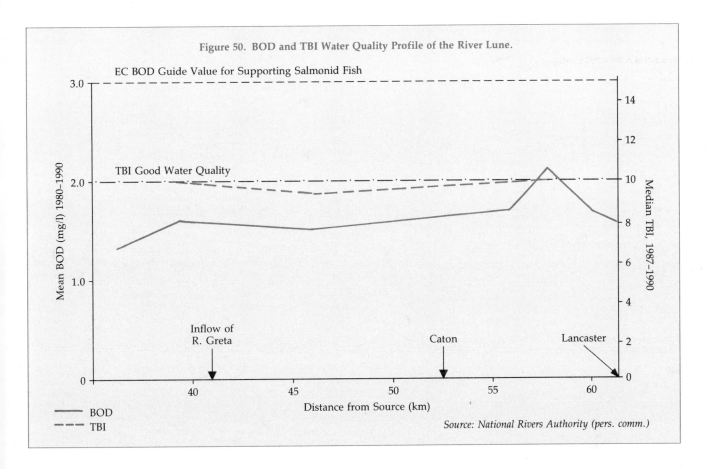

Figure 50. BOD and TBI Water Quality Profile of the River Lune.

Wenning has an annual mean daily flow of 840 Ml/day. The river (1989) is class 1b between the County boundary and Lune. In 1985, this stretch of the Wenning was class 1a. The salmonid phosphate standard is exceeded at Low Bentham, probably due to effluent inflow from both High Bentham sewage works and a fish farm at Low Bentham. But otherwise, the river meets all the salmonid standards (except nitrite). BOD is low and TBI scores are high, confirming the original classification of the river. It is, however, not an EC designated salmonid water.

4.81 The entire 10 km length of the River Hindburn is within Lancashire. It rises in the north of the Forest of Bowland and flows north-west to join the Wenning near Hornby, after receiving the waters of the Roeburn at Wray. It has an annual mean daily flow in its lower reaches of approximately 370 Ml/day and contributes significantly to the volume of the Wenning. It was classified as 1a for its whole length in 1985 and 1989 and does not exceed any of the standards for salmonid waters. It also has low BOD and high TBI. Nevertheless, like the Wenning, it is not itself a designated water, although 2.6 km of its tributaries are designated salmonid waters.

4.82 The River Roeburn rises in the next valley to the Hindburn and flows north to join it, some 11 km from its own source. Prior to its confluence with the Hindburn, it has an annual mean daily flow of 150 Ml/day. It was class 1a for its whole length in 1985 and 1989 and has low BOD and a high TBI. It is an EC designated salmonid water and does not exceed any of the salmonid standards. In addition to the main channel, a 1.1 km tributary stream is also a designated salmonid water.

4.83 The Rivers Conder and Cocker are small rivers which flow into the Lune estuary. The Conder rises in the hills east of Lancaster and flows approximately 8 km south-west to Galgate, 1 km below which, it turns north-west for 3 km, draining into the estuary at Glasson. It is tidal below Conder Green. The Cocker rises south of Galgate and also flows south-west, before turning north-east. It is only 8 km long and runs through Cockerham Marsh into the estuary and across Cockerham Sands to join the main channel of the Lune. The river is tidal in its lower stretches. Flow measurements are unavailable for both rivers.

4.84 The Conder was class 1b for its whole length in 1985 and 1989 and, apart from nitrite, meets salmonid standards. The upper half of the Cocker was class 1b in 1985, but class 2 in 1989. Its lower reaches were class 2 in 1985 and class 3 in 1989, because of higher BOD and ammonia levels. The Cocker exceeds the salmonid standard for BOD and the cyprinid standard for both ammonia and phosphate, indicating a high organic content and nutrient enrichment. It is not an EC designated water, although 11.4 km of the Conder above its tidal limit is a designated salmonid water.

4.85 Farmland on the southern edge of the Lune estuary is drained by two small rivers, Ridgy Pool and Pilling Water. Ridgy Pool flows northwards for 4 km to join the north-west flowing Pilling Water at Stake Pool. Pilling Water then continues northwards through Pilling Marsh crossing Cockerham Sands to the Lune. The entire 7 km length of Pilling Water was class 3 in 1985 and 1989 and Ridgy Pool was class 4 in both years. This very low quality is heavily influenced by agricultural

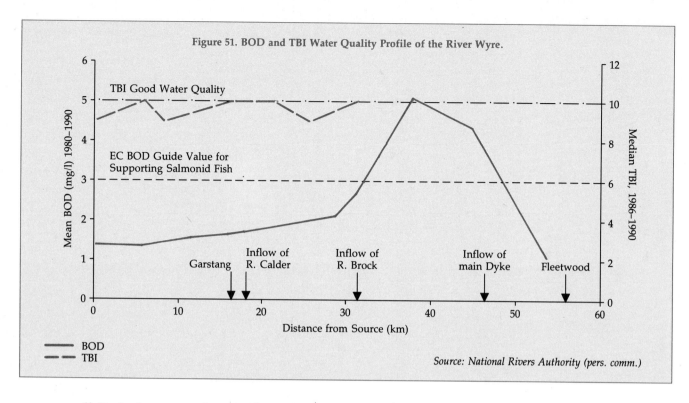

Figure 51. BOD and TBI Water Quality Profile of the River Wyre.

TBI Good Water Quality

EC BOD Guide Value for
Supporting Salmonid Fish

Mean BOD (mg/l) 1980-1990

Median TBI, 1986-1990

Garstang
Inflow of
R. Calder
Inflow of
R. Brock
Inflow of
main Dyke
Fleetwood

Distance from Source (km)

BOD
TBI

Source: National Rivers Authority (pers. comm.)

run-off. Both rivers exceed cyprinid standards for dissolved oxygen, ammonia, nitrite and phosphate. Pilling Water exceeds the salmonid standard for BOD, whereas Ridgy Pool exceeds the cyprinid standard for both BOD and suspended solids. Both are highly nutrient enriched and have a very high organic loading. Neither are designated fishery waters.

River Wyre and Tributaries

4.86   The River Wyre is formed by the confluence, at Abbeystead, of the Tarnbrook Wyre and the Marshaw Wyre, both of which run down from the western edge of the Forest of Bowland. Abbeystead Reservoir lies below the confluence and the Wyre really begins as the outflow from the reservoir. It then flows south through Garstang to St. Michael's on Wyre before turning west. It is tidal below Great Eccleston and its estuary turns northwards near Thornton, before discharging to the Irish Sea at Fleetwood.

4.87   The whole of the Wyre system lies in Lancashire and the Wyre itself stretches approximately 45 km from the source of the Tarnbrook Wyre to the tidal limit, and 15 km to the mouth of the estuary. In its middle reaches, it has an annual mean daily flow of 370 Ml/day, but by St. Michael's, this has increased to 660 Ml/day. There is a primary river gauging station at St. Michael's (Figure 44) and the measurements of flow in the River Wyre over the last ten years are shown in Figures 47–49.

4.88   The quality of the Wyre decreases downstream. In both the 1985 and 1989 surveys, it changes from class 1a in the upper reaches to 1b upstream of Catterall, becoming class 2 below St. Michael's (see Figure 45). These changes are underlined by the increase in BOD downstream, though the river does have a consistently high TBI (Figure 51). Very few of the standards for salmonid

waters are actually exceeded in the Wyre, except, once more, the nitrite standard.

4.89   In the upper Wyre, the water is naturally soft, so that many trace metal standards are lowered (as per Table 22) and concentrations of lead, zinc, copper and chromium are often close to, or slightly greater than, set limits. At Scorton, the minimum value for dissolved oxygen is below the cyprinid limit but the mean value is well above the 50% limit for salmonid waters. In its lowland stretches, farm discharges mean that the Wyre becomes nutrient enriched and high phosphate levels (above the cyprinid standard) are recorded.

4.90   The Wyre, nevertheless, is a locally important salmonid fishery and the whole of the Tarnbrook Wyre and Marshaw Wyre, plus 19.4 km of the Wyre from Abbeystead to below Garstang, are designated salmonid waters. Below Garstang, the 5.8 km to the tidal limit is a designated cyprinid water. Within the Wyre catchment, there is a total of 92.8 km of designated salmonid waters and 5.8 km of cyprinid waters.

4.91   The smaller of the County's two River Calders rises on Calder Fell and flows south-west through Calder Vale to join the Wyre at Catterall. It is 10 km long and has an annual mean daily flow of 31 Ml/day before joining the Wyre. It was class 1b over its whole length in 1985 and 1989 and exceeds the salmonid nitrite and phosphate standards, indicating modest nutrient enrichment. This corresponds with a downstream increase in BOD although a high TBI is maintained. The whole river is a designated salmonid water.

4.92   A wide area north of Preston is drained by several streams and small rivers flowing either north, or west, to join the Wyre near St. Michael's. The River Brock rises on the southern edge of Bowland and flows south-west to the village of Brock before turning west towards the Wyre. It is approximately 16 km long from its source to its confluence with the Wyre, where it has an annual mean daily flow of 165 Ml/day. In 1985 and 1989 the section between the Brock's confluence with the River Wyre and New Draught Brook was class 2, its upper 13.5 km remained class 1b in 1989. Below New Draught Brook, the River Brock exceeds the salmonid standard for BOD and cyprinid standards for ammonia, nitrite and phosphate. A high BOD and poor TBI confirm that the Brock is subject to organic pollution and nutrient enrichment in its lower reaches. Nevertheless, the whole river is a designated salmonid water.

4.93 The area between the Brock and Preston is drained by several brooks, which eventually join to form New Draught. Sparting Brook (3 km) and Westfield Brook (6 km) run over farmland north of Preston and join to form Barton Brook. Woodplumpton Brook drains the northern outskirts of Preston for 12 km, and joins the 7 km long Barton Brook to form New Draught, which then flows north for 3.7 km to enter the Brock just upstream of its confluence with the Wyre. Sparting Brook was classified 1b in 1985, but deteriorated to class 2 in 1989. Westfield, Barton and Woodplumpton Brooks were class 2 in 1985 and 1989, whilst the lower 3.1 km of Woodplumpton Brook was class 3 in 1985 and 1989. The first 2.7 km of New Draught improved from class 3 to class 2 over the same period, though its final kilometre stayed in class 3. There is a consistent exceedance of salmonid standards for both BOD (see Figure 52) and minimum dissolved oxygen concentration, and of the cyprinid standards for nitrite, ammonia and phosphate. It is perhaps surprising, therefore, that Sparting,

Westfield and Barton Brooks and New Draught are all designated salmonid waters.

4.94 Much of the area east of Blackpool is below sea level and is drained by a complex series of dykes and drains, which connect the Wyre and Ribble estuaries. One of the principal waterways is the Main Dyke, which runs east from Marton Mere for 3 km before turning north for 7.4 km to enter the Wyre estuary at Skippool. Approximately 40 Ml/day flow from Main Dyke into the Wyre at this point. It was class 3 for its entire length in 1985 and had not improved by 1989. Below its outflow from Marton Mere, the minimum salmonid oxygen limit is breached and the cyprinid ammonia and nitrite standard are exceeded. However, at Skippool, cyprinid standards for dissolved oxygen, BOD, ammonia, nitrite, suspended solids and phosphate are all exceeded. Main Dyke is not an EC designated water.

River Ribble and Tributaries

4.95 The Ribble is Lancashire's principal river and approximately 40% of the County lies within its catchment. Its source is in the Pennines from where it flows through Settle and Ribblesdale to the southeast, before turning south-west towards Lancashire. The Ribble enters Lancashire 33 km below its source, 2 km upstream of Paythorne. It then bisects the County, flowing a further 60 km southwest to its tidal limit at Walton-le-Dale. The estuary then extends a further 25 km to the Irish Sea beyond Lytham St. Annes. Its main tributaries are the Stock Beck, joining downstream of Paythorne, the Hodder and Calder, joining west of Clitheroe, the

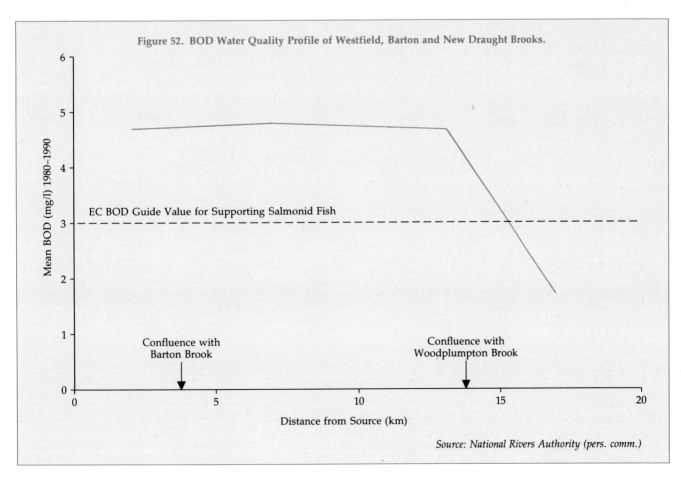

Figure 52. BOD Water Quality Profile of Westfield, Barton and New Draught Brooks.

EC BOD Guide Value for Supporting Salmonid Fish

Confluence with Barton Brook

Confluence with Woodplumpton Brook

Distance from Source (km)

Mean BOD (mg/l) 1980–1990

Source: National Rivers Authority (pers. comm.)

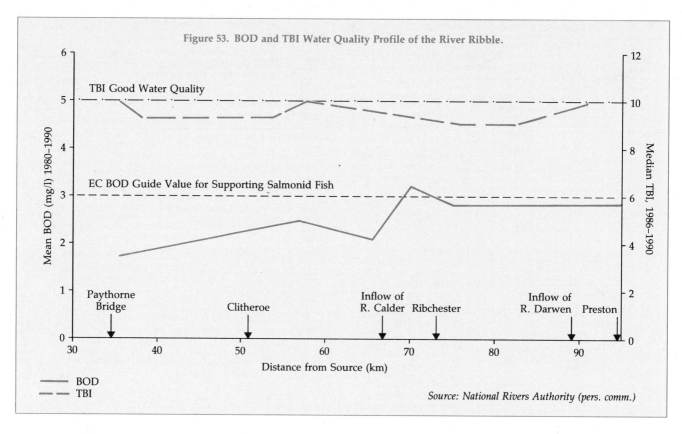

Figure 53. BOD and TBI Water Quality Profile of the River Ribble.

Source: National Rivers Authority (pers. comm.)

Darwen, entering at Bamber Bridge and the Douglas, flowing in opposite Freckleton.

4.96   The inflow of the Hodder and the Calder contribute significantly to the volume of flow of the Ribble. Above their confluences, at Mitton, the Ribble has an annual mean daily flow of approximately 1,200 Ml/day. At Dinckley (below the entry of the Hodder and Calder) this increases to 3,050 Ml/day. Below Ribchester, the river flows through a long series of meanders, which slows it down as it nears Preston. An annual mean daily flow of approximately 2,901 Ml/day is recorded at Samlesbury; the decrease presumably due to abstractions upstream. There is also a primary river gauging station on the Ribble at Samlesbury (see Figure 44) and Ribble flows are shown in Figures 47–49. These show similar patterns to the measured flows in the Lune. The patterns of monthly flows through the year are also very similar, although

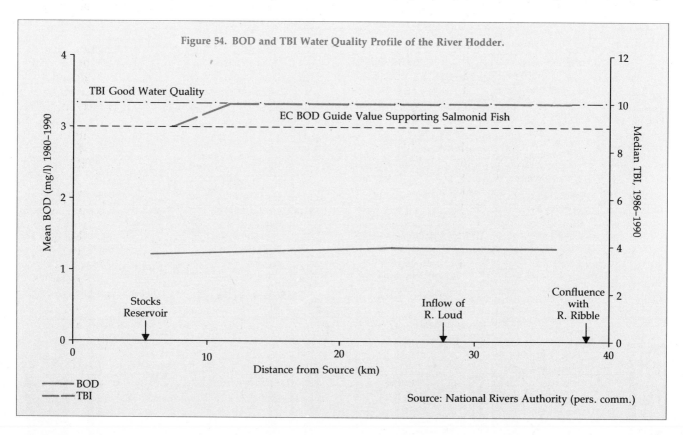

Figure 54. BOD and TBI Water Quality Profile of the River Hodder.

Source: National Rivers Authority (pers. comm.)

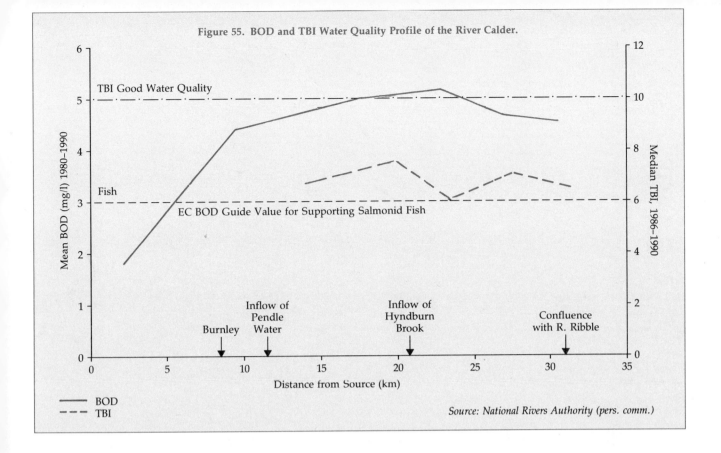

Figure 55. BOD and TBI Water Quality Profile of the River Calder.

minimum flow in the Ribble occurs in July, rather than May, as in the Lune.

4.97 The water quality classification of the Ribble changes several times as it flows through the County (see Figure 45). It was class 1b in 1985 and 1a in 1989 where it enters Lancashire, but changes to class 1b after receiving the mainly class 2 waters of Stock Beck. Below the inflow of Mearley Brook at Clitheroe, the Ribble improved from class 2 to class 1b since 1985. The remaining 52 km from the Calder to St.Annes is class 2 now, as it was in 1985.

4.98 The inflow of the Calder, with its high organic loading and trace metal contamination, is the major influence on the quality of the Ribble. Salmonid limits for lead and cadmium, and the cyprinid standard for copper, are all exceeded immediately below its confluence with the Ribble. There is also evidence of organic pollution, because BOD exceeds the salmonid limit, though mean oxygen concentration is above its salmonid limit for the whole of the river. Lower reaches show a slight improvement in water quality, indicated by a drop in BOD, although occasional low oxygen concentrations have been recorded. Nitrite and phosphate standards are, however, exceeded throughout the lower river, confirming its nutrient enriched state. Trends in BOD and TBI down the Ribble are shown in Figure 53.

4.99 The Ribble has reasonably good water quality and supports a diverse invertebrate community and an important salmonid and cyprinid fishery. The whole river upstream of the Calder is a designated salmonid fishery and the 19 km from Ribchester to the tidal limit are a designated cyprinid fishery. Within the Ribble catchment in Lancashire, there

are 138.7 km of EC designated salmonid waters and 19 km of cyprinid waters.

4.100 The Hodder rises in the north-east of Bowland and flows south-east into Stocks Reservoir. Below here, it flows south and then south-east to join the Ribble at Mitton. It receives the waters of Croasdale Brook at Slaidburn, Easington Brook at Easington, the River Dunsop at Dunsop Bridge, Langden Brook at Langden Bridge and the River Loud at Doeford Bridge. The Hodder is 40 km long and, prior to joining the Ribble, has an annual mean daily flow of 1,550 Ml/day.

4.101 The whole of the river and its tributaries were classified 1a in 1985 and 1989, except for a small length of the main channel immediately below Stocks Reservoir, and the whole of the River Loud (which were class 1b). Water quality data confirm these classifications and only the nitrite standards are exceeded. BOD is very low and the TBI is high along the whole length (Figure 54). The River Loud, at times, breaches the salmonid standards for minimum oxygen levels in its upper reaches, but has a mean oxygen concentration above the recommended limit. The Loud is also slightly nutrient enriched, and phosphate levels exceed the cyprinid standard. The whole Hodder system thus has a generally high water quality, comparable with the Lune. The entire length of the Hodder, including Stocks Reservoir, is a designated salmonid water, as are most of its tributaries. There are a further 40.8 km of designated salmonid waters in the system, which accounts for about 60% of all salmonid waters in the Lancashire Ribble catchment.

4.102 The East Lancashire Calder is 32 km long, and rises on the northern edge of the Forest of

Rossendale on Thievely Scout, flowing north-west to Burnley receiving the waters of the River Brun en route. Downstream of Burnley, it is joined by Pendle Water and flows westwards to Great Harwood where, after its confluence with Hyndburn Brook, it turns north-west to join the Ribble. At Padiham, the Calder has an annual mean daily flow of 435 Ml/day, which increases to 700 Ml/day by the time it enters the Ribble.

4.103   Near its source, the Calder was classed 1a in 1985 and 1989 but it quickly becomes class 4 (class 3 in 1985) at Holme Chapel after receiving polluted minewaters from Black Clough. There is a slight improvement to class 3, and then to class 2 (in 1985 and 1989) by the time the River Brun joins the main channel. The Calder then remains class 2 for 23.6 km until its confluence with the Ribble, except for a class 3 stretch of 6.2 km from the inflow of Hyndburn Brook. In 1985, this entire 23.6 km stretch was class 3.

4.104   The BOD profile (Figure 55) shows the difference in quality between most of the Calder and its headwaters. The fluctuation in TBI also reflects the distribution of polluting influences down the river (Figure 55). The headwaters have high lead (exceeding the salmonid standards) and copper (exceeding the cyprinid standard) concentrations due to the Black Clough minewaters, but meet other standards. Below the Brun, however, quality falls dramatically. Cyprinid limits for copper, cadmium, nitrite, suspended solids and phosphate are exceeded and salmonid standards for BOD and lead are also breached. This indicates significant organic pollution, nutrient enrichment and trace metal contamination below Burnley. At Padiham, the maximum concentrations of suspended solids and minimum oxygen concentrations are evidence of occasional organic pollution incidents, probably from Burnley sewage works. Sewage effluent also causes exceedance of the cyprinid ammonia standard at Padiham.

4.105   Organic pollutants remain high at Whalley and zinc exceeds the salmonid limit upstream of Sabden Brook. Prior to its confluence with the Ribble, salmonid standards for lead, zinc, BOD and minimum dissolved oxygen and cyprinid standards for copper, cadmium, ammonia, nitrite and phosphate are breached. The Calder, therefore, is one of the most seriously polluted rivers in Lancashire and, not surprisingly, is not a designated fishery. There are, however, 19.7 km of designated salmonid waters in the whole catchment. Sabden Brook, for example, is a designated salmonid water from Sabden, down to its confluence with the Calder.

4.106   The River Don rises in the moors east of Burnley, where it is initially called Thursden Brook. Thursden Brook flows west for 4.5 km (before it becomes the Don) which then flows south-west for only 2.5 km before entering the Brun at Rowley. The Brun rises on Worsthorne Moor and flows north-west for 7 km to join the Calder in the centre of Burnley. It receives the waters of Swinden Water and the Don, in close succession at Rowley. Prior to its confluence with the Calder, the Brun has

an annual mean daily flow of approximately 60 Ml/day.

4.107   Both rivers are clean in their upper reaches, the Brun being class 1a and the Don class 1b in 1985 and 1989. Below Worsthorne, however, the Brun becomes class 2 and, below Rowley, class 3. This decline is due to polluted water from coal mine spoil at Rowley. There is a large input of iron compounds which discolour the water and blanket the river bed, depleting the invertebrate community (Greenfield and Ireland, 1978). The salmonid standards for lead and phosphate and the cyprinid standards for copper and suspended solids are all exceeded at Rowley. By the time the Brun reaches the Calder, it also has a BOD higher than the salmonid standard and cadmium levels above the cyprinid standard. There are, however, no designated fisheries in the Don-Brun system.

4.108   Colne Water is formed by the junction of the River Laneshaw and Wycoller Beck at Laneshaw Bridge. Both rise on the moors east of Colne and, from their confluence, Colne Water flows west for 7 km before joining Pendle Water at Barrowford. It has an annual mean daily flow of 80 Ml/day when it joins Pendle Water. In 1989, Colne Water was classed 1b for its first 7.2 km. It deteriorates in quality to class 3, (class 2 in 1985) after passing Colne STW, and has consistently high phosphate and nitrite concentrations along its entire length. Below Colne, salmonid standards for minimum dissolved oxygen, lead and BOD and cyprinid standards for suspended solids, nitrite and phosphate are exceeded. The TBI also declines down the river. Colne Water itself is not a designated fishery, but 5.3 km of its tributary streams are salmonid waters.

4.109   Colne Water has been subject to several significant pollution incidents, the most notable of which occurred in 1989. Around 1,000 gallons of toxic caustic soda overflowed from the NWW water treatment plant at Laneshaw Bridge causing the death of over 5,000 trout (Pendle Pollution Control, 1990). This prompted the District Council to undertake a monitoring programme in the Pendle river basin. The first year's results show that Colne Water is recovering from the 1989 incident, but that it may be several years before it is restored to its former condition (Pendle Pollution Control, 1990).

4.110   Streams running off the eastern slopes of Pendle Hill feed Ogden reservoirs, the outflow from which forms Pendle Water. This runs roughly east for 7.5 km, from Barley towards Colne, before receiving Colne Water at Barrowford. After the confluence, Pendle Water flows south-west for 6.5 km before entering the Calder north of Burnley. Above its confluence with Colne Water, Pendle Water has an annual mean daily flow of 38 Ml/day, increasing to 200 Ml/day before of its confluence with the Calder.

4.111   The upper reaches of Pendle Water are class 1a as far as Higherford and 1b from here to the Colne Water confluence. The remaining 7.8 km deteriorates to class 3 up to its junction with the Calder. In 1985 the upper 3.3 km of this last 7.8 km stretch was class 2. The change from 1b to 3 is due to the poor quality of Colne Water. Quality above its

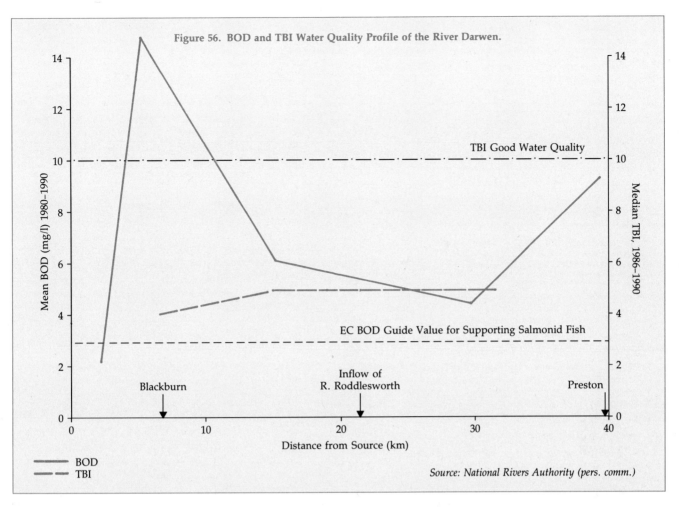

Figure 56. BOD and TBI Water Quality Profile of the River Darwen.

TBI Good Water Quality

EC BOD Guide Value for Supporting Salmonid Fish

Blackburn

Inflow of
R. Roddlesworth

Preston

Mean BOD (mg/l) 1980–1990

Median TBI, 1986–1990

Distance from Source (km)

—— BOD
- - - TBI

Source: National Rivers Authority (pers. comm.)

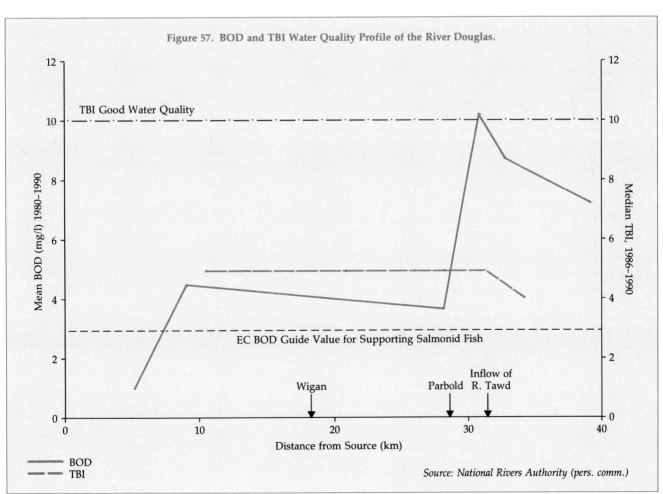

Figure 57. BOD and TBI Water Quality Profile of the River Douglas.

TBI Good Water Quality

EC BOD Guide Value for Supporting Salmonid Fish

Wigan

Parbold

Inflow of
R. Tawd

Mean BOD (mg/l) 1980–1990

Median TBI, 1986–1990

Distance from Source (km)

—— BOD
- - - TBI

Source: National Rivers Authority (pers. comm.)

confluence with Colne Water is much better, with only nitrite standards being exceeded. Below Barrowford, minimum oxygen concentrations and BOD breach salmonid standards and phosphate and nitrite exceed cyprinid standards. Further downstream, as it nears the Calder, Pendle Water reduces in quality. Salmonid standards for lead and for the minimum dissolved oxygen concentration are breached and cyprinid standards for BOD, ammonia, nitrite, phosphate, suspended solids and copper are all exceeded. There is a particularly high level of organic pollution in this part of the river. These changes are also reflected in the downstream decline in the invertebrate community. Median TBIs fall from 10 above Colne Water to 6 at the entry to the Calder. Only the upper reaches and tributaries of Pendle Water are suitable for supporting a good fishery and the 7.5 km of river above the entry of Colne Water, and 1.7 km of tributary streams, are designated salmonid waters.

4.112   Streams like Whams Brook and White Ash Brook flow down from Oswaldtwistle Moor and combine in Oswaldtwistle to form Hyndburn Brook. The River Hyndburn, which rises east of Accrington and flows through the town, enters Hyndburn Brook at Church. Hyndburn Brook flows north from Oswaldtwistle for 6.5 km to join the Calder north of Great Harwood. Above the entry of the River Hyndburn, the Brook has an annual mean daily flow of 22 Ml/day, to which the River Hyndburn contributes a further 18 Ml/day. By the time the Brook enters the Calder, it has a mean flow of 135 Ml/day.

4.113   Water quality along the length of Hyndburn Brook is poor. In 1989, its first 4 km were class 1b, whilst the 1.3 km to the inflow of the River Hyndburn was class 3 (an improvement from 1985, when it was class 4). Beyond the confluence, the final 5.8 km up to the Calder was class 3 in both 1985 and 1989. It has one of the most serious metal contamination problems in the County, exceeding the salmonid standard for lead and cyprinid standards for arsenic, copper and zinc at Oswaldtwistle. This arises mainly from mine drainage and industrial discharges. It also suffers from organic pollution and nutrient enrichment, exceeding the salmonid BOD limit and the cyprinid standards for ammonia, nitrite and phosphate. The River Hyndburn is similarly polluted and also has high cadmium levels. As it enters the Calder, Hyndburn Brook breaches salmonid standards for lead, BOD and minimum dissolved oxygen and exceeds cyprinid standards for cadmium, arsenic, copper, zinc, nitrite, phosphate and suspended solids. There is also an indication of mercury levels in excess of recommended limits. Consequently, the invertebrate fauna is poor and a median TBI of 5 is recorded throughout the Brook. Not surprisingly, no part of Hyndburn Brook or the River Hyndburn is a designated fishery.

4.114   The River Darwen is formed by the outflow of Jacks Key Reservoir south of Darwen and flows 40 km roughly north-west, past Blackburn, to join the Ribble near Preston, where it is tidal below Walton-le-Dale. On the outskirts of Blackburn, the Darwen receives approximately 20 Ml/day of highly polluted water from the River Blakewater, which flows through the centre of Blackburn, and at Pleasington it receives the waters of the River Roddlesworth. Prior to its confluence with the Ribble, the Darwen has an annual mean daily flow of 360 Ml/day.

4.115   Along with the Calder, Hyndburn Brook and parts of the Douglas, the Darwen is one of the most polluted of Lancashire's rivers. Its first 1.6 km were class 1b in 1989, but this deteriorated to class 2 up to Hollins Paper Mill. Between here and Darwen sewage works, the river declines to class 4, but is class 3 from the sewage works until the confluence with the River Roddlesworth, 8.7 km downstream (despite receiving the class 4 waters of the River Blakewater). The next stretch, 8.3 km to the inflow of Hole Brook, improves to class 2 (despite receiving a class 3 inflow from the River Roddlesworth). Beyond Hole Brook, the main channel deteriorates again to class 3 up to tidal limits at Walton-le-Dale (a kilometre before it joins the Ribble). Hole Brook, itself, reduces from class 2 to class 4 on passing Blackburn sewage treatment works. The Darwen's NWC classification has remained largely constant since 1985, apart from an improvement from class 3 to 2 along the 4.3 km stretch between the inflows of the Roddlesworth and Alum Brook.

4.116   Even near its source, the Darwen breaches minimum cyprinid dissolved oxygen concentrations and suffers high BOD and suspended solids. Below the town of Darwen, the river exceeds cyprinid standards for BOD, suspended solids, nitrite, phosphate and minimum dissolved oxygen concentration. The class 4 River Blakewater exceeds cyprinid standards for BOD, ammonia, suspended solids, nitrite, phosphate and minimum dissolved oxygen as it discharges to the Darwen. The River Roddlesworth also drains very poor quality water into the Darwen, due to effluent from the Star Paper Mills at Feniscowles.

4.117   By Samlesbury Bottoms, however, the Darwen has improved, and only exceeds cyprinid standards for nitrite, phosphate and minimum dissolved oxygen and the salmonid standards for BOD. Prior to joining the Ribble, it exceeds cyprinid standards for copper, BOD, nitrite, phosphate and minimum dissolved oxygen. The changes in the quality of the Darwen are illustrated by the fluctuations in BOD shown on Figure 56. The TBI, however, is consistently low (Figure 56), showing the poor quality of the invertebrate fauna. The river has no designated fisheries.

River Douglas and Tributaries

4.118   The River Douglas begins as the outflow of Lower Rivington Reservoir (which is fed by many streams off the western edge of the West Pennine Moors) south-east of Chorley and is the County boundary for 7 km before entering Wigan south of Adlington. It flows in a large 14 km loop through Wigan before it again forms the Lancashire border for 2 km south of Appley Bridge. The Douglas then enters the County and flows north for a further 26 km, entering the Ribble estuary opposite Freckleton. The 15 km below Rufford are tidal. The

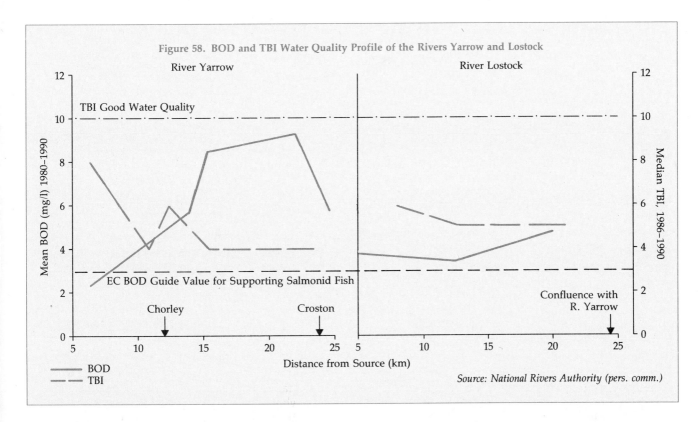

Figure 58. BOD and TBI Water Quality Profile of the Rivers Yarrow and Lostock

Source: National Rivers Authority (pers. comm.)

Douglas is a relatively small river for most of its length and has an annual mean daily flow of 365 Ml/day north of Parbold and 370 Ml/day at Rufford. There is a primary river gauging station on the Douglas at Wanes Blades Bridge between Parbold and Rufford (Figure 44). Variation in flow from 1979–1989 and monthly flow patterns (1983–1990) are shown in Figures 47–49.

4.119   The BOD profile for the Douglas (Figure 57) shows a variation in water quality, though the TBI is consistently low, indicating that occasional improvements in water quality along the river do not actually result in biological improvements. The Douglas suffers from high levels of nutrient enrichment and organic pollution. At Adlington, the salmonid BOD standard and the cyprinid standards for minimum oxygen concentration, ammonia, nitrite, suspended solids and phosphate are all exceeded. At Parbold, the same applies. This remains the case downstream of Hoscar sewage works at the inflow of the River Tawd, and, in addition, the cyprinid limits for BOD and copper and the salmonid lead standard are exceeded. Consequently, no part of the Douglas is a designated fishery. Two of the reservoirs in its catchment, Worthington and Rivington, are, however, designated salmonid waters. Below Lower Rivington Reservoir, the Douglas is class 1a for 1.5 km, but becomes class 2 after receiving effluent from Horwich sewage works via Pearl Brook. It remains class 2 until leaving the County, deteriorates to class 3 in Wigan but recovers to class 2 before re-entering Lancashire at Appley Bridge. Parbold sewage works effluent reduces the class to 3 for the next 4.6 km up to Rufford (this length was class 4 in 1985).

4.120   The River Tawd rises south of Skelmersdale and flows north for 10.5 km to join the Douglas between Parbold and Rufford. It is a small river, with an annual mean daily flow of 75 Ml/day at its

confluence with the Douglas. In 1985 and 1989 it was class 4 from Skelmersdale to Newburgh, and class 3 beyond this down to the Douglas. Water quality data for the Tawd show that it is both nutrient enriched and organically polluted. Prior to its confluence with the Douglas, it exceeds salmonid standards for BOD and phosphate and cyprinid standards for nitrite and copper.

4.121   The River Lostock rises above Whittle-le-Woods and flows in a wide loop around Leyland, before turning south to join the Yarrow at Croston. It is approximately 24 km long and has an annual mean daily flow of 190 Ml/day below Leyland. In 1985 and 1989 it was class 2 for most of its length but became class 3 below the Leyland Motor Works, returning to class 2 south of the town. It has the typical water quality of a small lowland river in the County, showing both nutrient and organic enrichment. Even above Whittle-le-Woods, the salmonid standard for BOD and the cyprinid standards for ammonia, nitrite and phosphate are breached. The same parameters are exceeded all the way to its confluence with the Yarrow. Changes in BOD and TBI are shown in Figures 58. The Lostock is not a designated fishery.

4.122   The River Yarrow rises on Anglezarke Moor and flows into Yarrow Reservoir, which is connected to Anglezarke and Upper Rivington Reservoirs. It emerges from the northern end of the latter and flows initially north-west towards Chorley, but then loops round the southern edge of the town before flowing west to the Douglas, receiving the waters of the Lostock at Croston, 1 km prior to its confluence with the Douglas. It is 24.5 km long and has an annual mean daily flow of 245 Ml/day at Croston.

4.123   Immediately below Upper Rivington Reservoir, the river is class 3 for 3 km, becoming class 2 and then class 1b up to Limbrick. Here, the inflow of the Black Brook reverts the Yarrow back to class 2. Effluent from Chorley sewage works reduces the river to class 3, though the final 7 km before the confluence with the Douglas is class 2. Like the Lostock, it is both nutrient and organically enriched. Upstream of Chorley sewage works, salmonid standards for BOD and phosphate and cyprinid standards for nitrite and minimum dissolved oxygen are breached. Below here, the river deteriorates significantly and also exceeds cyprinid standards for mean dissolved oxygen, BOD, ammonia, suspended solids and phosphate. The sharp rise in BOD and drop in the TBI associated with the sewage works can be seen in Figure 58. The Yarrow then remains largely unchanged, except for some improvement in dissolved oxygen concentrations, for the rest of its length.

4.124   The flat land south of the Ribble estuary and west of the Douglas is drained by a network of ditches and dykes. These drain mainly into the Three Pools Waterway and The Sluice. Three Pools Waterway forms the County boundary east of Southport and discharges to the Ribble estuary between the town and Banks. The Sluice runs north-west from Martin Mere reserve, past Tarleton Leisure Lakes (where it becomes Back Drain), and empties into Three Pools at Banks. Three Pools is class 3 for its entire 12 km length, and the 9 km Sluice/Back Drain is all class 2, except in its upper section where it is class 3. Both waterways are highly organically and nutrient enriched and consistently exceed cyprinid standards for dissolved oxygen, BOD, suspended solids, ammonia, nitrite and phosphate.

River Irwell and Tributaries

4.125   The Irwell rises on the moors above Bacup and flows down through the town before turning west towards Rawtenstall. It then turns south and flows out of the County at Ramsbottom. Approximately 15.5 km of the Irwell lies in Lancashire. Numerous tributary streams run down from the Moors to join the Irwell in the Rossendale valley. Thus, by the time the river leaves Lancashire, it has an annual mean daily flow of approximately 305 Ml/day.

4.126   In its upper reaches, the Irwell is class 3, due largely to mine washings entering the river but it improves to class 2 below Bacup. It becomes class 3 for a short stretch below Rossendale sewage works and then remains class 3 until it leaves the County. Water quality data show that the river exceeds the cyprinid nitrite and minimum dissolved oxygen standards and the salmonid BOD and phosphate standards between Bacup and Rawtenstall. As the Irwell leaves the County, it continues to breach the salmonid water standards for minimum dissolved oxygen and BOD and cyprinid standards for nitrite and suspended solids. Despite this generally poor water quality, 18.8 km of the upper tributaries of the Irwell are designated salmonid waters. This does not, however, include any of the Irwell itself.

4.127   Limy Water is the largest of the Irwell's tributaries. It is formed from the outflow of Clowbridge Reservoir and flows south for 8.7 km to join the Irwell at Rawtenstall. It is class 1a for its first 1.5 km, class 1b for a further 2.2 km and class 2 for the remainder of its length. Prior to joining the Irwell, Limy Water exceeds the salmonid standard for BOD and the cyprinid nitrite standard. It is, therefore, generally good quality water, but because of its size, does not significantly improve the Irwell after joining it at Rawtenstall.

Quality of Standing Waters

Lakes

4.128   There are only two natural lakes in Lancashire, Hawes Water near Silverdale and Marton

Table 24 Ownership and Capacity of Reservoirs in Lancashire. 1990

| Owner | Total Numbers | Total Surface Area (ha) | Total Capacity (m³) | Number with Capacity (m³) | | | |
				up to 100 000	100 000 to 500 000	500 000 +	No Data
NWW	82	976.3	27,092,890	13	48	19	2
NRA	1	1.4	55,000	1	0	0	—
BWB	6	89.4	9,510,369	0	4	2	—
YWA	1	11.7	866,000	0	0	1	—
Industry	9	10.6[1]	441,527[1]	3	2	0	4
Private	7	11.4[1]	213,000[1]	3	0	0	4
Local Authorities	3	20.9[1]	352,800[1]	nd	nd	nd	—
New Towns Commission	1	nd	nd	nd	nd	nd	—
Angling Clubs	6	nd	nd	nd	nd	nd	—
Fisheries	2	nd	nd	nd	nd	nd	—
LANCASHIRE	118	1,121.7[1]	38,530,786[1]				

Source: Various

Notes: [1] – incomplete data
      nd – no data

Figure 59
Distribution of Reservoirs in Lancashire .1990

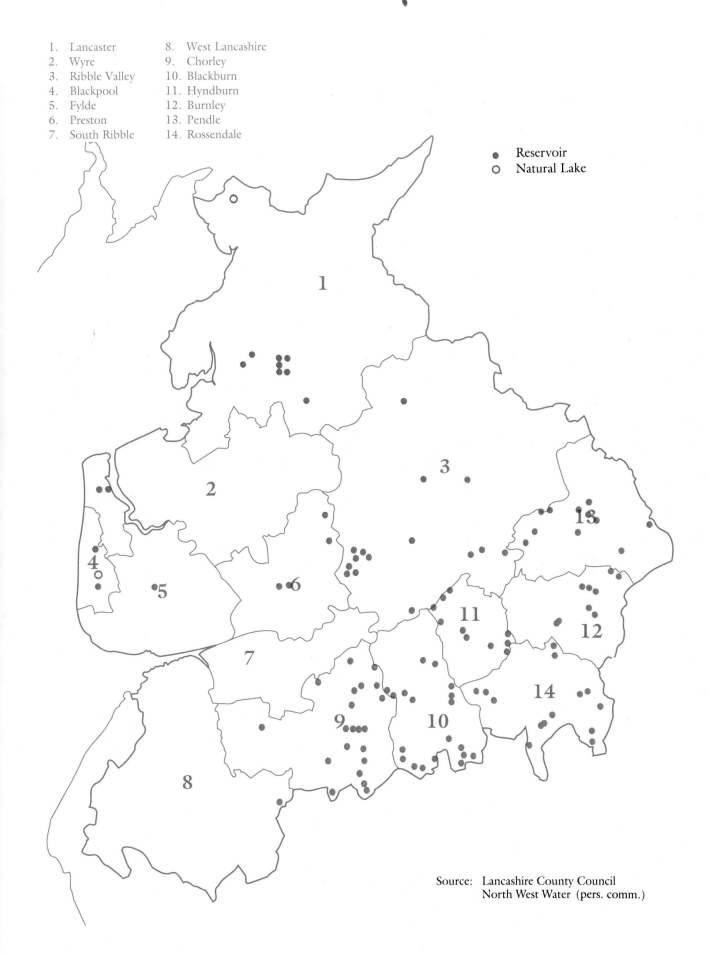

1. Lancaster
2. Wyre
3. Ribble Valley
4. Blackpool
5. Fylde
6. Preston
7. South Ribble
8. West Lancashire
9. Chorley
10. Blackburn
11. Hyndburn
12. Burnley
13. Pendle
14. Rossendale

● Reservoir
○ Natural Lake

Source: Lancashire County Council
North West Water (pers. comm.)

Mere in Blackpool (see Figure 59). The former is not monitored for water quality, but the inflow and outflow of Marton Mere are. These data indicate that Marton Mere is nutrient enriched. The Mere does not, however, seem to suffer from the algal problems which have beset the nearby Stanley Park Lake. Hawes Water is one of only three marl lakes in the north of England. It is highly calcareous and relatively low in nutrients, resulting in a high water quality. It supports a diverse plant and aquatic invertebrate community (see Chapter 9).

Reservoirs

4.129 There are 118 reservoirs in Lancashire, ranging in size from Stocks Reservoir (47.4 ha) to small angling club and fish farm reservoirs. They are an extensive aquatic resource and their distribution is shown in Figure 59. Most are found in the south-east of the County, scattered throughout the West Pennine Moors and the South Pennines. Many were built to supply water to growing Lancashire towns during the last century.

4.130 The main reservoir groups in the County are:

* Stocks (Ribble Valley);
* Anglezarke, Yarrow, Upper and Lower Rivington (Chorley);
* Entwistle, Wayoh and Jumbles (Blackburn);
* Holden Wood, Ogden, Calf Hey and Cowm (Rossendale);
* Foulridge, Ogden, Black Moss and White Moor (Pendle);

* Cant Clough, Hurstwood and Swinden (Burnley).

Stocks Reservoir is an important supply and recreational (fishing) reservoir. The various reservoir groups in the West Pennine Moors are also used for supply and provide collectively, one of the most important concentrations of water-based recreational facilities outside of the Lake District (see Chapter 11). Foulridge is also important for recreation and maintains water levels in the Leeds and Liverpool Canal.

4.131 Table 24 details the ownership, number and capacity of Lancashire's reservoirs. NWW is the major owner in the County, with 82, or 70%, of the total. Of these, 54 are used for drinking water supply. Supply reservoirs have been classified by NWW according to permissible recreational use as shown in Table 25.

4.132 Water quality information for reservoirs is not collected by the NRA, so there are no data from which to make a detailed assessment of reservoir quality. NWW monitors supply reservoir outflow quality, prior to its entry to the treatment works, for its own operational purposes, but this information is not publicly available. Reservoir water quality must therefore, be inferred from the nature of the reservoir catchment. The location of Lancashire's reservoirs and the nature of their catchments suggests that all main reservoirs are likely to have a reasonable water quality.

Ponds and Pits

4.133 These constitute a substantial, but little known, aquatic resource in Lancashire. On the Fylde in particular, there are large numbers of marl pits, which form an important network of ponds. Further information on their numbers and distribution is given in Chapter 9 and on Figure 142. Nothing is known about their water quality, although many must be subject to nutrient enrichment from farm run-off. Main pond concentrations coincide with intensive livestock-rearing areas (see Chapter 8 and Figures 127 and 128).

Canals

4.134 There are two canals in Lancashire, the Lancaster and the Leeds and Liverpool. The Lancaster Canal runs from Preston to Tewitfield on the Cumbria border, with a branch to the Lune estuary at Glasson. The Leeds and Liverpool Canal, which enters the County south of Downholland in West Lancashire, crosses into Wigan Metropolitan Borough at Appley Bridge, and re-enters Lancashire south of Chorley, from whence it flows north-east up the Calder Valley to Greenberfield, on the North Yorkshire border. Its Rufford Branch links into the Ribble Estuary. The total length of all canals is 164.8 km (72.3 km on the Lancaster and 92.5 km on the Leeds-Liverpool).

4.135 Both canals are owned by British Waterways Board (BWB), who are aiming to improve the water quality for aesthetic and recreational reasons. In 1988, NWW provided BWB with chemical water quality data for the canals. These 1988 data have been compared with 1989 NRA data in Table 26.

Table 25 Status of North West Water Reservoirs in Lancashire. 1990

Status	Permissible Recreational Activity	Number
Compensation	Swimming, paddling	6
Supply Classification A	Power boating, hovercraft, water skiing and all activities listed below.	8
Supply Classification B	Waterskiing by limited numbers using non-polluting boats, sub-aqua, windsurfing, sailing, canoeing, angling, model-boating.	0
Supply Classification C	Limited numbers: sailing, rowing, canoeing, angling, model-boating, windsurfing (club managed).	27
Supply Classification D	Angling from the shore only.	4
Supply Classification E	Generally none, though exceptions may occur.	3
Supply Classification F	Generally none, though exceptions may occur.	12
Not in use		1
Disused		5
Redundant		1
Industrial supply		1
Service		1
No information		13
LANCASHIRE		82

Source: NWW (pers. comm.)

4.136 Quality along the Leeds-Liverpool Canal has remained constant over the two year period, with 90% in class 2 and 10% in class 1a. The Lancaster Canal presents a more variable picture, particularly for the stretches between the Preston Branch and Catterall and between Glasson and Hest Bank. However, the NRA have confirmed (pers.comm.) that the reductions to class 2 reflect reclassifications based on several years data, correcting previous mis-classifications. BOD water quality profiles are presented for both canals in Figures 60 and 61.

Quality of Groundwaters

4.137 Groundwater collects in openings, cavities and spaces in rocks, and is derived either from water rising from deep underground, or from rain water seeping down. Aquifers (water-bearing strata) are the commonest form. These may be either porous, where water is held between grains in the rock, or pervious, where water occurs in joints and fissures. Water remains in the aquifer, because underlying strata are impermeable, preventing downward escape.

4.138 There are two main types of aquifer-bearing rocks in Lancashire, the Permio-Triassic Sandstones, and Carboniferous Limestone (see Figure 3). These form a Y-shaped belt extending northwards from the south-west of the County, and splitting into two arms north of Preston. One arm continues northwards to the Lune estuary and the other, composed of the limestone, north-eastwards. A smaller area of limestone occurs in the Carnforth

Table 26 NWC Classification of Canals in Lancashire. 1988 and 1989

Section of Canal	Length (km)	NWC Class 1988	NWC Class 1989
Leeds and Liverpool Canal:			
R. Douglas – Blackey Hall	83.6	2	2
Blakey Hall – Greenberfield	8.9	1a	1a
Lancaster Canal:			
Lune – Glasson Dock	0.8	1b	1b
Glasson – Hest Bank	21.1	1a	2
Hest Bank – Tewitfield	11.2	1a	1b
Preston Branch – Catterall	15.6	1a	2
Catterall – Swillbrook	11.9	1b	2
Swillbrook – Maudlands	11.7	2	3
LANCASHIRE	164.8	—	—

Sources: British Waterways (1989) and NRA (pers. comm.)

area. The NRA carries out limited borehole monitoring (see above), but unavailability of the data means that no indication of groundwater quality can be given here.

4.139 The Millstone Grit series (see also Figure 3), of which most of eastern Lancashire is comprised, gives rise to large numbers of springs. Springs

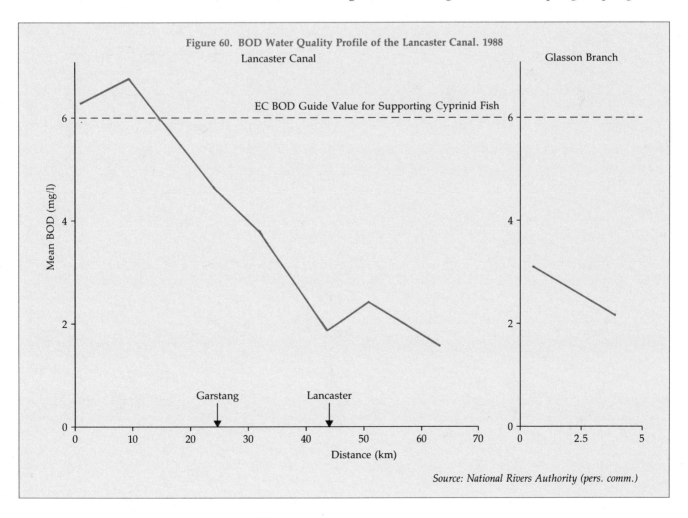

Figure 60. BOD Water Quality Profile of the Lancaster Canal. 1988

Source: National Rivers Authority (pers. comm.)

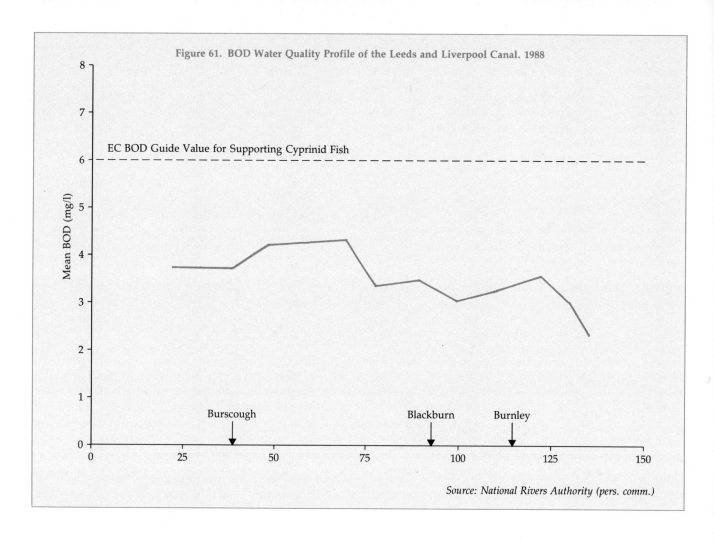

Figure 61. BOD Water Quality Profile of the Leeds and Liverpool Canal. 1988

EC BOD Guide Value for Supporting Cyprinid Fish

Burscough

Blackburn

Burnley

Mean BOD (mg/l)

Source: National Rivers Authority (pers. comm.)

essentially consist of groundwaters emerging at the surface. They arise when water seeping through the soil and surface rock strata encounters an impermeable rock layer. The water can no longer move downwards so it moves along the surface of this layer to emerge at the surface. Large numbers occur in east Lancashire and are used for private drinking supplies and agricultural purposes. Data on drinking water quality from springs are dealt with in the section on Private Water Supplies (below).

Quality of Estuarine and Coastal Waters

4.140 There are three major estuaries in Lancashire, the Lune, Wyre and Ribble. A large portion of Morecambe Bay also lies within the County, whilst the Rivers Keer and Cocker have small estuaries. In 1988, NWW examined 124 km of estuarine waters in the County (North West Water 1988). Estuaries are included in the NWC quality survey and have a separate, though similar, classification system to that for rivers, ranging from Class A (Good), to Class B (Fair), Class C (Poor) and Class D (Bad). Following the 1988 survey, NWW calculated the lengths of estuarine waters of different quality in the County (see Table 27). Figure 45 shows the position recorded by the NRA for 1989. It indicates that only minor changes occurred between 1988 and 1989.

4.141 The majority of estuarine water in Lancashire is thus of good to fair quality. As this quality is largely determined by inflows from rivers, and activities in their catchments, further improvements in Lancashire's estuary quality are heavily dependent upon changes upstream. Nevertheless, plans to improve the water quality of the Fylde coast and the Ribble estuary have been proposed by NWW.

4.142 Estuarine water chemistry is different to freshwater and the standards used for assessment of freshwater quality do not apply. Estuaries have naturally lower dissolved oxygen, and higher suspended solid concentrations than most freshwaters. There are no specific standards on which to base an assessment of estuary quality, so

Table 27 NWC Classification of Lancashire's Estuaries. 1988

NWC Class	Quality Description	1988 (km)	%
A	Good	46	37
B	Fair	65	53
C	Poor	10	8
D	Bad	3	2
LANCASHIRE		124	100

Source: North West Water (1988)

quality assessment is largely restricted to the NWC scheme.

Lune Estuary

4.143 The Lune estuary extends from the tidal limit of the River Lune, in Lancaster, out into the southern part of Morecambe Bay. It is Class A for the whole of its length, although it does receive some Class B waters from Overton Dyke and the River Conder and sewage effluent from Lancaster sewage works at Stodday. It is, nevertheless, a high quality estuary. It has consistently high dissolved oxygen concentrations and supports an important migratory fish population. The Lune is also the major contributor of freshwater to Morecambe Bay, accounting for almost 50% of the total input (Robinson and Pringle, 1987).

Wyre Estuary

4.144 The Wyre estuary extends from the river's tidal limit at Cartford Bridge, Great Eccleston to Wyre Light at the extreme southern edge of Morecambe Bay. The whole estuary is Class B. It receives effluent dishcarges from the ICI Hillhouse complex at Thornton and sewage effluent from the works at. Poulton-le-Fylde. Despite these, the estuary supports migratory fish and can be considered to have a reasonable water quality.

Ribble Estuary

4.145 The Ribble estuary extends from the tidal limit at Walton-le-Dale, near Preston, westwards to the Irish Sea. It can also be considered to include the tidal stretches of the Douglas, as far south as Rufford. The estuary is mostly Class B, although the Douglas between Rufford and Croston is Class C. At the extreme mouth of the estuary, beyond St. Anne's and Southport, where there is considerable dilution of the river water by seawater, it is Class A.

4.146 Despite the input of poor quality water from both the Darwen and Douglas, and sewage effluent from the large sewage works at Clifton Marsh, the estuary maintains a reasonable water quality. Dissolved oxygen concentrations remain quite high and the estuary carries migratory fish. Many more salmon move back and forth with the tides in the estuary than actually penetrate upstream (Priede et al., 1988), so it is important that the quality of the estuary is, at the very least, maintained.

Morecambe Bay

4.147 Morecambe Bay lies inland of a line between Walney Island, Cumbria and Rossall Point, Fleetwood. Thus, the north Lancashire coast comprises the whole of the eastern edge of the Bay. Four main rivers, each with their own estuary, drain into the Bay. The Cumbrian Leven and Kent enter the north of the Bay and the Lancashire Lune and Wyre flow into its south-eastern section. The whole of the Bay in Lancaster District is Class A.

4.148 Morecambe Bay receives direct discharges of sewage and industrial effluents, in addition to those arriving down its feeder rivers. In Lancashire, the major discharges to the Bay are sewage outfalls at Carnforth, Morecambe and Heysham and the Heysham Nuclear Power Station outfall. Despite these, which cause localised problems, the Bay has a high water quality throughout, with low concentrations of pollutants and very little nutrient enrichment (Robinson and Pringle, 1987).

Coastal Waters

4.149 There are 67 km of coastline in the County (NRA, pers.comm). This excludes all estuarial coastline and consists primarily of two main areas; the Fylde coast on the Irish Sea and the eastern edge of Morecambe Bay, from Fleetwood to Silverdale. There is limited monitoring of these coastal waters, most of which concentrates on radioactive or bacteriological parameters. General water quality information is less available.

4.150 The water quality of the surf-zone was assessed in a study carried out by the North Western and North Wales Sea Fisheries Committee in the early 1970's (Hinchcliffe, 1976). Several sites along the Lancashire coast were sampled and both bacteriological and physico-chemical parameters were assessed. These showed a consistent seasonal pattern with high salinity, high pH and low inorganic nitrogen concentrations in the summer months. Dissolved oxygen remained high all year and phosphate concentrations also varied little seasonally. Numbers of coliform bacteria were lower in summer than in winter, indicating a faster rate of die-off in the warmer summer months.

4.151 The major influence on Lancashire's coastal water quality is the River Mersey which strongly influences both salinity and concentrations of nutrients (nitrogen and phosphorus) (Hinchcliffe, 1976). There was evidence of increasing nutrient concentrations in coastal waters, possible leading to eutrophication problems, associated with algal blooms (Hinchcliffe, 1976). Nutrient levels were, however, thought already sufficient to support algal blooms and Hinchcliffe suggested that some other factor was limiting algal growth. This remains the case, because large algal blooms, leading to fish or bird deaths and shellfish poisoning, have not been reported.

4.152 Lancashire's coastal waters have a reasonably good chemical water quality, with some degree of nutrient enrichment, but insufficient to create a significant water quality problem. There is, however, a consistently poor bacteriological quality, indicating a high level of organic pollution associated with sewage inputs. Bacteriological quality is monitored by the NRA with regard to the requirements of the EC Bathing Water Directive.

Bathing Waters

4.153 The main concern over coastal water quality relates to their recreational use. Consequently, most analysis of coastal waters is restricted to bacteriological quality in relation to public health. The quality of bathing waters is currently a major issue, receiving widespread coverage with Lancashire's beaches at the forefront of this publicity. The persistent failure of the County's designated bathing waters to comply with EC standards, has led to the Commission instituting proceedings against the UK Government.

4.154 EC Directive 76/160/EEC required member States to designate waters widely used for bathing as bathing waters, and to monitor them regularly. The Directive lays down water quality standards for designated waters, including bacteriological and physico-chemical parameters. Bacteriological standards are given in Table 28. The assessment of bathing water quality is based on the standards for total and faecal coliforms, and is determined by the percentage of samples complying with the mandatory limits. A 95% compliance rate is required for a bathing water to meet EC standards. Anything less constitutes a failure.

4.155 The actual physical limits of designated bathing waters, either out to sea or along the shore, are not defined by the DOE and there is no requirement to do so in the Directive. At present, bathing waters are defined by a single point, i.e. the sampling point used by the NRA for monitoring water quality. The NRA is, however, proposing to define limits to bathing waters and has already suggested limits for the Fylde coast beaches to the DOE.

Table 28 EC Bacteriological Standards for Bathing Waters.

Parameter	Standard (95 percentile value)		Minimum sampling frequency
	Guide Value	Mandatory Limit	
Total coliforms per 100 ml	500	10000	Fortnightly
Faecal coliforms per 100 ml	100	2000	Fortnightly
Faecal streptococci per 100 ml	100	—	When presence suspected
Salmonella per litre	—	0	When presence suspected
Enteroviruses PFU per 10 litres	—	0	When presence suspected

Source: EC Directive 76/160/EEC

4.156 Figure 62 shows the location of bathing waters in Lancashire, with an informal estimate of how far they extend along the coast. The defined sampling points for each bathing water are given in Table 29. The percentage compliance of these waters with EC standards in 1989 is also given in Table 29. Ten out of the eleven bathing waters in Lancashire failed to meet EC requirements in 1989. However, all eleven failed in 1990 (NRA, pers.comm.). Assessment of NRA statistics for sample points along the Lancashire coast reveal that mandatory standards for coliform bacteria are frequently exceeded and guide values are rarely achieved. For example, maximum counts of five times the mandatory EC limit for coliforms have been recorded at Manchester Square, Blackpool, with an average of twice the mandatory limit and over four times the guide value. Bathing water

Figure 62

Compliance of Lancashire's Bathing Waters with the E.C. Standard for E. coli. 1989

Bathing Beaches

1. St. Annes South
2. St. Annes North
3. Blackpool South
4. Blackpool Central
5. Blackpool North
6. Bispham
7. Cleveleys
8. Fleetwood
9. Heysham
10. Morecambe South
11. Morecambe North

Note (a) Heysham was the only beach to pass in 1989.
     (b) All eleven beaches failed in 1990.

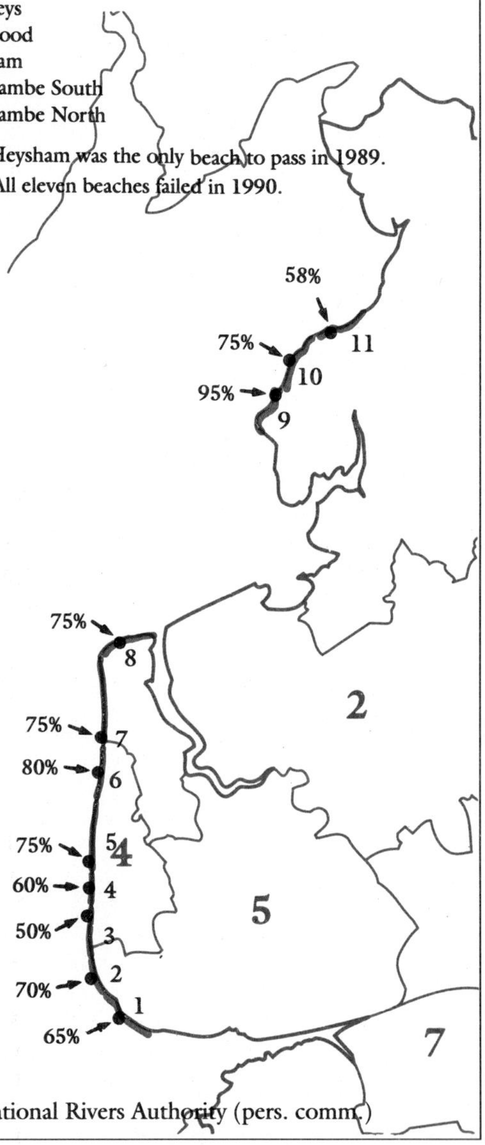

Source: National Rivers Authority (pers. comm.)

quality in Lancashire is, therefore, poor and is a significant water quality issue in the County.

4.157 Proposals to ensure compliance of the Blackpool and Wyre beaches by the 1995 or 1996 bathing season are currently being evolved by NWW, in partnership with the local authorities for the area. Schemes to achieve compliance for Fylde and Lancaster bathing waters are under discussion, working to a similar timescale. Interim measures to bring short-term improvements are also being

Table 29	Compliance of Lancashire's Bathing waters with the EC Standard for E. coli. 1989				
District	Bathing Water	Sampling Point	Grid Reference	Percentage Compliance	Pass/Fail
Lancaster	Morecambe North	Town Hall	441 650	58	Fail
	Morecambe South	West End	422 636	75	Fail
	Heysham	Half Moon Bay	413 618	95	Pass
Wyre	Fleetwood	Fleetwood Pier	336 485	75	Fail
	Cleveleys	Cleveleys	312 433	75	Fail
Blackpool	Bispham	Bispham	307 397	80	Fail
	Blackpool North	North Pier	305 364	75	Fail
	Blackpool Central	Central Pier	306 356	60	Fail
	Blackpool South	South Pier	304 338	50	Fail
Fylde	St. Anne's North	Convalescent Home	304 305	70	Fail
	St. Anne's	St. Anne's Pier	318 283	65	Fail

Source: NRA (pers. comm.). NWW (pers. comm.).

promoted. Final solutions for Lancashire's bathing waters seem set to be based on the incorporation of a minimum of secondary sewage treatment to replace current discharges of raw, or primary, effluent to estuaries and coastal waters. When all these measures are implemented, the bacteriological quality of the County's coastal waters will be radically improved.

Quality of Offshore Waters in the Irish Sea

4.158   Lancashire's coast forms part of the eastern boundary of the Irish Sea, which is a semi enclosed sea bounded by St. David's Head to the south and the Mull of Galloway to the north. Oceanic water enters the Irish Sea via St. Georges Channel, and outflow is via the North Channel. Freshwater inputs arise from river discharges, and direct sources (precipitation minus evaporation). The net freshwater input is 41.7 km³/year. The majority of this comes from the eastern margin of the Irish Sea, including the Lancashire rivers, Lune, Wyre, Douglas and Ribble.

4.159   Three primary forces are responsible for the movement of water in the Sea; the tides, the weather, and water density differences. The movements of water are important in distributing pollutants in the sea and along the coast. There is a larger tidal range on the eastern side of the Irish Sea than along the Irish coast. In most areas, tides are sufficiently energetic to mix water, creating a vertically homogeneous water column throughout the year. The eastern Irish Sea, however, develops significant stratification, especially in spring

and winter near the major estuaries of North West England. This may hinder the dispersal of contaminants entering the sea from rivers.

4.160   The effects of surface waves, formed by the wind, become significant during storms, especially affecting sediment movement in the shallow areas of the eastern Irish Sea. The time-averaged circulation of the Sea is relatively weak with no particularly coherent directionality over large areas. A tentative scheme of surface and bottom currents is shown on Figure 63. Circulation patterns do, however, vary seasonally and patterns in coastal waters receiving river outflows may not reflect those further offshore in the main body of water. For example, the plume entering from the River Mersey may, depending on the prevailing weather conditions etc., either pass directly out to sea, or move along either the North Wales or Lancashire coasts. Similarly, sludge dumped in Liverpool Bay can be washed towards the land by the bottom currents.

Inputs of Pollutants

4.161   The most up-to-date information about the Irish Sea was published by the Irish Sea Study Group in October 1990. Much of the ISSG report on Waste Inputs and Pollution (Irish Sea Study Group, 1990) has been condensed from the Dickson and Boelens (1988) report, 'The Status and Current Knowledge on Anthropogenic Influences in the Irish Sea'. Both sources have been used in the compilation of this section.

Figure 63

Schematic Distribution of Currents in the Irish Sea.

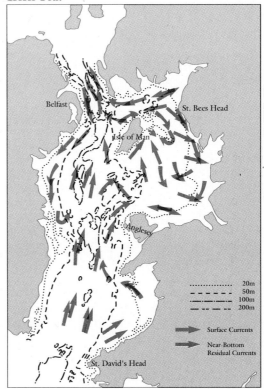

Source: Dickson and Boelens (1988)

4.162 The Irish Sea coast has been divided into sectors, to allow an assessment of riverine inputs by area (Figure 64). The estimated inputs from each division are shown in Table 30. This indicates that inputs from Lancashire and South Cumbria contribute 18% of biodegradable organic matter (as measured by BOD), 17% of ammonia, 31% nitrate, and 7% of phosphate to the eastern Irish Sea between the Solway and Cardigan Bay. Discharges from the sector, which includes Lancashire, contribute a high proportion of mercury, copper, and arsenic inputs. The worst source of most contaminants, however, is the Mersey estuary sector.

Figure 64
Coastal Sectors of the Irish Sea Relating to Table 30.

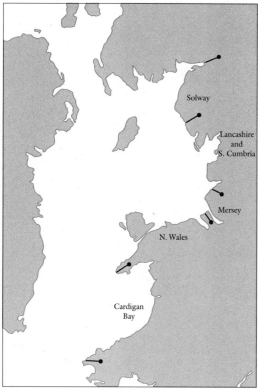

Source: Dickson and Boelens (1988)

4.163 By far the largest input of nutrients is through St. George's Channel. This brings about 100 million tonnes of nitrogen a year and 28 million tonnes of phosphorus. This is due to the enormous volume of water involved (Irish Sea Study Group, 1990). Even though concentrations are very low, the load is considerable, and predominantly 'natural'.

4.164 Though the total nutrient load from domestic and industrial wastes is not as great, these are concentrated at certain locations where they are substantially elevated. These point sources are also adjacent to areas which are widely used or heavily populated, and include Liverpool Bay and the Lancashire coast.

4.165 Rivers contribute approximately half of annual metal inputs to the Irish Sea (Irish Sea Study Group, 1990). Other sources are dumped dredge spoil, sewage and industrial wastes, and in some cases, the water which flows in through St. Georges Channel. Smaller contributions come from direct sewage and industrial discharges. The discharge of metals into Liverpool Bay has resulted in a more widespread, although still spatially localised, problem of metal contamination. There are many other coastal sites in the Irish Sea where human activity has led to locally elevated levels of metals, particularly in sediments.

4.166 The primary source of synthetic organic chemicals is run-off from land through major rivers, sewage discharges and dumping of sewage sludge. Precise information on levels of these potentially highly toxic substances is extremely limited (Irish Sea Study Group, 1990).

4.167 Very large quantities of degradable organic materials are generated and disposed of each day to surface waters. These are by-products of plant or animal origin excluding materials manufactured from fossil hydrocarbons (e.g. oils, gas and coal). Examples include domestic sewage and wastes from the food processing industry. Their main inpact is their effect on BOD. Table 30 shows that Lancashire and S.Cumbria jointly contribute 18% of the BOD to the eastern Irish Sea.

4.168 There are few sewage sludge and dredged material dumping sites in the Irish Sea, though the actual tonnage of material dumped per site is large. Table 31 gives the total weight and the weight of various components dumped in 1984. Liverpool Bay contributes 80% of the total weight dumped at sites and, also, to most of the heavy metal pollution (87% of mercury inputs).

4.169 The quantities of sewage sludge dumped in the Irish Sea have risen in line with population and the decrease in the number of sewage outfalls discharging directly to the sea. There are major dumping sites in the eastern basin, especially Liverpool Bay (see Figure 64). This contributes both organic and inorganic pollutants to the system. The concentrations of heavy metals in this sludge are within the limits set for primary settled sludges in the UK (Dickson and Boelens, 1988). In March 1990, the Secretary of State for the Environment announced that UK marine sewage sludge dumping will cease by 1998.

4.170 Surveys in 1979, 1982 and 1983 found total hydrocarbon concentrations in the eastern Irish Sea, in the range 2–74 ug/l, with concentrations greater than 10 ug/l in Liverpool Bay. These results indicate heavy contamination, which arises from a variety of sources, including river and atmospheric inputs, sea disposal of wastes and shipping operations (Irish Sea Study Group, 1990).

Impact of Pollutants

4.171 Information on the chemical quality of water, biota and sediments is limited, but general trends can be observed. The sea is mainly well oxygenated, though low oxygen levels are occasionally encountered in Liverpool Bay close to the sewage sludge dumping ground, or following large inputs of organic matter from the Mersey. Eastern Irish Sea waters are also enriched with human

Table 30 Estimated Inputs to Coastal and Estuarine Waters of the Irish Sea from English and Welsh Coasts.

Sector/Route	Flow (10³m³d⁻¹)	Tonnes per day				Grams per day				Kilograms per day							
		BOD	NH₄-N	NO₃-N	PO₄-P	YHCH	Drins	DDT	PCBs	Mercury	Cadmium	Arsenic	Chromium	Copper	Lead	Nickel	Zinc
Cardigan Bay																	
River	6853	9.6	0.4	8.2	0.3	83	30	56	56	0.6-1.3	2.7-4.6	11-14	24-74	37-61	30-87	67-88	720
Sewage	26	9.0	1.0	NS	0.2	1.0-3.6	0.3-1.1	0.4-2.1	0.2-1.5	–	0.1	0.1	0.8	2.4	1.6-1.8	0.4-0.5	8.2
Trade	–	–	–	–	–	–	–	–	–	–	–	–	–	–	–	–	–
TOTAL	6879	18.6	1.4	8.2	0.5	84-86.6	30.3-31.1	56.4-58.1	56.2-57.5	0.6-1.3	2.8-4.7	11.1-14.1	24.8-74.8	39.4-63.4	31.6-88.8	61.4-88.5	728
North Wales																	
River	5440	9.0	0.7	7.6	0.8	29	14	27	27	0.2-0.5	1.0-2.6	5.3	20-28	14-24	33-50	22-26	167
Sewage	76	7.1	1.3	0.7	0.5	3.4-7.7	2.6-3.3	3.8-7.6	2.6-7.6	–	0.7-0.9	0.6	4.6-4.7	7.9	5.8	2.3-2.7	210
Trade	16	5.8	0.1	NS	NS	–	–	–	–	–	0.9	–	5.8	6.0	9.1	3.5	966
TOTAL	5532	21.9	2.1	8.3	1.3	32.4-36.7	16.6-17.3	30.8-34.6	29.6-34.6	0.2-0.5	2.6-4.4	5.9	30.4-38.5	27.9-37.9	47.9-64.9	27.8-32.2	1343
Mersey																	
River	5918	31	31	24.2	6.7	41-76	max. 18	max. 34	max. 34	3.5	1.9	7-21	48-75	58	223	56	205
Sewage	515	176	11	0.6	1.6	14-52	12-19	9-14	1-20	0.2	1.7	1	51-63	131	192	27-99	639
Trade	113	48	2.3	0.2	NS	NS	NS	NS	NS	NS	0.5	NS	2	80	10	1-8	14-50
TOTAL	6546	255	44.3	25.0	8.3	55-128	12-37	9-48	1-54	3.7	4.1	8-22	101-140	269	425	84-163	858-894
Lancashire and South Cumbria																	
River	9271	26	2.5	21.6	2.7	14-68	max. 30	max. 58	max. 58	0.4-1.2	2.5	11-13	36-83	45	21-51	25	146
Sewage	226	48	7.1	NS	0.5	7-24	6-9	6-11	2-11	0.1	0.5	1	12-23	41-68	21	5-25	149
Trade	48	6	0.5	2.4	NS	NS	NS	NS	NS	0.5	NS	NS	4	3	2	4	5
TOTAL	9545	80	10.1	24.0	3.2	21-92	6-39	6-69	2-69	1.0-1.8	3.0	12-14	52-110	89-116	44-74	34-54	300
Solway																	
River	8813	18	0.5	11.6	0.8	9-53	max. 26	max. 49	max. 49	0.2-1.0	0.3-0.8	10	20-100	17	20-44	11	66
Sewage	34	5	0.7	NS	NS	1	0.3-0.6	0.2-0.4	max. 0.6	NS	NS	NS	1-2	6	9	1-5	25
Trade	92	36	0.2	NS	31.7	NS	0.3	NS	NS	0.5	44.1	NS	225	81	30	67	170
TOTAL	8939	59	1.4	11.6	32.5	10-54	0.6-26.9	0.2-49.4	max. 49.6	0.7-1.5	44.4-44.9	10	246-327	104	59-83	79-83	261

Source: Dickson and Boelens (1988)

Notes: NS = thought to be not significant.
Sector boundaries are illustrated in Figure 64
NH₄-N = Amoniacal nitrogen
NO₃-N = Nitrate nitrogen
YHCH = Hexachlorocyclohexane
Drins = aldrin, endrin, dieldrin, isoeldrin
PCBs = Polychlorinated biphenyls

derived nitrogen and phosphorous. Elevated levels are mainly attributable to riverine inputs.

4.172   Nitrogen may be a more important 'trigger' for increased productivity in the marine environment than phosphorus and the increasing number of reports of phytoplankton blooms in the Irish Sea might be linked to a greater supply of nutrients (Irish Sea Study Group, 1990). Plankton populations are highest off the Welsh, Lancashire and Cumbrian coasts and in Cardigan Bay. Abnormal algal blooms, which have occurred in the North Western Irish Sea and in Liverpool Bay, can kill fish, shellfish larvae and seabirds.

4.173   High trace-metal concentrations tend to occur in the eastern, less saline parts of the Irish Sea, in particular, Liverpool Bay and off the Lancashire coast. However, these are well below UK quality standards for sea water (Irish Sea Study Group, 1990). Available data for dissolved metal concentrations in surface waters are given in Table 32. Unusually high cadmium concentrations are found in Liverpool Bay and off St. Bees Head (western tip of Cumbria). In the former case, the main sources of dissolved cadmium are the Rivers Mersey and Ribble. Freshwater inputs are probably also the main sources of copper, zinc and nickel. Dissolved lead and mercury concentrations are also higher in the eastern waters of the sea than in central open waters. Dissolved reactive mercury concentrations

in Liverpool Bay are 1.0–2.0 ng/l, compared with 0.5–1.5 ng/l in open waters (Dickson and Boelens, 1988). Metals, especially lead and mercury, are also found in suspended particulate matter and there are usually more metals in the suspended particulates than in the bottom sediment. Reliable data for metals in sediment is only available in a few areas, but metal concentrations tend to be higher in muddy than sandy sediments.

4.174   Elevated mercury levels are found in the fish of Liverpool and Morecambe Bay (Table 33). In both areas, however, the concentration of mercury in a representative sample of fish flesh is below the Environmental Quality Standard set by the EC (0.3 mg mercury per kg fish flesh), although large individuals in some species may show higher concentrations. The ISSG report indicates that future decreases in mercury concentrations are difficult to predict, due to the reservoir of mercury remaining in estuarine and near shore sediments. These, together with continuing inputs, provide a continued source of mercury to the fish.

4.175   In contrast, there are no reports of elevated concentrations of copper, zinc or lead (Table 33) in fish tissues although metal concentrations in homogenised mussel tissues were elevated in localised areas around inputs. Levels of cadmium in the more contaminated coastal areas may be as high as 10% of the recommended UK quality standard for

Table 31 Inputs of Sewage Sludge, Industrial Wastes and Dumped Dredge Spoil to the NW Part of the Irish Sea. 1984

Location by Sector	Total Weight	Organics	Solids	Cd	Cr	Cu	Ni	Pb	Zn	Hg
Liverpool Bay										
Industrial	28 924	1 894	4 527	0	0	0.1	0.1	0	0.5	0
Sewage Sludge	1 279 050	49 303	49 303	0.6	41.1	26.4	3.1	47.4	143.1	0.3
Dredge Spoil	3 545 000	—	1 371 947	1.1	113.3	103.3	60.9	191.0	560.7	3.1
Holyhead										
Dredge Spoil	10 400	—	10 088	0	0.2	1.2	0.8	1.7	2.2	0
Outer Morecambe Bay										
Dredge Spoil	688 500	—	513 400	0	6.9	12.3	0	20.7	34.4	0.5
Cumbria Coast										
Dredge Spoil	558 800	—	279 400	0.2	10.0	12.6	17.7	40.0	15.9	0
TOTAL	6 110 674	51 197	2 228 665	1.9	171.5	155.9	82.6	300.8	756.8	3.9

Source: Dickson and Boelens (1988)

Notes: Cd = Cadmium. Cr = Chromium. Cu = Copper. Ni = Nickel. Pb = Lead. Zn = Zinc. Hg = Mercury.
All figures are given in Tonnes.

Table 32 Dissolved Metals in Surface Waters from the Irish Sea

Area	Mercury	Cadmium	Copper	Lead	Nickel	Zinc	Iron	Manganese
Liverpool Bay	–	(140–740)270	(0.90–3.0)1.45	(0.66–4.17)1.74	–	(2.3–48)12	–	–
Cardigan Bay	–	(480–2410)1110	(0.98–4.02)1.72	(1.12–3.53)2.24	–	(3.6–20)7.5	–	–
North Channel	–	(10–180)	(0.30–1.50)	(0.02–0.36)	–	–	–	–
Western Irish Sea	–	(10–520)110	(0.18–3.75)0.59	(0.05–1.20)0.19	(0.22–0.55)0.38	(0.8–9.0)3.0	(0.03–0.6)0.09	(0.15–2.6)0.53
Eastern Irish Sea	–	(10–620)40	(0.28–0.98)0.66	(0.05–1.00)0.11	(0.32–23)0.71	(2.3–7.5)4.2	(0.06–1.9)0.18	(0.22–15)1.95
Irish Sea	(6–22)13	(10–230)76	(0.08–1.32)0.44	–	(0.03–0.34)0.12	(1.0–13)2.6	–	–
South East Irish Sea	–	(11–220)	(1.01–2.48)1.73	(0.21–1.4)	–	–	–	–
Offshore of sewage sludge dump site	–	(77–78)77	(0.72–0.95)0.83	–	(0.27–0.34)0.30	(4.20–6.20)5.2	–	–
At dump site	–	(64–100)82	(0.87–1.25)1.1	–	(0.37–0.45)0.41	(6.46–8.93)7.7	–	–
Inshore of dump site	–	(87–160)120	(0.98–1.43)1.2	–	(0.51–0.57)0.54	(7.66–13.3)10.5	–	–
North East Irish Sea	–	(22–85)37	(0.32–1.28)0.49	(0.016–0.053)0.023	–	–	–	–

Source: Dickson and Boelens (1988)

Notes: Values are given in $ug.l^{-1}$, except for Cadmium and Mercury which are in $ng.l^{-1}$
Range values are shown in brackets. Mean values are outside brackets.

cadmium in sea water. However, throughout most of the Irish Sea cadmium levels are less than 2% of the standard.

4.176 The principal impact of synthetic organic chemicals in the Irish Sea is measurable quantities of organochlorine residues in waters, sediments and, more importantly, certain marine animals. MAFF surveys showed high (i.e., greater than 2 mg/kg) concentrations of total DDT in some liver samples of Liverpool Bay fish caught in 1983. Elevated organochlorine, pesticide and PCB concentrations, have also been detected in the livers of cod and whiting caught in Morecambe Bay.

4.177 The Irish Sea supports a diverse fauna, similar to other seas around the British Isles but fish yield (see Table 34) is lower than in other areas, including the North Sea. Detailed information on Lancashire fishing activity is given in Chapter 8.

Water Pollution Sources and Impacts

Introduction

4.178 Rivers, estuaries and coastal waters have traditionally been regarded as convenient places for the disposal of liquid waste, even though this can markedly reduce quality of the water concerned, and limit the uses to which water can be put. Table 35 shows the size and types of effluent discharges currently operating in Lancashire as a legacy of this approach.

4.179 Effluent discharges arise from three principal sources:

* sewage;
* trade (mainly industrial) operations;
* agricultural activities.

The effects of sewage discharges are particularly

important because they are the most numerous and contribute the largest, and most continuous, volumes. Effluents from industrial installations and farm pollution can be significant because of the range of potentially polluting elements that they can contain.

4.180   Principal discharges require consents from the NRA, who monitor against terms and conditions in the consents. The 'consented' discharges which currently exist in Lancashire are shown in Figure 65. There are 150 in all, of which 89 (60%) are from sewage and effluent treatment plants, 5 (3%) are coastal sewage outfalls, and 56 (37%) are from trade premises (a further three coastal outfalls discharge stormwater overflows). Figure 65 shows only the principal consented discharges. Many smaller ones exist, including farm, trade and tip effluent discharges.

Discharges

4.181   Sewage has such a profound impact on the aquatic environment because of the volumes produced. Each one of us generates between 135–200 litres every day, necessitating a large and complex sewage treatment and disposal system, with associated discharges. In its untreated state, sewage consists mostly of liquid (98% water), but also contains grit and solids. Solids are mostly derived from washing, food preparation, and excreta, in roughly equal proportions, whilst grit comes largely from paved surfaces. Sewage effluent contains both organic and inorganic matter, including enormous numbers of bacteria, of which coliforms are the most abundant. Other bacteria and viruses are also encountered and much attention is now focussed upon the public health implications of putting effluent, which has had only basic treatment, into water courses.

4.182   Comprehensive sewage treatment has three aims:

* the removal of faecal, organic and other solids by screening and/or settlement and the production of sewage sludges;

* the removal of dissolved and suspended organic material by its conversion to biological material and its subsequent settling to produce a secondary sludge;

* a final effluent with a low level of BOD and suspended solids to minimise impact on receiving waters.

4.183   To meet these aims, treatment works require preliminary and primary treatment to remove the bulk of the solids and grits. This is followed by a biological secondary phase, which uses a range of organisms including bacteria, fungi, protozoa and other invertebrates to remove more of the suspended solids and oxidise organic matter. Where even cleaner effluent is required, tertiary treatment, including disinfection, can be used to further reduce suspended solids and organic matter. Additional specialised treatment procedures can also remove ammonia and phosphorus. However, such sophisticated forms of treatment are comparatively rare as yet, and many discharges in the County

Table 33   Contaminants in Fish and Mussels from the Irish Sea

Contaminant		Range in concentration (mg kg^{-1} wet weight)			
		Western Channel	Liverpool Bay	Morecambe Bay	St. Bees' Head/ NE Isle of Man
Mercury	Fish (M)	0.05–0.11	0.21–0.35	0.17–0.60	0.10–0.22
	Mussels	0.04–0.07	0.06–0.12	0.06–0.10	0.05–0.06
Copper	Fish (M)	0.2–0.2	0.2–0.3	0.2–0.3	0.2–0.3
	Mussels	1.2–3.8	1.7–2.2	1.1–1.8	1.4–1.5
Zinc	Fish (M)	3.0–5.8	3.3–5.3	2.4–6.2	3.3–6.1
	Mussels	15–50	17–62	25–28	20–24
Cadmium	Fish (L)	0.2 (M)	0.2–0.4	0.2	0.2
	Mussels	0.3–0.5	0.4–0.5	0.3–0.6	0.5–2.0
Lead	Fish (L)	0.2 (M)	0.4	0.2	0.2
	Mussels	1.0–1.8	1.2–4.3	1.6–2.6	1.0–2.0
Dieldrin	Fish (L)	0.02–0.35	0.01–0.20	0.01–0.23	0.08–0.09
	Mussels	0.01	0.03	0.01	0.02
DDT	Fish (L)	0.06–1.0	0.27–2.8	0.03–3.4	0.21–0.42
	Mussels	0.01–0.08	0.08	0.01–0.02	0.01
PCBs	Fish (L)	0.2–4.0	0.9–8.4	0.4–6.4	0.18–2.0
	Mussels	0.05–0.1	0.15	0.05	0.05

Source: Dickson and Boelens (1988)

Notes: Fish species included – cod, whiting, plaice, dab, flounder and sole
(M) = muscle tissue analysed
(L) = liver tissue analysed

receive only preliminary or primary treatment. Some do not even receive this.

4.184   The conditions imposed on all discharges from sewage treatment works by the NRA indicate the quality of effluent each works can release into

Table 34   Total Biomass of the Main Commercial Demersal Species in the Irish Sea

Rank	Species	Biomass (tonnes)	Cumulative Percentage
1	Cod	18 056	29
2	Whiting	15 482	55
3	Sole	7 324	67
4	Plaice	6 241	77
5	Rays	6 198	87
6	Saithe	3 108	92
7	Hake	1 360	94
8	Monk Fish	1 026	96
9	Pollack	786	97
10	Ling	412	98
11	Haddock	376	99
12	Brill	303	99
13	Turbot	285	100
14	Megrim	205	100
15	Lemon Sole	198	100
TOTAL		61 360	100

Source: Dickson and Boelens (1988)

Figure 65

Principal Consented Discharges and Coastal Outfalls to Lancashire's Waters. 1990

1. Lancaster
2. Wyre
3. Ribble Valley
4. Blackpool
5. Fylde
6. Preston
7. South Ribble
8. West Lancashire
9. Chorley
10. Blackburn
11. Hyndburn
12. Burnley
13. Pendle
14. Rossendale

■ Treatment Works (ETW/STW)

■ Trade

◄ Combined Sewage Outfall

◄ Storm Overflow Outfall

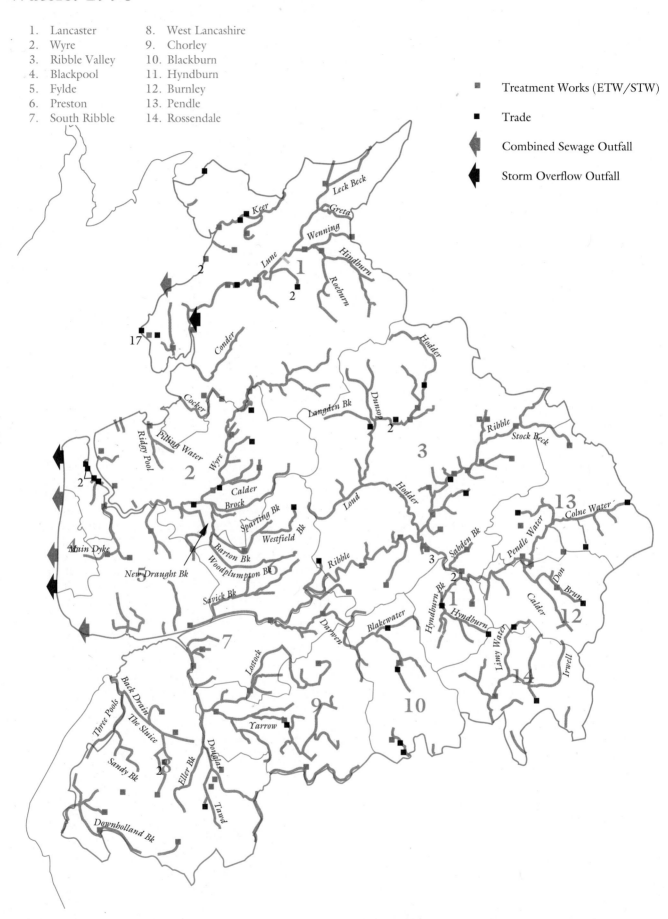

Source: National Rivers Authority (pers. comm.)

Table 35	Large Consented Effluent Discharges in Lancashire. 1990			
Discharger	Max flow rate (Ml/Day)			
	<10,000	10,000–100,000	>100,000	Total
Sewage (NWW)	46	22	21	89
Trade sewage	10	2	1	9
Heavy industry	12	10	5	27
Farming/light industry	0	0	2	2
Electricity industry	8	5	5	18
LANCASHIRE	72	39	34	145

Source: Liverpool University EAU, derived from data provided by NRA.

the environment. Discharge consent criteria are based on:

* the target water quality in the receiving water;

* existing water quality in the receiving water;

* the ability of an individual treatment works to produce a high quality effluent;

* the costs involved in making improvements in a sewage works so that better quality effluent can be produced.

4.185 The parameters used to define effluent quality from domestic sewage works are BOD, suspended solids and (sometimes) ammonia. Effluent must reach the prescribed parameter standard, 95% of the time, to comply with consent limits. The consent can also prescribe higher limits which, if exceeded, result in failure and render the operator of the works liable to prosecution.

4.186 Consent limits at inland sewage treatment works in Lancashire vary, though the majority are within the following ranges:

BOD 30 to 60 mg/l;
suspended solids 25 to 60 mg/l.

However most limit values for suspended solids are set at 45 mg/l.

4.187 Assessment of consent compliance is based on the analysis of samples taken by the NRA over a 12 month period. A number of samples are permitted to fail before a treatment works is judged to have performed outside its consent. The maximum number of permitted failures usually depends on the size of the works. The position applying in Lancashire is given in Table 36.

Table 36	Maximum Number of Permitted Failures at Lancashire Sewage Treatment Works. 1990	
Works Volume (Ml/day)	Annual Sampling Frequency	Maximum Permitted Number of Failures
Over 2.0	26	3
0.5–1.99	13	2
Up to 0.49	6	1

Source: NRA (pers. comm.)

4.188 Lancashire has 78 consented sewage treatment works, most of which are in the Ribble catchment (44%). Some have more than one outfall discharging effluent, and so there are 89 consented effluents. The number of works in each catchment are shown in Table 37. Four of Lancashire's 89 consented sewage effluents failed to comply with their consent conditions in 1989/90. These were the discharges at:

* Wittingham, in the Lune catchment;
* Chipping, in the Ribble catchment;
* Hillhouse, in the Douglas catchment;
* Burscough, in the Douglas catchment.

Table 37	Number of Sewage Works in Lancashire by Hydrometric Area. 1990	
Hydrometric Area	Number of Sewage Works	% of Total
Keer	4	5
Lune	12	15
Wyre	8	10
Ribble	34	44
Douglas	18	23
Irwell	2	3
LANCASHIRE	78	100

Source: NRA (pers. comm.)

4.189 Towards the end of 1989, however, thirteen treatment work effluents which were close to exceeding, or were breaching, their limits, were granted relaxations of their consents by the Secretary of State for the Environment. This was to allow remedial measures to be implemented. In eleven of the cases, the relaxed consents are time-limited to coincide with the completion of improvements. In two cases, however, the relaxations appear to be permanent. The thirteen works involved are:

* Nether Kellet, discharging to Nether Beck and River Keer;
* Burton in Lonsdale, discharging to River Greta;
* Halton East, discharging to River Lune (*no time limit*);
* Lancaster (Stodday), discharging to River Lune Estuary (*no time limit*);
* Garstang, discharging to River Wyre;
* Barton, discharging to Barton Brook;
* Weeton, discharging to Main Dyke tributary;
* Chorley, discharging to River Chor diversion and Yarrow;
* Skelmersdale, discharging to River Douglas;
* Ormskirk, discharging to Langleys Brook;
* Burscough, discharging to Boathouse Sluice;
* Westhead, discharging to Castle Brook and Eller Brook;
* Rossendale, discharging to River Irwell.

4.190 Sewage effluent outfalls have a marked impact on local river water quality, and this is revealed by changes in the NWC classification. The following treatment works discharges in the

County show how dramatic the deterioration can be:

* Hoscar discharge to R. Douglas, *change in class from 2 to 4;*
* Horwich discharge to R. Douglas, *change in class from 2 to 3;*
* Chorley discharge to R. Yarrow, *change in class from 2 to 3;*
* Darwen discharge to R. Darwen, *change in class from 2 to 4;*
* Samlesbury discharge to R. Darwen, *change in class from 2 to 3;*
* Colne (hospital) discharge to Colne Water, *change in class from 1 to 2;*
* Clitheroe discharge to R. Ribble, *change in class from 1b to 2;*
* Rawtenstall discharge to R. Irwell, *change in class from 2 to 4.*

The situation in the case of the Darwen is exacerbated by a paper mill which discharges nearby.

4.191   Figure 62 shows the consistently poor record of Lancashire's designated bathing waters in failing to comply with the bacteriological standards of the EC bathing water Directive. The reason for this is the outfalls, discharging largely untreated sewage to our coastal waters. There are eight such outfalls (each serving more than 10,000 people) along the Lancashire coast and nine treatment works providing only primary treatment before discharging effluent to estuarine waters. Their positions are indicated on Figure 65. Several of the outfalls discharge sewage after screening only. At Chatsworth Avenue (Fleetwood), the outfall discharges onto the beach without even screening.

4.192   A proposal was put forward by the former NWW Authority in 1988 to bring Fylde beaches up to the EC standard by 1993 by constructing a 5 km long sea outfall from Rossal Point to the edge of the Lune Deep. After preliminary treatment only, (screening and grit removal), the combined outputs from most of the Fylde (from a population of about a quarter of a million), up to three times dry weather flow, would have been discharged to the sea. All flows in excess of this (stormwater) would have been stored and discharged on favourable tides from existing outlets.

4.193   After widespread opposition, based on the view that the scheme required a higher degree of treatment, and the Secretary of State's announcement (March 1990) that no new marine sewage outfalls would be allowed unless the effluent going down them has received treatment, the long sea outfall proposal was refused discharge consent (May 1990). NWW, with local authorities, is now working towards achieving bathing water compliance at all Lancashire beaches, by the middle of the decade, on the basis of new proposals for the Fylde, Ribble and Morecambe Bay, using secondary treatment as a minimum.

Trade Discharges

4.194   Effluents from trade and industry can contain a wide range of potentially polluting elements. These can include heavy metals, chemicals, organic and inorganic wastes from the chemical industry, food processing wastes, oil and oil dispersants, wastes with high or low pH, heated waters and other organic rich material. Many such wastes can be treated to remove polluting elements, but preventing the discharge of all trade materials to our water system would be the most environmentally beneficial option of all. However, industry has traditionally discharged to rivers, both directly and via the sewage system, and current arrangements are based on this cheapest option.

4.195   Once released into rivers, estuaries and coastal waters, pollutants in effluents can affect the aquatic environment if levels are not kept within safe limits. Many chemical and metal-rich wastes in sufficient concentrations are toxic to aquatic organisms, or reduce their longer term chances of survival. Suspended solids can smother plants and animals and change the habitat. Organic-rich effluents can cause oxygen depletion, heated waters can alter the aquatic biota, and mine drainage water can be acidic.

4.196   The more significant trade discharges are consented, and monitored, by the NRA (most discharges) and HMIP (discharges involving red list substances). Lancashire has a total of 56 consented trade discharges, Table 35 summarises these by size. The electricity industry discharges are largely cooling waters which may have elevated temperatures. Their discharge consents set limits for temperature. Other effluents are related to industrial processes and can contain pollutants associated with these processes.

4.197   The commonest industrial effluents in the County range from metal plating works, (where water is used for cooling during processing), to much more complex discharges from chemical installations which have a high number of consented parameters. There are also a number of discharges from quarries and minewaters, which can be high in suspended solids and have this parameter consented. Paper manufacturers also produce effluents which can have high levels of suspended solids.

4.198   None of the discharges can to be associated with particularly large decreases in the NWC river classification. Although a paper mill in Darwen coincides with such a change, a sewage treatment works discharges in close proximity and contributes significantly to the decrease in quality. This apparent lack of correlation between river water quality, as presented in the NWC classification, may be partly due to the fact that discharges do not necessarily affect the parameters on which the NWC system is based. Furthermore, a number of outfalls on a river system can result in a more gradual decline in water quality.

Agricultural Discharges

4.199   Agricultural activities can affect the quality of water resources in two main ways. Firstly, applications of nitrate-rich fertilisers, pesticides and herbicides can impair the quality of water draining off fields into surface and groundwaters. The degree, and nature of, any alteration in quality is determined by the type of farming practised in an area. For example, upland sheep grazing areas in East Lancashire are less likely to receive fertiliser, pesticides or herbicides than lowland areas like West Lancashire and the Fylde, which are subject to cropping. Chapter 8 deals with potential environmental impact arising from the distribution of farm types in the County. However, no groundwaters in Lancashire are affected by high levels of nitrates, as occurs elsewhere in the UK.

4.200 The second way that farming affects water quality is through pollution incidents. These can result from uncontrolled discharge of animal wastes (slurry) from dairy farms, intensive pig and, occasionally, poultry units. Polluting liquors can also come from silage clamps, yard washings and land runoff following poor spreading of fertilisers. Further pollution problems stem from the release of sheep dip chemicals into water courses, oil spillage and vegetable washings on farms, which can have a locally damaging effect. All sources are more likely to pollute at times of high rainfall which increases the liquid content of slurry and silage. Most of these discharges have high levels of organic matter and also sometimes suspended solids. The main effect, when they reach rivers and streams, is to cause rapid deoxygenation which can lead to fish mortality. Several cases of this happening in Lancashire watercourses have been reported during 1989 and 1990.

4.201 A joint exercise by the Water Authorities Association (WAA) and MAFF (Water Authorities Association, 1986) considered the problem during 1986 for the North West region. Their report notes that a move towards stock rearing and associated silage production in recent years without, in most instances, adequate waste management procedures, has led to the avoidable release of silage liquor. In 1986, in the North West, a total of 491 farm pollution incidents were recorded, of which 162 were serious and 5 led to prosecution. The majority of incidents concerned dairy and silage production.

4.202 Over the last few decades, the production of 'farmed' salmonid fish has increased markedly. Recent statistics from the NRA indicate that there are about 26 fish farms in the North West, most of which are for rainbow trout production (NRA, pers.comm.), situated on rivers and occasionally on lakes. Effluents from fish farms can have low dissolved oxygen concentrations and cause oxygen depletion in rivers receiving the effluent. They can also contain elevated levels of nutrients and chemicals used in farm maintenance. Since fish farms require high quality water for successful production, they tend to be situated on unpolluted rivers and, occasionally, on lakes where comparatively minor changes in water quality can have a marked effect on aquatic biology. The position in Lancashire is unclear.

4.203 The NRA respond to all reported pollution incidents. If an incident is found to have occurred, action will be taken to minimise the damage caused and to determine the responsible party. Under powers granted in the WA 1989, the NRA can prosecute individuals, or companies, responsible for serious pollution incidents.

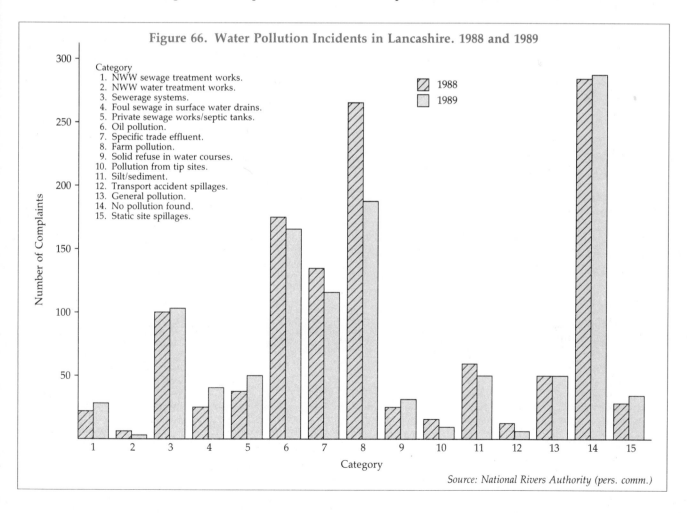

Figure 66. Water Pollution Incidents in Lancashire. 1988 and 1989

Category
1. NWW sewage treatment works.
2. NWW water treatment works.
3. Sewerage systems.
4. Foul sewage in surface water drains.
5. Private sewage works/septic tanks.
6. Oil pollution.
7. Specific trade effluent.
8. Farm pollution.
9. Solid refuse in water courses.
10. Pollution from tip sites.
11. Silt/sediment.
12. Transport accident spillages.
13. General pollution.
14. No pollution found.
15. Static site spillages.

Source: National Rivers Authority (pers. comm.)

4.204 In Lancashire, there were 1234 reported pollution incidents in 1988, reducing to 1158 in 1989. These included a wide range, arising from numerous sources (see Figure 66). The largest single category relates to inspections where no pollution was found, indicating either that the report was mistaken, or a small incident had occurred which quickly dispersed. The four most significant categories of confirmed pollution incident in Lancashire are farm pollution, oil pollution, trade effluents and breakdowns of sewerage system (either through collapse or overloading).

4.205 The 1158 incidents in 1989 amount to an average of more than three pollution events per day. Even discounting unconfirmed reports (283), there were still more than two confirmed incidents a day. Few would have been major incidents, but the scale of the impact upon the County's freshwater is clear. These incidents, of course, occur over and above regular inputs from consented discharges and unreported incidents.

4.206 The number of incidents which result in prosecution is small. In many cases, the expense of court action against a minor offender is prohibitive or the party responsible for the incident cannot be traced. In other cases, assurances about remedial measures may result in settlement out of court.

4.207 There were 10 prosecutions by the NRA in Lancashire in 1989, six of which were against farmers. The prosecutions of individual farmers are almost certainly related to particular pollution incidents, but those against industrial firms may be for persistent breach of consent limits. Comparing the number of prosecutions with the number of pollution incidents, reveals that less than 1% of incidents result in the polluter being prosecuted.

Water-Borne Infections

4.208 Gut, and various other, pathogens excreted by humans and animals enter the water environment either directly, or indirectly via sewage treatment works. Some species, when infected by such pathogens, do not show any symptoms of disease, and provide a continuing reservoir for infection. The removal of pathogens from sewage during treatment is limited in conventional works (Smith et al., 1978), and there are no biological standards controlling the output from sewage works. Water treatment works are often unable to remove all pathogens from the drinking water supply.

4.209 Pathogenic bacteria and protozoa (microscopic animals) can remain viable in freshwater for a variable length of time, depending on temperature, water quality and the type of pathogen. While viable, and if present in sufficient numbers, they can infect animals and humans who ingest them. Humans and animals may also be infected directly by ingesting excreta (urine and/or faeces) of an infected animal, and indirectly from muds, soils, or by eating contaminated animals.

4.210 There are three main water-borne pathogens that can occur in Lancashire: leptospire and salmonella (both bacteria) and the protozoan parasite Cryptosporidium.

4.211 Leptospirosis is the general term for diseases resulting from infection by leptospire bacteria. In Britain, three strains cause disease in humans. One is found in rats, another in dogs and the third, mainly in dairy herds. The strain that causes the most severe illness in humans is transmitted by rats (Weil's disease). Rats are found in, and around, most fresh waters and, consequently, this is also the most common source of infection. Weil's disease varies considerably in people from a mild flu-like illness with a severe headache to meningitis, renal failure and occasionally death.

4.212 Leptospires remain viable for up to three weeks in freshwater, but less than 24 hours in salt water or in the presence of detergent. They are widespread, but the incidence of disease is low. In 1989, there were less than 70 reported cases in the whole of the UK (and some of these were of overseas origin). Three of the cases were reported from Chorley, and contaminated water has been suggested as the likely source. Two were in young boys bathing in a stream and the third was a farm worker (the most commonly infected group of people). Rat control programmes have been initiated in the vicinity of the contaminated waters and no further cases reported.

4.213 Like leptospirosis, several different strains of salmonella can infect humans, causing nausea, vomiting, stomach pains and diarrhoea. Salmonella is the bacterium associated with food poisoning, but strains can occur in freshwaters. A study (Smith et al., 1978) found that 10 of 14 sites tested in Lancashire and Cheshire contained salmonella. Most appeared to have been contaminated by sewage and farm effluent, although one upland site was probably contaminated by gulls.

4.214 Cryptosporidium is a protozoan parasite, principally of farm livestock, which can infect humans. If water supplies become contaminated with excreta from infected livestock, the parasite can be ingested. It multiplies in intestines causing stomach pains, fever, vomiting and diarrhoea. Like leptospires, Cryptosporidium is widespread in the environment, but outbreaks of infection are relatively rare. There have been no reported outbreaks in Lancashire.

Bacteria and Viruses in Rivers

4.215 Evidence of the levels of bacteria in Lancashire's inland waters and estuaries is scarce. However, Preston Borough Council have been conducting their own monitoring programme of the bacteriological quality of the river Ribble as it flows through the town. Water samples have been examined since 1984 for various parameters included in the EC Bathing Waters Directive. These are total coliforms, E. coli, salmonella and campylobacter virus. The quantity of organisms found is so enormous, as to indicate gross pollution. Figure 67 shows the trend in concentrations of E. coli at various sampling points. The other pathogens sampled show similar trends.

4.216 Whilst there are no formal standards applying to non-designated bathing waters like this stretch of the Ribble, it is instructive to compare the

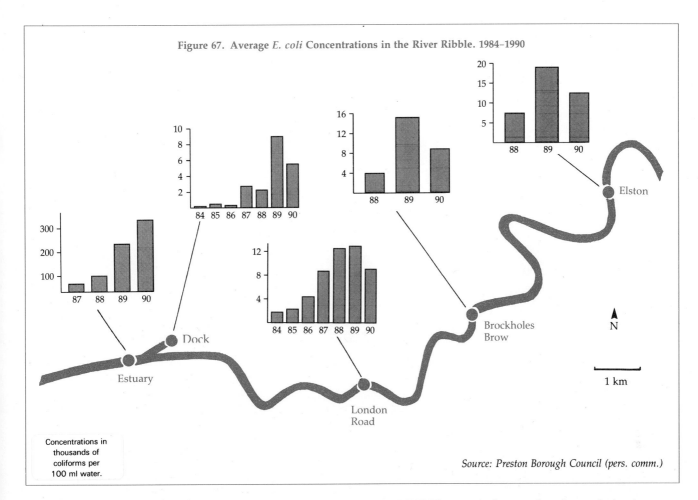

Figure 67. Average *E. coli* Concentrations in the River Ribble. 1984-1990

Concentrations in thousands of coliforms per 100 ml water.

Source: Preston Borough Council (pers. comm.)

findings with the EC Bathing Water Directive (76/160/EEC). Preston Dock and the Ribble in this part of Lancashire, are both subject to regular recreational and amenity use, including contact water sports and bathing, so ingestion of water must occur.

4.217 Table 28 lists the EC bacteriological standards for bathing waters. Comparing Preston Council's results with these, shows that the average total coliform concentration in Preston Dock (small basin), exceeded the Directive limit by 41.6 times: 416,000 coliforms per 100 ml. The maximum concentration recorded was 1,800,000, 180 times over the EC limit. Salmonella and campylobacter were recorded in nearly all samples and the EC Directive requires nil occurrence for compliance.

Acidification

4.218 Many upland waters are particularly suspectible to increases in acidity. Acid waters support only poor invertebrate communities, and fish are often sparse or absent. Such waters also have elevated levels of the toxic metal, aluminium. Acidification is therefore a potentially serious problem, greatly reducing the wildlife and amenity value of upland waters and restricting their use for drinking water supply. 'Acid rain' (see Chapter 3) is a primary cause, but the process may be accelerated by land uses such as coniferous plantations. The onset of acidification probably coincided with the start of the Industrial Revolution, but the process has only received national and international attention in the 1970s and 80s.

4.219 NWW has recently completed a study for the DOE, examining the extent and effects of acidification in Cumbria and the South Pennines (North West Water, 1989a). This included 13 sample sites in Lancashire and a further four on, or immediately, outside the County boundary. Water quality data for these sites from 1982–87 show that three Lancashire sites, and three of the boundary sites, have a mean pH of less than 6.0, (the lower EC limit for supporting fish).

4.220 Only two Lancashire sites had aluminium levels greater than 0.2 mg/l (the PCV for drinking water), but all four of the boundary sites exceeded that level (see Figure 68). Sites with both low pH (6.0) and high aluminium (2.0 mg/l) are worst affected and both fish and invertebrate populations can be reduced in such waters. This small number of samples, however, gives limited evidence of acidification in the upland areas, where acid waters occur naturally as a result of the poor buffering capacity of naturally acidic soils.

Eutrophication

4.221 'Eutrophication' is a natural process by which waters become nutrient enriched, particularly by nitrogen and phosphorus. The process can, however, be greatly accelerated by the impact of human-derived nutrients. This is termed hypereutrophication. The most common symptom of eutrophication is excessive growth of microscopic algae. Large numbers of algae may, in certain conditions, become concentrated at the surface or edges of lakes or reservoirs. They produce a dense green, or blue-green, coloration and a surface scum.

Figure 68
Acidification of Surface Waters and Sites Affected by Blue-Green Algae at NWW Monitoring Sites in Lancashire.

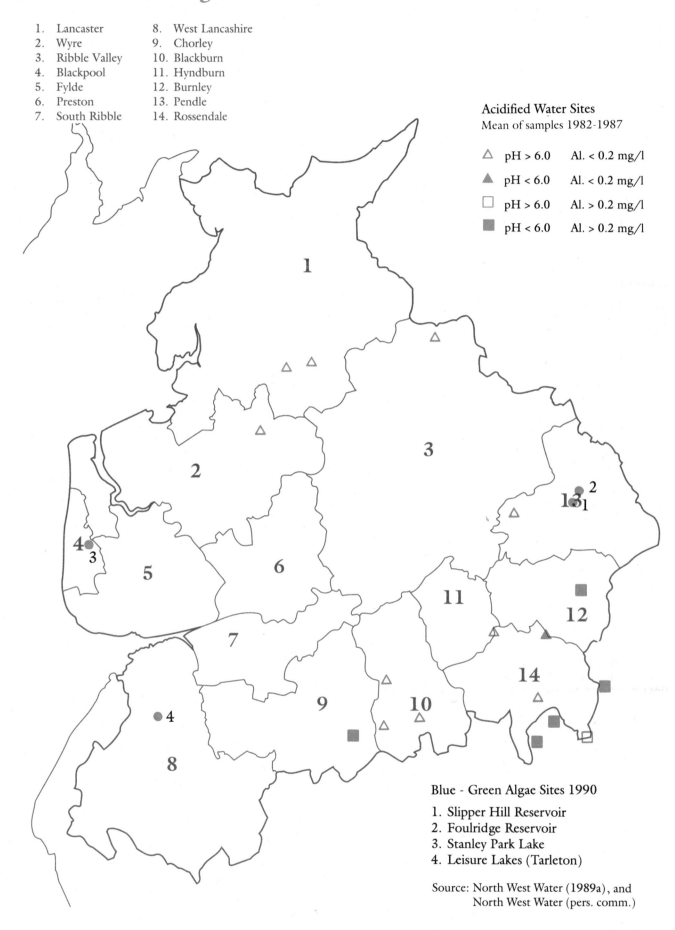

1. Lancaster
2. Wyre
3. Ribble Valley
4. Blackpool
5. Fylde
6. Preston
7. South Ribble
8. West Lancashire
9. Chorley
10. Blackburn
11. Hyndburn
12. Burnley
13. Pendle
14. Rossendale

Acidified Water Sites
Mean of samples 1982-1987

△ pH > 6.0   Al. < 0.2 mg/l
▲ pH < 6.0   Al. < 0.2 mg/l
☐ pH > 6.0   Al. > 0.2 mg/l
■ pH < 6.0   Al. > 0.2 mg/l

Blue - Green Algae Sites 1990

1. Slipper Hill Reservoir
2. Foulridge Reservoir
3. Stanley Park Lake
4. Leisure Lakes (Tarleton)

Source: North West Water (1989a), and
North West Water (pers. comm.)

4.222 Algal blooms cause substantial problems for water treatment works and can create unpleasant tastes and odours in drinking water. Blooms also cut off light to, and suppress the growth of, submerged plants and when the algae die their decomposition can use up oxygen at the lake or reservoir bottom. This can kill aquatic wildlife. Algae decomposing on the shore is also unsightly and smelly and may harbour the bacterium which causes avian botulism, a fatal disease of wildfowl and domestic animals. Some species of blue-green algae also produce toxins which, if consumed in sufficient quantities, can be lethal to domestic animals and cause illness to humans.

4.223 The incidence of algal blooms is due to a combination of factors. High nutrient concentrations in waters create the potential for blooms, but only in sustained sunny weather and still water conditions do algae multiply rapidly to create a bloom. These conditions have occurred in the last two years, resulting in numerous reports of algal blooms in the County.

4.224 The NRA have started a national programme to monitor for the presence of potentially toxic blue-green algae at 500 sites. Twelve of these are in Lancashire (see Figure 68). These are at:

* Pine Lake Resort (Carnforth);
* Stocks Reservoir (Slaidburn);
* Marton Mere (Blackpool);
* Stanley Park Lake (Blackpool);
* Leisure Lakes (Tarleton);
* Rivington Reservoir (Near Chorley);
* Anglezarke Reservoir (Near Chorley);
* Jumbles Reservoir Country Park (Edgeworth);
* Dean Clough Reservoir (Gt. Harwood);
* Rowley Lake (Burnley);
* Slipper Hill Reservoir (Foulridge);
* Foulridge Reservoir (Foulridge).

The waters at Stanley Park, Leisure Lakes, Slipper Hill and Foulridge were all affected by blue-green algae in 1990. The following waters were also affected in 1990, but they are not routinely sampled: Glasson Dock (Lancaster), Barrowford Reservoir (Pendle), Preston Dock, Grimsargh No.3 Reservoir (both Preston).

4.225 Lancashire remained relatively free of algal bloom problems until last year. At the end of May 1990, however, Stanley Park Lake in Blackpool was closed to the public because of a bloom. The vast majority of the algal population consisted of non-toxic green algae but toxic blue-green algae (the species *Microcystis* and *Anabaena*) were found. Toxic algae were also found in Barrowford Reservoir near Nelson, Grimsargh Reservoir near Preston, the Foulridge Reservoirs and at the Leisure Lakes, Tarleton, whilst a dense bloom of the filamentous blue-green alga, *Oscillatoria agardhii*, developed in Preston docks in June. The NRA and District Councils are co-operating in monitoring waters for toxic algae and in ensuring that the public are informed of potential dangers.

4.226 Blooms also develop in the sea, producing a brown or red coloration of the water. Blooms of the marine algae, *Phaeocystis*, may produce large quantities of foam which can accumulate on beaches.

Other marine algae can form toxic blooms which can poison fish directly or, when the poison accumulates in shellfish, seabirds. Humans can suffer from paralytic or diarrhetic shellfish-poisoning following consumption of contaminated shellfish. Further problems are caused when the blooms die and sink to the sea bottom. Decomposition consumes much oxygen, causing death of marine life. Such incidents have been reported for the European North Sea Coast but, though blooms have been reported off the Fylde Coast and in Morecambe Bay, they have not resulted in serious loss of wildlife.

Radioactive Discharges

4.227 International guidelines concerning the exposure of individuals to radiation are issued by the International Commission on Radiological Protection (ICRP). The NRPB is responsible for advising the Government on ICRP guidelines. Acceptable levels of exposure to radiation have been established. These are based on the 'critical group' concept. The critical group comprises those individuals in a particular area who are likely to receive the greatest exposure to radioactivity. In Lancashire, the critical group for external doses resulting from the discharges from Sellafield outside West Cumbria, and the liquid discharges from Springfield, are occupants of houseboats moored permanently in the muddy creeks of the Ribble Estuary.

4.228 The current dose rate for both those occupationally exposed to ionising radiation, and the general public, are specified in the UK by the Ionising Radiation Regulations, 1985. The Regulations are based on ICRP recommendations, and specify 5 mSv as the annual limit on effective dose equivalent. More recently, however, ICRP has recommended that the limit on effective dose equivalent for members of the public should be 1 mSv per annum, averaged over a lifetime. The NRPB consequently recommended that for practical purposes, the simplest way to ensure compliance with this lifetime limit was to restrict annual doses to a maximum of 1 mSv. For the 'critical group' the NRPB recommends that doses from effluent dishcharges from nuclear installations should not exceed an effective dose equivalent of 0.5 mSv per year for a single site.

4.229 Both nuclear installations in Lancashire, Heysham and Springfields, discharge liquid radioactive effluents to surface waters. BNFL Springfields discharge liquid effluents to the Ribble estuary, just upstream of Clifton Marsh sewage treatment works. Discharges are made through either or both of two enclosed pipelines which extend to the middle of the main drainage channel. The most recent data for 1988 indicate that annual discharge limits are 13.32 TBq of alpha activity and 444 TBq of beta activity. The actual amounts discharged were 0.42 TBq and 110 TBq beta activity, constituting 3.2% and 25% of the permissible limits respectively (see Table 38).

4.230 The exposure of the 'critical group' in 1988, was 0.27 mSv (Ministry of Agriculture, Fisheries and Food, 1989a), (See Table 39). This is less than

Table 38 Principal Discharges of Liquid Radioactive Waste from Lancashire's Nuclear Establishments. 1988

Establishment	Radioactivity	Discharge Limit (Annual Equivalent) (TBq)	Discharges During 1988 (TBq)	% of Limit
Springfields	Total alpha	13.32	0.42	3.2
	Total beta	444	110	25
Heysham Station 1	Total activity	4	0.033	<1
	Sulphur-35	7.5	0.27	3.6
	Tritium	1850	111	6.0
Heysham Station 2	Tritium	1200	0.00074	<1
	Sulphur-35	7	0.000011	<1
	Cobalt-60	0.036	0.000008	<1
	Other radionuclides	0.45	0.00007	<1

Source: Ministry of Agriculture, Fisheries and Food (1989a)

both the ICRP recommended principal dose limit of 1 mSv/year and the NRPB recommendation of 0.5 mSv/year. The majority of this dose comes from Sellafield effluent, and BNFL estimate that about 11% derives from Springfields discharges (Ministry of Agriculture, Fisheries and Food, 1989a). A recent report by Friends of the Earth (Watts and Green, 1990) suggested that if NRPB exposure limits were to be lowered, and increased occupation of the Lune and Wyre estuaries occurred, some members of the public may be put at risk. However, the report confirmed the MAFF view that current levels of exposure are below existing NRPB limits.

4.231 A report by RADMIL on exposure in the inter-tidal areas of the Lune, Wyre and Ribble also confirmed the MAFF measurements (RADMIL, 1990). RADMIL concluded that "the additional dose received by people who use the inter-tidal areas of the rivers is less than the differences found in the range of natural radiation exposures in different parts of Lancashire".

4.232 The nuclear power stations at Heysham discharge liquid effluent directly to Morecambe Bay. The potentially critical exposure pathways are through locally caught fish and shellfish, which are monitored by MAFF. Radioactive discharges from the two Heysham stations in 1988 are shown in Table 38. All comprise a small percentage of the permissible limit.

4.233 The NRPB have established public radiation exposure dose limits for several radioisotopes. These include the radioisotopes of strontium (Sr),

iodine (I), caesium (Cs), plutonium (Pu), americium (Am) and curium (Cm). Generalised Derived Limits (GDL) have been set for Cs, Pu, Am and Cm (Table 40), based on 'deliberately cautious assumptions'. These are used to assess the significance of low-level contamination. Where contamination exceeds a GDL, it does not automatically mean that the public dose limit has been exceeded. This can only be determined after an investigation of local occupancy factors, dietary and other habits, the conditions of discharge and prevailing weather conditions. The NRPB state that compliance with GDL ensures, with virtual certainty, compliance with dose limit. Comparison of GDL from Table 40 with radioactivity in environmental materials given in Tables 41 to 44, shows that none of the GDL were breached in Lancashire during the years specified.

4.234 Data concerning radionuclide concentrations in the aquatic environment and organisms are produced annually by MAFF. These place particular emphasis on organisms commonly used as food. Recent levels of radioactivity in materials near Springfields and Heysham are presented in Tables 41 and 42 respectively. The only radionuclides detected which were due to Springfields discharges, were isotopes of thorium and protactinium in concentrations of low radiological significance. Other radionuclides present were mainly from Sellafield (Ministry of Agriculture, Fisheries and Food, 1989). The results for 1988 around Heysham (Table 42) also reflect discharges from Sellafield, and exposures are within the ICRP recommended principal dose limit of 1 msv per year (Ministry of Agriculture, Fisheries and Food, 1989a).

4.235 In addition to the data collected close to Lancashire's nuclear facilities, results of monitoring fish and shellfish catches from the Irish Sea are available. Catches landed at Fleetwood and Morecambe are of greatest significance to consumers in Lancashire. Radionuclide concentration data for fish and shellfish for these ports are presented in Tables 43 and 44. These data have been used to calculate the effective dose equivalent for individuals consuming these foodstuffs given in Table 45.

4.236 By far the greatest source of artificial radioactivity in Lancashire waters, particularly in estuarine and coastal waters, is the Sellafield discharge. This has a major, (though reducing), impact on levels of radioactivity in the Irish Sea generally, with the Cumbrian and Lancashire coasts having the highest levels of all (see Figure 69). Dose rates, both in air

Table 39 Summarised Estimates of Critical Group Exposure in Lancashire from Discharges of Radioactive Waste. 1988

Establishment	Radiation exposure pathway	Critical group	Exposure (mSv/year)
Springfields	External	Houseboat dwellers (River Ribble)	0.27[1]
Heysham	Fish and shellfish consumption	Local fishing community	0.07 (0.11)[1][2]

Source: Ministry of Agriculture, Fisheries, Fisheries and Food (1989a)

Notes: [1]*Mainly due to discharges from Sellafield.*
[2]*The first value is based on a gut transfer factor for plutonium and americium of 0.0002; the value in brackets is based on a gut transfer factor of 0.0005.*
ICRP and NRPB exposure limit for the critical group is 1 mSv/year.

Table 40 Generalised Derived Limits for Radioisotopes in the Aquatic Environment, Including Seafoods.

Material	Unit	^{134}Cs	^{137}Cs	^{238}Pu	^{239}Pu	GDL ^{240}Pu	^{241}Pu	^{241}Am	^{242}Cm	^{243}Cm	^{244}Cm
Marine fish	Bq kg^{-1}	500	800	10	10	10	300	9	200^b	10	20
Freshwater fish	Bq kg^{-1}	3,000	4,000	60	50	50	2,000	50	1,000^b	70	90
Crustaceans	Bq kg^{-1}	3,000	5,000	60	60	60	2,000	60	1,000^b	80	100
Molluscs	Bq kg^{-1}	8,000	10,000	200	200	200	4,000	100	3,000^b	200	300
Freshwater sediment	Bq kg^{-1}	5,000	10,000	80,000	80,000	80,000	2,000,000	70,000	2,000,000	100,000	100,000
Marine sediment	Bq kg^{-1}	2,000	7,000	40,000	40,000	40,000	1,000,000	30,000	900,000	50,000	60,000
Freshwater	Bq m^{-3}	100	400	600	500	500	4,000	100	4,000	200	300
Freshwater (drinking only)	Bq m^{-3}	100,000	100,000	2,000	2,000	2,000	50,000	2,000	20,000^a	2,000^a	3,000^a
Seawater	Bq m^{-3}	700	2,000	30	30	30	100	5	90^b	5	7

Source: National Radiological Protection Board (1987)

Notes: GDL apply to conditions over a year and are based on the critical age group, which is adults except where indicated by:
(a) for infants aged 1 year;
(b) for children aged 10 years.

Table 41 Radioactivity in Environmental Materials near BNFL Springfields, Lancashire. 1988

Material	Sampling	Total beta	^{60}Co	^{106}Ru	^{134}Cs	^{137}Cs	^{154}Eu	^{155}Eu	^{228}Th
Bass	Ribble Estuary	150	ND	ND	1.5	60	ND	ND	0.0025
Eel	Ribble Estuary	75	ND	ND	1.0	40	ND	ND	0.0020
Grey Mullet	Ribble Estuary	150	ND	ND	0.78	24	ND	ND	0.0042
Sea Trout	Ribble Estuary	130	ND	ND	0.79	18	ND	ND	0.0019
Shrimps	Ribble Estuary	200	ND	ND	0.40	13	ND	ND	0.024
Cockles	Lytham	180	ND	ND	ND	11	ND	ND	0.56
Mud	Pipeline outlet	33 000	6.2	41	14	820	4.5	2.5	53
	Becconsall	37 000	6.4	71	17	1 100	13	4.2	NA
	Skippool Creek	2 000	7.6	120	19	1 300	13	6.2	37
	Penwortham	140 000	6.1	55	15	830	ND	ND	NA
Sand	Lytham	740	1.3	9.4	2.7	150	ND	3.0	17

Mean radioactivity concentration (wet)*, (Bq kg^{-1})

Material	Sampling point	^{230}Th	^{232}Th	^{234M}Pa	^{238}Pu	^{239}Pu + ^{240}Pu	^{241}Am	^{242}Cm	^{243}Cm + ^{244}Cm
Bass	Ribble Estuary	0.0010	0.00068	ND	NA	NA	ND	NA	NA
Eel	Ribble Estuary	0.0011	0.00078	ND	NA	NA	ND	NA	NA
Grey Mullet	Ribble Estuary	0.0010	0.0010	ND	NA	NA	ND	NA	NA
Sea Trout	Ribble Estuary	0.00081	0.0011	ND	NA	NA	ND	NA	NA
Shrimps	Ribble Estuary	0.022	0.010	ND	NA	NA	ND	NA	NA
Cockles	Lytham	1.4	0.37	ND	NA	NA	8.2	NA	NA
Mud	Pipeline outlet	290	67	75 000	36	172	234	0.28	0.66
	Becconsall	NA	NA	96 000	NA	NA	320	NA	NA
	Skippool Creek	83	39	ND	NA	NA	310	NA	NA
	Penwortham	NA	NA	340 000	NA	NA	220	NA	NA
Sand	Lytham	30	18	700	NA	NA	37	NA	NA

Source: Ministry of Agriculture, Fisheries and Food (1989a)

Notes: *except for sediment, where dry concentrations apply.
NA = not analysed. ND = not detected. Co = Cobalt. Ru = Ruthenium. Cs = Caesium. Eu = Europium. Th = Thorium.
Pa = Protactinium. Pu = Plutonium. Am = Americium. Cm = Curium.

and through the food chain, are, nevertheless, low in Lancashire, and do not constitute a matter of serious concern at present. Table 46 and 47 give the gamma radiation dose rates for the intertidal areas near Springfields and the Lancashire coast.

4.237 RADMIL monitors radiation and radio-activity in the County. Its programme includes the following measurements of the marine environment:

* gamma dose rates in coastal and intertidal areas;
* beach surveys;
* sand and sediment measurements;
* airborne particulates;
* fish and shellfish.

4.238 These measurements are reported in RADMIL's annual, and various ad-hoc, reports. The 5th Annual Report (1990) contains a number of relevant conclusions. Nuclear discharges to the marine environment continue to be detectable. Some measurements in fish, shellfish and sediments showed small amounts of radioactive contamination which were below GDL, and of the same order as in 1989. Gamma radiation monitoring on sandy beaches has shown values within the expected range for rocks, soil and sand in the UK attributable to natural radioactivity. Monitoring of objects in beach debris, which may be handled by the public, has indicated no radiological hazard.

4.239 As anticipated, silt and sand monitoring has shown that the former becomes more con-taminated, and this will continue to be monitored. Silt areas are not used commonly for amenity pur-poses, and people do not come into contact with them for lengthy periods. Radiation doses received by those who use intertidal areas are small. However, assessing doses-to-skin from direct contact with silt is more difficult. RADMIL has used

Table 42 Radioactivity in Environmental Materials and Gamma Dose Rates near Heysham Nuclear Power Station, Lancashire. 1988

| Material | No. of Samples | Mean radioactivity concentration (wet)*, (Bq kg^{-1}) | | | | | | | |
		Total beta	^{54}Mn	^{60}Co	^{95}Zr + ^{95}Nb	^{106}Ru	^{125}Sb	^{134}Cs	^{137}Cs
Plaice	4	120	ND	ND	ND	ND	ND	0.4	20
Bass	1	220	ND	ND	ND	ND	ND	2.5	126
Whitebait	1	150	ND	ND	ND	ND	ND	0.8	25
Cockles	4	110	ND	2.7	ND	6.0	0.3	0.3	14
Mussels	4	64	ND	0.7	ND	5.6	0.4	ND	5.4
Fucus vesiculosus	4	350	ND	0.7	ND	0.3	0.6	0.5	27
Samphire	1	120	ND	0.2	ND	ND	ND	0.4	26
Sediment: Sunderland Point	4	930	0.2	2.8	ND	32	0.7	3.9	300
Half Moon Bay	5	1200	ND	4.8	0.8	60	4.3	5.4	470
Turf: Tummer Hill Marsh	1	1200	ND	ND	ND	ND	ND	15	600

| Material | No. of Samples | Mean radioactivity concentration (wet)*, (Bq kg^{-1}) | | | | | | |
		^{154}Eu	^{155}Eu	^{238}Pu	^{239}Pu + ^{240}Pu	^{241}Am	^{242}Cm	^{243}Cm + ^{244}Cm
Plaice	4	ND	ND	NA	NA	ND	NA	NA
Bass	1	ND	ND	NA	NA	ND	NA	NA
Whitebait	1	ND	ND	0.055	0.25	0.35	ND	0.0009
Cockles	4	ND	0.3	0.9	4.3	10	0.017	0.041
Mussels	4	ND	ND	0.20	1.0	1.5	ND	0.0049
Fucus vesiculosus	4	ND	0.1	0.60	2.8	1.5	0.0050	0.0050
Samphire	1	ND	ND	NA	NA	ND	NA	NA
Sediment: Sunderland Point	4	2.0	3.9	NA	NA	88	NA	NA
Half Moon Bay	5	6.1	3.9	22	110	150	ND	0.44
Turf: Tummer Hill Marsh	1	ND	ND	NA	NA	65	NA	NA

Source: Ministry of Agriculture, Fisheries and Food (1989a)

Notes: *except for sediment, where dry concentrations apply.
NA = not analysed, ND = not detected. Co = Cobalt, Zr = Zirconium. Ru = Ruthenium. Sb = Antimony. Cs = Caesium.
Eu = Europium. Pu = Plutonium. Am = Americium. Cm = Curium.

Table 44 Transuranic Radioactivity in Shellfish from the Irish Sea. 1988

Sampling area/ landing point	Sample	^{238}Pu	^{239}Pu + ^{240}Pu	^{241}Pu	^{241}Am	^{242}Cm	^{243}Cm + ^{244}Cm
				Mean radioactivity concentration (wet), Bq kg^{-1}			
Morecambe Bay	Shrimps	0.0093	0.044	NA	0.063	0.00026	0.00026
	Cockles	0.82	3.7	68	8.4	ND	0.037
	Mussels	0.20	1.0	NA	1.5	0.0052	0.0050
Fleetwood	Cod	0.00014	0.0078	NA	0.0012	ND	ND
	Plaice	0.00039	0.0018	NA	0.0032	ND	0.00001
	Fish Meal	0.018	0.092	NA	0.13	ND	0.00049
	Whelks	0.12	0.56	NA	0.71	ND	0.0017

Source: Ministry of Agriculture, Fisheries and Food (1989a)

Notes: NA = Not analysed. ND = Not detected. Pu = Plutonium. Am = Americium. Cm = Curium.

Table 45 Individual Radiation Exposures due to Consumption of Irish Sea Fish and Shellfish. 1988

Exposed population	Consumption rate used in assessment, kg year^{-1}	No. of Samples	Nuclide	Committed effective dose equivalent, (mSv/year) A	B
Consumers in Morecambe Bay area	Fish (flounders + plaice):	50	^{137}Cs	0.038	0.038
	crustaceans (shrimps):	18	^{239}Pu + ^{240}Pu	0.007	0.017
	molluscs (cockles + mussels):	15	^{241}Am	0.015	0.037
	Others			0.010	0.018
			Total	0.07	0.11
Consumers associated with commercial fisheries: Fleetwood	Fish (plaice + cod):	82	^{137}Cs	0.025	0.025
	crustaceans (shrimps):	17	^{239}Pu + ^{240}Pu	0.009	0.023
	molluscs (cockles + whelks):	23	^{241}Am	0.020	0.050
	Others			0.016	0.022
			Total	0.07	0.12
Typical member of the fish-eating public consuming fish landed at Whitehaven/Fleetwood	Fish (plaice + cod):	15	^{137}Cs	0.004	0.004

Source: Ministry of Agriculture, Fisheries and Food (1989a)

Notes: IGRP and NRPB limit for critical group = 1 mSv/year
  A = Dose equivalent based on a gut transfer factor from seafood for Pu and Am of 0.0002
  B = Dose equivalent based on a more cautious gut transfer factor from seafood for Pu and Am of 0.0005
  Cs = Caesium. Pu = Plutonium. Am = Americium.

'cautious' models to predict the likely dose-to-skin of those using silt areas for amenity purposes. These predictions have shown the expected dose to be below national dose limits.

Drinking Water Quality

Introduction

4.240 The majority of homes in Lancashire are supplied with mains water by NWW, though many rely on private supplies from wells, or springs. The mains supply system consists of a vast network of water sources, aqueducts, supply pipes and service pipes. Water supply is a major industry in the UK.

4.241 Lancashire's mains drinking water comes from a variety of sources and NWW adjusts supplies and moves water through the distribution system as required. It is therefore difficult to define exactly where the water from a consumer's tap originates, it will probably be from a mixture of sources which will vary through the year. Major sources of Lancashire's water are Haweswater (in Cumbria), Stock's Reservoir, in Ribble Valley, the Lancashire Conjunctive Use Scheme on the Rivers

Table 43 Beta/Gamma Radioactivity in Fish from the Irish Sea. 1988

Sampling area/ landing point	Sample	Total beta	^{134}Cs	^{137}Cs
		Mean radioactivity concentration (wet) Bq kg^{-1}		
Morecambe Bay	Flounder	180	1.4	80
	Plaice	120	0.4	20
	Bass	220	2.5	130
Fleetwood	Cod	140	0.5	19
	Plaice	120	0.3	16
	Fish Meal	370	1.0	12

Source: Ministry of Agriculture, Fisheries and Food (1989a)

Note: Cs = Caesium.

Lune and Wyre, numerous small reservoirs in the south and east of the County, some river abstractions and groundwater sources (particularly north of Preston).

4.242 Water from these sources is piped to treatment works. The extent of treatment depends on the quality of water entering the works; some

Figure 69

Concentration of Caesium-137 in Filtered Water from the Irish Sea. 1988

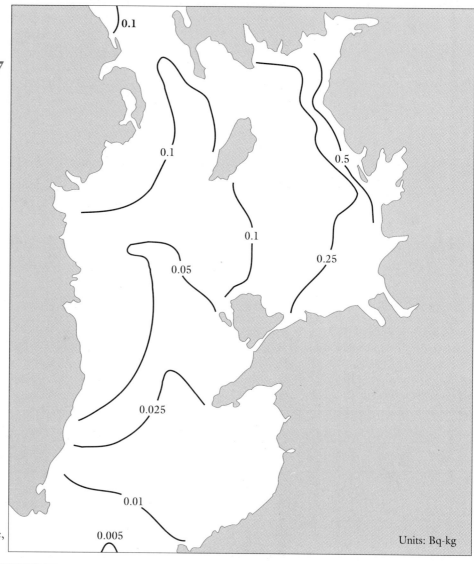

0.1

0.1

0.5

0.1

0.05

0.25

0.025

0.01

0.005

Units: Bq-kg

Source: Ministry of Agriculture, Fisheries and Food (1989a)

Table 46 Gamma Radiation Dose Rates in Air at 1 m Over Intertidal Areas near BNFL Springfields, Lancashire. 1988

Location	No. of Samples	Mean Gamma Dose Rate in Air at 1m.	
Pipeline outlet	4	0.14	(uGy/hr)
Freckleton	4	0.17	
Becconsall	5	0.17	
Lytham	4	0.16	
Penwortham	3	0.15	

Source: Ministry of Agriculture. Fisheries and Food (1989a)
Note: uGy/hr = Micro Grays per Hour.

4.244 The water supply system is organised into 'water supply zones' (WSZ), also termed compliance zones. Each WSZ is defined principally by a source of water with a generally uniform quality. The population of each zone must not exceed 50,000. WSZ may be supplied with water from more than one treatment works, and some works supply several zones. There are 76 WSZ wholly, or substantially, in Lancashire which are shown in

requires extensive treatment, some relatively little. Water from different sources is often mixed, using cleaner water to dilute lower quality water so as to meet appropriate standards.

4.243 From the works, treated water enters the distribution system. Water pipes run under most Lancashire streets, and service pipes run from the mains to each domestic property. NWW is responsible for the service pipe from the mains to the curtilage of a property (the communication pipe). On crossing the curtilage, the pipe becomes the responsiblity of the property owner and is known as the supply pipe.

Table 47 Gamma Radiation Dose Rates over Intertidal Areas of the Lancashire Coast. 1988

Location	Ground type	No. of samples	Mean Gamma Dose Rate in Air at 1m. (uGy/hr)
Becconsall	Mud	5	0.17
Skippool Creek	Mud	4	0.18
Fleetwood	Sand	4	0.074
Blackpool	Sand	4	0.060
Ainsdale	Sand	4	0.060
Tummer Hill Marsh	Salt Marsh	4	0.27
Sunderland Point	Mud	4	0.11
Freckleton	Mud	4	0.17

Source: Ministry of Agriculture, Fisheries and Food (1989a)
Note: uGy/hr = Micro Grays per Hour.

Figure 70
Drinking Water Supply Zones in Lancashire. 1990

1. Lancaster
2. Wyre
3. Ribble Valley
4. Blackpool
5. Fylde
6. Preston
7. South Ribble

8. West Lancashire
9. Chorley
10. Blackburn
11. Hyndburn
12. Burnley
13. Pendle
14. Rossendale

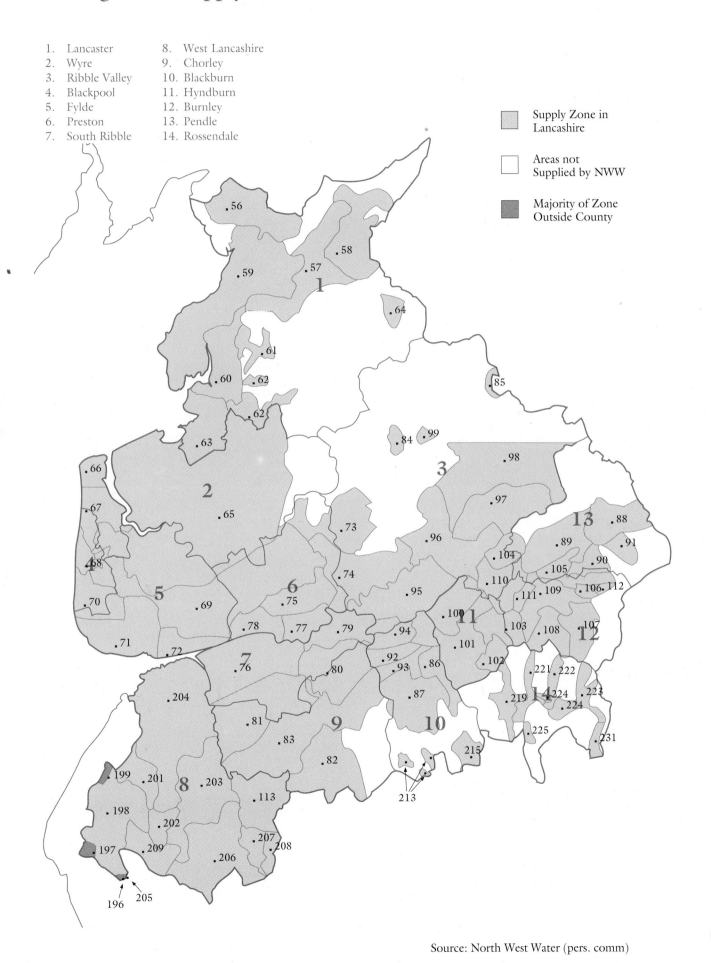

Supply Zone in Lancashire

Areas not Supplied by NWW

Majority of Zone Outside County

Source: North West Water (pers. comm)

Figure 70. Their names and reference numbers are given in Appendix D.

Prescribed Concentrations or Values

4.245 Drinking water quality standards are derived from information on life-long human exposures. EC Directive 80/778/EEC specifies water quality standards and preferred guidelines. These were implemented in the UK in 1985, with further clarification in The Water Supply (Water Quality) Regulations, 1989 in force since January 1990. These Regulations also supplement Part II of the WA 1989.

4.246 The Drinking Water Directive defines Maximum Admissible Concentrations (MAC) for various parameters, many of which have guideline values. For example, the MAC for aluminium is 200 ug/l, whilst the guideline value is 50 ug/l. The guidelines were seen, by some, as long term aims. Many of the MAC, and guidelines, are derived from World Health Organisation recommendations produced in 1984. The Regulations refer to Prescribed Concentrations or Values (PCV), which are usually equivalent to MAC. It should be noted that the guideline levels for each parameter given in the Drinking Water Directive are excluded from the UK Regulations.

4.247 Water quality is monitored by NWW at the consumer's tap. All parameters listed in the Regulations must be sampled and the results assessed against each PCV. Monitoring at the tap has one major drawback and places NWW in a particularly difficult position. It is possible for lead, zinc and copper concentrations in water to be significantly affected by the internal piping of a property. NWW is responsible for supplying wholesome water at the tap, but have no responsibility for supply pipes (and tanks) within properties. It thus has to ensure a sufficiently high quality such that internal piping does not reduce quality to cause a breach of standards.

4.248 The Regulations outline sampling frequencies to assess compliance with PCVs. Some parameters require single samples, whilst others are based on three monthly, or annual, means. Prior to 1987, the UK Government interpreted the EC Directive by comparing PVC with three-monthly means, rather than on a single sample basis. This allowed drinking water to contain greater overall concentrations for some parameters. The system now relies on the single sample approach. Parameters considered in this Audit are subject to single sample PCVs, rather than three monthly means.

4.249 NWW has supplied water quality information relating to samples taken at consumers' taps in Lancashire WSZ during the period 1/5/89 to 30/4/90 inclusive. Water companies are not obliged to supply data relating to sampling at water treatment works, so it has not been possible to compare raw and treated water data. A public register of drinking water quality was set up by NWW in January 1990.

Relaxations and Undertakings

4.250 To avoid enforcement action under the WA 1989, water undertakers can seek 'relaxations', or offer 'undertakings' to take appropriate steps to secure or facilitate compliance with a PCV. Relaxations apply to raw water and undertakings to treated waters. Part III of the Regulations allows the Secretary of State to authorise 'relaxations' ('derogations' under the EC Directive) of PCV which are caused by the nature or structure of the ground the supply comes from, exceptional weather conditions, or emergencies to maintain supply. Relaxations usually have time limits set for remedial action.

4.251 Where relaxations are allowed, the relaxed standard becomes the standard in force. Any failures against the relaxed standard could, therefore, trigger enforcement action. Parameters which fail the original PCV, but pass a relaxed standard, are not identified as failures. Relaxations affecting Lancashire involve 31 treatment works and 58 WSZ (out of 76 in the County). Issued in September 1989, these relaxations require that treatment should be improved by December 1994. Parameters frequently associated with relaxations include colour, iron, and manganese, which do not have known significant short, or long-term, public health implications. Relaxations relating to iron and manganese are given in Table 48.

4.252 Undertakings may be applied under Section 20(5)(b) of the WA 1989 when water quality contravenes the Regulations during treatment or distribution. All zones have undertakings for iron, colour, manganese and turbidity, due to deficiencies in the distribution system. NWW has also undertakings relating to aluminium for 34 WSZ in Lancashire, corresponding to those supplied from treatment works using aluminium compounds for treatment, (NWW, pers.comm.).

4.253 Section 52 of the WA 1989 places a duty on undertakers to provide water which is 'wholesome' at the time of supply. This is enforceable by the Secretary of State for the Environment under of the Act, who is required to take action where satisfied that the water company is contravening (or has contravened and is likely to again) a PCV, or a relaxed PCV. However, the Secretary of State is not required to take action in accordance with S.20(5) where he is satisfied that either:

* the contravention is 'trivial', or;
* the company has an undertaking, or;
* Part I of the Act precludes action.

4.254 Unfortunately, trivial has not been defined, and this is a cause of considerable uncertainty. At the Parliamentary Committee stage of the Water Act, the Water Minister stated that ' . . . it is very unlikely that circumstances giving rise to a danger to health could properly be regarded as trivial'. However, for lead and coliforms only, further guidance is contained in the 'Guidance on Safeguarding the Quality of Public Water Supplies' (Department of the Environment, 1990). For lead, the DOE have stated that:

* 'The risk may also be regarded as relating to an insignificant part of the supply zone when . . . less than 2% of the samples have exceeded the lead standard'.

For coliforms, the guidance is that:

* 'Remedial action must be taken in respect of each zone where more than 5% of samples contain coliforms'.

4.255 However, neither the WA 1989, its Regulations nor the DOE provide similar criteria for aluminium, iron, manganese and other parameters. The absence of formal guidance is unhelpful. For the purpose of this Audit, and so as to place the extent of PCV failures into some kind of context, the 2% failure criterion applying to lead has been adopted for aluminium and for all other parameters (except coliforms). Hence, PCV breaches for aluminium are only regarded as 'trivial' when less than 2% of the samples have failed the aluminium standard. Adoption of the 2% failure rate also accords with the principles of the precautionary approach. However, it is stressed that it has no legal or enforceable basis. When formal guidance is announced, future versions of the Audit will clearly be based upon such guidance. It is also emphasised, that adoption of the 2% criterion does not suggest that there is any evidence that the drinking water concerned is a risk to public health. It is a means of giving the data some reasonable perspective.

Lead

4.256 The PCV for lead is 50 ug/l. There are no relaxations pertaining to lead in Lancashire but, every WSZ has an undertaking which means the PCV can be exceeded, whilst areas at risk are identified. Of the 76 Lancashire supply zones, 52 (or 68%) had some samples which exceeded the PCV during the 1989/90 sample period.

4.257 Table 49 shows maximum and mean figures and the geographical areas affected for the 39 supply zones where samples exceeded the PCV for 2%, or more, of the time. Seven zones failed on more than 10% of the samples, although in each case the annual average was below the PCV. The highest maximum figure for lead occurred in the Sabden zone (No.104) with a level of 740 ug/l which is more than fourteen times the PCV.

4.258 Levels in supply zones where the PCV was exceeded in less than 2% of the samples are excluded from Table 49. However, this does not mean that maximum levels recorded in these zones were not high. For example, Ribble Valley (WSZ 096) shows a maximum value of 210 ug/l, which exceeds the PCV by over four times, but less than 2% of samples exceeded the PCV, so such exceedances are regarded as 'at risk but not significant'. The most frequent failures for lead occur at Aughton (209), with a 22.2% failure rate, and Wigan North West (113), failing on 26.7% of the samples. Other zones where failures were frequent, and maximum concentrations exceed the PCV were Dolphinholme/Welby Crag (062), Cockerham (063) and Wayoh North (215).

4.259 The natural lead content of freshwater resources world-wide has been estimated at 0.001–0.010 mg/l (World Health Organisation, 1984). Higher levels in supply can result when water has a low pH or is soft or 'aggressive', and dissolves lead from pipes and plumbing in domestic properties. Lead concentrations can vary widely after treatment due to the presence of lead pipes; depending on the length of pipe, the time the water has been standing in the pipe, whether the water is soft or aggressive, and vibrations caused by traffic.

Table 48 Relaxations for Manganese and Iron in Drinking Water in Lancashire.

Treatment Works	WSZs Supplied	Max. Permitted Conc. (ug/l) at Treatment Works	
		Manganese	Iron
Cliffe	100	784	581
Cantclough/Hurstwood	107	630	238
Hodder	66, 67, 69, 70, 71, 72, 84, 92, 94, 99	204	500
Oswestry	198, 201–204, 206–209	554	290
Chipping	73	180	—
Coldwell	72	1060	330
Dilworth	74	104	416
Laneshaw	88	169	—
Mitchells	102	370	242
Ogden (Barley)	89	55	400
Sunnyhurst	87	165	243
Whitebull	76–78	213	1089
Springs	213	202	335
Wayoh	215	226	—
Broughton	66, 67, 69–72	39	298
Fishmoor	86, 87, 92–94	1540	849
Franklaw	66, 67, 69–72, 75, 77, 79–83	204	1295
Scotsforth	59, 60	145	—
Langthwaite	59–61	727	—
Barnacre	63, 65–72	665	221
Blundell House	197, 198, 202, 204, 209	158	133
Dunmail Rise	47, 49, 54, 56–58, 62	54	300
Bickerstaffe	198, 202, 204, 209	226	—
Lowcocks	97	159	—
Worsthorne	109	192	262
Mill Brow	198, 201–204, 209	—	1050
Haslingden	219	261	—
Loveclough	221	293	—
Clough Bottom	222, 223	267	377
Cowpe	224	165	—
Cowm	231	1330	3410

Source: NWW (pers. comm.)

Notes: Manganese PCV is 50ug/l
Iron PCV is 200ug/l

WSZ	No. of Samples	% Failure	Mean Conc. (ug/l)	Max. Conc. (ug/l)
056 Silverdale/Yealand	46	2.2	8	60
057 Regional/Caton Filter House	47	2.1	9	100
058 Haweswater/Lune Valley	42	2.4	13	340
060 Lancaster General/Galgate	53	7.5	15	60
062 Dolphinholme/Welby Crag	44	18.2	24	80
063 Cockerham	23	13.0	23	250
067 Cleveleys & Thornton	141	2.1	9	90
068 Warbreck Tower	80	5.0	16	150
069 Stocks District	100	3.0	15	340
070 Blackpool South	55	7.3	21	150
071 Lytham St. Annes	91	7.7	15	150
076 Preston South	114	7.9	16	170
077 Preston Ribbleton/Fulwood	86	3.5	10	40
078 Preston West	72	2.8	11	60
080 Bamber Bridge	52	7.7	16	230
093 Blackburn South II	36	5.6	11	130
094 Blackburn West	78	3.8	10	130
095 Blackburn North	62	6.5	12	110
097 Lowcocks	116	3.4	10	170
098 Waddington	92	2.2	8	70
100 Cliffe	59	3.4	9	50
103 Burnley Road	107	4.7	11	110
104 Sabden	44	6.8	25	740
110 Simonstone on Altham	134	3.7	13	610
111 Padiham	22	4.5	16	110
113 Wigan North West	90	26.7	35	210
198 Ainsdale	29	2.0	38	160
201 Southport North	40	7.5	14	110
202 Halsall Lane Ormskirk	32	6.3	13	120
204 Tarleton	34	8.8	16	120
206 Skelmersdale Lower	35	2.9	15	90
208 Upholland	31	3.2	13	60
209 Aughton	36	22.2	40	260
213 Springs	15	6.7	16	70
215 Wayoh North	29	13.8	37	250
221 Loveclough	29	22.7	44	280
222 Clough Bottom Direct	29	6.9	16	70
223 Clough Bottom Bacup	38	7.9	25	120
224 Cowpe	26	11.5	20	80

Table 49 Lancashire Supply Zones where Lead Exceeded the PCV in more than 2% of Drinking Water Samples. May 1989 to April 1990

Source: NWW (pers. comm.)

Notes: All WSZ have undertakings for lead.
The PCV for lead is 50 ug/l

4.260 Drinking water is one of many pathways of lead ingestion by humans. Lead is well documented as a cumulative poison in humans, causing brain damage, particularly in children. In 1987, a Medical Research Council study concluded that there is no evidence of a safe level of lead in humans. This has recently been confirmed by the Water Research Centre, who suggest that the EC MAC for lead concentrations in drinking water might not be low enough to protect human health. FOE believe that there is no truly 'safe' level for lead and are lobbying for the PCV to be reduced to 10 ug/l , with a target level of zero (Friends of the Earth,1990).

4.261 Lead levels exceed the PCV in 60% of Lancashire's WSZ. This is a matter of great concern, because of both the frequency and degree of failures (up to fourteen times the PCV in one case). The major cause of the problem in the County is the widespread presence of lead pipes, since NWW states that no lead concentrations above 50 ug/l have been found in treated water from their plants (NWW pers. comm.). Communication pipes (owned by NWW), but largely, supply pipes (owned by the householder) cause elevated lead levels. The situation is more likely in older buildings, where older plumbing remains in use. A major concern here is older schools which still have lead piping, because young children absorb more lead from food and water than adults and are particularly at risk.

4.262 When street mains (which are not lead) are refurbished, lead communication pipes owned by NWW are now replaced as a matter of course (North West Water Annual Report, 1988–89). Supply pipes are entirely the responsibility of property owners. A large proportion of properties served by NWW have lead pipes (70%). By removing lead piping on private property (through the use of local authority grants) the householder obliges the water company to remove any lead communication pipe work. Action by householders is the main solution to the problem of lead in water.

4.263 By the end of 1991, areas with significant lead problems must be identified by NWW. They must also assess whether or not treatment is reasonably practicable and reductions can be achieved. A further application for an undertaking from the Secretary of State will then be submitted in the light of these investigations.

4.264 Resolving the contamination of water by removing piping is considered to be a long-term solution (NWW, pers.comm.). The problem can be temporarily treated by two methods. Firstly, buffers can be added to raise the pH, preventing uptake from lead pipes. Secondly, the solubility of lead in pipes can be reduced by chemicals (usually orthophosphate). The DOE have advised a further temporary measure in a 1983 report on the study of lead levels in Lancashire schools. This states that households and buildings that might expect elevated lead levels should 'flush', i.e.draw off, about 1 gallon of water before taking water for consumption.

Aluminium

4.265 The PCV for aluminium is 200 ug/l, although the guideline level cited in the Drinking Water Directive is 50 ug/l. There are no aluminium relaxations in Lancashire at present. However, undertakings apply to 34 WSZ coinciding with treatment works which use aluminium sulphate as a coagulant. Unlike lead, there are no fixed maxima relating to undertakings for aluminium in Lancashire, because there are no fixed maxima set nationally.

4.266 In total, there were 15 WSZ where aluminium exceeded the 200 ug/l PCV. Table 50 indicates the 18 zones that failed on 2% or more samples; two of these (Preston South (076); Trawden (091)) are not covered by undertakings because the treatment plants do not use aluminium. Trawden had the greatest maximum concentration of aluminium at 810 ug/l, over four times the PCV. These breaches are due to 'natural' aluminium and would be caused by heavy rain and classified as trivial.

4.267 A further supply zone not covered by an undertaking (Lowcocks (097)) failed the Regulations although the rate was less than 2%. The supply zone where aluminium concentrations exceed the PCV most frequently was Morecambe/Carnforth (059), at 12.2% of samples. For the first nine months of 1990, however, these two WSZ showed a 3.6% and 6.4% failure respectively.

4.268 Aluminium sulphate is commonly used in water processing as a coagulant to remove organic matter. It is removed at a later stage in the treatment process. The most intense use occurs at works receiving water rich in organic matter derived from upland areas. Past use, and the consequent levels in drinking water, assumed that aluminium does not represent a human health hazard. Aluminium is also ubiquitous in the environment. There are many pathways for ingestion of aluminium besides drinking water, since it is present in many foods. It is not, however, thought to be an essential trace nutrient for humans (World Health Organisation, 1984).

4.269 Over recent years, increasing concern has been expressed about a possible link between aluminium and the incidence of Alzheimer's disease. In spite of a great deal of research, the nature of the link is still uncertain and it is not known whether aluminium is a causative factor or is merely indicative in patients with the disease. One study (Martyn et al., 1989), however, indicated that the risk of contracting Alzheimer's disease was 1.5 times higher in areas where the mean aluminium concentration in drinking water exceeded 100 ug/l, compared to areas where concentrations were below 10 ug/l. If this relationship is validated by further research, the current PCV may not be set at a level which adequately protects public health for a lifetime.

4.270 There are two alternatives to the use of aluminium compounds as a coagulant. Ferric compounds are one possibility, though they can only be used at newer treatment works specially designed cater for them. There are no such plants in Lancashire at present. However, a number of works at the planning stage, will use ferric compounds, including Accrington (Mitchells), Burnley (Worsthorne), and Colne (Laneshaw Bridge). The timetable for the use of alternative coqulants is specified in undertakings documents.

4.271 Another alternative to aluminium compounds is the full or partial, utilisation of polyelectrolytes. These compounds can only be used at smaller and newer treatment works. NWW is using them as an interim measure because they are expensive. There is no objection to their use on grounds of public health (DOE, pers. comm.). NWW is in the process of modernising and replacing older treatment works and has also undertaken to improve control systems and efficiency at existing plant. Increased efficiency, and the use of alternative coagulants, is targeted for completion by the end of 1992, with construction finished by late 1994.

Table 50 Lancashire Supply Zones where Aluminium Exceeded the PCV in more than 2% of Drinking Water Samples. May 1989 to April 1990

WSZ	No. of Samples	% Failure	Mean Conc. (ug/l)	Max. Conc. (ug/l)
059 Morecambe/Carnforth	49	12.2	119	230
060 Lancaster	55	5.5	90	430
067 Cleveleys & Thornton	122	2.5	65	400
069 Stocks District	78	2.6	78	850
074 Dilworth*	50	6.0	245	620
076 Preston South	96	2.1	65	280
080 Bamber Bridge	50	4.0	64	290
084 Dunsop	43	2.3	79	210
086 Fishmoor Boosted	76	3.9	72	495
091 Trawden	41	2.4	59	810
093 Blackburn South II	21	4.8	91	340
100 Cliffe	60	5.0	115	250
102 Mitchells	61	9.8	91	260
213 Springs	18	5.6	84	210
215 Wayoh North	29	10.3	75	350
219 Haslingden Grane	67	9.0	99	260
221 Loveclough	23	4.3	59	250
224 Cowpe	27	3.7	73	520

Source: NWW (pers. comm.)

Notes: The PCV for aluminium is 200 ug/l
All above WSZ have undertakings for aluminium
*Now taken out of commission

Total Coliforms

4.272 The Regulations require that coliform bacteria should be entirely absent from drinking water. However, a proviso under Section 3(6) of the Regulations allows that the bacteria can be present in 5% of the samples, provided that the samples taken in the preceeding year (or the most recent 50 samples) showed complete absence. NWW has coliform undertakings for every WSZ in Lancashire.

4.273 There are 40 supply zones which transgress the regulations for total coliforms, eight failures being for faecal coliforms. Table 51 shows the five supply zones where samples fail for more than 5% of the time. Supply zones with maximum values of over 100 total coliforms per 100 ml are Lancaster Central (060), at 258 per 100 ml; Burnley mixed (109), at 112 per 100 ml and Upholland (208), at 110. per 100 ml.

4.274 Coliforms are derived from many sources, including plant and soil material. But the most important source in terms of human health are coliforms of faecal origin. Coliform bacteria are indicators of more dangerous organisms which can cause a variety of human health problems. Irritation of the throat, stomach upsets and diarrhoea may all result from their ingestion. It is impossible to identify the number of such complaints related to drinking water, because they can be caused by so many other factors and are also unlikely to be reported.

4.275 Bacterial levels in water are traditionally controlled by disinfection. Water is usually chlorinated for this purpose. Such measures are carried out at all Lancashire treatment works.

Table 51 Lancashire Supply Zones where Total Coliforms Exceeded the PCV in more than 5% of Drinking Water Samples. May 1989 to April 1990

WSZ	No. Samples	% Failure	Mean Conc. (Number per 100 ml)	Max. Conc. (Number per 100 ml)
058 Haweswater/Lune Valley	91	5.5	0.7	57.0
060 Lancaster Central/ Galgate House	168	7.7	1.8	258.0
215 Wayoh North	33	9.1	0.3	6.0
222 Clough Bottom Direct	29	6.9	0.2	5.0
231 Cowm	28	7.1	1.0	28.0

Source: NWW (pers. comm.)

Notes: PCV for total coliforms is zero (for 95% of samples)
All above WSZ have undertakings for total coliforms

Iron

4.276 There are undertakings for iron at all Lancashire WSZ. In addition, there are 21 relaxations (see Table 48). The PCV is 200 ug/l, whilst the Drinking Water Directive provides a guideline value of 50 ug/l. PCV were exceeded in 24 supply zones during the 1989/90 sampling period, with 18 having a more than 2% failure rate. The maximum failure rate was over 33%, at Cockerham (zone 063). However, these failures do not include supply zones which are subject to relaxations. The greatest relaxation is 238 ug/l at Cant Clough/Hurstwood treatment works, which feeds a number of supply zones.

4.277 Iron is an essential element in human nutrition. Objections to its presence in drinking water in quantity are on aesthetic grounds, because it tends to colour the water. The levels found in Lancashire are highly unlikely to constitute a health risk.

Manganese

4.278 The PCV for manganese is 50 ug/l, whilst the guideline value cited in the Drinking Water Directive is 20 ug/l. As with iron, there are undertakings for manganese covering every supply zone in Lancashire. There are also 30 relaxations. Relaxations for treatment works, and the WSZ which they supply, are detailed in Table 48. There are 22 zones which exceed the PCV for manganese, with 14 failing for 2%, or more, of the samples.

4.279 The presence of manganese in potable water is objectional for aesthetic rather than health reasons, and the levels found in Lancashire are extremely unlikely to have any adverse effect on humans. Manganese is an essential trace element for metabolic processes and is one of the least toxic elements (World Health Organisation, 1984).

Hydrogen Ion (pH)

4.280 There are no relaxations or undertakings relating to the pH of Lancashire water supplies. The pH range permitted by the Regulations was 5.5–9.5 until January 1990, when it was decreased to 6.5–8.5 in accordance with the Drinking Water Directive. Under the original limits, there were 17 failures, all at the top end of the range, between May 1989 and April 1990.

Colour and Turbidity

4.281 Colour and turbidity are particularly noticeable parameters and, along with 'taste', are those most likely to produce public complaints. Colour is measured as Hazen units and the PCV is 20 on the Hazen scale. Turbidity is measured as Formazin Turbidity Units (FTU) and the PCV is 4 FTU. There are undertakings for colour and turbidity for all WSZ in the County and relaxations for colour covering 46 zones. There were 11 zones where the PCV for turbidity was exceeded, five of which had a failure rate in excess of 2%. There was only one zone where a failure for colour was recorded, which was also greater than 2%.

4.282 Colour and turbidity are the result of materials suspended in the water and are particularly prevalent in upland waters with their naturally high natural levels of peaty compounds, iron and manganese. Many parts of Lancashire have this sort of water, particularly in the east of the County. It can be treated with coagulants, but excessive use of iron or aluminium creates its own problems. Coloured water may, therefore, often be diluted with clearer water to achieve the PCV. There are no real public health dangers associated with colour or turbidity, unless there are bacterial aggregations associated with suspended particles.

Trihalomethanes

4.283 Concern over concentrations of trihalomethanes (THM) has been expressed in the press and breaches of the PCV for THM (100 ug/l) have been reported for Hyndburn (The Observer, 6/8/89). THM are usually created when chlorine (used to remove bacteria from water during treatment) reacts with peat and other organic material found in water from moorland reservoirs and nutrient-rich rivers. The THM standard is a three-month average standard and failures on individual samples can be tolerated. A valid assessment of their extent in Lancashire's drinking water was not possible from data supplied by NWW, because records do not cover all supply zones. All 54 WSZ for which information is available, however, are satisfactory.

Private Water Supplies

4.284 Drinking water in the past largely came from individual wells, springs and streams. Properties not connected to the mains supply still rely on such 'private' supplies. Responsibility for ensuring their quality rests with District Councils, and the WA 1989 has given them powers to enforce the Water Supply (Water Quality) Regulations 1989 for these supplies. The extent to which they are able to fulfil this function is, however, dependent on the resources allocated to their sampling programme.

4.285 District Councils with only a small number of private supplies are able to sample annually, but those with large numbers may require several years to complete a sampling programme. The quality of supply, however, may vary considerably from day to day, depending on factors like rainfall. One sample may not provide an accurate indication of overall quality. Failed samples clearly indicate problems, but there is no way to be sure that a supply which passes on the day of sampling will be of the same quality the following day. This is a fundamental problem in designing local authority sampling programmes.

4.286 Supplies are sampled for bacteriological and chemical analysis. There is, however, a substantial difference in the breadth and depth of the two types of analysis and supplies are more frequently tested bacteriologically. Bacteriological tests are carried out by the Public Health Laboratory Service and the quality of the supply is determined from standards laid down by the DOE in 1982.

4.287 Samples are analysed chemically for 25 parameters by the County Analyst according to the Water Supply (Water Quality) Regulations (Table 52). When supplies are found to be unsatisfactory, District Councils are empowered to seek remedial action by the owner of the supply. Many people served by private supplies are, however, quite content with their supply and are reluctant to accept that it is unsatisfactory. District Council policy is to try and ensure the co-operation of all private supply owners in maintaining a satisfactory quality.

4.288 There are upwards of 1,300 private supplies in Lancashire (Table 53). Most are in the north and east of the County, where outlying farms continue to use springs and wells (Figure 71). Three Districts have no private supplies (Blackpool, Fylde and West Lancashire). The total number of supplies is not currently known for Ribble Valley and Rossendale Districts. The DOE has provided a classification system, based on the number of people served by a supply. The criteria for this are:

* Class I – Supplies regularly serving more than 500 people;

Table 52 Private Water Supply Parameters Analysed by the County Analyst.

Parameter	Prescribed Concentration or Value (unless otherwise stated)
Free Chlorine (Cl) mg/l	—
Fluorides (F) ug/l	1,500
Total Hardness (Ca) mg/l	60 (MRC)
Calcium (Ca) mg/l	250
Copper (Cu) ug/l	3,000
Iron (Fe) ug/l	200
Lead (Pb) ug/l	50
Manganese (Mn) ug/l	50
Aluminium (Al) ug/l	200
Magnesium (Mg) mg/l	50
Zinc (Zn) ug/l	5,000
Potassium (K) mg/l	12
Sodium (Na) mg/l	150
Nitrate (NO_3) mg/l	50
Sulphate (SO_4) mg/l	250
Nitrate (NO_2) mg/l	0.1
Odour Dilution Number	3 at 25°C
Taste Dilution Number	3 at 25°C
Oxidisability (O_2) mg/l	5
pH	5.5 (MRC) to 9.5
Turbidity (FTU)	4
Ammonium (NH_4) mg/l	0.5
Chlorides (Cl) mg/l	400
Colour (HU)	20
Conductivity uScm	1,500 at 20°C

Source: Lancashire County Council.

Note: MRC = Minimum Required Concentration

* Class II – Supplies regularly serving between 50 and 500 people;
* Class III –Supplies regularly serving less than 50 people (excluding Class IV);
* Class IV – Supplies serving one domestic property only;
* Class V – Supplies where untreated water is bottled for sale for the public that is not recognised as a Natural Mineral Water under the Natural Mineral Water Directive (80/777/EEC).

Almost all Lancashire's private supplies are Class III or IV (nearly 90%, see Table 53). Class I and II are generally restricted to public houses and other food establishments.

4.289 Table 53 shows the numbers of private supplies throughout Lancashire and the proportion of unsatisfactory supplies. Most of the problems which occur relate to bacteriological quality. This is potentially the most serious public health aspect of

Figure 71

Number of Private Water Supply Zones by District in Lancashire. 1990

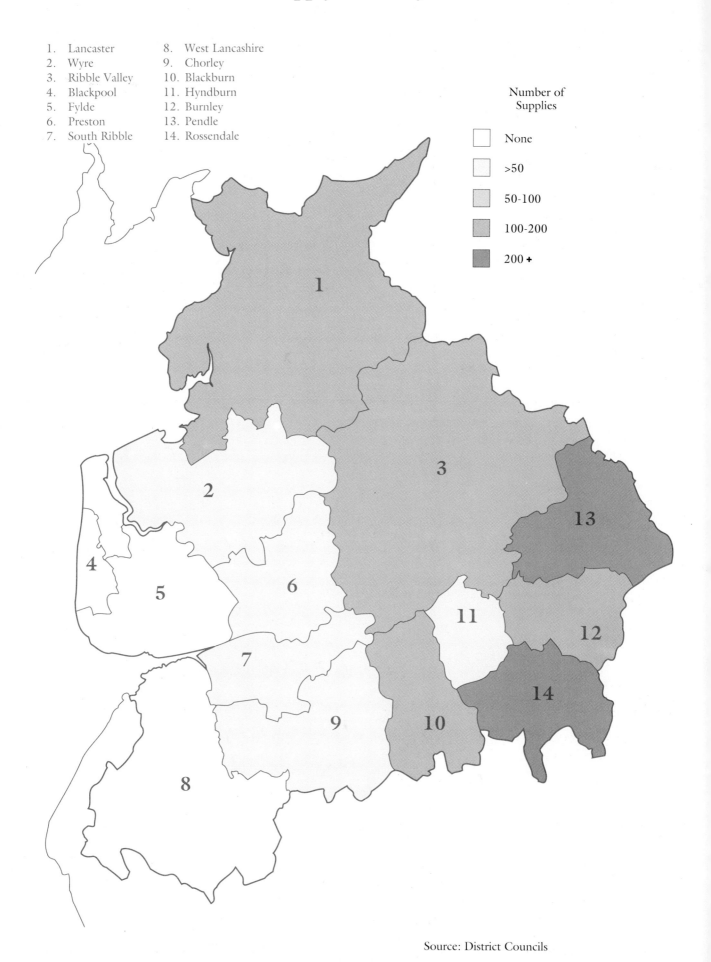

1. Lancaster
2. Wyre
3. Ribble Valley
4. Blackpool
5. Fylde
6. Preston
7. South Ribble
8. West Lancashire
9. Chorley
10. Blackburn
11. Hyndburn
12. Burnley
13. Pendle
14. Rossendale

Number of Supplies

None
>50
50-100
100-200
200 +

Source: District Councils

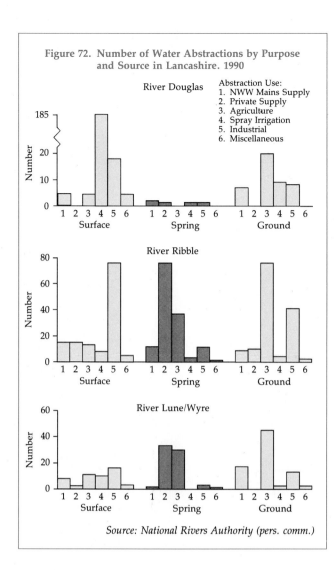

Figure 72. Number of Water Abstractions by Purpose and Source in Lancashire. 1990

River Douglas

Abstraction Use:
1. NWW Mains Supply
2. Private Supply
3. Agriculture
4. Spray Irrigation
5. Industrial
6. Miscellaneous

River Ribble

River Lune/Wyre

Source: National Rivers Authority (pers. comm.)

* Class II – Supplies which are suitable with treatment;
* Class III –A temporary classification for supplies which are unsuitable but could be improved by remedial work;
* Class IV – Supplies which are unsuitable for dairying purposes because they are subject or liable to dangerous pollution.

Treatment of Class II supplies consists of either hand-chlorination, chlorination plant or a filtration system. In Lancashire, 251 (16%) of the County's 1,570 dairy farms use a private water supply. MAFF are required to ensure that all supplies are maintained to acceptable bacteriological quality.

Water Abstractions

4.293 Abstractions from surface waters, springs and groundwater are controlled by the NRA. Under the Water Resources Act 1963, the NRA are required to "take any action necessary to conserve, redistribute or otherwise augment water resources and to secure the proper use of water resources in England and Wales". The NRA thus control all

private supplies. Following samples of supplies, action by Environmental Health Officers should ensure that appropriate remedial measures are taken by the supply owners and that quality improves. Many owners are, however, lax in maintaining treatment equipment and bacteriological problems are frequent.

4.290 Chemical quality is a long term problem and cannot be improved by the measures used to remove bacteria. The difficulties faced by NWW with public supply also confront private supplies. Iron and manganese concentrations are naturally high in the Pennine waters of East Lancashire. They do not comprise a public health risk, but the PCV (Table 53) is frequently exceeded.

4.291 Aluminium and lead are a different matter and do exceed their MACs in some areas. The aluminium is naturally derived, but the lead usually comes from piping. The potential problems of lead and aluminium discussed earlier, apply equally to private supplies.

4.292 MAFF are responsible for monitoring the bacteriological quality of private supplies used by dairy farms. Dairy water supplies are classified by MAFF according to their bacteriological suitability:

* Class I – Supplies which are suitable for dairying purposes without any treatment;

Table 53 Private Water Supplies in Lancashire. 1990

	Known Total	Class I	Class II	Class III	Class IV	% failures Bact.	% failures Chem.	Chemical parameters failing	Sampling
Lancaster	158	2	1	43	112	34	34	Al, Fe, Pb, Mn	3 year programme
Wyre	34	1	3	8	22	Not given	Not given	Not given	Annually
Ribble Valley*	146	2	8	43	93	63	45	Fe, Mn, Al	Continuing programme
Blackpool	0	–	–	–	–	–	.	–	–
Fylde	0	–	–	–	–	–	–	–	–
Preston	22	–	1	–	21	15	35	Pb, Fe, Mn	Annually
South Ribble	4	–	–	–	4	25	25	Not given	Annually
West Lancashire	0	–	–	–	–	–	–	–	–
Chorley	39	–	–	–	39	37	22	Fe, Mn	Annually
Blackburn	119	–	–	40	79	51	41	Pb, Mn, Fe, Al	Continuing programme
Hyndburn	40	–	–	6	34	62	26	Not given	Biannually
Burnley	118	–	118			Not given	Not given	Pb, Fe, Mn	2-3 times annually
Pendle	252	9	2	3	238	48	49	Al, Fe, Mn, Pb, Cu	Continuing programme
Rossendale*	400	–	–	50	350	58	50	Al, Pb, Mn	Continuing programme
LANCASHIRE	1,332	14	140	193	992	–	–	–	

Source: District Councils

Notes: Al = Aluminium   Pb = Lead
    Fe = Iron   Mn = Manganese
    Cu = Copper
    *Incomplete total.

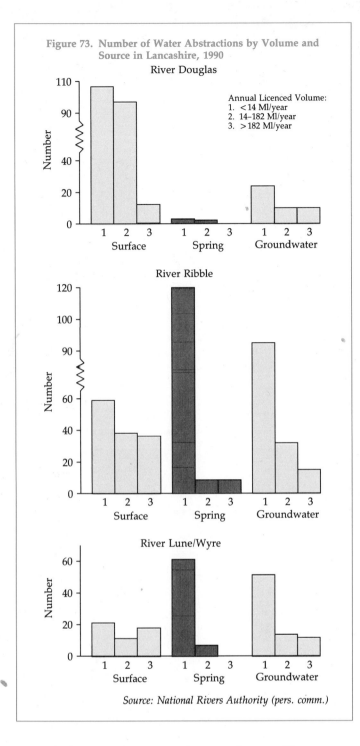

Figure 73. Number of Water Abstractions by Volume and Source in Lancashire, 1990

River Douglas

Annual Licenced Volume:
1. < 14 Ml/year
2. 14–182 Ml/year
3. > 182 Ml/year

River Ribble

River Lune/Wyre

Source: National Rivers Authority (pers. comm.)

* mains water supply;
* private water supplies;
* agricultural use (excluding spray irrigation);
* spray irrigation;
* industrial use:
* miscellaneous other uses.

4.296 NRA 'purpose codes' give some specific uses within these major categories. The different licenced uses of abstracted water within Lancashire are:

* North West Water mains supply;

* Private supplies (drinking, cooking, sanitation, washing), Commercial (hotels, etc.), Household (domestic), Industrial premises, Swimming pools;

* Agriculture (excluding spray irrigation), basic agriculture (livestock watering etc.), fish farming (farming and restocking), food processing and dairying, vegetable washing, slaughter houses;

* Spray irrigation, agriculture, other (e.g.public parks and gardens, golf courses);

* Industry, boiler feed, cooling water, process of manufacture, National Power power generation, power generation (water power), paper making, sand and gravel washing, steam raising, washing down floors and machinery;

* Miscellaneous, amenity, dust suppression, fire fighting, standby/emergency supply, transfer of water, vehicle washing, water supply (non private or mains), monitoring of water quality, conservation/rearing of wildfowl.

4.297 NWW and the electricity generating companies are the largest abstractors. The former regularly transfers large volumes of water over great distances. Wastage can arise from leakage from aqueducts and mains, overflowing service reservoirs and faulty valves and large quantities are lost from faulty domestic plumbing and fittings. Recent figures in the press claim that up to 30% of abstracted water can be lost (The Guardian, 20/7/90). Large abstractors can be set targets to reduct waste reduction (National Rivers Authority, 1990).

4.298 The different sorts of abstraction, in terms of source and use, vary considerably across Lancashire. This reflects both the distribution of the different water sources, and different human activities throughout the County. Lancashire falls mainly into the three hydrometric areas of the Lune/Wyre, Ribble and Douglas (see Figure 43). Abstractions in these hydrometric areas have been grouped by water source, purpose of abstraction, and the annual licenced volume of abstraction. The numbers of abstractions within each group are given in Figures 72 and 73.

4.299 Surface water abstractions are used mainly for spray irrigation in the agricultural parts of South and West Lancashire, and mostly for industrial uses in Central and East Lancashire. Springs are almost absent in the Douglas catchment, but are extensively used for private supplies and agricultural use

abstractions or impoundments of water. They can stipulate Minimum Acceptable Flows for watercourses and alter water resource control conditions in times of drought.

4.294 All regular abstractions require a licence, except for domestic or agricultural abstractions of less than 200 litres a day. Other exceptions to the licence requirements include one-off abstractions of less than 4,546 litres, or those in exceptional circumstances such as land drainage or fire fighting. Licences specify the exact location of the abstraction point, its purpose and limits on daily and annual volumes. The NRA charge for issuing or modifying abstraction licences, to cover administrative and other costs.

4.295 Water is abstracted for numerous purposes, though there are six main groups:

Figure 74

Location of Large Groundwater Abstractions in Lancashire. 1990

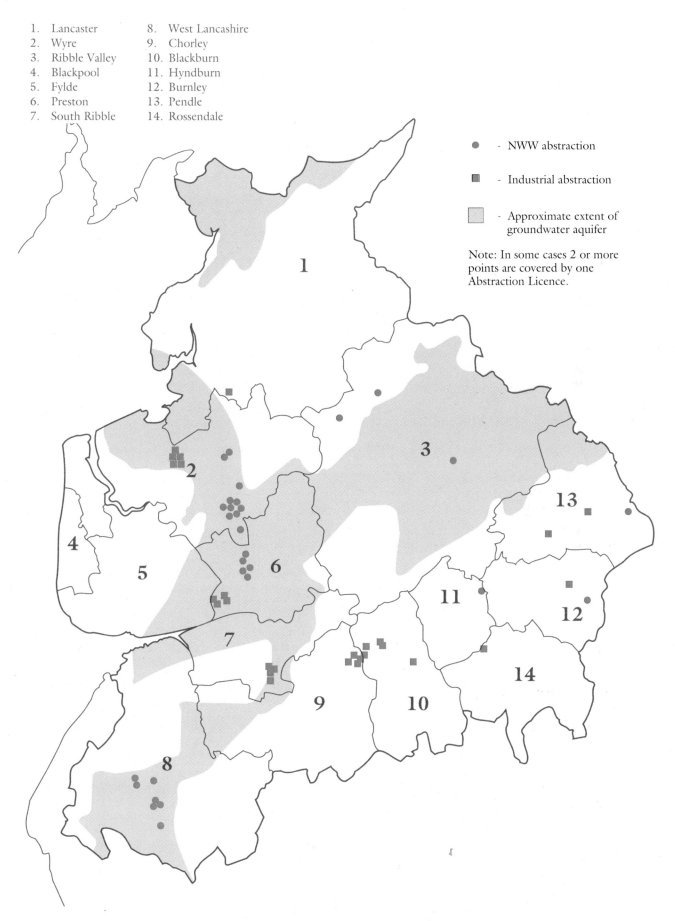

1. Lancaster
2. Wyre
3. Ribble Valley
4. Blackpool
5. Fylde
6. Preston
7. South Ribble
8. West Lancashire
9. Chorley
10. Blackburn
11. Hyndburn
12. Burnley
13. Pendle
14. Rossendale

● - NWW abstraction

■ - Industrial abstraction

▨ - Approximate extent of groundwater aquifer

Note: In some cases 2 or more points are covered by one Abstraction Licence.

Source: National Rivers Authority (pers. comm.)

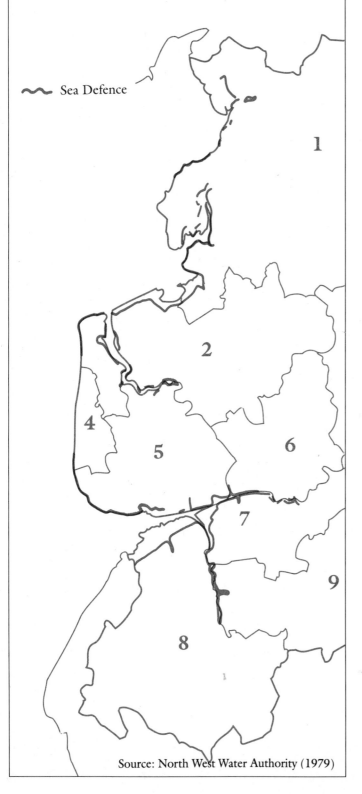

Figure 75
Sea Defences in Lancashire. 1979

∿ Sea Defence

1

2

4

5

6

7

9

8

Source: North West Water Authority (1979)

elsewhere. Groundwaters are used mainly for agricultural purposes throughout the County, although there is a concentration of industrial use in Central and East Lancashire.

4.300 NWW abstracts vast volumes of water for mains supply, mostly from reservoirs (which are included as surface waters) or groundwaters, through boreholes. Groundwater abstractions are usually only used to supplement surface water supplies under certain conditions, e.g.low reservoir levels in summer coinciding with high demand. The locations of major abstractions from groundwaters, both NWW and industrial, are shown in Figure 74. These correspond well to the distribution of likely aquifer bearing rocks in the County. Small abstractions consist mainly of private supplies or agricultural users.

Flood Defence

4.301 One aspect of water resources which traditionally receives little public attention except in response to major incidents, is flood defence. Awareness was heightened by the major flooding of North Wales, associated with gales and high tides early in 1990. Areas of Lancashire are also low-lying and susceptible to flooding, both along the coast and in inland river valleys, and the possibility of rises in sea level (see Chapters 2 and 3) add further urgency to the matter.

4.302 Flood defence in inland areas of Lancashire is largely the responsibility of the NRA. Along the coast, however, District Councils are also responsible for coastal protection. The NRA is in the process of determining who is responsible for which sections of the coast. Sea defences existing in 1979 are shown in Figure 75.

4.303 Areas at risk from flooding include low-lying areas in large river floodplains and coastal areas which actually lie below sea level. Rivers may burst their banks and flood surrounding fields but only rarely does this occur to such an extent that life and homes are threatened. There are, however, substantial and important residential areas on the Lancashire coast and a severe coastal storm or tidal surge leading to flooding could cause enormous damage. It is, therefore, very important that sea defences are regularly checked and maintained, and predictions regarding changes in sea level monitored constantly.

4.304 The NRA have a major capital works programme for improving flood defence and the current schemes in Lancashire are as follows:

	Start	Finish
Savick Brook, Preston	June 1990	March 1992
River Wyre channel works	April 1984	— 1990
Yarrow Wall, Croston	August 1990	March 1991
Bannister Brook	April 1989	March 1994
River Lostock	January 1989	March 1991
River Douglas (embankments)	April 1990	March 1993
Cocker Sands embankment	March 1991	April 1992
Brows at Glasson	April 1991	March 1992
River Yarrow at Croston	April 1992	March 1993
River Blakewater	April 1994	March 1997
Walton-le-Dale	April 1994	March 1996
Mearley Brook	April 1994	March 1996
Walverden Water	April 1994	March 1996
Tinker Brook	April 1995	March 1996

These schemes are largely restricted to inland areas at present because the policy with regard to sea defences has yet to be determined. Once the NRA have completed their nationwide review of sea defences, the capital works programme will no doubt be extended to include sea defence work, possibly in co-operation with local authorities.

References

British Waterways (1989). Water quality in canals; a summary of water authority data 1988. Environmental Bulletin 3/89. British Waterways Board.

Conlan K., Hendry K., White K.N. & Hawkins S.J. (1988). Disused docks as habitats for estuarine fish: a case study of Preston Docks. Fish Biology 1988, 33 (supplement A), p85–91. The Fisheries Society of the British Isles.

Dickson R.R. & Boelens R.G.V.(eds) (1988). The Status of Current Knowledge on Anthropogenic Influences in the Irish Sea. Co-operative Research Report No.155. International Council for the Exploration of the Sea (ICES).

Department of the Environment (1984). Classification of Potable Water Supplies. DOE Circular 25/84. HMSO.

Department of the Environment (1982). The bacteriological examination of drinking water supplies. Report 71. HMSO.

Department of the Environment, Welsh Office (1985). River Quality in England and Wales. HMSO.

Department of the Environment (1989). Guidance on Safeguarding the Quality of Public Water Supplies. HMSO.

Friends of the Earth (1990). Lead in drinking water. FOE.

Gardiner J. & Mance G. (1984). United Kingdom water quality standards arising from European community directives. WRC (Water Research Centre) Technical Report 204. WRC.

Greenfield J.P. & Ireland M.P. (1978). A survey of macrofauna of a coal-waste polluted Lancashire fluvial system. Environmental Pollution 16.

Hellawell J.M. (1978). Biological Surveillance of Rivers. Water Research Centre.

Hinchcliffe P.R. (1976). Surf-zone water quality in Liverpool bay. Estuarine and Coastal Marine Science (1976) 4:427–442.

Holdgate M.W.(1979). A Perspective of Environmental Pollution. Cambridge University Press.

Irish Sea Study Group (1990). The Irish Sea – Waste Inputs and Pollution. Liverpool University Press.

Ministry of Agriculture, Fisheries and Food (1989). Report on the Disposal of Waste at Sea, 1986 and 1987. HMSO.

Ministry of Agriculture, Fisheries and Food (1989a). Aquatic Environment Monitoring Report Number 21 –Radioactivity in Surface and Coastal Waters of the British Isles, 1988. MAFF.

Martyn, C.N. et al. (1989). Geographical relation between Alzheimer's disease and aluminium in drinking water. The Lancet 1:59–62.

National Radiological Protection Board (1987). Revised Generalised Derived Limits for Radioisotopes of Strontion, Iodine, Caesium, Plutonium, Americum and Curium. (NRPB-GS8).

National Rivers Authority North West Region (1989). Monitoring requirements – 1990; inland water quality. NRA.

National Rivers Authority (1990). North West Region Rivers Advisory Committee. Leakage. NRA.

North West Water (1979). First Report of Survey of Land Drainage Functions. NWWA.

North West Water (1988). County Review 1988 for Lancashire. NWWA.

North West Water (1989a). Acidification of Surface waters in Cumbria and South Pennines. NWWA.

North West Water (1989b). Annual Report 1988/89. NWWA.

Pendle Pollution Control (1990). Pendle rivers monitoring April 1989 to March 1990. Pendle Pollution Control.

Priede I.G., Solbet J.F., Nott J.E., O'Grady K.T. & Cragg-Hine D.(1988). Behaviour of adult salmon, Salmo salar, in the estuary of the River Ribble in relation to variations in dissolved oxygen and tidal flow. J. Fish Biology, 33, supplement A. The Fisheries Society of the British Isles.

RADMIL (1990). Fifth Annual Report of RADMIL 1989/90. RADMIL.

Robinson N.A. & Pringle A.W. (eds.) (1987). Morecambe Bay. An Assessment of Present Ecological Knowledge. Centre for North-West Regional Studies and the Morecambe Bay Study Group.

Smith P.J., Jones F. & Watson D.C. (1978). Salmonella pollution of surface waters. Journal of Hygiene, 81, 353–360.

Water Authorities Association and the Ministry of Agriculture, Fisheries and Food (1986) Water pollution from farm waste in England and Wales. Water Authorities Association.

Watts, P and Green, P. (1990) Unjustifiable Exposures – Sellafield contamination of the Rivers Lune and Wyre, Lancaster UK. FOE.

World Health Organisation (1984). Guidelines for Drinking Water Quality, World Health Organisation, Geneva.

Chapter Five
Waste

Introduction

5.1 Waste is anything unwanted or surplus. Everyone produces waste of some kind and in Lancashire, each of us generates about half a tonne every year. It is a reflection on the wastefulness of modern society that waste disposal is a major industry.

5.2 Most waste is presently disposed of by landfill. Monitoring and control of all landfill sites is the responsibility of the County Council as waste disposal authority. The County Council grants both the planning permission and site licence required for all such operations.

5.3 All methods of disposal have environmental impacts. These include potential contamination of ground and surface water and the generation of landfill gas, as waste rots or decays. Leachates are produced as liquid seeps through landfill picking up substances from the waste, whilst there is also potential for noise, dust and litter from sites. Waste incineration is also not without environmental consequences.

5.4 Before the Control of Pollution Act (COPA) 1974 there was very little legislation controlling waste disposal operations. As a result, we have inherited many old, completed landfill sites with environmental problems.

5.5 The best way to reduce the need for disposal, and associated environmental problems, is by waste avoidance, recycling and recovery. At present, Lancashire has a number of transfer stations, waste treatment plants, household waste disposal centres and recycling collection schemes in operation. But these account for only a small percentage of the total waste handled. There is clearly scope for a much greater proportion of waste recycling, but changes in social attitudes and market conditions are required before major advances can be made.

5.6 Litter is a further manifestation of society's attitude to waste. It has a serious impact on the quality of our landscape and townscape and can have public health implications, particularly if allowed to accumulate over time. Very little local detailed information exists on the problem of litter in the County. Sadly, all too often, it is accepted as a part of modern life.

5.7 This Chapter deals firstly with the legislative and organisational framework for waste in Lancashire. After defining the main waste categories data are presented on the amounts arising in each category and how these are disposed of. Details are then given about the amount of waste recycled and the type and location of recycling facilities. A section on environmental effects follows with a description of how waste operations are managed. A final section deals with litter, describing the groups and schemes involved in Lancashire.

5.8 The convention adopted for this Green Audit is for data to be presented by District Council boundaries. However, major waste facilities are located according to population catchments which often extend over a number of District boundaries. The text of this Chapter reflects this fact.

Legislation

European

5.9 European Community (EC) waste legislation is contained mainly in the 1975 Council Directive on Waste (75/442/EEC). This requires member States to establish waste disposal authorities (WDA) which must prepare waste disposal plans and regulate disposal activities. The Directive also incorporates the 'polluter pays' principle, with the cost of disposal falling upon the waste producer, or those undertaking the disposal.

5.10 A further Directive on the Disposal of Waste Oils (75/439/EEC) states that their collection and disposal should not damage health and the environment and that, wherever possible, waste oils should be recycled. A 1976 Directive regulates the disposal of PCBs, (76/403/EEC), whilst measures to control substances like arsenic, lead, mercury and asbestos are contained in the Directive on Toxic and Dangerous Waste (78/319/EEC). The Directive on the Transfrontier Shipment of Hazardous Waste (84/631/EEC) concerns the trans-boundary movement of hazardous material by road, water or air.

5.11 The use of sewage sludge in agriculture is regulated by the Directive on the Protection of the Environment when Sewage Sludge is Used in Agriculture (85/469/EEC). The discharge of dangerous substances into water is controlled by the Directive on Pollution Caused by Certain Dangerous Substances Discharged into the Aquatic Environment (76/464/EEC). This lists substances that must be licensed for discharge and regulated by member States. Discharges into groundwater are controlled by the Directive on the Protection of Groundwater Against Pollution Caused by Certain Dangerous Substances (80/68/EEC). Of major significance at present, is the consideration being given by the EC to new Directives on landfill waste and municipal waste waters.

United Kingdom

5.12 Until very recently, the Control of Pollution Act (COPA) 1974 was the principal legislation for waste. This required County Councils, as the WDA, to prepare a waste disposal plan, and for all waste disposal operations to be licensed. The Act also dealt with consents required for all discharges to water.

5.13 The Refuse Disposal (Amenity) Act 1978 makes it the duty of the County Council to provide Household Waste Centres. Local authorities are also authorised to remove and dispose of abandoned vehicles and other refuse. Certain wastes are also controlled through the Control of Pollution (Special Waste) Regulations 1980. These are concerned with wastes that threaten public health. A comprehensive record system has been developed through these regulations to monitor the transportation and disposal of special waste.

5.14 The Environmental Protection Act (EPA) 1990 re-enacts much of the COPA 1974 waste legislation and gives local authorities revised duties. Its major changes stem from its separation of the waste regulating and operating functions currently practised by County Councils. In future, regulation of all waste disposal activities and licences wil be handled by new Waste Regulation Authorities, (WRA), provided by County Councils. WRA will also prepare and implement waste disposal plans. A parallel, but separate WDA, also established by County Councils, will let and manage contracts for domestic waste disposal. In doing so, WDA will have to have regard to minimising pollution and maximising recycling. Waste collection remains a District Council function. WDA will also provide Household Waste Disposal Centres, (HWDC), and, as landowner, will maintain, restore and monitor completed sites.

5.15   County Councils will no longer carry out disposal operations, and their present facilities will be transferred to an 'arms-length' Local Authority Waste Disposal Company, (LAWDC), sold entirely to existing private companies or operated on a joint basis with private industry.

5.16   Under the EPA 1990, District Councils are required to prepare a register of contaminated land for their area. As Waste Collection Authorities (WCA), Districts must also produce a Recycling Plan. The Act introduces a new 'duty of care' requirement on all waste producers, carriers and disposers.

5.17   Planning permission is required for most waste facilities, and this is controlled by the Town and Country Planning Act (TCPA) 1990. The Local Government Acts 1972 and 1985, and the TCPA (Amended) 1977 are also used by Planning Authorities for the control of waste disposal operations. The Town and Country Planning General Development Order 1988 requires District Councils to consult the WDA regarding planning applications for any development within 250 m of the boundary of a waste disposal site.

5.18   The Food and Environment Protection Act 1988 requires that licenses must be issued by the Ministry of Agriculture, Fisheries and Food (MAFF) for sewage sludge dumping. The Collection and Disposal of Waste Regulations 1988 define clinical, household, industrial and commerical waste. They prescribe the cases where a charge can be made for the collection of household waste. These regulations also state when a waste disposal licence is not required. Under the Local Government Act 1988, District Councils were obliged to put their Waste Collection Service out to compulsory competitive tender.

5.19   The Control of Pollution (Amendment) Act 1989 provides for the compulsory registration of vehicles used for transporting controlled waste. Under this measure, vehicles suspected of being used for the illegal disposal of waste can be impounded. Its principal aim is to restrict fly-tipping and it is likely to take effect at the same time as the EPA 1990.

5.20   The Public Health Acts 1936 and 1961 and the Public Health (Recurring Nuisances) Act 1969 deal with the accumulation of rubbish that is prejudicial to health or causing a nuisance. District Councils can serve abatement notices and remove such material when it is detrimental to the amenities of the neighourhood. The 1961 Act defines rubbish as 'rubble, waste paper, crockery, metal and any other kind of refuse'.

5.21   The Radioactive Substances Act 1960 regulates the keeping and use of radioactive material on premises and provides for the disposal and accumulation of radioactive waste.

5.22   The Highways Act 1980 gives local authorities the power to install litter bins along streets and highways. The dropping of litter was made a summary offence by the Litter Act 1983 with a possible fine of up to £1,000. It also makes it the duty of litter authorites to maintain and empty litter bins provided by them. This Act also defines litter as including derelict vehicles, vessels and scrap metal and rubbish of any description.

5.23   The EPA 1990, rationalises street cleaning responsibilities, making all streets and highways the responsibility of District Councils (other than motorways). Local Authorities are under a duty to keep clean all land in their control. An individual now has the power to apply to the Magistrates Court for a Litter Abatement Order directed at District or County Councils who fail to do this. District Councils may also serve Litter Abatement Orders on other landowners and designate Litter Control Zones.

5.24   Under the Mines and Quarries (Tips) Act 1969, a tip is defined as an accumulation or deposit of refuse from a mine or quarry, whether in solid or liquid state. Local Authorities are given powers to ensure that disused tips are not a danger to the public, and may serve notices requiring owners to carry out remedial operations. The Mines and Quarries (Tips) Regulations 1971 control the actual operation of tips, and makes specifications for the monitoring of closed tips.

Organisations

Central Government

5.25   The Department of the Environment (DOE) is responsible for national policy on waste disposal and the formulation of legislation. The Department of Transport is responsible for cleaning motorways, whilst British Rail are responsible for their land. HMIP monitors certain disposal operations, whilst the National Radiological Protection Board monitors sites containing radioactive waste on request. NRA water quality monitoring also encompasses leachate from tips.

Local Government

5.26   In 1974, County Councils were made WDA and given the responsibility for administering the waste disposal function in their areas, whilst the collection of waste from households was confirmed as a District Council responsibility. At the same time, the COPA 1974 provided WDA with additional regulatory powers and responsibilities.

5.27   The WDA had a dual rôle. They were providers and operators of landfill sites and HWDC whilst also being responsible for regulating waste facilities. The major changes in these duties introduced by the EPA 1990 have been described above.

5.28 In addition to their waste management responsibilities, County Councils are also the planning authority for all waste facilities. Control is exercised through conditions and restrictions placed on planning consents and by refusing planning permission for unsuitable sites, developments or processes. The County Council has established the Tidy Up Lancashire Campaign together with the Tidy Britain Group to promote and assist litter abatement in response to the Litter Act 1983. As Highway Authorities, County Councils may also provide litter bins in streets, and must empty and maintain them.

5.29 District Councils are responsible for all refuse collection, street and highway cleansing, and have a duty to keep clean all land in their control, including parks and amenities. Districts also have the power to install litter bins, bring in byelaws to control dogs and dog-owners, and may introduce fixed penalty schemes for littering. All Lancashire Districts are represented on the Tidy Up Lancashire Campaign steering group.

Other Organisations

5.30 The private sector plays a major rôle in waste disposal. Companies large and small provide landfill sites, though most small operators are only licensed to accept inert waste and cannot accept commercial, industrial or household waste. Recently, through the Local Government Act, 1988, District Councils have been obliged to subject the household waste collection service to compulsory competitive tendering. This has resulted in a number of private companies taking over collection, with District Councils remaining as the WCA.

5.31 WCA are only responsible for the collection of domestic waste which represents a small portion of all controlled waste handled. Most of the rest is collected and transported by private companies. This includes the operation of skips and heavy vehicles for the collection of industrial, commercial, household clearance, demolition and construction waste.

5.32 North West Water is responsible for the treatment and disposal of sewage and sewage sludge in Lancashire. Responsibilities for consenting and monitoring effluent discharges from sewage works rest with the NRA. Where disposal is to land, a waste disposal licence may be required.

5.33 The commercial sector plays an important rôle in the control of litter by sponsoring litter bins around their premises or through various litter collection centres. There are many voluntary groups involved with litter prevention operating individual clean up and enhancement schemes in their own areas. These include conservation groups, church organisations, schools, Parish Councils and neighbourhood/resident groups. The Tidy Britain Group (TBG) is the major national organisation charged with promoting measures to reduce the problem. They are involved in specific campaigns. In Lancashire, such schemes operate with Pendle, Blackpool and Chorley District Councils.

Waste and Litter in Lancashire

Definition of Waste

5.34 Waste is divided into categories according to type to aid in the identification, disposal and licencing of disposal sites. The principal types are:

* Household Waste, defined by the COPA 1974 as waste from a private dwelling or residential home, education establishment or hospital;

* Commercial Waste, defined by COPA 1974, as waste from shops, offices, businesses and places of entertainment;

* Industrial Waste, defined by COPA 1974 as waste from any factory or industrial process, including clinical waste, sewage sludge and scrap metal, arising from industry;

* Special Wastes are defined by the Control of Pollution (Special Waste) Regulations 1980, as those which are sufficiently hazardous to present a threat to human health. Appendix E shows the 31 substances presently covered. Wastes are also classed as Special if they are prescription medicines or have a combustion threshold (flashpoint) of 21°C or less. The Regulations are currently under review and consideration is being given to the inclusion of wastes which present an immediate, delayed or accumulative risk to the environment;

* Construction and Demolition Waste, which consists of masonry and rubble from demoliton or reconstruction;

* Clinical Waste, defined by the Collection and Disposal of Waste Regulations 1988, includes any waste arising from medical, nursing, dental, veterinary, pharmaceutical or similar practice, and all human and animal tissue, blood, swabs, drugs, dressings, syringes and needles, including that which may arise in the home;

* Sewage Sludge which results from the treatment of raw sewage. This typically contains up to 98% water prior to any de-watering process;

* Radioactive Waste which consists of radioactive material, or a substance or article contaminated by the production, storage, or use of radioactive material;

* Mines and Quarry Waste is that produced from normal mining or quarrying operations;

* Agricultural Waste is that arising from farmland and premises, and includes waste from farm buildings and animals.

Waste Arising

5.35 In 1989, a total of 7.81 million tonnes of waste arose in Lancashire. This represents approximately 5.5 tonnes per person per year. However, of this total, only 3.27 million tonnes was 'controlled' waste subject to the provisions of the COPA 1974 and the EPA 1990. The remaining 4.54 million tonnes 'non-controlled' waste, was material from agricultural and mines and quarrying sources. Controlled waste is defined by COPA 1974 as 'household, industrial and commercial waste, or

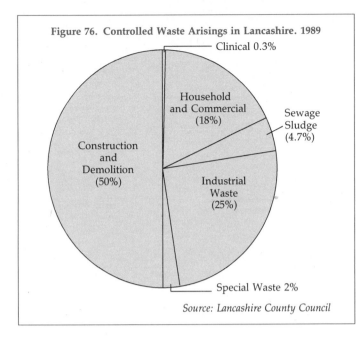

Figure 76. Controlled Waste Arisings in Lancashire. 1989

Clinical 0.3%

Household and Commercial (18%)

Sewage Sludge (4.7%)

Construction and Demolition (50%)

Industrial Waste (25%)

Special Waste 2%

Source: Lancashire County Council

any such waste'. A summary of the controlled waste arising from Lancashire is presented in Figure 76, and the arisings from the separate categories are now dealt with in turn.

Household and Commercial Wastes

5.36 In 1989/90, the quantity produced was estimated to be 587,575 tonnes, (about 0.5 tonnes for each resident in the County). This includes household waste taken by the public to HWDC, commercial waste from offices and retail premises, and all household waste collected by District Councils or their agents. Figure 77 indicates how this waste arises by District. Blackpool produces the largest quantity of household and commercial waste with approximately 49,000 tonnes. This is brought up to a total of over 67,000 tonnes by waste from HWDC. Lancaster has the next highest total

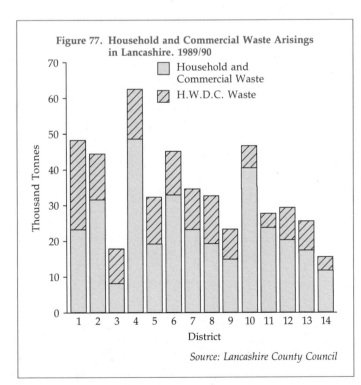

Figure 77. Household and Commercial Waste Arisings in Lancashire. 1989/90

Household and Commercial Waste

H.W.D.C. Waste

Source: Lancashire County Council

with over 47,000 tonnes; however, the figures suggest that over half of this is collected through HWDC which is the largest proportion for any District. Rossendale and Ribble Valley both produced less than 20,000 tonnes of domestic and commercial waste in the year.

Industrial Waste

5.37 Non-special industrial waste is collected by private contractors from factories, offices and shops. It is disposed of either at County Council facilities or private sites, including landfills within a factory's own boundary. In 1989, the quantity produced was estimated to be 794,607 tonnes. Some was deposited outside the Lancashire boundary, and the figures given are based on an assumption as to how much is 'exported'. This is assumed to be about 40,000 tonnes (North West Waste Disposal Officers, 1988).

Special (Industrial) Waste

5.38 Special Waste includes substances like asbestos, most acids and alkalis, chlorinated solvents, heavy metal sludges, various organic wastes, and pharmaceutical products and by-products. A full list is given in Appendix E. Because of their nature, they require specialised disposal methods which include chemical treatment and high temperature incineration. Some are suitable for landfill, (e.g. asbestos). In comparison with non-special waste the quantities of special waste produced are small. In 1989, their arisings represented just 2% of all waste generated in Lancashire. Only a few treatment plants and high temperature incinerators are required nationally and so special wastes are commonly exported out of the County.

5.39 Transport of special waste is covered by a complex documentation system which records the point of arising, transportation details, final disposal site and the nature and quantity of these wastes. The County Council is responsible for monitoring the transport of such arisings in Lancashire.

5.40 A total of 68,057 tonnes of special waste was produced in the County in 1989. A further 9,300 tonnes was imported through ports in Lancashire, and most was taken to other parts of the country. At the same time, chemical recovery plants in the County accept waste from all over the country, importing 26,564 tonnes into Lancashire from the rest of the UK. In addition, 900 tonnes of material was imported into the country from abroad to be handled at these plants, of which 696 tonnes comes through Lancashire ports and 204 tonnes from other ports in the country.

5.41 Table 54 indicates the arisings of special waste in 1989. This shows that Wyre produces the largest quantity (25,680 tonnes), due to the ICI Hillhouse plant at Thornton Cleveleys. Chorley and Lancaster also produce significant proportions and with Wyre, contribute 67% of the County's production.

Construction and Demolition Waste

5.42 This category includes materials deposited at both County Council and private facilities. A limited amount will be exported and some will be imported. The estimated figure of 1.6 million tonnes of demolition and excavation arisings assumes a net import of 60,000 tonnes. (North West Waste Disposal Officers, 1988). In addition, an appreciable amount is deposited at sites exempt from licensing provisions for which records do not exist. This applies particularly to situations where such material is being used for building work, or where demolition waste is disposed of on the demolition site.

Clinical Waste

5.43 An estimated total of 10,700 tonnes of clinical waste is produced in Lancashire each year (Lancashire County Council, 1987), some of which is incinerated. Some is chemically sterilized and disposed of to landfill. The disposal of clinical waste is currently under consideration by the Lancashire Waste Management Officers Group, who are also looking at veterinary waste, (for which very little information presently exists). Veterinary wastes are either collected by District Councils as industrial waste, or by specialist contractors who dispose of it by incineration.

Sewage Sludge

5.44 Sewage sludge in its original state contains about 98% water and quantities are presented in terms of their 'wet weight'. When raw sewage undergoes treatment, water is removed and the remaining sludge is termed 'dry', and is measured by 'dry weight'. Lancashire-specific data for either forms are difficult to obtain, because NWW information is regionally based. In 1987, for instance, the former NWWA dumped 1,626,000 tonnes (wet weight) of sewage sludge into Liverpool Bay (Ministry of Agriculture Fisheries and Food, 1988). A total of about 120,000 tonnes of dry sludge are produced each year in the region.

5.45 As far as Lancashire is concerned, it is estimated that 156,000 tonnes of wet and 24,500 tonnes of dry sludge are passed to landfill sites each year. Clifton Marsh, Freckleton, (Fylde), takes most of this, comprising primary-treated sludge from the adjacent NWW sewage treatment works and secondary treated sludge from elsewhere. The rest goes to the County's river system, or to coastal waters by various sea outfalls, (see Chapter 4). An unknown quantity goes to agricultural land and other uses after treatment. In 1988, a volume of 520 Ml of sewage was treated at Lancashire's treatment works every day, and 135 Ml per day were discharged untreated to the sea. (North West Water, 1988.)

5.46 In May 1990, the Secretary of State for the Environment announced that all sewage sludge dumping to sea will cease by 1998, and that all sewage disposed of through sea outfalls must first receive treatment. NWW have indicated that by 1995/96, all discharges to sea in Lancashire, from the Ribble to the Cumbrian border, will be subject to secondary treatment. These changes will produce a considerable increase in the amount of sewage sludge needing alternative disposal, whether by incineration, land disposal, or other means. But the benefits in terms of improved water quality, will be considerable.

Table 54 Special Waste Arising by District in Lancashire. 1989

District	Total Arising (Tonnes)	Remaining in Lancashire	Exported
Lancaster	8,550	3,847	4,703
Wyre	25,680	25,507	173
Ribble Valley	330	247	83
Blackpool	211	90	121
Fylde	544	116	428
Preston	5,344	752	4,592
South Ribble	2,326	100	2,226
West Lancashire	471	8	463
Chorley	10,572	34	10,538
Blackburn	2,810	732	2,078
Hyndburn	1,465	505	960
Burnley	2,782	249	2,533
Pendle	1,758	92	1,666
Rossendale	409	54	355
Various	4,805	785	4,020
LANCASHIRE	68,057	33,118	34,939

Source: Lancashire County Council.

Note: "Various" comprises small arisings taken to chemical treatment plants.

Radioactive Waste

5.47 Some wastes arising from British Nuclear Fuels (BNFL) are deposited in the County. The Radiochemical Inspectorate of the DOE sets a limit on the materials that can be deposited at any particular site. Other waste materials, of an activity higher than that specified for local disposal are exported to specialised sites. In 1989, a total of 14,784 tonnes low level waste was produced in Lancashire, of which 14,643 tonnes were deposited at Clifton Marsh landfill site (British Nuclear Fuels Limited, 1990). Clifton Marsh is the only site in Lancashire currently receiving low level radioactive waste. It is sampled and monitored by the National Radiological Protection Board, the Radiochemical Inspectorate and BNFL, to ensure its compliance with regulations.

Non-Controlled Waste

5.48 Mines and quarry and agricultural waste types are not controlled by the COPA 1974. They make up the bulk of all waste generated each year in the County (about 60%) and are mostly not dealt with as part of any formal disposal system. Any arisings of the former taken to landfill sites are usually classed as construction and demolition waste, and are included in the figure of 1,703,015 tonnes for 1989/90 (shown in Table 55). There are no figures available for the amount of other mining waste, though large amounts are deposited at a variety of excavation sites.

Table 55 Controlled Waste Disposed of in Lancashire. 1989/90

District	Household and Commercial	Industrial	Construction and Demolition	Liquids and Sludges	Total
Lancaster	93,421	104,788	121,153	4,715	324,077
Wyre	67,088	96,231	185,398	58,848	487,549
Ribble Valley	12,306	24,635	7,574	—	44,515
Blackpool	—	—	—	—	—
Fylde	136,629	143,917	311,526	5,418	597,490
Preston	—	3,754	97,588	—	101,342
South Ribble	23,577	15,962	7,811	—	47,350
West Lancashire	235,639	44,003	97,474	—	377,116
Chorley	164,916	35,511	402,899	1,277	604,603
Blackburn	—	32,447	36,861	2,186	71,494
Hyndburn	74,011	98,995	104,963	2,180	280,149
Burnley	39,122	78,493	216,720	—	334,335
Pendle	7,498	28,172	40,376	—	76,046
Rossendale	17,620	43,419	72,688	—	133,719
LANCASHIRE	871,827	750,327	1,703,015	74,616	3,399,785

Source: Lancashire County Council.

5.49 Estimates produced from MAFF data given in Chapter 8, suggest that 4.3 million tonnes of agricultural waste are produced each year in Lancashire. The bulk of this is returned to the land as animal waste and crop residue. Small quantities of diseased crops are deposited at landfills in the County. Five landfill sites are authorised by MAFF to accept the carcasses of animals slaughtered as a result of disease, which includes the headless carcasses of cows affected by Bovine Spongiform Encephalopathy. These are Clifton Marsh (Preston), Salt Ayre (Lancaster), Jameson Road (Wyre), Rowley (Burnley) and Whinney Hill (Accrington). However, MAFF commissioned an incinerator at Wrexham for the disposal of BSE carcasses and after October 1990 all BSE carcasses will be disposed of in this way.

Waste Deposited

5.50 Table 55 and Figure 78 show the quantities of each category of controlled waste disposed of within each District. They show that Blackpool has no disposal site accepting controlled waste. Chorley, Fylde and Wyre accept the greatest quantities of controlled waste, amounting to a half of the County total. Fylde's position is explained by the existence of Clifton Marsh (Freckleton). A total of almost 3.4 million tonnes of controlled waste is disposed of within the County each year, compared with a total waste production of almost 3.3 million tonnes (Figure 76). The difference is due to the disposal of waste imported into the County. Figure 79 shows the importance of both inert waste (demolition and construction waste), household and commercial waste and industrial waste, which together form 98% of all waste disposed of to landfill in Lancashire. Inert waste on its own represents 50% of total waste deposited. These figures include information for both privately owned and County Council sites.

Waste Management Facilities

5.51 The type and number of waste disposal facilities in Lancashire are given in Table 56. Public

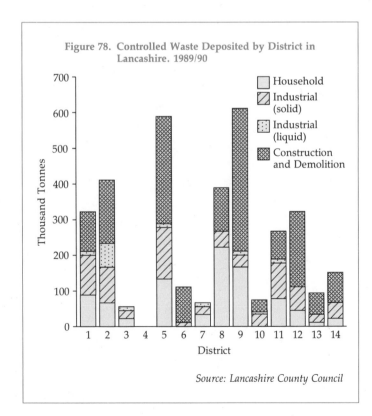

Figure 78. Controlled Waste Deposited by District in Lancashire. 1989/90

Source: Lancashire County Council

and private facilities are included. Their location is shown on Figures 80 and 81. Table 56 shows that there are 75 landfill sites open at present, with a further 66 licenced but temporarily closed. In addition, there are 22 open transfer stations, 20 HWDC, three chemical recovery plants, one private incinerator and 194 waste reclaimers. The 29 clinical waste incinerators in the County have been excluded from Table 56 as they are not currently licenced. This will change with the removal of Crown immunity in 1991.

5.52   It can be seen that landfill facilities predominate. Indeed, the only controlled wastes in Lancashire that are not landfilled are those which are recycled, or which are unsuitable for landfill, e.g. pesticides, strong acids and solvents.

Landfill Sites

5.53   Landfill describes the disposal of waste on, or in, land. It is the most economical method of disposal in terms of capital and operating costs which explains why over 90% of controlled waste in the UK is disposed of in this way. In Lancashire, at 98%, the proportion is even higher, and includes all household and commercial waste. Lancashire has a valuable tipping resource in the many former quarries and excavated areas.

5.54   In 1987, the County Council published a Draft Waste Disposal Plan (as required by the COPA 1974) with the overall objective of achieving ''. . . the disposal of waste at the least possible cost to the community with due regard being given to the safeguarding of the environment and the use of waste as a resource''. The draft Plan details and

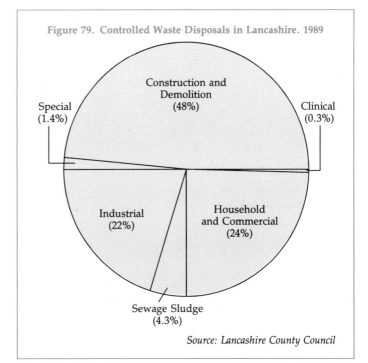

Figure 79. Controlled Waste Disposals in Lancashire. 1989

Special (1.4%)

Construction and Demolition (48%)

Clinical (0.3%)

Industrial (22%)

Household and Commercial (24%)

Sewage Sludge (4.3%)

Source: Lancashire County Council

examines all available disposal methods and concludes that controlled landfill will continue to be the principal ultimate method of waste disposal in Lancashire during the Plan period (up to 1997). However, because of recent legislation, and the likelihood of even more stringent controls, the cost of landfill will almost certainly increase. More careful site preparation will be required before landfill can proceed and the amount of environmental monitoring required during and after landfill will also grow.

Table 56   Summary of Waste Disposal Facilities in Lancashire. 1990

District	Landfill Sites Private	Landfill Sites LCC	Transfer Stations Private	Transfer Stations LCC	HWDC	Chemical Recovery Plants	Incinerators	Waste Reclaimers
Lancaster	2 (4)	2 (—)	3 (1)	—	2	1	1	15
Wyre	5 (2)	1 (—)	1 (—)	—	2	—	—	21
Ribble Valley	5 (4)	1 (1)	— (—)	—	3	—	—	2
Blackpool	— (—)	— (—)	2 (1)	1	1	—	—	13
Fylde	2 (1)	1 (1)	— (—)	—	2	—	—	6
Preston	2 (6)	— (—)	4 (2)	—	1	1	—	23
South Ribble	— (2)	1 (—)	2 (—)	—	1	1	—	9
West Lancashire	2 (11)	1 (—)	2 (—)	—	3	—	—	8
Chorley	5 (4)	1 (—)	1 (—)	—	1	—	—	14
Blackburn	11 (13)	— (—)	1 (—)	—	2	—	—	28
Hyndburn	8 (7)	1 (—)	— (—)	—	1	—	—	22
Burnley	4 (5)	1 (—)	1 (—)	—	1	—	—	15
Pendle	2 (—)	1 (—)	2 (—)	1	2	—	—	10
Rossendale	4 (5)	2 (—)	1 (—)	—	2	—	—	9
LANCASHIRE	62 (64)	13 (2)	20 (4)	2	24	3	1	194

Source: Lancashire County Council.

Note: Figures in brackets refer to temporarily closed facilities.

Figure 80

County Council Waste Management Facilities. 1990

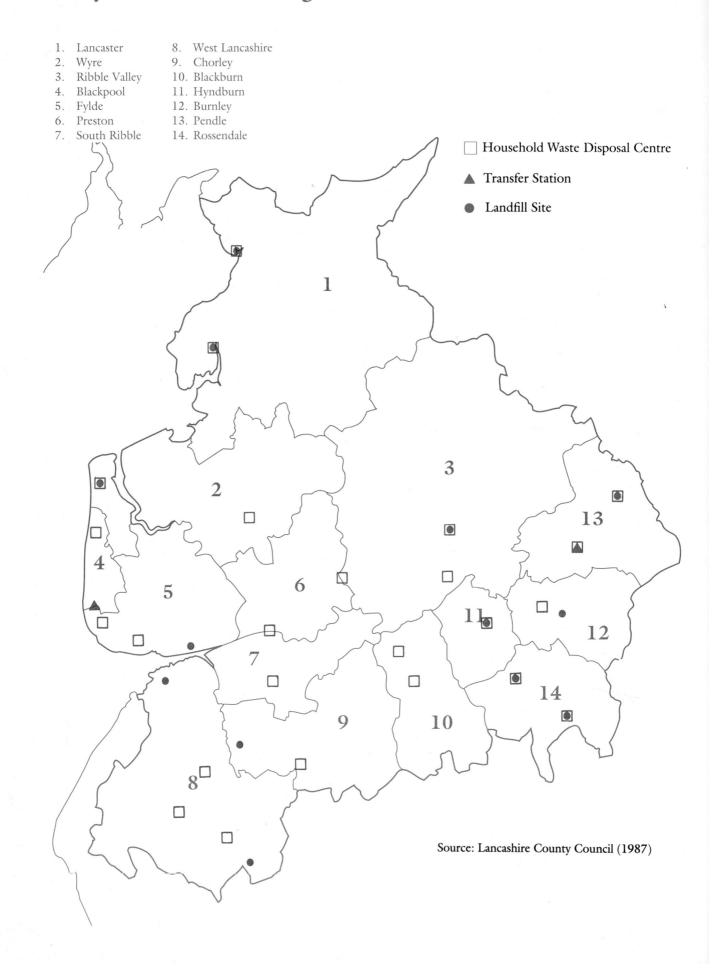

1. Lancaster
2. Wyre
3. Ribble Valley
4. Blackpool
5. Fylde
6. Preston
7. South Ribble
8. West Lancashire
9. Chorley
10. Blackburn
11. Hyndburn
12. Burnley
13. Pendle
14. Rossendale

☐ Household Waste Disposal Centre

▲ Transfer Station

● Landfill Site

Source: Lancashire County Council (1987)

Figure 81
Private Waste Management Facilities in Lancashire. 1990

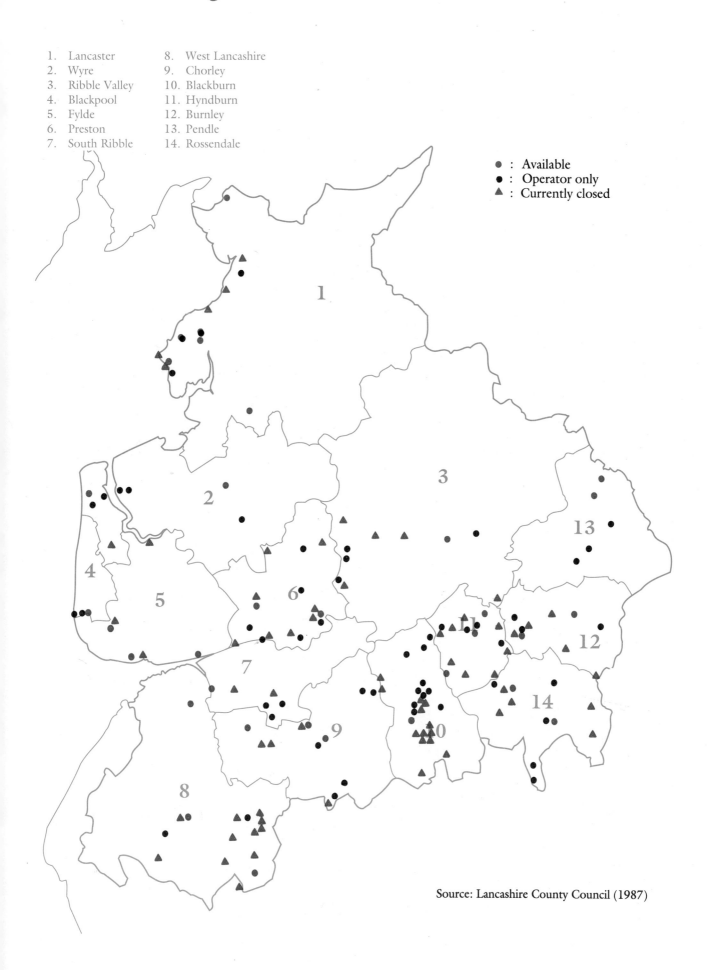

1. Lancaster
2. Wyre
3. Ribble Valley
4. Blackpool
5. Fylde
6. Preston
7. South Ribble
8. West Lancashire
9. Chorley
10. Blackburn
11. Hyndburn
12. Burnley
13. Pendle
14. Rossendale

● : Available
● : Operator only
▲ : Currently closed

Source: Lancashire County Council (1987)

5.55 Two main types of landfill sites exist in the County, based on the principles of 'containment' and 'disperse and attenuate'. Containment sites are designed to hold all polluting material within the site itself. This is done either by artificial impermeable liners, or by locating the site in strata like clay or shale. Disperse and attentuate sites allow the migration of leachate through the base and sides of the site. The theory has been that surrounding rocks will absorb and filter out the harmful constituents of leachate, though this is now being questioned. As a result, it is likely that future landfill sites will be engineered as containment sites. The design, operation and management of landfill operations is constantly being improved as technological advances are made to prevent adverse environmental effects.

5.56 Alternatives to landfill include composting, resource recovery and incineration. At present, no controlled waste is composted within the County and there are no major resource recovery centres, other than transfer stations, HWDC, paper mills, scrap yards, and plastic and solvent plants that recover certain wastes. Only a relatively small amount of waste is recovered in this way. There is only one licensed waste incinerator in Lancashire, (but 29 clinical unlicensed incinerators exist).

Transfer Stations and Household Waste Disposal Centres

5.57 Transfer Stations are intermediate facilities where waste is delivered or stored. This is then bulked up prior to 'transfer' to a disposal site.

They offer certain advantages, which include:

* the potential for recycling;

* a reduction in vehicle movements when the disposal site is a long distance from the area producing the waste;

* economies of scale;

* a permanent location giving stability to the users.

5.58 Transfer stations in Lancashire are used for a wide variety of wastes, from household to hazardous chemical types. The County Council operates two transfer stations for household waste, whilst the private sector operates a further 24. Their distribution is shown in Table 56. There is a marked trend towards the establishment of transfer stations.

5.59 The County Council provides and manages 24 HWDC spread evenly throughout Lancashire. These allow individuals to dispose of a wide variety of redundant material. Table 57 shows the different types of waste recovered at these. Bric-a-brac is any household, or other, item with a re-sale value. In 1989/90, a total of £7,539 was paid for this type of waste, whilst £22,699 was paid for non-ferrous scrap metal. A total of 2,822 tonnes of ferrous scrap was recovered, with a value of £95,408. Waste paper, used oil and glass are also collected. Chlorofluorocarbons (CFCs) are recovered from fridges taken to HWDC. It is estimated that over 8,000 fridges were treated in this way in 1990.

Table 57 Recycling Activity at County Council Household Waste Disposal Centres. 1989/90

District	Ferrous Scrap 89/90 (Tonnes)	Waste Paper 89/90 (Tonnes)	Used Oil 89/90 (Tonnes)	Glass (Tonnes)	Non Ferrous Scrap '89 (£)	Bric-a-Brac '89 (£)	CFC No. of Fridges '90
Lancaster	229	99	8	—	2,029	263	—
Wyre	224	161	9	14	1,633	342	284
Ribble Valley	214	161	6	—	1,820	1,297	—
Blackpool	319	159	9	15	2,317	478	1,040
Fylde	263	274	13	34	4,516	516	1,126
Preston	218	169	5	—	1,285	580	1,040
South Ribble	305	189	14	—	766	395	1,386
West Lancashire	199	199	7	—	898	385	433
Chorley	188	89	5	—	1,161	335	381
Blackburn	192	119	5	—	704	347	918
Hyndburn	83	68	1	—	1,250	312	—
Burnley	114	73	3	—	826	446	866
Pendle	156	141	8	—	2,648	1,418	381
Rossendale	118	105	3	—	846	425	537
LANCASHIRE	2,822	2,006	95	63(1)	22,699	7,539	8,392(2)

Source: Lancashire County Council.

Notes: (1) These figures do not include glass collected by District Councils at Household Waste Disposal Centres. No subsidity is paid for this glass, which amounts to a total of 1,132 tonnes in Lancashire.
(2) These figures are extrapolated from a sample 3-week period 24/4/90 to 15/5/90 when 472 fridges were collected. The scheme started in April 1990.

Waste Reclaimers

5.60   There are 194 known waste reclaimers within Lancashire, and Table 58 shows their location by District. Most are now subject to licensing and control, though waste paper and rag contractors are presently exempt. Collectively, reclaimers form the largest example of waste recycling in the County, salvaging a wide range of ferrous and non-ferrous metals, plastics and waste oil. Licences seek to control their environmental impact and will be important in seeking to prevent the ground contamination associated with a number of existing scrapyards.

Table 58   Waste Reclaimers in Lancashire. 1990

District	Number of Waste Reclaimers
Lancaster	15
Wyre	20
Ribble Valley	2
Blackpool	13
Fylde	6
Preston	23
South Ribble	9
West Lancashire	8
Chorley	14
Blackburn	28
Hyndburn	22
Burnley	15
Pendle	10
Rossendale	9
LANCASHIRE	194

Source: Lancashire County Council.

5.61   In addition to licensed reclaimers, there are a great number of independent operators, spread throughout the County, that do not require licensing under present legislation. These collect a wide range of material from the public and industry, but there are no data on the quantities involved.

Chemical Recovery Plants

5.62   There are three licensed facilities in Lancashire which specialise in the recovery of solvents for re-use. These are located in Heysham (Lancaster), Preston and Leyland (South Ribble). A modest amount of reclaiming goes on in Ribble Valley and Hyndburn too. Table 59 shows that the vast majority of the waste treated in this way is brought into the County (98%). This contrasts sharply with the origin of special waste deposited, where the position is reversed. Chemical recovery plants remove an appreciable quantity of what would otherwise be difficult waste, unsuitable for landfill and requiring incineration. Recovered chemicals are sold as raw materials for production processes. There is always a small amount of

Table 59   Special Waste Treated or Deposited in Lancashire. 1989

District	Treated Arising Within County	Treated Imported	Deposited Arising Within County	Deposited Imported	Total
Lancaster	204	17,548	3,860	12	21,624
Wyre	—	—	25,789	1	25,790
Ribble Valley	—	1,660	—	—	1,660
Fylde	—	—	1,818	—	1,818
Preston	249	4,852	—	—	5,101
South Ribble	210	2,020	—	—	2,230
Hyndburn	—	437	988	34	1,459
LANCASHIRE	663	26,517	32,455	47	59,682

Source: Lancashire County Council.

Note: Figures are in Tonnes.

residue that cannot be reclaimed. Some is incinerated and some goes to landfill.

Incinerators

5.63   There are no household refuse incinerators in Lancashire, though there is a small incinerator handling liquid waste with some organic

Table 60   Lancashire County Council Waste Disposal Facilities. 1990

District	Site	Status	Remaining capacity (tonnes) Up to 100,000	100,000 to 500,000	Over 500,000
Lancaster	Cotestones	A		★	
	Salt Ayre	A			★
Wyre	Jameson Road	A			★
Ribble Valley	Henthorne	A		★	
	Thornley-with-Wheatley	C	Not applicable		
Blackpool	Chapel Road TS	A	Not applicable		
Fylde	Clifton Marsh	A			★
South Ribble	Much Hoole	A		★	
West Lancs	Pimbo	A	★		
Chorley	Ulnes Walton	A		★	
Hyndburn	Whinney Hill	A			★
Burnley	Rowley	A			★
Pendle	Rainhill Rock	A	★		
	Corporation Street TS	B	Not applicable		
Rossendale	Duckworth Clough	A	★		
	Rakehead	A		★	

Source: Lancashire County Council.

Notes: TS = Transfer Station
A = Accepts waste from any contractor
B = Accepts waste produced by site operator or specified contractor only
C = Currently closed

Table 61 Private Waste Disposal Facilities Licensed in Lancashire. 1990

District	Status			Remaining Capacity				Total
	A	B	C	NA	I	II	III	
Lancaster	2	4	5	8	2	—	1	11
Wyre	1	5	2	5	1	2	—	8
Ribble Valley	—	5	3	3	4	1	—	8
Blackpool	—	2	—	2	—	—	—	2
Fylde	2	—	1	1	1	1	0	3
Preston	2	5	8	13	1	—	1	15
South Ribble	—	3	3	4	2	—	—	6
West Lancashire	2	2	11	4	4	5	2	15
Chorley	2	4	4	4	4	1	1	10
Blackburn	1	12	13	11	15	—	—	26
Hyndburn	4	4	12	11	8	—	1	20
Burnley	4	3	8	4	8	2	1	15
Pendle	1	2	1	2	2	—	—	4
Rossendale	—	6	5	5	5	1	—	11
LANCASHIRE	21	57	76	77	57	13	7	154

Source: Lancashire County Council.

Notes: A = Licensed and accepting waste from any waste disposal contractor.
B = Licensed but only accepting waste produced by site operator or other specified contractors.
C = Licensed but currently closed for the reception of waste.
NA = Not applicable or completed.
I = Up to 100,000 tonnes.
II = Between 100,000 and 500,000 tonnes.
III = Over 500,000 tonnes.

contamination in use at a site in Lancaster. The expected throughput in 1990 is 4,700 tonnes. There are 29 clinical waste incinerators at hospitals and nursing homes (see Figure 29).

County Council Waste Disposal Facilities

5.64 The County Council is the major waste disposal operator in Lancashire and at 1 June 1990 operated 13 landfill sites, 2 transfer stations and 24 HWDC. Figure 80 shows their location. The ownership and management of these will be either sold or transferred to a private company under the EPA 1990. Table 60 shows details of their current status and an estimate of remaining capacity. However, it is not possible to predict accurately the remaining life of any site, due to variations in the quantities and type of waste deposited.

Private Waste Disposal Facilities

5.65 At 1 June 1990, there were 154 licensed waste management facilities operated in the County by the private sector. They range from large landfills accepting household refuse, to small sites accepting only sub-soil, and from complex chemical recovery plants to sealed skips for the storage of asbestos waste. Under the EPA 1990, and the system of Integrated Pollution Control which is introduced under this Act, chemical treatment plants will become a scheduled process and, will in future, be monitored and controlled by HMIP.

5.66 For a variety of technical, operational and economic reasons, not all facilities are available at any one time for the disposal of waste. The location of all private facilities is shown on Figure 81, which also shows the current status of each facility. Many of the closed sites are completed and will not accept further waste. Table 61 shows the number of currently licensed facilities in Lancashire and their present status, with an indication of remaining capacity.

Special Waste Disposal Facilities

5.67 Due to its hazardous nature, all phases of the disposal of special waste are carefully monitored. Its transportation has already been discussed. The disposal, storage and treatment of special waste is limited to 14 sites within the County. Table 59 summarises the amounts of this waste treated or deposited by District. A very high proportion of solvent waste is recovered from the quantity treated and the cleaned solvent re-used. The sites in Lancashire where special waste is landfilled, subject to special handling and aftercare are:

* Salt Ayre, Lancaster;
* Jameson Road, Wyre;
* ICI Hillhouse, Wyre;
* Clifton Marsh, Fylde
* Blythe's, Church (private), Hyndburn;
* Whinney Hill, Hyndburn.

5.68 All landfill sites accepting special waste are engineered to prevent public health or environmental problems. Monitoring programmes are stipulated in the site licence to ensure that problems arising from special waste disposal are detected and corrected immediately. Some special wastes are mixed with other, less difficult, materials to reduce the concentration of the hazardous component. This is known as 'co-disposal'. Other options available include incineration, which is both expensive and causes environmental problems through air pollution, and produces ash and residues that also require disposal.

Site Licensing

5.69 The COPA 1974 required all sites and facilities handling or disposing controlled wastes to be licenced by the WDA. The County Council, as the WRA under the EPA 1990 will be responsible for the issue and enforcement of these licences. Most licensed sites also require a valid planning permission granted by the County Council. Applications for both site licences and planning permissions require site investigations to establish the suitability of the proposed development. This includes geological survey works, surface and groundwater investigations and geographical surveys. Each site operator is required to prepare a comprehensive working plan.

5.70 Planning applications may be refused for any number of reasons, including the unsuitability of the waste type proposed, inadequate access, and detrimental environmental impacts. A site licence may only be refused under COPA 1974 where what is proposed would cause water pollution or endanger public health, or where no valid planning permission has been granted. The EPA 1990 extends this to include the fitness of the applicant to hold a waste licence; but this will not be introduced before 1992.

5.71 Both licences and planning consents include conditions to control site preparation, operation, restoration and aftercare. These can include restrictions on the hours and days of operation, the types of waste to be deposited, the type of vehicles allowed, site screening, tipping operations and environmental controls to prevent windblown litter, water pollution, noise and dust. Planning permissions define a period within which restoration must take place. Beyond this, there is a five year aftercare period within which activities such as replacing dead trees or making good any subsidence, are carried out.

5.72 Under recent regulations, all site operators must now monitor for surface water contamination and landfill gas. Monitoring programmes are included within the working plan and are enforced through licence conditions.

Enforcement and Complaints

5.73 The County Council, as WDA, was responsible for enforcing the relevant parts of COPA 1974. The County Council will retain their enforcement rôle as the new WRA under the EPA 1990. The County Council will be able to prosecute anybody who deposits, or allows the deposit of controlled waste, on land which is not licenced to receive waste, or where licence conditions are not complied with. The County Council remains the planning authority for waste disposal.

5.74 As WRA, the County Council can require that waste is removed from any location where it has been illegally deposited, or that action is taken to minimise the consequences. A further power allows the WRA to modify the conditions of any site licence, provided this will not cause unreasonable expense to the licence holder. Since 1980, a total of 50 successful prosecutions have been made.

5.75 Members of the general public regularly complain about the operation of both licensed and unlicensed sites. Table 62 shows the number of complaints received over the last three years, associated with private waste disposal.

5.76 Complaints have risen over the period, as a result of a doubling in the unlicensed category. Generally, these relate to odour, mud deposited on roads, litter blowing from sites, and operating outside permitted hours. Such matters are covered by licence conditions and are dealt with by site visits and, if necessary, enforcement action. Unlicensed site complaints usually relate to the fact that disposal is occurring. In many instances, it is not possible to find the person responsible or take any action. Illegal sites are generally remote, with difficult access or visibility, and are often used for a short period of time or intermittently.

Table 62	Complaints about Private Waste Disposal Sites in Lancashire. 1987–1989		
Year	Licensed Sites	Unlicensed Sites	All Sites
1987	61	59	120
1988	77	58	135
1989	50	124	174
TOTAL	188	241	429

Source: Lancashire County Council.

Waste Recycling

5.77 Many items of waste disposed to landfill can be reclaimed, recycled or put back into regular use. It is estimated that about 56% of waste from our dustbins could be recycled. This is made up of 30% paper and card, 4% plastic, 3% textiles, 10% glass and 9% metals (Lancashire County Council, 1989). The recycling of this waste would bring three main benefits:

* the conservation of energy;
* the preservation of basic raw material resources;
* the reduction in the quantity of waste requiring disposal.

Aluminium recycling produces a 95% energy saving, and there is a 50% energy reduction when paper is produced from waste as opposed to virgin pulp (Friends of the Earth and the Daily Telegraph, 1989). The environmental implications are also significant. Not only are the problems associated with waste disposal reduced, but damage arising from the extraction of raw materials, or their processing, can be prevented.

5.78 Recycling of household waste in Lancashire is undertaken in a variety of ways. The County Council employs a recycling officer, who co-ordinates recycling initiatives and acts as a liaison between industry and the local community. Aluminium can collections, bottle bank usage and paper re-use are promoted and information and advice is given to groups who wish to undertake recycling activities. A Recycling Directory exists to help organisations find outlets for the material that they collect. District Councils are required to produce Recycling Plans under the EPA 1990, and some are beginning to appoint their own Recycling Officers (e.g. Chorley).

5.79 The major initiatives include a payment by the County Council of a subsidy, (calculated as 50% of current disposal costs) to organisations and District Councils collecting paper and glass. In 1989, £5,696 was paid for 3,000 tonnes of glass and £3,968 for 12,128 tonnes of paper. Recycling is also a principal activity at County Council HWDC. Table 57 shows the amount of waste recycled at the 24 centres during 1989/1990.

5.80 Nearly all of the glass collected is returned to PLM Redfearn and Co., in Barnsley, where it is re-used. Metal is sold to scrap metal merchants. Depending on type and quality this will be melted down for use in a wide variety of products. Paper

District	Paper	People Per Collection Point	Glass	People Per Collection Point
Table 63 Recycling Collection Points in Lancashire. 1989				
Lancaster	16	8,000	21	6,000
Wyre	9	11,000	6	17,000
Ribble Valley	—	—	4	13,000
Blackpool	—	—	2	71,500
Fylde	2	36,000	5	14,000
Preston	2	64,000	7	18,000
South Ribble	4	25,000	6	17,000
West Lancashire	7	15,000	12	9,000
Chorley	7	14,000	11	9,000
Blackburn	—	—	6	22,000
Hyndburn	—	—	7	11,000
Burnley	—	—	3	30,000
Pendle	—	—	8	11,000
Rossendale	5	13,000	4	16,000
LANCASHIRE	52	26,700	102	13,600

Source: Lancashire County Council.

is recycled by various merchants and the final use depends on the type of paper and the degree of contamination by other products. Waste oil is collected by 13 recycling companies which operate within the County. This is processed to remove impurities to make it suitable for vehicle lubrication, or low grade fuel for industrial use. Bric-a-brac is purchased by various dealers for re-sale through their own outlets.

5.81   District Councils are also actively involved in the collection of recyclable materials like paper and glass. Table 63 shows how these local collection points are distributed. Some are organised and run by voluntary groups or by commercial enterprises. A joint scheme between a waste disposal contractor and Lancaster City Council has been developed for the collection of alluminium cans at ten sites.

5.82   It is important to note that recycling of waste is only viable when a market exists for the material that is collected. Such markets have traditionally been volatile. In June 1990, a glut developed in the paper market and merchants became reluctant to accept the quantities of waste paper available. The price dropped considerably, making collection less economic. As a result, a lot of paper collected for recycling ended up on landfill sites.

5.83   From April 1990, all fridges and freezers taken to HWDC have been taken to a specialist contractor where they are either re-furbished and re-used, or have their CFC coolant removed. This is stored and then returned to ICI for re-use. Recycling in this way prevents release of the gas to the atmosphere, and minimises the risk of damage to the ozone layer.

5.84   The recycling and reclamation of waste on a large and comprehensive scale could make a major environmental contribution by preventing problems created by production of raw materials and the disposal of waste. However, to be done with most effect waste should be separated at source i.e. at the home and factory. This will require a major reorganisation of both the waste collection and disposal industry. Several interesting experiments are currently taking place in various parts of the country which focus on separation at source. These include the Recycling City initiatives in Sheffield and Cardiff.

Environmental Effects

5.85   Landfill accounts for 98% of waste disposal in Lancashire. It is now known that there are many environmental problems associated with the process (Department of the Environment, 1988). The most significant relate to potential contamination of ground and surface water by leachate, the contamination of land, and the production and migration of landfill gas on some sites. Both leachate and landfill gas are produced by the decay of wastes in sites that have accepted biodegradable waste. Leachate is produced when water, such as rainwater, flows through the fill material picking up soluble pollutants. When this leaves the site, it can be highly contaminated. However, not all landfill sites create these environmental effects. Many, and certainly the more recent ones, are engineered to prevent their occurrence, and measures are provided to control both leachate and landfill gas.

Ground Water and Surface Water Contamination

5.86   The uncontrolled discharge of leachate from one landfill site in Lancashire has caused two fish-kill incidents in an adjacent watercourse. Various other instances of leachate affecting streams at several sites have been identified in inspection reports. Remedial action was taken at all of these sites under the enforcement of licence conditions, which corrected the situation. The NRA also monitors surface water, and will prosecute in situations where pollution is occuring. Site licences now include conditions which make operators responsible for monitoring surface water on, and around, their site, and for reporting any contamination to the WRA. Groundwater, however, is far more difficult to monitor and the consequences of contamination can be far more serious. The DOE have stated that landfill sites are a major threat to groundwater quality, and that a number of cases of groundwater pollution attributable to landfill have been recorded in the UK (Department of the Environment, 1988). They also state that landfills, and their wide range of contaminants, threaten many sources of drinking water, but that there are very few examples where these sources have been lost due to contamination. A recent FOE report, based on an Institute of Geological Science Survey carried out for the DOE in 1974 (Gray et al., 1974) identified some 20 contaminated sites in Lancashire as posing 'some risk' to groundwater. However, no conclusive evidence exists at present to show that this is the case.

5.87 The absence of information is worrying, because the problem could be extensive. There are a large number of disperse and attenuate sites which, over the years, have accepted waste that will rot or decay. Figure 82 shows the location of almost 600 sites in Lancashire which may have accepted waste that could cause groundwater contamination. Investigations will have to be carried out to establish the full extent of the situation and to identify remedial measures where necessary. The preparation of registers of contaminated land by District Councils under the EPA 1990, provides the starting point for this process.

Landfill Gas

5.88 Landfill gas is produced by the breakdown of biodegradable waste over a long period of time. The gas, (which contains methane), can migrate undergound from a landfill site and may accumulate in nearby buildings. In this situation, there is a risk of explosion, as occurred in Lancashire in 1980 at Platts Lane Landfill Site (West Lancashire) where one man was injured, and outside North Quarry, Appley Bridge, (also West Lancashire) where structural damage was caused (Lancashire County Council, 1988).

5.89 There are 11 sites in Lancashire currently operating active gas extraction systems where landfill gas is pumped out of the site and either used as an energy source (see Chapter 7) or burned off. These are listed in Table 64. Several other sites have proposals to install gas extraction systems. Many others operate some form of gas venting system, where trenches are provided around the site to allow the passive venting of migrating gas. However, the installation of such a system will not necessarily prevent gas problems. Recent waste disposal advice recommends that all landfill operations incorporate a landfill gas monitoring programme. Details of the gas monitoring carried out on County Council landfill sites are given below. All planning authorities are currently legally obliged to consult the WDA about any planning application for land within 250 m of any known landfill site.

5.90 District Councils are now obliged under the EPA 1990, to produce a register of all areas of contaminated land. This will help to reveal, for the first time, the extent of environmental problems associated with contaminated land in the County. Our current knowledge is very poor. Desk studies in Lancashire have identified 587 sites (Figure 82) that are potentially contaminated. Information about their size, and the types of waste deposited, usually only exists for sites which operated after 1974, when the COPA 1974 was introduced. Information becomes sparser as the age of sites increases.

5.91 All contaminated sites require extensive investigation into their chemical nature and gas status before any redevelopment occurs. Instability, due to the differential settlement of waste following the completion of waste disposal, can also be a problem.

5.92 Land and water contamination can also arise from the activities and operations of waste reclaimers and waste transfer stations. Reclaimers

Table 64 Landfill Sites with Active Gas Extraction in Lancashire. 1990

District	Site Name	Location	Private/LCC
Lancaster	Salt Ayre	Lancaster	LCC
Blackpool	Midgeland Farm	Blackpool	LCC
West Lancashire	Platts Lane	Burscough	LCC (Closed)
	West Quarry	Appley Bridge	Private
Chorley	Withnell Quarry	Withnell	Private
	Lower Burgh	Chorley	LCC (Closed)
Blackburn	Stockclough	Blackburn	LCC (Closed)
Burnley	Rowley	Burnley	LCC
Pendle	Waidshouse	Nelson	LCC (Closed)
	Rainhill Rock	Barnoldswick	LCC
Rossendale	Rakehead	Bacup	LCC

Source: Lancashire County Council.

are often based on the same site for many years. Unless the ground-surface is sealed, soil can be contaminated with oils, metals, acid from batteries and any other chemicals present in waste brought onto the site. Contaminants may also seep into adjacent watercourses, and land. These sites are now being progressively licensed and their environmental impacts brought under control. However, they have existed in the community for many years and, whilst the potential problems are recognised, the scale and the best remedies have not yet been fully identified.

Nuisance

5.93 Nuisance occurs where landfill, or other waste management operations, intrude upon the lives of the people who live and work around them. It is created by diverse factors like litter spread from sites, mud on the road, increased traffic movements, vehicle noise or odour. Additional problems arise from the presence of pests and birds. Rodents and flies used to be a serious problem on old sites. Modern operational techniques (including the compaction and daily coverage of waste, and the use of pest controls) have largely eliminated these problems from well run sites. Gulls are an inevitable accompaniment of landfill operations, often in considerable numbers. They are potential transmitters of disease and have been linked with the spread of salmonella.

Effects on Landscape and Wildlife

5.94 Waste disposal can have a very direct impact on wildlife. Leachate and water contamination can kill aquatic and terrestrial organisms. Although only two instances of fish kills have been recorded in Lancashire, others may have occurred. Landscape quality is invariably reduced by operations, though careful site preparation, and the use of screening and bunding can reduce this. The potential development of land may also be restricted by the presence of landfill, or other waste management operations.

Figure 82
Land Contaminated by Biodegradable Waste in Lancashire. 1990

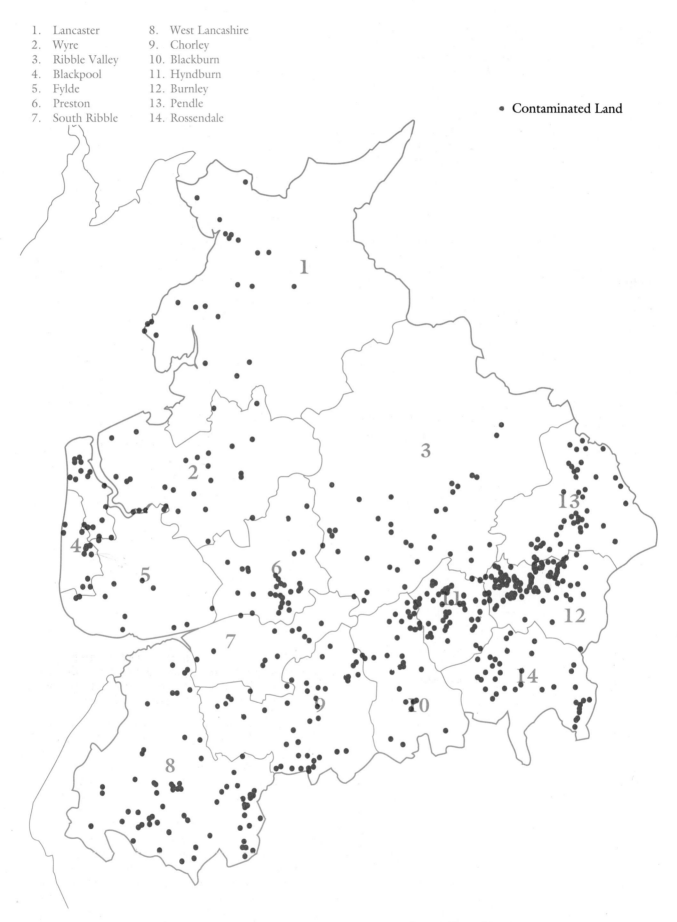

1. Lancaster
2. Wyre
3. Ribble Valley
4. Blackpool
5. Fylde
6. Preston
7. South Ribble
8. West Lancashire
9. Chorley
10. Blackburn
11. Hyndburn
12. Burnley
13. Pendle
14. Rossendale

• Contaminated Land

Source: Lancashire County Council.

5.95 The concept of landfill is being subjected to increasing scrutiny, and, in some places, is being radically reconsidered. In America, Holland and Germany, for example, toxic landfilled materials are being excavated and incinerated, because of the problems associated with the containment of contaminants arising from the waste types deposited (ENDS,1990). Britain has recognised many of the problems, and is attempting to improve controls and prevention through the EPA 1990. However, the true scale of the environmental damage arising from old landfill sites will not emerge until the new contaminated land registers are completed and extensive monitoring and assessment has been carried out at every site.

Restoration and Aftercare

5.96 Upon completion of landfill, it is possible for sites to be restored and returned to productive use. Generally, small sites accepting inert wastes can be readily grassed over and returned to grazing. All landfill site licences require that sites are covered with an adequate layer of soil. With larger, modern sites, restoration is an integral part of the whole operation. First, a water-tight layer of clay (or plastic) is placed over the final layer of waste to stop rainfall entering the landfill, thus reducing leachate. Secondly, the land will be restored, commonly to pasture or arable farmland.

5.97 Figure 83 shows the extent of restored landfill sites completed over the last 15 years. Table 65 lists some of the sites on which restoration has been undertaken in Lancashire with the type of restoration carried out. Some of the sites are still

Table 65 Landfill Sites in Lancashire on which Restoration is Known to Have Taken Place. 1990

District	Site	After-Use	Area Restored (ha)
Lancaster	Cotestones	P	8
	Sunderland Point	P	1
Wyre	Jameson Road	G/T	1
Ribble Valley	Abbots Brow	P	4
	Chatburn	T	2
	Henthorne	P	5
	Thornton-in-Wheatley	P	1
Blackpool	Midgeland Farm	A	32
Fylde	Grange Farm I and II	P/G	81
Preston	Mellings	G	2
South Ribble	Much Hoole	P	12
West Lancashire	Pimbo	G	10
	Platts Lane	G	12
Chorley	Lower Burgh	G	20
	Ulnes Walton	G	4
Blackburn	Feniscowles	P	2
	Bull Hill	G/T	10
	Bog Height	G	2
	Duckworth Hall	G/T	2
Burnley	Rowley	G/T	6
	Old Barn Farm	G/T	1
Pendle	Rainhall Rock	G	3
	Knotts Lane, Colne	G	3
	Waidshouse, Nelson	G	7
	Winewalls, Trawden	G	2
	Catlow	T	1
	Nelson STW	G	4
	Bunkers Hill	G	1
Rossendale	Meadowhead	G	3
	Rakehead	P	3
LANCASHIRE			245

Source: Lancashire County Council.

Note: P = Pastureland
G = Grassland
T = Trees
A = Agriculture

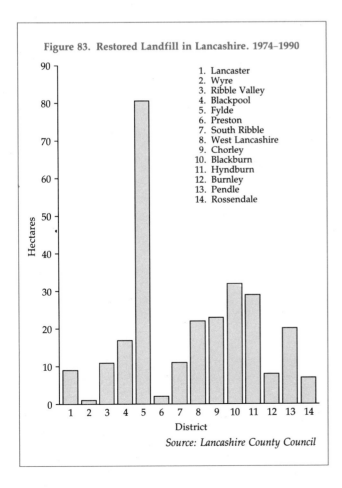

Figure 83. Restored Landfill in Lancashire. 1974–1990

1. Lancaster
2. Wyre
3. Ribble Valley
4. Blackpool
5. Fylde
6. Preston
7. South Ribble
8. West Lancashire
9. Chorley
10. Blackburn
11. Hyndburn
12. Burnley
13. Pendle
14. Rossendale

Source: Lancashire County Council

operational and restoration is being undertaken gradually. Aftercare is carried out for a defined period, usually five years, to ensure that the restoration schemes become properly established.

5.98 Land contaminated by old gas works waste is often located close to urban centres, providing a valuable resource for redevelopment. The waste from these sites needs to be removed, or treated, before development can take place. In most cases, the contaminated material is taken to a licensed site. This is a very expensive operation. Recently, in-situ biological treatment of old gas works waste was carried out at the Greenbank site, Blackburn. Microbes were specially cultured and seeded into the contaminated land. This greatly accelerated the normally slow, natural degradation of coal tars and organic compounds. This process resulted in the land being de-contaminated without creating an extra burden on landfill sites. Such bio-engineering solutions are only possible with organically based pollutants. However, they could have significant impacts on the waste disposal industry if they were adopted more widely.

Monitoring

5.99   Waste management monitoring is carried out predominantly by County Councils waste licensing staff, who visit all sites to ensure compliance with conditions attached to licences. In 1989, 1,893 inspections were made. Table 66 and Figure 84 detail these by District and type. The inspections include both public and private sites.

5.100   A wide range of other monitoring activity takes place on, and around, waste facilities. This includes monitoring by:

* the County Council, who enforce planning permissions;
* North West Water, who monitor leachate discharges to sewer;
* the NRA, who inspect landfill sites and monitor any adjacent watercourses;
* the National Radiological Protection Board, commissioned to undertake an annual survey of radiological emissions from the Clifton Marsh landfill site.

Other bodies which monitor from time to time include HMIP, the Health and Safety Executive, District Council Environmental Health Departments, and the Fire Brigade.

5.101   Specific scientific monitoring is also undertaken. On sites for which the County Council is responsible this is carried out to detect gas or leachate present within, and outside, the site and to establish any effects on ground or surface water.

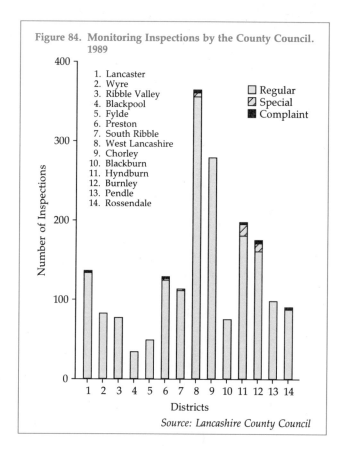

Figure 84. Monitoring Inspections by the County Council. 1989

1. Lancaster
2. Wyre
3. Ribble Valley
4. Blackpool
5. Fylde
6. Preston
7. South Ribble
8. West Lancashire
9. Chorley
10. Blackburn
11. Hyndburn
12. Burnley
13. Pendle
14. Rossendale

□ Regular
▨ Special
■ Complaint

Source: Lancashire County Council

Sampling of waste arriving at the site is also carried out to ensure that it is satisfactory for disposal.

5.102   Table 67 details the monitoring programme for landfill gas, leachate and surface water in effect at 1 April 1990 and Table 68 indicates the numbers of samples taken for laboratory analysis between 1984 to 1990. The latter table shows a marked increase in sample analysis in the last three years, especially in water sampling. This information is also summarised in Figure 85. Landfill gas is monitored for methane and carbon dioxide and, usually also for oxygen and atmospheric pressure.

Table 66	Waste Monitoring Inspections Made by the County Council in 1989.			
District	Regular	Special	Complaint	Total
Lancaster	134	1	—	135
Wyre	83	—	—	83
Ribble Valley	77	—	—	77
Blackpool	34	—	—	34
Fylde	49	—	—	49
Preston	124	1	1	126
South Ribble	112	1	—	113
West Lancashire	356	4	3	363
Chorley	279	—	—	279
Blackburn	76	—	—	76
Hyndburn	181	14	3	198
Burnley	162	9	1	172
Pendle	98	—	—	98
Rossendale	87	3	—	90
LANCASHIRE	1,852	33	8	1,893

Source: Lancashire County Council.

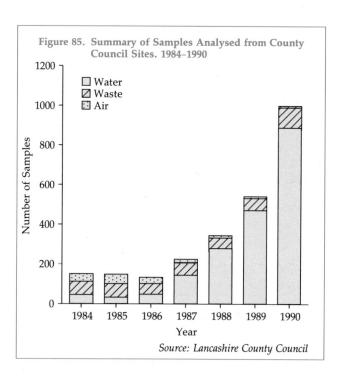

Figure 85. Summary of Samples Analysed from County Council Sites. 1984–1990

□ Water
▨ Waste
▨ Air

Source: Lancashire County Council

Table 67 Monitoring Programme on County Council Landfill Sites from April 1990

District	Site Name		Water Sampling			Gas Monitoring		
			Boreholes	Others	Visits a Year	Boreholes	Probes	Visits a Year
Lancaster	Salt Ayre	★	31	—	24	11	—	24
	Cotestones	★	9	2	12	2	—	12
Wyre	Jameson Road	★	12	—	24	8	—	24
	Valients Farm		—	1	1	—	3	4
Ribble Valley	Henthorne	★	13	4	12	9	—	24
	Chatburn Scott		1	—	4	5	—	12
	Scott Laithe		—	1	4	2	1	12
	Abbey Brow		—	—	—	—	3	12
Blackpool	Midgeland Farm		27	—	4	27	—	12
Fylde	Clifton Marsh	★	56	5	4	15	3	4
	Saltcotes		9	2	4	4	2	12
South Ribble	Much Hoole	★	1	3	12	1	—	12
	Hennel Lane		—	—	—	8	—	12
West Lancashire	Pimbo	★	14	—	12	20	—	24
	Platts Lane		4	2	4	10	—	36
	Rufford		—	—	24	8	—	24
Chorley	Lower Burgh		—	—	—	21	—	48
	Ulnes Walton	★	10	2	12	5	2	12
Blackburn	Feniscowles		8	—	12	17	—	24
	Bull Hill		5	—	4	8	—	12
	Duckworth Hall		—	—	—	—	5	14
Hyndburn	Whinney Hill	★	4	2	12	12	2	24
	Church		2	2	12	6	—	12
	Cunliffe		2	—	6	3	—	6
	Enfield		—	—	—	8	—	12
	Huncoat		—	—	—	—	4	12
Burnley	Rowley	★	5	2	12	50	—	48
Pendle	Rainhall Rock	★	12	2	12	17	—	24
	Knotts Lane		1	—	4	2	—	12
	Wadeshouse Road		—	—	—	26	8	48
	Catlow		—	—	—	3	—	12
Rossendale	Rakehead	★	13	2	24	22	—	24
	Duckworth Clough	★	4	2	12	6	—	12
	Meadowhead		—	2	12	—	—	—
LANCASHIRE			243	36	279	334	33	616

Source: Lancashire County Council.

Note: ★Active Landfill Site.

Groundwater and leachate samples are analysed for a variety of chemical compounds; including ammonia, nitrates, nitrites, chlorides, sulphates and metals, with tests for pH, conductivity and Chemical Oxygen Demand.

5.103 Waste monitoring is undertaken on all County sites by random inspections of loads to check that no dangerous materials are inadvertently accepted. At Clifton Marsh, (Fylde) and Salt Ayre, (Lancaster) small laboratories exist to allow more detailed checks. All sites accepting asbestos have regular air monitoring to check that no harmful levels of fibres are released. The only landfill site accepting waste in drums is Clifton Marsh, where every drum of controlled waste is opened and the contents verified against documentation carried with the load before being placed in a trench for burial.

5.104 Monitoring at private landfill sites is generally undertaken in order to comply with site licence

Table 68 Summary of Samples from County Council Waste Disposal Sites Analysed by the County Analyst. 1984–1990

Year	Water	Waste	Air	Total
1984	47	68	46	161
1985	34	67	51	152
1986	47	65	24	136
1987	142	67	15	224
1988	281	46	10	337
1989	467	68	5	540
1990	890	103	5	998
TOTAL	1,908	484	156	2,548

Source: Lancashire County Council.

Note: 1990 Figures are for January to May.

Table 69 Monitoring Undertaken on Private Waste Disposal Sites in Lancashire. 1990

District	Site	Boreholes/Probes	Comment
Lancaster	Ellel	1 deep borehole	Groundwater monitored, no result yet available.
Wyre	ICI Borehole	—	Pressure checks done twice yearly on pipeline. Samples analysed for mercury and iron.
	Gift Hall Farm	4 shallow probes	Site not yet operational.
	Poulton Railway Cutting	5 shallow probes	Site Licence expired. Checked by LCC staff. Gas migration occurring.
Ribble Valley	Hollins Hall Farm	3 shallow probes	Landfill gas checked. No results to date.
	Chapel Hill	16 shallow probes	Landfill gas is being produced.
Fylde	Westby	8 boreholes	Monitoring for gas and leachate to be undertaken (new site).
Preston	Lea Marsh	4 boreholes	Groundwater monitoring undertaken by County Analyst on regular basis for Preston BC.
	Cottam Hall	6 shallow probes	Gas levels to be checked monthly. Site not yet open (June 90).
	Lightfoot Green Farm	6 shallow probes	Monthly checks for gas. Twice monthly checks on water-course. Site not yet open (June 90).
South Ribble	Distillex	—	Surface Water checked for chlorinated solvents before discharge.
West Lancashire	Alder Lane	5 boreholes	Only leachate levels checked.
	Parbold Quarry	28 boreholes	Checked weekly for landfill gas. Surface water checked weekly.
	West Quarry	14 boreholes	Checked twice weekly for landfill gas.
	Sandfield Quarry	18 shallow probes	Checked monthly by LCC staff. Gas being produced.
	Alty's Brickworks	8 deep boreholes	Monthly checks for methane – low levels being found.
Chorley	Withnell Quarry	18 boreholes (gas)	Gas checked weekly, migration occurring.
		8 boreholes (groundwater)	Groundwater checked for levels weekly and full analysis quarterly.
	Castlehouse Quarry	6 shallow probes	Low levels of gas detected. Surface water checked for conductivity weekly, full analysis quarterly.
	Dawber Quarry	4 shallow probes	Monthly checks for methane. No migration detected.
Blackburn	Bog Height Quarry	1 borehole 5m deep	Licence surrendered when more work requested. Migration occurring.
	Stockclough Quarry	Required by licence	Site currently closed and no monitoring undertaken.
	Springside Mill	10 probes to 1.5m	Migration occurring.
	Goosehouse Quarry	Required by licence	Site has been closed for 8 years but not yet full. No monitoring done.
	Heightside Farm	2 shallow probes	No gas detected, more work required.
	Bent Hall Farm	Several shallow probes	Low levels of gas found.
Hyndburn	Duckworth Hall	30 Shallow probes Some boreholes	Gas being produced, migration not detected.
	Stanhill	Some monitoring being undertaken	Gas migration is occurring. Site closed.
Burnley	Old Barn Farm	1 Borehole	No gas detected.
Rossendale	Holden Vale	Shallow probes	Landfill gas is migrating but Company no longer exists.
	Wham Hill	Survey for gas carried out using shallow probes	Low levels of gas are migrating.

Source: Lancashire County Council.

conditions. All sites which have taken, or wish to take, biodegradable wastes are subject to gas monitoring. Results are sent to the WRA at regular intervals. However, such conditions were only enforceable under COPA 1974 whilst the site licence was current. Several operators returned their licences rather than comply with monitoring conditions when the site has been substantially completed. This major loophole has been closed by the EPA 1990. A few sites are required to undertake monitoring for water pollution. Table 69 details the sites and the monitoring currently carried out.

5.105   Monitoring for landfill gas migration is also undertaken by several District Councils on household waste sites closed prior to the introduction of the COPA site licensing in 1976, and on some private landfill sites where the licenses have been returned.

Litter

5.106   Litter is a widely spread waste-related problem, though there is an absence of reliable information relating to Lancashire. However, the Tidy Britain Group (TBG) has conducted some sample research, nationally. There are many definitions of litter, from the dictionary's 'Untidy Refuse' to the TBG's 'Waste in the Wrong Place'. The EPA 1990 contains a new power for the Secretary of State to add animal faeces, including dog faeces, to the duty of local authorities to keep relevant land clear of litter and refuse. This suggests that dog faeces are now considered to fall within the definition of litter.

5.107   The results of a recent TBG Survey of Litter collected during individual projects are shown in Figure 86. These show that nationally, 49% of litter is made up of small fragments, including cigarette

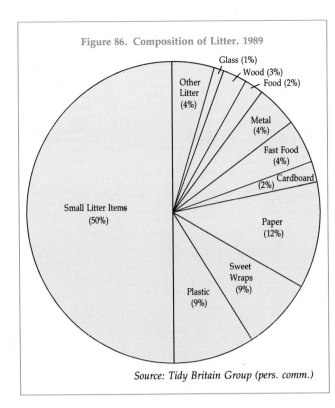

Figure 86. Composition of Litter. 1989

Glass (1%)
Wood (3%)
Food (2%)
Other Litter (4%)
Metal (4%)
Fast Food (4%)
Cardboard (2%)
Small Litter Items (50%)
Paper (12%)
Sweet Wraps (9%)
Plastic (9%)

Source: Tidy Britain Group (pers. comm.)

Litter Schemes

5.108 Lancashire County Council is one of only two County Council groups in Britain to become actively involved with the TBG. This has led to the formation of the Tidy Up Lancashire Campaign (TUL). The TBG and the County Council work to promote public awareness of Lancashire's own litter problem and, with District Council and voluntary organisations, to organise and establish litter abatement schemes. Through TUL, funds have been made available from donations by British Telecom and the County Council for local litter enhancement schemes. Table 70 shows how grants have been distributed following their launch in April 1989. A total of £23,066 has been granted so far, and new funds have recently been made available. 83% of applications for this grant have been supported.

5.109 TBG and Pendle Borough Council launched the 'Give Nelson a Clean Sweep' Campaign in December 1988. Litter weighing formed part of this campaign to quantify the weights being deposited in a specified area. Figure 87 shows the average quantities of litter collected from eleven bins, and from street sweepings, over five months. During the period, 66% of litter was deposited in the bins, leaving 34% dropped in the street.

5.110 In Blackpool, the Keep Blackpool Tidy Group, co-ordinated by the Borough Council since February 1989, has actively promoted local anti-litter initiatives, and has organised various litter picking events.

related items. Paper and sweet wrappers make up to 21%, leaving 29% divided between the other categories listed. In addition to the types shown in Figure 86, abandoned vehicles, fly-tipped waste and refuse sacks deposited long term are also included within the scope of litter. Legislation has now been strengthened to combat these problems.

Table 70	Grants from the Tidy Up Lancashire Campaign. 1989–1990		
District	Applications Made	Applications Granted	Total Amount Granted (£)
Lancaster	28	26	2,300
Wyre	3	3	250
Ribble Valley	9	8	720
Blackpool	13	12	1,145
Fylde	8	8	695
Preston	24	21	2,600
South Ribble	13	12	996
West Lancashire	13	12	1,265
Chorley	47	17	2,470
Blackburn	31	30	3,510
Hyndburn	14	12	1,105
Burnley	16	15	1,515
Pendle	26	25	2,820
Rossendale	19	18	1,675
LANCASHIRE	264	219	23,066

Source: Tidy Up Lancashire Campaign (pers. comm.).

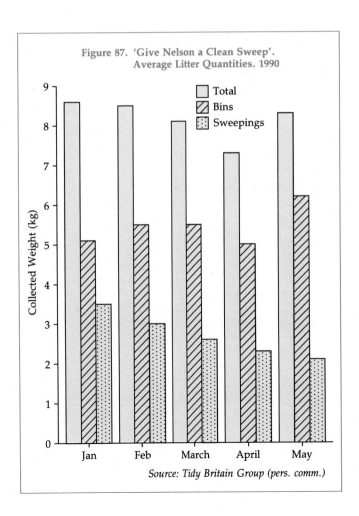

Figure 87. 'Give Nelson a Clean Sweep'. Average Litter Quantities. 1990

Total
Bins
Sweepings

Source: Tidy Britain Group (pers. comm.)

5.111 Chorley Borough Council and TBG have been involved with a campaign in Adlington, where a survey was carried out to assess people's attitude to litter. 70% of the people questioned believed litter to be an individual responsibility, whilst 46% thought it was a Local Authority responsibility. 95% of people questioned thought it was never acceptable to drop litter in a clean place, and 89% thought it was never acceptable in an already littered place.

5.112 All District Councils are involved on the TUL Steering Group, and with various local schemes to promote a clean litter-free environment.

Litter Removal

5.113 Most litter is deposited on the roads and pavements of our towns. An effective street cleaning programme is therefore essential. From April 1991, District Councils will be responsible for all street and road cleansing under the EPA 1990. From the same date, all local authorities will have to keep all land in their control, to which the public has access, clear of litter and refuse. This extends existing responsibilities to other potential litter black spots like parks, playing fields, Country Parks and picnic sites, urban commons, other amenity areas, car parks and shopping precincts.

5.114 Litter is not only an urban problem. The improved accessibility of the countryside has resulted in litter despoiling previously clean areas. These are often difficult to clear and have a lower frequency of cleansing. In these situations, litter can also pose a serious risk to wildlife and farm livestock. Fly-tipping involves larger items and accumulations of rubbish other than litter. District Councils have powers under the Public Health Acts 1936 and 1961 to serve an abatement notice on offenders, (in the unlikely event that they can be found) and to remove any rubbish. County and District Councils have powers under the Refuse Disposal (Amenity) Act 1978 to prosecute any person who abandons anything on any land in the open air.

Prosecutions

5.115 Dropping litter is a summary offence under various Acts of Parliament, though only limited use is made of this legislation. The maximum permitted fine under the Litter Act 1983 was £400 (increased from April 1991 under the EPA 1990 to £1,000). The national average in 1988 for litter fines under this Act was £39.68. The average for Lancashire, for the same year, was £52.50, with 52 people being found guilty of the offence (Home Office).

References

British Nuclear Fuels Limited (1990). Annual Monitoring Report. BNFL.

Department of the Environment (1971). (Circular 42/71) The Dangerous Litter Act. HMSO.

Department of the Environment (1986). Waste Management Paper 26. HMSO.

Department of the Environment (1988). Assessment of Groundwater Quality in England and Wales. HMSO.

Department of the Environment (1989). Waste Management Papers 4 and 27. HMSO.

Department of the Environment (1990). Pilot Survey of Potentially Contaminated Land in Cheshire – A Methodology for Identifying Potentially Contaminated Sites. HMSO.

ENDS (1990). Report 180. Contaminated Land Gets Its Proper Place On The Environmental Agenda. Environmental Data Services Ltd.

Friends of the Earth and The Daily Telegraph (1989). Recycling 1990 Lancashire Directory. The Daily Telegraph.

Garner J.F. (1990). Control of Pollution Encyclopedia. Butterworths.

Gray D.A. Mather J.P. and Harrison I.B. (1974). Review of groundwater pollution from waste disposal sites in England and Wales, with provisional guidelines for future site selection. Quarterly Journal of Engineering Geology Vol. 7.

Lancashire County Council (1987). Draft Consultative Document Waste Disposal Plan. LCC.

Lancashire County Council (1988). Minutes of the Waste Disposal Sub-Committee (12.1.88).

Lancashire County Council (1989). Waste Recycling Directory. LCC.

Lancashire County Council (1990). Minutes of the Waste Disposal Sub-Committee (28.2.90).

Ministry of Agriculture Fisheries and Food (1988). Report on the Disposal of Waste at Sea 1986/87. HMSO.

North West Water (1988). County Review 1988 (Incorporating The Way Ahead) for Lancashire County. NWW.

North West Waste Disposal Officers (1988). Forward Planning Sub-group First Report. Unpublished.

Chapter Six
Noise

Introduction

6.1   Sound is caused by pressure fluctuations in the air. If these are intense enough, and within the human audible frequency range, then people with normal hearing can detect them. The human ear is sensitive to a wide variety of sounds. Some sounds are acceptable and pleasant. When a sound is unwanted, or becomes annoying, it is called noise.

6.2   There are many reasons why a sound becomes annoying to people. The commonest causes are the type of sound, the intermittency of the sound or the nature of the environment into which the sound is introduced.

6.3   The effects of noise on people are various. It can cause annoyance by disturbing sleep, interfering with conversations, interrupting work or enjoyment of the TV or radio. This can lead to stress, behavioural changes and related physiological changes. Exposure to very high noise levels can also lead to noise-induced hearing loss or ringing in the ears – a condition known as tinnitus.

6.4   Public concern about noise has grown in recent years, reflecting a growth in sources of noise – particularly in terms of road and air traffic – and a decline in tolerance of noise intrusion into the environment. Statistics on public complaints to District Council Environmental Health Officers (EHOs) across the UK indicate that complaints about noise increased by 80% between 1977 and 1987/8 (Department of the Environment, 1990).

6.5   This Chapter firstly outlines the legal and organisational framework for noise in the County, describes how noise is measured and then examines sources of noise in Lancashire. Where noise levels from particular sources have been measured, these are presented. Otherwise, descriptions are given of the noise sources together with examples of sources and locations. Noise complaints data are also presented for each type of noise source, together with details of monitoring arrangements operating in the County.

Legislation

European

6.6   The EC has produced a number of Directives aimed at reducing noise in the environment, which the UK must implement. EC Directives set standards for noise from humans, vehicles, aircraft, lawnmowers, construction plant and for noise in the work place. They have a dual purpose; firstly, to ensure that noise limits imposed by individual member States do not create barriers to trade, and secondly, to progressively reduce noise levels for environmental reasons.

6.7   Directive 84/424/EEC sets limits for noise from cars, buses and lorries, whilst Directive 87/56/EEC sets limits for motorcycle noise. Aircraft noise is covered by two EC Directives, 80/51/EEC and 83/206/EEC (amendment), which require member States to ensure that the relevant categories of civil aircraft registered in their territories are not used unless certified in accordance with the Convention on International Civil Aviation. Directive

87/252/EEC set noise limits for lawn mowers according to the cutting width of the mower. In 1986, the European Community adopted a Directive (86/188/EEC) to protect workers from the risks related to noise exposure at work, which member States had to implement by January 1990.

United Kingdom

Neighbourhood Noise

6.8   Part 3 of The Control of Pollution Act (COPA) 1974, contains most of the legislation for noise control in the UK. It is the principal law giving District Councils powers to protect people against the adverse effects of noise pollution and mainly deals with local (i.e. neighbourhood) noise problems; it does not deal with road traffic noise or aircraft noise.

6.9   Under Section 57 of COPA 1974, Districts have a duty to inspect their areas from time to time to detect whether noise amounting to a nuisance exists, or is likely to occur, or recur. Where the local authority is satisfied that there is a level of noise which amounts to a nuisance, it can serve a notice under Section 58 of COPA 1974, requiring abatement of the nuisance. This does not necessarily mean that the noise nuisance will then cease. For a noise caused by a trade or business, if it can be shown that the 'best practicable means' (BPM) for preventing or counteracting the effects of the noise have been used, then this is a defence against prosecution.

6.10   Under Section 59 of COPA 1974, an individual has the right to take proceedings for noise nuisance. The individual should make a complaint to a magistrate, who will issue a summons if it is shown that a case exists. If the court is satisfied that a nuisance exists, it may make an order to abate the nuisance, and to execute any necessary works. Again, the defence of BPM exists for noise from a trade or business.

6.11   Noise from construction sites is controlled under Section 60 of COPA 1974. When construction work is being, or is going to be carried out, a District Council may serve a notice imposing requirements concerning plant or machinery to be used, hours during which the work may be carried out and the level of noise which may be emitted. Prior consent to carry out construction site work can be obtained by the contractor under Section 61 of COPA 1974, by submitting an application giving particulars of the work to be carried out, the methods to be used, and the steps taken to minimise noise.

6.12   Under Section 62 the use of loudspeakers is banned in streets at night and closely controlled for advertising sales of perishable foods. However, emergency services (fire, police, ambulance, water) are exempted from this rule, as would appear to be charities and political activities.

6.13   Also, under Section 57 of COPA 1974, a District Council may designate all, or part, of its area as a 'Noise Abatement Zone', the purpose of which is the long-term control of noise from fixed premises. The local authority measures noise from premises within the zone and records them in a register, according to the Control of Noise (Measurements and Registers) Regulations 1976. Once the noise level has been registered it cannot be exceeded, except with the local authority's consent. Over a period of time, the local authority may seek to reduce the levels by serving a reduction notice under Section 66 of COPA 1974.

Road Traffic Noise

6.14 Maximum noise levels for vehicles when new and in use, are set out in the Motor Vehicle Construction and Use Regulations 1986 and the Motor Vehicle (Type Approval) (Great Britain) Regulations under the Road Traffic Act 1972. Maximum levels for motor cycles are set out in the Motorcycles (Sound Level Measurement Certificates) Regulations 1980. The Type Approval Regulations currently set maximum limits for new goods vehicles of 84 dB(A), 77 dB(A) for cars, and 82 dB(A) maximum for motorcycles according to the requirements of the EC Directives.

6.15 The Motor Vehicle Construction and Use Regulations also impose fines in respect of any vehicle making excessive noise and restrictions on the use of motor horns etc. Most prosecutions brought by the police are for use of vehicles with defective silencers.

6.16 The Noise Insulation Regulations of the Land Compensation Act 1973 impose a duty on the highway authority to offer a grant to provide noise insulation for householders if they experience increased noise levels as a result of a new or altered road, and the resulting noise level reaches or exceeds 68 dB(A) L_{10} (18 hours) (see Noise Measurement and Noise Units). The same Act provides for compensation where property values have fallen because of increased traffic noise. The Noise Insulation Regulations do not provide for grants to householders affected by increased traffic resulting from re-routing or traffic management schemes from a general increase in traffic flow. (See Chapter 12.)

Aircraft Noise

6.17 Section 78 of the Civil Aviation Act 1982 gives the Secretary of State for Transport wide powers to enforce noise standards on aircraft, apply restrictions on aircraft movement, control flight paths and apply their operational controls. Local authorities have no powers to act on complaints about aircraft noise. The Air and Air Traffic Control Regulations 1981 cover general rules as to flight, not permitting aircraft to fly below 457 m (1500 feet). Landing and take-off routes are prescribed by air traffic control procedures and these usually include a requirement for the rate of height gain or loss and turning to minimise noise over built-up areas. Near international airports, aircraft are frequently restricted to formal 'minimum noise routes', but aircraft are generally high when flying over Lancashire, so that adherence to these routes does not apply.

6.18 Reductions in noise nuisance have largely resulted from improved jet engine design. Standards drawn up by the International Civil Aviation Organisation are implemented in the UK through the Air Navigation (Noise Certification) Order 1986. Aircraft are only permitted to use UK airports if they have a noise certificate, which is issued if noise levels on take-off and landing are below prescribed limits. Legal liability in respect of nuisance by military aircraft is excluded by statute.

Railway Noise

6.19 No legislation currently exists to govern noise emissions from railways. However, in its planning of high speed rail links with the Channel Tunnel, British Rail has said it will adopt a policy similar in effect to that of the Noise Insulation Regulations governing road traffic noise. British Rail states that it will act to reduce noise or mitigate its effects where a level of 70 dB(A) is exceeded at affected buildings (Technica, 1990). At the moment, there is no high speed rail link to the North West and no plans by British Rail to join Lancashire to the high speed route from London to the Tunnel.

Planning and Noise

6.20 Guidelines are given to local planning authorities by the Department of the Environment regarding new developments in noisy areas. Circular 10/73 'Planning and Noise' ensures District Councils control development where noise is likely to be a problem. The Noise Working Party has recommended, (1990), that the Circular needs updating and revising.

Occupational Noise

6.21 The EC Directive relating to noise exposure at work has been implemented in the UK through the Noise at Work Regulations 1990 under the Health & Safety at Work Act, 1974. The Regulations require that, where average daily noise exposures exceed 85 dB(A), personal ear protectors are to be made available to workers and they must be informed of the risks to their hearing. Above 90 dB(A), the use of personal ear protectors is compulsory and measures to reduce noise exposure must be implemented.

Organisations

Central Government

6.22 The Department of the Environment is responsible for the co-ordination of noise policy in the UK, whilst the Department of Transport is responsible for the overall control of noise from motor vehicles, aircraft and ships. The Civil Aviation Authority is responsible for implementing the requirements of the Civil Aviation Act 1982 with respect to noise certification of aircraft, noise abatement procedures during take-off and landing and aircraft routeing along Minimum Noise Routes. The Ministry of Defence is responsible for noise from military aircraft. The Department of Employment is responsible for noise within work places, regulation of which is carried out by the Health and Safety Executive.

Local Government

6.23 The rôle of Local Government is to take practical action to prevent, or abate, noise nuisance. This is the responsiblity of District Council Environmental Health Departments, who control neighbourhood noise using the relevant sections of COPA 1974. Sound measurements may be taken by Environmental Health Officers (EHOs) in response to complaints, especially if there are serious or persistent problems with noise. These measurements will then be used to determine whether the noise constitutes a statutory nuisance. If not, the EHO may make an informal request to the person responsible for the noise in order to seek a reduction in the noise level.

6.24 EHOs may also conduct noise monitoring with regard to planning consents for new industrial or commercial developments, or domestic developments near existing noise sources. Local authority planning departments consult EHOs about planning applications. In most cases, the EHO will make certain recommendations concerning noise control, but there may be a necessity to conduct noise monitoring in some circumstances. The additional contribution of the new development to the existing sound level may then be assessed.

6.25 The Highways Laboratory of the County Council conducts traffic noise monitoring with respect to new road schemes as required by the Noise Insulation Regulations of the Land Compensation Act, 1975 (see Chapter 12). They have a responsibility to predict the likely noise nuisance from traffic using the new roads within a period of fifteen years from the date of completion. Areas around the new road are designated, within which the noise level at the exteriors of properties is predicted, to assess eligibility for noise insulation grants. Every new road scheme in the County will include such a designated area. Properties adjacent to existing roads are, however, not eligible for noise insulation grants, even if increases in traffic volumes cause a noise nuisance.

6.26 The Lancashire Constabulary is responsible for enforcing the Motor Vehicle Construction and Use Regulations to control the noise emission from individual vehicles in use.

Other Organisations

6.27 British Rail are responsible for noise from railway lines in the County. Noise from civilian or commercial aircraft comes under the juristiction of the Civil Aviation Authority. Local aircraft noise may emanate from Blackpool Airport which is owned by Blackpool Borough Council or from Warton or Samlesbury Aerodromes owned by British Aerospace Corporation. The Noise Abatement Society is the principal national voluntary organisation campaigning on noise issues in the UK. Recently, the National Society for Clean Air has extended its remit to include noise matters and is changing its name to the National Society for Clean Air and Environmental Protection.

Noise Pollution in Lancashire

Noise Units and Indices

6.28 The sound pressure level of the threshold of pain is over a million times that of the quietest audible sound. In order to reduce the size of the numbers involved when measuring sound, a logarithmic scale of decibels (dB) is used based on a reference level of the lowest audible sound.

6.29 The human ear responds differently to different frequencies of sound. It is therefore usual to weight the measured frequencies to imitate the human response. This is done by using electronic noise level meters fitted with an 'A' weighting device that makes the instrument respond in a similar way to the human ear.

6.30 The resulting 'A' weighted decibel reading – dB(A) – has been set so that 0 dB(A) is the threshold of hearing and 100 dB(A) corresponds to a loud noise (typically, noise from a pneumatic drill at 10 m). Figure 88 shows the sound level in dB(A), for a range of common sounds. In daily life, noise levels generally vary between 30–40 dB(A) and 80–90 dB(A), or even more. The loudness of a sound doubles each time the sound level increases by 10 decibels, so that 60 dB(A) is 'twice as loud' as 50 dB(A), and 90 dB(A) is twice as loud as 80 dB(A).

6.31 Whilst the majority of noise measurements are made in dB(A) units, many noises vary with time. Noise rating indices have been formulated which take time variation into account and these are used for noise assessment in connection with grant schemes etc. For road traffic noise, an index has been devised to show the noise level in dB(A) exceeded for 10% of the time, which is expressed as the L_{10}. The average of the hourly readings between 0600 and 2400 hrs gives the L_{10} (18 hour). This index is used to assess the eligibility for grants under the Noise Insulation Regulations.

6.32 When assessing hearing damage risk due to exposure to occupational noise, the equivalent continuous sound level L_{Aeq} is used. This is a notional level in dB(A) which, over the measured period, would deliver the same amount of sound energy as the actual fluctuating level. It enables fluctuating levels to be described in terms of single sound levels over a set exposure period. The L_{Aeq} over 24 hours is used as a measure of railway noise, for example, in applications for planning consents for developments near railway lines.

6.33 Aircraft noise has traditionally been treated differently to other sources of noise pollution. An index called the perceived decibel (PNdB), which purports to be a measure of the 'noisiness' of jet aircraft, is used to measure the noise from individual aircraft. The Noise and Number Index (NNI) is used to assess the eligibility of houses for grants towards insulation under airport grant schemes. The NNI value depends on the number of aircraft over-flights and the average perceived noisiness level of the aircraft.

Noise Nuisance

6.34 The extent to which noise causes a nuisance will vary considerably. The main factor determining

Figure 88

Typical Sound Levels in Lancashire.

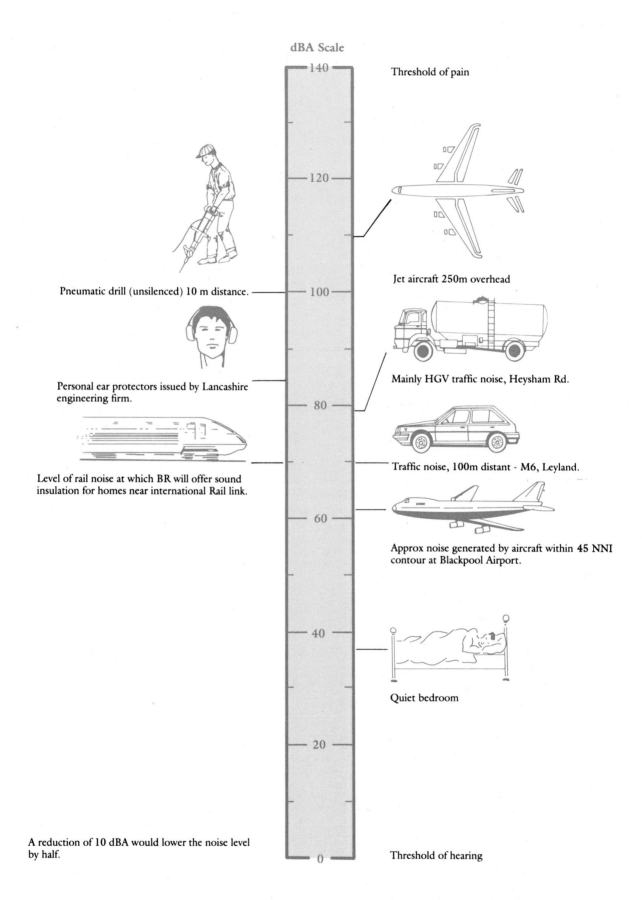

dBA Scale

- 140 — Threshold of pain
- 120 —
- 100 — Jet aircraft 250m overhead
- 80 — Mainly HGV traffic noise, Heysham Rd.
- 60 — Traffic noise, 100m distant - M6, Leyland.
- 40 — Approx noise generated by aircraft within **45 NNI** contour at Blackpool Airport.
- 20 — Quiet bedroom
- 0 — Threshold of hearing

Pneumatic drill (unsilenced) 10 m distance.

Personal ear protectors issued by Lancashire engineering firm.

Level of rail noise at which BR will offer sound insulation for homes near international Rail link.

A reduction of 10 dBA would lower the noise level by half.

Source: Lancashire County Council

the noise level from any source, is the distance of the hearer from the source. Other factors such as physical obstacles between the hearer and the source, and the level of perception and tolerance of the individual, will also affect whether the noise is considered a nuisance. Frequently, it is a 'different' noise which results in complaints. People become accustomed to a level of background noise, most of which is generated by road traffic. Only when an unaccustomed sound is heard does it become intrusive and constitute a noise. The time of day is also very important in determining nuisance; night-time noise being far more likely to be a nuisance than day-time noise. Thus, unaccustomed and night-time occurrences generate the greatest number of complaints to District Council Environmental Health Departments, even though they may not necessarily have high 'sound levels'.

6.35   There are no precise legal sound levels defining a noise nuisance. The policy of District Councils in the County is to try and resolve noise complaints informally, especially domestic complaints. Many EHOs are understandably reluctant to intervene in domestic situations due to the personal grievances which can arise between neighbours. The two parties are usually encouraged to reach an agreement between themselves, without involving the EHO.

6.36   A similar informal approach is also preferred in instances of industrial and commercial noise complaints, although EHOs are more prepared to impose restrictions on industrial offenders than on domestic offenders. It is also much easier to monitor industrial noise and confirm a noise nuisance. In some cases, the complaints procedure has led to successful prosecutions against persistent offenders.

Noise Complaints

6.37   Information on noise in the County is derived from two sources. Firstly, from records of public noise complaints maintained by District Council EHOs and secondly, from various noise level measurements taken by EHOs, the County Council as highway authority and by other bodies. The number of noise complaints received by all Lancashire Districts is presented in Figure 89.

6.38   Public complaints are registered according to the type of noise to which they relate:

* domestic noise;
* industrial and commercial noise;
* construction site noise;
* noise in streets;
* transport noise.

The first four are controlled by COPA 1974. Transport noise from road traffic, aircraft and railways is not controlled by this Act and therefore not dealt with by EHOs, although complaints are still received and recorded and then passed on to the highway authority, the Department of Transport, British Rail or relevant airport.

6.39   A total of 4,120 complaints were recorded in Lancashire in 1988/89. The numbers recorded in each District are shown in Figure 89. A remarkably

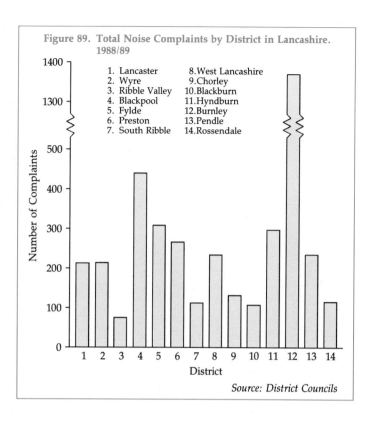

Figure 89. Total Noise Complaints by District in Lancashire. 1988/89

1. Lancaster
2. Wyre
3. Ribble Valley
4. Blackpool
5. Fylde
6. Preston
7. South Ribble
8. West Lancashire
9. Chorley
10. Blackburn
11. Hyndburn
12. Burnley
13. Pendle
14. Rossendale

Source: District Councils

high number of complaints (1371) were recorded in Burnley, due to a combination of reasons that may include low public tolerance of noise or several high noise point sources in the District. Blackpool (440) recorded the second highest number whilst Ribble Valley (76) could be regarded as Lancashire's 'quietest' District.

6.40   Total recorded noise complaints in Lancashire according to source are presented in Figure 90. Noise complaints according to source by District are shown on Figure 91.

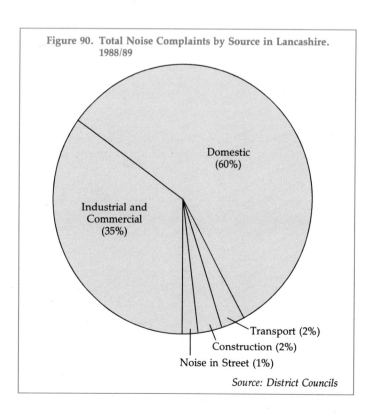

Figure 90. Total Noise Complaints by Source in Lancashire. 1988/89

Domestic (60%)

Industrial and Commercial (35%)

Transport (2%)
Construction (2%)
Noise in Street (1%)

Source: District Councils

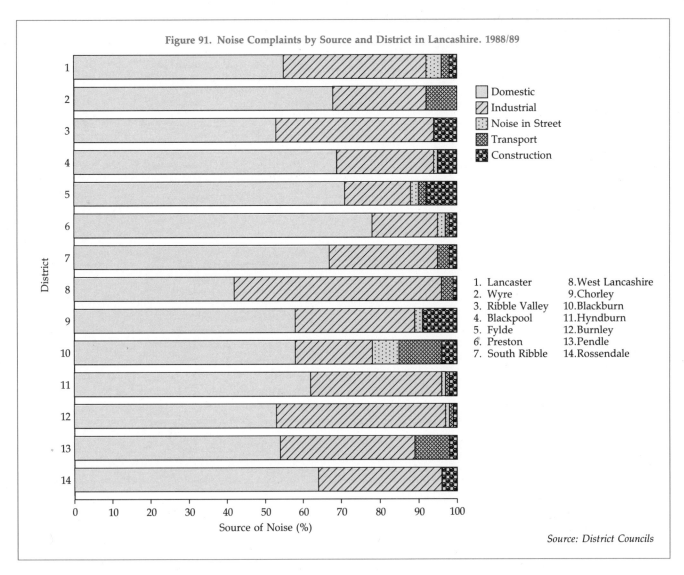

Figure 91. Noise Complaints by Source and District in Lancashire. 1988/89

Legend:
- Domestic
- Industrial
- Noise in Street
- Transport
- Construction

1. Lancaster   8. West Lancashire
2. Wyre   9. Chorley
3. Ribble Valley   10. Blackburn
4. Blackpool   11. Hyndburn
5. Fylde   12. Burnley
6. Preston   13. Pendle
7. South Ribble   14. Rossendale

X-axis: Source of Noise (%) — 0 to 100
Y-axis: District

Source: District Councils

Domestic Noise

6.41 The largest proportion (60%) of noise complaints in the County, (see Figure 90) concern domestic noise. These range from 78% of the total in Preston to 42% in West Lancashire. Domestic noise was the greatest source of complaint in every District except West Lancashire. EHOs state that the main cause of these domestic complaints is barking dogs. They also think that there is a rising trend of complaints, possibly as people become less tolerant of intrusive noise and more aware of their right to complain and of the complaints procedure.

6.42 Although noisy neighbours may not create a high level of sound generally, it can seem high and intrusive in adjacent properties. Banging and drilling from DIY activities and loud music from hi-fi systems may cause vibration as well as a noise nuisance, and these problems can be worsened by poor quality buildings. A national survey conducted by the Buildings Research Establishment found that, for homes built in the early 1970s, 55% of party walls and 44% of party floors failed to meet the Building Regulations requirements for noise. These Regulations require new houses and flats to have sound insulation to prescribed standards limiting noise between dwellings to acceptable levels given normal day-to-day noise.

6.43 Neighbourhood noise problems are compounded in summer when doors and windows are open and the noise intrudes onto the street. People are usually tolerant of some noise from neighbours for short periods of time, but persistent or anti-social noise (e.g. late at night) is understandably unacceptable.

Industrial and Commercial Noise

6.44 Operation of almost any industrial machinery will generate noise. This will normally be confined to industrial premises but, in some cases, may cause annoyance to local residents. Factory owners can be forced by law to ensure that, within the BPM, any noise issuing from their site does not constitute a nuisance. Planning applications for new or extended plant must also take account of appropriate noise control measures.

6.45 Industrial noise caused 35% of total noise complaints in 1988/89. Industrial sources were second in order of importance in terms of complaint in every District except West Lancashire, where they formed the largest source (54%), (Figure 90). They related generally to a wide range of industries such as paper, textile and plastics works, metal foundries, engineering and manufacturing.

6.46 Industrial noise will cause particular nuisance if it continues through the night. Factory expansion to include a night shift has resulted in complaints in Rossendale. Such night time noise may cause sleep disturbance which has public health implications. Other sources of noise associated with industrial premises apart from the actual machinery noise, are 24 hour fans or air conditioning units and tannoy systems. Such noise has caused complaints in Chorley.

6.47 Shops and business premises can cause a noise nuisance to local residents, particularly when the noise continues through the night. For example, all-night operation of washers and dryers in laundries has been reported in Preston. In addition to noise generated on the premises, however, there are often other noise sources associated with commerical activities. Commercial traffic is referred to below, whilst noise from late night establishments like public houses, or food (chip) shops has caused some complaints from nearby residents. The latter is a common problem in Blackpool.

Construction Site Noise

6.48 Construction sites caused 2% of all County noise complaints in 1988/89, with Chorley recording the highest levels, (9%). They have a great potential for noise being usually quite open and, unlike industrial premises, without the means to confine the noise. As well as high sound levels from machinery, powered tools and heavy traffic, there may also be 'impact' sounds, such as hammering, and pile-driving. Another major source of noise disturbance is road works. Where a road has to be dug up for new cables, water mains or pipes, consent may be required from the local authorities before commencement of works which are likely to generate high levels of noise.

6.49 Quarrying can also generate noise, principally by blasting operations and movements of heavy traffic. Blast noise may also have an 'impact' effect on the hearer if close enough to the quarry. In some parts of the County, e.g. Ribble Valley and Chorley, quarries do create a nuisance through a combination of the noise and dust they generate.

Noise in Streets

6.50 Noise in streets accounted for 1% of all County noise complaints in 1988/89. This category includes noise from loudspeakers, ice-cream chimes, street trading, playing of radio cassettes or noisy conduct taking place in the street and causing nuisance to homes nearby. The highest proportion of complaints occurs in Blackburn, with 7% of all complaints recorded in that District.

Transport Noise

6.51 Transport noise is the most widespread source of noise nuisance in the UK. However, because it is neither covered by COPA 1974, nor is it the responsiblity of EHOs, it results in only 2% of all complaints recorded in the County in 1988/89. The highest proportion (11%) of complaints were recorded in Blackburn.

6.52 Transport noise forms most of our background noise and is something to which much of the population has become accustomed. However,

Table 71	Measured Road Traffic Noise in Lancashire. 1989	
Site	Distance from source (m)	Measured level dB(A) L_{10} (18 hour)
M6 Leyland	100.00	69.9
M61 Leyland	100.00	59.0
B6243 Longridge	6.64	72.0

Source: South Ribble BC, Ribble Valley BC (pers. comms.)

it does produce high noise levels which cause nuisance to those who live close to roads and railways or beneath flight paths. Because of the nuisance that it causes, and because of the legislation that exists to prevent or ameliorate noise from roads and aircraft particularly, more specific data in terms of noise level measurements exist for this source of noise in the County.

Road Traffic Noise

6.53 Road traffic is the most consistent and continous source of noise in the modern urban environment. Virtually all 'background noise' is generated by traffic and Lancashire's 7,400 km network of roads and motorways constitute probably the greatest source of noise throughout the County. Examples of the sort of sound levels produced by road and motorway traffic are shown in Table 71.

6.54 Figure 92 shows the daily fluctuation in M6 motorway noise near Leyland. Major roads and motorways generate the greatest sound levels due to their volume of traffic, but may not constitute a major nuisance because there are usually few properties immediately adjacent to them. A smaller road with only a moderate volume of traffic (e.g. the B6243 at Longridge), may constitute more of a nuisance than a motorway, because houses are much closer to the road (see Table 71).

6.55 EHOs in Blackpool report seasonal patterns to traffic noise in the town, but acknowledge that this is marked by the far greater daily variation in noise. Measurements of noise taken in Preston town centre also showed great variation over time and space.

6.56 Perhaps the major source of complaints about transport noise in Lancashire is industrial and commercial freight traffic. Movements of HGV lorries to and from sites like slaughterhouses, factories, quarries or docks, can create a serious nuisance in the immediate vicinity. This sort of nuisance has been reported in Wyre, Chorley and Hyndburn, but certainly has a wider coverage throughout the County.

6.57 One area that suffers, particularly from lorries, is Lancaster/Heysham, where traffic between the expanding port of Heysham and the M6 motorway has to pass through built-up areas. As part of a national study into the environmental effects of lorries, (see Chapter 12), noise measurements were taken at four locations in Lancaster and two in Heysham. Noise profiles generated at two of these locations are shown in

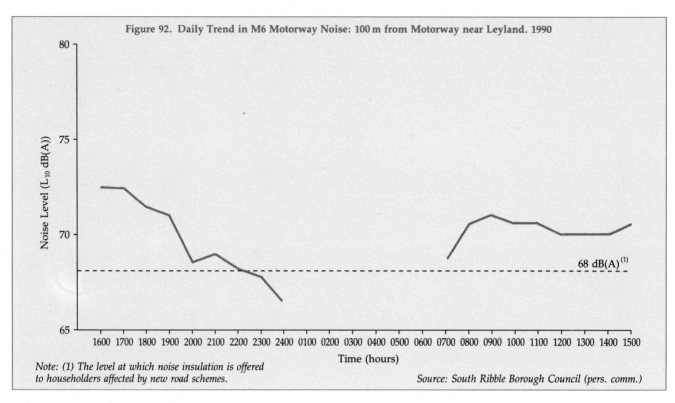

Figure 92. Daily Trend in M6 Motorway Noise: 100 m from Motorway near Leyland. 1990

Note: (1) The level at which noise insulation is offered
to householders affected by new road schemes.

Source: South Ribble Borough Council (pers. comm.)

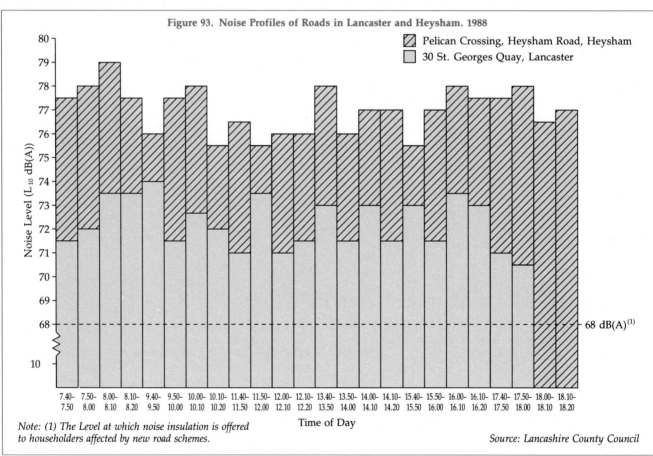

Figure 93. Noise Profiles of Roads in Lancaster and Heysham. 1988

Pelican Crossing, Heysham Road, Heysham
30 St. Georges Quay, Lancaster

Note: (1) The Level at which noise insulation is offered
to householders affected by new road schemes.

Source: Lancashire County Council

Figure 93. It can be seen that the dB(A) L_{10} level at both sites consistently exceeded 68 dB(A) – the level at which noise insulation is offered to householders affected by new road schemes. These high levels were recorded at four of the six sites monitored.

6.58 The vibration caused by heavy traffic movements may also add to the nuisance. There are likely to be very good grounds for complaint if such

traffic movements continue through the night. Problems reported in Hyndburn concern noise from large vehicles with refrigerator units, which remain switched on even when the vehicle is parked at night.

Aircraft Noise

6.59 Aircraft noise is a feature of only a small area

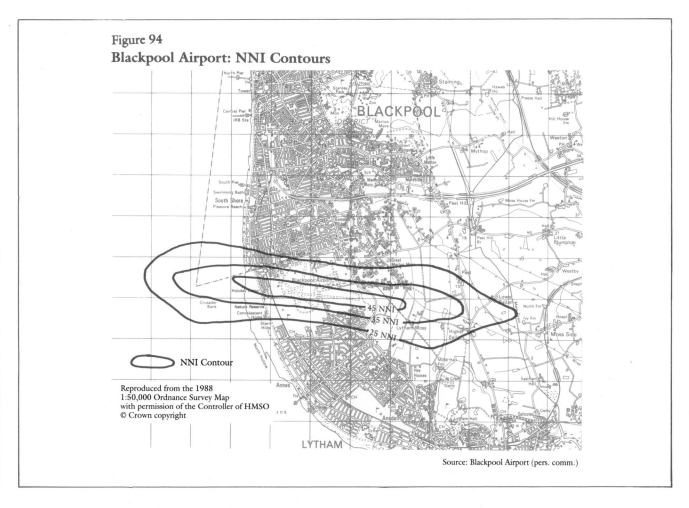

Figure 94
Blackpool Airport: NNI Contours

NNI Contour

Reproduced from the 1988
1:50,000 Ordnance Survey Map
with permission of the Controller of HMSO
© Crown copyright

45 NNI
35 NNI
25 NNI

Source: Blackpool Airport (pers. comm.)

of the County. Lancashire has only three airfields, Blackpool Airport and Warton and Samlesbury Aerodromes. However, RAF Woodvale in Formby is just outside the County boundary and military jets also fly over the County from bases in the UK and Europe heading for the Lake District. Jet aircraft create a very high level of sound but only low numbers of jets operate from Blackpool Airport (see Chapter 12). Furthermore, the main runway at the airport is orientated in an east-west direction so aircraft approach and take-off either over the sea or over sparsely populated Fylde farmland (Figure 94). The majority of traffic consists mainly of light aircraft or helicopters. Figure 94 also shows the NNI contours for the airport.

6.60   The Wilson Committee (1963) found that aircraft noise becomes a reason for complaint at 35 NNI, intrusive at 40–50 NNI, annoying at 50–60 NNI and very annoying at 60 NNI. It can be seen from Figure 94 that there are only a few dwellings within the highest 45 NNI contour at Blackpool Airport. The Airport itself receives, on average, only two–four complaints a month from the public about aircraft noise (Blackpool Airport, pers. comm.). Helicopter traffic at the airport reached very high levels when the Morecambe Bay drilling platform was set up. There were almost continuous helicopter movements and engines were kept running whilst on the ground. This led to numerous complaints and an investigation by Blackpool Borough Council in 1985.

6.61   Local residents have recently become concerned over the growing helicopter training activity

at Blackpool Airport, particularly when hover training is concentrated in one area. However, variation of helicopter training areas by Air Traffic Control has reduced the number of noise complaints (Blackpool Airport, pers.comm.).

6.62   Samlesbury Aerodrome is only used for light aircraft and is situated in a predominantly rural area where noise is unlikely to be a major problem. Warton Aerodrome, however, is very close to Warton and Freckleton and also has the greatest quantity of jet traffic. Military jet testing from Warton creates high sound levels in the area and flight paths include parts of West Lancashire (across the River Ribble) as well as Fylde and Preston. There appears, however, to be a high tolerance level amongst the local population to these jet movements, because very few complaints are made to District Councils or to British Aerospace.

Railway Noise

6.63   In common with other regular transport noise, people living near railway lines seem to develop a high tolerance to noise. Complaints are usually dealt with by local British Rail managers, but, in exceptional circumstances, noise specialists from the British Rail research laboratory may be called in. Most complaints relate to maintenance work, or to changes in rolling stock when sound may not actually be louder but appears so because it is different from usual. Railway noise only affects those living within a narrow corridor either side of the lines – a very small proportion of the County population.

6.64   Following general advice given in the DOE Circular 10/73 'Planning and Noise', many local planning authorities have adopted standards and guidelines in respect of railway noise and new residential development. Of a sample of authorities that have used the 24-hour L_{Aeq} index nearly all are below 65 L_{Aeq} and many are at or below 60 L_{Aeq}. At these noise levels there would be a general presumption to refuse development.

Entertainment and Leisure Noise

6.65   Numerous leisure pursuits have the potential for creating noise nuisance. Transport-based activities like power-boating, water-skiing, car rallies, motorcycle scrambling, microlight aircraft and powered hang-gliders can produce irritating engine noise. Many of these however, will be restricted to particular areas or dates. Activities such as motorcycle scrambling (particularly if the silencers have been removed) and low flying microlights have caused complaints in Cuerden Valley Park, Chorley, and the West Pennine Moors area respectively. Microlight noise disturbance to wildlfowl and wading birds has been reported by the Nature Conservancy Council, (Nature Conservancy Council pers.comm.) as a source of concern on the Lune Estuary (particularly on the Wyre-Lune Sanctuary area and Middleton Sands).

6.66   Clay pigeon shooting has also caused nuisance in some areas. Shoots with less than 28 meets per year do not require planning consent and may thus take place without the knowledge of any other party. Shoots planning more than 28 meets per year must take account of noise control in their planning application to the local authority.

6.67   Similarly, licences for public entertainment at pubs, clubs or discotheques (and particular outdoor

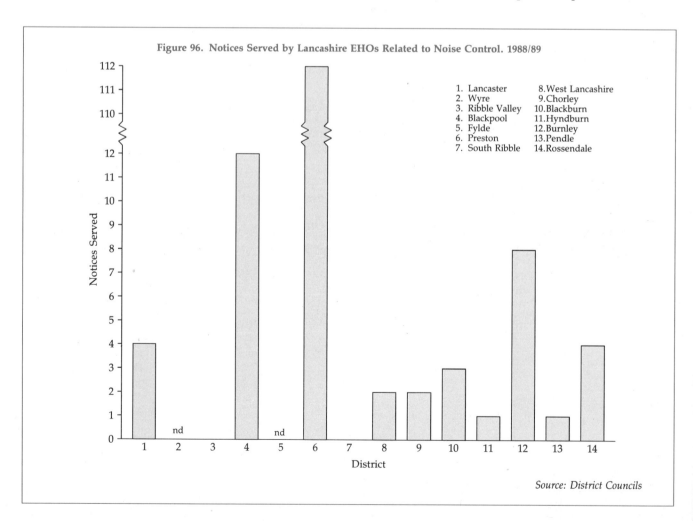

Figure 95. **Premises Licenced for Public Entertainment in Lancashire. 1989**

1. Lancaster
2. Wyre
3. Ribble Valley
4. Blackpool
5. Fylde
6. Preston
7. South Ribble
8. West Lancashire
9. Chorley
10. Blackburn
11. Hyndburn
12. Burnley
13. Pendle
14. Rossendale

Source: Chartered Institute of Public Finance and Accountancy (1989)

Figure 96. **Notices Served by Lancashire EHOs Related to Noise Control. 1988/89**

1. Lancaster
2. Wyre
3. Ribble Valley
4. Blackpool
5. Fylde
6. Preston
7. South Ribble
8. West Lancashire
9. Chorley
10. Blackburn
11. Hyndburn
12. Burnley
13. Pendle
14. Rossendale

Source: District Councils

events like pop concerts), are only granted by local authorities after noise issues have been considered in the planning process. The numbers of premises licensed for public entertainment in the County are shown in Figure 95.

6.68 Public entertainment, however, still causes complaints despite such planning procedures, particularly if the noise continues late into the night. Apart from pubs, clubs and discos, other entertainment noise is generated from amusement parks, principally through patron noise (screams, shouts, etc.) and public fireworks displays. This has been a particular problem in Blackpool.

Occupational Noise

6.69 It is estimated that about 1 million people in the UK are working in conditions that may damage their hearing unless precautions are taken (National Society for Clean Air,1990). People typically at risk are those in the steel or engineering industries, paper and board manufacturing or those who operate wood-working machinery. Since the Noise at Work Regulations were implemented in January 1990, the Health & Safety Executive has served three notices on firms in Lancashire requiring measures to be undertaken to reduce noise exposure of workers. One was to a chicken slaughterhouse in Ribble Valley, one to a West Lancashire engineering firm making bulk containers for lorries, and one to a Blackburn firm making body panels for cars. A noise measurement was taken at the firm making bulk containers and the reading of 110 dB(A) was 100 times the upper legal limit of 90 dB(A) (HSE, pers. comm.).

Noise Abatement Notices

6.70 The number of Notices served by District Councils in Lancashire in 1988/89 requiring abatement of noise nuisances is presented in Figure 96. A total of 149 Notices were served in the year, which corresponds to 3.6% of all recorded complaints. Preston had the highest number of Notices, issuing 75% of all those served in the County.

Noise Abatement Zones

6.71 One solution to the problem of noise in an area is for the District Council to designate a Noise Abatement Zone (NAZ), where noise limits can be set and where it becomes an offence to exceed them. While NAZ provide a means of controlling community noise without having to prove that the noise amounts to a nuisance, it is a little used method of control. To date, no NAZ have been designated in Lancashire.

6.72 Another solution to noise problems is to avoid noise becoming a nuisance by anticipating problems at the planning stage, and ensuring that noise generating developments are either suitably located or incorporate noise reduction features. This latter case is often encountered with new roads, where noise barriers may be included as part of the road scheme.

6.73 A general solution to aircraft noise has been to phase out aircraft with older, more noisy jet engines, and to operate them in a way that reduces or localises the noise heard on the ground. Aircraft like the Trident are no longer used in the UK, whilst the older Boeing 707 and the BAe 1–11 can only be used if fitted with silencing devices (Department of Transport, 1988).

References

Chartered Institute of Public Finance and Accountancy (1988). Environmental Health Statistics 1987–89 Actuals. CIPFA

Department of the Environment (1990). Digest of Environmental Protection and Water Statistics. HMSO

Department of Transport (1988). Transport and the Environment. HMSO

Fields J.M. & Hall F.L. (1988). Community effects of noise. in: Transportation Noise Reference Book. (Ed. Nelson) Butterworths.

National Society for Clean Air (1990). 1990 Pollution Handbook. NSCA

Nelson P. (Ed.) (1988). Transportation Noise Reference Book. Butterworths.

Sewel E.C. & Scholes W.E. (1978). Sound insulation performance between dwellings built in the early 1970's. Building Research Establishment Current Paper CP20/78.

Taylor S.M. & Wilkins P.A. (1988). Health Effects. in: Transportation Noise Reference Book (Ed. Nelson). Butterworths.

Technica (1990). Railway noise standards – lets get them right. Technician Consulting Scientists and Engineers Technical document.

Wilson Committee (1963). Committee on the problem of noise. Final Report 1963.

Chapter Seven

Energy

Introduction

7.1 Society cannot function without energy. We rely on a regular and plentiful supply for our heat, light and power and hence production and supply is a major industry. Energy occurs in many forms, including light, heat (thermal), electrical, potential, kinetic or stored chemical (energy trapped between, or within, atoms). Energy can be changed from one form into another. For example, when coal is burnt, stored chemical energy is converted to light and heat. There is a continuous loss of light, and especially heat, from the earth to space which would exhaust the earth's energy supply were it not for the Sun. The light and heat generated by the Sun continually replenish our energy sources.

7.2 The rôle of plants in trapping this sunlight and converting it into stored chemical energy by photosynthesis is fundamental to our energy supply. The chemical energy stores of wood, coal, oil and gas are all derived directly from plants. The burning of these fuels, either directly to drive machinery, or to generate electricity, provides the bulk of our supply. Other sources, like kinetic energy from wind and water, or the chemical energy stored in radioactive materials, are also exploited, but not nearly as widely.

7.3 Our continuing level of energy consumption, with its reliance on fossil fuels lies at the heart of our most serious environmental problems. Concerns about these, coupled with rising energy costs, have prompted a major re-evaluation of the way in which energy is produced and used, with a strong emphasis on maximising efficiency of use. It has led also to an increasing interest in alternative and renewable sources of energy.

7.4 This Chapter presents the legislative framework for regulation of the energy industry and goes on to discuss the production, supply and consumption of energy in Lancashire. The major energy sources supplying Lancashire's needs are considered in detail and the consequences of reliance on fossil fuels are explored. The potential for exploiting alternative sources and initiatives on efficient use of energy are also examined.

Legislation

European

7.5 There is relatively little EC legislation concerning the energy industry. A 1976 Directive (76/491/EEC) established a procedure for information and consultation on the prices of crude oil and petroleum products within the Community. The EC Environmental Assessment Directive (85/337) procedures apply to the establishment of major new energy installations or mining and drilling operations. The Directive has been implemented in the UK through the Town and Country Planning (Assessment of Environmental Effects) Regulations 1988.

United Kingdom

7.6 The Energy Act 1976 provided broad controls over electricity, crude liquid petroleum (oil), natural gas, petroleum products and any other substance used as fuel. It also included specific provisions for the maintenance of fuel reserves, the exploitation of offshore natural gas and requirements for information on passenger car fuel consumption. Specific legislation controls each of the principal components of the UK energy industry.

7.7 The electricity industry is being reorganised under the provisions of the Electricity Act (EA) 1989. At the core of the EA 1989 are its provisions for privatising the electricity industry. Electricity suppliers are required to be licensed by the Secretary of State for Energy and have a duty to "develop and maintain an efficient, co-ordinated and economical system of electricity supply". A licence is also required to transmit electricity and the duties of licence-holders are to "develop and maintain an efficient, co-ordinated and economical system of electricity transmission"; and to "facilitate competition in the supply and generation of electricity".

7.8 The EA 1989 includes conditions for charging and setting tariffs, requirements for planning consents for new construction and overhead lines and performance standards to ensure consumer protection. There are also provisions for the establishment of local consumers' committees and a National Consumers' Consultative Committee. A Public Electricity Supply Code is contained in a Schedule to the Act. Section 32 of the EA 1989 states that electricity generated by non-fossil fuel generating stations must be utilised by electricity supply companies.

7.9 Nuclear power stations and other nuclear sites must be licensed by the Secretary of State according to the Nuclear Installations Act 1965. This Act also details the duties of licencees with regard to operating procedure and safety standards. British Nuclear Fuels Ltd. (BNFL) was established as a separate company from the United Kingdom Atomic Energy Authority (UKAEA) under the provisions of the Atomic Energy Authority Act 1971. UKAEA itself subsequently had its finances put on a trading fund basis in the Atomic Energy Authority Act 1986. Provisions for control and funding of nuclear electricity generation are being developed in the light of changes brought about through the EA 1989. Other details on the law relating to the nuclear industry appear in Chapter 3.

7.10 The Gas Act (GA) 1986 also contains regulations controlling gas supply and provisions for privatising the industry. Public gas suppliers must be authorised by the Secretary of State, whilst their duties are "to develop and maintain an efficient, co-ordinated and economical system of gas supply; and to comply, subject to certain conditions, with any request to supply gas" and, "to avoid any undue preference in the supply of gas to persons entitled to a supply".

7.11 The GA 1986 also specifies the basis for charges, quality standards (for pressure, purity and uniformity of calorific value) and safety regulations. A Public Gas Supply Code is given in a Schedule of the Act. Consumer protection will be further ensured through the establishment of a Gas Consumers' Council.

7.12 The UK coal industry is nationalised, although there are also numerous small private mines. Operations in all mines are subject to safety regulations given in the Health and Safety at Work etc. Act 1974 and the Mines and Quarries Act 1954. The coal industry was reorganised under the Coal Industry Act 1987 which created the British Coal Corporation (BCC) from the National Coal Board. The Act also made provisions for financial support of BCC through grants and trusts extended by the Coal Industry Act 1990.

7.13 Control of land-based and offshore oil and gas production was originally established in the Petroleum (Production) Act 1934. The laws concerning licensing of production sites were amended in the Petroleum Act (PA) 1987. Exploration and drilling activities are subject to the provisions of the Oil and Gas Enterprise Act 1982. The PA 1987 made further provisions for the establishment of safety zones around offshore installations. Transport of oil and gas by pipeline is covered by the Oil and Pipelines Act 1985. This established the Oil and Pipelines Agency to replace the British National Oil Corporation as the national regulatory body.

7.14 Though UK energy production supply policy is now well defined in law, there are no specific provisions in the Electricity or Gas Acts for the promotion of energy conservation. The Energy Conservation Act 1981 contained some provisions for regulating the "design, construction and operation of certain energy-consuming appliances" (so as to ensure their efficiency) and for the testing of certain heat generators. This Act also made provision for grants for purposes of energy conservation schemes.

Organisations

European

7.15 The Energy Directorate of the Commission has interests in energy supply, consumption and efficiency throughout the Community. It is responsible for Community energy policy, as outlined in Council Resolutions, and also commissions studies. A study of the North West Region of the UK was commissioned by the Directorate in 1985 and published in 1987 (Commission of European Communities, 1987). Data from this report are included in this Chapter.

Central Government

7.16 The Department of Energy (DEn) is responsible for all energy-related issues in the UK. It publishes annual statistics on production and use (Department of Energy, 1989c) and papers and guidance on specific issues.

7.17 The Energy Efficiency Office (EEO), established by DEn in 1984 with a Regional Office in Manchester, promotes efficient energy use in the domestic, commercial and industrial sectors. It gives information and advice on energy conservation and is involved in research and development, and conservation schemes, through the Building Research Energy Conservation Support Unit (BRECSU). The Energy Technology Support Unit (ETSU) of DEn is actively involved in research into alternative energy sources through its Renewable Energy section.

Local Government

7.18 Local authorities are major users of energy and influence matters in other ways – for example, through their rôles as planning and highway authorities. In the case of Lancashire, the County Council's energy policy is formulated and implemented through its Energy Management Unit (EMU). This produces an annual Energy Performance Review and promotes energy conservation measures. EMU also gives technical advice to Council Departments on energy conservation measures. District Councils have developed and implemented their own individual energy policies, similar to those of the County Council.

Other Organisations

7.19 Apart from that supplied by BCC and Nuclear Electric, all energy in the UK now comes from private companies. The EA 1989 created three new generating, transmission and supply Companies: Powergen, National Power and Nuclear Electric. These provide electricity to the national grid which is controlled by the National Grid Company. Electricity is then distributed by the Regional Electricity Boards, who pay the generating companies for the electricity they use. Lancashire's electricity is supplied by the North Western Electricity Board (NORWEB).

7.20 British Gas North Western are responsible for gas supplies to the County and are authorised as a public gas supplier, subject to the conditions in the GA 1986. Hydrocarbons (GB) Ltd.(a subsidiary of British Gas plc) are responsible for operations in the Morecambe Bay gas field.

7.21 Solid fuels are supplied by BCC and numerous private companies. Oil and petroleum supplies to the County are distributed entirely by the private sector ranging from small, local companies to the large multi-nationals.

7.22 The GA 1986 and EA 1989 established groups to ensure consumer protection. Local consumer committees will be formed in Regional Electricity Board areas and there is also a national Gas Consumers' Council. Gas and electricity supply companies are obliged to consult their respective consumers' organisations and to ensure that consumer views are taken into account.

7.23 The Institute of Energy is the professional body for the industry. It and DEn have jointly established the Centre for Research, Education and Training in Energy, (CREATE), to promote energy education at primary, secondary and tertiary levels.

7.24 The Watt Committee on Energy is a charitable body which provides technical advice and publishes reports on specific energy issues. Organisations such as the Electricity Association also produce statistical information. The Association for the Conservation of Energy was established in 1982 by Companies involved in energy conservation as a further source of advice and information. The charity, Neighbourhood Energy Action (NEA) actively supports community energy conservation schemes.

Energy in Lancashire

Energy Sources, Production and Supply

7.25 There are many sources of energy in Lancashire. There are deposits of fossil fuels: coal, oil and natural gas beneath the County and Morecambe Bay. There are fast flowing streams, tides and waves. Strong winds blow onto the coast and in the uplands. Hot dry rocks and deposits of hot water in aquifers lie far below the surface of the County. The sun shines strongly in the early summer months, particularly on the coast. Woodlands cover 5% of the County's land surface, producing timber which could be used as fuel. Meanwhile, millions of tonnes of agricultural, industrial, household and commercial waste are produced every year by human activities in the County. These could be burnt to produce heat or, the 'landfill gas' they produce could be used to create heat or electricity. At Springfields, uranium fuel is produced for the nuclear power stations at Heysham and for other stations in the UK and abroad. Of all these 'native' sources, those most exploited to produce energy are natural gas from Morecambe Bay and the nuclear fuel from Springfields.

Electricity

7.26 There are two electricity generating stations in Lancashire, at Padiham and Heysham (see Figure 97). Padiham Power Station is owned by National Power and currently uses coal and oil to fire its steam generators. However, this is likely to change because Padiham is one of three UK sites where National Power are planning to install a combined-cycle gas turbine.

7.27 Heysham Power Station is a nuclear power station owned by Nuclear Electric. Uranium

Table 72 Generating Capacity of Lancashire Power Stations. 1990

Station	Gross generating capacity (MW) Sets	Net Capability (MW)	Type of Fuel	Generating Company
Padiham	2×120	224	Coal/oil	National Power
Heysham 1	2×660	1,020	UO_2	Nuclear Electric
Heysham 2	2×660	1,230	UO_2	Nuclear Electric
Heysham (Auxillary)	4×17.5	—	Gas	Nuclear Electric
Heysham 2 (Auxillary)	4×6.7+ 4×5.3	47.6	Diesel	Nuclear Electric

Sources: NORWEB (pers. comm.). Nuclear Electric (pers. comm.) and The Electricity Council (1989).

Table 73 Small Scale Electricity Generation in Lancashire. 1989

District	Operator	Site	Fuel	Generator site (kW)	Combined Heat and Power
Wyre	ICI	Hillhouse	—	48,000	—
Ribble Valley	NWW	Stocks	Hydro	0	—
Blackpool	Blackpool Health Authority	Victoria Hospital	Diesel	464	—
Fylde	Fylde Borough Council	Kirkham Baths	Natural Gas	15	YES
	Toby Restaurants	Grand Hotel St. Annes	Natural Gas	15	YES
Preston	Barclays Bank	Garstang Road Preston	Natural Gas	15	YES
	NWW	Preston Effluent Treatment Works, Broughton	Natural Gas	0	—
South Ribble	Leyland Vehicles	Spurrier/Farrington Works, Leyland	Diesel	7,500	—
	Whitbread	Samlesbury	Diesel	2,800	—
West Lancashire	West Lancashire District Council	Park Pool, Ormskirk	Natural Gas	40	YES
Chorley	Chorley Borough Council	Baths, Union Street	Natural Gas	15	YES
	Royal Ordnance Factory	Chorley	—	8,250	—
Burnley	Burnley Borough Council	Padiham Pool	Natural Gas	40	YES
	Burnley Borough Council	William Thompson Centre, Burnley	Natural Gas	120	YES
	Smurfit Paper Mills	Calverdale Road, Burnley	Steam	980	—
Rossendale	NWW	Ewood Bridge Effluent Treatment Works, Haslingden	Natural Gas	40	YES

Source: North Western Electricity Board (1989)

Figure 97
Energy Production and Potential in Lancashire. 1990

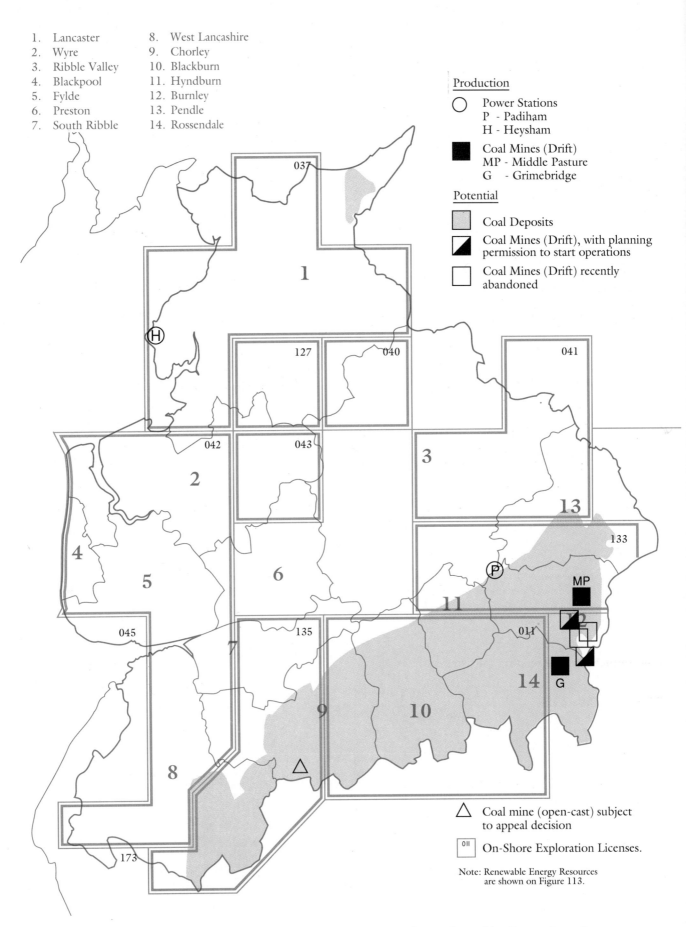

1. Lancaster
2. Wyre
3. Ribble Valley
4. Blackpool
5. Fylde
6. Preston
7. South Ribble
8. West Lancashire
9. Chorley
10. Blackburn
11. Hyndburn
12. Burnley
13. Pendle
14. Rossendale

Production

○ Power Stations
P - Padiham
H - Heysham

■ Coal Mines (Drift)
MP - Middle Pasture
G - Grimebridge

Potential

Coal Deposits

Coal Mines (Drift), with planning permission to start operations

Coal Mines (Drift) recently abandoned

△ Coal mine (open-cast) subject to appeal decision

On-Shore Exploration Licenses.

Note: Renewable Energy Resources are shown on Figure 113.

Source: Lancashire County Council

dioxide, supplied by BNFL at Springfields, is its main fuel. Heysham has two generating stations, Heysham 1 and 2. Both are Advanced Gas Cooled Reactors (AGRs), commissioned in 1983 and 1988 respectively. Heysham 1 also has auxillary gas turbines which can be used for on site emergency supplies, whilst Heysham 2 has diesel generators for emergencies.

7.28   The maximum generating capacities of Padiham and Heysham are given in Table 72. However, neither operates at full capacity throughout the year. The actual power generated annually by the two Lancashire stations is not available.

7.29   Both stations supply electicity to the national grid. Any electricity supplied to the grid becomes available nationally and its source cannot be distinguished. Therefore, electricity generated within Lancashire is not necessarily used within the County.

7.30   Lancashire's electricity is supplied and distributed by NORWEB from the grid. NORWEB also supply all of Cumbria and Greater Manchester. Lancashire contains 586,000 (28%) of NORWEB's 2,096,000 customers.

7.31   There is also some small scale electricity generation in Lancashire, (see Table 73) used to supply the localised power needs of the individual generators.

Gas

7.32   The UK is virtually self-sufficient in natural gas, principally from offshore drilling platforms in the North Sea and Morecambe Bay. In 1988, 975 million m^3 of natural gas were extracted from the Morecambe Bay gas field, sufficient to supply approximately 350 million therms of energy. Two new platforms for the Morecambe Bay gas field have been built and will begin production towards the end of 1990.

7.33   Gas from these fields enters the national distribution system, making it impossible to identify a particular source of Lancashire's gas. Gas is distributed throughout Lancashire by British Gas North Western. It is supplied at an elevated pressure to the outskirts of towns and villages and the pressure is then reduced before feeding into street mains.

Solid and Liquid Fuels

7.34   Very little coal is now mined in Lancashire. The extent of deposits and mining activity are shown on Figure 97. There are no active open-cast mines in the County, although BCC applied to extract 1 million tonnes from a 162 ha site at Ellerbeck West near Coppull, Chorley. This proposal went to a second public inquiry in January 1990. The Secretary of State for the Environment subsequently rejected the appeal on ecological and landscape grounds.

7.35   Two small, privately owned drift mines, Grimbridge (SD 852 248) and Middle Pasture (SD 887 303), are currently extracting coal in East Lancashire. Their combined output is probably less than 100 tonnes per week. Two other drift mines have been granted planning permission to commence operations, whilst a further two have closed in recent years (see Figure 97).

7.36   Virtually all coal consumed within the County is imported and then distributed by numerous private wholesalers. Padiham Power Station is currently the largest single consumer. However, coal is still an important domestic fuel in East Lancashire. Many of these areas are covered by Smoke Control Orders, which have been instrumental in reducing pollution levels associated with fossil fuel burning (see Chapter 3).

7.37   All liquid fuels consumed in Lancashire are imported through a variety of wholesalers and distributors. These provide heavy fuel oils, gas oils (diesel), petrol and aviation fuel.

Other Reserves

7.38   The potential for exploitation of oil and gas reserves has been explored in parts of the County. Exploration licences have been granted by the DEn to the Amoco, Pendle, Enterprise, British Gas, Teredo, Clyde, Sovereign and Edinburgh Companies for exploratory wells to be drilled. None have yet applied for an appraisal licence. Areas in Lancashire licensed for exploration are shown on Figure 97. The greatest potential is thought to lie in the Fylde and Ribble estuary area, which is being explored by British Gas.

Energy Consumption

7.39   Energy consumption data specific to Lancashire are largely unavailable, because the energy industry is structured nationally and regionally.

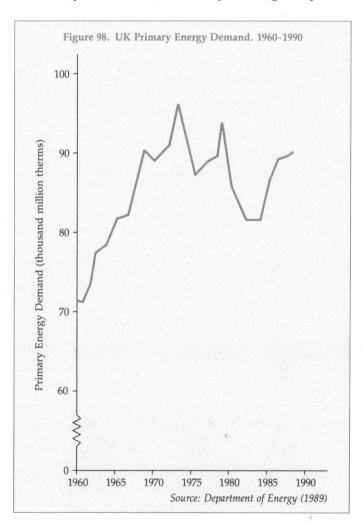

Figure 98. UK Primary Energy Demand. 1960–1990

Source: Department of Energy (1989)

Regional statistics have to be used on the assumption that Lancashire's position is typical of the region. The County may not account for as much of the region's energy consumption relative to area as the Merseyside and Greater Manchester conurbations, but the proportional consumption by different user groups is likely to be similar throughout the North West.

7.40   UK primary demand increased throughout the 1960s, but has fluctuated widely in recent years without showing any particular trend (Figure 98). Demand by source, however, shows clearer trends (Figure 99). There was a notable rise in the use of gas throughout the 1970s and 1980s, coupled with a decline in the use of coal. There has also been an increase in electricity demand since 1960, whilst

petrol demand has declined after peaking in 1970. It is more than likely that Lancashire's energy demand has mirrored these trends.

7.41   The 1987 study of energy use in the North West (Commission of European Communities, 1987) includes records of energy consumption in the region for 1985/86. Corresponding information was supplied by British Gas. This provides the most recent information on total energy demand in the North West.

7.42   Figure 100 shows the proportional contribution of different fuel sources to North West energy demand for the domestic, transport, commercial and industrial sectors. Energy use by individual sectors is shown in Figure 101. Gas dominates domestic fuel consumption and is also the major energy source for industry. Solid fuels are only used to a limited extent in these sectors. Liquid fuels (oil, or its derivatives) supply the greatest proportion of commercial energy demand and virtually all transport demand. In the transport sector, only electrified railway lines do not use liquid fuel and these

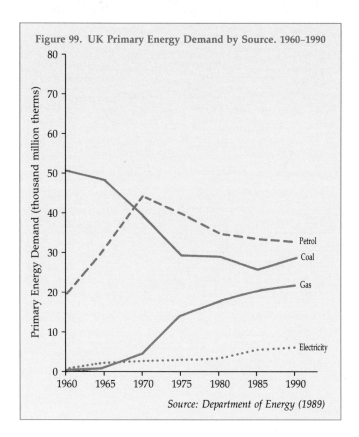

Figure 99. UK Primary Energy Demand by Source. 1960–1990

Source: Department of Energy (1989)

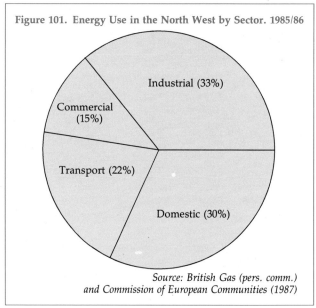

Figure 101. Energy Use in the North West by Sector. 1985/86

Source: British Gas (pers. comm.)
and Commission of European Communities (1987)

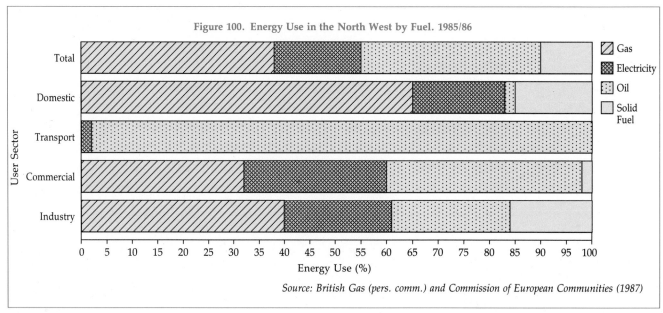

Figure 100. Energy Use in the North West by Fuel. 1985/86

Source: British Gas (pers. comm.) and Commission of European Communities (1987)

account for only a very small percentage of transport energy consumption. Electricity provides roughly similar proportions of the Region's domestic, commercial and industrial needs.

Electricity

7.43 Sales of electricity by NORWEB in the North West have increased substantially in the 1980s (see Figure 102). Present consumption in Lancashire is not available as such figures are regarded as 'commercially sensitive'. By far the greatest number of NORWEB customers are domestic consumers (Figure 103) but, despite this, the domestic sector accounts for a lower proportion of sales than the industrial sector. The latter constitutes only 0.5% of NORWEB's customers, but accounts for 37.6% of all sales (Figure 104).

7.44 Electricity demand throughout the UK shows a marked daily trend (Figure 105) with constantly higher demand in winter than in summer. Demand also rises sharply at the start of the day, but then declines and remains steady before an evening peak (around 6 p.m.), corresponding with the increase in domestic activity. Demand then declines through the night. Use of storage heaters causes a rise in demand between midnight and 3 a.m. in winter. This daily trend shows the impact of domestic sector energy needs on the supply system.

7.45 Domestic consumption (which constitutes 34% of NORWEB's sales) consists of numerous components (Figure 106). In households using electricity for all their needs, heating of both water and living space consumes the greatest amount (35.3% of total). After heating, appliances which are run

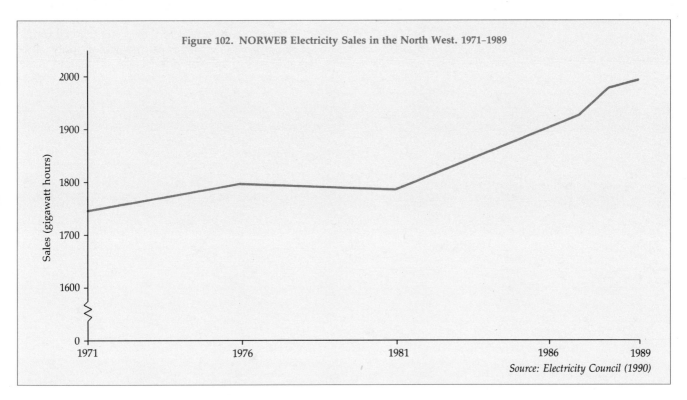

Figure 102. NORWEB Electricity Sales in the North West. 1971-1989

Source: Electricity Council (1990)

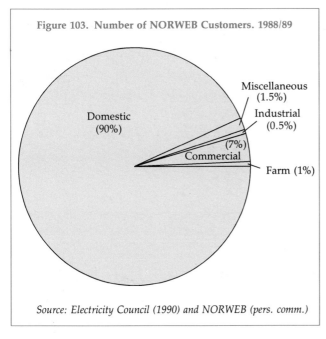

Figure 103. Number of NORWEB Customers. 1988/89

Source: Electricity Council (1990) and NORWEB (pers. comm.)

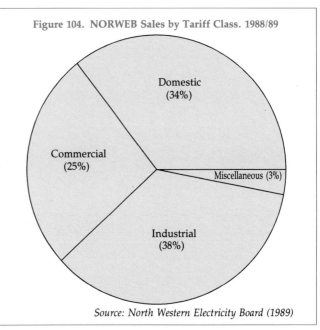

Figure 104. NORWEB Sales by Tariff Class. 1988/89

Source: North Western Electricity Board (1989)

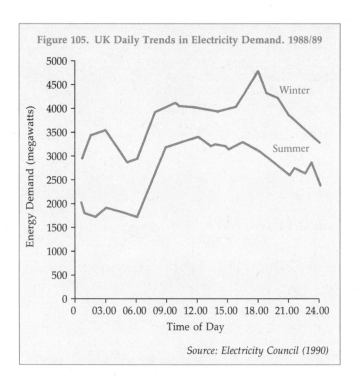

Figure 105. UK Daily Trends in Electricity Demand. 1988/89

Source: Electricity Council (1990)

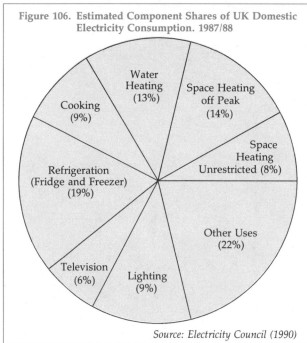

Figure 106. Estimated Component Shares of UK Domestic Electricity Consumption. 1987/88

Source: Electricity Council (1990)

continuously, or frequently, (e.g. refrigerators, freezers and cookers), consume the most electricity.

Gas

7.46 Though the production and use of all fossil fuels damage the environment, gas is a cleaner fuel than most. Increased use of gas therefore will help Lancashire's, and the wider, environment to some degree. UK consumption has, in fact, grown three-fold in the last 20 years (Figure 107) but now appears to be tailing off, although the number of customers continues to rise. Gas sales in Lancashire comprise approximately 2.6% of total UK sales. Figure 108 shows the proportion of Lancashire gas sales to each tariff (or consumer) sector. Unlike electricity, the domestic sector gas sales constitute a greater proportion than both the industrial and commercial sales put together.

7.47 Gas consumption varies throughout the County, reflecting the character of each District (Figure 109). Domestic consumption is particularly high in more densely populated districts like Lancaster, Preston, Blackburn and Blackpool and is lowest in the sparsely populated Ribble Valley. Industrial consumption is greatest in Lancaster and Blackburn.

7.48 Gas is continuing to increase in importance as an energy source in all sectors of the community, as more homes and business premises instal gas central heating and factories switch from coal and oil to gas-fired boilers. Gas is also the fuel used for the energy efficient combined heat and power (CHP) systems and the combined space and water-heating systems which are being increasingly used by industry and the public sector. This involves the use of electricity generating plant fitted with heat

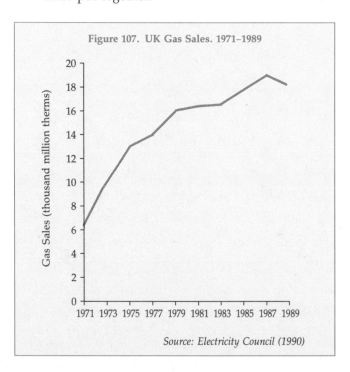

Figure 107. UK Gas Sales. 1971–1989

Source: Electricity Council (1990)

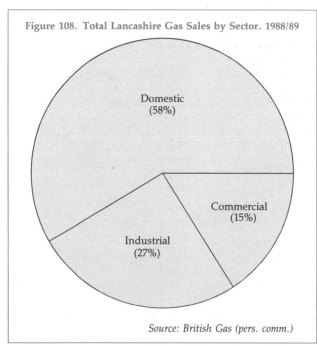

Figure 108. Total Lancashire Gas Sales by Sector. 1988/89

Source: British Gas (pers. comm.)

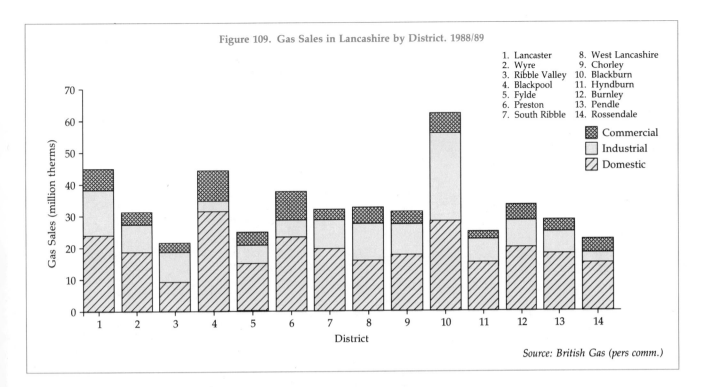

Figure 109. Gas Sales in Lancashire by District. 1988/89

1. Lancaster   8. West Lancashire
2. Wyre   9. Chorley
3. Ribble Valley   10. Blackburn
4. Blackpool   11. Hyndburn
5. Fylde   12. Burnley
6. Preston   13. Pendle
7. South Ribble   14. Rossendale

Commercial
Industrial
Domestic

Source: British Gas (pers comm.)

recovery facilities, thus providing both electricity and useable heat. Table 73 shows eight organisations that have adopted the CHP system in Lancashire.

Liquid and Solid Fuels

7.49 Transport relies almost exclusively on liquid fuels, and road traffic is by far the greatest consumer in the region (Figure 110). Transport accounts for two thirds of the total fuel oil consumption in the North West with most of the rest being consumed by industry and commerce. Assuming that this proportion applies to Lancashire, the total annual fuel oil consumption in the County is in the order of 1,224 million gallons.

7.50 Comparable estimates for solid fuel consumption in Lancashire are impossible to obtain. Solids do, however, account for a much smaller proportion of energy use in the North West than liquid fuels (Figure 100). They are used principally in the industrial and domestic sectors, particularly in East Lancashire. Smoke control restrictions, and the increasing use of gas central heating systems, are contributing to a decline in domestic solid fuel use. Many industrial consumers are also converting to gas in preference to solid fuel. These changes have an important environmental effect, as gas produces less air pollution than solid fuel, giving rise to no ash, dust or smoke and lower levels of SO_2 and NO_2 (see Figures 111 and 112).

Renewable and Alternative Resources

7.51 Renewable energy is defined as 'those continuous energy flows that occur naturally and repeatedly in the environment'. Because they usually do not give rise to emissions of gases, such sources are generally far less damaging to the environment (though there can be visual problems). Current policy, however, remains firmly fixed in favour of traditional, non-renewable energy

resources. But the major pollution problems associated with the latter are focussing more and more attention on renewable sources. As finite resources of fossil fuels dwindle, they will become more expensive thus making other, currently uneconomic resources more commercially viable. Although this problem can be ameliorated by more energy efficient technology, the rôle of renewable resources looks set to become increasingly important in future years. Indeed, with privatisation, the electricity supply companies will be obliged to purchase at least some energy from non-fossil fuel sources. This includes both renewable and nuclear forms.

7.52 This section summarises the renewable energy resources already in use, or having potential, for electricity generation in Lancashire (shown on Figure 113) (Energy Technology Support Unit,

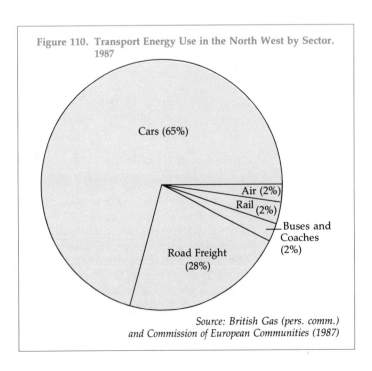

Figure 110. Transport Energy Use in the North West by Sector. 1987

Cars (65%)

Air (2%)
Rail (2%)
Buses and Coaches (2%)
Road Freight (28%)

Source: British Gas (pers. comm.)
and Commission of European Communities (1987)

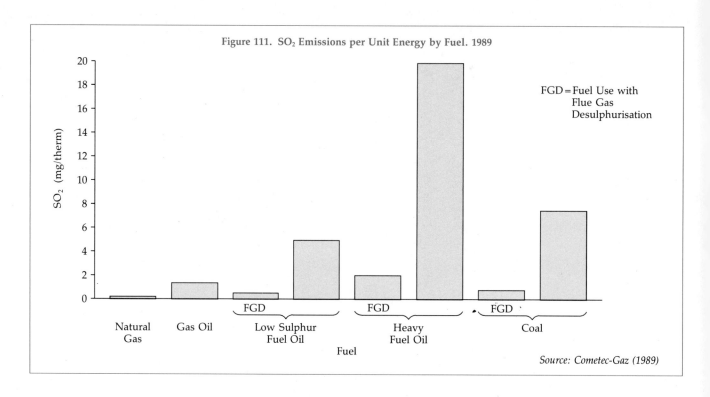

Figure 111. SO$_2$ Emissions per Unit Energy by Fuel. 1989

FGD = Fuel Use with Flue Gas Desulphurisation

Source: Cometec-Gaz (1989)

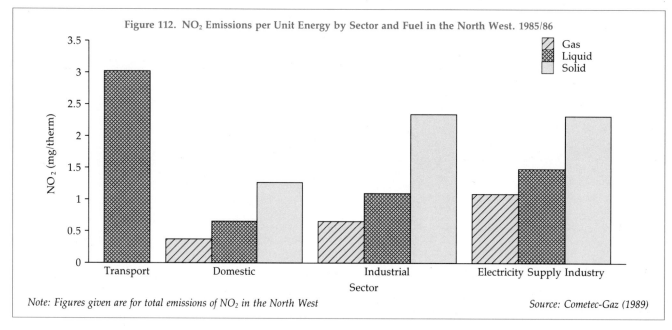

Figure 112. NO$_2$ Emissions per Unit Energy by Sector and Fuel in the North West. 1985/86

Gas
Liquid
Solid

Note: Figures given are for total emissions of NO$_2$ in the North West

Source: Cometec-Gaz (1989)

1989). Energy from water, the sun, wind, biofuels and geothermal sources are considered in turn. Some forms of energy are not renewable as such, but relate to large natural resources (for example, geothermal energy), whilst others relate more to recycling activity (for example, the use of landfill gas). It is, however, convenient to consider them all together.

7.53   In 1988 NORWEB and ETSU initiated a joint study on renewable energy in the North West (North Western Electricity Board/Energy Technology Support Unit, 1989). The report assesses the current status and future trends of renewable resources in the region from the stance of a private sector organisation, and not necessarily from the point of view of the environmental benefits involved.

Energy from Water

7.54   There are three forms of water-generated energy currently, or potentially, exploitable in Lancashire: hydro-electric power (HEP), tidal power, and wave energy.

7.55   Though the County is not considered to have potential for the large scale production of HEP locally, conditions exist where it could be economic to generate power at sites which have heads of water of 3 m, or more, (i.e. where running water falls a vertical distance of 3 m, or more, within a short horizontal distance). There are no sites currently used although NORWEB/ETSU (1989) identify three possible locations. These are Barnacre Reservoir (Wyre), Belmont Reservoir and Blackburn Effluent Treatment Works (both in Blackburn). All three sites are owned by North

Figure 113
Existing and Potential Renewable Energy Resources in Lancashire . 1990

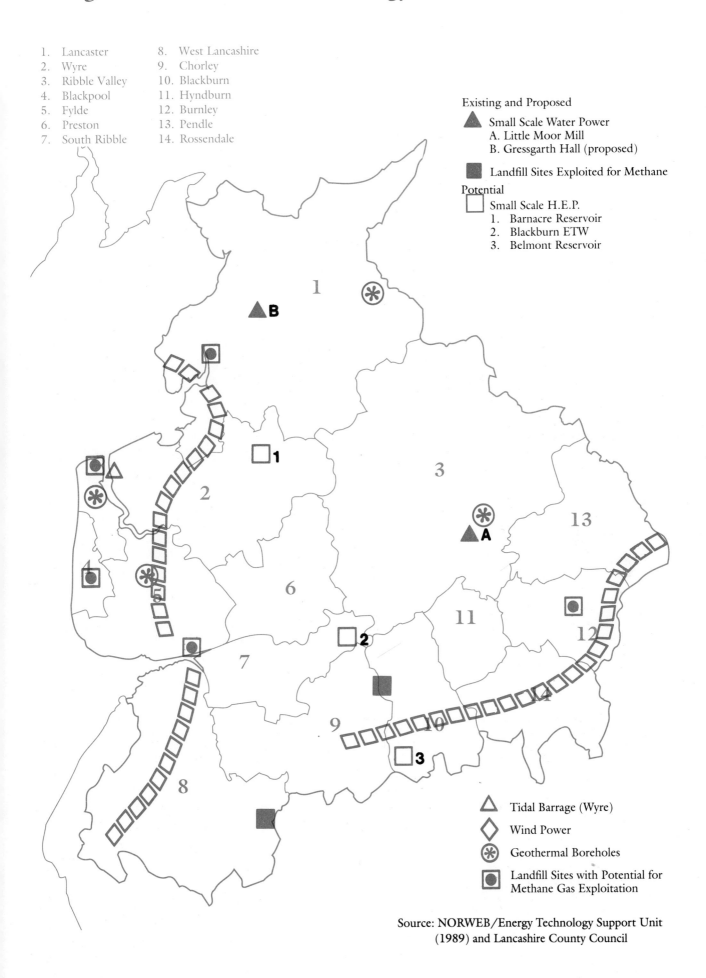

1. Lancaster
2. Wyre
3. Ribble Valley
4. Blackpool
5. Fylde
6. Preston
7. South Ribble
8. West Lancashire
9. Chorley
10. Blackburn
11. Hyndburn
12. Burnley
13. Pendle
14. Rossendale

Existing and Proposed

▲ Small Scale Water Power
A. Little Moor Mill
B. Gressgarth Hall (proposed)

■ Landfill Sites Exploited for Methane

Potential

□ Small Scale H.E.P.
1. Barnacre Reservoir
2. Blackburn ETW
3. Belmont Reservoir

△ Tidal Barrage (Wyre)

◇ Wind Power

✳ Geothermal Boreholes

◉ Landfill Sites with Potential for Methane Gas Exploitation

Source: NORWEB/Energy Technology Support Unit
(1989) and Lancashire County Council

West Water. They could contribute 0.33 megawatts of the total estimated maximum output of 3.6 megawatts (that is 9% of the total estimated maximum output), at an average of 2.2 pence per kilowatt hour. The use of small-scale HEP schemes is generally considered economically attractive by the Energy Technology Support Unit (1989a).

7.56 The National Association of Water Power Users (NAWPU), formed in 1975, promotes the use of water power for energy production. Principal methods are water-driven mill wheels or turbines. Under the Water Act 1989, charges for the abstraction of water solely on a volume basis were abolished. This has made smaller scale water power generation more attractive. Before the advent of large-scale coal production in the nineteenth century, Lancashire's industry was powered by hundreds of water wheels on the fast-running streams which flow down from our moors and fells. Widespread water-generated power ceased long ago and today there is one private water power generator in Lancashire (registered with NAWPU). This is Littlemoor Mill, Clitheroe (Ribble Valley), which has two water powered turbines. There is also a proposal, to instal a single turbine at Gressgarth Hall, Caton, (Lancaster).

7.57 Tidal movements can be exploited by the construction of barrages across estuaries. Such barrages contain turbines driven by the movement of the tides. The NORWEB/ETSU study does not consider a Morecambe Bay barrage to be a serious proposition, because it would be so large that its output would be impossible to integrate exclusively into the NORWEB area. It would exceed the non-fossil fuel requirements contained in the EA 1989. With an annual energy output of 5,400 gigawatt hours, it would provide the third highest estimated output behind the Severn and Solway Firth (Energy Technology Support Unit, 1989a). Together, these three estuaries could produce 12% of the current total UK generation (Energy Technology Support Unit, 1989b).

7.58 Other, smaller-scale sites with potential have been identified on the Wyre and Lune estuaries (Energy Technology Support Unit, 1989b) (see Figure 113). The Wyre estuary is viewed as the best prospect. Estimates of the cost of electricity from a Wyre barrage are 4.0–4.9 pence per kilowatt hour. It would have an estimated installed capacity of 27 megawatts and an annual output of 90,000 megawatt hours per year. A feasibility study for a Wyre barrage has recently been approved at an estimated cost of £200,000, of which two-thirds has been provided by DEn. The remainder will be provided by NORWEB, Lancashire County Council, Lancashire County Enterprises Ltd., and the National Rivers Authority. The feasibility study will investigate the potential effects of a barrage on the natural and man-made environments of the river, its estuary and surrounding land. It will also establish the engineering design, cost and energy output of the barrage and its economic feasibility as an electricity generating scheme. This investigation is only a first stage. If the barrage is found to be feasible, more detailed work will be required to finalise a scheme.

7.59 This is the first major proposal in Lancashire to investigate power generation from alternative sources. However, all potential environmental impacts including impact on wildlife habitats, flooding and water quality will have to be studied and balanced against the benefits of energy production before development can be considered.

7.60 There are two potentially exploitable forms of wave energy – inshore and offshore. Energy from wave resources is discounted by the North Western Electricity Board/Energy Technology Support Unit study due to the unsuitable nature of the Lancashire coast. The high tidal range, shelving coastline, lack of a long wave reach, combined with the limitations of existing technology, render the development of inshore and offshore wave resources unlikely in the forseeable future.

Solar Energy

7.61 There are three main methods of harnessing energy from the sun: passive, active and photovoltaic.

7.62 Passive solar heating involves heating the air inside buildings by solar radiation from large glass panels on south facing walls (like a greenhouse). This is not so much a form of electricity production, as a means of securing energy efficiency. Heat loss can be minimised by well insulated floors, roofspace and walls with a much smaller glazed area on the north facing walls. Passive solar design technology is considered as economically attractive by the Energy Technology Support Unit (1989a).

7.63 Active heating, using solar panels on roofs and south-facing facades, is currently expensive and at present seems unlikely to become cost-effective in the UK on a widespread basis. It does, however, have potential for special applications, like heating of swimming pools. The extent of any application of either passive or active technology in Lancashire is not known.

7.64 Photovoltaics involves the use of photo-electric cells to generate electricity from sunlight. Costs are currently high and its wider application depends upon a decrease by a factor of 10 or 20 before it can compete economically with other sources (Energy Technology Support Unit, 1989a). The method is most efficient in cloud free conditions but still operates with reasonable efficiency on cloudy days. Figure 11 shows Lancashire's average hours of sunshine throughout the year and a reasonable level of efficiency could be expected from a photovoltaics system in Lancashire.

Wind Energy

7.65 Wind is regarded as a highly promising energy resource within the NORWEB area (North Western Electricity Board/Energy Technology Support Unit, 1989). Its energy can be harnessed from both onshore and offshore sources.

7.66 The exposed nature of Lancashire's coast, combined with high ground inland, results in higher than average windspeeds (see Figure 14). These make the County potentially favourable for wind power developments. NORWEB estimate that in their area as a whole approximately 283 square km could be available for up to 2,300 turbines generating 1–2 terawatts per annum, at a cost of 2–4 pence per kilowatt hour. These areas are free from major physical constraints like towns, villages, woods and lakes. Other constraints include major road and rail systems, and sensitive landscapes like Areas of Outstanding Natural Beauty.

7.67 However, turbines have an appreciable environmental impact. Large areas are required for wind parks, because individual turbines cannot be located too close to one another due to the disruption of wind patterns. The two main impacts are visual and the generation of noise. Most of Lancashire's coast is dominated by urban development and is therefore unsuitable for large wind parks. However, the area around Morecambe Bay, the Fylde, West Lancashire and the uplands of East Lancashire are relatively undeveloped, making them potential sites for wind turbines. But, their suitability at a local level would need to be investigated very carefully indeed.

7.68 The prospects for offshore wind energy are not as promising, because of high installation and maintenance costs. Indeed, NORWEB/ETSU (1989) do not include offshore wind resources in their study. In terms of environmental impact, this option is preferable to onshore wind energy development as aesthetic intrusion and noise problems would both be negligible.

Geothermal Energy

7.69 Geothermal energy is derived from heat currents in the earth's mantle and can be harnessed either from aquifers or 'hot, dry rocks'.

7.70 The latter is achieved by passing water over the surface of impermeable hot rocks in the earth's crust (like granite) and pumping the heated water back to the surface. There is no known potential for this technique in Lancashire, because the relevant geological formations lie too far below the surface.

7.71 Geothermal aquifers with temperatures less than 150°C, are not considered to be commercially viable at present. Higher temperatures are found only in active volcanic regions and are therefore not relevant to the UK. The West Lancashire aquifer is unlikely to attain temperatures greater than 40°C (North Western Electricity Board/Energy Technology Support Unit, 1989), and does not provide a viable option. Four exploratory boreholes were sunk in Lancashire to determine the feasibility of geothermal heat energy (see Figure 113), but these preliminary investigations have not been taken any further forward.

Biofuels

7.72 Biofuels are derived from solid, liquid or gaseous substances produced from organic matter; the principal forms being timber and various types of waste.

7.73 NORWEB/ETSU (1989) identified two principal uses of wood for energy: 'residue from conventional forestry practices' and 'energy forestry' (where trees are grown specifically for fuel). The former involves the combustion of branches, stumps, bark, roots and tree tops discarded after conventional forestry practice, whilst the latter consists of managing timber on a short-term rotational basis (e.g. coppicing).

7.74 NORWEB/ETSU estimate that wood harvesting in the UK will nearly double to 8.5 million m^3 per annum as post-war plantations mature. In addition, incentives to plant, (e.g. under the farm set-aside scheme) and other concessions will ensure that more trees continue to be planted. However, because of the very low area of woodland in Lancashire, our potential contribution to both these energy sources is limited. A small experiment in coppicing and marketing farm timber for wood-burning stoves began in the Forest of Bowland a few years ago. It has proved a viable venture, though the initiative has not been taken up elsewhere.

7.75 The digestion of wet waste by anaerobic bacteria results in the generation of methane-rich biogas. Methane can be generated from animal waste and crop residue, or from landfill sites. The gas can be used to generate electricity, or as a direct replacement for fossil fuels in boilers or furnaces. It can also be upgraded for use as a high quality fuel.

7.76 The disposal of domestic and industrial waste to landfill tips creates the appropriate conditions for bacteria to degrade the waste and produce methane. As 98% of all refuse is presently landfilled (see Chapter 5), a considerable resource has been created. It is estimated that, given proper design, around 75% of the gas available in any site is recoverable (North Western Electricity Board/Energy Technology Support Unit, 1989). Nearly 50% of UK landfill gas exploited up to 1989 was used for power generation (gas engines and generators), whilst the remainder was used to fuel boilers (18%) or kilns (32%).

7.77 Difficulties in using landfill gas arise because of low and inconsistent pressure and impurity. It cannot, therefore, be used for direct public supply, but sufficient pressure can be achieved to fuel boilers in local buildings.

7.78 In 1989/90, a total of 1.38 million tonnes of household, commercial and non-special industrial waste were generated in Lancashire. This was landfilled, and 15 sites accounted for over 200,000 tonnes of waste each. It is estimated that this landfill waste could potentially produce a gas resource of up to 37 million therms per year.

7.79 Biffa Environmental operate a landfill site at Withnell, Blackburn, and are currently installing a gas extraction system. The methane extracted will be used by the company and a system is being installed to supply electricity into the national grid. At Appley Bridge, West Lancashire, Wimpey Waste Management use landfill methane to fuel two 1 megawatt generators which supply electricity to the national grid and heat a local factory. These sites, and those which have potential, are shown in Table 74 and Figure 113. They represent a large potential for recycled energy in Lancashire. However, such developments have to be properly designed and engineered and gas production will decrease when the majority of waste within the site has degraded. NORWEB has shown interest in this form of energy production, but no site investigations have yet been carried out to establish the suitability of individual sites.

7.80 Household and commercial solid waste contains combustible material like paper, cardboard and wood. The incineration of solid waste is a cost-effective alternative to landfill in large urban areas. The potential of this resource in the NORWEB region is 86 megawatts, producing 602,000 megawatt hours per year at a cost of 3.5 pence per kilowatt hour. The process requires a continual supply of high volumes of waste to be economic so incinerators must be located close to a conurbation. At present, the system is not economically viable in Lancashire and there are no proposed domestic and commercial waste incinerators in the County.

7.81 Incineration of scrap tyres and clinical waste has potential in Lancashire for producing a further 40,000 megawatt hours per year at a cost of 1 pence per kilowatt hour. This could reduce disposal problems associated with landfilling this waste, and produce recycled energy. However, its burning produces toxic fumes, if the process is not carefully designed. It is essential that high temperatures are maintained at the required level throughout the combustion process and that any waste gases are treated to remove pollutants before emission to the atmosphere.

7.82 Clinical hospital waste incineration costs between £60–£150/tonne and is currently done on a fairly small-scale at individual hospitals. Incineration is likely to become more expensive as flue emissions are more closely regulated. The potential in the NORWEB area is estimated to lie between 8,400–24,000 megawatt hours per year. Various chemical waste incinerators in Lancashire already practice heat recovery for local use.

Overview

7.83 The DEn has a continuing programme of research and development into renewable energy resources. Annual expenditure on this programme was only £3.6 million in 1978/79 rising to £17.3 million in 1981/82. In 1983/84, spending was reduced to £11.3 million, but, by 1988/89, it had climbed back to £16.0 million. Table 75 summarises the UK and Lancashire potential for the different sources, based on ETSU's research programme.

7.84 In the North West, the total potential output is estimated at 15,000 gigawatt hours per year,

Table 74   Landfill Sites in Lancashire with Gas Potential. 1989

District	Site and Location	Operator
Lancaster	Salt Ayre, Lancaster [1]	Lancashire CC
Wyre	Jameson Road, Fleetwood[1]	Lancashire CC
Ribble Valley	Henthorn, Clitheroe	Lancashire CC
Blackpool	Midgeland Road, Blackpool[1]	Lancashire CC
Fylde	Grange Farm I and II, Clifton Marsh	Lancashire CC
South Ribble	Much Hoole, Longton	Lancashire CC
West Lancashire	Appley Bridge, near Skelmersdale[2]	Wimpey/ Mainsprint
	Pimbo, Skelmersdale	Wimpey/ Mainsprint
	Platts Lane, Burscough	Wimpey/ Mainsprint
Chorley	Lower Burgh, Chorley	Lancashire CC
Blackburn	Withnell Quarry, Blackburn[2]	Biffa Environmental
Hyndburn	Whinney Hill, Accrington	Lancashire CC
Burnley	Rowley, Burnley[1]	Lancashire CC
Pendle	Waidshouse Road, Nelson	Lancashire CC
Rossendale	Rakeshead, Bacup	Lancashire CC

Source: North Western Electricity Board/Energy Technology Support Unit (1989)

Notes: [1]Due to restrictions imposed by the commercial confidentiality of data held by ETSU it is not possible to give individual site potential. However, sites marked [1] might merit Norweb's further attention.
[2]Operating gas utilisation system in place.

Table 75   Assessment of Renewable Energy Scheme Potential in the UK and Lancashire. 1989

Type of Power	Type of Production	UK Prospects	Most favourable prospects for Lancashire
Water	Small-scale Low Head Hydro Power at heads of water less than 3m	Promising but Uncertain	–
	Small-scale Low Head Hydro Power at heads of water above 3m	Economically Attractive	Yes
	Tidal Energy	Promising but Uncertain	Yes
	Shoreline Wave Energy	Promising but Uncertain	–
	Large-scale Offshore Wave Energy	Long Shot	–
Solar	Passive Solar Design	Economically Attractive	Yes
	Active Solar Heating	Long Shot	–
	Photovoltaics	Long Shot	–
Wind	Wind Energy – on land	Promising but Uncertain	Yes
	Wind Energy – offshore	Long Shot	–
Geothermal	Hot Dry Rocks	Promising but Uncertain	–
	Geothermal Aquifers	Long Shot	–
Biofuels	Energy Forestry	Promising but Uncertain	–
	Anaerobic Digestion e.g. Landfill Gas	Economically Attractive	Yes
	Combustion of Dry Wastes	Economically Attractive	–

Source: North Western Electricity Board/Energy Technology Support Unit (1989).

though not all of this is commercially exploitable immediately. About 2,500 gigawatt hours per year could be produced relatively quickly at a cost of about 3 pence per kilowatt hour, mostly from biofuels and onshore wind energy. However, the majority of this potential lies in Cumbria. Lancashire does have potential, though, for contributions in the short to medium term from tidal energy, onshore wind and landfill gas.

7.85 It is essential that the development of any renewable sources in the County is preceded by an in-depth analysis of the environmental consequences. Though most alternative energy sources are environmentally desirable in themselves, they can also have disbenefits. The consequences of wide-scale alteration of estuaries for tidal barrages, use of land for wind farms, and the burning of waste can be considerable. Effects can include impacts on wildlife habitats, landscape quality and, in some circumstances, the creation of atmospheric pollution. Environmental Impact Assessment is a fundamental requirement of any feasibility study for developing all renewable (as well as non-renewable), energy schemes.

Environmental Effects

7.86 Combustion of any fossil fuel will produce a mixture of waste gases, including SO_2, NO_x and CO_2. When released into the atmosphere, these can have significant accumulative effects. In addition to waste gases, burning heavy fuels like oil and coal produces particulate wastes as smoke. The incidence of these pollutants in Lancashire, and their contribution to a range of environmental conditions, has been discussed in Chapter 3.

Acid Rain

7.87 SO_2 is the main gas associated with acid rain. It is produced primarily by the combustion of coal and fuel oils (Figure 111). Coal and oil fired power stations have been major emitters of SO_2 because of the large quantities of fuel they consume. The Government has made a commitment to the EC to reduce SO_2 emissions from power stations. This was initially to be achieved by the installation of flue gas desulphurisation (FGD), whereby sulphur is removed from waste gases prior to emission. But FGD is expensive to instal, and, despite the long-term benefits, the Government now favours the use of coal with a low sulphur content. Padiham is the only power station in Lancashire currently using coal and oil. Proposals to convert this station to a gas turbine are under consideration and, if these proceed, there will be no need for a FGD system. There are no plans at present to install a FGD system at Fiddlers Ferry, near Warrington, a large power station close to Lancashire's southern border. Drax power station in Yorkshire is the only power station in Great Britain currently being fitted with FGD equipment.

7.88 Natural gas contains very little sulphur, but small quantities of organic sulphur compounds are added to give it its distinctive smell (for safety reasons). Emissions of SO_2 from burning gas are relatively low (see Figure 111).

7.89 Combustion processes also release NO_x which contribute to acid rain, global warming and smog formation. Transport is the major contributor to NO_x emissions (Figure 112). Indeed, if the rate of NO_x emission per unit of energy produced is multiplied by total energy consumption per sector, transport produces approximately 4,535 kg of NO_2 or more than twice the amount from industry (approximately 2,014 kg), and almost five times the domestic amount (approximately 930 kg).

Global Warming

7.90 Global warming has also been considered in Chapter 3. Energy production results in emissions of several 'greenhouse gases', CO_2, methane, ozone and nitrous oxide. The latter two arise primarily from transport use (i.e. petrol burning). Natural gas is methane and so any leakage or venting, contributes to methane emissions. Something between 3% and 10% of the natural gas used by British Gas is estimated to leak to air, and add to global warming.

7.91 Most forms of energy production release CO_2, the main greenhouse gas. Thus the major emphasis of proposals for reducing CO_2 emissions is targetted at electricity generation and energy efficiency. The Department of Energy (1989b) suggests that reductions may be achieved by increased use of nuclear energy, alternative/renewable sources and energy efficient systems like CHP. Promotion of efficient energy use and conservation is also needed in the domestic, industrial and commercial sectors and implementation of such measures will have financial as well as environmental benefits.

Other Environmental Effects

7.92 The energy industry also has a significant environmental impact through its use of land. Large areas of derelict, or contaminated, land can result from production activities, requiring reclamation and decontamination before redevelopment can occur.

7.93 Coal fired power stations produce large quantities of pulverised fuel ash, which contains high concentrations of arsenic and boron. These toxic elements, combined with a very fine particle structure, make PFA very difficult to reclaim. Five Lancashire coal fired power stations have been decommissioned since the late 1970s; Fleetwood (Wyre), Lancaster, Penwortham (Preston), Blackburn and Huncoat (Hyndburn). The Fleetwood site has been partially reclaimed, the Penwortham site has been reclaimed and landscaped as recreational openspace, the Blackburn site has been reclaimed and commercially developed, the Huncoat site is undergoing redevelopment for tourism and recreation and the Lancaster site is undergoing redevelopment as a vehicle testing centre.

7.94 Gasworks used to be a feature of all Lancashire towns but they were closed with the advent of natural gas. They do, however, present serious reclamation problems, because of tar pits and waste dumps containing high concentrations of toxic metals, spent oxides, phenols, sulphates and sulphides. Their reclamation can be complex, because these contaminants must be removed before development can occur. The traditional approach is to excavate contaminated material and transport it to landfill – a process followed at Water Street, Chorley and North Road, Preston. The use of microbes to digest contaminants in-situ was pioneered and used on the Greenbank site in Blackburn. This process is discussed further in Chapter 5. Many former gas works sites have now been reclaimed and redeveloped, but others remain as contaminated sites requiring treatment.

7.95 The nuclear power industry produces radio-active waste which must be dealt with. Some is discharged directly to the atmosphere or to estuaries and coastal waters (see Chapters 3 and 4). The disposal of radioactive waste is discussed further in Chapter 5. 14,784 tonnes of low level radioactive waste were deposited at landfill sites in the County, principally at Clifton Marsh, in 1989. All 'high level' waste is processed and put into long-term storage at sites such as Drigg.

7.96 The transportation of fuels, waste products or electricity also has impacts on the environment. Heavy vehicle transport of coal and oil by road con-tributes to traffic pollution. The laying and main-tenance of pipelines and overhead wires can damage habitats and landscape and cause general disturbance to residents. The potential impact of fuel transport is particularly serious because of the risk of a major accident.

7.97 In addition to their aesthetic intrusion, it has been shown that overhead power lines emit electro-magnetic radiation. This is restricted to the imme-diate vicinity of the power line. Research on the public health effects of this form of radiation is still in its infancy but preliminary work has shown a pos-sible correlation between miscarriages, childhood cancer, tumours, headaches and nausea. Clearly, more research is required in this field.

Energy Efficiency

7.98 Great emphasis is now being placed on the efficient use and conservation of energy for both economic and environmental reasons. Improved energy efficiency is essential to reducing the emis-sion of gases that contribute to the greenhouse effect and acid rain. It is estimated that there is potential for energy savings of up to 60% in the UK with present technology (though only 20% is cur-rently economically viable) (Department of Energy, 1989). Friends of the Earth claim that the DEn's esti-mate is too pessimistic and predict that a 70% saving could be achieved over the next 15 years, with existing technology.

Domestic Sector

7.99 Domestic sector consumption is limited to a range of end uses which have been successfully modelled by the Building Research Establishment in a computer programme. This shows the measures which have the greatest impact on domestic energy use and evaluates the effects of implementing them. The most important measures for the North West are cavity wall insulation, loft insulation, draught proofing and heating controls. If these were implemented with maximum effect, it is estimated that domestic comsumption in the region could be reduced by one third (Commission of European Communities, 1987). Further savings could be achieved by the use of more efficient domestic appliances and lighting.

Industrial and Commercial Sector

7.100 The extent to which energy efficiency measures can be, or have been, implemented in this sector varies greatly. Some firms have considered energy management to be a worthwhile investment but others give it a low priority (Commission of European Communities, 1987). Many companies have implemented energy saving through 'good housekeeping', although not many have set attain-ment targets or employed full-time energy managers (Commission of European Communities, 1987).

7.101 The EEO have supplied a list of ten Lancashire-based companies, who have made sig-nificant efforts through the implementation of an energy saving policy, or through employing energy managers:

* British Telecom plc   Preston;
* Leyland Daf Ltd.   Leyland, South Ribble;
* Daniel Thwaites plc   Blackburn;
* Scapa-Porritt Ltd.   Blackburn;
* Sun Paper Mill Ltd.   Feniscowles, Blackburn;
* Enfield Manufacturing Co. Ltd.
                          Oswaldtwistle, Hyndburn;
* Wm. Blythe & Co. Ltd.   Church, Hyndburn;
* Lucas Aerospace Ltd.   Burnley;
* Rolls Royce plc   Barnoldswick, Pendle;
* Smith & Nephew Textiles Ltd.
                              Brierfield, Pendle.

Public Sector

7.102 The public sector is a major energy con-sumer, with considerable potential and incentive for implementing energy saving measures. Hospitals, schools, street lighting, public adminis-tration and other public services can all benefit from such schemes. For example, the annual energy con-sumption of the Blackburn, Hyndburn and Ribble Valley Health Authority amounts to 76,137 megawatts, which is greater than the total con-sumption of street lighting throughout the County. An example of how public agencies can implement energy reduction measures is given in paras. 7.111–7.113.

Transport Sector

7.103 There is considerable scope for improve-ment in the efficiency of transport energy use through new technology like advanced lean burn engines and improved maintenance. Driver habits are also critical. Individual drivers can affect fuel consumption by as much as 20% in identical cars (Commission of European Communities, 1987). At present, cars are sold on the basis of high perfor-mance rather than high energy efficiency. However, these priorities are changing due to cost and environmental concern. Many manufacturers are working towards better fuel economy through improved aerodynamics, engine and transmission development and reductions in vehicle weight.

7.104 Energy efficiency in the transport sector would also be achieved through a reduction in emphasis on private road transport. A switch to more public transport, reducing vehicle numbers, and a shift from road to rail haulage would have a significant impact on consumption and expenditure.

Energy Efficiency Initiatives

7.105 A number of initiatives have been introduced to improve energy efficiency and to spread public awareness of the benefits. All consumers are now being encouraged to use energy efficiently. The government give advice and encouragement via the EEO and the DOE. The former provides information and practical demonstrations to Local Authorities and Housing Associations. They also support and monitor new building schemes which adopt innovative energy saving techniques.

7.106 The main thrust of government initiatives is directed at the domestic sector and particularly at heating costs. The Homes Insulation Scheme (HIS), run by the DOE, started in 1978 and gave grants to householders towards the cost of loft, pipe and hot water tank insulation. The scheme changed in 1988 to concentrate on 'low income households' and has now been discontinued. The expenditure on HIS grants in Lancashire is shown in Figures 114 and 115. A total of £5,197 million was spent in Lancashire between 1983 and 1988.

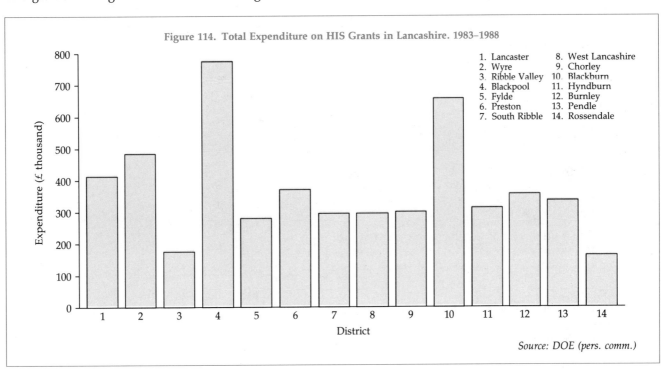

Figure 114. Total Expenditure on HIS Grants in Lancashire. 1983–1988

1. Lancaster	8. West Lancashire
2. Wyre	9. Chorley
3. Ribble Valley	10. Blackburn
4. Blackpool	11. Hyndburn
5. Fylde	12. Burnley
6. Preston	13. Pendle
7. South Ribble	14. Rossendale

Source: DOE (pers. comm.)

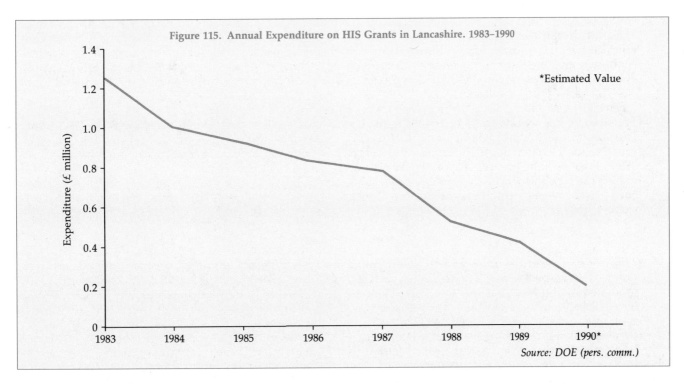

Figure 115. Annual Expenditure on HIS Grants in Lancashire. 1983–1990

*Estimated Value

Source: DOE (pers. comm.)

7.107 The scheme will be succeeded by the Home Energy Efficiency Scheme at the end of 1990. This will provide insulation and draughtproofing grants to 'low income households'. Registered network installers will be recommended to carry out the work for the householder; but there will also be provision for householders to undertake work themselves, or contract other private installers.

7.108 The government also provides support for the Community Insulation Scheme (CIS), through the charity, Neighbourhood Energy Action (NEA). CIS provides grants for the establishment of insulation projects mainly through Employment Training. All projects must be registered with NEA and are unique to their particular area. There are nine Lancashire based projects; these are the Blackpool Energy Action Team, the Burnley Energy Project, Heatsave Lancaster, Heatsave Lancaster 2, Hyndburn Energy Conservation Project, Keeping Wyre Warm, the Ormskirk and District Energy Project, Rossendale Valley Training Ltd.and the West Lancashire Energy Project. NEA are also involved in other energy efficiency initiatives like Winter of Action on Cold Homes and promoting energy efficiency in urban regeneration and housing improvement schemes.

7.109 The EEO also advises businesses about energy efficiency, whilst further support comes from energy suppliers, through advisory services and provision of awards. The electricity industry gives national Power for Efficiency and Productivity (PEP) Awards and building efficiency awards (BETA). British Gas sponsor the Gas Energy Management (GEM) Awards, both nationally and regionally. Preston Area Health Authority won this year's regional Space Heating and Hot Water GEM Award, following installation of a new system at Whittingham Hospital. A company in Skelmersdale (Tolona Pizza Products Ltd.) won the regional Process Heating GEM award. This competition has run for 15 years, during which time 564 entrants have made a cumulative saving of 436 million

therms per year. The suppliers also promote energy efficiency in the domestic sector through public information and sales campaigns e.g. the 'Use Gas Wisely' campaign.

7.110 The County and District Councils also encourage energy efficiency in the domestic sector through public information campaigns, and sometimes through insulation grants. A number of Lancashire local authorities encourage energy efficiency and conservation within their own properties. The County Council's policy is implemented by its Energy Management Unit (EMU). This is explained here as an example of the energy savings that can be made by local authorities through careful planning and expenditure.

7.111 In 1981, the County Council set itself a target of saving 25% of total energy consumption by the year 2000, from a base year of 1978/79. In 1985, the Audit Commission were asked to report on performance so far. They recommended that the 25% saving could be achieved by April 1992. Energy performance is reviewed annually by the EMU and the performance over the last 10 years (1979–89) was also reviewed in the 1990 report (Lancashire County Council, 1990).

7.112 Total monetary saving on costs since 1979–89 has been over £15 million. County energy performance, (at 1988/89 prices), despite falling below the target in 1986/87 and 1987/88, has now returned to the revised target level (Figure 116). Targets have been set for consumption of heating fuels and electricity. The heating fuel saving targets for both 1988/89 and the last 10 years have been exceeded, with actual savings of £10.35 million, but those for electricity have not. The level of electricity saving has, however, increased steadily since 1985/86 with actual savings over the last ten years of £4.83 million.

7.113 Several schemes have been adopted to help the programme. The '50/50 scheme' enables schools which make energy savings to retain half of the total

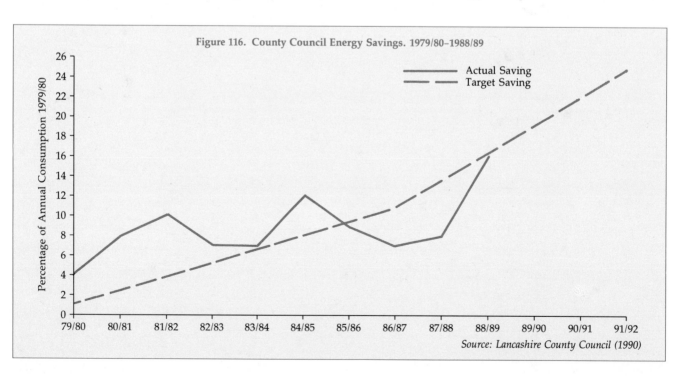

Figure 116. County Council Energy Savings. 1979/80–1988/89

Source: Lancashire County Council (1990)

amount of money saved for school funds. £166,000 was recovered by schools in this way in 1988/89. There are plans to extend the scheme to non-education buildings. The County Council has also provided training programmes for building managers, and introduced energy performance contracts, in partnership with private contractors, and energy management systems. The EMU is also actively involved in assessing new technologies like CHP and evaluating their application in Council buildings.

References

Chartered Institute of Public Finance and Accountancy (1989). Environmental Health Statistics 1987–88 Actuals – Statistical Information Service. CIPFA.

Cometec-Gaz (1989). Gas and the Environment. Brochure prepared as a contribution to the European Year of the Environment (EYE). COMETEC-GAZ.

Commission of European Communities (1987). Study for the Commission of the European Communities Directorate General for Energy, contract No. 85/13/706/11/004.1. Energy study of the North West Region of the UK (March Consulting Group). CEC.

Department of Energy (1989a). Review 9, Autumn 1989. HMSO.

Department of Energy (1989b). An evaluation of energy related greenhouse gas emission and measures to ameliorate them. Energy Paper No.58. UK country study for the Intergovernmental Panel on Climate Change. HMSO.

Department of Energy (1989c). Digest of United Kingdom Energy Statistics, 1989. HMSO.

Electricity Council (1990). Handbook of Electricity Supply Statistics 1989. The Electricity Council.

Energy Technology Support Unit (1989a). Renewable Energy in the UK. ETSU.

Energy Technology Support Unit (1989b). The UK Potential for Tidal Energy from Small Estuaries. ETSU.

Lancashire County Council (1989). Lancashire at Work 1990. An Industrial and Commercial Directory. LCC.

Lancashire County Council (1990). Energy Performance Review 1988/89. Report to the Land and Buildings Sub-Committee, 11th January 1990. LCC.

North Western Electricity Board/Energy Technology Support Unit (1989). Prospects for Renewable Energy in the Norweb Area. NORWEB/ETSU.

North Western Electricity Board (1989). Statistical Information 1988/89. NORWEB/ETSU.

Chapter Eight
Land and Agriculture

Introduction

8.1　Land is a finite resource that has to supply our needs for homes, jobs, food, transport, fuel, building materials, recreation and so on, whilst at the same time preserving landscape features and wildlife habitats.

8.2　Lancashire's 306,951 ha serve the needs of a population of 1,390,800, representing 0.22 ha (roughly half a football pitch) per person. Land must be used to satisfy as many as possible of the legitimate needs and desires of the population and this necessitates a system of land use planning to secure its most efficient and effective use. The type of land use that takes place, and where it takes place, greatly influences other aspects of the environment, for example, air quality and water quality. This makes the study of land use fundamental to the County's Green Audit.

8.3　The pattern of land use in the UK is the result of the action and interaction of a variety of natural, economic and social factors over time and there are usually very good reasons for the existing use of land. However, not every piece of land is being put to its most productive or best use and some uses are inappropriately located. Correcting these problems, and resolving land use conflicts is the responsibility of, and a challenge to, both Central and Local Government.

8.4　The five basic human needs that land must satisfy are a home, food, work, recreation and communication. Housing has a high priority in its demand for land. Although population increase in the County is small, the growing number of households means that more homes are required for the same number of people. Chapter 10 makes reference to the location of housing in the County with regard to its impact on the landscape. Food is produced by farming which is the dominant land use in the County. Its location and extent are determined by topography, soils, climate, land quality and economic factors. The type of farming practised affects the landscape and potential for pollution in particular areas. Another crop from the land is timber and forestry, a small but important land use in the County. Industry has been, and continues to be, important in influencing environmental conditions in Lancashire. Some industries are fixed in location due to the presence of minerals or water resources and other industries may be closely connected with these. Some, like the textile industry in Lancashire, are closely tied by historical tradition and the availability of skilled workers. Recreation is a use to which land can be put in addition to other primary uses, and this is discussed in Chapter 11. The use of land for communications – by road, railway, tram, canal or air is covered in Chapter 12. Dominant amongst the uses is the road system which, having developed from Roman times, now reaches the remotest areas of the County.

8.5　This Chapter describes land use in Lancashire. It uses data of the land cover in the County collected by satellite, discriminating nine discrete categories. The area of the County falling into each of these categories is presented together with a further breakdown by District. Agriculture – as the dominant land use in Lancashire – is examined in detail, firstly in terms of land quality and then with details of the dominant farm types. Commercial forestry and fisheries are then described, followed by the environmental effects of land use, particularly with respect to farming.

Legislation

European

8.6　The single most important European policy having an impact on land use is the Common Agricultural Policy (CAP) which is defined in Article 39 of the Treaty of Rome. This seeks to maintain prices through farm subsidy, import restrictions and commodity control. It has secured the maintenance of upland and marginal agriculture, a reduction in dairying and a strong market in meat and cereals. It is impossible to assess its precise land use effects in Lancashire, although they have undoubtedly been profound. It is still too early to identify the effect of the decline caused by the CAP, and reductions in price support, although it is likely that much land, especially marginal land, could go out of production in due course.

8.7　To facilitate the transition to a unified market, the European Commission published a White Paper in 1985 with almost 300 detailed proposals, mainly Directives, for adoption by 1992. Most have been adopted with some additional proposals. EC Regulation 797/85 includes provision for a Farm and Conservation Grant Scheme aimed at improving the structure of agriculture within the Community. This provides for payment of compensatory allowances previously made under Council Directive 75/268/EEC for mountain and hill farms and those in other Less Favoured Areas.

8.8　EC Regulation 1760/87 aims to maintain the viability of farming communities and contribute to environmental protection and the conservation of natural rural resources. It makes funds available for specific measures to protect the environment and landscape, and to assist hill farming and Less Favoured Areas.

8.9　Grants for afforestation (Directive 85/337/EEC), farm modernisation (Directive 72/159/EEC), farm amalgamation (Directive 72/160/EEC) economic guidance and skill training for agricultural workers (Directive 72/161/EEC) have all been designed to stabilise enterprises in marginal areas. They follow a tradition in Britain of farm subsidy which has maintained marginal and hill farming.

8.10　Systems of quotas, subsidies and standards have helped to control dairy, meat and cereal production. Milk quotas and meat export controls (Directive 64/432/EEC) have helped to restrict these industries. The Milk Act (1985) makes provision for payments to be made in compensation for losses.

8.11　Other EC Directives affecting land use are referred to in appropriate Chapters.

United Kingdom

8.12 In Britain, the framework for land use is largely provided by the town and country planning system. The Town and Country Planning Act (TCPA) 1990 has recently repealed and consolidated most previous planning Acts. Planning decisions rest principally with local authorities at County and District level working to overall guidance set by the Government. In the countryside, farm land and buildings are currently exempt from planning control, though the Government's White Paper on the environment suggests extending controls to the siting, design and external appearance of farm and forestry buildings. Otherwise, Agricultural Acts are the only major ones which affect land use.

8.13 The Agriculture Act 1986 gives Ministers a legal duty to balance farming interests with rural and environmental interests. Such interests include economic and social welfare, conservation and enhancement of natural beauty, wildlife and historic interest and public enjoyment of the countryside. The Farmland and Rural Development Act 1988 allows the introduction of various schemes for alternative farm uses. The Capital Allowances Act 1990 also makes provision to enable allowances to be made for farm buildings and forestry. Various other schemes have been introduced which have important environmental implications. They include Less Favoured Areas, Hill Livestock Compensatory Allowance, Set Aside, the Farm Woodland Scheme, Farm and Conservation Grant Scheme, Farm Diversification Grants and the designation of Environmentally Sensitive Areas.

8.14 Specific regulations on food and hazardous substances were subject to stricter controls under the Food and Environmental Protection Act 1986. This allowed for regulations on the Control of Pesticides 1986 and for Maximum Residue Levels 1988 as well as for the Control of Substances Hazardous to Health 1988. Control of the latter is also provided by the Health and Safety at Work Act 1974. Other controls of hazardous and polluting substances and practices come under the Control of Pollution Act 1974 (which relates to Water, Air and Noise) and the Environmental Protection Act 1990.

8.15 The Water Act 1989 lays down general duties to privatised water industries on conservation, access and recreation on land in their ownership and use. It also established the National Rivers Authority, whose job is to protect and improve the quality of inland, coastal and underground waters, including their protection from farm operations.

8.16 The Wildlife and Countryside Act 1981 gives various degrees of protection to wild plants and animals and their habitats. Under the Act the Nature Conservancy Council (NCC) is required to identify areas of the countryside of special interest for various environmental and scientific reasons including Sites of Special Scientific Interest (SSSI) and Areas of Special Protection for Birds. In addition, Areas of Outstanding Natural Beauty were set up under the National Parks and Access to the Countryside Act 1949.

8.17 Control of woodland and forest activities is provided under the Forestry Acts 1967, 1979 and 1986 and subsequent regulations. The 1986 Act requires the Forestry Commission to achieve a reasonable balance between afforestation, timber production and nature conservation. The TCPA 1985 and 1971, the Local Government Planning and Land Act 1980 and the Town and Country Amenities Act 1974 and their regulations provide for preservation of trees.

8.18 The principal Acts governing fishing are the Sea Fish (Conservation) Act 1967, the Sea Fisheries Act 1968 and the Fisheries Act 1981, whilst the Salmon and Freshwater Fisheries Act 1975 applies to inland fishing and the sea up to six miles from the territorial baseline. Inshore fish and shellfish industries are also subject to the Sea Fisheries Regulation Act 1966 and the byelaws of the North West and North Wales Sea Fisheries Committee (NWNWSFC). These define and regulate fisheries boundaries, fishing methods, boat size and type of net. They also control the levels of fishing in certain areas through closure orders and seasonal limits. In broad terms, inshore fisheries are also bound by the Food and Environmental Protection Act 1985.

Organisations

Central Government

8.19 There are a number of government departments which influence land use. The Ministry of Agriculture Fisheries and Food (MAFF) administers the agriculture, horticulture and fisheries policy. It implements the CAP in terms of subsidies, quotas, restrictions and various regulations. MAFF has direct links with the farming industry through Regional Panels which are non-statutory liaison bodies.

8.20 Under MAFF, the Agricultural Development and Advisory Service (ADAS), deals directly with farmers and the industry. Its work includes research and development, advising farmers and performing statutory and regulatory work on behalf of MAFF. Under ADAS are the Farm and Countryside Service and the Research and Development Service.

8.21 The Forestry Commission is a government department which exists to undertake forestry and promote forestry interests. It now has the duty to create a balance in its operations between the interests of forestry and conservation. Information, training, research and advice are important functions of the Commission. In addition it administers various grants related to forests and woodlands and issues licences and permits for felling.

8.22 The Department of Environment (DOE) has overall responsibility for land use planning, housing and construction, environmental protection, water and recreation.

8.23 Two national statutory agencies whose activities are concerned with, and have an impact on, land use are the Countryside Commission (CoCo) and the NCC. CoCo is concerned with landscape conservation and informal recreation. It is an advisory and promotional body, neither owning land nor managing facilities. The NCC is the government body responsible for promoting and securing nature conservation. It gives advice to Government and all those whose activities affect wildlife. It defines areas of particular conservation value and interest, manages National Nature Reserves and undertakes research, including the NCC Phase I Habitat Survey of Lancashire.

Local Government

8.24   Lancashire County Council co-ordinates strategic land use planning through the Lancashire Structure Plan. This contains broad policies on the scale and location of housing, industrial and commercial development, landscape protection, the rural economy, strategic transport planning, minerals, conservation, recreation, waste disposal and land reclamation. The County Council is, itself, a major landowner and manager. It controls a County Farms Estate and is responsible for managing a wide range of recreational and conservation/ amenity sites.

8.25   At District level, Councils are responsible for implementing the Structure Plan through Local Plans and development control policies. They also have responsibility for many other land use related aspects, including housing, waste collection, open spaces, environmental health, derelict land reclamation, cemeteries and allotments.

Other Organisations

8.26   At the regional level a major land owner is North West Water plc. It has inherited a large estate in Lancashire which, under the Water Act 1989, must be managed with due regard to environment and amenity. Some 8,419 ha are involved (see Chapter 11). Other large landowners in the County are the Duchy of Lancaster and the Duke of Westminster. Most of the land, however, is controlled by an enormous number of smaller, individual owners. Collectively, their stewardship is the major factor determining land use, and changes in use, in the County. Many owners belong to, and are advised by, the local branches of the Country Landowners Association and the National Farmers Union.

8.27   Lancashire Trust for Nature Conservation is a voluntary organisation which promotes wildlife and conservation issues, creates and manages nature reserves and offers a range of services including publications and organisation of projects.

8.28   There are many other non-statutory and charitable or voluntary organisations involved in conservation and environmental issues. Some, like Friends of the Earth and the Council for the Protection of Rural England, are national. Others, such as the Blackburn and the Rossendale Groundwork Trusts, operate only in the County. Their rôle is increasingly important in forming public opinion about environmental issues.

Land and Agriculture in Lancashire

Land Cover

8.29   It is not easy to distinguish precisely the use to which each piece of land is being put. It is often easier to identify 'land cover' which is derived from an analysis of the physical appearance of land. In this Chapter data for both land cover and use are presented where best appropriate or available. It is important to avoid interpreting maps and data of land cover as though they give a precise indication of land use, and vice-versa.

8.30   The value of a survey of land use or cover rests primarily on the system of land classes or divisions employed. There is no universal system. The one adopted for the Green Audit is based on broad categorisation of urban and non-urban types which is designed to:

* establish the broad pattern of land use across Lancashire as a whole;
* assist in evaluating the overall environmental impact of agriculture and forestry.

8.31   The main data presented are a land use inventory compiled from two sources, the 1985 LANDSAT 5 satellite and the 1988 MAFF Parish Farm Census returns. Analysis of both was conducted by specialists at Salford University, and the results form the basis of this Chapter. Satellite data are ideal for surveys of large areas in which the land parcels are made up of woods, fields, moors and other extensive features. Unfortunately, the best available LANDSAT image for Lancashire is five years old and some land use changes will inevitably have occurred, especially in farm rotations. In addition there are cases where the classification of land use is ambiguous or undecided. No survey is without error, even one conducted in the field by trained observers. Experience shows, however, that land use surveys from satellites are of the order of 80–90% accurate; a similar order to manual survey. Only very detailed field checking would reveal where errors actually are. On balance, satellite data provides the most versatile, complete and accurate means of surveying large areas.

8.32   LANDSAT series satellites are designed for observing land cover. They orbit the Earth at an altitude of 700 km and revisit the same part of the Earth's surface every 16 days. Instruments on board the satellites record the sun's radiation reflected back from the earth, either as visible light or infrared radiation. This is picked up in different wavebands. Reflected radiation is measured for small areas (called pixels) of the Earth's surface of about 30 m square and this information is relayed back to Earth. Lancashire is represented by about three and a half million pixels. These are recorded by the satellite in the twenty seconds it takes to pass over the County. A satellite photograph of Lancashire can be seen on the front cover of this Report.

8.33   The measurements of reflected radiation can be used to identify the land cover of an area. This is because different surfaces reflect back different amounts of radiation in varying wavebands. Thus, sand reflects more radiation than peat and improved grassland reflects more than unimproved grassland. By taking readings from small sample areas where land cover has been established by field survey, it is possible to identify other parts of the image with similar readings and thus produce a total picture of where in the County the cover type occurs.

Figure 117

Extent of Lancashire Covered by Buildings. 1985

1. Lancaster
2. Wyre
3. Ribble Valley
4. Blackpool
5. Fylde
6. Preston
7. South Ribble
8. West Lancashire
9. Chorley
10. Blackburn
11. Hyndburn
12. Burnley
13. Pendle
14. Rossendale

• Building Cover

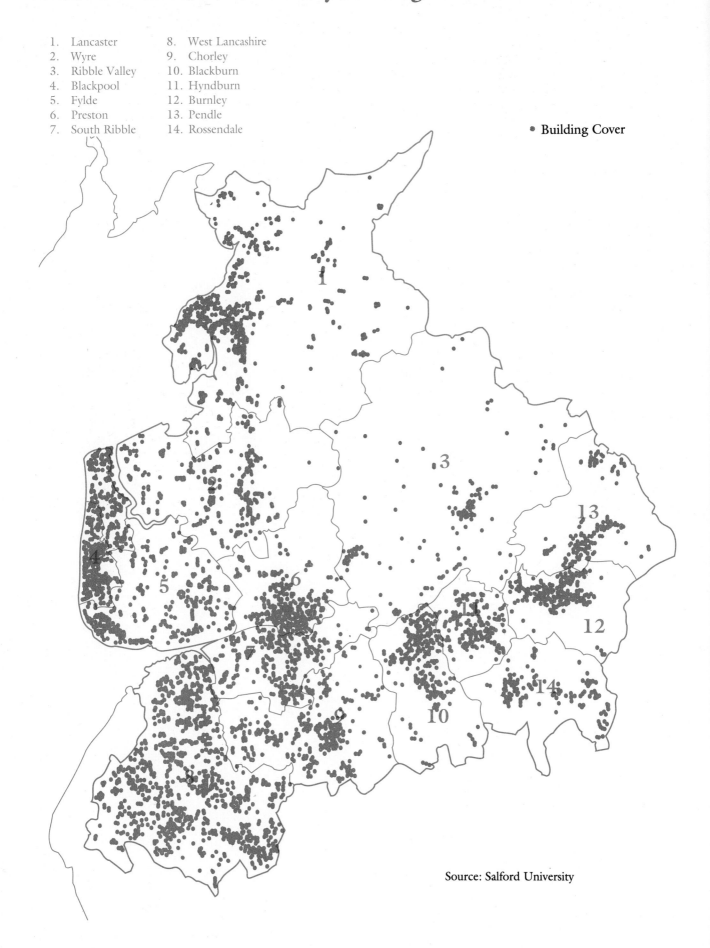

Source: Salford University

8.34 However, not all land cover types can easily be discriminated by satellite. For example, well managed grassland, arable land and playing fields reflect solar radiation in a similar way to dark rocks and the slate roofs of houses. For these reasons, errors in the computer classification of land cover are unavoidable, but are generally found to be of the same order as the error involved in manual survey. The advantage of the satellite is that it gives land use at one point in time for the whole County, which would be impossible to do by field survey for such a large area.

8.35 The pixels on the satellite image of Lancashire have been classified into nine land cover categories. These are:

* Buildings;
* Improved Grassland and Arable Land;
* Unimproved Grassland;
* Moorland;
* Coniferous Woodland;
* Broadleaved Woodland;
* Marsh and Wetland;
* Sand;
* Inland Water.

The distribution of each of these categories in the County is presented in Figures 117–125. A statistical breakdown of the areas by District, and the proportion which each cover type forms of the County area, are given in Tables 76 and 77.

Buildings

8.36 Building cover includes all the built-up and suburban areas of towns and villages together with the small parks, gardens and other green spaces that exist between the buildings. Individual building groups in the countryside covering most of, or more than, a 30 m square pixel are also included. All industrial and commercial buildings and areas with extensive hard surfaces, whether in urban or rural areas, are also in this category. The distribution of this cover type (Figure 117) closely corresponds with the urban areas and buildings identified on Ordnance Survey maps. The total area of the County covered by buildings is 58,200 ha or 18% of Lancashire. However, there are considerable differences between the fourteen Districts. Blackpool is the most densely built-up District with 70% of its area covered by buildings. Ribble Valley, in contrast has only 2% of its area covered by buildings. The high figure for West Lancashire is explained partly by the existence of many large farm complexes but also by radiation discrimination problems between this cover category and the next one.

Improved Grassland and Arable Land

8.37 This land cover category identifies the most intensively farmed areas in the County where either arable crops, horticultural crops or improved grassland for dairying or livestock rearing exists. It can be seen from Figure 118 that there is a wide distribution of this cover type across the Coastal Plain with noticeable concentration in the major river valleys and on the Fylde. In total it covers 76,901 ha or 25% of the County area. The Districts of Wyre, Fylde, Preston and Chorley have the largest proportions of their areas in improved grassland or arable cover. However, West Lancashire and South Ribble are less well represented than MAFF data (see below) indicate. This is probably due to a misclassification of bare fields (which can have a similar

Table 76 Land Cover in Hectares by District in Lancashire. 1985

District	Buildings	Improved Grassland/ Arable	Unimproved Grassland	Moorland	Coniferous Woodland	Broadleaved Woodland	Marsh	Sand	Inland Water	Total
Lancaster	5,017	15,110	10,900	20,992	1,269	2,249	865	1,038	231	57,671
Wyre	6,720	8,905	5,161	4,425	340	766	568	1,277	170	28,332
Ribble Valley	1,403	16,725	12,690	21,520	2,807	2,398	351	293	291	58,478
Blackpool	2,444	80	63	14	—	—	49	827	21	3,498
Fylde	5,418	5,848	1,982	562	49	182	1,354	1,106	—	16,501
Preston	3,825	5,963	2,909	272	171	400	528	114	57	14,239
South Ribble	4,856	2,920	1,120	373	91	385	905	623	34	11,307
West Lancashire	13,961	5,308	812	879	473	439	4,158	7,672	68	33,770
Chorley	4,271	5,399	2,238	4,687	244	975	1,342	670	466	20,292
Blackburn	3,073	1,702	1,221	6,039	439	507	165	234	343	13,723
Hyndburn	2,113	1,478	1,017	1,646	67	271	176	432	102	7,302
Burnley	1,939	1,406	1,130	5,758	100	366	34	255	89	11,077
Pendle	1,695	4,923	3,360	5,549	135	899	51	169	169	16,950
Rossendale	1,465	1,134	1,106	9,111	69	388	83	359	96	13,811
LANCASHIRE	58,200	76,901	45,709	81,827	6,254	10,225	10,629	15,069	2,137	306,951

Source: Salford University.

Figure 118
Extent of Lancashire Covered by Improved Grassland and Arable Land . 1985

1. Lancaster
2. Wyre
3. Ribble Valley
4. Blackpool
5. Fylde
6. Preston
7. South Ribble
8. West Lancashire
9. Chorley
10. Blackburn
11. Hyndburn
12. Burnley
13. Pendle
14. Rossendale

• Improved Grassland and Arable Land Cover

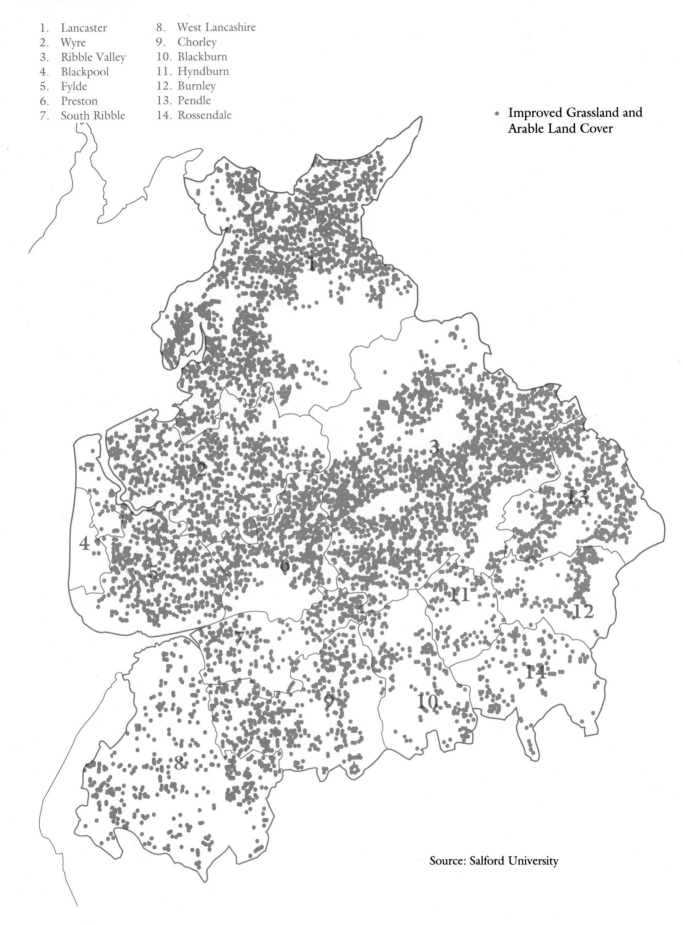

Source: Salford University

Figure 119

Extent of Lancashire Covered by Unimproved Grassland.1985

1. Lancaster
2. Wyre
3. Ribble Valley
4. Blackpool
5. Fylde
6. Preston
7. South Ribble
8. West Lancashire
9. Chorley
10. Blackburn
11. Hyndburn
12. Burnley
13. Pendle
14. Rossendale

• Unimproved Grassland Cover

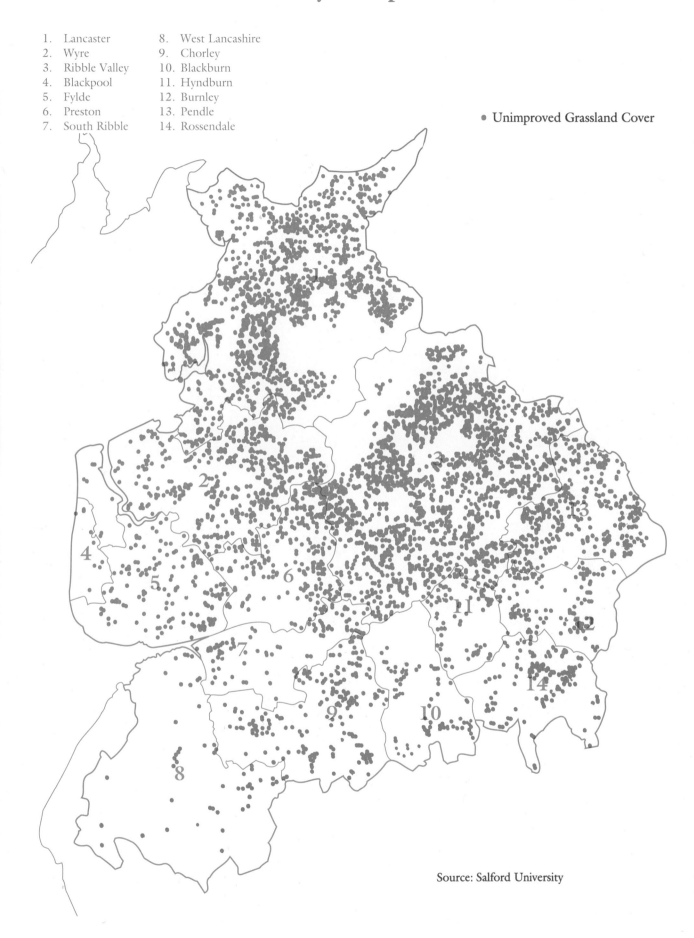

Source: Salford University

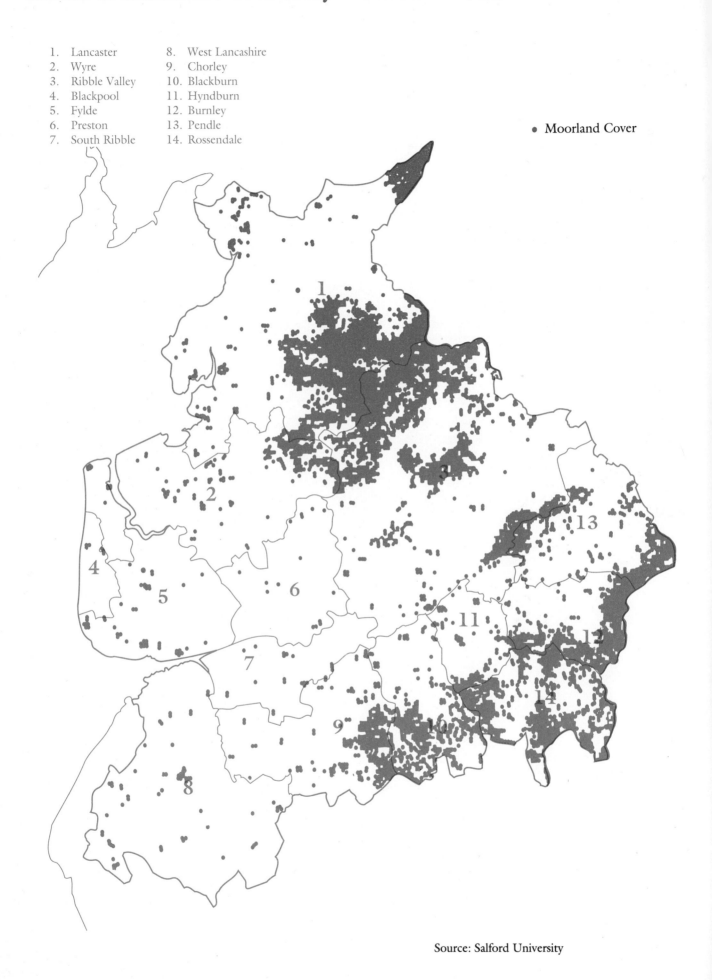

Figure 120
Extent of Lancashire Covered by Moorland . 1985

1. Lancaster
2. Wyre
3. Ribble Valley
4. Blackpool
5. Fylde
6. Preston
7. South Ribble
8. West Lancashire
9. Chorley
10. Blackburn
11. Hyndburn
12. Burnley
13. Pendle
14. Rossendale

• Moorland Cover

Source: Salford University

reflectance to hard surfaces) into the building land cover category in these Districts.

Unimproved Grassland

8.38 This land cover category identifies less intensively managed pasture land. It shows a similar distribution (Figure 119) to improved grassland cover but has a greater concentration in upland areas. It covers a total of 45,709 ha or 15% of the County area. It forms a large proportion of the area of Ribble Valley (Table 77) and only a small proportion of the area of West Lancashire.

Moorland

8.39 This category includes both enclosed and unenclosed moorland and incorporates areas of rough grassland and upland peat. Small areas of 'derelict' or unmanaged vegetation in lowland areas have also been classified in this category. Moorland distribution (Figure 120) is picked out very clearly and lies in extensive upland tracts in the Forest of Bowland, West Pennine and South Pennine areas and on Leck Fell in the north of the County. It covers 81,827 ha or 27% of the County. Rossendale, Blackburn and Burnley have high proportions of moorland whilst Preston and Blackpool (Table 77) have the least.

Coniferous Woodland

8.40 This land cover type is also well picked out (Figure 121) and can be seen to consist of small scattered stands over much of the County with a single large stand of woodland in Ribble Valley (Gisburn Forest). In total, coniferous woodland covers 6,254 ha or 2% of the County. Ribble Valley and

Lancaster have the highest proportions within their areas whilst Blackpool has none (Table 77).

Broadleaved Woodland

8.41 The map of this land cover type (Figure 122) shows that there are no large stands of predominantly broadleaved woodland in the County. However, small stands do occur in a fairly uniform distribution across the County with the exception of the upland areas and the coastal plain. Broadleaved woodland covers 10,225 ha or 3% of the County area. Ribble Valley and Lancaster again have high proportions of this type of woodland and Blackpool once again has none (Table 77).

Marsh and Wetland

8.42 This land cover category includes mudflats, zones of inundation and wet vegetation on inland sites, as well as coastal marsh. Distribution of marsh (Figure 123) in the County shows a wide scatter of small sites in lowland areas with concentrations along the Ribble and Wyre estuaries and around Morecambe Bay. Hesketh Marsh and Warton Bank at the mouth of the Ribble and Leighton Moss in Lancaster are well picked out. Marsh covers a total of 10,225 ha or 4% of the County. West Lancashire has a high proportion of marsh land cover but Burnley and Pendle have very little (Table 77).

Sand

8.43 The sand category includes areas of exposed dry sand in both coastal and inland locations. The distribution of sand in the County (Figure 124) shows deposits along the coast, as expected, and also areas of glacial sand and sandy soils in the north

Table 77 Percentage Land Cover by District in Lancashire. 1985

District	Buildings	Improved Grassland/ Arable	Unimproved Grassland	Moorland	Coniferous Woodland	Broadleaved Woodland	Marsh	Sand	Inland Water
Lancaster	9	26	19	36	2	4	1	2	<1
Wyre	24	31	18	16	1	3	2	4	<1
Ribble Valley	2	29	22	37	5	4	<1	<1	<1
Blackpool	70	2	2	<1	—	—	<1	24	<1
Fylde	33	35	12	3	<1	1	8	7	—
Preston	27	42	20	2	1	3	4	<1	<1
South Ribble	43	26	10	3	<1	3	8	5	<1
West Lancashire	4	16	2	3	1	1	12	23	<1
Chorley	21	27	11	23	2	5	7	3	<1
Blackburn	22	13	9	44	3	4	1	2	2
Hyndburn	29	20	14	22	1	4	2	6	2
Burnley	17	13	10	52	1	3	<1	2	1
Pendle	10	29	20	33	1	5	<1	1	<1
Rossendale	11	8	8	65	<1	3	<1	3	1
LANCASHIRE	18	25	15	27	2	3	4	5	<1

Source: Salford University.

Figure 121
Extent of Lancashire Covered by Coniferous Woodland. 1985

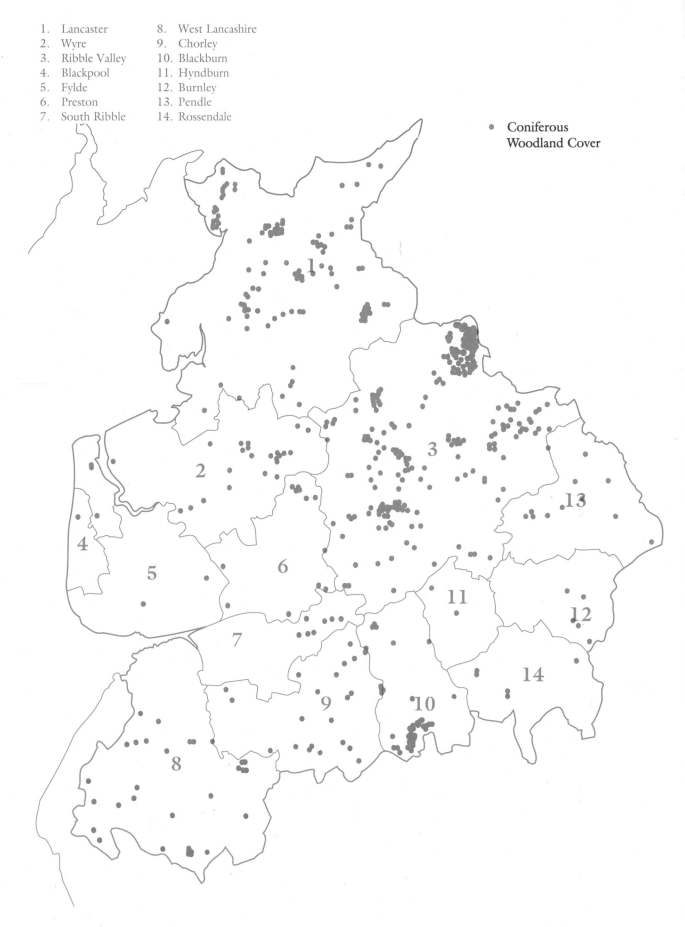

1. Lancaster
2. Wyre
3. Ribble Valley
4. Blackpool
5. Fylde
6. Preston
7. South Ribble
8. West Lancashire
9. Chorley
10. Blackburn
11. Hyndburn
12. Burnley
13. Pendle
14. Rossendale

• Coniferous
  Woodland Cover

Source: Salford University

Figure 122

Extent of Lancashire Covered by Broadleaved Woodland. 1985

1. Lancaster
2. Wyre
3. Ribble Valley
4. Blackpool
5. Fylde
6. Preston
7. South Ribble
8. West Lancashire
9. Chorley
10. Blackburn
11. Hyndburn
12. Burnley
13. Pendle
14. Rossendale

• Broadleaved Woodland Cover

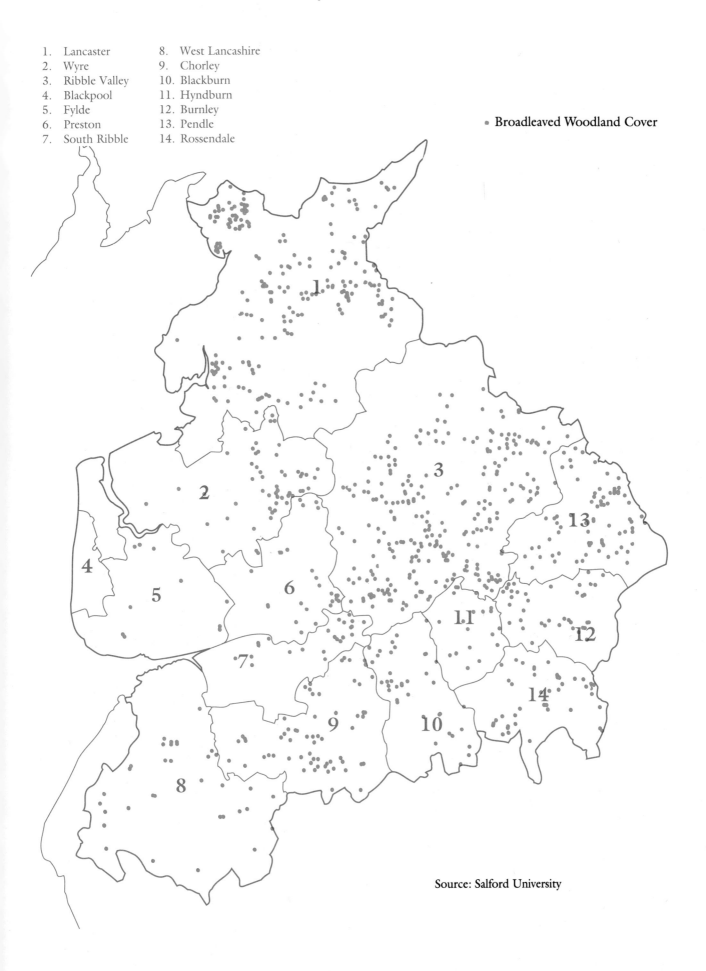

Source: Salford University

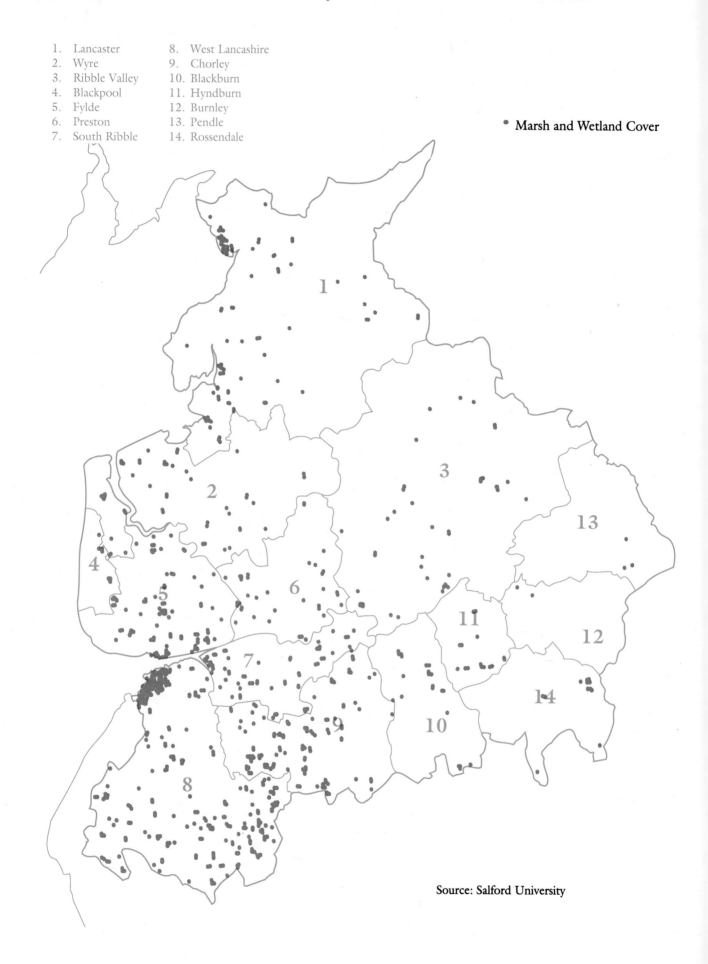

Figure 123

Extent of Lancashire Covered by Marsh and Wetland . 1985

1. Lancaster
2. Wyre
3. Ribble Valley
4. Blackpool
5. Fylde
6. Preston
7. South Ribble
8. West Lancashire
9. Chorley
10. Blackburn
11. Hyndburn
12. Burnley
13. Pendle
14. Rossendale

• Marsh and Wetland Cover

Source: Salford University

Figure 124

Extent of Lancashire Covered by Sand . 1985

1. Lancaster
2. Wyre
3. Ribble Valley
4. Blackpool
5. Fylde
6. Preston
7. South Ribble
8. West Lancashire
9. Chorley
10. Blackburn
11. Hyndburn
12. Burnley
13. Pendle
14. Rossendale

● Sand Cover

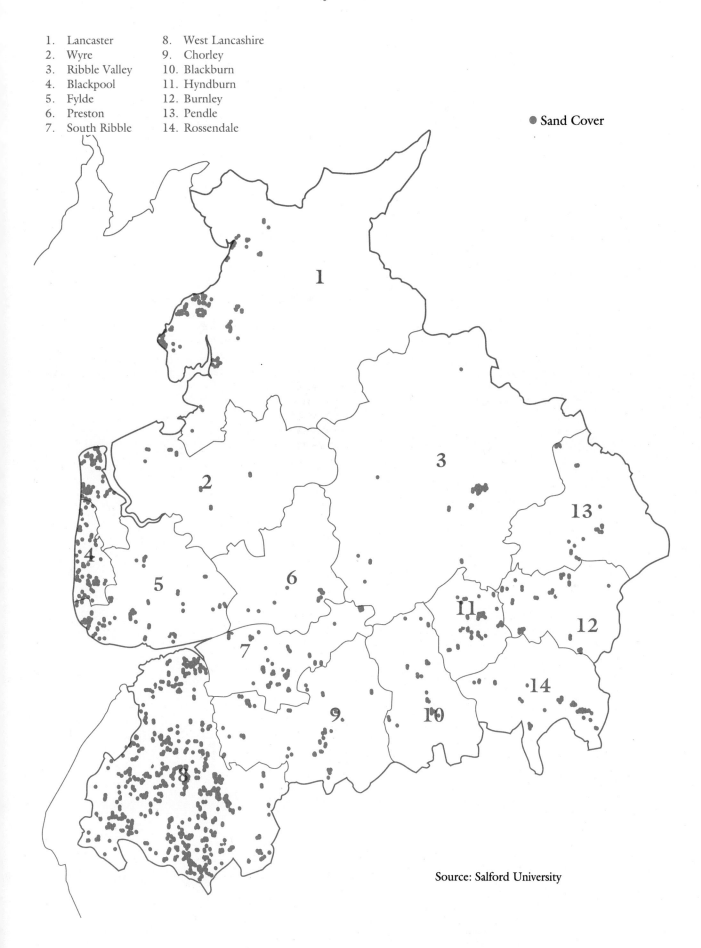

Source: Salford University

Figure 125
Extent of Lancashire Covered by Inland Water. 1985

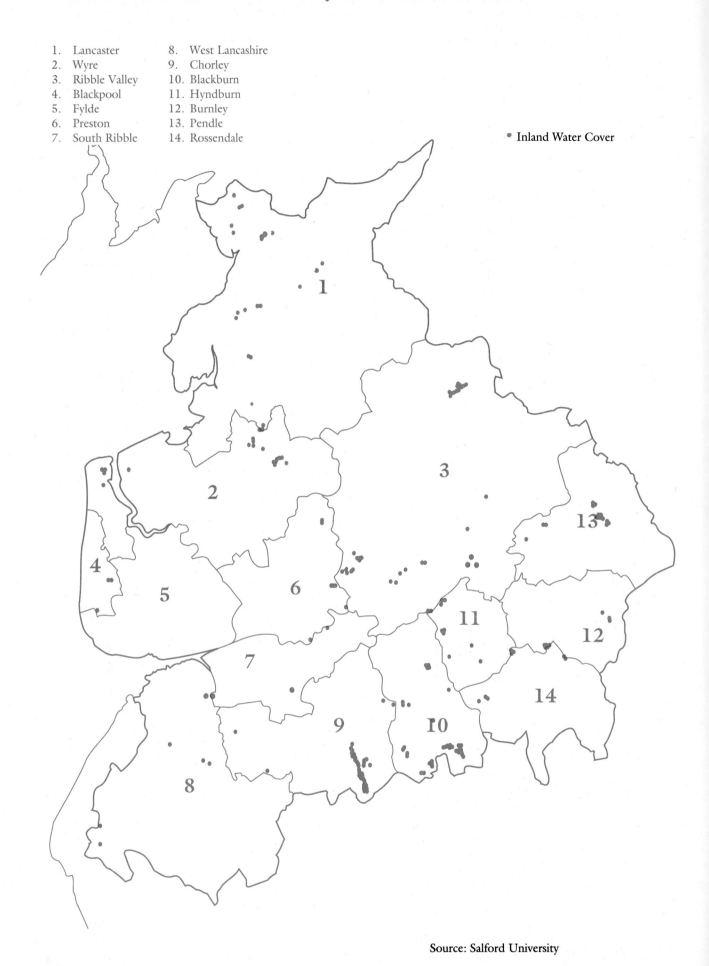

1. Lancaster
2. Wyre
3. Ribble Valley
4. Blackpool
5. Fylde
6. Preston
7. South Ribble
8. West Lancashire
9. Chorley
10. Blackburn
11. Hyndburn
12. Burnley
13. Pendle
14. Rossendale

• Inland Water Cover

Source: Salford University

west and particularly south west of the County. Isolated sand deposits inland are probably old or new quarries and pits. Sand covers 15,069 ha or 5% of the County. Blackpool and West Lancashire have large proportions of their areas in this category whilst Ribble Valley and Preston have very little (Table 77).

Inland Water

8.44 This category includes reservoirs, lakes and large ponds but excludes most of Lancashire's large number of small field ponds, and all rivers and canals. The distribution of inland water (Figure 125) is scattered widely but distinctly shows the large water supply reservoirs. This is the smallest land cover type covering only 2,137 ha or 0.7% of the County. Blackburn and Chorley containing the Anglezarke and Rivington, Turton and Wayoh series of reservoirs have large proportions of inland water in their areas whilst Fylde has none (Table 77).

Summary

8.45 In summary, the estimates of land cover in Lancashire show the high proportion of moorland (27%) and improved grassland and arable land (25%) in the County, plus the large area (18%) covered by buildings. Unimproved grassland (15%) is another large category. It also reveals the relatively small area of woodland (5%) and inland water (0.7%). Land cover that is in agricultural use will include the grassland categories together with moorland and marsh; in all a total of 71% of the County. This is close to the figures given from MAFF data (see below). Figures for moorland and woodland cover derived from satellite analysis compare well with those from ecological surveys given in Chapter 9.

Agricultural Land Classification

8.46 The ADAS Agricultural Land Classification (ALC) is a grading of land according to the degree to which physical characteristics limit potential for agricultural production. There are five main grades, which, along with two classes for urban and non-agricultural land, produces a seven fold division of land. These are:

* Grade 1 land with minor or no physical limitations to agricultural use;
* Grade 2 land with some minor limitations to agricultural use;
* Grade 3 land with moderate limitations from soil, relief, climate;
* Grade 4 land with severe limitations from soil, relief, climate;
* Grade 5 land with very severe limitations;
* Class 6 urban area;
* Class 7 non-agricultural land.

8.47 ALC provides only a crude means of describing the farming potential of land. It is broadly based and the boundaries between classes are not fixed by field survey. For these reasons, ALC should strictly be used only for broad comparisons between large areas. The distribution of ALC classes in Lancashire is shown on Figure 126.

8.48 The main physical factors limiting agricultural production and taken into account in the ALC are topography, climate and soil type. It can be seen from the topography map (Figure 5) that extensive parts of Bowland exceed 305 m, whilst Longridge Fell and the West Pennines areas are over 229 m. These uplands have similar characteristics of high rainfall, exposure, short growing season and poor soils. The combination of these factors means that almost all of the uplands are Grade 5 merging gradually with Grade 4 as altitude decreases to the west.

8.49 Land in the Fylde region rarely exceeds 30 m and the bulk is under 15 m. This flat or gently undulating land is sheltered by uplands to the east and north and is comparatively little damaged by the cold and snow-bearing easterly winds of winter months. Favourable coastal conditions, together with versatile soils derived from glacial and post-glacial deposits, means that Grade 2 and Grade 1 land is widespread here.

8.50 Land in the Ribble Valley varies from 46–183 m increasing in altitude towards Bowland and the Pennines. The land is rounded and not heavily dissected, the flood plain is narrow and physical factors cause a predominance of Grades 3 and 4 land.

8.51 Data on the amounts of land in each grade and class by District are presented in Table 78 and Table 79. Only 14% of the County falls in Grades 1 and 2, compared with 17% nationally. 56% of Lancashire is Grade 3 or 4 and 20% is of the lowest quality, Grade 5.

Table 78 Agricultural Land Class Areas by District in Lancashire. 1970

| District | ALC Grades/Classes | | | | | | | |
	1	2	3	4	5	6	7	Total
Lancaster	—	625	21,329	14,922	16,361	2,464	—	55,701
Wyre	—	8,237	12,172	2,427	2,955	2,231	55	28,077
Ribble Valley	—	28	15,217	24,277	15,996	425	1,782	57,725
Blackpool	—	186	512	—	—	2,686	49	3,433
Fylde	—	7,560	5,565	358	—	1,793	869	16,145
Preston	—	141	10,919	421	218	2,541	—	14,240
South Ribble	252	993	7,149	678	—	1,950	—	11,022
West Lancashire	19,697	4,405	4,476	1,724	—	2,958	70	33,330
Chorley	1,327	379	12,335	2,125	2,366	1,318	325	20,175
Blackburn	—	—	1,329	4,616	4,661	2,614	167	13,387
Hyndburn	—	—	184	4,800	666	1,662	—	7,312
Burnley	—	—	1,125	4,257	4,750	1,514	11	11,657
Pendle	—	—	890	10,183	3,957	1,693	—	16,723
Rossendale	—	—	—	6,357	7,160	—	12	13,529
LANCASHIRE	21,276	22,554	93,202	77,145	59,090	25,849	3,340	302,456

Source: Ministry of Agriculture, Fisheries and Food (1970) and Salford University.

Note: Areas given in ha.

Figure 126

Agricultural Land Classification in Lancashire. 1970

1. Lancaster
2. Wyre
3. Ribble Valley
4. Blackpool
5. Fylde
6. Preston
7. South Ribble
8. West Lancashire
9. Chorley
10. Blackburn
11. Hyndburn
12. Burnley
13. Pendle
14. Rossendale

Grade/Class

Grade 1
Grade 2
Grade 3
Grade 4
Grade 5
Class 6
Class 7

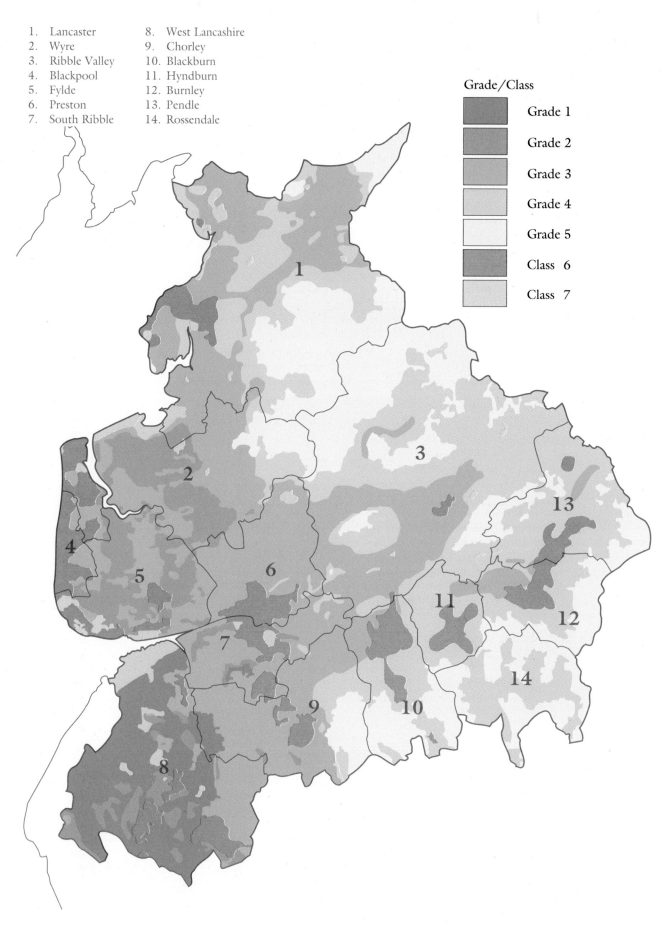

Source: Ministry of Agriculture,
Fisheries and Food (1970)

8.52 District comparisons show an uneven nature of the distribution of land classes particularly of Grades 1 and 2. 93% of Grade 1 land in the County and 20% of Grade 2 land is in West Lancashire. Fylde (34%) and Wyre (37%) account for most of the rest of the Grade 2 land. Thus, the highest quality agricultural land is concentrated in a semi-continuous belt along the coast north and south of the Ribble Estuary.

8.53 In other Districts, the proportions of land in each Grade strongly reflect the elevation of the land and the degree of urbanisation. Grade 3 land is most widespread in Wyre (43%), Chorley (61%), Ribble Valley (65%), Preston (77%) and Lancaster (38%). These Districts contain extensive tracts of coastal lowland or broad valleys. Lancaster has an even balance of land Grades 3, 4 and 5, reflecting its range of elevation. Districts predominantly in higher parts show correspondingly higher proportions of their areas in Class 4 or 5 although only Rossendale (53%) has more than half of its area in Class 5.

8.54 The urban cover from ALC is 8.55%. This compares with the estimate of 18.9% for buildings cover from satellite data. However, ALC ignores built-up areas outside the major urban agglomerations. Also, ALC analysis was done in the mid-1960s, and urban development has expanded since then.

Farming

8.55 Farming has had an impact on the environment since it began in prehistoric times, but great changes have come about in the period since the end of the last war. The trend in agriculture since 1945 has been to maximise production, with increasing intensity and specialisation of land use, chemicals and machinery. There has been a general trend towards monoculture and away from the old mixed farm; increases in arable land and improved grassland at the expense of unimproved pasture; removal of hedges, woodlands and other landscape features; and a removal of livestock from the fields to covered yards and specialised intensive units.

8.56 The effects on the environment have been to reduce wildlife habitats, alter the landscape, increase environmental pollution (particularly of water), and reduce the amenity and recreational value of the countryside. Further details of these effects are dealt with below, and in Chapters 9, 10 and 11.

8.57 The types of farming that take place differ in their impact on the environment. Intensive agriculture, based on high input/high output, tends to cause the greatest damage. Intensive arable farming is particularly associated with problems from the application of pesticides and fertilisers. Intensive livestock farming causes problems with the disposal of wastes from silage and slurry. In recent years, there has been a move towards more 'environmentally friendly' farming or low input/low output farming which carries out the production of food in a manner which furthers environmental, recreational and social interests. This trend is being driven partly by a growing demand for food produced by more 'natural' methods.

Table 79 Percentage of Each Agricultural Land Class by District in Lancashire. 1970

District	ALC Grades/Classes						
	1	2	3	4	5	6	7
Lancaster	—	1	38	27	29	5	—
Wyre	—	29	43	9	11	8	<1
Ribble Valley	—	<1	26	42	28	1	3
Blackpool	—	6	15	—	—	78	1
Fylde	—	47	35	2	—	11	5
Preston	—	1	77	3	1	18	—
South Ribble	2	9	65	6	—	18	—
West Lancashire	59	13	14	5	—	9	<1
Chorley	7	2	61	10	12	6	2
Blackburn	—	—	10	34	35	20	1
Hyndburn	—	—	2	66	9	23	—
Burnley	—	—	10	36	41	13	<1
Pendle	—	—	5	61	24	10	—
Rossendale	—	—	—	47	53	—	<1
LANCASHIRE	7	7	31	25	20	9	1

Source: Ministry of Agriculture, Fisheries and Food (1970) and Salford University.

8.58 This section details the type of farming that takes place in Lancashire and then moves on to consider the environmental effects of these farming practices upon particular areas of the County. Steps that have been taken in the County to better integrate farming with environmental protection are then detailed.

8.59 MAFF Agricultural Census Statistics for 1988 (Ministry of Agriculture, Fisheries and Food, 1988) reveal that of the total land area in Lancashire, 73% (226,711 ha) is farmed. Grassland forms the dominant part of this land and covers 145,492 ha (48%) of the County. The vast majority of this grassland is permanent or semi-permanent. Cereals and crops for stockfeeding cover 20,351 ha (7%) of the County. Horticultural crops, mainly vegetables, cover 5,349 ha. Potatoes, sugar beet and oilseed rape add an additional 3,903 ha to this area forming 3% of land in the County. The selected items in the statistics for Lancashire do not reveal the use of all farmland.

8.60 The Census analysis of farm type shows the dominance of livestock rearing in the County. Cattle and sheep farming covers 30% (91,502 ha) of all land, a large part of the land being given Less Favoured Area status. Dairy farming covers 27% (82,749 ha), whilst cropping covers 8% (25,625 ha) of the area. Pig and poultry farms occupy only 2% (6,503 ha) of the County, whilst horticulture takes up 1.5% (4,712 ha) of land.

8.61 The distributions of dominant farm types in the County are shown in Figures 127–132. These maps are constructed from MAFF Agricultural Census data on numbers of holdings in each

County parish. It is instructive to compare them with the Lancashire soils map, (Figure 6), which shows the importance of soils in determining farm type. They show the dominant type of farming in each Parish i.e. where a particular type of farming comprises more than 50% of holdings. Where no single type dominates, a mixed type is recorded. Pigs and poultry are recorded slightly differently; a black dot in a parish indicates where either or both 500 pigs or 20,000 fowl per 1,000 ha are found in a parish but nowhere do they form the dominant farming type. The maps ignore urban land use and record the dominant use of holdings in urbanised parishes. Unclassified holdings, which are the dominant number in many parishes, are ignored.

8.62 Cattle and sheep rearing is the dominant farm type in the County, (Figure 127), most prevalent in the eastern part of the County and the Lune Valley. It occurs on fairly steep slopes and corresponds mainly with Grade 4 land.

8.63 The second most dominant farm type in the County is dairying (Figure 128) which occurs in the lowlands of the Fylde Plain, the Ribble and Calder Valleys and the foothills of the West Pennines. The distribution of dairying correlates closely to Grade 3 land which supports some of the best quality permanent grassland.

8.64 Rough grazing for sheep (Figure 129) is restricted to fells and moorland in Bowland, the West Pennines, Pendle Hill and the South Pennines. The very steep slopes, excessive rainfall and exposure, poor drainage, shallow and poor soils make this the lowest quality agricultural land (Grade 5), suitable only for this type of farming.

8.65 Cropping (Figure 130) comprising those farms where the production of cereals, crops for stockfeeding, potatoes, sugar beet or rapeseed is dominant, occurs in the Fylde, West Lancashire, South Ribble and Chorley. It corresponds with areas of Grade 1 and Grade 2 agricultural land developed on peat and alluvial soils.

8.66 Horticulture (Figure 131) comprising those farms where the production of horticultural crops (mainly vegetables) is dominant, occurs in West Lancashire, Lytham St. Annes and one parish in Fylde. Horticultural holdings have developed near Lytham partly because of versatile Grade 2 soils and partly because of demand from the holiday trade. In West Lancashire, the Grade 1 land comprises deep, well drained loams or peat lying on level sites or gentle slopes. Yields are consistently high and most crops can be grown.

8.67 Pigs and poultry (Figure 132) holdings are numerous and widespread in the lowland areas of the County but cover a relatively small area of land and are not the dominant farm type. They are therefore represented as points (or spots) on the map.

8.68 Table 80 breaks down the farm size of holdings in Lancashire. Even allowing for the significant number of non-classified holdings, it is clear that the County is dominated by small, or modest, sized farms. Over 40% of holdings are less than 20 ha whilst 72% are less than 100 ha. Given the very small average size of the non-classified holding, it is reasonable to add these to the 'under 20 ha' category, increasing the proportion for the County to 63%.

Commercial Forestry

8.69 The only available data on commercial forestry in Lancashire relates to Forestry Commission land of 1,992.5 ha owned by the Commission, 1,765.6 ha is in plantation woodland (89%), 98.4 ha is in non-plantation woods (5%), and 128.5 ha is in 'non-forest' estate (6%). Of the first two categories, (plantations and non-plantations totalling 1,864 ha), 1,660.9 ha are currently used for timber production.

8.70 Satellite data provides an estimate of predominantly coniferous woodland of 6,643 ha composed of several large upland tracts and many smaller areas elsewhere. The larger areas are Forestry Commission and North West Water plantations. The many smaller conifer dominated woodlands are not large enough to be fully commercial.

Game

8.71 Over a quarter of the County is covered by moorland (Figure 120) and it is known that some of it is managed for game. However, no data were made available on the extent of game management, the number of shoots or the productivity of shoots. It is known that the management of heather moorland for game can be beneficial in providing a habitat for other upland bird species (see Chapter 9).

Commercial Fisheries

8.72 Lancashire's rivers, canals and ponds are important for both coarse and game fisheries. Most fresh water fishing is recreational on a 'catch and put' basis. Production figures for such fishing have little meaning. Salmon catches for Lancashire rivers however showed a large rise in 1988 to over 1400 from the previous ten years, which averaged about 500. It is difficult to know if this figure will be sustained and whether it is due to water quality improvements, more intensive fishing, or more assiduous catch reporting. There are commercial fisheries for salmon and sea trout in the estuaries of the River Lune and Ribble, 37 people being licenced to net salmon in the Lune and six in the Ribble (NRA, pers. comm.).

Table 80	Farm Size in Lancashire. 1988			
Size in ha.	Number of Holdings	% of All Holdings	Area (ha)	Average Holding Size (ha)
Under 20	3,239	41	22,182	6.8
20–99.9	2,457	31	113,046	46.0
100–299.9	364	5	53,575	147.2
300 ha +	57	1	34,260	601.1
Not classified	1,770	22	3,648	2.1
LANCASHIRE	7,887	100	226,711	28.7

Source: Ministry of Agriculture, Fisheries and Food (1988)

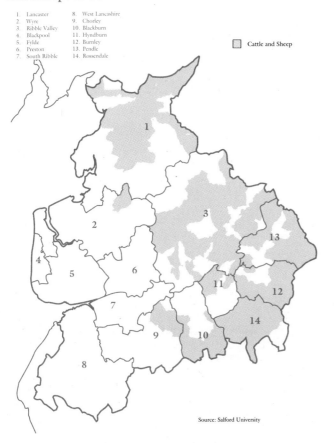

Figure 127

Lancashire: Dominant Farm Type - Cattle and Sheep. 1988

1. Lancaster
2. Wyre
3. Ribble Valley
4. Blackpool
5. Fylde
6. Preston
7. South Ribble
8. West Lancashire
9. Chorley
10. Blackburn
11. Hyndburn
12. Burnley
13. Pendle
14. Rossendale

☐ Cattle and Sheep

Source: Salford University

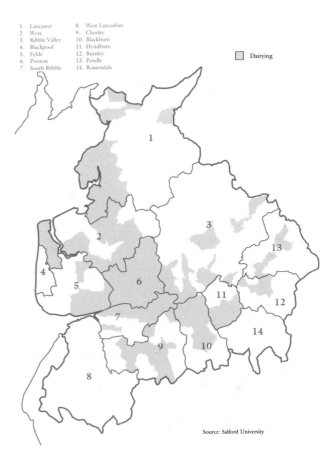

Figure 128

Lancashire: Dominant Farm Type - Dairying. 1988

1. Lancaster
2. Wyre
3. Ribble Valley
4. Blackpool
5. Fylde
6. Preston
7. South Ribble
8. West Lancashire
9. Chorley
10. Blackburn
11. Hyndburn
12. Burnley
13. Pendle
14. Rossendale

☐ Dairying

Source: Salford University

Figure 129

Lancashire: Dominant Farm Type - Sheep and Rough Grazing. 1988

1. Lancaster
2. Wyre
3. Ribble Valley
4. Blackpool
5. Fylde
6. Preston
7. South Ribble
8. West Lancashire
9. Chorley
10. Blackburn
11. Hyndburn
12. Burnley
13. Pendle
14. Rossendale

☐ Sheep and Rough Grazing

Source: Salford University

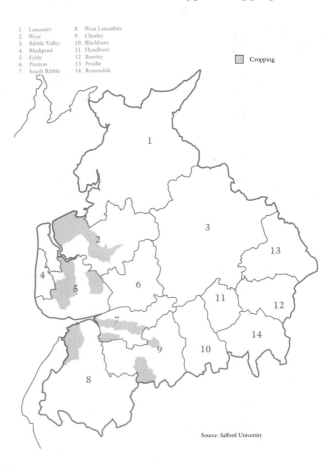

Figure 130

Lancashire: Dominant Farm Type - Cropping. 1988

1. Lancaster
2. Wyre
3. Ribble Valley
4. Blackpool
5. Fylde
6. Preston
7. South Ribble
8. West Lancashire
9. Chorley
10. Blackburn
11. Hyndburn
12. Burnley
13. Pendle
14. Rossendale

☐ Cropping

Source: Salford University

Figure 131

Lancashire: Dominant Farm Type - Horticulture. 1988

1. Lancaster
2. Wyre
3. Ribble Valley
4. Blackpool
5. Fylde
6. Preston
7. South Ribble
8. West Lancashire
9. Chorley
10. Blackburn
11. Hyndburn
12. Burnley
13. Pendle
14. Rossendale

Horticulture

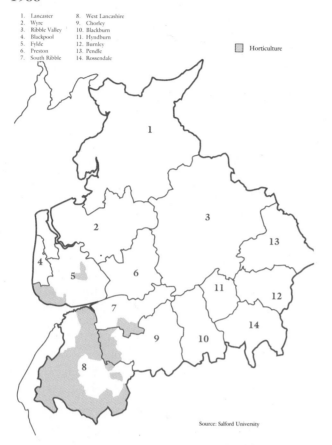

Source: Salford University

Figure 132

Lancashire: Dominant Farm Type – Pigs and Poultry. 1988

1. Lancaster
2. Wyre
3. Ribble Valley
4. Blackpool
5. Fylde
6. Preston
7. South Ribble
8. West Lancashire
9. Chorley
10. Blackburn
11. Hyndburn
12. Burnley
13. Pendle
14. Rossendale

Pigs and Poultry

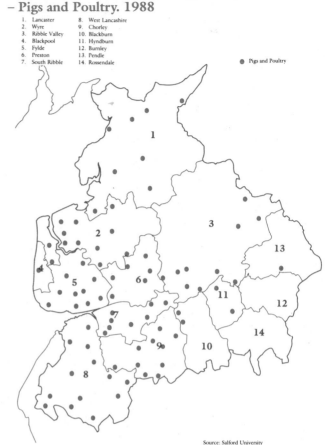

Source: Salford University

8.73 'Inshore' fishing takes place within a three mile limit of the coast. Lancashire's inshore fisheries form part of the North Western and North Wales Sea Fisheries (NWNWSF) District, which extends from Haverigg Point in Morecambe Bay to Cemaes Head, Dyfed. The principal areas involved in the County are around Morecambe, Heysham, the Lune and Wyre estuaries, Fleetwood, Blackpool, Lytham and Southport. These relate predominantly to shellfish harvesting, although sea fish landings are recorded at some sites. Shellfish of importance are clams, cockles, mussels, oysters, periwinkles and shrimps. No commercial crab or lobster production takes place.

8.74 During 1989, commercial fishing in Lancashire supported 221 men full-time, using 82 boats and 28 vehicles. However, 158 men and over half the boats were employed in offshore trawling; the

remainder pursuing netting, shrimping and cockling. Part-time employment supported a further 71 men, 20 boats and 31 vehicles; almost wholly in inshore activity.

8.75 Fishery production levels are reported by MAFF and in the quarterly reports of the NWNWSFC. These offer only a partial indication of production. This is because not all landings can be recorded and those that are do not always give an indication of source. Thus, shellfish caught outside Lancashire may be landed at Lancashire ports due to weather conditions, market demand, etc. The same applies to some sea fish landings. The tonnages of recorded landings for 1989 are given in Table 81.

8.76 Table 81 shows how Fleetwood dominates all fishing activity but that shellfish harvesting is more widespread. 57% of fish landings at Fleetwood comprised cod, plaice, mackerel and whiting, with a mixture of inshore species making up the remainder. Shellfish landings vary between localities, but shrimps and prawns are important generally, representing 14.7% of all landings. Mussels constitute 34% of all landings but are restricted to Morecambe. The catch at Fleetwood comprises nephrops, queens, scallops and squid, which together account for 51% of all shellfish landings. The total value of all fish landings for the County in 1989 was £5.9 m, with Fleetwood landings representing 98% of this figure. Shellfish contributed £0.6 m, predominantly at Morecambe (19.8%) and Fleetwood (75.6%).

Table 81 Fish Landings at Lancashire Ports. 1989

	Morecambe	Lune	Fleetwood	Blackpool	Lytham	Total
Demersal species	27.12	14.31	5,193.24	–	–	5,234.67
Pelagic species	6.18	0.1	3.63	–	–	9.91
Shellfish	272.85	5.45	317.32	2.74	14.17	612.53
LANCASHIRE	306.15	19.86	5,514.19	2.74	14.17	5,857.11

Source: North Western and North Wales Sea Fisheries Committee (1989).

Notes: All figures are in Tonnes.

8.77 In terms of land use and economy, inshore fishing might be considered a minor activity. But it is an important indicator of marine pollution, most of which arises as a consequence of other land uses in the County.

Environmental Effects

8.78 Land is a precious natural resource susceptible to degradation by the uses which are made of it. These uses can also affect other parts of the environmental system like air and water. Land in Lancashire is used for housing, industrial development, waste disposal, road building, mineral working and so on, but about 75% of the County is taken up by agriculture and forestry. These uses therefore exert a dominant influence on our land resource.

8.79 Two main environmental effects have been experienced in Lancashire. Firstly, landscape and habitat changes have been brought about since the war, as hedgerows have been removed, land drained and moorland reclaimed due to the intensification of agriculture. These aspects are dealt with more fully in the next two Chapters.

8.80 Secondly, agriculture contributes to the pollution of land and water. Pollution occurs principally because of fertiliser and pesticide applications on crops and organic waste products from livestock. Fertiliser run-off and leaching has caused the hyper-eutrophication of watercourses which has brought about ecological changes in water bodies (see Chapter 4). It has also affected drinking water supplies as nitrates from nitrogen-based fertilisers have percolated down to groundwater aquifers drawn for public water supply. This appears to be more of a problem in East Anglia, the Midlands and the South-West of England where arable farming is more prevalent. Pollution from farm waste can occur in major spillages leading to fish kills or in a large number of minor leakages to watercourses which collectively downgrade river quality. Descriptions of river water quality in the County including both chemical and biological analyses are given in Chapter 4.

8.81 Intensive livestock production in the form of dairy farming or beef fattening cause some of the major sources of farm pollution. The main problems are silage (fermented grass) liquor, farm yard washings and slurry. Silage use has increased massively since the late 1960s and now 90% of all farmers (other than pure arable) are making and feeding silage. Grass is ensiled in farm yards, waste ground or on the edges of fields from which silage liquor can seep. Such liquor is acidic, corrosive and 200 times as polluting as untreated domestic sewage. It is impossible to dilute silage liquor sufficiently to prevent damage and it should be kept away from streams or underground water supplies altogether.

8.82 Farm yard washings and dairy parlour washings constitute another pollution source since they contain dung and urine. They should not be allowed to run directly into a watercourse but instead taken into a soakaway · or settling tank (Ministry of Agriculture, Fisheries and Food 1973).

Table 82	Annual Waste Production by Populations of Cattle, Pigs and Chickens in Lancashire. 1988	
	Population	Waste Production (tonnes/year)
Cattle	265,490	3,963,353
Pigs	218,202	358,394
Chickens	4,323,943	216,197
LANCASHIRE	4,807,635	4,537,944

Source: Ministry of Agriculture, Fisheries and Food (1973, 1988).

8.83 Farm slurry consists mainly of excreta from livestock. Quantities vary with types of animal and the type of feed they eat. MAFF estimate that an adult cow produces 40.9 kg of excreta per day, a pig 4.5 kg per day and a chicken 0.05 tonnes a year (Ministry of Agriculture, Fisheries and Food 1973). MAFF Agricultural Census data give 1988 population of cattle, pigs and chickens in Lancashire. When multiplied by the amount of waste each animal produces it would appear that over 4.5 million tonnes of animal excreta a year need to be disposed of in the County (Table 82).

8.84 MAFF suggest that between 90–95% of all livestock excreta is disposed of in accordance with good agricultural practice. At the higher level of good practice (95%), some quarter of a million tonnes of farm excreta are disposed of each year in Lancashire without due care. The position is underscored by statistics on water pollution incidents from the NRA which show that farm pollution was the main source of incident in the County in 1988/89 (Chapter 4) and that slurry was the main cause of farm pollution incidents in 1989. The reasons were principally inadequate storage design capacity, collapsing and leaking of stores, and poor operation of stores (National Rivers Authority/Ministry of Agriculture, Fisheries and Food 1990). In the North West Region of NRA farm pollution incidents from cattle or cows in 1989 were greatest for silage, followed by slurry, yard washings and dairy/parlour washings. The NRA report that in the North West, as in previous years, the pattern of pollution incidents shows the highest proportion arising from dairy farming and beef fattening practices in the lowland areas of the Fylde Plain, Ribble Valley and lower catchments of the River Lune. (Compare with Figures 127 and 128).

8.85 Pigs were the second highest source of farm pollution incidents in the North West in 1989. Slurry stores and yard washings were the principal causes. Poultry were the third highest source of pollution incidents (National Rivers Authority/Ministry of Agriculture, Fisheries and Food 1990). Figure 132 shows the distribution of pig and poultry farming in the County. They occur in parishes along the Lune, Ribble, Calder, Douglas and Wyre valleys and are therefore likely to be a potential source of pollution in these areas.

8.86 The least pollution from livestock can be expected in the areas of rough grazing for sheep (Figure 129) which have relatively low intensity stocking and waste production. However, sheep dips are a widespread source of localised water pollution incidents and because of the chemicals (pesticides) used, can be quite damaging.

8.87 There was only one water pollution incident related to mineral fertilisers in the North West in 1989 (National Rivers Authority/ Ministry of Agriculture, Fisheries and Food 1990). However, as outlined earlier, the long-term effects of fertiliser use and run-off in terms of eutrophication may be significant on the watercourses and groundwater in parts of the Fylde and West Lancashire where cropping and horticulture are predominant (Figures 130 and 131). In this context, there is a need to be vigilant of drinking water quality where supplies are drawn from aquifers or surface water sources where pollution may be a problem. Chapter 4 outlines quality of drinking water supplies in the County.

8.88 Pesticides and fertilisers are also used in forestry, but application rates are much lower and less frequent than for farming. Losses of nutrients and soil from forested areas occurs when trees are felled during preparation of drainage systems and during planting. Cutting of stands leads to oxidation of soil organic matter with loss of soluble nutrients and erosion of exposed, disturbed soil. Gullying in forests following drainage is common. However, the area of commercial forest in Lancashire is so small that these problems are likely to be negligible.

Complaints

8.89 Complaints regarding the effects of farming on the environment usually concern impacts near urban areas. Most are about odours (see Figure 33 and Table 9) and farm waste disposal.

8.90 West Lancashire has a variety of complaints arising from horticulture and intensive livestocking. Odours are a general problem, but particular complaints (six in 1989/90) concern odours from manure used in mushroom production. Some 50 complaints regarding 23 incidents of slurry spreading and emptying or overflowing slurry tanks were recorded in 1989/90. Blackpool also records complaints about smells from mushroom farms close to the town, amounting to about six per year.

8.91 Fylde has similar types of complaint related to smells especially from pig farms and slurry production. Complaints have also been made about horseflies and rats around such areas. Crop spraying and water course pollution complaints are also recorded. Most problems in Blackburn relate to general odour from pig farms and muck spreading though there have been some complaints about maggot farming. Problems in other Lancashire Districts are generally few and intermittent. Where complaints are referred to District Council Environmental Health Officers, these are usually resolved by discussions with the offender and the complainant.

Environmental Solutions

8.92 In recent years the Government has introduced several schemes for farmers to encourage better protection of the environment. Some are only in their pilot stages whilst others are directed more at areas of over-production in arable crops in the south and east of the UK. However, some are relevant to Lancashire, although take-up on certain schemes has been limited.

Less Favoured Areas

8.93 A large proportion of the County is designated as Less Favoured Areas (LFA). The area involved is 143,152 ha (47% of the County), of which 81,722 ha (or 27%) is 'severely disadvantaged' and 61,430 ha (20%) is disadvantaged (MAFF, pers. comm.). The purpose of this designation is to maintain a minimum population level and conserve the countryside by sustaining farming in an area where agriculture is practically and economically more difficult. This is achieved by selective financial incentives. One of these is the Hill Livestock Compensatory Allowance (HLCA), which is made on the number of breeding cattle and sheep on farms within the LFA that have at least three hectares of usable agricultural land. There are approximately 1,100 claimants in the County. (MAFF, pers. comm.) Although, on the one hand, the HLCA contributes to landscape maintenance, on the other it has led to over-stocking, causing damage to valuable and sensitive habitats like heather moorland and features like hedges, ponds and stone walls. Damage to moorland, upland grassland and woodland floras by overgrazing has been noted in the County with problems being highlighted on upland limestone grassland at Leck Fell and on moorland in the West and South Pennines (see Chapter 9).

8.94 The Government in its Environment White Paper states that, because of damage arising from the HLCA, they are to examine whether the environmental benefits afforded by the scheme should be made more specific, and will be consulting on these ideas.

Set-Aside

8.95 The set-aside scheme offers farmers an incentive to reduce agricultural production. There are eleven participants in the County (MAFF, pers. comm.). They receive payments for taking at least 20% of their arable land out of production for five years and putting it to fallow, woodland or non-agricultural use. Maintenance of hedges, ditches, ponds and other features on, or adjacent to, set-aside land is also encouraged. Because only a small area of Lancashire is used for arable production the potential take-up of this scheme is limited.

Farm and Conservation Grant Scheme

8.96 Introduced in 1989, the Farm and Conservation Grant Scheme replaced earlier incentives aimed at supporting capital investment in the agriculture industry. It is mainly targeted at bringing about environmental improvements on farms. It is not clear how many recipients there are in Lancashire, though MAFF has 138 approved plans in its local division and has received 445 notifications on the 'non-plan' side against which 263 claims have been made. (MAFF, pers. comm.) 50% grant aid is available for the replacement or improvement of waste handling facilities, including silage and slurry stores, and grants are available for the regeneration of native woodlands and heather moors. Grants for repairs to traditional agricultural buildings are available which top up existing grants for hedges, stone walls and shelter belts.

Farm Woodland Scheme

8.97 The Farm Woodland Scheme funded by MAFF aims to reduce agricultural surpluses, provide environmental benefits, contribute to farm income and rural employment and encourage on-farm timber production. Annual payments are made at different rates for different areas, with the most generous grants for arable/improved grassland not covered by LFA status and the smallest grants for unimproved land in LFAs. The payments are made for between 10–40 years depending on the nature of the woodlands planted. Largest payments are given to woodlands with the most broadleaves. Take-up of this scheme in Lancashire is limited to a single case. A similar scheme, the Woodland Grant Scheme, is run by the Forestry Commission with the aim of encouraging timber production.

Farm Diversification Grant Scheme

8.98 The Farm Diversification Grant Scheme run by MAFF is intended to aid farmers in developing alternative commercial uses for agricultural buildings and land. It can include schemes for tourism, recreation and leisure or commerce and industry. The local MAFF division has received 54 applications for capital investment items and 21 applications for feasibility or marketing studies (MAFF, pers. comm.).

Other Schemes

8.99 There are several other schemes which are available nationally but do not at present operate in Lancashire. There are now 19 Environmentally Sensitive Areas (ESA) in the UK covering 3.5% of all agricultural land, ranging from mountains and moorland in Perthshire to wetlands in Somerset and Suffolk. The special qualities of ESA, some of which are in National Parks or AONB, are protected through incentive payments to farmers for the maintenance of traditional farming practices. ESA have been popular with farmers and conservationists and, in 1991, the Government will be assessing their value and deciding whether to extend the scheme. When the scheme was originally announced, the County Council asked the Countryside Commission to recommend to the Government that both of Lancashire's AONB, and the West and South Pennines, be declared ESA. However, the proposal was not accepted.

8.100 Nitrate Sensitive Areas (NSA) have been set up by the Government in ten pilot areas in England with the aim of reducing the amount of nitrate leaching from agricultural land. Farmers in these areas receive free advice on regulating operations like cropping and fertiliser use to reduce the risk of nitrate leaching into water. They also qualify for annual payments to help them make changes, like switching from arable to low intensity grassland cultivation. In a further nine areas, non-designated NSA, farmers get similar free advice on reducing nitrate leaching. There are unlikely to be any NSA designated in Lancashire in the foreseeable future.

References

Ministry of Agriculture, Fisheries and Food (1970). Agricultural Land Classification of England and Wales. Sheet 94, Preston. MAFF.

Ministry of Agriculture, Fisheries and Food (1973). Farm Waste Disposal. Short-term leaflet no. 67. MAFF.

Ministry of Agriculture, Fisheries and Food (1988). Agricultural Statistics, United Kingdom, 1988. HMSO.

National Rivers Authority/Ministry of Agriculture, Fisheries and Food (1990). Water Pollution from Farm Waste 1989, England & Wales. NRA.

North Western and North Wales Sea Fisheries Committee (1989). Quarterly Reports of the Clerk and Chief Fishery Officer. NWNWSFC.

Chapter Nine
Wildlife

Introduction

9.1 We need wild plants and animals. They can tell us a great deal about the quality of our environment as a whole, and many kinds of wildlife are sensitive indicators of pollution. Indeed, much of our awareness of pollution hazards comes from the study of wildlife and its habitats. Wild plants and animals are an integral part of the County's ecosystems: they are often a conspicuous element in our most cherished landscapes and can enrich people's lives in towns and in the countryside. Wild places like ancient woods or peat bogs can yield fascinating insights into the past – including our human past – going back hundreds or even thousands of years.

9.2 Wild plants and animals depend for their survival on very specific and diverse kinds of habitat, like estuarine mud flats, ancient woodlands or farm ponds. Much concern has been expressed about the loss of such habitats nationally, and globally, which could lead to the extinction of species in the next few decades on an unprecedented scale. Thus, the following sections look at the principal habitats in Lancashire and the wildlife that depends on them; what is happening to them, and what sort of protection they receive.

9.3 Wildlife habitats vary enormously in terms of their age; their origin; the extent to which they are man-made; and their importance. A lot of emphasis is placed in this account on semi-natural habitats, because these are generally the most valuable for wildlife and are most in need of protection. But it should be borne in mind that these include sites of national importance which did not exist 70, or even 10, years ago. Moreover, most of the common wildlife – the plants and animals which we come into contact with most regularly – do not live on special sites, but in the wider countryside, as well as in, and around, our towns. It should also be remembered that transitions between one habitat and another, (for example, the change from reedswamp to open water), and intricate mixtures of habitats, (like glades or rides in woodland), can be just as important to some animals and birds as the principal habitat types that are described here.

9.4 Our wildlife depends upon every part of Lancashire's Environmental System, and the wider world, for food, shelter and survival. Soils, climate and topography are the major determinants of vegetation type and cover. Plants of all kinds, in turn, provide the base material for animal life. Air and water quality are also critical for most species and the impact that human activity has upon this quality, emphasises the crucial rôle that we play in the survival, or otherwise, of wild plants and animals.

9.5 After dealing with the legislation for wildlife protection, and the organisations in Lancashire concerned with this, the Chapter examines the distribution of the principal habitats in the County and the plants and animals associated with them. This is followed by an analysis of the protection given to specific habitats and species, of the threats and changes affecting wildlife resources, and the arrangements which exist for monitoring.

Legislation

European

9.6 A number of international agreements and directives apply in the UK. Britain is a contracting party to the Convention held in Ramsar, Iran in 1971. Under this, the DOE is responsible for designating wetlands of international importance for their wildfowl, wading birds, or other wild animals or plants, in accordance with agreed scientific criteria. Such designations are termed Ramsar sites.

9.7 The Convention of the Conservation of European Wildlife and Natural Habitats (Bern Convention) came into force in June 1982. The UK, as a contracting party, is required to:

* legislate to conserve the habitats of specified endangered flora and fauna;

* protect areas important for specified migratory species;

* prohibit the deliberate damage to, or destruction of, breeding or resting sites of certain species.

9.8 EC Directive (79/409/EEC) on the Conservation of Wild Birds came into force in April 1981, and requires member States to maintain populations of certain species and to preserve a sufficient diversity of habitats for their conservation. The Directive requires that member States:

* classify the most suitable habitats for listed species as Special Protection Areas;

* formulate and implement plans for the conservation and use of listed wetlands;

* establish nature reserves for wetlands, whether included in the list or not, and provide adequately for their wardening.

9.9 EC Directive (85/799/EEC) is applied to secure habitat conservation within UK farming landscapes by the designation of Environmentally Sensitive Areas. Under this, MAFF pays farmers to adopt traditional management practices, designed to farm land productively, but in accord with landscape and habitat conservation objectives.

United Kingdom

Habitat Protection

9.10 The Wildlife and Countryside Act, (WCA) 1981 forms the basis of almost all statutory protection of wildlife in Britain. It consolidated and extended previous wildlife law, contained principally in the National Parks and Access to the Countryside Act (NPACA) 1949. Part I of the WCA 1981, deals with the protection of animals and plants, and includes 'schedules' listing the species afforded particular protection. Part II of the Act addresses general nature conservation requirements and habitat, or site protection. Sites of Special Scientific Interest (SSSI), National Nature Reserves (NNR), Limestone Pavement Orders (LPO) and Management Agreements are the main measures included for habitat protection.

9.11   SSSI are the most widely used protection measure. Responsibility for their designation rests with the Nature Conservancy Council (NCC), the statutory body for nature conservation in the UK. SSSI include the best examples of our natural heritage of wildlife habitats, geological features and landforms. A few are nature reserves, but the majority are privately owned and often managed primarily for purposes other than nature conservation.

9.12   Under the WCA 1981, SSSI must be formally 'notified' by NCC to the owners and occupiers of the land, the Secretary of State for the Environment and the local planning authority. The relevant water company and the National Rivers Authority are formally notified about the existence of SSSI under Section 9 of the Water Act, 1989. Owners and occupiers must give NCC notice in writing if they intend to carry out any operations which have been notified to them by NCC as likely to damage the special interest of the site concerned. Local planning authorities are required to consult NCC when considering granting planning permission for any proposed development on SSSI. The NCC is empowered to enter into management agreements with owners and occupiers, involving financial payments where appropriate, in order to conserve the special interest of these sites.

9.13   NNR are areas of outstanding importance declared by the NCC under Section 19 of the NPACA 1949. Some are owned and leased by NCC, but many are established under agreements with the owners and occupiers. All are managed in the interests of nature conservation, and provide opportunities for study and research. Under the WCA 1981, NNR can also be held and managed by approved bodies other than NCC. Visitors are welcome on most NNR, but permits are often required for access away from public rights of way.

9.14   Local authorities have powers under Section 21 of the NPACA 1949 to declare Local Nature Reserves (LNR) in consultation with the NCC. LNR must normally be of high nature conservation interest, or have a high natural history value in a District or County context for formal education and public enjoyment, to be considered for designation in consultation with NCC. Before a declaration can be made, the local authority must either own or lease the site, or obtain agreement from the owner. Local authorities are empowered to acquire land for LNR by compulsory purchase if necessary, and also to apply byelaws to assist in site protection and management.

9.15   Under Section 39 of the WCA 1981, local planning authorities are empowered to enter into Management Agreements with owners or occupiers of land in order to conserve and enhance the natural beauty or amenity (including wildlife value) of that land. Similarly the NCC may enter into management agreements with owners/occupiers under Section 15 of the Countryside Act (CA) 1968.

9.16   The WCA 1981 makes provision for the protection of limestone pavements. Under Section 34 where the NCC or the Countryside Commission are of the opinion that a pavement is of special interest, they will inform the local planning authority. The local planning authority may then make a LPO, prohibiting the removal or disturbance of limestone. Further working of any limestone requires planning permission from the County planning authority.

9.17   Along with government departments, local authorities are required by Section 11 of the CA 1968 'to have regard to the desirability of conserving the national beauty and amenity of the Countryside'. This statement is amplified by the government Circular 27/87 'Nature Conservation', which states that 'This duty embraces the conservation of flora, fauna, geological and physiological features and extends to urban as well as rural areas.' Authorities are particularly urged to ensure that where they hold or own land for any purpose, their own estate management practices take nature conservation considerations fully into account. It also urges local authorities to have regard for nature conservation when determining planning applications and developing land use policies in Local Plans.

9.18   The Town and Country Planning Act, (TCPA) 1990 ensures that any operations which constitute development, including mineral extraction, require the consent of the local authority. However, many acts of agricultural development, including drainage, removal of vegetation, cultivation, etc., do not require planning consent. If planning permission is required for development, the local authority can apply conditions to the consent requiring the developer to undertake operations which may be in the interest of nature conservation.

9.19   The minerals section of the TCPA 1990 is of direct relevance to the conservation of remnant lowland peat mosses. Under the Act, the mineral planning authority are empowered to deal with inadequate, poorly conditioned planning consents for mineral extraction and have a duty to review working sites on a regular basis. Where new methods of peat working are contemplated, the original planning permission on sites (perhaps now inactive) may be revoked. This requires a peat company to re-apply for planning consent, and allows the re-negotiation of restoration conditions and proposed after uses and even the termination of operations.

9.20   Under the TCPA 1990, tree preservation orders (TPO) can be made by District or County Councils. These are made principally on landscape grounds, but small woods (which may be important habitats) can be covered by a TPO.

9.21   The felling of trees in Great Britain is controlled by the Forestry Commission under the Forestry Acts 1967 and 1986. A licence from the Forestry Commission is normally required to fell growing trees, but in any calendar quarter, up to 5 m³ of timber may be felled without a licence, providing that no more than 2 m³ are sold. There are also a number of special case exemptions. The Forestry Act 1986 enables the Forestry Commission to replace trees, other than those covered by a TPO, felled without authority. Amendments to the Forestry Acts 1967–1976 require the Commission to achieve a reasonable balance between forestry practices and nature conservation interests.

9.22 Under the Protection of Birds Act 1954 wildfowl refuges or sanctuaries could be designated. Even though the Act has been repealed, the Interpretation Act, 1976 allows statutory Wildfowl Refuges designated under the Act, to remain valid.

9.23 Inheritors of land may be exempted from Capital Transfer Tax if the land concerned is assessed by the NCC to be of special wildlife value. In practice, this usually means that the land is notified as an SSSI or is of comparable quality. Tax exemption is awarded in return for the owner agreeing to manage the land to conserve its features of special interest. A parallel arrangement exists with the Countryside Commission over land of special landscape value.

Species Protection

9.24 Schedules 5 and 8 of the WCA 1981 list the wild animals and plants which are afforded full legal protection. Under Section 9 of the Act, it is normally an offence to kill, injure, take, possess or sell scheduled animals (whether live or dead), or to disturb or destroy their place of shelter and protection. Under Section 13 of the Act, it is normally an offence to pick, uproot, sell or destroy scheduled plants.

9.25 Special measures to protect birds are also contained in the WCA 1981. Under Section 1, it is normally an offence to kill, injure or take any wild bird; to take, damage or destroy the nest of any wild bird while its nest is in use or being built; or to take or destroy an egg of any wild bird. In addition, it is normally an offence to disturb any Schedule 1 species while it is building a nest or is in, on or near a nest containing eggs or young; or to disturb the dependent young of any Schedule 1 species.

9.26 The Badgers Act 1981 gives legal protection to the badger, but not to its sett. The Protection of Badger Setts Bill, currently before Parliament, seeks to protect setts which are in use, whether or not badgers are in residence.

9.27 'Red Data' books are non-statutory lists of plant or animal species which are rare, endangered or vulnerable in a particular geographical area, together with their habitat requirements, the threats they face, and the extent to which existing populations are protected. British Red Data Books have so far been produced for flowering plants, insects and birds, though none exist for Lancashire. The Landscape and Wildlife Strategy for Lancashire proposes that a Red Data Book should be prepared for such species in the County.

Organisations

Central Government

9.28 The NCC is the body responsible for advising government on nature conservation in Great Britain. Its work includes the selection, establishment and management of NNR, the selection and management of Marine Nature Reserves, the identification and notification of SSSI, the provision of advice to others and dissemination of knowledge about nature conservation and the support and

conduct of research relevant to these functions. NCC may also fund management agreements on notified sites and grant-aid other projects of nature conservation value.

9.29 The DOE, although primarily concerned with other aspects of the environment, through its revised arrangements on grants for the treatment of derelict land with a nature conservation after-use, is relevant to nature conservation in Lancashire. The DOE is also responsible for the designation of wetlands as Ramsar sites and of Special Protection Areas (SPA) which are both considered to be of international importance.

9.30 The Countryside Commission contributes significantly to the conservation and creation of wildlife habitats in the wider environment, in terms of advice and grant-aid for landscape conservation works. MAFF is also growing in importance as a provider of funds and advice to encourage conservation on farms. It provides grants under the Farm and Conservation Grant Scheme and the Farm Woodland Scheme to provide facilities which can benefit wildlife conservation.

Local Government

9.31 County and District Councils have been actively involved in wildlife conservation for many years. This has involved the protection of habitats through development control and Structure and Local Plan provisions, as well as the active promotion of conservation through sympathetic land reclamation and improvement schemes, and practical support for local communities and the volunteer nature conservation sector.

9.32 In Lancashire, existing and proposed areas of activity are integrated and given new momentum in the County Council's recent 'Landscape and Wildlife Strategy for Lancashire'. This was approved by the County Council in July 1990 and sets out practical strategies for:

* landscape conservation;
* semi-natural habitats and species protection;
* man-made and urban landscapes;
* County Council land holdings;
* derelict land;
* increasing public awareness, the rôle of the voluntary sector and community involvement.

Other Organisations

9.33 Under Section 8 of the Water Act 1989, NWW and the NRA have a duty to conserve flora, fauna, geological and physiographical features of special interest on their land. Under Section 9 of the Act, NWW and the NRA also have a duty to have regard to SSSI notified to them by the NCC and to receive written consent from the NCC before carrying out any works, operations or activities which are likely to destroy, damage or significantly prejudice any of those aspects of the special interest referred to in the notification.

9.34 These conservation duties are embodied in NWW's own Code of Practice on Conservation, Access and Recreation (revised 1990). The Water Company's predecessor, the North West Water

Authority, contributed significantly to nature conservation on its holdings in terms of woodland reinstatement, habitat creation and the provision of informal nature conservation areas. It also licensed areas to voluntary bodies to manage.

9.35 The Lancashire Trust For Nature Conservation (LTNC) is the main independent charity concerned with the conservation of all wildlife in the County. With a membership of over 3,400, presently growing at a rate of over 20% per year, the Trust manages 35 reserves and carries out surveys, practical tasks and education and community projects. LTNC is also responsible for a number of urban wildlife projects in which the development of links with local communities is an important element.

9.36 The Royal Society for the Protection of Birds (RSPB) is Europe's largest voluntary wildlife conservation body, supported by a subscribing membership of over half a million. The Society manages a network of reserves in Great Britain, actively campaigns on environmental issues as they affect wild birds and undertakes conservation research. It owns and manages reserves in Lancashire at Leighton Moss, Morecambe Bay and Warton Crag.

9.37 The Woodland Trust is a national charity concerned with the conservation of native and broadleaved trees and woodland, through the acquisition of existing woods and the planting of new ones. The Trust presently owns over 350 woods nationally, including eight in Lancashire.

9.38 The British Trust for Conservation Volunteers (BTCV) is a national charity aiming to involve people of all ages and backgrounds in practical conservation work. This can vary from hedge laying and drystone walling to pond restoration and tree planting. The Trust has a residential volunteer centre near Chorley which caters for 'Natural Break' working holidays and weekend groups from schools and colleges. BTCV works closely with local volunteer groups and does invaluable work for local authorities in the County.

9.39 The Lancashire Farming and Wildlife Advisory Group (FWAG) is an independent forum of farmers, landowners, conservation bodies, MAFF, local authorities and other environmental and local interests. FWAG aims to reconcile the differences between modern farming methods and landscape and wildlife conservation. It employs a full-time adviser, and offers free advice to farmers and landowners on all aspects of conservation that can be part of an efficient farming unit.

9.40 The work of Groundwork Trusts and of the Lancashire branch of the Council for the Protection of Rural England are important, whilst the activities of the Wildfowl and Wetland's Trust at Martin Mere near Burscough has helped create a site of international importance. The very significant work undertaken by local wildlife societies, field clubs and amateur naturalists cannot be underestimated. These often provide the initial sources of information that enable the larger bodies like NCC, LTNC and local authorities to execute their duties.

Wildlife in Lancashire

Sources of Information

9.41 The main difficulty in auditing Lancashire's wildlife is that the kind of information which is really needed is only partly available. As yet, there are only incomplete estimates of the total County areas of certain major habitats. There is little quantitive information on population sizes or trends, except for bird or butterfly counts on certain reserves and other key areas. Moreover, the results of different surveys carried out using different methods are generally incompatible. Fortunately, the last decade has seen increased activity in survey and recording and this looks set to continue in the 1990s.

9.42 The principal sources of information on wildlife habitats in the County are:

* 'Phase 1' habitat surveys, which map all habitats in an area using a nationally adopted methodology developed by the NCC. Sites and features of particular interest are also identified and described in accompanying 'target notes'. Total areas for the different habitats mapped can be calculated on a District basis, and a County data base thus established. So far in Lancashire, surveys have been completed for Ribble Valley, Blackburn, Hyndburn, Burnley, Pendle and Rossendale. Surveys are currently in progress in Preston, South Ribble, Chorley, Fylde and West Lancashire, and it is anticipated that they will be completed in 1991. At the present time, therefore, it is not possible to present comparable, quantitive data for the County as a whole. Nevertheless, data for those Districts where survey and analysis is complete have been presented in this version of the Audit to illustrate particular points;

* the National Vegetation Classification (NVC) has been developed by Lancaster University under contract to the NCC. Using plant species and habitat data obtained in the field, it aims, for the first time, to provide a comprehensive classification of British vegetation. The NVC is, in its simplest of terms, a system of classifying the vegetation communities of habitats on the basis of plants (whether trees, shrubs, flowering plants, mosses, etc.) that commonly occur together. These commonly occurring plants give their names to the communities of the habitat to which they belong. For example, the common oak–bracken–blackberry community is one of several NVC communities to occur among Lancashire's woodland habitat. The NVC is being prepared for publication at the time of writing. It is hoped that future Audits will draw upon the NVC in much greater detail;

* Sites of Special Scientific Interest notification papers;

* NCC publications and internal reports, including the Invertebrates Sites Register for Lancashire;

* RSPB publications, reserve reports, estuary and bird species summaries;

* NCC and LTNC site and species files;

* the County Council's own ecological research.

Sources of information relating to specific habitat types are referred to in the relevant habitat sections.

Woodland Habitat

9.43 This section firstly examines the extent of present total woodland cover, and then the proportions of ancient, pre-1945 and post-1945 woodland which make up this total. This is followed by a brief examination of the botanical diversity of Lancashire's woodlands, using the NVC classification and an outline of their principal plant and animal species. This general pattern of coverage and composition is adopted for each of the main habitat types described below.

Present Woodland Cover

9.44 The history of Lancashire's woodland goes back much further than any written record. Pollen grains preserved in peat tell us that 5,000 years ago by far the greater part of Lancashire, in common with the rest of Britain, was covered in broadleaved forest. However, today only 5% of the County is covered by woodland (see Table 77) compared to a UK average of 9%. This is one of the most eloquent testimonies we have to the influence of people upon the environment of the County.

9.45 3.3% of woodland is composed of approximately 1,226 woods over 2 ha, amounting to some 10,134 ha in all (see Table 83). The total area is made up of approximately 28% 'ancient', 54% pre-war secondary and 18% post-war secondary woodland.

9.46 Little woodland occurs in the east of the County above the 300 m contour, and over large areas of highly productive agricultural land in the west. However, the resource is generally scattered over the County as a whole. In terms of Districts over 62% of the total woodland area lies in Lancaster (2,592 ha), and Ribble Valley (3,729 ha) Wyre, Chorley, West Lancashire and Blackburn each support over 500 ha, whilst the least woodland is found in Blackpool, Rossendale, Hyndburn and Fylde. Only three Districts have a higher percentage of woodland than the County average: Lancaster (4.5%), Ribble Valley (6.4%) and Blackburn (4.1%) (see Table 83). The figures of 10,134 ha given above relate to woods of 2 ha and above in area. But Lancashire has many much smaller stands and copses. Precise figures for their extent do not exist. However, the satellite estimates indicate that these may total over 6,300 ha.

Ancient Woodland

9.47 Ancient woodland originated at least as long ago as 1600. Although the actual trees now standing in such woods may all be younger than this, it means that the site has been continuously wooded at least since that time. Indeed, such woods may be directly descended from the original 'wildwood';

District	Total No. Woods	Total Area (ha)	% Woodland Cover
Lancaster	280	2,592	4.5
Wyre	99	549	1.9
Ribble Valley	342	3,729	6.4
Blackpool	–	–	–
Fylde	49	197	1.2
Preston	36	319	2.2
South Ribble	36	199	1.8
West Lancashire	90	620	1.8
Chorley	78	540	2.7
Blackburn	66	563	4.1
Hyndburn	32	141	1.9
Burnley	53	347	3.1
Pendle	34	210	1.2
Rossendale	31	128	0.9
LANCASHIRE	1,226	10,134	3.3

Table 83 Total Woodland in Lancashire. 1986

Source: Lancashire County Council (1986).

Note: Only Woodlands over 2ha are included in this Table.

the natural woodland cover which re-established itself over most of the British Isles after the last Ice Age 10,000 years ago. Because of their continuity, ancient woodlands are usually of much greater ecological value than their more recent counterparts. As landscape features of great antiquity, these also have a much-undervalued historical significance.

9.48 There are 2,802 ha of existing woodland on ancient sites, including plantations on ancient sites (Table 84 and Figure 133). These occur in most parts of the County, but are strongly associated with river and stream side sites – often on steep slopes – in the valleys of the Ribble, the Lune and the Wyre (and to a lesser extent the Douglas and the headwaters of the Irwell) and their tributaries. The major exception to this rule is the important collection of woodland in the Arnside-Silverdale AONB. Rarely does ancient woodland now occur above the 150 m contour. With around 38% of the County's ancient woodland, Lancaster contains more than any other District; but a further 25.7% occurs in Ribble Valley. Very little exists in West Lancashire, Pendle or Rossendale, and there is none in Fylde or Blackpool. Ancient woodlands which have been regarded as semi-natural show a similar distribution, concentrated in the north and centre of the County.

Pre-1945 Secondary Woodland

9.49 Secondary woods originated after 1600, on sites that had previously been cleared of trees, usually many centuries earlier. They may be either plantations of broadleaved or coniferous trees, or of

Figure 133
Ancient Woodland in Lancashire, 1988

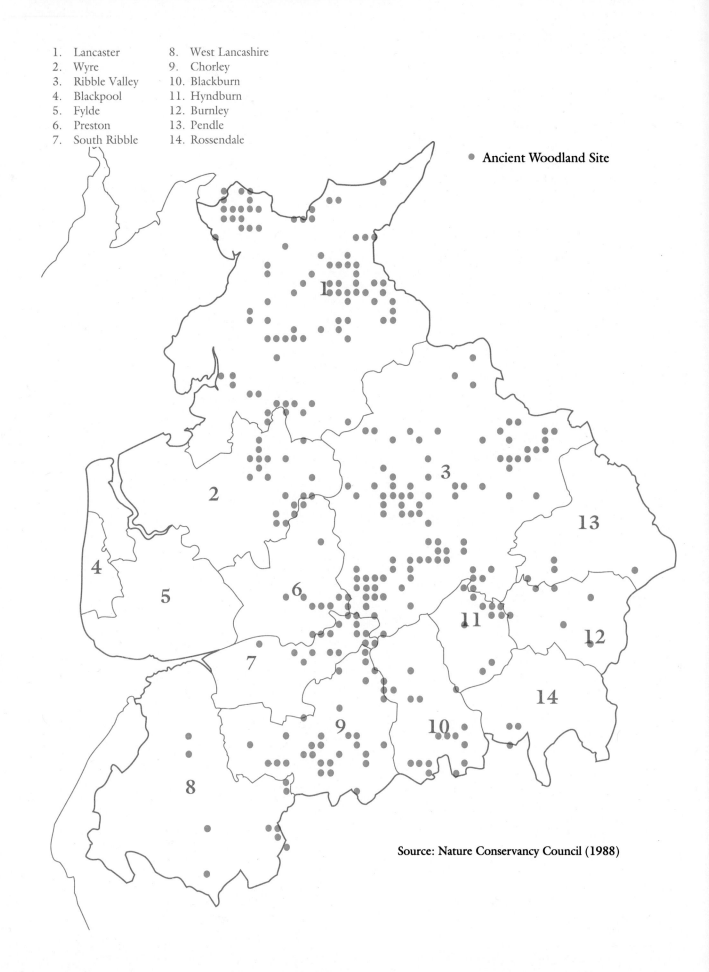

1. Lancaster
2. Wyre
3. Ribble Valley
4. Blackpool
5. Fylde
6. Preston
7. South Ribble
8. West Lancashire
9. Chorley
10. Blackburn
11. Hyndburn
12. Burnley
13. Pendle
14. Rossendale

● Ancient Woodland Site

Source: Nature Conservancy Council (1988)

both, or may have grown up naturally within this period on non-woodland sites.

9.50 Secondary woods have been established in all parts of the County, including areas, and sites, which no longer support any ancient woodland such as the Fylde (except for Blackpool) and on the Bowland Fells. About 35% of all such woodland in the County is in Ribble Valley; the larger part of which is coniferous plantations. Other Districts with relatively large areas of secondary woodland include Lancaster, West Lancashire (mostly broadleaved) and Blackburn and Chorley (mostly coniferous). (See Table 85 and Figure 134).

Post-1945 Secondary Woodland

9.51 Since the last war, about 1,864 ha of new woodland have been planted (Table 86 and Figure 135), which forms about 18.4% of the total County area of woodland over 2 ha in size. Some 62% of this increase is coniferous, and a further 38% is mainly broadleaved – largely the result of planting by the Forestry Commission, water undertakings and private owners in the Forest of Bowland, and to a lesser extent to the south of Blackburn. Little new woodland has been planted in the west of the County, particularly in South Ribble whilst none at all has occurred in Fylde and Blackpool.

Size Distribution of Woodland

9.52 Lancashire is a County of small woods. Woods larger than 100 ha are very rare, and, with a

Table 85 Pre-1945 Secondary Woodland in Lancashire. 1986

District	Total No. Woods	Area Mainly Broadleaved (ha)	Area Mainly Coniferous (ha)	Total Area (ha)
Lancaster	182	1,139	132	1,271
Wyre	73	251	60	311
Ribble Valley	206	742	1,163	1,905
Blackpool	—	—	—	—
Fylde	49	197	—	197
Preston	24	85	31	116
South Ribble	14	86	—	86
West Lancashire	76	522	5	527
Chorley	37	233	36	269
Blackburn	29	228	8	236
Hyndburn	11	48	12	60
Burnley	43	249	23	272
Pendle	24	87	69	156
Rossendale	19	53	9	62
LANCASHIRE	787	3,920	1,548	5,468

Source: Lancashire County Council (1986)

Note: Only Secondary Woodlands over 2ha are included in this Table.

Table 84 Ancient Woodland in Lancashire. 1988

District	Total No. Woods	Area Ancient Semi-Natural (ha)	Area Plantation on Ancient Sites (ha)	Total Area (ha)
Lancaster	122	872	182	1,054
Wyre	22	177	7	184
Ribble Valley	114	670	50	720
Blackpool	—	—	—	—
Fylde	—	—	—	—
Preston	12	161	—	161
South Ribble	21	93	18	111
West Lancashire	10	47	26	73
Chorley	38	223	7	230
Blackburn	25	123	42	165
Hyndburn	14	50	—	50
Burnley	6	11	20	31
Pendle	5	17	—	17
Rossendale	3	5	1	6
LANCASHIRE	392	2,449	353	2,802

Source: Lancashire County Council (1986) and Nature Conservancy Council (1988)

Note: Only Ancient Woodlands over 2ha are included in this Table.

Table 86 Post-1945 Secondary Woodland in Lancashire. 1986

District	Total No. Woods	Area Mainly Broadleaved (ha)	Area Mainly Coniferous (ha)	Total Area (ha)
Lancaster	24 (14)	233	34	267
Wyre	10 (10)	45	9	54
Ribble Valley	57 (46)	145	959	1,104
Blackpool	— (—)	—	—	—
Fylde	— (—)	—	—	—
Preston	5 (5)	13	29	42
South Ribble	1 (1)	2	—	2
West Lancashire	4 (4)	20	—	20
Chorley	10 (5)	41	—	41
Blackburn	13 (13)	90	72	162
Hyndburn	9 (9)	28	3	31
Burnley	7 (7)	31	13	44
Pendle	6 (6)	27	10	37
Rossendale	11 (11)	39	21	60
LANCASHIRE	157 (131)	714	1,150	1,864

Source: Lancashire County Council (1986)

Notes: Brackets = New woodland
Only Secondary Woodlands over 2ha are included in this Table.

Figure 134
Secondary Woodlands (Pre-1945) in Lancashire. 1986

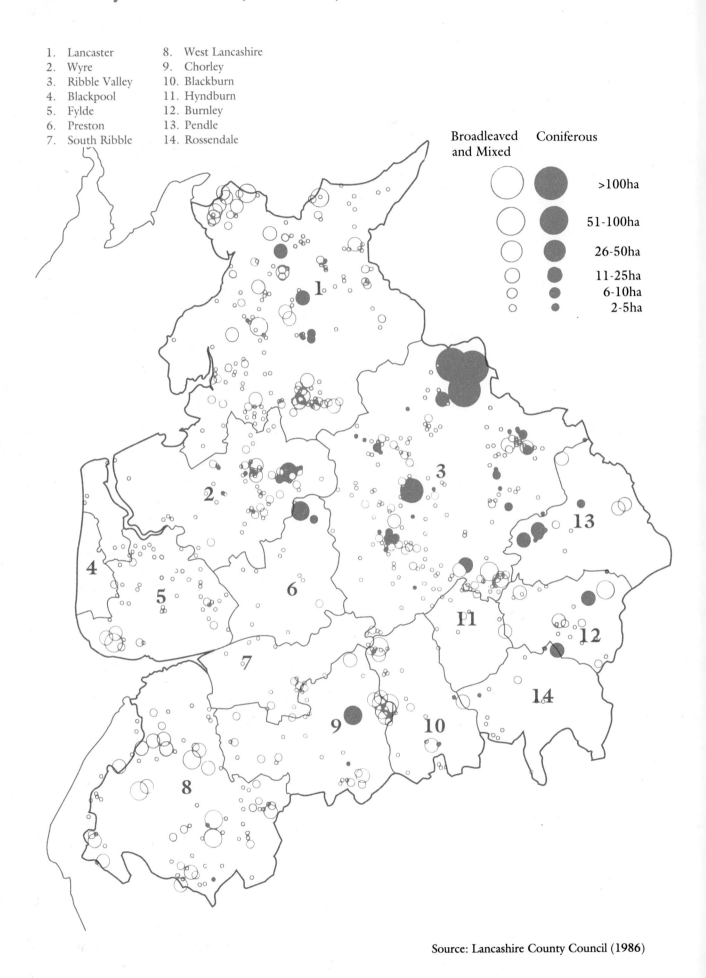

1. Lancaster
2. Wyre
3. Ribble Valley
4. Blackpool
5. Fylde
6. Preston
7. South Ribble
8. West Lancashire
9. Chorley
10. Blackburn
11. Hyndburn
12. Burnley
13. Pendle
14. Rossendale

Broadleaved and Mixed   Coniferous

>100ha
51-100ha
26-50ha
11-25ha
6-10ha
2-5ha

Source: Lancashire County Council (1986)

Figure 135
Secondary Woodlands (Post - 1945) in Lancashire . 1986

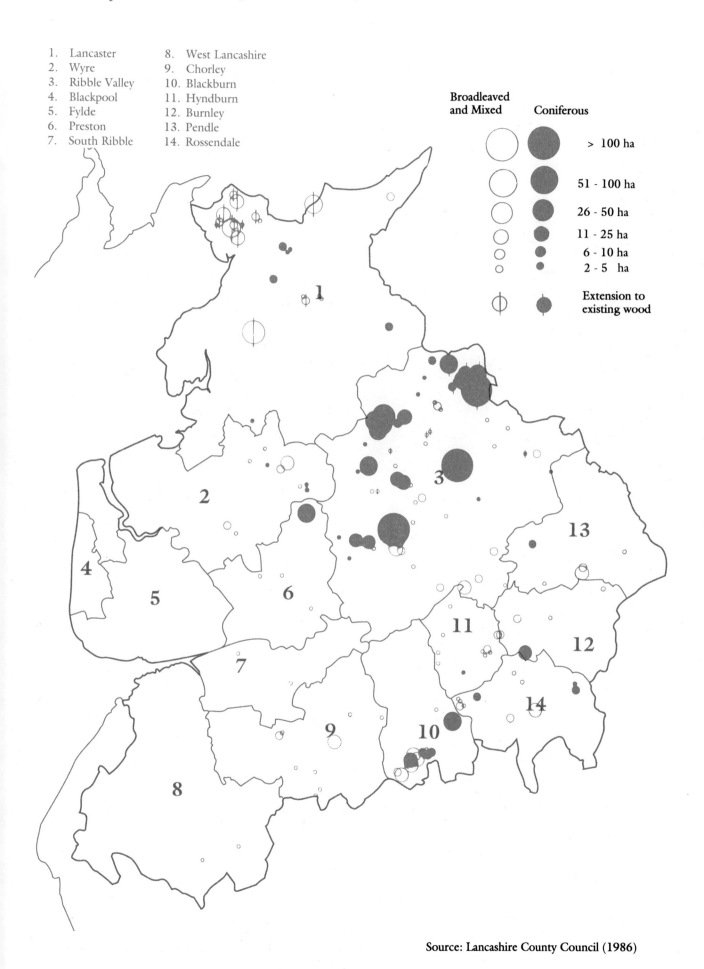

1. Lancaster
2. Wyre
3. Ribble Valley
4. Blackpool
5. Fylde
6. Preston
7. South Ribble
8. West Lancashire
9. Chorley
10. Blackburn
11. Hyndburn
12. Burnley
13. Pendle
14. Rossendale

Broadleaved and Mixed   Coniferous

> 100 ha
51 - 100 ha
26 - 50 ha
11 - 25 ha
6 - 10 ha
2 - 5 ha

Extension to existing wood

Source: Lancashire County Council (1986)

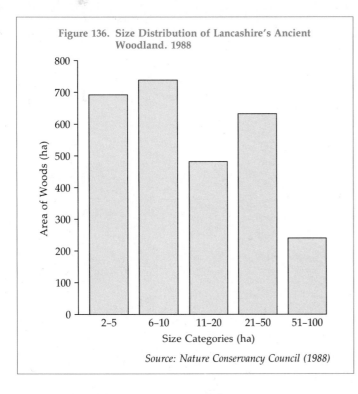

Figure 136. Size Distribution of Lancashire's Ancient Woodland. 1988

Area of Woods (ha)

Size Categories (ha)

Source: Nature Conservancy Council (1988)

single exception, are coniferous plantations on and around the Bowland Fells. Indeed, there are only nine woods over 50 ha, of which only two are mainly ancient (semi-natural): Gait Barrows, in Silverdale, (Lancaster) and Red Scar and Tun Brook Woods, (Preston). Until fairly recently, Old Park Wood, Osbaldeston, near Preston was a third ancient wood which exceeded 50 ha, but felling has now reduced it below this. Over 80% of all woods are less than 10 ha and over 65% smaller than 5 ha. Ribble Valley, especially, has a very large number of small woods; the majority of them secondary. This is the general pattern north of the Ribble. In the south of the County, although there are no woods larger than 50 ha (and far fewer woods generally), woods larger than 5 ha make up to a greater proportion of the total than they do in the north. Figure 136 shows the size distribution of remaining ancient woodlands. It is apparent that there is very little above the 21–50 ha size category, and only a very small amount in blocks greater than 51 ha (9%).

Woodland Diversity

9.53   Largely because of its geographical location at the boundary between upland and lowland Britain, Lancashire is a transitional zone between varying woodland types. Species at the southern end of their northern distribution, and species at the northern end of their southern distribution provide much of Lancashire's woodland diversity. Five woodland types dominated by characteristics groups of botanical species occur in Lancashire, representing some ten NVC communities.

9.54   Alder woodland occurs in floodplains, spring lines along valley sides and rivers and tributaries. Three NVC communities occur in Lancashire: alder-panicled sedge, alder-stinging nettle and alder-ash-yellow pimpernell.

9.55   Ash – Elm woodlands are a widespread and diverse group of woodlands occurring throughout

the County. The two NVC communities found here are ash-field maple-dog's mercury and ash-rowan-dog's mercury.

9.56   The oak woodlands of Lancashire can be divided into two NVC communities. Common oak-bracken-blackberry is essentially of southern distribution in Great Britain, whilst the sessile oak-birchwood-sorrel community is principally distributed in north and west Britain. The distributions of the two communities overlap in Lancashire – a principal contributor to the ecological diversity of woodlands in the County.

9.57   Oak – birch woodlands contain two NVC communities, both of which occur in Lancashire. The common oak-birch-wavy hair grass community occurs in the upper parts of Lancashire valleys, while the sessile oak-downy birch-*Dicranum majus* (moss) community is present, but often poorly developed, in North Lancashire.

9.58   Only one of the four British NVC beech woodland communities occurs in Lancashire, this being the beech-wavy hair grass group. This occurs as semi-natural stands within the south of England, but essentially similar planted stands occur on the fringes of the Lancashire Pennines.

Flora and Fauna

9.59   The County's woodlands are a permanent, or temporary, home for a large range of wildlife. A particularly large number of plant species is associated with our woods, including many which are rare or declining. As far as mammals are concerned, most of those which occur in the County are also found in woodlands. The badger, woodmouse and red-squirrel (only in Silverdale, and in a thin belt between Formby and Chorley) are largely confined to woods, but species like red and roe deer, fox, bank and short-tailed voles, mole, common shrew, hedgehog, rabbit, brown hare, grey squirrel and bats (especially the noctule bat) frequent woods for food and shelter.

9.60   Birds are even more reliant on the County's woods and many species breed and nest there by preference. Different species often rely on specific parts of the habitat, as follows:

* Blackcap, garden warbler, whitethroat, lesser whitethroat, wren, chiffchaff, long-tailed tit, robin, woodcock – clearings, or trees adjacent to clearings, with moderate low shrub and herb cover;

* Woodpigeon, turtle dove, collared dove, jay, songthrush, blackbird, chaffinch, greenfinch, redpoll, sparrowhawk – tall shrub layer;

* Kestrel, tawny owl, barn owl, little owl, jackdaw, great tit, marsh tit, blue tit, redstart, pied flycatcher, starling, tree sparrow, nuthatch, tree creeper – holes in trees;

* Green woodpecker, great spotted woodpecker, lesser-spotted woodpecker, willow tit – holes excavated in trees;

* Carrion crow, heron, rook, magpie, siskin, crossbill – tree canopy.

Woodlands along the Lune Valley (Lancaster), Fair Oak Woods (Ribble Valley) and Roddlesworth Woods (Blackburn and Chorley) are important for redstart and pied flycatcher. Tree pipit has a stronghold in Roddlesworth Woods. Wood warbler breed mainly in woodlands to the east of the County (Lancashire and Cheshire Fauna Society, 1988).

9.61 Probably more than half of the County's butterflies and moths are to be found in woodlands. Lancashire has several nationally important species (including the high brown fritillary, pearl bordered fritillary, Duke of Burgundy, northern brown argus, white letter hairstreak and ruddy carpet) which are associated with woods. Three rare and notable species of cranefly and hoverfly are also found.

Scrubland Habitat

9.62 Scrub is vegetation dominated by native shrub species, which in Lancashire are usually hawthorn, blackthorn, gorse, bramble and grey willow. It is a transitory habitat, usually resulting from the colonisation of grassland or wetland. If allowed to develop naturally, in time, scrub becomes woodland dominated by tree species.

Location and Extent

9.63 Because scrub can arise and develop into woodland quickly, it is difficult to measure its extent. Nevertheless, the Phase 1 survey for North-East Lancashire gives some indication of the amounts to be expected. It shows how limited the overall extent of scrub is as a habitat. District areas so far available are given in Table 87.

9.64 Scattered areas of scrub colonisation on upland fringes, coincided with times of agricultural depression and reduced grazing pressure earlier this century. More recently scrub cover has also increased locally on disused and derelict land, and on railway banks and cuttings where regular burning no longer takes place. But by far the largest area of scrub in the County has grown up over the last 30 years in the Arnside-Silverdale AONB, where an increase of 225 ha of 'woodland' was recorded between 1965 and 1980 (Woolerton, 1983). In fact, this is largely scrub which has colonised areas of limestone grassland and other unimproved open land as a result of lower sheep grazing, and a much reduced rabbit population following the introduction of myxomatosis. The true picture here, and in the County as a whole, will emerge in 1991 when the full Phase I habitat survey has been completed.

Scrubland Diversity

9.65 The NVC recognises ten vegetation communities dominated by scrub species. The diversity of Lancashire's scrub is shown by the presence of seven of these NVC communities within the County. They are as follows: grey willow-marsh bedstraw scrub, grey willow-downy birch-reed scrub, hawthorn-ivy scrub, blackthorn-bramble scrub, gorse-bramble scrub, bramble-Yorkshire fog scrub, bracken-bramble underscrub.

Table 87 Area of Scrub in Six Lancashire Districts. 1988

District	Area (ha)
Ribble Valley	15.6
Blackburn	31.3
Hyndburn	1.7
Burnley	2.6
Pendle	9.5
Rossendale	1.5
TOTAL	62.2

Source: Phase 1 Habitat Survey

Flora and Fauna

9.66 Scrub is an unstable dynamic habitat, and this is reflected in its associated flora and fauna. Its dominant shrubs are mostly thorny, which discourages grazing. As the shrubs, and then trees, grow and multiply, competition for water, nutrients and light reduces the number of low-growing herbs, and different herbaceous species may invade.

9.67 Animals are much influenced by the constantly changing nature of the habitat. Linnet and yellowhammer will colonise open scrub, but leave as the cover closes in. Chaffinch, on the other hand, breed only in tall, dense scrub, whilst willow warbler, dunnock and common whitethroat remain common throughout the succession from open to closed canopy.

9.68 Over 230 species of insects have been recorded feeding on hawthorn, whilst gorse in particular is favoured by spiders. The abundant insect life on willows attracts insectivorous birds migrating in autumn. Butterflies and hoverflies favour scrub areas when it is too windy in more exposed places. The high proportion of berry-bearing shrubs provides abundant food, (including insects), for small mammals and birds, and scrub is one of the favoured habitats for a number of breeding birds. These include willow warbler and other warblers, linnet, long-tailed tit and turtle dove. Reed bunting and grasshopper warbler favour wet scrub, whilst gorse and bracken are the choice of stonechat and whinchat.

Grassland Habitat

9.69 Old meadows and pastures which have not been intensively managed with fertilisers and herbicides, or recently re-seeded, are often of special nature conservation interest. Although maintained by cutting and/or grazing, they are composed of wild plant species which form stable communities under traditional management, dating back continuously for decades and even centuries. However, most grasslands in Lancashire are not of this kind, but have been improved to varying extents for greater agricultural productivity.

Figure 137
Neutral and Limestone Grasslands in Lancashire. 1986 and 1988

1. Lancaster
2. Wyre
3. Ribble Valley
4. Blackpool
5. Fylde
6. Preston
7. South Ribble
8. West Lancashire
9. Chorley
10. Blackburn
11. Hyndburn
12. Burnley
13. Pendle
14. Rossendale

Limestone Grassland (1988) ■

Neutral Grassland (1986) { Class I ● Class II ○

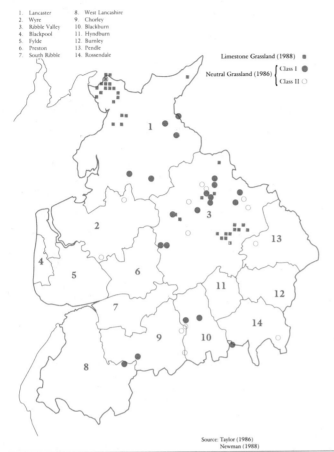

Source: Taylor (1986)
Newman (1988)

Table 88 Areas of Principal Limestone Grasslands in Lancashire. 1988

District	Location or Type	Area (ha)
Lancaster	Arnside–Silverdale AONB	27.1
Ribble Valley	Reef Knolls	46.5
	Quarries and Kilns	3.8
	Roadside Verges	1.4
TOTAL		78.8

Source: Newman (1988)

Table 89 Areas of Species-Rich Neutral Grasslands in Seven Lancashire Districts. 1990

District	Grade 1 Sites (ha)	Grade 2 Sites (ha)	Total Area (ha)
Lancaster	19.2	9.4	28.6
Ribble Valley	46.4	16.2	62.6
West Lancashire	1.3	—	1.3
Chorley	3.0	—	3.0
Blackburn	4.9	27.8	32.7
Pendle	—	6.5	6.5
Rossendale	9.7	4.5	14.2
TOTAL	84.5	64.4	148.9

Source: NCC (pers. comm.)

9.70 Based on the NVC, grasslands in Lancashire can be divided into three groups:

* Limestone Grasslands;
* Neutral Grasslands;
* Acidic Grasslands.

Acidic grasslands are normally moorland and moorland fringe habitats and are dealt with more fully below. This section deals with 'unimproved' neutral and limestone grasslands which are of special interest for their wildlife. Good examples of either are now rare in Lancashire, and they are arguably the County's most threatened habitats.

Limestone Grasslands

9.71 Limestone grassland in Lancashire occurs only on soils developed either directly over the Carboniferous limestone (see Figure 3) or on drift derived from it. It is restricted as a result to Arnside-Silverdale AONB (extending south to Carnforth and Over Kellet), the Clitheroe area in Ribble Valley, and on Leck Fell in Lancaster (see Figure 137). The last-named is the only locality in Lancashire which has truly upland limestone grassland (Newman, 1988). The total area surviving at present is unknown, but figures for the principal locations (surveyed by Newman in 1988) are given in Table 88. The largest single area of limestone grassland is some 17.5 ha at Worsaw Hill, near Clitheroe.

Neutral Grasslands

9.72 Unimproved neutral grasslands were formerly commonplace in all stock-raising areas. Now rare in Lancashire, as elsewhere, surviving sites are widely scattered in the north, east and south of the County as shown on Figure 137. The best examples are found in river valleys remote from urban areas, notably the Hodder and its tributaries, with other important sites in Hindburndale in Lancaster and along the Tarnbrook in Wyre. Such grassland also occurs occasionally in East Lancashire where agricultural grassland has not been intensively managed. However, the Tarnbrook meadows comprise the only known surviving example of a group of adjacent unimproved meadows of high nature conservation value. Table 89 is not complete, since it does not include additional sites identified from recent and ongoing Phase 1 surveys. Grade 1 sites are the very best remaining examples, whilst Grade 2 are of significant, but lower, interest in a County context. Wet neutral grasslands, important for breeding birds, are predominantly coastal, with a few notable sites further inland in the Lune Valley and in Pendle.

Non-agricultural Grasslands

9.73 Species-rich limestone and neutral grasslands are generally associated with traditional agricultural management. However, with the advent of intensive grassland management, non-agricultural sites – mainly railway banks and cuttings, and roadside verges – are becoming increasingly important as refuges for plant communities of this kind and some of the wildlife associated with them. Although information is incomplete, certain disused railway lines in the County are known to have developed interesting neutral, and more rarely, limestone, grassland communities. Known sites include the former Colne-Earby (Pendle), Preston-Bamber Bridge via Todd Lane (South Ribble), and Haskayne (West Lancashire) lines, as well as the operational line between Clitheroe and Hellifield. Roadside verges of interest are recorded from a few scattered localities in Lancaster and Ribble Valley districts, and elsewhere.

Grassland Diversity

9.74   Despite the rarity of unimproved limestone grasslands, Lancashire probably has as great a variety of types as it has ever had. Four of the fourteen British NVC communities occur, these being the sheep's fescue-meadow foxtail, the hairy oatgrass, the blue moor grass-limestone bedstraw, and the sheeps fescue-common bent-wild thyme communities.

9.75   Of the 18 NVC neutral grassland communities, eight occur in Lancashire. These are the false-oat-grass, the sweet vernal-grass-wood cranesbill meadow, the meadow foxtail-great burnet, the knapweed-crested dog's-tail, the ryegrass-marsh marigold flood pasture and the Yorkshire fog-tufted hair grass communities.

Flora and Fauna

9.76   Limestone and neutral grasslands are a botanist's paradise, and provide the habitat for many once commonly spread plants. They also tend to be colonised by a large number of species, which adds to their interest. Up to 70 species can occur at individual sites of both habitat types. In Lancashire, rare or unusual species found include:

* Limestone – spring sandwort, spring cinquefoil, spring sedge, lesser butterfly orchid, autumn lady's tresses, field gentian, bird's eye primrose, bee orchid, fly orchid;

* Neutral – globe flower, saw-wort, dyersgreenweed, northern marsh orchid, meadow cranesbill, wood cranesbill, melancholy thistle, brown sedge, lesser tussock-sedge.

9.77   The limestone grasslands of Silverdale are of outstanding importance for their butterflies. Twenty-six species, (1/3 of the British total), have been recorded from this area. These are the large skipper, dingy skipper, pearl-bordered fritillary, small pearl-bordered fritillary, high brown fritillary, dark green fritillary, orange tip, green hairstreak, small copper, red admiral, large white, small white, green-veined white, brown argus, scotch argus, small blue, common blue, holly blue, meadow brown, wall brown, painted lady, peacock, small tortoiseshell, small heath, grayling and Duke of Burgundy. Most of the rarer ones are specifically dependent on this habitat. Butterflies of neutral grasslands are less numerous but typical species include meadow brown, small copper, common blue, small heath, small skipper and large skipper, whilst the day-flying chimney sweeper moth is commonly seen. Grasshoppers are amongst a host of insects and spiders which occupy these sites.

9.78   Though few mammals live permanently in meadows and pastures, invertebrates like earthworms, leather jackets and beetles are a major food source for many. The abundant insect life also attracts bats and a variety of birds.

9.79   Damp lowland neutral (and moderately acidic) grasslands are the principal breeding habitat for some birds, especially waders, but also species like yellow wagtail, meadow pipit and skylark. A nationwide survey of wet meadow breeding birds (British Trust for Ornithology and the Royal Society for the Protection of Birds, 1982) identified major breeding sites for lapwing, snipe, curlew, redshank and oystercatcher. The study demonstrated the national importance of these Lancashire habitats. Despite being one of the less well surveyed Counties, (data being submitted for only twelve sites), the total number of breeding waders in Lancashire was exceeded by only seven other Counties in England and Wales. Lancashire emerged amongst the top ten counties for every wader species studied, and, in terms of the number of breeding birds per site produced one of the highest rates of any County.

9.80   Traditional hay meadows are favoured by common partridge and corn bunting and were once the habitat of the corncrake. Calling male corncrakes have been present in very small numbers at one location in the County in recent years, but the status of the species in the County is unclear (RSPB pers.comm.). Its demise has been attributed to farm mechanisation and a change from hay to silage production.

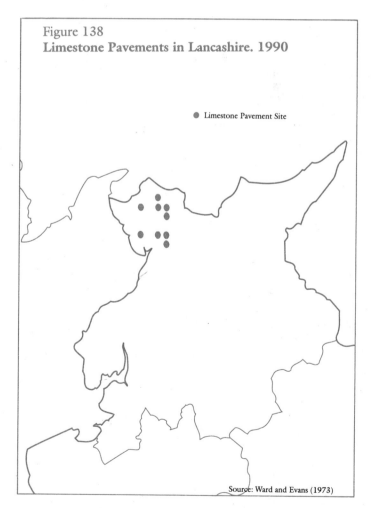

Figure 138
Limestone Pavements in Lancashire. 1990

● Limestone Pavement Site

Source: Ward and Evans (1973)

Limestone Pavement Habitat

9.81 Limestone pavements consist of the fossilised remains of countless minute creatures which inhabited the sea about 300 million years ago. Earth movements raised them to the surface where they were smoothed by glaciation during the last Ice Age over 8,000 years ago. Since then rain water and humic acids from subsequent vegetation cover, acting on bedding planes in the limestone, have created the characteristic clint and grike features that can be seen on the surface of Lancashire's limestone pavements today.

Location and Extent

9.82 Limestone pavements in Lancashire are confined to the Arnside–Silverdale AONB in Lancaster, between Morecambe Bay and to the west of the A6 trunk road. Their location is shown in Figure 138. The Warton Crag pavements occur at the highest altitude, some 130 m above sea level, but most lie between 30 and 100 m. Although pavements exist at 25 distinct locations, it is convenient to group them into geographically similar sites (see Table 90). Other pavements are covered entirely by woodland, their extent remaining unknown, and have been excluded from this account (which is based on Ward and Evans, 1973). The NCC is currently surveying the Limestone Pavements of Lancashire; including open and wooded pavements, which will advance their knowledge of pavement distribution, extent and condition.

Flora and Fauna

9.83 Ash and yew are the most abundant tree species, with silver birch and rowan frequent. Scots pine and holly are common on the Gait Barrows pavements. Hazel is the most abundant shrub, accompanied by hawthorn, ivy, juniper, privet, buckthorn, dogrose, blackberry, great and common sallow and elder. Four nationally rare herbaceous species, – the lily-of-the-valley, dark-red helleborine, pale St. John's-wort and angular seal, – are found at Gait Barrows. Other uncommon species which are frequent are hemp-agrimony, wood melick, betony, rigid-buckler fern, dropwort, northern bedstraw, bloody crane's-bill, tutsan,

ploughman's-spikenard, saw-wort, and hairy violet. Fauna associated with limestone pavements has already been described in the woodland, scrub and grassland sections.

Moorland Habitat

9.84 This section is concerned principally with the treeless unenclosed uplands of North and East Lancashire, known popularly as 'moorland'. This is a vernacular term which is not easy to define. Moorland forms by far the most extensive area of semi-natural habitat in the County. A number of different types are represented, including heaths, bogs (or mires), acidic grasslands and tall herb and fern communities. Each type is made up of distinct vegetation communities, but most moorland ecosystems are a mosaic of these groups. The relationship between them, through the agency of moorland management, is central to an understanding of their wildlife importance. The location of moorland boundaries is problematical since some moorland vegetation is (or was) divided into large enclosures. Indeed, many fields which were formerly enclosed are now in various stages of reversion back to moor.

Location and Extent

9.85 Large areas of moorland habitat occur in North and East Lancashire, principally in the Forest of Bowland, the West Pennine Moors and the South Pennines, with additional areas on Leck Fell (Lancaster) and elsewhere in East Lancashire. With a total area of approximately 41,000 hectares, unenclosed moorland comprises some 13.5% of the County area. Its distribution is shown in Figure 139 whilst the extent of heather moorland is shown in Figure 140.

9.86 The transition from enclosed grassland to unenclosed moorland occurs typically between 300 m and 350 m, although a broad band of marginal land is frequently present. However, the exposed western edges of both the Bowland Fells and the West Pennine Moors depress the altitude of this boundary substantially, down to as low as 150 m to 200 m at Harrisend Fell and White Coppice, for example. Land has been enclosed to unusually high altitudes in Rossendale, however, particularly around Bacup. Here, the transition to moorland is at altitudes as high as 400 m or more, although presently lower in some localities due to reversion. Moor and fell top altitudes vary from 449 m at Thieveley Pike and 456 m at White Hill, to 557 m on Pendle Hill and 560 m at Ward's Stone, Bowland. By far the highest land in the County is at Leck Fell, which reaches 627 m.

9.87 Phase 1 habitat categories have been grouped in Table 91 for the Districts of Ribble Valley, Chorley, Blackburn, Hyndburn, Burnley, Pendle and Rossendale. These Districts include some 65% of the total unenclosed moorland area of the County and an unknown proportion of the total area of marginal land. The Table shows that within this area, bog and mire and marshy grassland communities cover the largest areas. However, whilst bog is virtually confined to open moorland, about one third of the marshy grassland occupies marginal land on the moorland edge.

Table 90 Limestone Pavements in Lancashire. 1973		
Pavement Group	Number of Separate Sites	Area (ha)
Cringlebarrow Wood	2	3.28
Eaves Wood	1	0.11
Gait Barrows	2	11.40
Heald Brow	3	0.97
Thrang End	5	1.39
Warton Crag	8	10.15
Yealand Hall Allotment	4	4.54
TOTAL	25	31.84

Source: Ward and Evans (1973)

Figure 139

Moorland Habitat in Lancashire .

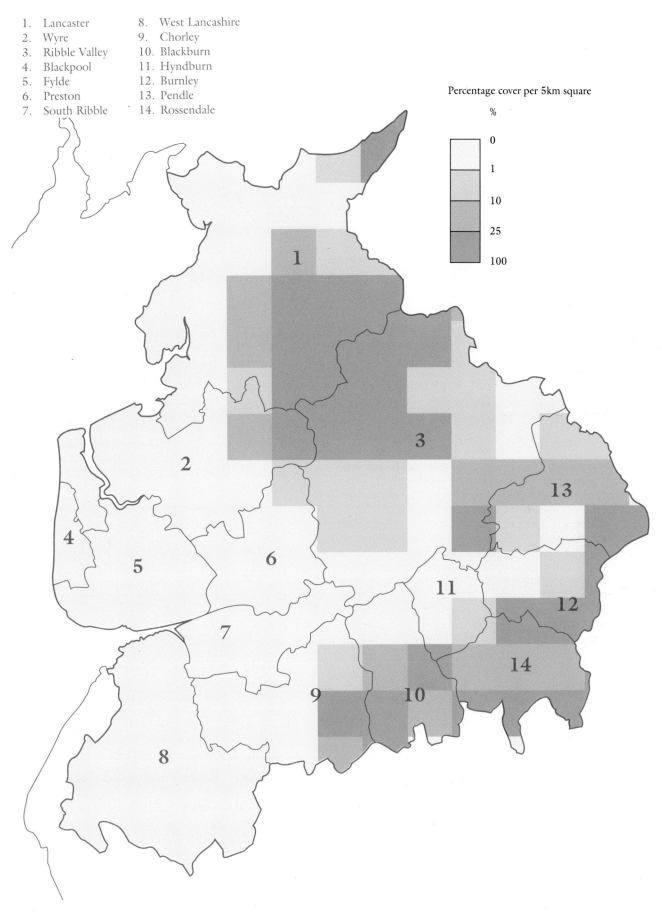

1. Lancaster
2. Wyre
3. Ribble Valley
4. Blackpool
5. Fylde
6. Preston
7. South Ribble
8. West Lancashire
9. Chorley
10. Blackburn
11. Hyndburn
12. Burnley
13. Pendle
14. Rossendale

Percentage cover per 5km square

%

0
1
10
25
100

Source: Nature Conservancy Council
Phase 1 habitat survey

Figure 140

Heather Moorland in Lancashire.

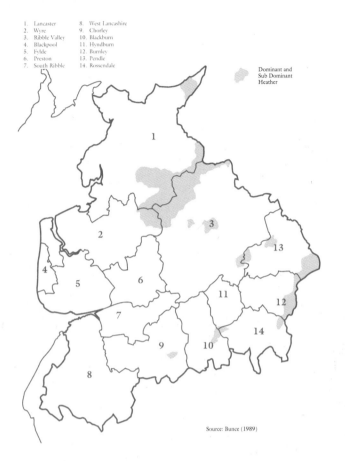

1. Lancaster
2. Wyre
3. Ribble Valley
4. Blackpool
5. Fylde
6. Preston
7. South Ribble
8. West Lancashire
9. Chorley
10. Blackburn
11. Hyndburn
12. Burnley
13. Pendle
14. Rossendale

Dominant and
Sub Dominant
Heather

Source: Bunce (1989)

9.88 Relatively small areas of heath and bracken occur in marginal or enclosed landscapes. In fact, most heather in these situations is associated with abandoned sandstone quarries subject to light, or no, grazing by stock. Significant areas of bracken are found only in the Forest of Bowland and in Pendle (see Table 92). Flushes and springs are widely scattered over the various moorland areas from base-rich systems on Leck Fell to acidic ones

Table 91 Moorland and Marginal Vegetation in Seven Lancashire Districts. 1988

Vegetation Type	Unenclosed Moorland (ha)	Marginal Land (ha)	Total Moorland (ha)	Marginal/ Total Ratio (%)
Bog and Mire[1]	7,972	6	7,978	—
Flush and Spring	157	1	158	<1
Heath[2]	5,451	118	5,569	2
Bracken	1,210	39.	1,249	3
Acid Grassland	6,143	866	7,009	12
Marshy Grassland[1]	5,607	2,635	8,242	32
TOTAL[3]	26,540	3,665	30,205	12

Source: Phase 1 Habitat Survey.

Notes: [1]*Purple moor-grass mires and rush pastures on mineral soils and thin peat are excluded from bog and mire and included in marshy grassland.*
[2]*Excludes dwarf shrub communities on deep peat.*
[3]*Total County area of unenclosed moorland is 41,000 ha.*

Table 92 Areas of Continuous Bracken and Flush & Spring in Six Lancashire Districts. 1988

District	Continuous Bracken (ha)	Flush & Spring (ha)
Ribble Valley	1,123.6	105.2
Blackburn	9.4	11.6
Hyndburn	0.4	0.2
Burnley	9.3	19.0
Pendle	111.5	16.4
Rossendale	9.8	13.6
TOTAL	1,264.0	166.0

Source: Phase 1 habitat survey.

in West Pennine Moors. Total areas recorded so far are shown in Table 92.

9.89 NVC mire types include a wide variety of bog, bog pool, wet heath, fen-meadow, rush-pasture, spring and other peat-based vegetation, in both upland and lowland situations. Some 36 of these NVC communities are represented in Lancashire, emphasising the complexity and range of our total moorland resource.

Flora and Fauna

9.90 Though the County's total moorland resource sustains many specialised, characteristic plant species, individual tracts of moorland can be quite low in diversity, even over large areas. On the other hand, very small sites like flushes and springs can sustain a rich variety of species. Common moorland plants include bilberry, (or whinerry), crowberry, common cotton-grass, heather, wavy hair-grass, cowberry, matt-grass and purple moorgrass. Rarities which occur in Lancashire are bog rosemary, bog asphodel, broad-leaved cottongrass, lesser twayblade, pale forget-me-not, lesser clubmoss and fir clubmoss. Chickweed, wintergreen and hay-scented buckler-fern are very rare, each surviving at a single site.

9.91 Vertebrate animals are typically confined to the common frog, field vole, field mouse, weasel, stoat and fox. The principal faunal interest of the moorlands lies in their birds. Indeed, the Bowland Fells are of international importance for their breeding birds. Maintenance of heather moorland for game purposes, provides an ideal habitat not only for red grouse and the rare black grouse but also for other birds, including several raptors. Of these, the hen harrier is of major significance, since the Bowland Fells is the only locality in England where it regularly breeds. Other raptors breeding in Lancashire include merlin (for which Bowland is an important English stronghold), peregrine falcon and short-eared owl. The much more common kestrel and sparrowhawk are also found on the moors, whilst heather is particularly favoured by ring ouzel and twite.

9.92 Of the upland bird species which breed regularly in the County, only black grouse, (now confined to a single 'lek'), and hen harrier appear confined to the Forest of Bowland. Golden plover, merlin, short-eared owl and ring ouzel all occur at other moorland sites in the County, though in limited numbers. Bowland also supports one of the five largest breeding colonies of lesser black-backed gull in Great Britain; with up to 7600 nesting pairs forming 11% of the national, and 7% of the EC, populations.

Lowland Remnant Peat Moss Habitat

Location and Extent

9.93   Raised bogs should not be confused with the upland blanket peat bogs of East Lancashire, which resulted from high rainfall levels. By contrast raised bogs are usually formed on flat lowland flood plains associated with larger river systems. The past and present day locations of Lancashire's lowland mosses are shown in Figure 141. These lowland raised bogs lie generally below the 80 m contour along the Coastal Plain and were once very extensive. The total County area of these 'remnant' mosses is approximately 400 ha; the best example of which is at Winmarleigh Moss covering approximately 88 ha. However, Heysham Moss (Lancaster) and Fenton's Moss near Pilling (Wyre) have recently been shown to be of very high conservation value. Other types of lowland peats include valley and basin mires such as White Moss near Tosside. The NCC view this as the best remaining example of a lowland basin mire in the County.

Flora and Fauna

9.94   Lancashire's lowland mosses were typical raised bogs originally covered by bog mosses, fen vegetation and reed swamp with a great variety of marsh plants, reeds and sedges. Most of this variety has now vanished. Only Winmarleigh Moss resembles anything like original conditions. Other remnant uncultivated mosses no longer support raised bogs because they have dried out and are degraded. However, they still have considerable nature conservation value, despite a limited flora. Remnant mosses provide the only lowland habitat for heather, bell heather, hair's-tail cotton grass, common cotton grass and purple moor grass.

9.95   The animal life of the mosses was, and to some degree remains, highly distinctive. Nesting birds include skylark, meadow pipit, reed bunting, curlew, cuckoo, snipe and mallard. The hummocks and drier vegation of raised bogs support many insects and invertebrates. Butterflies and moths of interest include the large heath, (formerly abundant but now with only two colonies left in Lancashire) large skipper and green hairstreak. Over one-third of the British species of moths have been recorded in Lancashire mosses. Important species include the large emerald, garden tiger, ruby tiger, oak eggan, fox, Manchester treble bar, purple bordered gold, rare emperor and the particularly rare purple hook tip. The bog bush-cricket is another invertebrate found at only one mossland site in the County. Lancashire's remnant lowland mosslands have some notable dragonflies and damselflies. The common darter can be found in most bog pools in

Figure 141

Past and Present Distribution of Lowland Moss Habitat in Lancashire. 1852 and 1989

☐ Extent of Peat (1852)

▨ Extent of Peat (present day)

Source: Lancashire Trust for Nature Conservation (1989)

Table 93	Areas of Swamp and Fen in Seven Lancashire Districts. 1988
District	Area (ha)
Lancaster	94.1
Ribble Valley	1.8
Blackburn	1.6
Hyndburn	1.4
Burnley	0.7
Pendle	5.7
Rossendale	1.6
TOTAL	106.9

Source: Phase 1 Habitat Survey and RSPB (pers. comm.)

the County. Outstanding species recorded include the southern hawker and the golden-ringed dragonfly.

Swamp and Fen Habitat

Location and Extent

9.96 Most present-day areas of swamp and fen are fragmentary and associated with man-made features like ponds, canals, reservoirs and abandoned mill lodges. More extensive areas are rare, but of outstanding wildlife value and are a reminder of a once more extensive Lancashire landscape. Table 93 shows total swamp and fen recorded for those Districts where Phase 1 surveys had been completed by 1988.

9.97 By far the largest single area of swamp and fen is the RSPB reserve at Leighton Moss, Silverdale, in

Table 94	Proportion of Ponds by District in Lancashire.
District	%
Lancaster	6
Wyre	14
Ribble Valley	12
Blackpool	1
Fylde	15
Preston	12
South Ribble	9
West Lancashire	9
Chorley	13
Blackburn	4
Hyndburn	1
Burnley	1
Pendle	1
Rossendale	2

Source: Second Edition 1:25,000 OS Maps (Various dates)

Lancaster, where there are at present some 79 ha. This is the only large reedbed in Lancashire, and the largest in North-West England. Most other areas of nature conservation significance are also in North Lancashire, including Hawes Water, Silverdale (14.5 ha); Crag Bank, Carnforth; Cinderbarrow Tarn, Borwick (all Lancaster); and Greenhalgh Castle Tarn, Garstang (Wyre). Other sites are small and widely scattered on the coastal plain, including newly-created reedbeds at Martin Mere, Burscough in West Lancashire; the margins of field ponds, ditches, rivers and canals, and occasional seasonally flooded depressions. Linear reedbeds have also developed along the foot of railway embankments at Croston and Rufford, in West Lancashire. The habitat also occurs on a localised, small scale basis in the towns and urban fringe of East Lancashire, where reedswamp has often colonised disused mill lodges.

Flora and Fauna

9.98 A total of 28 different types of British swamp and fen are recognised by the NVC and 25 of them have been recorded in Lancashire. Sedges, reed, rush and flag species predominate. Several NVC types recorded, and some of the species they support, are rare in the County and overall diversity could be significantly affected by the loss of just a few small sites. This is certainly true of tufted-sedge swamp, great fen-sedge swamp and the common reed-hemp agrimony fen sites.

9.99 The fauna of the reedbeds at Leighton Moss include all the three rarest breeding birds of this habitat in Britain; bittern, bearded tit and, (since 1986), marsh harrier. The populations of each are of national significance, and this is their only major breeding site in Britain outside the broadlands of East Anglia. Other birds breeding or feeding in the larger reedbeds include reed warbler (here close to its northern limit in Britain), sedge and grasshopper warblers, reed bunting, water rail, heron, moorhen, and a small number of spotted crake. Leighton Moss is also one of the very few places in Lancashire where otter still regularly breed, whilst swamp and fen provide the traditional breeding habitat for the harvest mouse. In recent years, this has been recorded from two other sites in Lancashire – in Chorley and in Wyre.

9.100 Leighton Moss and Hawes Water are known to support a very diverse invertebrate fauna. This includes species entirely dependent on swamp conditions, such as the wainscot moth. The fen wainscot moth also occurs at Martin Mere (West Lancashire).

Freshwater Habitat

9.101 Freshwater habitats are divided into standing and running waters. The former comprise lakes, reservoirs, lodges and ponds, whilst the latter include rivers and their tributaries. Canals are also considered to be standing waters.

Location and Extent

9.102 Lancashire has just two remaining natural lakes, Hawes Water (Lancaster District) and Marton

Figure 142
Pond Distribution in Lancashire

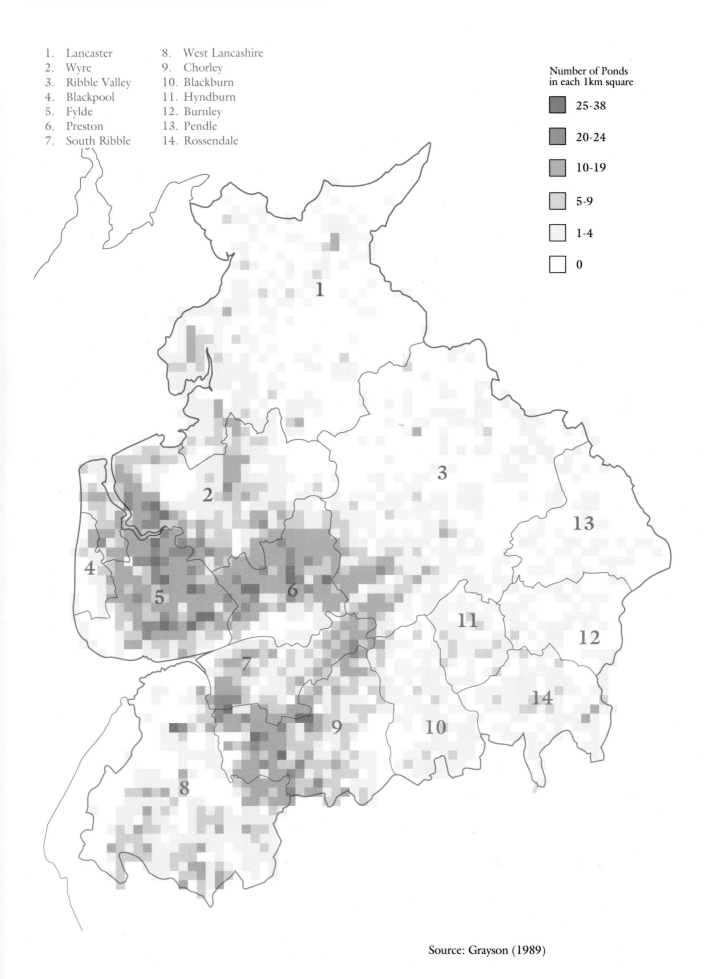

1. Lancaster
2. Wyre
3. Ribble Valley
4. Blackpool
5. Fylde
6. Preston
7. South Ribble
8. West Lancashire
9. Chorley
10. Blackburn
11. Hyndburn
12. Burnley
13. Pendle
14. Rossendale

Number of Ponds
in each 1km square

25-38
20-24
10-19
5-9
1-4
0

Source: Grayson (1989)

Mere (Blackpool). However, there are 118 public supply reservoirs, covering an approximate area of 1,122 ha. Figure 59 shows their distribution. In addition Lancashire has several man-made lakes which do not serve as reservoirs. These include Martin Mere (occupying part of the original lake, which, prior to drainage, was probably the largest in Lancashire), and Leighton Moss.

9.103   Field ponds form one of the County's largest and most under-rated wildlife resource. There were about 12,000 ponds in 1965 though numbers have fallen dramatically since (see below). Figure 142 shows the densities of ponds by 1 km squares. This reveals that the Fylde (including the Districts of Fylde, Wyre, Blackpool and Preston) contains high pond densities of national importance. Table 94 breaks the pond distribution down by District.

9.104   The eastern half of the County contains significantly fewer ponds than the west. There is a close geographical fit between the areas of high pond density and soil type; namely the Salop and Salwick/Flint Associations (shown on Figure 6) which both occur in the western half of the County where the practice of excavating marl-pits was widespread.

9.105   Lancashire's running water habitat is based on six main catchment rivers, joined by a multitude of tributaries, covering a total length of 1,032 km, as classified by North West Water Authority (1988). These are shown in Figure 44. In addition, there are two canals which contribute 164.8 km of standing water.

Flora and Fauna

9.106   There are 189 plants considered truly aquatic that are native to Britain. A wide variety of these occurs in Lancashire's standing and running freshwater habitats, though supply reservoirs are generally poor for water flora. Indeed, the Lancaster Canal supports 59 out of the 189 aquatic species (32%). There is a dearth of specific information on the flora of running water. Plants typical of the shallow marginal zone of the County's ponds include soft rush, reed grasses, branched bur-reed, greater water plantain, yellow flag and watercress. In deeper water, common water-crowfoot, spiked water milfoil, fennel-leaved pondweed, broad-leaved pondweed and yellow water lily are often found. Uncommon marginal zone plants include water violet, lesser reedmace and several species of water dropwort (fine leaved, tubular and parsley). Uncommon plants of the deeper zones are common clubrush, mare's-tail, water soldier, frogbit and stonewort.

9.107   Representatives of all the major animal groups – protozoa, invertebrates, fish, amphibians, reptiles, birds and mammals occur in, or around, Lancashire's freshwaters. The most widely studied group are birds, lakes and reservoirs being especially good for wildfowl.

9.108   Marton Mere (Blackpool) for example, supports some 35 breeding waterfowl and wetland birds. It is the most important breeding site in Lancashire for little grebe and is of County importance for great crested grebe, coot, mallard, pochard and

shoveler. Martin Mere (West Lancashire) supports nationally important numbers of winter migrant birds. Over 100 species over-winter on the Mere, but its populations of pink-footed geese (up to 18,000), teal (5,000 to 10,000) and pintail (1,000 to 2,500) are especially important. Martin Mere also supports important populations of wintering Bewick's and whooper swans, shoveler, gadwall and mallard – well in excess of 1% of the total UK wintering population. Leighton Moss (Lancaster) is of outstanding ornithological value. It contains the largest reedbed in England with nationally important breeding populations of bittern and bearded tit, with a further 65 species breeding regularly. A study of East Lancashire reservoirs revealed some 82 bird species associated with 114 water bodies (Spencer, 1969).

9.109   There are six amphibians native to Britain, all of which occur in Lancashire; the common frog, common toad, smooth or common newt, palmate newt and great crested, or warty newt. The natter-jack toad exists at just one Lancashire site, and is extremely vulnerable here with just three females being found in 1990.

Coastal Habitat

9.110   Lancashire's coastline consists of six basic habitat types: mudflats and sandflats, saltmarshes, sand beaches and dunes, low clay cliffs, a small stretch of rocky cliff at Heysham and areas of limestone cliff around the Arnside/Silverdale area of Morecambe Bay. Sand dunes are restricted to southern Fylde, whilst the three cliff types are even more limited. But the County's estuarine mud and sand-flats are by far and away our most significant wildlife habitats, playing an internationally important rôle in the global migration patterns of a large proportion of certain wildfowl and wading birds. The County occupies a focal point on the so-called East Atlantic Migration Flyway which has been described as one of the great wonders of the natural world. Wildfowl and wading birds breed around the northern hemisphere making the most of the short but productive Arctic summer. As the days shorten and the food supplies dwindle the birds must move south. Countless thousands of birds from as far afield as Canada, Greenland and Siberia channel down the East Atlantic and arrive on Britain's estuaries. Many birds will spend the entire winter on Lancashire's estuaries but others will just pause to refuel on their way to warmer climes. (Boyd and Pigot, 1989.)

Location and Extent

9.111   The Ribble and Lune estuaries and Morecambe Bay provide the majority of the mud and sandflat habitat. Because of its significance, it is all protected as SSSI, amounting to an area of more than 47,000 ha. Just under a half of the habitat – 20,585 ha, lies within the boundary of Lancashire, and is shown on Figure 143. This map also shows the locations of Lancashire's saltmarsh, sand dune and marine habitats.

9.112   The Nature Conservancy Council (1986) Saltmarsh Survey of Great Britain describes Lancashire as having five geographically distinct saltmarsh areas. These are Carnforth Marsh, River Lune, Cockerham and Pilling Marsh, River Wyre Estuary and the River Ribble. Their combined area in 1983 was approximately 4,600 ha or some 10% of the total area of saltmarsh around the British coast (estimated at 44,900 ha – Gray, 1979). The Wyre marshes, (Barnaby Sands and Burrows Marsh) totalling 104 ha, are particularly valuable, because they are the only ones not subject to grazing.

9.113   The Fylde sand dune system is the remnant of Lancashire's once extensive sand dune habitat. The dunes between Granny's Bay (Lytham) and Squires Gate (Blackpool) cover an area of around 150.8 ha. This total can be broken down into seven, distinct habitat types (according to Nissenbaum, 1989):

* Sand Dune Flats (82.0 ha);
* Yellow Dunes (14.2 ha);
* Grey Dunes (20.0 ha);
* Dune Slack (5.5 ha);
* Dune Meadow (1.7 ha);
* Scrub (0.4 ha);
* Disturbed Land (27.0 ha).

Flora and Fauna

9.114   These coastal habitats collectively sustain a wide range of plant species, highly adapted to the saline, exposed and often water-logged conditions. However, it is their value for birdlife for which they are especially noteworthy. The rôle played by Lancashire estuaries in global bird migration is emphasised by Figure 144. A site is considered to be internationally important for a bird species if it regularly supports more than 1% of the North West European population of that species. Morecambe Bay, the Lune estuary and the Ribble estuary all hold internationally important numbers and species of birds. Their mudflats are rich in invertebrates on which the waders feed, whilst adjacent saltmarshes provide roosting sites at high tide.

9.115   The international importance of the Ribble Estuary for birds is illustrated by Tables 95 and 96, whilst Table 97 places both Morecambe Bay and the Ribble into their national context as sites for waders. The Ribble estuary is the second most important UK estuary for wildfowl. It plays a vital rôle in the survival of sanderling and black-tailed godwit, supporting greater numbers than any other site in Britain. The Ribble also holds internationally important populations of bar-tailed godwit, grey plover, oyster catcher, redshank, pink-footed goose, whooper and bewick's swan, shelduck, teal and wigeon. During autumn, over 100,000 wading birds have been counted.

9.116   Morecambe Bay holds internationally important populations of pink-footed geese, shelduck, pintail, oystercatcher, ringed plover, grey plover, knot, dunlin, bar-tailed godwit, curlew, redshank and turnstone. In addition, the Bay supports nationally important populations of sanderling, great crested grebe, red-breasted merganser, goldeneye and cormorant. Oystercatchers, curlews and turnstone are found in greater numbers in Morecambe Bay than any other

Figure 143
Saltmarsh, Sandflat, Mudflat, Sand Dune and Marine Habitat in Lancashire. 1990

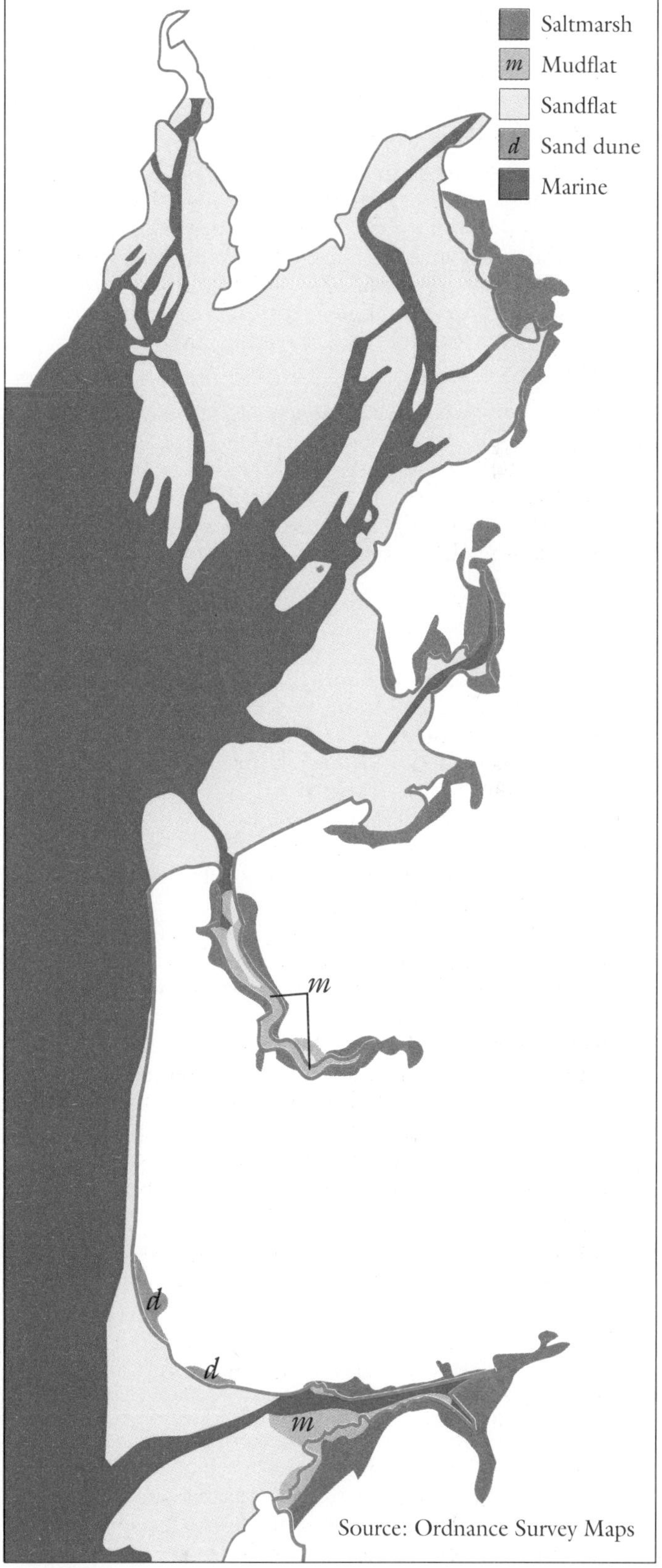

Saltmarsh
m Mudflat
Sandflat
d Sand dune
Marine

Source: Ordnance Survey Maps

Table 95 Birds of International and National Importance on the Ribble Estuary. 1984/85–1988/89

Species	Mean Peak Count	% NW European Population	% UK Population
Pink-footed goose	22,822	20.7	20.7
Bar-tailed godwit	19,366	11.4	18.6
Knot	34,299	9.8	15.6
Wigeon	28,604	3.8	11.4
Bewick's swan*	469	2.8	6.7
Black-tailed godwit	1,587	2.3	31.7
Sanderling	2,207	2.2	15.8
Grey Plover	2,719	1.8	13.0
Whooper swan	289	1.7	4.8
Shelduck	3,989	1.6	6.0
Oystercatcher	12,409	1.4	10.2
Teal	4,781	1.2	4.8
Redshank	1,576	1.0	2.1

Source: Salmon et al. (1990)

*Population of Bewick's swan shared with Martin Mere

site in Britain. These huge winter flocks of wading birds regularly exceed 150,000 making Morecambe Bay the second most important estuary for waders in the UK. Table 98 shows the international importance of Morecambe Bay for these species.

Table 96 Top UK Sites for Wildfowl. 1984/85–1988/89

Estuary	Mean Peak Count	Peak 1988/89
Loughs Neagh/Beg	91,885	67,924
The Wash	67,691	63,438
Ouse Washes	50,500	56,473
RIBBLE ESTUARY	55,160	48,967
Loch of Strathbeg	44,493	40,723

Source: Salmon et al. (1990)

Table 97 Top Estuaries for Waders in the UK. 1984/85–1988/89

Estuary	Peak Winter Count 1988/89	Average Peak Winter Count 1984/85 to 1988/89
The Wash	225,180	199,947
MORECAMBE BAY	171,516	157,051
RIBBLE ESTUARY	152,399	97,778
The Thames	87,650	85,408
Humber	97,536	84,984

Source: Salmon et al. (1990)

9.117 The saltmarshes of Lancashire provide important roosting sites for waders at high tide as well as supporting a number of important breeding bird communities. In addition to waders, the Ribble saltmarshes also support a diverse breeding community which includes redshank, common tern, black-headed gull, skylark, lapwing, teal, shoveler, ringed plover and snipe. The Morecambe Bay saltmarshes provide a nesting habitat for breeding oystercatcher, ringed plover, lapwing, curlew, redshank, shelduck, snipe, black-headed gull, wheatear, reed-bunting, common tern, sedge warbler and linnet.

Marine Habitat

Location and Extent

9.118 Defining a precise landward boundary for Lancashire's marine habitat is not easy. It is usually taken as the sea and seabed below the median low water mark out to territorial limits three miles from the 'baselines' (the legal definition of baselines is 'the low water line along the coast except in the case of bays and island groups') (Nature Conservancy Council, 1979). Figure 143 shows the location of Lancashire's marine habitat.

9.119 Lancashire's inter and sub-tidal habitat has been little studied, and information about its flora and fauna is limited. Most of the available material comes from the work of the Morecambe Bay Study

Table 98 Birds of International and National Importance in Morecambe Bay. 1984/85–1988/89

Species	Mean Peak Count	% NW European Population	% UK Population
Pink-footed goose*	8,469	7.7	7.7
Knot	24,675	7.1	11.2
Oystercatcher	54,126	6.0	19.3
Redshank	6,880	4.6	9.2
Bar-tailed godwit	3,539	3.5	5.8
Pintail	2,294	3.3	9.2
Dunlin	41,879	3.0	10.0
Curlew	10,357	3.0	11.4
Turnstone	1,952	2.8	4.3
Shelduck	3,671	1.5	4.5
Grey Plover	2,018	1.3	9.6
Ringed Plover	604	1.2	2.6
Eider	4,846	–	6.9
Cormorant	525	–	2.6
Goldeneye	359	–	2.4
Red-breasted merganser	217	–	2.2
Lapwing	14,544	–	1.5

Source: Salmon et al. (1990)

*The pink-footed goose population is shared with the Fylde.

Origin of Wintering and Passage Birds on Lancashire Estuaries. 1981

Source : Prater (1981)

Wildfowl

1. Bewicks Swan
2. Whooper Swan
3. Pink-footed Goose
4. Shelduck
5. Wigeon
6. Teal
7. Pintail
8. Shoveler

Waders

9. Oystercatcher
10. Ringed Plover
11. Grey Plover
12. Knot
13. Sanderling
14. Dunlin
15. Black-tailed Godwit
16. Bar-tailed Godwit
17. Curlew
18. Redshank
19. Turnstone

Group (Robinson and Pringle, 1987). Nothing of particular ecological significance has yet been reported. There are some 64 species of macroscopic algae occurring in Morecambe Bay, whilst the phytoplankton found is described as 'unremarkable' (Evans, 1987). Some 207 invertebrate species were noted, (Adams, 1987), which form a considerable part of the food supply of waders and wildfowl.

9.120 Morecambe Bay is exceptional for the size and regularity of its intertidal colonies of the common mussel, whilst its shallow waters are an important nursery ground for many species of young fish. Two groups are of particular importance: flatfish (plaice, dabs, flounders and sole) which concentrate in mud flat channels in their first year of life, and young herring and sprat (known as whitebait) which concentrate in the open water in their first year. On the outer part of the Bay, in the deeper channel between Heysham and Fleetwood, plaice, sole, skate, rays and cod occur. Virtually all the rivers draining into Morecambe Bay have runs of salmon and/or sea trout and eels. The Lune is one of the major salmon and sea trout rivers in England and supports extensive commercial and sport fisheries. Thus, the Bay forms part of the migratory route for salmon, sea trout and eels.

Urban and Industrial Habitat

9.121 Towns are the home of a surprisingly wide variety of plants and animals, some of which actually thrive in the urban environment. In some places interesting plant and animal species have developed. Indeed, some industrial wastes have provided unique habitats, including calcareous pulverised fuel ash colonised by orchids, demolition rubble colonised by poppies and tall buildings providing nest sites for kestrels which hunt for prey amongst unsprayed grasslands. However, whilst a plethora of information exists describing what one may find in towns, there are, as yet, no data on the position in Lancashire.

9.122 Generally, though, buildings, walls, gardens, parks and open spaces, road and railway banks, derelict land and industrial wasteland, streams, rivers, canals and reservoirs provide a huge variety of habitats. The mainly linear nature of these habitats provides green corridors and networks that are vital to wildlife. These are valuable habitats in themselves, but perhaps more importantly, they enable wildlife to move around towns and to link with the countryside.

9.123 Important habitats have also arisen as a by-product of various industrial activities. Abandoned limestone quarries are not only frequently of high geological value, but can also develop grassland communities of outstanding wildlife interest. Two such quarries have recently been declared Local Nature Reserves in the Clitheroe area (see below). Sandstone quarries are much more numerous in the County. Although rarely as rich in plant species they can develop scrub, heath, acidic and neutral grasslands, and wetland habitats in places where these are scarce. The more mature sites can support large insect and amphibian populations, whilst inaccessible quarry ledges can provide nesting habitats as a substitute for upland cliffs which are rare in the County.

9.124 Clay-pits are frequently slightly calcareous and often retain open water and wetland habitats. They can be very valuable for plants, insects, birds and amphibians including rare species like the great-crested newt. Sand and gravel pits of recent origin are concentrated in the Wyre Valley and near Carnforth. Generally flooded, they are potentially extremely valuable wildlife habitats. However, most worked-out sites have been developed primarily for recreational use, which can restrict wildlife value.

9.125 Industrial waste tips of significant botanical interest are rather rare in Lancashire. The best surviving examples are iron works waste tips at Carnforth and Lower Darwen. The flora of both is very rich with over 250 species being recorded at the latter site alone. Some plants are otherwise absent from the districts concerned, and include County rarities. Industrial buildings themselves may be of value. Peregrines, for example, bred successfully on one cotton mill chimney in 1990. Reservoirs, lagoons, canals and railways and roadside verges are other urban man-made habitats of potential wildlife significance which are considered elsewhere.

Linear Habitat

9.126 Much of the biological diversity in lowland agricultural areas is associated not with the farmed land itself (which is usually arable or intensive grassland), but with linear features. The most common are stream (or ditch) sides, hedgerows and roadside verges. In 1978, a stratified random survey of these was undertaken throughout the County, noting plant species and habitat factors. The data were analysed by the Institute of Terrestrial Ecology (ITE) at Merlewood Research Station, and helped give a picture of ecological diversity in the wider countryside.

Streamsides

9.127 Streamsides were the most diverse of the three types. In terms of the total length of streamside habitat in Lancashire, it was estimated that 3% are saltmarsh channels; moorland streamsides account for 12%, whilst banks with tree, shrub or other plants associated with woodland affinities make up 20%. As much as 50% lacked much tree or shrub cover, and were generally species-poor, usually being associated with man-made grasslands or arable land. The final 15% were richer in species, including plants of marshes and semi-natural grasslands, sometimes with trees or shrubs, and generally showing less human influence. The total number of plant species recorded was 262; significantly more than for hedges or roadsides.

Hedgerows

9.128 Hedgerows have been likened to the edges of woodland, and can be a major wildlife habitat in open agricultural landscapes, provided they are not cut too low. They provide food and shelter for birds, mammals, amphibians and insects, as well as singing posts for birds, and allow some movement of wildlife from one semi-natural habitat to another. The ITE confirmed that most Lancashire hedges contain hawthorn. Many, especially in the 'recent' landscapes of the Fylde and West Lancashire, are less than 200 years old and relatively poor in woody species. Nevertheless, perhaps 10% of the County's hedges are comparatively species-rich, frequently with hazel as an important component. These are often associated with old boundaries or traditional hay meadows, in areas of 'ancient' landscape and are most common in the Forest of Bowland AONB. They also occur locally elsewhere, including the fringes of the West Pennine Moors.

9.129 The abundance of stinging nettle is a reminder that hedgerows are a habitat for a large number of insects. Hedge bottoms are valuable for small mammals like shrews, bank vole and field mouse, as well as over-wintering beetles and amphibians like the great crested newt. Mature, overgrown hedgerows attract a wide range of birds, from resident finches and tits to summer visitors like willow warbler and whitethroat. Yellowhammer, now scarce over much of East Lancashire is much more common in areas with a high density of well-grown hedges. Sparrowhawks favour hedges for hunting, and winter berries provide food for thrushes, fieldfare and redwing.

Roadside Verges

9.130 Of the three linear habitat types, roadside verges show the most influence of human activity. Some 45% of surveyed sites were largely artificial communities, dominated by rye-grass or clover, or by open ground 'weed' species like dandelion or annual meadow-grass. By contrast, 25% are more natural (though probably cut occasionally), with scattered trees shrubs and shade-bearing herbs. Some verges are adjacent to hedgerows and about half of this 'semi-natural' group are especially species-rich, tending to resemble unimproved pasture or meadow. Verges of this kind occur most commonly at low to moderate altitudes in the Forest of Bowland, but locally elsewhere. A further 30% are intermediate in character, with cock's-foot, false oat-grass, cow parsley and hogweed. A total of 181 species was recorded at all sites.

Habitat and Species Protection

9.131 This section examines the overall position with regard to sites and species protection in Lancashire and the protection afforded to the specific habitats which have just been described. Figure 145 shows the location of the principal areas protected for wildlife in the County.

Sites Protection

9.132 Two Lancashire sites totalling 244.2 ha have been considered important enough to merit international designation as Ramsars and Special Protection Areas (SPA). These are:

* Leighton Moss, Lancaster (also SSSI). 124.9 ha;
* Martin Mere, West Lancashire (also SSSI). 119.3 ha.

Table 99 Sites of Special Scientific Interest in Lancashire. 1990

District	Site Name	Predominant Habitat Interest	Area (ha)	District (ha)
Lancaster	Artle Dale	Woodland	42.0	
	Bowland Fells (part)[1]	Moorland	7,457.0	
	Burton Wood	Woodland	17.7	
	Clear Beck Meadow	Grassland	0.5	
	Cockerham Marsh	Coastal	10.0	
	Crag Bank	Grassland	3.5	
	Cringlebarrow and Deepdale	Woodland	49.8	
	Eaves Wood	Woodland	51.5	
	Gait Barrows	Limestone Pavement	68.6	
	Hawes Water	Various/ Mixed	90.2	
	Leck Beck Head	Grassland	466.2	
	Leighton Moss	Swamp and Fen	124.9	
	Lune Estuary	Coastal	7,928.0	
	Morecambe Bay (part)[2]	Coastal	5,820.0	
	Robert Hall Moor	Grassland	18.8	
	Roeburndale Woods	Woodland	41.7	
	Tarnbrook Meadows	Grassland	10.8	
	Thrang End & Yealand Hall Allotment	Limestone Pavement	49.1	
	Trowbarrow Quarry	Geology	7.1	
	Warton Crag	Grassland	73.0	22,330.4
Wyre	Bowland Fells (part)[1]	Moorland	1,745.3	
	Barnaby Sands Marsh	Coastal	67.0	
	Burrows Marsh	Coastal	36.5	
	Rough Hey Wood	Woodland	5.9	
	Winmarleigh Moss	Lowland Peat Moss	57.5	1,912.2
Ribble Valley	Bowland Fells (part)[1]	Moorland	6,601.5	
	Clitheroe Reef Knolls	Geology	115.3	
	Cockwood Gorge	Geology	2.5	
	Coplow Quarry	Geology	4.9	
	Hodder River Section	Geology	7.4	
	Langcliffe Cross Meadow	Grassland	5.3	
	Light Clough	Geology	0.8	
	Little Mearley Clough	Geology	6.0	
	Mytton Meadows	Grassland	10.0	
	Salthill & Bellman Park Quarries	Geology	18.0	
	White Moss	Moorland	10.3	6,782.0
Blackpool	Marton Mere	Freshwater	38.5	38.5
Fylde	Newton Marsh	Coastal	65.5	
	Ribble Estuary (part)[3]	Coastal	1,930.0	1,995.5
Preston	Red Scar & Tunbrook Woods	Woodland	63.9	63.9
South Ribble	Darwen River Section	Geology	5.6	
	Ribble Estuary (part)[3]	Coastal	455.0	460.6
West Lancashire	Downholland Moss	Geology	21.2	
	Martin Mere	Freshwater	119.3	
	Mere Sands Wood	Freshwater	42.4	
	Ravenhead Brickworks	Geology	4.6	
	Ribble Estuary (part)[3]	Coastal	4,345.0	4,532.5
Chorley	Charnock Richard Pasture	Grassland	1.2	
	White Coppice Flush	Grassland	0.5	1.7
Blackburn	Gale Clough and Shooterslee	Woodland	2.8	
	Oak Field	Grassland	20.7	23.5
Hyndburn	Harper Clough & Smalley Delph	Geology	2.9	2.9
Burnley	Haworth Moor (part)[4]	Moorland	220.6	220.6
Pendle	Haworth Moor (part)[4]	Moorland	1,089.4	1,089.4
Rossendale	Hodge Clough	Geology	2.3	2.3
LANCASHIRE			39,456.0	39,456.0

Source: NCC (pers. comm.).

Notes: [1] *Falls partly into Lancaster, Wyre and Ribble Valley.*
[2] *Further part falls into Cumbria.*
[3] *Falls partly into Fylde, South Ribble, West Lancashire and Sefton.*
[4] *Falls partly into Burnley, Pendle, Bradford and Calderdale.*

Consultations are in hand to extend SPA status to the Bowland Fells SSSI (15,803.8 ha). The Ribble Estuary, Lune Estuary and Morecambe Bay also qualify for Ramsar SPA status and consultations are to commence shortly.

9.133 There are 50 SSSI in the County, covering a range of habitats and totalling 39,456 ha. These are listed in Table 99, which reveals that Lancaster has both the largest number of sites (20) and area protected (22,330.4 ha). In terms of area, Ribble Valley (6,782 ha), West Lancashire (4,532.5 ha) and Fylde (1,995.5 ha) come next. In terms of sites, Ribble Valley has eleven, although most of these have been notified because of their geological significance. The Districts most poorly protected are Hyndburn (2.9 ha), Rossendale (2.3 ha) and Chorley (1.7 ha), due in part to the fact that ecological diversity is lower in East Lancashire than in the north and along the coast, whilst the human impact on wildlife has perhaps been greater.

9.134 Site protection by statutory nature reserves (NNR and LNR) is extremely limited. There are only two NNR and five LNR, and two of the latter were declared in 1990. The sites are shown in Table 100.

9.135 No use has been made in Lancashire of management agreements under Section 39 of the WCA 1981. However, four large estates have entered into the Capital Transfer Tax Exemption scheme. Two are in Ribble Valley, one in Lancaster and one in Chorley. Exemptions have been given mainly on landscape grounds, though wildlife reasons have also featured.

9.136 To a degree, the deficiency in statutory nature reserve protection is offset by the number of non-statutory reserves acquired, or leased/licensed and managed by a variety of largely voluntary bodies. The LTNC has been to the fore in this movement, with the Woodland Trust and RSPB also prominent. There are now 43 non-statutory reserves in the County, listed in Table 101.

9.137 The LTNC has also listed some 459 sites which they consider to be Sites of Biological Importance. These are largely non-statutory designations, but include overlaps with statutory sites. Their numbers by District are given in Table 102.

Table 101	Non-Statutory Nature Reserves in Lancashire. 1990		
District	Reserve	Managing Body	Public Access
Lancaster	Burton Wood	LTNC	permit
	Eaves Wood	NT	yes
	Heysham Power Station	LTNC	no
	Hyning Scout Wood	WT	yes
	Leighton Moss	RSPB	yes*
	Lord's Lot Bog	LTNC	no
	Morecambe Bay	RSPB	yes*
	Oxcliffe Marsh	LTNC	yes
	Warton Crag	LTNC/RSPB	yes
Wyre	Armhill and Barnaby's Sands Marsh	LTNC	yes
	Burrows Marsh	LTNC	yes
	Fleetwood Marshes	LTNC	no
	Scorton	County Council	yes
Ribble Valley	Clough Lane Wood, Simonstone	WT	yes
	Moor Piece	LTNC	no
	Stocks Reservoir	NWW	permit
Fylde	Great Plumpton Sidings	LTNC	no
Preston	Boilton Wood	LTNC	yes
	Brockholes Wood	Preston BC/local group	yes
	Red Scar and Tun Brook Woods	LTNC	no
South Ribble	Cop Lane, Penwortham	LTNC	permit
	Cuerden Valley Park	LTNC/CNT	yes
	Dog Kennel Wood	WT	yes
	Longton Brickcroft	South Ribble BC	yes
	Shruggs Wood	South Ribble BC	permit
West Lancashire	Alex Wood, Lathom	WT	yes
	Haskayne Cutting	LTNC	permit
	Marton Mere, Burscough	WWT	yes*
	Mere Sands Wood	LTNC	yes*
Chorley	Croston Marsh	LTNC	no
	Dean Wood, Rivington	LTNC	no
Blackburn	Longworth Clough and Oakfield	LTNC	permit
	Pleasington Old Hall Wood	LTNC	yes
	Wayoh Reservoir	LTNC	yes
Hyndburn	Foxhill Bank	LTNC	permit
	Laund Clough	WT	yes
Burnley	Fother Royd Wood	WT	yes
	Hagg Wood	WT	yes

Source: Various

Notes: yes*: major visitor provision
CNT: Commission for the New Towns
LTNC: Lancashire Trust for Nature Conservation
RSPB: Royal Society for the Protection of Birds
NT: National Trust
WT: Woodland Trust
WWT: Wildfowl and Wetlands Trust

Table 100	Statutory Nature Reserves in Lancashire. 1990			
District	Site	Type of Reserve	Date Declared	Area (ha)
Lancaster	Gaitbarrows	NNR	1977	70.0
	Warton Crag	LNR	1984	19.4
Ribble Valley	Crosshill Quarry	LNR	1990	8.8
	Salthill Quarry	LNR	1990	9.3
Fylde	Lytham St. Annes dunes	LNR	1968	15.7
West Lancashire	Ribble Marshes	NNR	1981	2,226.0
Rossendale	Healey Dell	LNR	1976	33.9
LANCASHIRE				2,383.1

Source: NCC (pers. comm.)

Species Protection

9.138 Under Schedule 5 of the WCA 1981, several animal species which occur in Lancashire, are protected in various ways. Over 20 species are involved:

* Full Protection – bats (all species), red squirrel, otter, great crested newt;

* Protected from Killing, Injury and Sale – viviparous lizard, slow-worm, grass snake;

* Protected from Taking and Sale – adder, palmate and smooth newts, and the northern brown argus, small blue, Duke of Burgundy, large heath, high brown fritillary, pearl-bordered fritillary, and white-letter hairstreak butterflies.

Figure 145

Sites of Special Scientific Interest and Nature Reserves in Lancashire. 1990

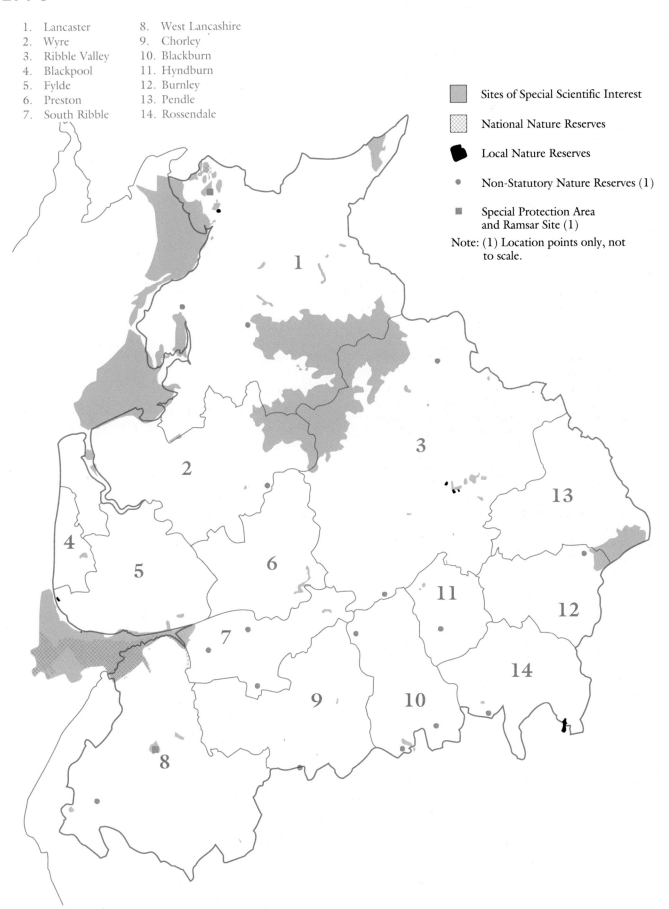

1. Lancaster
2. Wyre
3. Ribble Valley
4. Blackpool
5. Fylde
6. Preston
7. South Ribble
8. West Lancashire
9. Chorley
10. Blackburn
11. Hyndburn
12. Burnley
13. Pendle
14. Rossendale

Sites of Special Scientific Interest

National Nature Reserves

Local Nature Reserves

Non-Statutory Nature Reserves (1)

Special Protection Area and Ramsar Site (1)

Note: (1) Location points only, not to scale.

Source: Lancashire County Council

Table 102 Sites of Biological Importance in Lancashire Notified by LTNC. 1990

District	No. of sites (including statutory sites)
Lancaster	79
Wyre	24
Ribble Valley	82
Blackpool	5
Fylde	17
Preston	5
South Ribble	9
West Lancashire	38
Chorley	30
Blackburn	60
Hyndburn	18
Burnley	16
Pendle	14
Rossendale	62
LANCASHIRE	459

Source: LTNC (pers. comm.)

9.139 Thirteen bird species found in the County are protected by the special penalties contained in Schedule 1 of the WCA 1981. These are the barn owl, bearded tit, bittern, corncrake, goshawk, hen harrier, kingfisher, little ringed plover, marsh harrier, merlin, peregrine, quail and spotted crake. None of the plant species included in Schedule 8 of the WCA 1981 occurs in the wild in Lancashire.

Habitat Protection

9.140 Table 103 divides the area in the County protected by SSSI into the major habitat types described in this Chapter. It should be noted that SSSI often encompass more than one habitat, and so the division is based on the predominant interest of each site. The figures show that two habitats – moorland and coastal – comprise the overwhelming area. This is due to the importance of these types in County terms, (particularly true with regard to coastal), and the fact that by nature they are extensive habitats. In contrast, most other habitat types have their principal features of interest gathered into much smaller areas.

9.141 Supplementary data exist for the protection afforded to some of Lancashire's habitats. As far as woodlands are concerned, for example, the felling of woodland trees is generally subject to controls exercised by the Forestry Commission. A variety of other measures, ranging from Tree Preservation Orders (TPO) to nature reserves and SSSI have been adopted to protect Lancashire's woods (see Table 104). This shows that woodland TPO are widely, if thinly, scattered over the County. It also reveals how limited the protection afforded to ancient woods is, whether by statutory nature reserve status, or SSSI notification.

9.142 The general position with regard to the degree of protection afforded to other habitats is as follows:

* Grassland – Gaitbarrows NNR (Lancaster), contains meadows of interest, whilst three LNR have significant areas of limestone grassland (Crosshills and Salthill Quarries in Ribble Valley and Warton Crag in Lancaster). Four non-statutory reserves include valuable grassland (Great Plumpton Sidings, Fylde; Heysham Power Station, Lancaster; Longton Brickcroft, South Ribble and Haskayne Cutting, West Lancashire);

* Limestone Pavement – no Limestone Pavement Orders have been established in Lancashire yet, though all significant examples are protected by a combination of SSSI, NNR and LNR;

* Moorland – over 40% of Lancashire's unenclosed moorland is protected as SSSI. There are no moorland NNR and LNR, though LTNC manage three small non-statutory reserves, (Moor Piece in Ribble Valley, Lord's Lot Bog in Lancaster and Oakfield in Blackburn);

* Lowland Remnant Peat Mosses – only five of Lancashire's scarce and fragile lowland mosses are protected. These are Winmarleigh Moss (our best and only intact example) in Wyre, Hawes Water and Leighton Moss, both Lancaster, and White Moss and Downholland Moss, both West Lancashire. All are parts of SSSI.

Table 103 Sites of Special Scientific Interest in Lancashire by Predominant Habitat. 1990

Predominant Habitat	Area (ha)	Number of SSSI
Woodland	275.3	8
Scrubland	—	—
Grassland	610.5	11
Limestone Pavement	117.7	2
Moorland	17,124.1	4
Lowland Remnant Peat Moss	57.5	1
Swamp and Fen	124.9	1
Freshwater	200.2	3
Coastal	20,657.0	7
Marine	—	—
Urban and Industrial	—	—
Linear	—	—
Various/mixed	90.2	1
Geological	198.6	12
LANCASHIRE	39,456.0	50

Source: NCC (pers. comm.)

* Swamp and Fen – the majority of the most important examples of this habitat are statutorily protected by a combination of SSSI and nature reserve status;

* Freshwater – this group is poorly protected. The County's only two natural lakes, (Hawes Water, Lancaster and Marton Mere, Blackpool) are SSSI, as are the wetlands and waters at Leighton Moss and Martin Mere. Forty-five reservoirs and water-bodies are included in the LTNC list of Sites of Biological Importance, but this affords no legal protection. No ponds or running waters are legally protected; but stretches of the Lancaster Canal are shortly to be notified as SSSI.

* Coastal – all outstanding estuarine mud and sand flats and saltmarshes are protected by SSSI, whilst the Ribble Marshes are also NNR. Surprisingly, given their international significance, none of the County's estuarine habitats are afforded Ramsar or Special Protection Area status. Consultations are, however, taking place. On the other hand, only 10% of the County's scarce sand-dune habitat is protected, (some 16 ha out of 152 ha); The NCC are currently pursuing the SSSI notification of Lytham St. Annes LNR, together with the areas of dune to the seaward side of this.

* Marine – no protected areas;

* Urban and Industrial – there are no statutorily protected wildlife areas, but five quarries and mineral working sites have been notified as SSSI by virtue of their geological interest. A number of non-statutory sites are related to urban fringe sites or former industrial locations.

* Linear – Again, there is no statutory protection, apart from features in sites which have been designated for other purposes. A number of non-statutory sites exist, usually related to abandoned railway lines.

Threats to Wildlife

9.143 Lancashire's habitats and species are subject to a variety of influences which threaten or diminish their value. There are no precise statistical data on this broad set of problems. With limited exceptions, the evidence which exists is generalised and anecdotal. This section gives, therefore, only an outline of the nature of the threats involved. The section which follows presents firmer material on the consequences of these threats by way of changes recorded in the extent of some of the County's habitats.

9.144 The principal factors threatening the County's habitats are:

* Woodland – clearance and felling, coniferisation and the loss of native species, reductions in species and canopy/shrub layer diversity, stock grazing preventing natural regeneration, management neglect, air pollution, development;

* Grassland – agricultural improvements including the application of nitrogen-rich fertilisers, drainage of wet grassland sites, overgrazing, scrub encroachment, quarrying,

Table 104	Number of Protected Woodlands in Lancashire. 1990								
District	TPO	NT	SSSI	SBI	NNR	LNR	ONR	Ancient Woods Total	All Woods Total
Lancaster	n.d.	1	10	23	1	1	3	122	161
Wyre	26	–	1	3	–	–	–	22	52
Ribble Valley	61	–	–	41	–	–	3	114	219
Blackpool	–	–	–	–	–	–	–	–	–
Fylde	16	–	–	–	–	–	–	–	16
Preston	3	–	1	3	–	–	1	12	20
South Ribble	22	–	–	2	–	–	1	21	46
West Lancashire	25	–	–	15	–	–	2	10	52
Chorley	16	–	–	19	–	–	–	38	73
Blackburn	2	–	2	12	–	–	1	25	42
Hyndburn	35	–	–	7	–	–	2	14	58
Burnley	20	–	–	4	–	–	3	6	33
Pendle	7	–	–	3	–	–	–	5	15
Rossendale	5	2	–	22	–	1	–	3	33
LANCASHIRE	238	3	14	154	1	2	16	392	820

Source: Lancashire County Council, District Councils.

road-building, unsympathetic vergeside management, development;

* Limestone Pavement – removal of pavements for agricultural improvement and for sale in garden centres, scrub encroachment;

* Moorland – overgrazing, reclamation of marginal land, air pollution, peat extraction, access and recreation, illegal persecution of birds of prey, management neglect, drainage, afforestation, uncontrolled fires;

* Lowland Mosses – drainage, including changes in the water table brought about by draining adjacent land, peat extraction for garden use, air pollution;

* Swamp and Fen – drainage, nutrient enrichment caused by the inflow of polluted water, natural succession and scrub encroachment, land reclamation, land fill and illegal tipping, recreation;

* Freshwater – discharges of pollutants from sewage, industry and farms, fluctuations in water level, acidification, hypereutrophication, air pollution, reclamation of ponds for farming and development, tipping, access and recreation, natural succession and scrub encroachment;

* Coastal – discharges of pollutants from sewage industry and farms on the coast and inland, sand extraction, recreation and tourism, development, estuarine barrages, reclamation for agriculture, coastal defences, illegal tipping, encroachment by Spartina, sea-level rise;

* Marine – discharges of pollutants, marine accidents and spillages, lack of knowledge of the habitat, the absence of any clear management responsibilities;

* Urban and Industrial – development, reclamation, public disturbance, traffic pollution, invasive plants (e.g. Japanese knotweed);

* Linear – streamsides as for Freshwater, Hedgerows (clearance for farming and development, lack of management, severance), roadside verges as for Grassland, invasive plants.

Habitat Changes

Woodland

9.145   Since the last war, 1864 ha of new woodland have been planted in the County representing 18.4% of the present total County woodland area of woods over 2 ha. Some 62% of the new planting is coniferous, and a further 38% is mainly broadleaved –largely the result of planting by the Forestry Commission, water undertakings and private owners in the Forest of Bowland and, to a lesser extent, to the south of Blackburn. Little new woodland has been planted in the west of the County, particularly in the Fylde and South Ribble districts. The 1979–82 Forestry Commission census shows that conifer planting peaked in Lancashire between 1951 and 1960. The Commission's figures include planting on new sites and replanting of existing woodlands. They show that over 1,000 ha of mainly broadleaved woodland was established, or restocked, between 1951 and 1960, (more than in any decade since 1900).

This must refer largely to replanting of existing woods. However, the trend has since dramatically reversed, since the corresponding figure for 1971 to 1980 (67 ha) is the lowest for any decade since 1860 (Forestry Commission,1984). As far as woodland established by natural regeneration is concerned, only Silverdale (Lancaster) has witnessed any significant increase in recent years.

9.146   Some 601 ha of woodland have been lost since 1945, almost all of it broadleaved or mixed. This figure excludes woods smaller than 2 ha, which will also have been lost. About 76 ha have disappeared from ancient sites, representing about 2.7% of the County's 1945 stock of ancient woodland, whilst nearly 9.6% of the broadleaved and mixed secondary woodland that existed in 1945 has also been cleared. The largest losses are from Lancaster, Ribble Valley (both had the highest total to start with) and West Lancashire. Predominantly broadleaved woodland is involved in each case, but West Lancashire is exceptional in having lost a quarter of its broadleaved woodland since the war. Most of the ancient woodland loss has also been from Lancaster, Ribble Valley, Hyndburn and Burnley. Least clearance is recorded from the centre of the County, in Fylde, Preston, South Ribble and Chorley.

9.147   The net result of these changes (Table 105) is an overall increase in total woodland of 1,263 ha, largely from conifer planting. The totals for each District show an even spread. There has been a net increase north of the Ribble, a slight increase in East Lancashire and a decrease in the south west of the County. In terms of woodland type, this has meant an increase of over 62% in the area of coniferous woodland, which now comprises more than 26% of the County total.

9.148   Most woodland loss relates to areas of less than 5 ha, and do not involve the complete loss of the woods concerned. Of 53 woods completely lost, four were larger than 5 ha. Only six of the other 153 cases of recorded loss involved areas greater than 5 ha (three of them in West Lancashire). On the other hand, most new woodland is in the form of completely new woods rather than extensions to existing ones; the only real exceptions being Gisburn Forest and those growing up adjacent to existing woods in Silverdale. Thus the total number of woods recorded has increased from 1,148 to 1,226 over this period.

Grasslands

9.149   It has been estimated that, nationally, some 95% of species-rich lowland netural grasslands have been lost, and that only 3% of the former area now remains unchanged. Comparable data for Lancashire are not available, but with an estimated area of neutral grassland of significant nature conservation interest of the order of only 100–200 ha, it can be assumed that the County has probably suffered a loss of a similar order. Loss of limestone grassland is likewise undocumented, but this rare habitat has been much reduced by agricultural improvement, especially in Ribble Valley and Silverdale, and by encroachment of scrub in Silverdale.

Table 105   Woodland Clearance in Lancashire. 1945–1986

District	Total No. of Sites Cleared	Area Ancient (ha)	Area Secondary (ha)	Area Total (ha)
Lancaster	45 (9)	9	129	138
Wyre	12 (5)	11	21	32
Ribble Valley	47 (12)	25	104	129
Blackpool	– (–)	–	–	–
Fylde	– (–)	–	–	–
Preston	5 (–)	–	7	7
South Ribble	8 (2)	6	9	15
West Lancashire	23 (7)	8	109	117
Chorley	9 (1)	4	11	15
Blackburn	13 (4)	1	24	25
Hyndburn	14 (2)	12	25	37
Burnley	14 (3)	–	37	37
Pendle	4 (3)	–	16	16
Rossendale	12 (5)	–	33	33
LANCASHIRE	206 (53)	76	525	601

Source: Lancashire County Council (1986).

Note: Brackets = completely cleared woods.

Limestone Pavement

9.150   Data relating to limestone pavement loss are limited to old records. The NCC was initiating a limestone pavement survey at the time of writing, the results of which will be published at a later date. Ward and Evans (1973) estimated that 40% of the limestone pavements on the Gait Barrows site had been completely destroyed. Losses between 1973 and 1977, might have amounted to a further reduction of 25%. Estimates of loss at other pavement sites suggest, though, that almost half of the 2,150 ha of limestone pavement in Britain have been damaged to some degree (Nature Conservancy Council, 1980).

Moorland

9.151   In the absence of County-wide data, it is impossible to give more than an indication of trends so far as changes in moorland habitat is concerned. In the early nineteenth century, the need to feed the expanding population stimulated much enclosure, sometimes up to quite high altitudes in East Lancashire. As imported foodstuffs became widely available, much of this marginal farmland was abandoned in the late nineteenth, and the early part of the present, century. Most of this land has continued to revert to moorland, comprising rush-pasture, acidic grassland and significant areas of purple moor-grass. Much more recently, some of this reverted land has been reclaimed with agricultural grant-aid, and this has occasionally also extended onto unenclosed moorland. Nevertheless, the areas of marginal land and moorland proper which have been reclaimed in recent years probably remain quite small in relation to the total area.

9.152   From a wildlife point of view, changes in moorland vegetation may be as important as absolute losses or gains. Some types of moorland, including purple moor-grass, cotton-grass mires, calcifugous grasslands and rush-pastures, have probably increased over the last 200 years, whilst dwarf shrub communities have probably declined. *Sphagnum*-based blanket bog has virtually disappeared. The decline of the latter, and its replacement with cotton-grass or heather-bilberry-cotton-grass bog, appears to date back at least 500 years, and is probably the result of intense grazing and burning (Tallis, 1989; Birks, 1988). Drainage and atmospheric pollution have also played key roles in the disappearance of *Sphagnum* mosses. (Press, Woodin and Lee, 1986.)

9.153   There is very little quantitative data of more recent changes. Estimates of the area of heather moorland prepared for the DOE (see Table 106) show little change in the north-west over the post-war period (Bunce, 1989).

9.154   Table 106 and Figure 140 accord with the results of the only critical study of moorland habitat change known to have been carried out locally, in the South Pennines on the Lancashire-West Yorkshire border. (Haworth and Sykes, 1986). This concluded that little change had occurred in the actual areas of different types of moorland habitat, since the beginning of this century. However, there

Table 106	Changes in the Area of Heather Moorland in NW England. 1947–1984		
Source of Data	Year	Area Existing (ha)	Changes (in %)
Aerial Photographs	1947	19,600	—
Aerial Photographs	1969	18,800	−4
Aerial Photographs	1980	18,000	−4
Landsat Satellite Image	1984	20,250	+12

Source: Bunce (1989).

has been a considerable change in the spatial distribution of these habitats within the moorland. These were attributed to management practices, and a strong correlation emerged between healthy heather moorland and active game management. Elsewhere, informal observations indicate that heather cover has been almost completely lost over the last 50 years (e.g.in the West Pennine Moors), particularly as a result of overgrazing. The fact that recovery can and does take place under the correct management conditions serves to show that this is a dynamic situation, and one where local research is urgently required.

Lowland Remnant Peat Mosses

9.155   In the mid-nineteenth century, the one inch Geological Survey maps show that approximately 17,000 ha of uncultivated peat, and peat derived soils, existed in Lancashire. Today, a mere 400 ha remain. This represents a staggering loss of 98% in a little over a hundred years. Figure 141 illustrates the dramatic decline. Surviving areas include not only the remaining 'virgin' mossland, but also those sites currently having peat extracted and any other known areas of uncultivated peat – many of which now support semi-natural or plantation woodland and bear little resemblance to the original wet mosslands. Indeed Lancashire now has just one site that resembles the original wet mossland, which is at Winmarleigh Moss, north west of Garstang (Wyre and Lancaster Districts).

Swamp and Fen

9.156   This habitat has experienced both gains, and losses, in recent years. Perhaps the most serious loss has been at Mere Brow, (West Lancashire), where valuable reedbeds were destroyed in the early 1970s to make way for a water-based leisure complex. However, the area of reedbed at Leighton Moss has increased from 70 ha in 1965, to nearly 80 ha today, achieved largely through active management. This emphasises the dynamic nature of this particular habitat. Further increases could arise from sand and gravel operations, with proper planning controls over extraction and subsequent management.

Freshwater

9.157   There are no data concerning changes in the extent of the County's running waters, though the resource is likely to be one of the most constant of

Table 107	Field Pond Losses in Lancashire. 1845–1988		

No. of Ponds per 1 km OS grid square	Percentage of Ponds Lost (1845–1965)	Percentage of Ponds Lost (1965–1988)	Percentage of Ponds Lost (1845–1988)
1 to 4	48	34	66
5 to 9	39	48	68
10 to 19	32	41	60
20 to 24	12	45	51
25 to 38	11	51	57
LANCASHIRE	35	42	63

Source: Lancashire County Council (using OS 6" maps for 1845 and 1965 and aerial photographs for 1988).

all habitats. Principal variations are seasonal changes in river flows, and these have been given for main rivers in Chapter 4. Canal-based habitats have also remained largely intact. The only recent changes have been the loss of a 1 km branch linking to the Leeds-Liverpool Canal at Rainhill Rock, near Barnoldswick (Pendle) now used for landfill, and minor reclamations at Whittle-le-Woods (Chorley) and Walton Summit (South Ribble).

9.158 Most of the County's reservoirs were built in the last century and the early part of this. Most remain, though some small examples, of limited surface and marginal area, have been abandoned in recent years. Old mill lodges now constitute a significant biological resource. No data are available for them, but there are many hundreds scattered throughout the old textile parts of the County.

9.159 More information exists about the coverage of field ponds. Table 107 shows the reductions which have taken place since the middle of the last century. OS six inches to the mile maps for the 1845 period show some 17,324 ponds in the County. By the 1965 editions of the OS pathfinder maps, some 6,086 of these had been lost, leaving a total of 11,238. This represents a decrease of some 35% over the 120 year period. However, by 1988 the pond total had reduced to 6,476. This constitutes an even greater degree of loss, (42%), over a much shorter period (23 years), pointing to a major acceleration in the loss of County ponds. The total loss over the entire

Table 108	Changes in Saltmarsh Extent (Carnforth Group). 1845–1967				

Locality/Sub-group	1845	1888	(ha) 1910	1946	1967
Silverdale Marsh	7	128	40	109	244
Warton Marsh	7	197	255	485	506
Marshes to south of River Keer	15	22	16	87	80
Total	29	347	311	681	830
Change	–	+318	–36	+370	+149

Source: Gray and Scott (1987).

period (1845 to 1988) was 63%, representing 10,758 ponds.

9.160 A unique characteristic of the pond loss study is that it examines losses within, and between, different pond density classes. Of particular note, are the large percentage losses in high pond density areas between 1965 and 1988. Table 107 shows that over half the ponds in the 25 to 38 density category have disappeared. Moreover, the percentage loss in this category has grown by the greatest amount – some ten times – between the 1845–1965 and the 1965–1988 periods.

Coastal

9.161 Comprehensive information of losses and gains is unavailable for all of Lancashire's saltmarsh. However, data do exist for the Carnforth group. Table 108 shows the considerable fluctuations which occurred between 1845 and 1967. These stem from changes in the positions of the low-water channels of rivers flowing into Morecambe Bay. Over the entire period, the extent of saltmarsh increased dramatically in all three sub-groups. Growth of saltmarsh at Silverdale has been influenced by the lateral migrations of the main Kent channel. However, in the late 1970s the accretional trend of Silverdale Marsh was sharply reversed. In 1977, south-westerly gales, combined with high spring tides produced an eastward shift of the main channel in the Kent Estuary. By June 1981, the saltmarsh width had reduced from 1,000 m to 500 m, and in January 1989 it was 230 m at its widest extent.

9.162 Other significant saltmarsh losses have occurred as a result of coastal reclamation and sea defence. Hesketh Out marsh, on the Ribble Estuary has recently lost approximately 350 ha and the Pilling-Cockerham sea defence wall was responsible for the loss of a further 230 ha along that section of the coast.

9.163 There are no hard data on losses in sand dune habitat. However, dunes once extended along the entire coast between Lytham St. Annes and Fleetwood in the north. Only 150 ha remains intact today.

Linear

9.164 In an attempt to analyse hedgerow loss, the County Council examined aerial photographs of 1963 and 1988. This revealed that on average around 25% of the County's hedgerows had been lost over this period. Patterns of loss are as yet difficult to identify, but localised areas of very high loss are widely scattered, especially in parts of West Lancashire where there were rather few hedges to start with.

Monitoring

9.165 There is no consistent, comprehensive system for monitoring Lancashire's wildlife habitats and species. Monitoring, as opposed to initial surveying, usually takes place as a response to a particular problem. NCC monitor especially sensitive areas, particularly where consent has been given for activities which affect SSSI (Eaves Wood is a case in point). The only sites where monitoring does occur regularly, are non-statutory nature reserves such as those owned by the RSPB, LTNC or the Wildfowl and Wetlands Trust. Such reserves form a very small percentage of the County area, however.

References

Adams, C. (1987). Invertebrates of the Intertidal Zone. Morecambe Bay: An Assessment of Present Ecological Knowledge (Eds. Robinson and Pringle, 1987).

Birks, H.J.B. (1988). Long term ecological change in the British Uplands. Ecological Change in the Uplands. BES Symposium no. 7.

British Trust for Ornithology and the Royal Society for the Protection of Birds (1982). Breeding Birds of Wet Meadows. BTO/RSPB.

Boyd, M.and Pigot, J.Y. (1989). Flyways and Reserve Networks for Water Birds. IRWB publication no. 9.

Bunce, R.G.H. (1989). Heather in England and Wales. HMSO.

Evans, D. (1987). Phytoplankton. Morecambe Bay: An Assessment of Present Ecological Knowledge (Eds. Robinson and Pringle, 1987).

Forestry Commission (1984). County of Lancashire. Census of Woodlands and Trees, 1979–1982. FC.

Gray, A.J. (1979). The banks of estuaries and their management. Tidal Power and Estuary Management. Bristol, Scientechnica, 235–44. (Eds. Severn, R.T., Dineley, D. L. and Hawko E.L.)

Gray, A.J., and Sott, R. (1987). Saltmarshes. Morecambe Bay: An Assessment of Present Ecological Knowledge (Eds. Robinson and Pringle, 1987).

Grayson, R.F. (1989). The distribution and conservation of the ponds of North West England. Unpublished.

Haworth, P.and Sykes, J. (1986). A Study of Moorland Change in the Bronte Corridor Area of South Pennines.

Lancashire and Cheshire Fauna Society (1988). Lancashire Bird Report 1988. Lancashire and Cheshire Fauna Society.

Lancashire County Council (1986). Lancashire's Woodland Heritage. LCC.

Lancashire Trust for Nature Conservation (1989). Lancashire Mossland: past, present and future? Lapwing 48: 7–9. LTNC.

Nature Conservancy Council (1979). Nature Conservation in the Marine Environment. NCC/NERC.

Nature Conservancy Council (1980). The Conservation of Limestone Pavement. NCC.

Nature Conservancy Council (1986). Saltmarsh Survey of Great Britain – Lancashire. NCC.

Nature Conservancy Council (1988). Lancashire Inventory of Ancient Woodlands (Provisional). NCC.

Newman, J.R. (1988). A Botanical Survey of Limestone Grasslands in Lancashire. NCC.

Nissenbaum, D. (1989). A Management Plan for the Fylde Coastal Sand Dunes. MSc Thesis, University of London.

North West Water (1988). County Review 1988 for Lancashire. NWWA.

Prater, A.J. (1981). Estuary Birds of Britain and Ireland. Poyser.

Press, M.C., Woodin, S.J. & Lee, J.A. (1986). The potential importance of an increased atmospheric nitrogen supply to the growth of ombrotrophic Sphagnum species. New Phytologist 103: 45–55.

Robinson, N.A. and Pringle, A.W. (1987). Morecambe Bay: An Assessment of Present Ecological Knowledge. Centre of North West Regional Studies and the Morecambe Bay Study Group.

Salmon, D.G., Priest-Jones, R.P. and Kirby, J.S. (1990). Wildfowl and Wader Counts. W&WT.

Spencer, K.P.G. (1969). East Lancashire Reservoirs: An Ornithological Survey. Unpublished MSc Thesis, University of Salford.

Tallis, J.H. (1987). Fire and flood at Holme Moss: erosion process in an upland blanket mire. Journal of Ecology 75: 1099–1029.

Taylor, I. (1986). A Botanical Survey of Mesotrophic Grasslands in Lancashire. NCC.

Ward, S.D.and Evans, D.F. (1973). The Limestone Pavements on the Eastern Side of Morecambe Bay: Based on Botanical Criteria. ITE.

Woolerton (1983). The Arnside-Silverdale AONB – Land Management Study. Woolerton-Truscott Landscape Architects.

Chapter Ten
Landscape and Townscape

Introduction

10.1 Landscape and townscape are qualitative terms used to describe the visual scenery of our countryside and built-up areas. Because they are a visual phenomenon whose evaluation involves a large degree of subjectivity on behalf of the individual, they differ from other Green Audit subjects which are largely based on objective, scientific data. Wherever possible in this Chapter however, objective data has been presented to give estimates of landscape and townscape quality.

10.2 Difficulties in evaluating landscape and townscape quality, in no way lessen their importance, nor the contribution they make to overall environmental quality in the County. Indeed, landscape and townscape are the things that many Lancastrians value most, since we come into direct contact with them everyday and they are immediately obvious to us. Three quarters of Lancashire's population live in towns, (see Chapter 2) and the decision as to where we make our homes may be influenced by the townscape in particular areas, or the proximity to areas of attractive landscape.

10.3 The landscape is composed of a number of different elements; geology, topography, climate and vegetation, overlain by human activity (see Chapter 2). Very little of the County's landscape is truly natural. It has been shaped over centuries by people, who have had as much of an influence on the character of the countryside as they have on the creation and appearance of towns and villages. Townscape is also influenced by factors like geology which determines the availability, type and use of local building materials. These materials influence the scale and appearance of buildings in the towns and villages and how they blend into the landscape.

10.4 Lancashire has a rich and diverse landscape because of its varied geology, topography and the influences of climate and vegetation. The County lies at the transition between lowland and upland Britain, having landscape characteristics that are typical of both zones. This geographical position explains why Lancashire is so diverse. In terms of vegetation, the County is poor in woodland and rich in moorland. It has an ancient landscape pattern comprising woodlands, ponds, stone walls, hedgerows, pastures, archaeological features, hedges, quarries, settlements and other features. The townscape of the County is characterised by a similar range and variety. Most towns consist of mixtures of buildings of differing styles and ages, creating a variety of views, vistas and characters, though there are also strong unities arising from traditional regional styles.

10.5 There is general acceptance of the need for good landscape and townscape, and for efforts to be made to conserve them where they exist and enhance them where they are degraded. Much of the burden lies with individual landowners, both public and private. These people are the custodians of our rural and urban heritage. Their rôle is vital, because good landscape and townscapes add to quality of life, encourage tourism and aid economic regeneration.

10.6 This Chapter describes the legislation and organisations governing these topics and then presents data related to the landscape resource of the County, landscape protection and historic features in the landscape. It then moves onto landscape change and factors involved in the degradation of landscape followed by the ways in which it is enhanced. The second part of the Chapter deals with the townscape resource, giving data on features which can be used as a measure of townscape quality. It then deals with the degradation and enhancement of townscape in the County.

Legislation

European

10.7 Environmentally Sensitive Areas (ESA) were introduced into the Common Agricultural Policy by EC Regulation 85/797/EEC. Under this scheme, farmers are paid by MAFF to adopt traditional management practices that conserve landscape and natural habitats. Although several Areas have been established in the UK there are none as yet in Lancashire (see Chapter 8).

United Kingdom

10.8 The National Parks and Access to the Countryside Act 1949 established a framework for landscape designation and protection based upon the National Parks and Areas of Outstanding Natural Beauty (AONB). It also set up the National Parks Commission which provided a framework for the administration, protection and enhancement of these areas. The Countryside Act 1968 established the Countryside Commission which succeeded the National Parks Commission and is now the Government agency most directly concerned with landscape conservation.

10.9 Town and Country Planning legislation provides a comprehensive framework for land use planning and the control of development. The Town and Country Planning Act (TCPA) 1990 enables local authorities, under the guidance of the Secretary of State for the Environment, to set out and implement land-use policies and improve the physical environment of their areas. This Act repeals and re-enacts in consolidated form the Town and Country Planning Act 1971 and subsequent amending legislation. Broad land-use policies are laid out in the County Structure Plan and detailed elaborations of these are included in District Local Plans. The Act also permits local authorities to make Tree Preservation Orders (TPO) on individual trees, groups of trees or woodlands in the interest of amenity.

10.10 The Wildlife and Countryside Act 1981 excluded major development from AONB and gave greater prominence to protection of Sites of Special Scientific Interest (SSSI). The Act also allows for conservation and enhancement of AONB to take place by means of Management Agreements between landowners and local authorities or other bodies.

10.11 The Derelict Land Act 1982 allows for the designation of Derelict Land Clearance Areas and the payment of grants by Government towards the costs of reclaiming derelict land.

10.12 The National Heritage Act 1983 amended the Ancient Monuments and Archaeological Areas Act 1979 and contains legislation with respect to the scheduling and protection of ancient monuments in the UK. The Planning (Listed Buildings and Conservation Areas) Act 1990 re-enacts the provisions of the Town and Country Planning legislation for buildings and areas of special architectural or historic interest. This Act enables statutory instruments, made under previous Acts concerning listed buildings and conservation areas, to continue to have effect as if made under the new Act.

10.13 The Inner Urban Areas Act 1978 is used for the administration of the Government's Urban Programme scheme, which in Lancashire operates within the Districts of Preston, Blackburn and Burnley. The Housing Act 1985 enabled local authorities to designate General Improvement Areas (GIA) and Housing Action Areas (HAA) within residential areas that they identify as being in need of improvement. The Local Government and Housing Act 1989 terminates GIA and HAA from 1 April 1991 and replaces them with Housing Renewal Areas (HRA) to be designated by local authorities.

Organisations

Central Government

10.14 The Department of the Environment (DOE) is most closely concerned with landscape and townscape issues at Central Government level. It provides guidance in the form of Circulars, funds specialist agencies to carry out conservation work and directs grant aid through the Urban Programme and Derelict Land schemes. The DOE also maintains a Schedule of Monuments to which statutory protection is afforded. The Secretary of State for the Environment plays a key rôle in planning policy by approving the contents of County Structure Plans and District Local Plans. He also plays a major part in development control decisions by determining planning appeals.

10.15 The Countryside Commission are the Government's advisers on countryside matters with special responsibility for designating National Parks and AONB. They provide grants and advice for projects which conserve the natural beauty of the countryside and make it more accessible for public enjoyment. The Forestry Commission is a Government department responsible for promoting the interests of forestry in Great Britain. English Heritage is the statutory agency responsible for heritage conservation in the UK. It is the Government's official adviser on conservation legislation for the built environment and provides grants for rescue archaeology, town schemes, and repairs to historic buildings and ancient monuments. MAFF funds the Agricultural Development and Advisory Service (ADAS) and administers landscape improvement grants to farmers.

Local Government

10.16 Lancashire County Council, in addition to preparing policies in the County Structure Plan and other policy documents, undertakes practical action on townscape and landscape protection and enhancement in co-operation with the District authorities and other agencies. It helps fund Countryside Management Services in the Forest of Bowland and Arnside and Silverdale AONB and in the West Pennine Moors. The County Council also implements a programme of derelict land reclamation and carries out environmental enhancement schemes on its own and other land. It provides a Countryside Ranger Service over the County protecting the countryside and managing visitor pressure. It contributes to five town schemes in the County, working with and funding other agencies and voluntary groups involved in landscape and townscape work.

10.17 District Councils set out detailed policies for land use in Local Plans and use these policies in the control of development. Districts designate Conservation Areas and provide grant aid for the improvement of historic buildings and Conservation Areas. Three Districts are Urban Programme authorities and all Districts are involved in enhancement of townscapes and landscapes either through GIA, HAA, town schemes, or other environmental improvement schemes. As housing authorities, all Districts have a major rôle to play in the upkeep of residential estates in their control.

10.18 Several local authorities work together jointly in the Standing Conference of South Pennine Authorities (SCOSPA) to bring landscape improvements to the upland areas of the County within the SCOSPA area. Such co-operation between local authorities also takes place within the Forest of Bowland and the West Pennine Moors areas.

Other Organisations

10.19 Numerous voluntary organisations are involved in townscape and landscape work. The Council for the Protection of Rural England (CPRE) and the Civic Trust are major organisations campaigning on landscape and townscape conservation issues at a national level and through their local branches and affiliated societies in Lancashire. There are many local amenity groups and societies in Lancashire's towns which carry out improvement works, or campaign for these. Rossendale and Blackburn Groundwork Trusts, the Farming and Wildlife Advisory Group (FWAG), the Lancashire Trust for Nature Conservation (LTNC) and the British Trust for Conservation Volunteers (BTCV) are some of the larger ones involved in practical landscape work.

10.20 Private landowners, from small farmers to large estates and land owning companies like North West Water, play a major rôle in landscape protection and enhancement in Lancashire. The farming community are the stewards of most of the landscape of the County. Farming and landowners' organisations such as the National Farmers Union and the County Landowners Association also assist by advising and representing members.

10.21 Local authorities also help fund the Lancaster University Archaeological Unit (LUAU) which gathers data on archaeological sites in the County and maintains the County's Sites and Monuments Records database. LUAU advises planning authorities on planning applications that affect archaeological sites.

Landscape and Townscape in Lancashire

The Landscape Resource

10.22 It has been stated that Lancashire contains "some of the finest countryside in Britain" (Lancashire County Council, 1990a). In order to give an objective assessment of landscape quality, a systematic Scenic Quality Survey of the rural areas of the County was carried out and completed in 1980 (Lancashire County Council, 1985).

10.23 The Survey was based on a technique (devised by C.V.R. Tandy, 1971) which applies numerical values to aspects of the landscape. It involved a visual appraisal made by a landscape architect systematically recording his assessment of scenic elements comprising the landscape, at observation points related to the Ordnance Survey kilometre grid. Numerical values were assigned to these elements and an overall score produced for the landscape viewed from each observation station. The overall values range from 0, for particularly poor landscape under considerable urban influence, to 9 and above for landscapes of very exceptional quality (Figure 146).

10.24 Although now ten years old, the Survey is still the only comprehensive assessment of landscape quality carried out in the County (and one of the few completed in the UK). It has since been used to confirm the landscape quality of the AONB and to designate Areas of Special Landscape and Countryside Areas in the Structure Plan. As can be seen from Figures 146 and 147 Scenic Quality Values of 6.0–8.9 correspond closely to the extent of designated Areas of Outstanding Natural Beauty (AONB) in the Forest of Bowland and Arnside and Silverdale. Significant tracts of similar high quality lie outside AONB boundaries in the Leck Fell, Upper Ribble Valley and West Pennine Moors areas. Generally, the survey indicates lower landscape quality in the west of the County, particularly in northern Fylde, Over Wyre and the Heysham peninsula. The poorest landscapes occur around the County's principal urban areas.

Landscape Protection

Areas of Oustanding Natural Beauty

10.25 Lancashire contains two of the UK's 39 AONB in the Forest of Bowland and Arnside and Silverdale. Together, they cover 78,950 ha, or 25% of the County's total land area (Table 109). The main purpose of AONB designation is to conserve and enhance natural beauty, which includes flora, fauna, geological and landscape features.

10.26 The Forest of Bowland lies partly in Lancashire (73,550 ha) and partly in North Yorkshire with the Districts of Ribble Valley, Lancaster, Pendle, Preston and Wyre containing part of the

AONB within their boundaries (Figure 147). The Scenic Quality Survey confirmed it as the major area of scenic quality in Lancashire with more than two-thirds of the County's exceptional landscape (9.0 and above) and approximately three quarters of Lancashire's very attractive and varied landscape (6.0–8.9) being found within its boundary (Figure 146) (Lancashire County Council, 1985).

10.27 Bowland illustrates well the relationship between geology, topography, vegetation and landscape quality referred to in Chapter 2. It lies mainly above 240 metres (800 feet) and is dominated by a central upland core of deeply incised gritstone fells and tracts of peat moorland. The landscape character is one of grandeur and isolation. The core is fringed by foothills dissected by steep-sided river valleys. These have a subdued, wooded, cultivated and picturesque character in contrast to the dramatic open scenery of the fells (Lancashire County Council, 1985).

10.28 The Arnside and Silverdale AONB, occupying the north-westernmost part of Lancashire covers 5,400 ha of the County, the rest being in Cumbria (Figure 147). The area is characterised by highly distinctive small-scale, well-wooded limestone hills and rare limestone pavements – featuring the characteristic crags of Arnside Knott and Warton Crag – together with sheltered valleys and an attractive coastline. It's landscape is quite different to any other part of Lancashire.

Areas of Special Landscape

10.29 Areas of Special Landscape have been identified in the County Structure Plan (Lancashire County Council, 1987) based on the Scenic Quality Survey. These cover some 127,767 ha, or 42% of the total County area (Table 109), and comprise varied rural landscapes with some parts of exceptional scenic quality such as the upper Lune Valley, and parts of the Ribble Valley (Figures 146 and 147). These areas are said in the Structure Plan to be worthy of conservation and enhancement but are not thought to possess the uninterrupted high landscape quality of the AONB.

Countryside Areas

10.30 Countryside Areas (Figure 147) are also identified in the Structure Plan. They cover approximately 60,442 ha of the County, or 20% of the total County area (Table 109). Countryside Areas are the remaining rural landscapes outside of the AONB and Areas of Special Landscape, where landscape quality is unremarkable and may have deteriorated due to the intrusion of urban influences or the impact of modern agricultural practices. This designation embraces a wide range of landscape quality. Certain areas, particularly on the edge of towns, have been particularly degraded by motorways, new industrial estates, electricity pylons, mineral workings and other intrusions. One important point about Countryside Areas is that they form the countryside and landscape which is closest to where 75% of Lancashire's population lives. This makes them of great value for recreation and amenity but also puts them under growing pressure from human activity.

Figure 146
Scenic Quality Survey of Lancashire. 1980

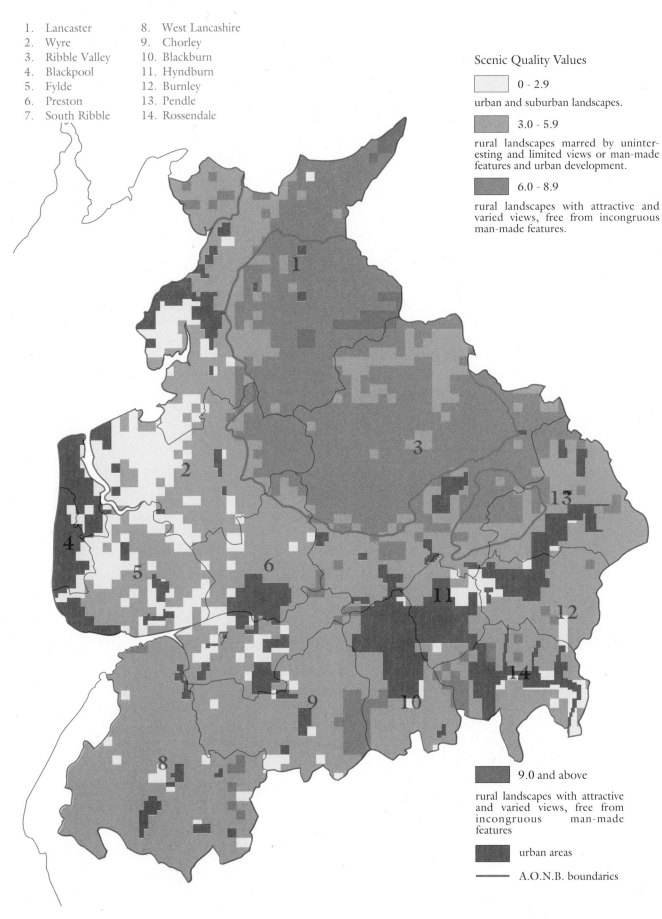

1. Lancaster
2. Wyre
3. Ribble Valley
4. Blackpool
5. Fylde
6. Preston
7. South Ribble
8. West Lancashire
9. Chorley
10. Blackburn
11. Hyndburn
12. Burnley
13. Pendle
14. Rossendale

Scenic Quality Values

0 - 2.9
urban and suburban landscapes.

3.0 - 5.9
rural landscapes marred by uninter-
esting and limited views or man-made
features and urban development.

6.0 - 8.9
rural landscapes with attractive and
varied views, free from incongruous
man-made features.

9.0 and above
rural landscapes with attractive
and varied views, free from
incongruous man-made
features

urban areas

A.O.N.B. boundaries

Source: Lancashire County Council (1985)

Figure 147
Areas of Landscape Protection in Lancashire. 1990

1. Lancaster
2. Wyre
3. Ribble Valley
4. Blackpool
5. Fylde
6. Preston
7. South Ribble
8. West Lancashire
9. Chorley
10. Blackburn
11. Hyndburn
12. Burnley
13. Pendle
14. Rossendale

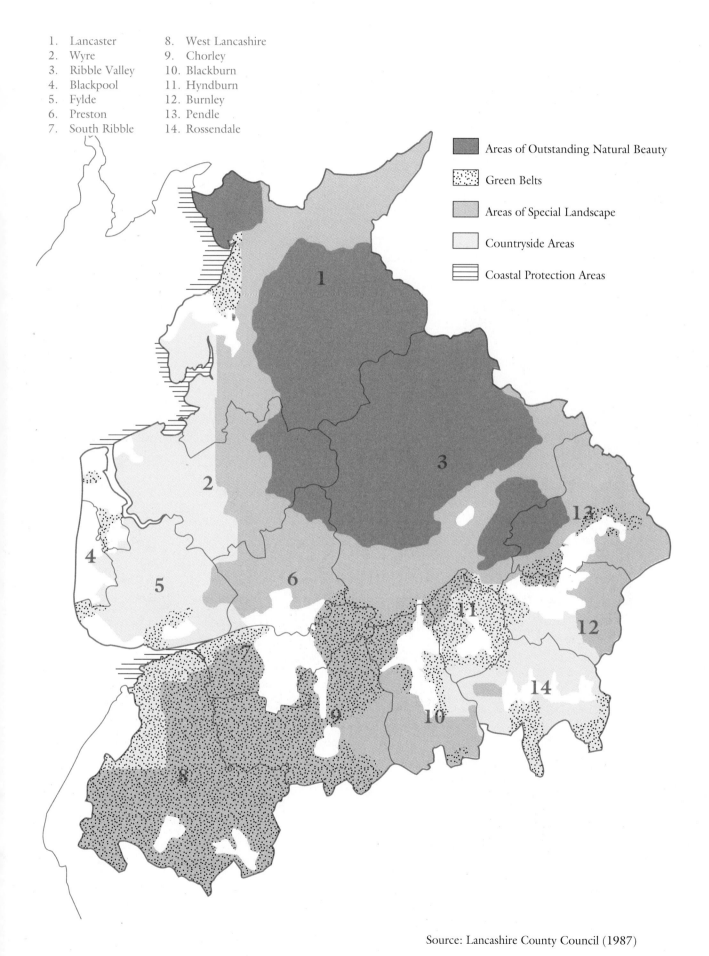

Areas of Outstanding Natural Beauty
Green Belts
Areas of Special Landscape
Countryside Areas
Coastal Protection Areas

Source: Lancashire County Council (1987)

Table 109	Areas of Landscape Protection in Lancashire. 1990	
Landscape Designation Protection	Approx. Areas (ha)	Approx. Proportion of County Area (%)
AONB	78,950	25
Areas of Special Landscape	127,767	42
Countryside Areas	60,442	20
(Green Belt) (1)	(34,145)	(11)
Urban Areas and Other Land	39,792	13
LANCASHIRE	306,951	100

Source: Lancashire County Council

Note: (1) Green Belt overlaps both Areas of Special Landscape and Countryside Areas. Its total has been excluded from the Lancashire total in the Table. The figures given for Green Belt relate to areas defined in Local Plans.

10.31 Lancashire has 108 km of coastline. Pressure for development is great, and threatens to further deteriorate an already low general scenic quality (see Figure 146). In order to protect landscape along the coast, Coastal Protection policies have been included in the Structure Plan. Some 29 km or 27% of the County's coastline is protected in this way (Figure 147).

Coastline

10.32 The Lancashire coastline forms the western edge of a plain that sweeps down from the edge of the Pennines. Comprising predominantly Permo-Triassic sandstones and marls, except for Carboniferous Limestone in the north, and masked by glacial and post-glacial deposits (Figures 3 and 4) the coastline is low and undramatic. The highest scenic quality landscapes occur in the Arnside/Silverdale AONB and at Hesketh Marsh according to Figure 146.

Green Belts

10.33 Green Belts are not a landscape protection device. They were originally conceived, and remain predominantly, as a policy to retain the character of towns and prevent their outward spread and coalescence. However, Government Circulars now include an objective for Green Belts to "safeguard the countryside from encroachment". (Elson, 1986)

10.34 Structure Plan policies seek to safeguard the Green Belts from development and restore and enhance neglected landscapes within them. The justification for Green Belts in the County is to safeguard open land areas and prevent the coalescence of settlements. However, as can be seen in Figure 147, some areas of Green Belt are also Areas of Special Landscape and some are Countryside Areas, indicating that they have some landscape quality.

10.35 Roughly 20% of the County is designated Green Belt in the Structure Plan. Just over a half of this broadly defined area has been identified more precisely in District Local Plans. Some of this Green Belt is contained in adopted Local Plans, (14,335 ha), whilst the rest is defined in draft only in plans awaiting adoption (19,810 ha). The combined total of adopted and non-adopted green belt amounts to 34,145 ha, or 11% of the area of Lancashire (Table 109).

Historic Landscape Features

10.36 Lancashire's landscape is not 'natural' but has been created by human influence for as long as people have been present in the County (see Chapter 2). The result is that in many parts of the County, there are important archaeological features forming part of the landscape. Archaeological remains contain irreplaceable information about past civilisations and are important for their own sake and for their rôle in education, leisure and tourism (Department of the Environment, 1990).

10.37 Archaeological sites in the County range from prehistoric occupation sites to nineteenth century industrial monuments; from sites preserved in lowland mosses and upland moors to urban buildings. There are over 12,500 known archaeological sites in the County, of which only 113 are Scheduled Ancient Monuments (LUAU, pers. comm). Scheduled Ancient Monuments (Figure 148 and Table 112) are nationally important and have statutory protection. The remaining 99% of Lancashire's archaeological heritage lacks formal protection, and must rely upon the goodwill of owners.

10.38 Although protection of the landscape for historical reasons is not enshrined in law, it does not

Figure 148
Scheduled Ancient Monuments in Lancashire. 1990

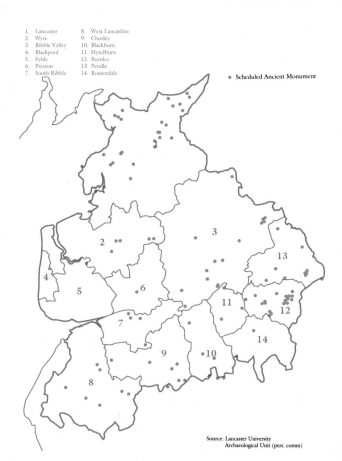

1. Lancaster
2. Wyre
3. Ribble Valley
4. Blackpool
5. Fylde
6. Preston
7. South Ribble
8. West Lancashire
9. Chorley
10. Blackburn
11. Hyndburn
12. Burnley
13. Pendle
14. Rossendale

• Scheduled Ancient Monument

Source: Lancaster University Archaeological Unit (pers. comm)

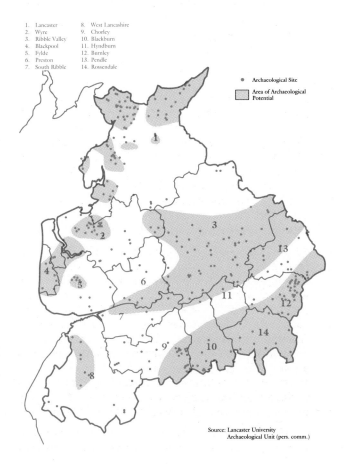

Figure 149
Pre-historic Sites in Lancashire. 1990

1. Lancaster   8. West Lancashire
2. Wyre   9. Chorley
3. Ribble Valley   10. Blackburn
4. Blackpool   11. Hyndburn
5. Fylde   12. Burnley
6. Preston   13. Pendle
7. South Ribble   14. Rossendale

● Archaeological Site
▢ Area of Archaeological Potential

Source: Lancaster University
Archaeological Unit (pers. comm.)

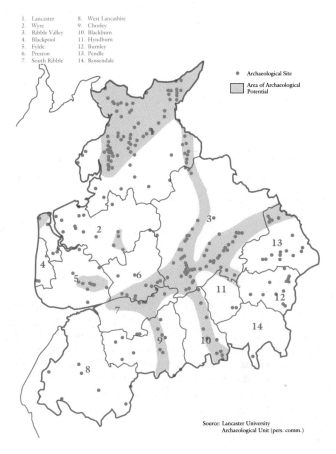

Figure 150
Roman Sites in Lancashire. 1990

1. Lancaster   8. West Lancashire
2. Wyre   9. Chorley
3. Ribble Valley   10. Blackburn
4. Blackpool   11. Hyndburn
5. Fylde   12. Burnley
6. Preston   13. Pendle
7. South Ribble   14. Rossendale

● Archaeological Site
▢ Area of Archaeological Potential

Source: Lancaster University
Archaeological Unit (pers. comm.)

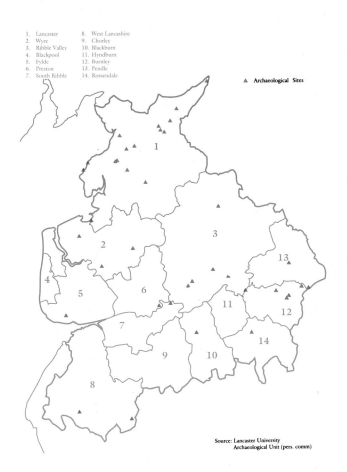

Figure 151
Early Medieval Sites in Lancashire. 1990

1. Lancaster   8. West Lancashire
2. Wyre   9. Chorley
3. Ribble Valley   10. Blackburn
4. Blackpool   11. Hyndburn
5. Fylde   12. Burnley
6. Preston   13. Pendle
7. South Ribble   14. Rossendale

▲ Archaeological Sites

Source: Lancaster University
Archaeological Unit (pers. comm)

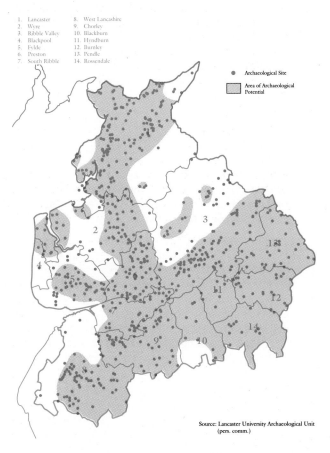

Figure 152
Medieval Sites in Lancashire. 1990

1. Lancaster   8. West Lancashire
2. Wyre   9. Chorley
3. Ribble Valley   10. Blackburn
4. Blackpool   11. Hyndburn
5. Fylde   12. Burnley
6. Preston   13. Pendle
7. South Ribble   14. Rossendale

● Archaeological Site
▢ Area of Archaeological Potential

Source: Lancaster University Archaeological Unit
(pers. comm.)

make its conservation any less important. The overlays of social and economic history embodied in our landscape are a key part of our cultural heritage. The location of all known sites from each main archaeological period, together with the areas of the County where further sites might be found, are shown in Figures 149–152.

10.39 Prehistoric archaeological sites (up to AD 43) are shown in Figure 149. They are generally better preserved on the high moorlands and under peat mosses where cultivation has not eroded them. The most substantial remains are 160 identified barrows (23 are Scheduled Ancient Monuments) and three hill forts (all Scheduled). Settlement sites have only been located in the Lune Valley so far and all six are Scheduled, as are the few small stone circles in the south of the County. There have been over four hundred finds of stone and flint tools from the whole of this period.

10.40 Roman sites (AD 43–fifth century) are shown in Figure 150. Military sites at Ribchester, Lancaster, Over Burrow and Walton-le-Dale are Scheduled Ancient Monuments (Figure 148). In addition, substantial lengths of Roman road are still traceable and in some cases the routes can be followed as earthworks.

10.41 The early Medieval period (fifth century–1066) has left few specific archaeological remains (Figure 151). Those that do exist consist of a single Viking barrow burial, various religious sites, seven crosses or remains of crosses, three gravestones associated with the churches and 17 coinhoards. Large areas of the County were first settled at this time and the same basic field patterns and much of the communications network remain today.

10.42 The Medieval period (1066–1540) is much richer in sites (Figure 152). Most of the larger towns in the County – Blackburn, Chorley, Clitheroe, Lancaster, Leyland, Ormskirk and Preston were substantial settlements in this time and many smaller towns and villages also contain Medieval remains – particularly in their churches – 134 of which are of Medieval date. About 30 villages are known to have existed which now exist only as earthworks, or in documentary reports. Medieval castles, tower houses, over 40 moated sites and some 80 substantial houses and halls along with many mills and farmsteads, enclosures and kilns are recorded in the County.

10.43 Almost all the buildings and features to be seen in the County today are post-Medieval and are further discussed under Townscape.

Landscape Change

10.44 The County Council's Landscape and Wildlife Strategy states that "as in the rest of Britain the overall landscape quality of the County is in decline" (Lancashire County Council, 1990a). However, there is no procedure in operation to monitor landscape change although the Scenic Quality Survey formed the basis for one when it was completed in 1980. Individual components of the landscape such as wildlife habitats, trees, hedgerows and woodlands are well catalogued but the overall change in landscape quality, due to changes in land use and development, is not monitored in the County.

Degradation of Landscape

10.45 The aesthetic quality of the landscape is largely a product of the use to which land is put, and how it is managed. The main land uses in the County have been described in Chapter 8. The farming and forestry industries are custodians of much of the rural landscape in Lancashire and landscape change is related in a large part to more intensive production on behalf of these industries (Lancashire County Council, 1990a). The extension of urban influences into the rural landscape is generally of detriment to landscape quality and was one of the main criteria reducing scores in the Scenic Quality Survey (Lancashire County Council, 1985).

10.46 It can be seen from Figure 146 that a large part of the County is covered by towns, urban fringe landscapes (values 0–2.9), and attractive but spoiled landscapes (values 3.0–5.9). Spoiled landscapes generally being where man-made features and urban development intrude into the view (Lancashire County Council, 1985).

10.47 Green Belts and the urban fringe are particularly subject to landscape degradation from land uses like mineral extraction, waste disposal, agricultural buildings and uses, together with electricity pylons, sewage works and so on which need a location near to towns but which are not subject to planning restrictions in the Green Belt.

Mineral Extraction

10.48 Mining has a long history in the British Isles and the landscape shows the effects of this activity over extensive areas. However, with the Industrial Revolution the whole scale of mining changed and so did its impact on the landscape. Some of the earliest coal mines in the County can be found in Rossendale, Burnley and Blackburn, where shallow coal seams and surface workings date back to the eighteenth century. Signs of these in the form of pit heaps, mine shafts and tramways can still be seen. Associated with mines came persistent environmental effects like water pollution, in addition to effects on landscape and nature conservation.

10.49 Current mineral extraction sites in the County are shown in Figure 153. There are presently 48 active sites working nine types of minerals in four different types of working. Inevitably, mineral workings have an "injurious impact on the landscape" (Lancashire County Council, 1987). However, minerals can only be worked where they occur and many are important national resources whose exploitation is necessary to prosperity and our quality of life (Department of the Environment, 1988). In some cases their environmental effects are temporary, but in others they are irreversible; adequate restoration and aftercare can reduce the impact and secure a beneficial after use.

10.50 The impact of the mineral working upon the landscape depends upon:

* where the site is located;
* whether the site is hidden or open to view;

Figure 153
Active Mineral Workings in Lancashire. 1990

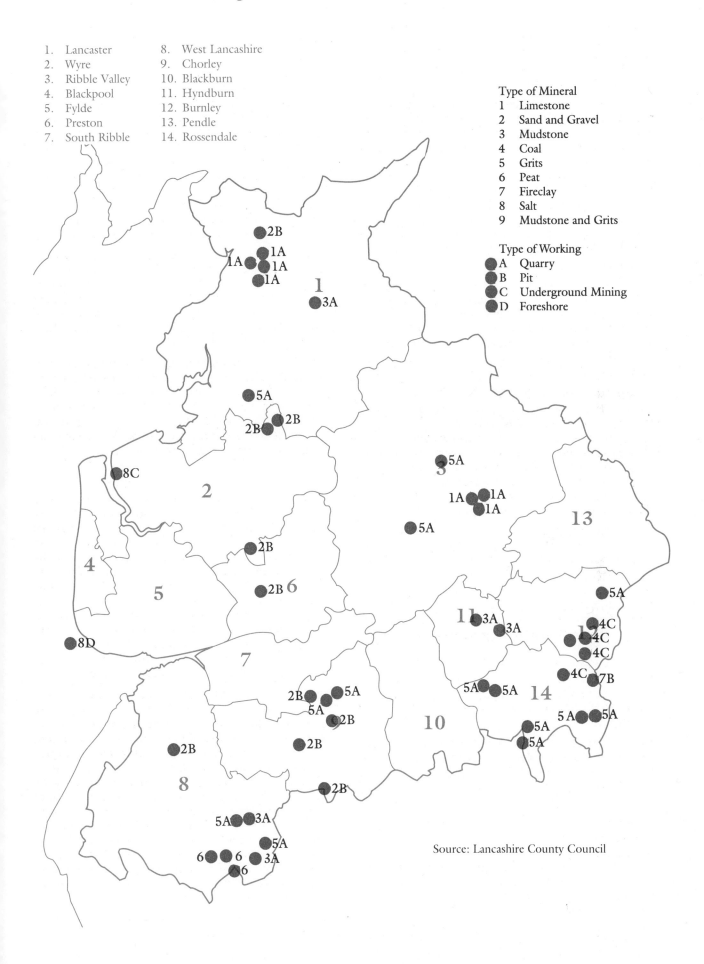

1. Lancaster
2. Wyre
3. Ribble Valley
4. Blackpool
5. Fylde
6. Preston
7. South Ribble
8. West Lancashire
9. Chorley
10. Blackburn
11. Hyndburn
12. Burnley
13. Pendle
14. Rossendale

Type of Mineral
1 Limestone
2 Sand and Gravel
3 Mudstone
4 Coal
5 Grits
6 Peat
7 Fireclay
8 Salt
9 Mudstone and Grits

Type of Working
A Quarry
B Pit
C Underground Mining
D Foreshore

Source: Lancashire County Council

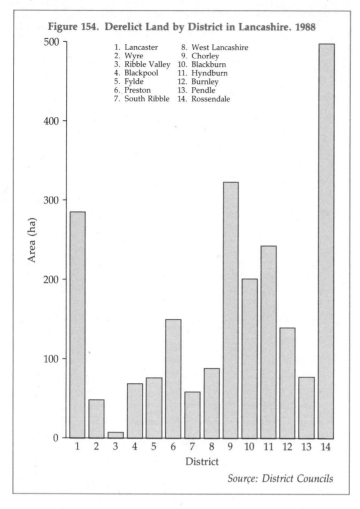

Figure 154. Derelict Land by District in Lancashire. 1988

1. Lancaster
2. Wyre
3. Ribble Valley
4. Blackpool
5. Fylde
6. Preston
7. South Ribble
8. West Lancashire
9. Chorley
10. Blackburn
11. Hyndburn
12. Burnley
13. Pendle
14. Rossendale

Area (ha)

District

Source: District Councils

* whether the working is new or old;
* the type of mineral extraction;
* screening or landscaping around the site.

10.51 It can be seen from Figure 153 that the majority of active mineral workings in Lancashire are quarries or pits. The location of mineral sites in relation to landscape protection areas can be seen by comparing Figures 153 and 147. Three mineral sites are located in the Forest of Bowland AONB. One is

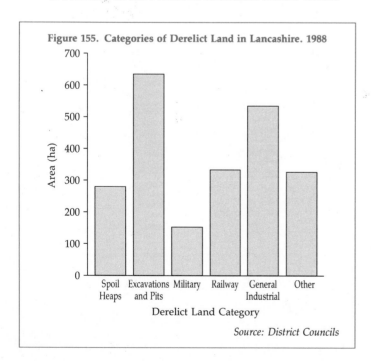

Figure 155. Categories of Derelict Land in Lancashire. 1988

Area (ha)

Spoil Heaps | Excavations and Pits | Military | Railway | General Industrial | Other

Derelict Land Category

Source: District Councils

a quarry and associated brickworks at Claughton Moor (Lancaster), whilst the other two are sandstone quarries at Waddington Fell and Leeming (Ribble Valley). Reference to Figure 146 shows the marked impact that Claughton brick works has in reducing the scenic quality of this part of the AONB.

10.52 AONB designation does not prevent minerals from being worked but Government policy requires that minerals applications in these areas "should be subject to the most rigorous examination". (Department of the Environment, 1988.) Lancashire Structure Plan policies also seek to protect the AONB together with Sites of Special Scientific Interest, Nature Reserves, Ancient Monuments and Listed Buildings from the consequences of mineral operations (Lancashire County Council, 1987).

10.53 The same degree of protection is not afforded to Areas of Special Landscape except for two areas; the Upper Lune Valley and Leck Fell and the valleys of the River Ribble and Lower Calder. Restrictions are not placed on mineral workings in the Area of Special Landscape more generally because this covers such a large part of the County (Table 109). Neither Countryside Area or Green Belt policies restrict the working of minerals for landscape protection reasons.

Derelict Land

10.54 Derelict land is defined as land so damaged by industrial or other development that it is incapable of beneficial use without treatment (DOE, pers.comm.). It is not surprising that a County which was a cradle of the Industrial Revolution, but has since suffered industrial change, should have a legacy of derelict land and redundant buildings.

10.55 A breakdown of derelict land by District (Figure 154), shows that the old industrial Districts of Lancaster, Preston, Chorley, Blackburn, Hyndburn, Burnley and Rossendale contain the majority of derelict land in the County. Much of Rossendale's results from mineral extraction, Lancaster has a legacy of old industrial sites and buildings whilst Chorley's derelict land is largely associated with the Royal Ordnance Factory.

10.56 Whilst the worst manifestations of dereliction in Lancashire have been removed, the County still has the third highest incidence of derelict land of any County in England and Wales. Some 2,260 ha remained in 1988 compared with 2,742 ha in 1982. The amount remains high despite the reclamation of approximately 800 ha during this period. The net reduction in derelict land of 492 ha, compared with 800 ha reclaimed, is a clear indication that dereliction is still being created or identified.

10.57 Derelict land occurs in both town and countryside thus having an affect on both townscape and landscape. In fact, some 60% lies in the rural areas (Lancashire County Council, 1990a) and 40% consists of excavations and tips (Figure 155) relating to former mineral workings. In many cases these occur in upland areas and are either out of sight, starting to re-vegetate naturally, or have become a longstanding and accepted part of the landscape (Lancashire County Council, 1990a). Some are now important wildlife and recreation sites having escaped reclamation for agriculture or industrial uses.

Housing Development

10.58 An analysis of DOE figures for land use change in the UK by the CPRE looked at the contributions of major land uses to changes in our countryside (Council for the Protection Rural England,1989). This revealed that between 1985 and 1987 residential development made up 66% of the land uses which had increased; way above the figures for uses like transport (13%), outdoor recreation (9%), industry and commerce (8%) and health and education (4%). Meanwhile over the same period, farmland contributed 61% of land uses which had decreased; way above the figures for vacant land (17%), woodland (16%), minerals (3%) and defence land (3%). CPRE concluded that the switch from farmland to residential use is still the biggest current change in land use in the UK.

10.59 The loss of farmland to housing development is a matter of concern in terms of landscape protection since it indicates that houses are being built in the countryside to a greater extent than on vacant land in towns and could therefore be having a detrimental impact on the landscape.

10.60 To see whether these national statistics apply to Lancashire, an analysis was carried out of the location of housing sites for which planning applications were made between 1986–89 and for which planning permission was given up to 1989 (Lancashire County Council, 1990b). Since Structure Plan policies seek to guide development to the main urban areas and away from the open countryside (Lancashire County Council, 1987) there should be comparitively little new greenfield development if the policies are being adhered to.

10.61 Planning applications are a measure of the demand for land and the pressure for development. Table 110 shows that 83% of all planning applications between 1986 and 1989 were for sites in the main urban areas, towns and villages, whilst 17% were for sites in rural areas. However, the analysis of planning permissions granted shows that Structure Plan policies are being implemented, because 93% of permissions were given in main urban areas, small towns and villages and only 7% in rural areas (Table 110).

10.62 A closer look at what is happening in each District (Table 111) shows that, with regard to the location of housing sites, the pattern of most sites being in the main urban area exists in most Districts, although there are variations. For example, 75% of Ribble Valley's housing sites are into settlements specified in the Structure Plan (Clitheroe, Longridge, Whalley/Billington) since it has no large urban areas. This is also the case with Fylde, where 50% of housing sites are concentrated into Freckleton/Warton and Kirkham/Wesham, and with Pendle where 40% are in Colne, Barnoldswick and Earby.

10.63 Development in rural settlements and the open countryside is greatest in Ribble Valley,

Table 110	Comparison of Locations of Housing Applications and Permissions in Lancashire. 1986–1989			
Location	Dwellings in Planning Applications (1986–89)		Dwellings with Planning Permission (1986–89)	
	Number	% of Total	Number	% of Total
Main Urban Areas	23,400	65	30,800	79
Towns	4,700	13	4,200	11
Towns and Villages	1,600	5	1,100	3
Rural Areas	6,300	17	2,600	7
LANCASHIRE	36,000	100	38,700	100

Source: Lancashire County Council (1990b).

Rossendale, Fylde and Wyre. However, Green Belt policies appear to be working with very few housing sites located in the Green Belt. The proportion for this rises above 1% in only two Districts, Chorley and West Lancashire, whilst the percentage for the County is only 0.6%. However, there are signs of growing pressure for development in the countryside, with some Districts inclined to favour these proposals even though they are contrary to the Structure Plan policies (Lancashire County Council, 1990b).

Landscape Enhancement

10.64 Enhancement of landscape in Lancashire is carried out within the framework of the areas of

Table 111	Location of New Housing Sites by District In Lancashire. 1986–89				
	Percentage of Dwellings in Each Area				
District	Main Urban Areas	Specified Settlements	Rural Settlements and Open Countryside	Villages in Green Belt	Green Belt
Lancaster	81.0	6.6	8.6	3.3	0.5
Wyre	68.3	14.2	12.4	—	0.1
Ribble Valley	2.1	75.0	22.8	—	0.1
Blackpool	100.0	—	—	—	—
Fylde	35.9	50.7	12.7	—	0.9
Preston	98.7	—	1.3	—	—
South Ribble	88.1	10.1	0.4	1.2	0.2
West Lancashire	64.9	28.7	—	3.8	2.6
Chorley	86.8	6.4	3.7	1.6	1.5
Blackburn	96.5	—	2.7	0.1	0.7
Hyndburn	88.6	10.9	—	—	0.5
Burnley	87.4	—	3.2	9.4	—
Pendle	52.2	42.2	5.2	0.1	0.5
Rossendale	70.2	11.7	14.6	3.1	0.4
LANCASHIRE	79.6	13.6	4.6	1.6	0.6

Source: Lancashire County Council (1990b).

protected landscape identified in Figure 147. The AONB are generally well managed and represent relatively stable agricultural landscapes requiring less attention, in the form of planting and woodland management to conserve the present landscape quality, than those of lesser quality (Lancashire County Council, 1987). The Forest of Bowland Countryside Management Service works with farmers and owners to implement small-scale landscape and ecological improvements.

10.65   The Areas of Special Landscape are also generally well managed agricultural areas but often under pressure from development and agricultural intensification. The Structure Plan targets these areas as being in need of enhancement where landscape quality is in danger of degenerating. Within Countryside Areas, where landscape quality has deteriorated, there is a policy to improve the quality of landscape by positive management of existing woodland and establishment of new woodland (Lancashire County Council, 1987). The Countryside Recreation Strategy 1988 identifies six Countryside Management Areas (CMA) which have potential for improved, co-ordinated recreational management and landscape enhancement and receive resources to achieve these aims (Figure 166). A number of practical measures operate in CMA, based on joint working between County, District and other authorities.

10.66   There is a long history of derelict land reclamation in Lancashire. The County Council was a pioneer in the field, and began work in the early 1950's. A large part of the County is identified as a Derelict Land Clearance Area where the DOE will provide up to 100% grant for local authority derelict land reclamation. The Leeds/Liverpool Canal Corridor, has been identified as amongst the worst problem areas in Europe. The Corridor has Rolling Programme status which means that its extensive dereliction is recognised by the DOE who will agree to fund schemes up to three years ahead. Lancashire County Council's bid to the DOE for grant in 1990/91 in the Rolling Programme Area totals £4.5 million whilst in other areas of the County the bid totals £1.75 million.

10.67   Because of the number of different agencies undertaking enhancement work in the County, and because there is no common system for measuring what is carried out, it is impossible to give any data on the success, or otherwise, of what is being achieved.

The Townscape Resource

10.68   Townscape is concerned with the aesthetic quality of built-up areas and consists mainly of the conservation of the architectural, historical and archaeological heritage of towns, but also includes factors like litter, impact of traffic, the presence of trees and landscaping, street furniture, planning and design and openspace. Townscape quality is not confined solely to old buildings. New buildings, including those in housing estates and suburbs, can also create good townscape. Townscape is about design, layout, scale, visual awareness, the appropriate use of materials and the juxtaposition of land uses. The factors which created good townscape in the past are just as important today, though many feel that we are not as good as our ancestors were in achieving consistently good quality.

10.69   One of the most unifying characteristics of towns in the past was a similarity of materials, which related to the surrounding landscape: local stone, bricks made from local clay, colour washing with local pigments, etc. Local materials also dictated the scale and proportion of the buildings. These unifying constraints have now disappeared (Montford, 1987).

Listed Buildings

10.70   The base measurements we have to estimate the townscape resource are the number of Listed Buildings of special architectural or historic interest in the County and the number of Conservation Areas. Table 112 summarises Lancashire's total resource of these. Listed status depends largely on age but any building more than 30 years old may be listed. Just about all buildings which pre-date 1700, and the majority of buildings of the period 1700–1840, are worthy of inclusion on a Statutory List – provided they approximate to their original condition.

10.71   However, only buildings of definite quality and character from the period 1840–1914 are listed, apart from those in a group. Selection is designed to include the major works of the principal architects. Only the most outstanding buildings of the inter-war and post-war periods are likely to be listed.

10.72   In addition, buildings and structures of any period which are particularly important illustrations of social or economic history – for example,

Table 112   Protection of the Built Heritage in Lancashire. 1990

District	Listed Buildings			Conservation Areas	Scheduled Ancient Monuments
	Grade I	Grade II*	Grade II		
Lancaster	23	57	1,033	33	18
Wyre	2	6	287	9	19
Ribble Valley	18	45	723	16	17
Blackpool	1	2	24	2	—
Fylde	2	10	127	7	—
Preston	1	1	127	10	1
South Ribble	3	14	284	4	3
West Lancashire	6	21	411	26	7
Chorley	5	23	392	9	8
Blackburn	2	15	188	7	6
Hyndburn	1	9	97	7	1
Burnley	4	14	287	8	22
Pendle	3	18	273	7	10
Rossendale	—	7	257	6	2
LANCASHIRE	71	242	4,510	151	114

Source: Lancashire County Council.

almshouses, schools, and railway stations – or which show technological innovations, virtuosity or are associated with well-known characters or events, are normally regarded as listworthy.

10.73   Listed Buildings are classified in grades to shown their relative importance, as follows:

* Grade I – buildings of exceptional interest whose preservation is in the national interest;

* Grade II* – particularly important buildings in Grade II;

* Grade II – buildings of special interest, which warrant every effort being made to preserve them.

10.74   There are 4,823 Listed Buildings of all grades in Lancashire of which 71 (about 1.5%) are Grade I. The majority of these occur in Lancaster and Ribble Valley (Figure 156 and 157). These Districts also have the largest number of Listed Buildings in the County, Blackpool has the least.

10.75   There is a rough correlation between the size of the District and number of Listed Buildings i.e. the bigger the District the greater the number of listings. However, contemporary administrative boundaries do not coincide with the boundaries of the geographical sub-regions within which settlement was taking place 150–200 years ago and it is these areas that contain the spread of buildings.

10.76   Lancaster District is outstanding in its number of Listed Buildings because of the wealth of the city between the late seventeenth century and early nineteenth century, and the wealth of the Lune Valley until the late nineteenth century. This led to the building of fine gentry houses and middle class villas which are worthy of protection today.

10.77   On the other hand, the mosslands both north and south of the Ribble were agriculturally poor until the nineteenth century and had little urban development. Consequently there are few fine old buildings or Victorian farm buildings in the Districts of Wyre, Fylde and West Lancashire which now cover this area. Before the Industrial Revolution and the drainage of the mosslands in the late eighteenth century, the wealthiest parts of the County were the areas of better agricultural land where mixed farming was possible. In these areas, churches of some quality were built in the later Middle Ages and substantial farmhouses were built from the late seventeenth century onwards. These areas now coincide roughly with the Districts of Lancaster, Preston, Ribble Valley, West Lancashire, Blackburn, Hyndburn, Burnley and the eastern parts of Wyre and Chorley.

10.78   A better indication of the location of Listed Buildings, and hence townscape quality in the County, can be gained from Figure 158 which shows the number of Listed Buildings by Parish. The richest Parishes are Lancaster, Clitheroe, Burnley, Preston, Rawtenstall, Bacup and Up-holland. Ramsgreave, North Meols and Dunnock-shaw are parishes without any Listed Buildings.

Conservation Areas

10.79   Conservation Areas protect an area as a whole – not just individual buildings. Conservation

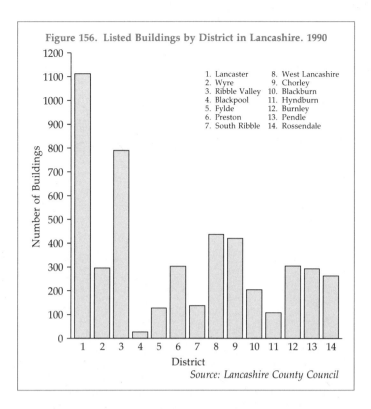

Figure 156. Listed Buildings by District in Lancashire. 1990

1. Lancaster   8. West Lancashire
2. Wyre   9. Chorley
3. Ribble Valley 10. Blackburn
4. Blackpool   11. Hyndburn
5. Fylde   12. Burnley
6. Preston   13. Pendle
7. South Ribble   14. Rossendale

Source: Lancashire County Council

means protecting an area not merely from neglect and decay, but also from the harmful effects of unsympathetic alterations or redevelopment. This is achieved through the stringent application of development control procedures in the planning process and the channelling of funds for enhancement of buildings.

10.80   The distribution of Conservation Areas in Lancashire is shown in Figure 159 and District numbers are listed in Table 112. The map illustrates the fact that Conservation Areas are not confined to towns but also occur in villages. In fact, nearly 60%

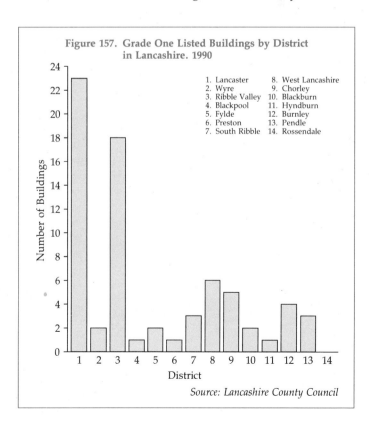

Figure 157. Grade One Listed Buildings by District in Lancashire. 1990

1. Lancaster   8. West Lancashire
2. Wyre   9. Chorley
3. Ribble Valley 10. Blackburn
4. Blackpool   11. Hyndburn
5. Fylde   12. Burnley
6. Preston   13. Pendle
7. South Ribble   14. Rossendale

Source: Lancashire County Council

Figure 158
Distribution of Listed Buildings by Parish in Lancashire. 1990

1. Lancaster
2. Wyre
3. Ribble Valley
4. Blackpool
5. Fylde
6. Preston
7. South Ribble
8. West Lancashire
9. Chorley
10. Blackburn
11. Hyndburn
12. Burnley
13. Pendle
14. Rossendale

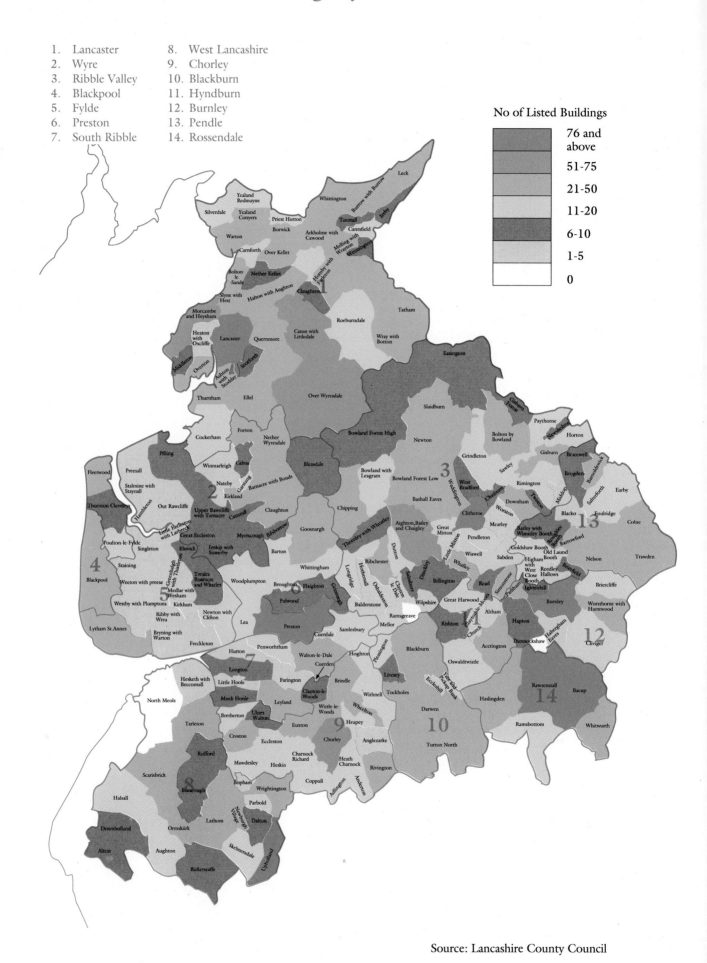

No of Listed Buildings

76 and above
51-75
21-50
11-20
6-10
1-5
0

Source: Lancashire County Council

Figure 159
Conservation Areas in Lancashire. 1990

1. Lancaster
2. Wyre
3. Ribble Valley
4. Blackpool
5. Fylde
6. Preston
7. South Ribble
8. West Lancashire
9. Chorley
10. Blackburn
11. Hyndburn
12. Burnley
13. Pendle
14. Rossendale

● Conservation Area

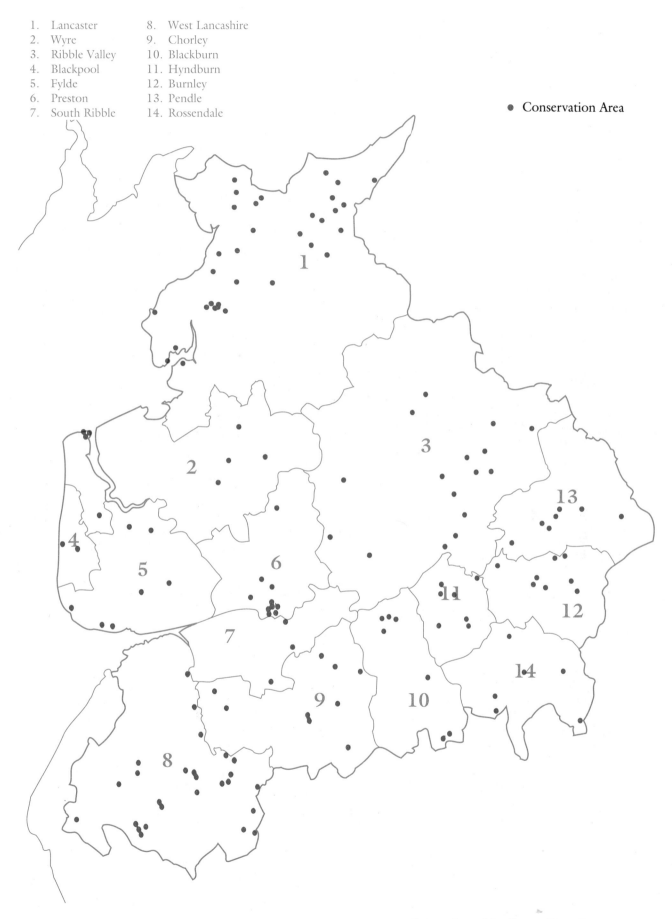

Source: Lancashire County Council

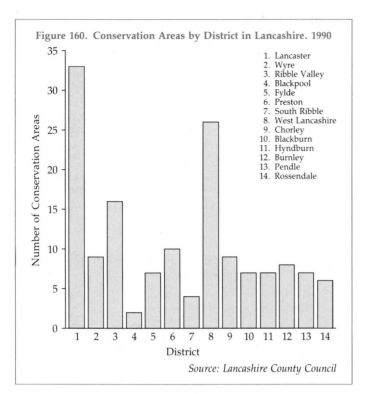

Figure 160. Conservation Areas by District in Lancashire. 1990

1. Lancaster
2. Wyre
3. Ribble Valley
4. Blackpool
5. Fylde
6. Preston
7. South Ribble
8. West Lancashire
9. Chorley
10. Blackburn
11. Hyndburn
12. Burnley
13. Pendle
14. Rossendale

Source: Lancashire County Council

are in 'traditional villages' in the County. These were the typical form of lowland settlement until the eighteenth century and beyond. In addition, most of the market towns which retain something of their traditional character, or have fine Victorian buildings in their centres, contain a designated Conservation Area.

10.81   Lancashire has a total of 151 Conservation Areas. Lancaster, Ribble Valley and West Lancashire

have the highest number (Figure 160). Most Districts have designated their Conservation Areas in villages, market towns, or in industrial villages and town parks, but West Lancashire have consciously designated a number in pleasant late nineteenth century and early twentieth century suburbs. This explains the high number here. Blackpool has the smallest number of Conservation Areas because its development took place mainly in the nineteenth century and is generally of limited architectural quality. This is also the reason for its small number of Listed Buidings.

Townscape Trees

10.82   Trees are another important element of townscape. They provide visual amenity in built-up areas and can be protected using Tree Preservation Orders (TPO). Trees in Conservation Areas are subject to the same controls as TPO. There are no comprehensive records for the Countywide coverage of TPO. However, Table 104 in Chapter 9 shows that there are 238 woodlands in the County which are protected by TPO.

Townscape Change

Degradation of Townscape

10.83   Townscape is degraded in a similar way to landscape – by inappropriate or insensitive land use, or by over-intensity of land use leading to a lack of variety in appearance. As with landscape, there is no procedure in operation for measuring change in townscape quality.

Enhancement of Townscape

10.84   The number of schemes to enhance townscape in each District in Lancashire is summarised in Table 113.

Urban Programme Areas

10.85   The Boroughs of Blackburn, Burnley and Preston are given assistance under the Government's Urban Programme scheme to carry out environmental improvements to help regenerate the local economy and tackle social needs. Resources are targeted to the areas of greatest need and each Borough identifies an 'Inner Area Partnership' area within the Borough where projects are carried out. Environmental improvement and housing schemes carried out under Urban Programme include the landscaping of vacant sites, tree planting, tackling eyesores, removing graffiti, and refurbishing buildings. All add to physical improvement of the area, and improve townscape.

10.86   Town Schemes cover specified buildings in Conservation Areas and are in operation in Lancaster, Clitheroe, Preston, Bacup and Padiham. They channel grant aid from English Heritage, the County and relevant District Councils towards the structural renovation of deteriorating buildings within the Town Scheme area.

Town Centre Improvements

10.87   In much the same way as with Town Schemes, some Districts allocate money to grant-aid

Table 113   Townscape Enhancement Areas in Lancashire. 1990

District	Urban Programme Area	Town Scheme	GIA	HAA	Proposed Housing Renewal Area
Lancaster	—	1	—	2	—
Wyre	—	—	2	1	—
Ribble Valley	—	1	3	—	—
Blackpool	—	—	11	—	—
Fylde	—	—	—	—	—
Preston	1	1	15	21	1
South Ribble	—	—	5	2	—
West Lancashire	—	—	—	1	—
Chorley	—	—	6	1	—
Blackburn	1	1	22	5	1
Hyndburn	—	—	15	10	1
Burnley	1	1	7	4	—
Pendle	—	—	4	10	1
Rossendale	—	1	9	4	1
LANCASHIRE	3	6	99	61	5

Source: DOE (pers. comm.)

improvement of the external appearance of properties within Town Centres, but not necessarily within Conservation Areas. Pendle is one District where such a scheme is in operation.

General Improvement Areas

10.88 General Improvement Areas, (GIA), were introduced in 1969 as the first move in an area-based approach to housing improvement programmes. They were designated in areas of high owner-occupation and basically sound stock. GIA are areas of physically poor housing which are made capable of 30 years extra life through grants to occupiers and environmental improvements. There are a total of 99 in Lancashire (Table 113). Preston and Hyndburn have the largest number designated whilst the Districts of Lancaster, Fylde and West Lancashire have none.

Housing Action Areas

10.89 Where poor housing conditions were accompanied by social stress, GIA were found to be inadequate and further legislation was introduced. Housing Action Areas (HAA) were introduced to facilitate rapid improvement in areas of the worst housing, effective management of accommodation, and improvement of the well-being of residents. HAA are areas of poor private housing combined with an incidence of socio-economic deprivation. Almost invariably, the houses are pre-1919, but through grant availability and environmental improvements the life of the property can be extended by 30 years. There have been 61 HAA established in Lancashire (Table 113). The District of Preston had the largest number whilst Ribble Valley, Blackpool and Fylde had none.

Housing Renewal Areas

10.90 The Housing and Local Government Act 1989 introduced the concept of Renewal Areas to replace existing GIA and HIA. This requires local authorities to produce a comprehensive ten year renewal strategy encompassing housing renovation and redevelopment, commercial and industrial development and environmental enhancement. A number of Lancashire authorities are proposing to declare Renewal Areas in 1990/91, including Blackburn, Burnley, Hyndburn Pendle and Rossendale.

Other Townscape Improvements

10.91 Many one-off environmental enhancement schemes are also undertaken in towns, ranging from town centre improvements like pedestrianisation and traffic calming schemes (see Chapter 12) to environmental art works. All can have a positive effect on townscape. No data on the existence of these schemes countywide has been collated.

References

Council for the Protection of Rural England (1989). Annual Report. CPRE.

Department of the Environment (1988). Minerals Planning Guidance. HMSO.

Department of the Environment (1990). Draft Planning Policy Guidance: Archaeology and Planning. HMSO.

Elson M.J. (1986). Green Belts. Heinemann.

Lancashire County Council (1985). Forest of Bowland. Statement of Intent. LCC.

Lancashire County Council (1987). Lancashire Structure Plan. Explanatory Memorandum. LCC.

Lancashire County Council (1988). A Countryside Recreation Strategy for Lancashire. LCC.

Lancashire County Council (1990a). Landscape and Wildlife Strategy for Lancashire. LCC.

Lancashire County Council (1990b). Monitor No. 52. LCC.

Marshall J.D. (1974). Lancashire. David & Charles.

Montford S. (1987). Townscape in: Town and County Planning Vol. 56 No. 2. TCPA.

Tandy, C.V.R. (1971). 'Landscape Evaluation'. In: Proceedings of a Symposium on Methods of Landscape Research Landscape Analysis held on 3 May 1967, London. Landscape Research Group.

Chapter Eleven
Openspace

Introduction

11.1 Openspace is vital to the well-being of Lancashire's population. From playspace for the under-fives in towns to long distance footpaths in the countryside, the provision and maintenance of openspace facilities is an essential component of the County's townscape and landscape. It is difficult to quantify their importance to social well-being, but such facilities are essential to the human need for play and relaxation for people of all ages. Access to openspace, whether urban or rural, formal or informal, adds not only to the quality of life of Lancastrians; it makes a significant contribution to wildlife and landscape creating important habitats and attractive greenspaces. The maintenance of these also helps to secure open land from development.

11.2 Leisure time and mobility have dramatically increased the numbers who visit Lancashire's countryside for recreation and this has stimulated a range of facilities to cater for them. Country Parks have been developed on the urban fringe, providing quiet activities like walking and picnicking within easy reach of the 75% of our people who live in towns. Access to large tracts of open land has increased opportunities for rambling. Picnic sites and special routes for walkers, cyclists and horseriders have also been developed throughout the County.

11.3 But in terms of everyday use, the most valuable openspace is that found in our towns and villages. Facilities like urban parks, playing fields and children's playgrounds, allotments, local footpath links and circuits, informal spaces, gardens, village greens and church yards are in constant use and make a major contribution to our way of life.

11.4 Many agencies are involved in providing and managing openspace in Lancashire; including public, private and voluntary agencies. This Chapter concentrates mainly on the facilities made available by the major providers: local authorities and landowners like North West Water (NWW). Rural and urban Commons, and nature conservation areas, are also covered. The large number of small, private facilities has not been included because comprehensive information is lacking. Data presented are generally confined to land which is freely available for public use. Exceptions are rural Commons (which do not have public rights of access, unless owned by a public agency) and educational land (which is only available through formal arrangement).

Legislation

European

11.5 There are no EC Directives, or other legal provisions, which have a significant impact on openspace in the County.

United Kingdom

11.6 The law governing openspace goes back many years. Indeed, there are Common Law, and some statutory, measures concerning access rights which date from medieval times. The most significant legislation is now contained in general Local Government law, the National Parks and Access to the Countryside Act (NPACA) 1949, and the Countryside Act (CA) 1968. Important provisions regarding the rights of way network appear in various Highway Acts (HA), whilst rights to Commons, and their protection, are covered by the Commons Registration Act (CRA) 1965.

11.7 As far as urban openspace is concerned, many facilities like parks were provided in earlier times by public subscription or benefactors. They have since passed to District Councils for upkeep and maintenance. The Physical Training and Recreation Act 1937 gave local authorities powers to provide facilities for sport and recreation, whilst S.111 of the Local Government Act 1972, enables Councils to develop a wide range of facilities related to the discharge of their leisure functions.

11.8 The law on Commons, rights of way, and rural openspace is more extensive. The Commons Act 1899 gives local authorities the power to improve Common land and impose bye-laws to govern its use. The Openspaces Act 1906 gave landowners the power to transfer openspaces and burial grounds to either a County or a District Council and allows Councils to make bye-laws relating to this land. The Law of Property Act (LPA) 1925 prohibits any building or fencing works on Common land unless it will benefit both private interests and the public. A County or District Council and any Commoner may ensure removal of any illegal works through a County Court.

11.9 Members of the public enjoy a free right of access under the LPA 1925 to all 'urban' Common land which lay within the boundary of an Urban or Borough District Council before 1974. This right was maintained after the abolition of the old Urban and Borough Districts in that year. Rural Commons, however, do not have automatic public access rights. The Acquisition of Land (Authorisation Procedure) Act 1946 provides that if a local authority purchases Common land by compulsory purchase, or wishes to use such land for other purposes, it must give adequate alternative land in its place, or go through Special Parliamentary Procedure. The CRA 1965 organised the collection of information on Common land and required that all eligible land should be registered. Where this was not done, the land ceased to be Common. A register of Commons and Village Greens must be maintained under this Act by County Councils.

11.10 The NPACA 1949 was a milestone in establishing and protecting rural recreation rights. It rationalised the extremely fragmented pre-existing law governing footpaths and bridleways and set up a comprehensive system for them. It also introduced Access Orders and Agreements to allow the public to recreate in 'Open Country'. The Act required local authorities to record all rights of way on a statutory map called the Definitive Map. Maintenance of the footpath, bridleway and byway network is the responsibility of the Highway Authority under the HA 1980. The Wildlife and Countryside Act 1981 strengthened the law relating to public rights of way, including the regulation of traffic and the appointment of wardens to advise and assist the public. Its principal measures concern the streamlining of procedures to modify the Definitive Map.

11.11 The CA 1968 established the Countyside Commission (CoCo) in place of the National Parks Commission. This Act promotes the conservation and enhancement of the natural beauty and amenity of the countryside and contains measures to develop and improve facilities for open air recreation. It also strengthened and extended the law relating to Access to Open Country. Local authorities were given the power to provide Country Parks, camping and picnic sites and to develop Common land for recreational purposes. Statutory water undertakers were also allowed to promote recreational use of their land and water, a power that was extended and strengthened by the Water Act 1973.

11.12 The Water Act (WA) 1989 makes it a duty for privatised water companies to have regard to the preservation of public access to land in their ownership. The Act also requires companies to promote recreational use of their resources and to conserve wildlife. The NRA, also established by the 1989 Act, is responsible for maintaining sea and river defences, which often have recreational value, for managing and controlling fisheries and for developing recreation on their land.

Organisations

Central Government

11.13 The DOE is the principal Government Department responsible for openspace. It coordinates policies on urban and countryside planning, sport, public access to the countryside, and Common land. Much of the detailed implementation of policy is carried out at national and regional levels by CoCo and the Sports Council (SC).

11.14 The CoCo have a duty to keep under review all matters relating to the provision and improvement of facilities for the enjoyment of the countryside, the conservation and enhancement of the natural beauty and amenity, and the need to secure public access for open air recreation. They conduct national surveys to assess use of and attitudes towards the countryside, and grant aid facilities. In 1989, for example, £428,413 in grant aid was allocated to agencies in Lancashire.

11.15 The principal aims of the SC are to encourage mass participation in sport, the development of excellence, the provision of facilities, and promoting the general understanding of the importance of sport and physical recreation. They also provide grant aid through regional offices. The North West Council for Sport and Recreation was established in 1976. In 1987–88, £502,354 was given to sports development in Lancashire, falling to £384,556 in 1988–89, and £242,508 in 1989–90. The North West Federation for Sport, Recreation and Conservation represents the governing bodies of

sport and District Sport Councils in the Region, including voluntary organisations.

Local Government

11.16 Recreational provision is a function common to both County and District authorities. The County Council provides and maintains many openspaces and recreational facilities.It is the prime mover in a number of joint countryside management initiatives and is responsible for negotiating and looking after Access Agreements and Orders made under the NPACA 1949. Bye-laws and other management arrangements have been introduced, to secure effective control and enjoyment of some of these openspaces. The County Council also maintains the Commons Register under the CRA 1965. As Local Education Authority, it is responsible for managing school land, including playing fields, and for arranging for use of this land via a letting scheme. As Highways Authority, the County Council maintains the rights of way network and funds various improvements and promotions from its recreation budget. Publications are produced to give information about facilities in the County.

11.17 District Councils also provide and manage rural facilities. However, their major contribution lies within towns and settlements. They manage the majority of Lancashire's urban parks, playing fields and playgrounds, and other public spaces like allotments and picnic sites. Bye-laws are introduced to control the use of these spaces and to avoid interference with public enjoyment.

11.18 Parish Councils and Meetings have long been responsible for providing and looking after local spaces. Though this responsibility has now largely been taken over by District Councils, some Parishes still maintain small parcels of land, sometimes on behalf of the District Council.

Other Organisations

11.19 A number of major landowners in the County play an important rôle in openspace provision. Foremost is NWW, whose extensive upland gathering grounds and reservoirs are Lancashire's paramount countryside recreational areas. Other organisations who contribute in a direct way are the National Trust, the NRA and British Waterways Board (BWB).

11.20 Nature conservation and wildlife groups also manage wildlife areas, to which they allow public access. Such access is carefully controlled, because the principal purpose of these sites is wildlife conservation. Lancashire has two Groundwork Trusts which are locally based organisations, concerned with the practical maintenance of rights of way, greenspace and recreation on the urban fringe and within towns.

11.21 There are many national and local recreation groups who actively campaign for the protection and improvement of openspace in Lancashire. These are too numerous to mention in detail, but include The Ramblers Association, cycling and horseriding groups, anglers, boating enthusiasts and motor-cycle groups.

Openspace in Lancashire

Urban Openspace

11.22 The fourteen District Councils are responsible for the majority of openspace and recreation facilities in our towns. This includes parks, playing fields, recreation grounds, allotments, childrens' playgrounds, golf courses and other public openspace. Table 114 shows the amount of urban openspace entirely under District Council control.

Use

11.23 In 1984, the Countryside Commission conducted a National Countryside Recreation Survey which included data on visits to urban parks and Openspace. Results show that 20% of people visit urban parks regularly, which means that up to 278,160 Lancastrians use town parks in this way. Recent surveys (Office of Population Censuses and Surveys, 1985 and 1988) show that 31% of the population participated in outdoor sport in 1983, and that this rose to 32% in 1986. When applied to Lancashire, outdoor sports participants were 427,056 in 1983 and 441,824 in 1986. The Sports Council (1988) estimate that by 1988 this use had risen by another 1%, representing 456,000 people in the County.

Standards

11.24 The 1925 National Playing Fields Association (NPFA) standard for play space has been adopted for this Report. This recommends the provision of 2.4 ha of playing space per thousand population, and covers the following facilities:

*   pitches, courts and greens for public, private, industrial and commercial use by all age groups;
*   childrens' playgrounds;
*   areas for casual play;
*   athletics facilities;
*   pitch and putt golf courses.

It excludes:

*   educational openspace;
*   grounds of Her Majesty's Services;
*   verges, woodlands, Commons and ornamental gardens;
*   full-length 9 and 18 hole golf courses;
*   large areas of water;
*   indoor facilities.

11.25 In the First Review of the Lancashire County Development Plan (1962), the 2.4 ha was apportioned to include 1.6 ha 'playing fields', 0.6 ha 'amenity openspace' and 0.2 ha for 'playgrounds'. Many Districts have also adopted these standards.

Parks

11.26 Lancashire's town parks originated in Victorian and Edwardian times, as formal, maintained areas of greenspace for expanding industrial population. Their regimented layout restricted use to strolling, relaxing, boating and childrens' play activities. Parkland management has since diversified, with many now offering football and rugby pitches, bowling greens, tennis courts and adventure playgrounds. Some are relaxing maintenance

Table 114 Total Urban Openspace Managed by District Councils in Lancashire. 1990

District	Parks (ha)	Playing Fields (ha)	Playgrounds (ha)	Other Public Openspace (ha)	Total (ha)
Lancaster	92	35	10	42	179
Wyre	40	50	7	296	393
Ribble Valley	26	30	11	20	87
Blackpool	145	21	11	86	263
Fylde	47	17	4	42	110
Preston	398	101	36	52	587
South Ribble	140	72	13	35	260
West Lancashire	206	73	6	89	374
Chorley	105	92	5	48	250
Blackburn	190	71	11	149	421
Hyndburn	106	55	5	30	196
Burnley	136	69	20	62	287
Pendle	46	41	3	100	190
Rossendale	39	45	9	32	125
LANCASHIRE	1,716	772	151	1,083	3,722

Source: District Councils.

Note: Data for Fylde are incomplete.

régimes to create more 'natural' parkscape, of greater value for wildlife. All parks provide valuable openspace for both formal and informal recreation. Urban parks are especially important, as they form 'green lungs' within otherwise built-up environments. They are also accessible and convenient for the majority of the population.

11.27 Lancashire has a total of 1,716 ha of urban parkland divided unequally between the fourteen Districts. Figure 161 shows that whilst Preston contains 24% of the County's town parks, Ribble Valley only has 1%. This further highlights the historic nature of provision, in that most park creation accompanied the early days of municipal planning in towns like Preston, Blackburn, Burnley and Blackpool. These Districts, together with West Lancashire, now have the highest percentages of town parks. However, the West Lancashire figure is inflated by the more recent addition of Tawd Valley Park, a large urban-fringe park on the edge of Skelmersdale.

11.28 Applying the County Development Plan 1962 recommendation of 0.6 ha per thousand population for amenity openspace, and assuming that parkland equates to amenity openspace, produces Table 115. This shows that all Districts except Wyre, Ribble Valley and Pendle achieve, and in most cases surpass, the recommended standard. By way of compensation, Wyre has a large extent of other Public Openspace (see Table 114), whilst Ribble Valley and Pendle have extensive and accessible countryside areas. There is an overall

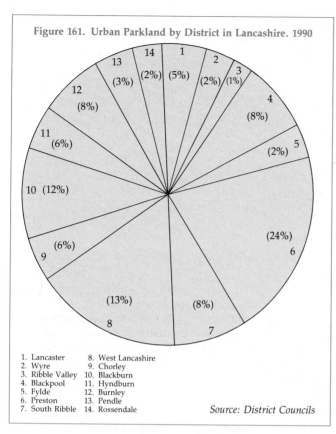

Figure 161. Urban Parkland by District in Lancashire. 1990

1. Lancaster (5%)
2. Wyre (2%)
3. Ribble Valley (1%)
4. Blackpool (8%)
5. Fylde (2%)
6. Preston (24%)
7. South Ribble (8%)
8. West Lancashire (13%)
9. Chorley (6%)
10. Blackburn (12%)
11. Hyndburn (6%)
12. Burnley (8%)
13. Pendle (3%)
14. Rossendale (2%)

Source: District Councils

provision of 1.2 ha of urban parkland per thousand population in Lancashire, which is double the recommended standard.

Playgrounds

11.29 These are the smallest, most localised form of openspace with unique requirements due to the age of children using them. Playgrounds vary greatly in size and the range of equipment provided. Different ages require different facilities (Department of the Environment, 1973). Under-fives need small areas close to home, whilst older children need larger and more varied spaces which can be further from home.

11.30 Some new housing developments include informal playspaces and playgrounds. Unfortunately, in many cases, these are inadequate and often unsafe, consisting of a small concrete or tarmacadamed area with one or two items of architectural equipment. Maintenance passes to the District Council when the housing development is completed. These sites then have to be made safe to meet the needs of the community. Sadly, vandalism and litter problems, including dog fouling, are frequent occurrences at playground facilities.

11.31 Table 116 shows the amount and distribution of playgrounds throughout the County. Preston has the highest provision with 36 ha or 24%, of the County total (Figure 162), whilst Pendle has 3 ha or 2%. The NPFA recommends 0.2 ha per thousand population. Table 116 shows that only Ribble Valley, Preston and Burnley achieve this. All other Districts fall far below. This drags the County-wide provision down to 0.1 ha per thousand population, exactly half the recommended standard.

Other Public Openspace

11.32 Districts provide many other types of openspace. This is not covered by the NPFA standards and so cannot be set against it. It includes areas like allotments, picnic sites, 'nature areas', beaches and promenades. Some incidental

Table 115	Urban Parks Provision in Lancashire. 1990	
District	Total Parkland (ha)	Parkland per Thousand Population (ha)
Lancaster	92	0.7
Wyre	40	0.4
Ribble Valley	26	0.5
Blackpool	145	1.0
Fylde	47	0.6
Preston	398	3.1
South Ribble	140	1.4
West Lancashire	206	2.0
Chorley	105	1.0
Blackburn	190	1.4
Hyndburn	106	1.3
Burnley	136	1.5
Pendle	46	0.5
Rossendale	39	0.6
LANCASHIRE	1,716	1.2

Source: District Councils.

Note: Data for Fylde are incomplete.

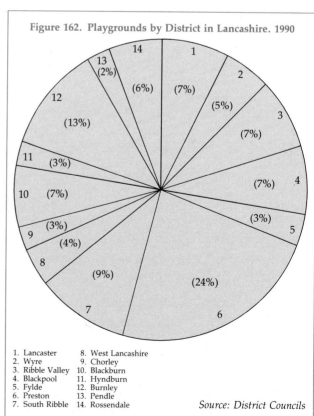

Figure 162. Playgrounds by District in Lancashire. 1990

1. Lancaster (7%)
2. Wyre (5%)
3. Ribble Valley (7%)
4. Blackpool (7%)
5. Fylde (3%)
6. Preston (24%)
7. South Ribble (9%)
8. West Lancashire (4%)
9. Chorley (3%)
10. Blackburn (7%)
11. Hyndburn (3%)
12. Burnley (13%)
13. Pendle (2%)
14. Rossendale (6%)

Source: District Councils

Table 116	Playground Provision in Lancashire. 1990	
District	Playgrounds (ha)	Playgrounds per Thousand Population (ha)
Lancaster	10	0.08
Wyre	7	0.07
Ribble Valley	11	0.2
Blackpool	11	0.08
Fylde	4	0.05
Preston	36	0.3
South Ribble	13	0.1
West Lancashire	6	0.06
Chorley	5	0.05
Blackburn	11	0.08
Hyndburn	5	0.06
Burnley	20	0.2
Pendle	3	0.03
Rossendale	9	0.1
LANCASHIRE	151	0.1

Source: District Councils.

Note: Data for Fylde are incomplete.

openspace, such as grassed areas within housing development and landscaped urban areas, are also included. Roadside verges are excluded, as they are not generally used as recreational purposes. Figure 163 shows the distribution of this type of openspace

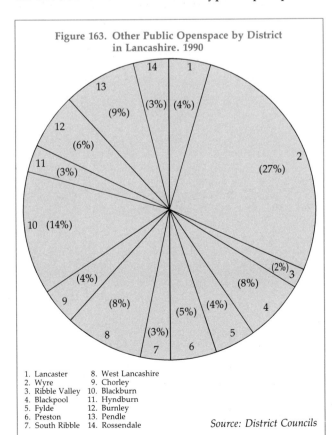

Figure 163. Other Public Openspace by District in Lancashire. 1990

1. Lancaster
2. Wyre
3. Ribble Valley
4. Blackpool
5. Fylde
6. Preston
7. South Ribble
8. West Lancashire
9. Chorley
10. Blackburn
11. Hyndburn
12. Burnley
13. Pendle
14. Rossendale

Source: District Councils

throughout the County. Wyre contains 27% of the entire County stock, whilst Blackburn has 14% and Pendle 9%. Ribble Valley has the least area available, with only 2% of the total.

11.33 Table 117 shows the District provision of other public openspace per thousand population. On this basis, Wyre provides 2.8 ha per thousand, Pendle 1.2 ha and Blackburn 1.1 ha and have the largest amounts. It is stressed that this provision cannot be assessed against the NPFA standard. However, it constitutes a very important recreational resource, especially in Wyre and Pendle, where other openspace is relatively low.

Playing Fields

11.34 Playing fields provide formal space for organised sport. They include football, hockey and rugby pitches, tennis courts, bowling greens, cricket wickets, athletic tracks and netball courts. Many such facilities are provided and maintained by District Councils, principally in urban areas. Preston, Chorley, South Ribble, West Lancashire, Blackburn and Burnley each have 10% (or more) of the County's playing fields (Figure 164). Districts like Lancaster, Blackpool and Wyre with high populations have correspondingly low provision.

11.35 Playing fields are important to large sectors of the population including young children and adults. Use is not confined to the formal sports for which they are designed, as they serve as unofficial play areas when not required for formal sport. The 1962 sub-division of the NPFA standard reflects this, by recommending 1.6 ha (out of the total of

Table 117	Other Public Openspace Provision in Lancashire. 1990	
District	Other Openspace (ha)	Other Openspace per Thousand Population (ha)
Lancaster	42	0.3
Wyre	296	2.8
Ribble Valley	20	0.4
Blackpool	86	0.6
Fylde	42	0.6
Preston	52	0.4
South Ribble	35	0.3
West Lancashire	89	0.8
Chorley	48	0.5
Blackburn	149	1.1
Hyndburn	30	0.4
Burnley	62	0.7
Pendle	100	1.2
Rossendale	32	0.5
LANCASHIRE	1,083	0.8

Source: District Councils.

Note: Data for Fylde are incomplete.

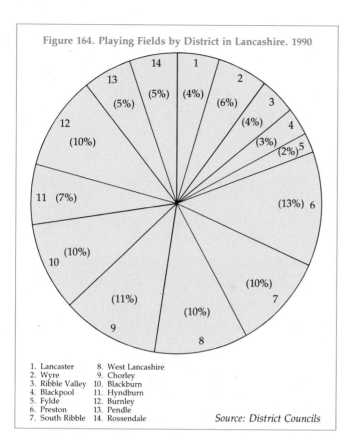

Figure 164. Playing Fields by District in Lancashire. 1990

1. Lancaster
2. Wyre
3. Ribble Valley
4. Blackpool
5. Fylde
6. Preston
7. South Ribble
8. West Lancashire
9. Chorley
10. Blackburn
11. Hyndburn
12. Burnley
13. Pendle
14. Rossendale

Source: District Councils

Table 119 Education Openscape in Lancashire 1990

District	Total Area (ha)
Lancaster	110
Wyre	101
Ribble Valley	47
Blackpool	107
Fylde	37
Preston	120
South Ribble	121
West Lancashire	133
Chorley	87
Blackburn	130
Hyndburn	66
Burnley	70
Pendle	64
Rossendale	49
LANCASHIRE	1,242

Source: Lancashire County Council.

2.4 ha) per thousand population. Table 118 shows the levels of provision existing in District areas, confirming that no District achieves the standards. Chorley comes closest with 1 ha per thousand population. For the County as a whole, only 0.6 ha

per thousand are available, which falls well below the standard. However, the figures do not include private sports facilities, as comprehensive data are not available. Use of these, of course, is nearly always restricted to members of clubs or associations owning private facilities.

11.36 The North West Council for Sport and Recreation published a Regional Recreation Strategy in 1980 identifying many deficiencies in playing field provision. This found that private facilities were being lost to other uses and public pitches were subject to intensive use and subsequent damage.

Educational Openspace

11.37 A total of 1,242 ha of playing fields are maintained around County Council Primary and Secondary Schools. Table 119 shows how these divide by District. They provide green space within many urbanised parts of the County. However, there is no automatic public right of access. The recreational potential of this land has to be reserved primarily for the benefit of school children. Over-use can be detrimental to its educational purpose and is, therefore, avoided.

11.38 In many cases, schools make their playing fields available to private clubs and the local community through leasing schemes. Any lease must be approved by the County Education Department and the individual school before it can go ahead. A survey is being carried out at present by the County Council and the SC to establish how many secondary schools and communities are taking advantage of this scheme. Preliminary results show that out of 116 secondary schools surveyed, 40 offer outdoor

Table 118 Playing Fields Provision in Lancashire. 1990

District	Playing Fields (ha)	Playing Fields per Thousand Population (ha)
Lancaster	35	0.3
Wyre	50	0.5
Ribble Valley	30	0.6
Blackpool	21	0.1
Fylde	17	0.2
Preston	101	0.8
South Ribble	72	0.7
West Lancashire	73	0.7
Chorley	92	1.0
Blackburn	71	0.5
Hyndburn	55	0.7
Burnley	69	0.7
Pendle	41	0.5
Rossendale	45	0.7
LANCASHIRE	772	0.6

Source: District Councils.

Note: Data for Fylde are incomplete.

Table 120	Number of Secondary Schools Making Sports Facilities Available in Lancashire. 1990		
District	Outdoor Facilities	Indoor Facilities	No Facilities
Lancaster	2	1	2
Wyre	2	—	3
Ribble Valley	3	1	1
Blackpool	4	1	—
Fylde	—	—	2
Preston	5	4	1
South Ribble	4	2	1
West Lancashire	5	—	1
Chorley	4	—	1
Blackburn	2	1	4
Hyndburn	1	1	—
Burnley	2	—	3
Pendle	2	—	4
Rossendale	4	—	1
LANCASHIRE	40	11	24

Source: Lancashire County Council.

Note: These results are based on 75 replies from 116 schools contacted (June 1990).

Table 121	Type of Sports Facilities Made Available by Secondary Schools for Public Use in Lancashire. 1990
Facility Type	Number Available
Football	36
Tennis	7
Rugby	18
Cricket	21
Artificial	4
Netball	5
Hockey	26
TOTAL	117

Source: Lancashire County Council.

Note: Most schools offer more than one sports facility.

facilities to non-school users. This represents 34% of the schools investigated, and compares favourably with 1980 when only 10% of Lancashire schools made their playing fields available (North West Council for Sport and Recreation, 1980). Table 120 shows the present position by District and includes the number of schools offering indoor facilities. Table 121 shows the type of facility offered.

11.39 Following the Education Reform Act 1988, schools have become responsible for their own budgeting. Dual use of school sports facilities can continue under this Act in a variety of ways. However, it is too early to say whether the new system will enhance, or reduce, dual use provision.

Total Urban Openspace

11.40 Table 122 combines all the elements (except educational space) described thus far, to give a total picture of the amount of urban openspace currently available in Lancashire. To give this picture, and allow comparison with the full NPFA standard of 2.4 ha per thousand population, separate figures are presented which include and exclude data for other public openspace and parks. Only the latter figures can be compared directly against the NPFA standard.

11.41 Lancashire has a total of 3,722 ha of all forms of urban Openspace. In District terms, Preston has by far the highest, followed by Blackburn, Wyre and West Lancashire. With only 87 ha in all, Ribble Valley has the lowest amount. In terms of meeting the NPFA standard, Lancashire Districts range

between 0.2 ha (Blackpool) and 1.1 ha (Preston) of 'eligible' openspace per thousand population (i.e. excluding other public openspace and parks). Table 122 shows, in fact, that none of the Districts attain the standard. If allowance is made for other public openspace and parks, the position improves markedly. Eight Districts (Wyre, Preston, South Ribble, West Lancashire, Chorley, Blackburn, Hyndburn and Burnley) meet the target, but

Table 122	Total Urban Openspace Provision in Lancashire. 1990			
District	Openspace (ha)		Urban Openspace per Thousand Population (ha)	
	All Openspace	Excluding Other Public Openspace and Parks	All Openspace	Excluding Other Public Openspace and Parks
Lancaster	179	45	1.4	0.3
Wyre	393	57	3.8	0.5
Ribble Valley	87	41	1.7	0.8
Blackpool	263	32	1.8	0.2
Fylde	110	21	1.5	0.3
Preston	587	137	4.6	1.1
South Ribble	260	85	2.5	0.8
West Lancashire	374	79	3.6	0.8
Chorley	250	97	2.6	1.0
Blackburn	421	82	3.1	0.6
Hyndburn	196	60	2.4	0.8
Burnley	287	89	3.1	0.9
Pendle	190	44	2.2	0.5
Rossendale	125	54	1.9	0.8
LANCASHIRE	3,722	923	2.7	0.7

Source: District Councils.

Note: Fylde data are incomplete.

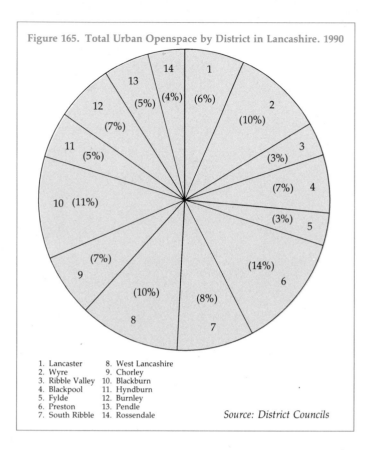

Figure 165. Total Urban Openspace by District in Lancashire. 1990

14 (4%)
13 (5%)
1 (6%)
2 (10%)
3 (3%)
4 (7%)
5 (3%)
6 (14%)
7 (8%)
8 (10%)
9 (7%)
10 (11%)
11 (5%)
12 (7%)

1. Lancaster
2. Wyre
3. Ribble Valley
4. Blackpool
5. Fylde
6. Preston
7. South Ribble
8. West Lancashire
9. Chorley
10. Blackburn
11. Hyndburn
12. Burnley
13. Pendle
14. Rossendale

Source: District Councils

Lancaster, Ribble Valley, Blackpool, Fylde, Pendle and Rossendale remain just below.

11.42 Figure 165 shows the distribution of total urban openspace, including Education land, between Districts. Preston contains the most, with 14% of the total area, whilst Blackburn (11%), Wyre (10%) and West Lancashire (10%) all contain significant amounts. Ribble Valley and Fylde have the lowest provision with only 3% of the total but have substantial rural areas within their boundaries by way of compensation.

Rural Openspace

Use

11.43 The 1984 National Countryside Recreation Survey (Countryside Commission, 1984) established how many people use the countryside for recreation and leisure activities. Half the population visit the countryside at least once in winter, rising to 60% in spring and 70% in summer. The number making frequent visits (five or more) varies from 20% of the population in winter, to 28% in spring and 38% in summer. 84% visit the countryside at least once a year, with 17% of the population making 68% of the trips. These figures suggest that about a quarter of a million people make frequent leisure use of Lancashire's countryside. The 1984 survey also showed that the most popular activities are drives, outings, picnics, rambling, visiting friends and informal sports.

11.44 Thus, countryside recreation is a major cultural and social phenomenon throughout the year. Whilst urban openspace and the seaside are also important destinations, the local countryside is even more popular. Countryside recreation shows no signs of declining and continues to attract a broad span of the population. The nature of demand is also changing, however, with greater interest in active outdoor sports. These have more potential for causing conflict between different users, between visitors and landowners and between visitors and the resource that they come to enjoy. Thus, the need for effective management has also increased so that the human and environmental consequences of demand in popular rural areas can be properly controlled.

Countryside Management

11.45 Formal management of recreation within defined areas – or Countryside Management Areas (CMA) – has been developed to a greater degree in Lancashire than in any other County. Table 123 shows that over 192,000 ha or 63%, of the County, is now subject to CMA schemes, based on joint-working between local authorities, government agencies, voluntary groups and private landowners.

11.46 Six CMA have been established so far:

* the West Pennine Moors;
* the Forest of Bowland;
* Arnside-Silverdale;
* Lower Ribble;
* Leeds-Liverpool Canal Corridor;
* the South Pennines.

In each CMA, the County Council collaborates with Districts, neighbouring Authorities, CoCo and a wide range of others to jointly plan, provide and manage facilities. An overall framework is developed which details proposals for facilities like Country Parks, picnic sites, information centres, trails and circular walks, wardening wildlife conservation and landscape improvements. Figure 166 shows the distribution of CMA and shows that six Districts, (South Ribble, Chorley, Blackburn, Hyndburn, Burnley and Rossendale) are totally covered, as is most of Ribble Valley and Pendle. Only Blackpool and Fylde have no CMA within their boundaries.

11.47 Two smaller countryside management schemes exist in the County. The Worsthorne Moor Scheme covers 1,265 ha of moorland owned by NWW in Burnley District. The Pendle Management Scheme also involves a number of NWW sites in Pendle District.

11.48 The Groundwork movement also implements countryside management projects. Two Groundwork Trusts, (GWT), have been established in Lancashire. Rossendale GWT has existed since 1983, and covers the whole of that District (13,811 ha). A new GWT was formed in Blackburn last year and this also operates throughout the whole Borough, (13,723 ha). A further Trust is being set up for the Leeds-Liverpool Canal Corridor CMA mentioned earlier. Adding its area to those of the existing Trusts, could mean that 72,339 ha (just under a quarter of Lancashire) could be subject to Groundwork status. Figure 167 shows the location of these areas.

Figure 166.
Countryside Management Areas in Lancashire. 1990

1. Lancaster
2. Wyre
3. Ribble Valley
4. Blackpool
5. Fylde
6. Preston
7. South Ribble

8. West Lancashire
9. Chorley
10. Blackburn
11. Hyndburn
12. Burnley
13. Pendle
14. Rossendale

1   South Pennines

2   Leeds - Liverpool Canal Corridor

3   Forest of Bowland

4   West Pennine Moors

5   Lower Ribble

6   Arnside - Silverdale

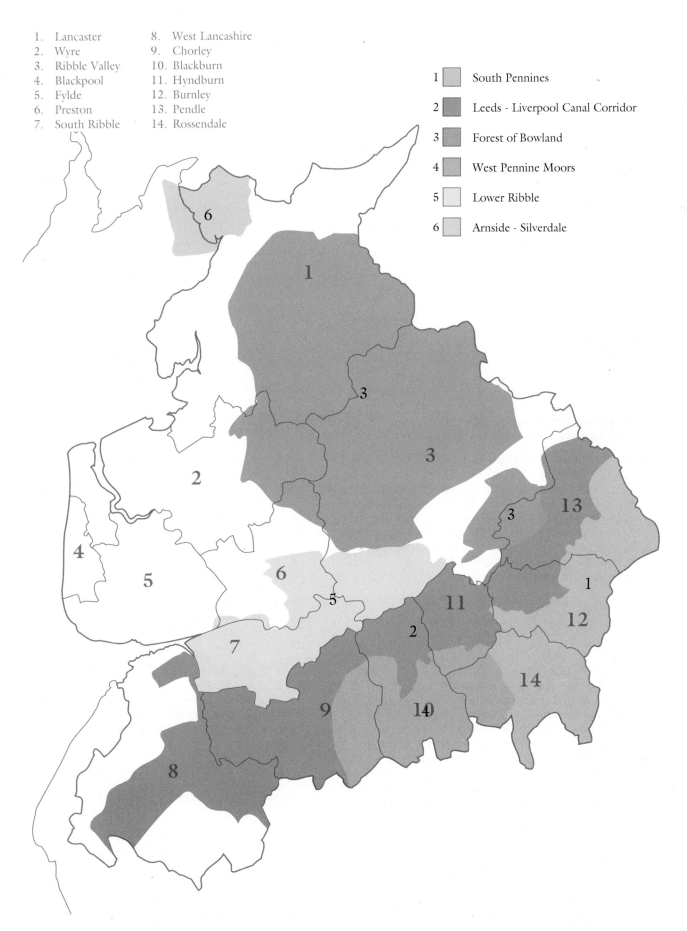

Source: Lancashire County Council

District	West Pennine Moors	Forest of Bowland	South Pennines	Lower Ribble	Leeds–Liverpool Canal	Arnside–Silverdale	Total (ha)
Lancaster	—	25,870	—	—	—	5,400	31,270
Wyre	—	5,130	—	—	—	—	5,130
Ribble Valley	—	38,920	—	8,642	—	—	47,562
Blackpool	—	—	—	—	—	—	—
Fylde	—	—	—	—	—	—	—
Preston	—	1,390	—	3,813	—	—	5,203
South Ribble	—	—	—	11,307	—	—	11,307
West Lancashire	—	—	—	—	13,836	—	13,836
Chorley	5,620	—	—	—	14,672	—	20,292
Blackburn	8,690	—	—	—	—	—	8,690
Hyndburn	1,512	—	—	—	5,790	—	7,302
Burnley	—	—	7,940	—	3,137	—	11,077
Pendle	—	2,280	6,820	—	7,430	—	16,530
Rossendale	2,830	—	10,981	—	—	—	13,811
LANCASHIRE	18,652	73,590	25,741	23,762	44,865	5,400	192,010

Table 123 Countryside Management Areas in Lancashire. 1990

Source: Lancashire County Council.

Note: All areas are in ha.

Figure 167

Existing and Proposed Groundwork Trust Areas in Lancashire.1990

1. Lancaster
2. Wyre
3. Ribble Valley
4. Blackpool
5. Fylde
6. Preston
7. South Ribble
8. West Lancashire
9. Chorley
10. Blackburn
11. Hyndburn
12. Burnley
13. Pendle
14. Rossendale

⊠ Existing Groundwork Trust
▓ Proposed Groundwork Trust

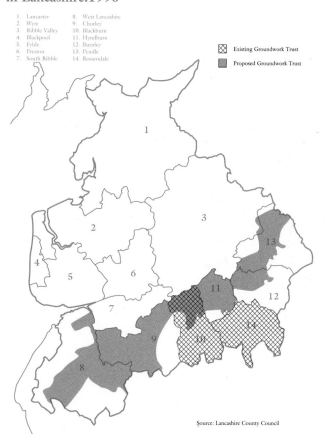

Source: Lancashire County Council

Country Parks and Picnic Sites

11.49 Country Parks were created by the CA 1968. They are large, accessible facilities, in attractive rural surroundings, given over generally to relaxation. They are specifically intended to meet the great demand from townspeople for access to the countryside. Seven have been established in Lancashire (Figure 168), covering an area of 962 ha (see Table 124). The sites concerned are:

* Rivington, (161 ha), on the south western edge of the West Pennine Moors CMA, in Chorley District;

* Beacon Fell, (110 ha), at the south western corner of the Forest of Bowland CMA, in Preston District;

* Jumbles, (26 ha), on the boundary between Blackburn District and Bolton, in the West Pennine Moors CMA;

* Wycoller, (143 ha), in the South Pennines CMA, Pendle District;

* Beacon Park, (149 ha), to the north east of Skelmersdale, in West Lancashire District;

* Witton, (90 ha), in Blackburn District;

* Cuerden Valley, (283 ha), in Chorley District, part of the Leeds-Liverpool CMA.

11.50 According to the CoCo (Countryside Commission, 1984), only 4% of the population visit Country Parks when they go into the countryside. However, Beacon Fell receives over 350,000 visitors every year (Lancashire County Council, 1988).

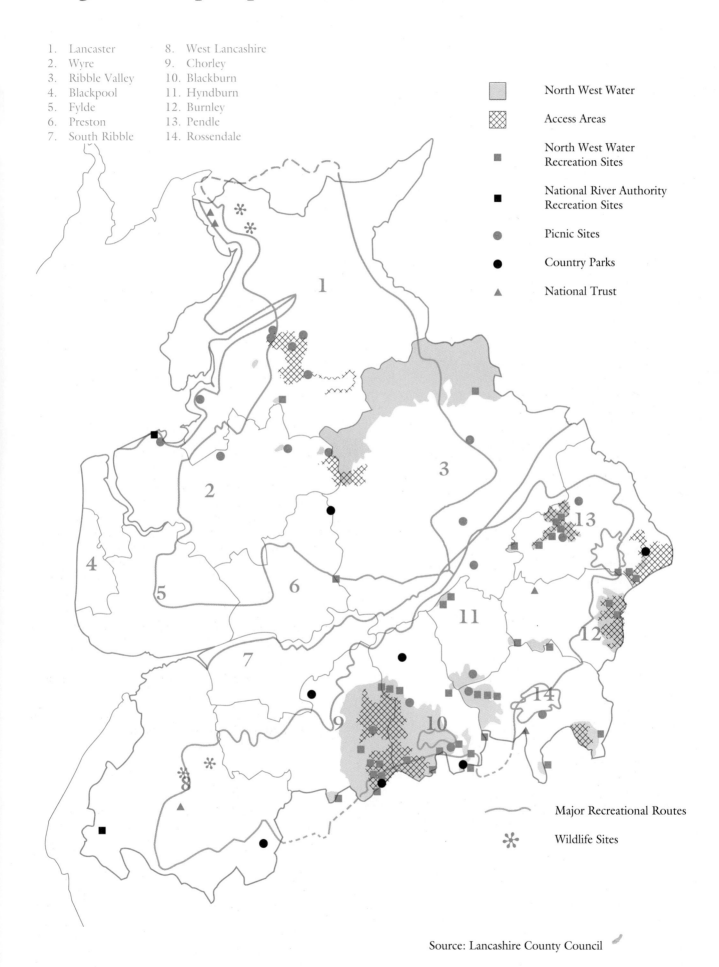

Figure 168

Managed Rural Open Space in Lancashire. 1990

1. Lancaster   8. West Lancashire
2. Wyre   9. Chorley
3. Ribble Valley   10. Blackburn
4. Blackpool   11. Hyndburn
5. Fylde   12. Burnley
6. Preston   13. Pendle
7. South Ribble   14. Rossendale

North West Water

Access Areas

North West Water
Recreation Sites

National River Authority
Recreation Sites

Picnic Sites

Country Parks

National Trust

Major Recreational Routes

Wildlife Sites

Source: Lancashire County Council

Table 124	Country Parks and Picnic Sites in Lancashire. 1990		
District	Country Parks (ha)	Picnic Sites (ha)	Total (ha)
Lancaster	—.	22[6]	22
Wyre	—	9[7]	9
Ribble Valley	—	18[8]	18
Blackpool	—	—	—
Fylde	—	—	—
Preston	110[1]	—	110
South Ribble	—	—	—
West Lancashire	149[2]	—	149
Chorley	444[3]	14[9]	458
Blackburn	116[4]	2[10]	118
Hyndburn	—	1[11]	1
Burnley	—	—	—
Pendle	143[5]	2[12]	145
Rossendale	—	6[13]	6
LANCASHIRE	962	74	1,036

Source: County and District Councils.

Notes: [1] *Beacon Fell.* [2] *Beacon.* [3] *Cuerden and Rivington.* [4] *Witton and Jumbles.* [5] *Wycoller.* [6] *Crook o' Lune; Conder Green; Birk Bank; Jubilee Tower; Bull Beck; Little Crag.* [7] *Scorton; Lane Ends Pilling; Brock Bottoms.* [8] *Springwood; Stocks Reservoir; Edisford Bridge;* [9] *Anglezarke.* [10] *Slipper Lowe; Entwistle Reservoir.* [11] *Cocker Cobbs.* [12] *Barley; Foulridge Wharf.* [13] *Clough Head Quarry; New Hall Hey.*

Because of its location on the edge of the Greater Manchester connurbation, Rivington Country Park receives even more visitors, though accurate figures are not available.

11.51 The CA 1968 also gives local authorities the powers to provide picnic sites. These generally take the form of small car parks with landscaped sitting areas and links to local footpaths. There are 20 main sites in Lancashire (see Figure 168), covering a total area of 74 ha. Eleven are managed by the County Council, five by Districts, two by NWW and one each by the NRA and Rossendale GWT. In addition to formal sites, there are many informal roadside pull-offs and viewpoints regularly used by walkers and picnickers.

Access to Open Country

11.52 Access to areas of Open Country can be established under Part V of the NPAC 1949. This is done by Access Agreement or, where agreement cannot be reached, by Access Order. An Agreement or Order is a legal arrangement which allows the public to walk freely on private land, without fear of prosecution for trespass, provided they abide by the terms of any bye-laws which apply.

11.53 Lancashire County Council was one of the pioneering Authorities in securing Access Agreements and began the process in the early 1950s. Since then, seven Agreements and one Order have been confirmed and the County Council has provided both financial and management assistance for the land involved. Much of the area subject to open access is now owned by NWW and joint arrangements have been established to allow harmonious use for recreation, water catchment and supply.

11.54 Lancashire's seven areas are Worsthorne Moor (Burnley), Rooley Moor (Rossendale), Anglezarke/Rivington/Withnell Moors (Chorley), Bromiley Pastures (Blackburn), Fairsnape and Saddle Fell/Wolf Fell (both Ribble Valley) and Clougha (Lancaster). These are shown on Figure 168. The total area of land managed under Access Agreements is 4,526 ha. An Access Order covers land at Wolf Fell in Bowland (its 208 ha lie between the Fairsnape and Saddle Fell Agreements). The total Access land amounts therefore to 4,734 ha.

11.55 In addition to these formal arrangements, NWW has allowed a number of 'concessionary' footpaths across its catchment land. Three exist in the Forest of Bowland and 'de-facto' access is permitted to 890 ha on Boulsworth Hill and 1,943 ha on Pendle Hill (Pendle). A total of 7,486 ha of Open Country is available for free public access via these formal Agreements and concessions. Their area and location is shown in Table 125.

Commons

11.56 There are over 9,697 ha of Common Land and Village Greens registered under the CRA 1965 in Lancashire. This includes 3,599 ha of urban Common, 6,082 ha of rural Common and 16 ha of Village Green. Commons are remnants of the Manorial system introduced in the Middle Ages. Rights of Common are registered to individual Commoners and an official record of them is maintained by the County Council. There are six rights: pasture (grazing), pannage (feeding pigs on acorns and beech mast), estovers (taking underwood or bracken), turbary (digging turf or peat), piscary (fishing) and common in the soil (taking sand, gravel, stone or minerals).

Table 125	Access to Open Country in Lancashire. 1990		
District	Name(s)	Type	Area (ha)
Lancaster	Clougha	Agreement	695
Wyre	Fairsnape	Agreement	262
Ribble Valley	Saddle Fell; Wolf Fell	Agreement and Order	353
Chorley	Anglezarke and Withnell; Rivington	Agreements	1,980
Blackburn	Bromiley Pastures	Agreement	354
Burnley	Worsthorne Moor	Agreement	893
Pendle	Pendle Hill; Boulsworth Hill	Concession/ de-facto	2,752
Rossendale	Rooley Moor	Agreement	197
LANCASHIRE			7,486

Source: Lancashire County Council and North West Water.

Figure 169
Commons and Village Greens in Lancashire. 1990

1. Lancaster
2. Wyre
3. Ribble Valley
4. Blackpool
5. Fylde
6. Preston
7. South Ribble
8. West Lancashire
9. Chorley
10. Blackburn
11. Hyndburn
12. Burnley
13. Pendle
14. Rossendale

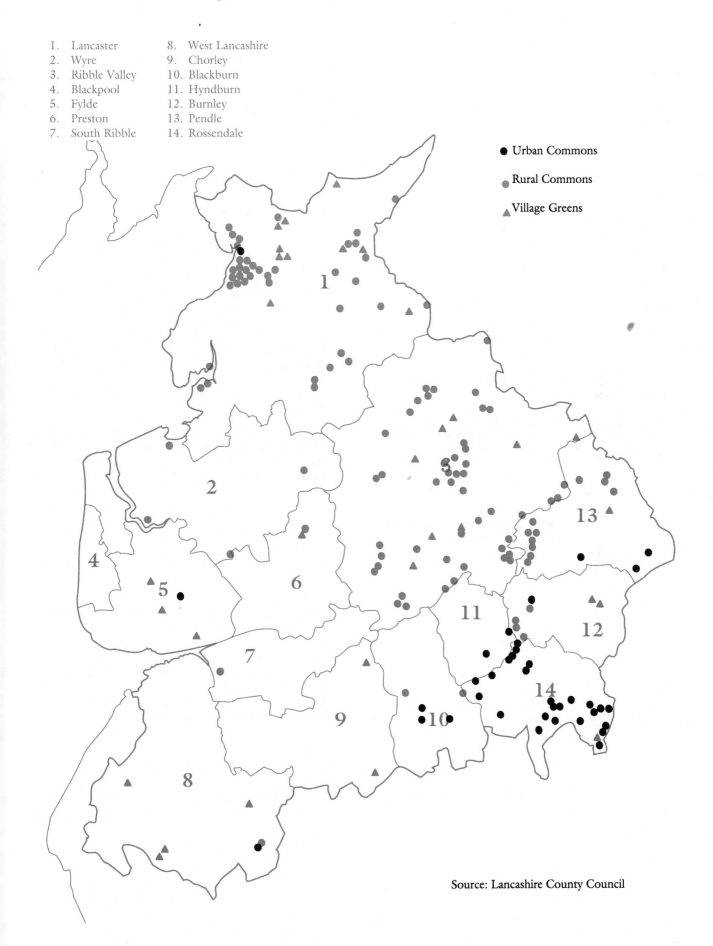

● Urban Commons
● Rural Commons
▲ Village Greens

Source: Lancashire County Council

Table 126	Urban and Rural Commons and Village Greens in Lancashire. 1990			
District	Urban Common (ha)	Rural Common (ha)	Village Greens (ha)	Total (ha)
Lancaster	10	3,936	4	3,950
Wyre	—	35	—	35
Ribble Valley	—	1,423	2	1,425
Blackpool	—	—	—	—
Fylde	1	—	3	4
Preston	—	1	1	2
South Ribble	—	38	—	38
West Lancashire	1	4	1	6
Chorley	—	—	1	1
Blackburn	257	50	—	307
Hyndburn	45	—	—	45
Burnley	18	207	2	227
Pendle	152	388	1	541
Rossendale	3,115	—	1	3,116
LANCASHIRE	3,599	6,082	16	9,697

Source: Lancashire County Council.

11.57 The LPA 1925 gave the public a legal right of access for 'air and exercise' to all Commons lying within the boundaries of Boroughs and Urban Districts. These are now known as urban Commons and the public retains the right of access.

11.58 However, rural Commons, (formerly within Rural District Council areas), have no public right of access, unless an Access Agreement has been made. Some in Lancashire have passed into the ownership of Parish and District Councils and public access has been given (for example Carr House Green Common, Inskip; Old Ball Green, Pilling; The Salt Marsh, Hambleton; and Delph Quarry, Claughton, all in Wyre District, and totalling 34 ha).

11.59 The distribution of Commons is shown on Figure 169, whilst Table 126 gives a breakdown of areas by District. Figure 170 shows that 86% of urban Commons are in Rossendale District, whilst Wyre, Ribble Valley, Preston, South Ribble and Chorley Districts have none. Lancaster has 65% of Lancashire's rural Commons, shown in Figure 171 whilst Ribble Valley has 23%, Fylde, Chorley, Hyndburn and Rossendale have none. Chorley and Blackpool have no Common Land at all.

11.60 Village Greens are also registered under the CRA 1965. The County has thirty-six in all (see Figure 169). They account for very little land, with Lancaster having 33% of the County's total with just over 4 ha. Wyre, Blackpool, South Ribble, Blackburn and Hyndburn have no registered Village Greens.

11.61 Many organisations (including the CoCo, the Commons Open Spaces and Footpaths Preservation Society and the County Council) believe that all Common land should be made available to the public for recreational use. A commitment to this effect was contained in the Government's last election manifesto, but measures have yet to be enacted.

Rights of Way Network

11.62 By far the most important and most frequently used recreational resource in Lancashire is

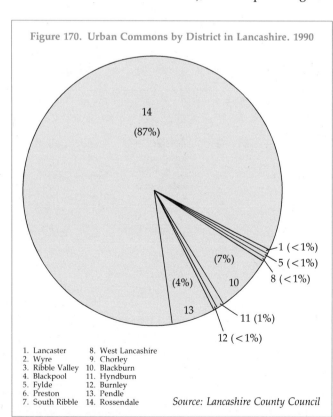

Figure 170. Urban Commons by District in Lancashire. 1990

14 (87%)

1 (<1%)
5 (<1%)
8 (<1%)
(7%) 10
(4%)
13
11 (1%)
12 (<1%)

1. Lancaster
2. Wyre
3. Ribble Valley
4. Blackpool
5. Fylde
6. Preston
7. South Ribble
8. West Lancashire
9. Chorley
10. Blackburn
11. Hyndburn
12. Burnley
13. Pendle
14. Rossendale

Source: Lancashire County Council

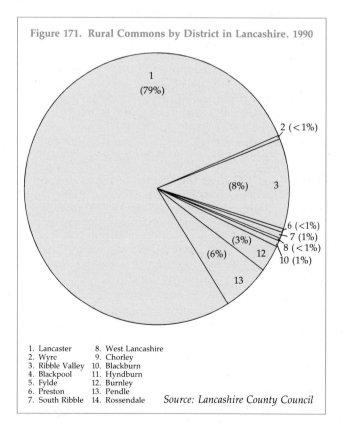

Figure 171. Rural Commons by District in Lancashire. 1990

1 (79%)
2 (<1%)
(8%) 3
6 (<1%)
7 (1%)
8 (<1%)
10 (1%)
(3%)
(6%) 12
13

1. Lancaster
2. Wyre
3. Ribble Valley
4. Blackpool
5. Fylde
6. Preston
7. South Ribble
8. West Lancashire
9. Chorley
10. Blackburn
11. Hyndburn
12. Burnley
13. Pendle
14. Rossendale

Source: Lancashire County Council

District	Footpaths (km)	Bridleways (km)	Byways (km)	Total (km)	% of County Total
Lancaster	624	72	8	704	11
Wyre	391	17	—	408	6
Ribble Valley	1,202	146	—	1,348	21
Blackpool	19	—	—	19	<1
Fylde	109	10	—	119	2
Preston	280	16	2	298	5
South Ribble	203	10	3	216	3
West Lancashire	500	5	2	507	8
Chorley	475	35	—	510	8
Blackburn	463	5	—	468	7
Hyndburn	233	18	5	256	4
Burnley	332	10	6	348	5
Pendle	603	32	2	637	10
Rossendale	615	11	2	628	10
LANCASHIRE	6,049	387	30	6,466	100

Table 127 Public Rights of Way Network in Lancashire. 1990

Source: Lancashire County Council.

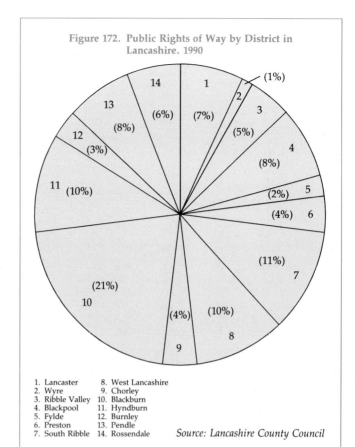

Figure 172. Public Rights of Way by District in Lancashire. 1990

1. Lancaster
2. Wyre
3. Ribble Valley
4. Blackpool
5. Fylde
6. Preston
7. South Ribble
8. West Lancashire
9. Chorley
10. Blackburn
11. Hyndburn
12. Burnley
13. Pendle
14. Rossendale

Source: Lancashire County Council

the rights of way network. This includes footpaths, bridleways and byways shown on the Definitive Map maintained by the County Council under the NPACA 1949 (see also Chapter 12). Lancashire has 6,466 km of statutory routes, comprising 6,049 km of footpaths, 387 km of Bridleways and 30 km of byways.

11.63 These routeways allow public access through most of the County and provide Lancashire's greatest recreational resource. Access is available freely to everyone, and is protected by legislation. In practice, though, blockages stemming from a combination of illegal actions, neglect and the problem of maintaining such a large, widely spread and often remote system, mean that some routes can be difficult to use. The CoCo have set a target for bringing all rights of way into good useable order by the end of this Century.

11.64 Table 127 gives the lengths of rights of way in each District, whilst Figure 172 shows their distribution. Ribble Valley has the best provision, with 21% of the County total, (it is, however, the largest District in area). Lancaster, Pendle and Rossendale come next, each having about a tenth of the system. Blackpool, which has the County's smallest area and is the most urbanised District, has the lowest provision of all with a mere 19 km of footpath. Relatively low provision in Wyre and Fylde means that the Fylde Peninsula generally has the least dense coverage in the whole of Lancashire.

Recreational Routes

11.65 Specific improvements have been carried out in many places to provide linear or circular recreational routes that can take heavy use and assist in tourism promotion. These are based largely on rights of way, though new, connecting links have been required in some cases. Some routes cater for walkers, some for horse-riders and some for cyclists. Lancashire has many recreational

Name of Route	Length (km)	District(s)	Managed by
The Lancashire Cycleway	420	All Districts except Blackpool	County Council
Lune Estuary Coastal Path	22	Lancaster	County Council
Ribble Way	64	Preston, Ribble Valley	County Council
Fylde Walks	25	Fylde	District Council
Cheshire Lines	8	West Lancashire	District and NRA
The North Turton Trail	35	Blackburn	County Council
Brontè Way	14	Pendle	County Council
Pendle Way	86	Pendle	District Council
Rossendale Way	72	Rossendale	District and County Council
Irwell Valley Way	44	Rossendale	County Council
LANCASHIRE	790		

Table 128 Major Recreational Routes in Lancashire. 1990

Source: Lancashire County Council.

routes, established by the County Council, District Councils or local organisations. Table 128 shows the main ones, with their lengths. They cover a variety of terrain and distance and cater for a variety of demand.

11.66   In addition to the 790 km provided by these facilities, there are many shorter routes, like nature trails and circular walks in the County. These include:

* Eaves Wood (Lancaster);
* Brock Valley Nature Trail (Wyre);
* Salthill Quarry Geology Trail (Ribble Valley).
* Spring Wood (Ribble Valley);
* Witch Wood (Fylde);
* Squire Anderton Wood (Preston);
* Tawd Valley (West Lancashire);
* Anglezarke Woodland Trail (Chorley);
* Birkacre Valley Trail (Chorley);
* Lead Mines Clough Trail (Chorley);
* Great Harwood Nature Trail (Blackburn);
* Roddlesworth Nature Trail (Blackburn);
* Sunnyhurst Woods (Blackburn);
* Shedden Clough Trail (Burnley);
* Wycoller Walks (Pendle);
* Calf Hey Trail (Rossendale);

Total Rural Openspace

11.67   Lancashire has a total of 21,135 ha of formally-provided rural openspace. This is made up of the Country Parks, picnic sites, Open Country Access land and Commons described above, plus openspace made available by NWW, the National Trust and others.

11.68   Table 129 shows how unevenly distributed this space is between Districts. Lancaster, with 5,058 ha, has just under a quarter of the County total, whilst Blackpool and Fylde account for only 18 ha between them. Lancaster, Ribble Valley and Rossendale totals are high due to the significant contribution made by Commons, whilst Chorley, Burnley and Pendle are boosted by large areas opened up by Access arrangements. Chorley also has the largest area of Country Parks. Picnic sites do not contribute very much to the total, providing only 73 ha in all.

11.69   NWW contributes an additional 2,032 ha to the total concentrated mainly in Pendle, Rossendale, Ribble Valley and Hyndburn. The National Trust manages 308 ha of openspace, with sites in Lancaster, West Lancashire, Burnley and Rossendale. The 576 ha of 'other' space consists of four wildlife reserves with public access. These are located in Lancaster and West Lancashire Districts.

Total Openspace in Lancashire

11.70   There are of 26,099 ha of urban and rural recreational openspace in the County, which is shown on Table 130. This gives an average of 18.8 ha per thousand population. The resource is distributed unevenly throughout the County. Table 130 shows that whilst Lancaster contains 5,347 ha of openspace, Fylde has only 151 ha. Two-thirds of the total is shared between four Districts, Lancaster (20%), Chorley (12%), Pendle (18%) and Rossendale (16%). However, these Districts have the bulk of the County's extensive Open Country Access Areas and Commons within their boundaries.

Table 129   Total Rural Openspace Provision in Lancashire. 1990

District	Country Parks	Picnic Sites	Access to Open Country	Commons and Village Greens	NWW Land not included elsewhere	National Trust	Other	Total (ha)
Lancaster	—	22	695	3,950	11	87	293	5,058
Wyre	—	9	262	35	18	—	—	324
Ribble Valley	—	18	353	1,425	271	—	—	2,067
Blackpool	—	—	—	—	—	—	—	—
Fylde	—	—	—	4	—	—	—	4
Preston	110	—	—	2	8	—	—	120
South Ribble	—	—	—	38	—	—	—	38
West Lancashire	149	—	—	6	—	6	283	444
Chorley	444	14	2,334	1	14	—	—	2,807
Blackburn	116	2	—	307	1	—	—	426
Hyndburn	—	1	—	45	200	—	—	246
Burnley	—	—	893	227	—	38	—	1,158
Pendle	143	2	2,752	541	982	—	—	4,420
Rossendale	—	6	197	3,116	527	177	—	4,023
LANCASHIRE	962	74	7,486	9,697	2,032	308	576	21,135

Source: Various.

Note: All areas are in ha.

Table 130	Total Openspace in Lancashire. 1990			
District	Urban	Rural	Total (ha)	% of County Total
Lancaster	289	5,058	5,347	20
Wyre	494	324	818	3
Ribble Valley	134	2,067	2,201	8
Blackpool	370	—	370	1
Fylde	147	4	151	1
Preston	707	120	827	3
South Ribble	381	38	419	2
West Lancashire	507	444	951	4
Chorley	337	2,807	3,144	12
Blackburn	551	426	977	4
Hyndburn	262	246	508	2
Burnley	357	1,158	1,515	6
Pendle	254	4,420	4,674	18
Rossendale	174	4,023	4,197	16
LANCASHIRE	4,964	21,135	26,099	100

Source: Various.

Note: All areas are in ha.

Table 131	Management of Openspace in Lancashire. 1990		
Agency	Urban (ha)	Rural (ha)	Total (ha)
District Councils	3,722	243	3,965
County Council	1,242	4,344	5,586
North West Water	—	5,678[1]	5,678
Others[2]	—	10,870	10,870
LANCASHIRE	4,964	21,135	26,099

Source: Various.

Notes: [1] NWW own a further 2,741 ha which is available for rural recreation and is managed by the County Council under joint-working arrangements in CMAs. This land is credited to the County Council's total because of this.
[2] Predominantly private owners of Commons (9,697 ha.).

North West Water

11.74   Following the WA 1973, the former NWW Authority opened up much of its land for public access and recreation. It did this by working jointly with the County and District Councils and other agencies. A total area of nearly 8,500 ha is involved, largely made up of catchment land and reservoirs in the uplands of South East and East Lancashire. This

Management of Openspace

11.71 Ownership and the responsibility for looking after Lancashire's stock of openspace falls to a variety of organisations in the public, private and voluntary sectors. The main ones involved have been mentioned already, and the extent of their rôle is summarised in Table 131. Locations of all rural sites and areas managed by these agencies is given on Figure 168.

District Councils

11.72   The paramount rôle of Districts in managing urban space has been acknowledged earlier. Despite this, a number of Districts also provide, and look after, rural facilities. Blackburn and West Lancashire, who manage Witton and Beacon Country Parks respectively, are notable examples. Just under 4,000 ha of openspace is managed by Lancashire's Districts – the bulk of which (94%) is urban.

County Council

11.73   Conversely, the County Council is principally involved in managing rural sites and areas. Over three quarters of the 5,586 ha under County control are in the countryside. Urban land managed by the County Council is comprised of mainly educational openspace. The County Council actually owns only 1,603 ha (or 37%) of the rural openspace that it manages. The balance belongs to NWW and is looked after on behalf of that Company, and other partners, involved in joint CMA arrangements.

Table 132	Rural Openspace in Lancashire Owned and Managed by North West Water. 1990	
District		(ha)
(a) Land owned by NWW but managed by LCC[1]		2,741
(b) Land owned and managed by NWW		
	Lancaster	11
	Wyre	18
	Ribble Valley	272
	Blackpool	—
	Fylde	—
	Preston	8
	South Ribble	—
	West Lancashire	—
	Chorley	14
	Blackburn	—
	Hyndburn	200
	Burnley	893
	Pendle	3,735
	Rossendale	527
	LANCASHIRE	8,419

Source: North West Water and Lancashire County Council.

Note: [1] The great majority of this area is in the West Pennine Moors, encompassing land in the Districts of Blackburn, Chorley, Hyndburn and Rossendale.

represents nearly 40% of all rural openspace in the County, falling mainly into the Districts of Blackburn, Burnley, Chorley, Pendle and Rossendale (see Table 132). This area forms, with the County's rights of way network and the rural space owned by the County Council, one of the largest and most important outdoor recreational resources available in any County in the UK.

11.75 With the passage of the WA 1989, NWWA land (with minor exceptions) moved to the ownership of the new private Company. The total area is shown on Figure 168. The Code of Practice on Conservation, Access and Recreation (1989) produced under the WA 1989, states that Water Companies should continue to allow public access to land and reservoirs of natural beauty or of amenity or recreational value. Wherever water supply and related functions require changes to public access, the Code states that recreational organisations should be consulted and proposals formulated to minimise any restrictions on access. In AONB like the Forest of Bowland, special arrangements require Companies to discuss proposals to sell land having recreational and wildlife interest with the CoCo and the Nature Conservancy Council. Their views have to be taken into account and where the land is of particular value, steps can be taken to safeguard it. However, these special protections do not apply to land-sales in other areas. Most of NWW rural openspace land in Lancashire falls into this 'non-protected' category.

Other Agencies

11.76 Nearly half of all rural openspace in Lancashire is managed by private owners. This consists of the 9,697 ha which make up Common land. Public access does not exist to 6,098 ha of this area though footpaths cross some Commons and 'informal' access is available in places. Access is available to the 3,599 ha of urban Common.

11.77 The balance of the 'other' category shown in Table 131 (1,173 ha) is divided between the NRA, the National Trust and various wildlife groups like the Royal Society for the Protection of Birds and Lancashire Trust for Nature Conservation. In addition, there are many unquantified small areas made available by private owners, Parish Councils and other groups, plus the 'linear' resource of Lancashire's two canals, maintained by the BWB.

11.78 The NRA manages only 11 ha for recreation at two sites. The first is the Lane Ends Picnic Site at Pilling, (Wyre) at 4 ha and the second is a 7 ha footpath, bridleway and cycleway, the former Cheshire Lines railway line at Downholland Moss (West Lancashire). The NRA also manages areas with fishing rights at Mitton Fishery, River Ribble, (a 500 m length), the River Douglas Flood Embankment, Becconsall (Near Preston) which offers 3 km of footpaths, and the River Lune Skerton and Halton Fisheries (NRA pers. comm.).

11.79 The National Trust owns a number of historic buildings and maintains the gardens and lands around these for public enjoyment. Some 308 ha are available in four areas located on Figure 168.

11.80 Wildlife organisations manage four large sites primarily for the preservation of wildlife and wildlife habitat. However, public access is available for recreational pursuits compatible with conservation (e.g. walking and birdwatching). The sites cover a total area of 576 ha comprising Leighton Moss, (184 ha in Lancaster), Martin Mere, (240 ha in West Lancashire) Warton Crag, (109 ha Lancaster) and Mere Sands Wood, (43 ha West Lancashire). There are over 20 smaller sites in Lancashire to which varying degrees of access is permitted. Further details on protected wildlife sites has been given in Chapter 9.

11.81 The BWB owns and manages inland waterways for both commercial and recreational use. In Lancashire, the Lancaster and the Leeds and Liverpool canals (shown on Figure 176) provide a total of 164.8 km of towpath and waterway for walking, cruising, canoeing and fishing. The Lancaster Canal has the highest density of pleasure craft per mile of any inland waterway outside London (British Waterways Board, 1988).

11.82 Many Parish Councils manage small parcels of openspace for recreation. This land is either owned by the Parish or the Parish acts as an agent for another landowner. Unfortunately, there is no central register of this land, and the area involved is not known. Many Parish Councils are also actively involved in maintaining rights of way in their area.

Landowners

11.83 The vast majority of land in Lancashire is privately owned. But private owners, and particularly the farming community, make two enormous contributions to public enjoyment of the countryside. Firstly, their stewardship of land creates the landscape character that is an essential component to the general enjoyment of leisure in rural areas. Secondly, landowners have responsibilities for the rights of way that cross their land, and are prevented by legislation from blocking them.

Environmental Impact

11.84 There are no comprehensive data on the environmental impact of openspace provision or use in Lancashire. Much anecdotal, and site-specific evidence is gathered by management agencies and, where serious impacts arise, these are dealt with. It is only possible, therefore, to give a general outline of the position.

11.85 In rural locations in particular, pressure from visitor numbers causes localised problems. Beacon Fell Country Park gets over 350,000 visitors every year, whilst the figure for Rivington Country Park must be far higher. Too many people regularly using paths, and popular sites, leads to unsightly erosion. Both of the above Country Parks are places where this has been of serious concern, though measures have been taken to deal with the matter. Congestion from trippers' cars in attractive villages, and along narrow rural lanes, also occurs in a number of popular areas. Disturbance to wildlife is a further consequence at some sites. Particularly serious problems can arise on the coast at bird roosting and nesting sites at critical times of the year, affecting Lancashire's internationally important colonies of waders and wildfowl. Landowners, farmers and other people who live in the countryside experience a further range of problems, including trespass, vandalism and general disturbance.

11.86 Openspace sites in towns are also prone to damage by vandals, whilst litter is a feature common to most sites in town and country. Many of these difficulties are dealt with on a day-to-day basis by maintenance staff and countryside wardens, within the limits of financial budgets. But at some sites, the scale and regularity of problems are matters of growing environmental concern.

11.87 On the positive side, and especially when well-managed, openspace is a major environmental asset in its own right. Lancashire's 26,000 ha forms a major landscape resource, and its green and open area add immeasurably to townscape and landscape. Their collective wildlife value is also important. But their principal value lies in the contribution they make to the social and physical well-being of Lancastrians, and visitors to the County, through the range of leisure opportunities they provide.

Threats

11.88 Again, only general observations can be made because detailed, specific data do not exist. Three principal categories of threat exist: potential loss of openspace to development, maintenance difficulties and deliberate damage and vandalism.

11.89 Urban sites are most at risk from development. Small, local openspaces, sportsfields and educational openspace are probably most threatened, though no specific data exists about the extent of any losses. Given the financial pressures under which many managing agencies now operate, there can be situations where capitalising on the development value of open land is viewed as an easy way of replenishing budgets. Such short-term gains are at the expense of permanent loss of recreational space.

11.90 Concern has also been expressed at potential changes in the status of rural openspace owned by NWW. No longer a public agency, and controlling 40% of all such resources in Lancashire, the Company operates primarily as a commercial organisation responsible to its shareholders. Under these circumstances, there is a fear that economic considerations may override public access needs, leading to changes in land management or disposals of land. The Code of Practice referred to earlier and the positive statements of the new Company that it will continue the excellent recreational and conservation policies of the former Water Authority, are grounds for concluding that Lancashire's rural spaces are secure for the foreseeable future. Maintaining co-operative working between local authorities, other agencies, and the Water Company will provide a further important safeguard.

11.91 Maintaining such a large and widespread openspace resource is both difficult and costly.

Many facilities are located in remote countryside, whilst the most difficult element of all to keep in good order are the 6,500 km of rights of way which cover all parts of the County. The position is not helped by the fact that almost 40% of all of Lancashire's openspace is looked after by local authorities, who do their best from budgets which have many more pressing calls made upon them.

11.92 Vandalism is a widespread feature of modern society. Openspaces in town and country are prime targets, and frequently suffer the consequences. Discarded litter, uncontrolled dogs and their faeces and other inconsiderate actions are also common, and add to the general devaluation of openspaces. Another problem encountered, is deliberate damage to footpaths, which in places constitutes an obstruction rendering the route impassible.

Monitoring

11.93 No consistent, comprehensive monitoring is carried out of the use made of Lancashire's rural openspace, or of the changes affecting it. The data presented in this Chapter are the first attempt ever to establish the overall extent of the resource. The CoCo commissions periodic National Household Surveys to identify general trends in the use of rural facilities, whilst the SC evaluate specific sports, outdoor activities and provision. Local authorities also do occasional surveys, nearly always in connection with a specific purpose or in response to complaints or incidents reported by the public, about a specific site. But these are too infrequent to provide comprehensive information. Given the enormous value that is derived from the resource, the lack of any monitoring activity is a matter of particular concern.

11.94 Urban openspace monitoring has also been inconsistent over the years, and no County-wide perspective has been taken before now. At the District level, the position is now changing because of the survey work required following the Local Government Act 1988. This has made it the responsibility of each District to accurately assess and measure all recreational openspace they maintain in preparation for competitive tendering. This assessment includes land like roadside verges and incidental gardens and openspace within housing estates. In a relatively short period, an even more complete inventory of District Council openspace than is presented here will be available.

References

Audit Commission (1989). Sport for Whom? HMSO.

British Waterways Board (1988). National Count. BWB.

Burnley Borough Council (1982). Worsthorne Moor Recreation Management Plan – Discussion Draft. Burnley Borough Council.

Campbell I. (1972). A Practical Guide to the Law of Footpaths. Commons, Open Spaces and Footpaths Preservation Society.

Campbell I. (1973). A Guide to the Law of Commons. Commons, Open Spaces and Footpaths Preservation Society.

Countryside Commission (1984). National Countryside Recreation Survey. Countryside Commission.

Countryside Commission and The Sports Council (1986). Access to the Countryside for Recreation and Sport. CoCo and SC.

Countryside Commission (1988). Sites of Conservation and Recreation Value Currently in the Ownership of Water Authorities. CoCo.

Department of the Environment (1973). Design Bulletin 27, Children at Play. HMSO.

Department of the Environment (1989). The Water Act 1989, Code of Practice on Conservation Access and Recreation. HMSO.

Lancashire County Council (1962). County Development Plan Review. LCC.

Lancashire County Council (1982). Lancashire Tourism Inventory. LCC.

Lancashire County Council (1988). A Countryside Recreation Strategy for Lancashire. LCC.

Marshall J.D. (1974). Lancashire. David and Charles.

National Playing Fields Association (1971). Outdoor Playing Space Requirements – Review of the National Playing Fields Association Playing Space Target. NPFA.

North West Council for Sport and Recreation (1980). Regional Recreation Strategy Technical Report No. 5. Position Statement on Outdoor Recreation in Urban Areas. NWCSR.

North West Water (1989). Draft Recreation and Access Directory. Unpublished.

Office of Population Censuses and Surveys (1985). General Household Survey 1983. HMSO.

Office of Population Censuses and Surveys (1988). General Household Survey 1986. HMSO.

The Sports Council (1968). Planning for Sport. SC.

The Sports Council (1976). Playing Fields: A New Approach to Assessing Requirements. Draft Report. SC.

The Sports Council (1988). Sport in the Community: Into the 90s. SC.

Chapter Twelve
Transport

Introduction

12.1 A good transport system is vital for the efficient functioning of society, but transport has an enormous impact on the environment and some modes of transport on established routes cause more damage than others. Because an efficient transport system is so important to the national economy, decisions about transport have traditionally been made taking into account mainly economic, rather than environmental, factors. In recent years there has been growing concern about the environmental effects of transport, (particularly roads and cars), and the Government has indicated that in the future greater priority will be given to measures which allow for economic growth but at the same time minimise environmental damage. However, the provision of all transport facilities has environmental implications of some type and degree.

12.2 The transport system in Lancashire is a product of human activity dating back to prehistoric times (see Chapter 2) but the greatest changes have come about since the invention of the motorcar, and the growth in popularity of private road transport. The amount of road traffic and its predicted future growth remain the main problem. Government forecasts are that by the year 2025 there will be between 83% and 142% more traffic than today (Department of Transport, 1989a).

12.3 Government priorities in transport policy currently favour roads and the private motorist over alternative transport modes. Public expenditure on roads went up by 2% between 1985/6 and 1988/9 but on rail declined by 45% and on buses and London underground went down by 19% (House of Commons Transport Committee, 1989). As a consequence public transport becomes even less attractive and more people choose to drive. Cycling and walking receive little attention or encouragement.

12.4 This Chapter looks at, and details methods of monitoring, the existing transport network in the County, its use and the purpose, origin and destination of those who use the network. It looks at the environmental effects and describes traffic management methods introduced in the County and the measures taken to promote public transport.

Legislation

European

12.5 EC Directives on transport relate mainly to air and noise pollution. Directive 85/210/EEC requires that all new cars now have to be capable of running on unleaded fuel and that unleaded petrol should be widely available. Directive 70/220/EEC sets limits for emissions from the engines of motor vehicles, which have since been amended several times. The most stringent standards are for large cars (with engines bigger than 2 litres) and the least stringent for small cars (with engines smaller than 1.4 litres). The new standards applicable for all new large cars from 1992 have been set at a level (for carbon monoxide, hydrocarbons and nitrous oxides) that require the use of catalytic converters. New small cars will also require catalytic converters from 1992. Excluded from these Directives are motorcycles, most petrol and diesel vans, and heavy goods vehicles.

12.6 EC Directive 84/424/EEC sets noise limits for cars, buses, and goods vehicles. Directive 87/56/EEC covers motorcycle noise. Aircraft noise is covered by Directive 80/51/EEC amended by 83/206/EEC and ensures that member States implement the noise standards for subsonic aircraft which have been agreed within the International Civil Aviation Organisation.

12.7 Directive 85/337/EEC asked member States to implement, within current land use planning systems, a method for assessing the effects of certain public and private projects upon the environment. This method has become known as 'Environmental Impact Assessment' and can be applied to road and other transport schemes.

United Kingdom

12.8 The main legislation covering the largest component of the transport network in Lancashire – the road network – is the Highways Act 1980. The Act contains the procedures for approving motorways and trunk roads and empowers Highway Authorities to construct, maintain and improve highways. It also contains powers for Authorities to stop up, or interfere with, highways, make up private streets, acquire land and maintain the footpath, bridleway and byway network. The Rights of Way Act 1990 also requires landowners to maintain and reinstate paths interfered with by agricultural operations.

12.9 The Road Traffic Regulation Act 1984, gives the Highway Authority a duty to promote road safety and empowers it to make Traffic Regulation Orders to control the movement or parking of the various classes of vehicles which use the roads, or the speed at which they may travel, in order to ensure that the road system operates safely and efficiently.

12.10 The Town and Country Planning Act 1990, the Town and Country Planning General Development Order 1977 and the Town and Country Planning General Development Order 1985 relate to the County Council's rôle as the Highway Authority with regard to development in Lancashire.

12.11 The Transport Act 1985 defines the County Council's powers and duties in respect to public transport. This Act de-regulated bus services and required Highway Authorities to invite tenders for services which it intends to subsidise (on social needs grounds). It also empowers Highway Authorities to make capital grants for British Rail projects.

12.12 Section 8 of the Railways Act 1974 allows Government to give grants for rail freight handling facilities resulting from a switch from road to rail transport. Section 35 of the Civil Aviation Act 1982 allows for airport consultative committees to be set up comprising users of the airport, local authorities and other organisations.

12.13 The Highways (Assessment of Environmental Effects) Regulations 1989 require the Secretary of State to publish an environmental statement for preferred routes of motorways and trunk roads which do not require planning permission. Those roads that do require planning permission have environmental assessments carried out under the Town and Country Planning (Assessment of Environmental Effects) Regulations 1988. Both sets of Regulations are enactments of the EC Directive 85/337/EEC.

Organisations
Central Government

12.14 The Department of Transport (DTp) is responsible for all transport matters that are functions of Central Government. It sets the legislative and regulatory framework for transport, promotes the provision of infrastructure for roads, railways, ports and airports and determines the organisational framework within which transport operators work. It is responsible throughout the UK for merchant shipping, civil aviation, vehicle licencing and registration and, (excepting Northern Ireland), for airports policy, railways, major ports, road traffic law, testing of road vehicles and licencing of bus operators. The Department is directly responsible for capital investment in motorways and other trunk roads and provides subsidies for socially necessary rail services.

Local Government

12.15 The DTp works closely with local highway authorities, like Lancashire County Council, who are responsible for all roads other than the motorways and trunk roads. The County Council acts as the Department's agent in maintaining most of the trunk road network in the County.

12.16 About 95% of roads in England are non-trunk roads, many handle long distance and industrial traffic and are of economic benefit to the nation. In recognition of this, the DTp pays a Transport Supplementary Grant (TSG) to highway authorities for expenditure on roads of more than local importance. Lancashire County Council submits an annual Transport Policies and Programme (TPP) Report to the Department with details of the money it would like to spend on highway improvements, car parking and public transport.

12.17 Lancashire County Council, in turn, has agency agreements with all District Councils, except Ribble Valley and Fylde Borough Councils, to undertake highway maintenance and traffic management functions in the built-up 'urban areas' of their Districts.

12.18 The County Council's TPP submission reflects the County land use and transport policies laid down in the Lancashire Structure Plan (1987) which was approved by the Secretary of State for the Environment in 1989. This is required in order to enable the Government to assess County Councils for capital expenditure and decide the way in which TSG, Annual Capital Guidelines and Supplementary Credit Approvals should be distributed in the ensuing years. Individual District Councils within the County prepare statutory Local Plans, covering all or parts of their Districts. The County Council certifies that the policies contained in each Local Plan, including transport policies, conform with the Structure Plan policies.

12.19 The County Council's rôle in the planning of public transport services has changed following the de-regulation of bus services. However, the County Council still plays a part in promoting and stimulating good public transport provision by both road and rail in the County.

Other Organisations

12.20 There are many national and local voluntary organisations, pressure groups, private companies and interest groups involved in transport. One of the largest and most influential of these is the 'road lobby'. The road lobby comprises four main industries; the motor industry, the road freight industry, the oil industry and the road building industry and joined with them are the motoring organisations. Together the road lobby campaigns for more road building.

12.21 There are many 'rival' pressure groups, mainly environmental organisations, that are generally anti-road and pro-public transport. The largest UK groups are Friends of the Earth (FOE) and the Council for the Protection of Rural England (CPRE), both of which are represented in Lancashire. Transport 2000 also has branches in the County. There are also many smaller local transport issue groups like the Ormskirk to Preston Travellers Association (OPTA) and Support the East Lancashire Line Association (STELLA).

Transport in Lancashire
The Transport Network, Development and Use
Roads

12.22 The County Structure Plan calls for a road network hierarchy to be established to reflect the function and importance of the roads and help in the implementation of strategic transport policies (Lancashire County Council, 1990a). The hierarchy consists of:

* Primary Routes – roads forming part of the national network of high quality routes linking all major centres of population. They comprise all motorways, non-motorway national roads and the more important class 'A' roads;

* Other Main Routes – roads which act as links between the main towns in Lancashire not lying on the Primary Routes and link these to the Primary Routes;

* Distributor Roads – these function as distributors of traffic within towns and to rural settlements. They cater for movements from locality to locality and link these areas to the Primary and Other Main Routes;

* Local Roads – these provide access to adjoining land or development. They also link small rural communities.

Figure 173
Roads and Traffic Flows in Lancashire . 1989

1. Lancaster
2. Wyre
3. Ribble Valley
4. Blackpool
5. Fylde
6. Preston
7. South Ribble
8. West Lancashire
9. Chorley
10. Blackburn
11. Hyndburn
12. Burnley
13. Pendle
14. Rossendale

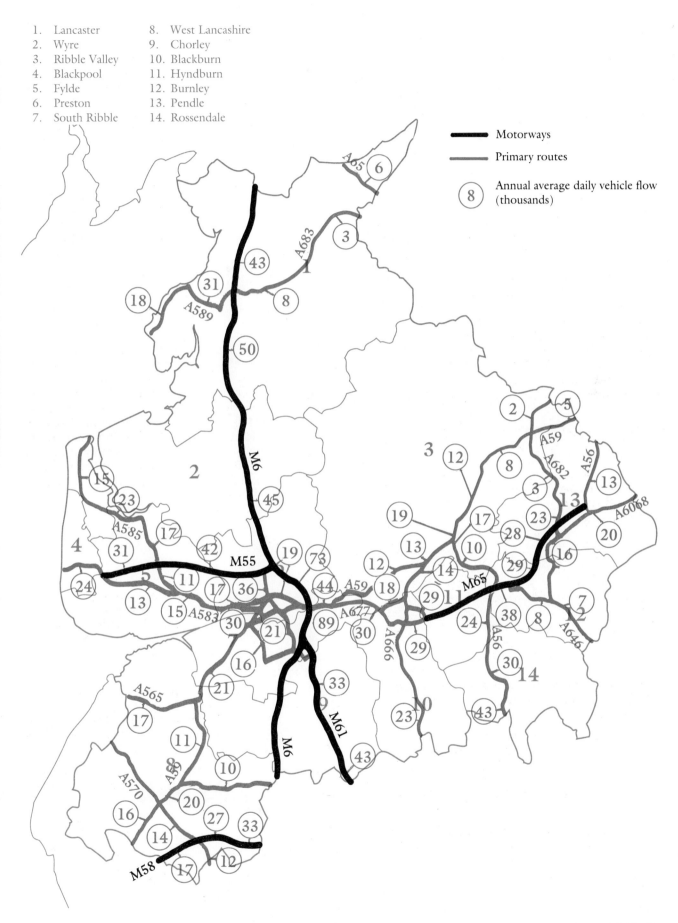

Source: Lancashire County Council (1990d)

12.23 Figure 173 shows the location of the Primary and other Main Routes of the County road network whilst Table 133 gives a statistical breakdown of the total road network length by District. There are a total of 7,400 km (4,600 miles) of roads in the County. This forms 2.7% of the 270,000 km (168,000 miles) of roads in England as a whole (Department of Transport, 1989b).

12.24 South, Central and North Lancashire are served by the M6 motorway and by the M61 which links Preston with Greater Manchester. The M55 provides a direct connection between Blackpool and the regional motorway network. In North East Lancashire, the M65 is primarily an internal high quality road link serving the Calder Valley towns but it has always been perceived as part of the motorway network providing ultimately a link to Yorkshire. The M58 connects South Lancashire with Merseyside. The A59 provides a direct connection between Merseyside and the North East of England and the A56/M66 links North East Lancashire with the Greater Manchester conurbation. The principal connections with Yorkshire are the A6068, A56 and A646.

12.25 The road network in Lancashire has continued to grow since 1949, when the first strategic road plan for the County was published. This led to the opening of Britain's first section of motorway – the M6 Preston By-Pass – in 1958. This eventually became part of the Birmingham-Carlisle M6 Motorway. The motorway network, as envisaged in 1949, is largely complete and, in addition, the M61 has been built to link Greater Manchester with the M6 at Preston. Many by-passes have been built to divert through – traffic from unsuitable roads in town centres (Lancashire County Council, 1988b).

12.26 The highways listed below are likely to be opened to traffic between January 1991 and December 1991, adding a further 4 km to the network:

* Kirkham and Wesham Bypass 1.9 km;
* Blackburn Inner Relief Road Phase 1 0.9 km;
* Penwortham Bypass Extension to Preston 1.2 km.

In addition to the above, a further 18.2 km of new unclassified roads, mainly estate roads, are expected to be added to the highway network by 31 March 1991.

12.27 Virtually every house, farm, office and factory in Lancashire has access to the national road system. Once a road is in place, unless restricted by an Order, it is open for use by pedestrians, bicycles, motorcycles, cars, taxis, buses, coaches, vans, lorries and other specialised vehicles. Most of us are pedestrians and many own bicycles, many more own cars. So the road system is instantly accessible to us in a way that rail, air, waterway and sea transport are not. Roads offer a means by which goods and people can move from door to door at any time that suits the convenience of the person or business.

12.28 Given these advantages, it is not surprising that roads account for approximately 92% of passenger transport and 60% of freight transport in the UK (Department of Transport, 1988). In terms of the composition of traffic journeys, cars and vans account for 90% of all traffic, journeys by goods vehicles 7%, journeys by motorcycles 2% and journeys by buses and coaches 1% (Department of Transport, 1988). However, although the car is the dominant mode of transport overall, public transport, walking and cycling play an important rôle in people's mobility.

Cars

12.29 Car ownership and car traffic levels have risen steadily in recent years but the 1981 Census found that 41% of households in Lancashire still did not have the use of a car and the overall County car ownership level was still below the national average (Lancashire County Council, 1988a) (Table 134).

12.30 The 1981 Census revealed wide local variations in car ownership within the County (Table 134). The old urban areas of North East Lancashire have low car ownership levels compared with the more affluent Central and West Lancashire areas and the Ribble Valley. Car ownership is primarily a function of income, but in rural areas like Ribble Valley, mobility will be more dependant on private transport than in urban areas and it is likely that higher priority will be given to car ownership here than elsewhere. As a consequence, Ribble Valley has the highest car ownership in the County at 1.02 cars per household and 73% of households owning cars in 1981 (Lancashire County Council, 1988a).

12.31 Comprehensive data on car ownership levels is only collected in the national Census of Population, the last being in 1981 and the next being in 1991. It is predicted that the 1991 Census will

Table 133	Road Network by District in Lancashire. 1990					
District	Motorways (km)	Other Trunk Roads (km)	Principal Roads (km)	Other Classified Roads (km)	Unclassified Roads (km)	Total (km)
Lancaster	26.75	4.90	90.52	292.71	517.97	932.85
Wyre	12.70	9.73	50.40	202.15	361.81	636.79
Ribble Valley	–	35.25	29.18	289.50	263.43	617.36
Preston	0.47	–	34.88	32.16	469.92	537.43
Fylde	12.10	9.52	54.01	115.75	223.11	414.49
Blackpool	6.11	0.18	35.45	123.52	373.78	539.04
South Ribble	10.00	18.55	27.18	83.92	315.36	455.01
West Lancs	12.70	45.57	47.38	258.65	421.45	785.75
Chorley	26.40	1.31	65.99	130.74	312.69	537.13
Blackburn	–	6.54	53.92	79.09	395.02	534.57
Hyndburn	8.20	5.80	34.95	39.45	236.58	324.98
Burnley	6.70	14.35	40.08	43.69	308.98	413.80
Pendle	18.80	2.80	37.06	80.72	278.65	418.03
Rossendale	–	9.72	46.04	41.71	163.67	261.14
LANCASHIRE	140.93	164.22	647.04	1,813.76	4,462.42	7,408.37

Source: Lancashire County Council.

show a very different car ownership situation to that of 1981, with a significant increase in the number of cars per household, including ownership in East Lancashire.

12.32   The total number of vehices licensed in Lancashire has grown from 373,000 in 1975 to 552,000 in 1985, 571,000 in 1987 and latest available figures from the DTp put the total for 1988 at 604,000 vehicles. This represents a rise of 62% in vehicle ownership in the County from 1975 to 1988. Of the 1988 total, 495,000 were cars (Department of Transport, 1989c).

12.33   The 1981 Census revealed that 55% of Lancashire's workforce travels to work by car (compared with a national average of 50%). This is despite a slightly lower rate of car ownership in Lancashire. Commuter belts can be defined around the major urban centres of Lancaster, Blackpool, Preston, Blackburn and Burnley. Commuting by car is especially important for those living in the villages of the Ribble Valley, Central Lancashire and the Fylde. The area around Lancaster tends to form a distinct commuter zone with especially high values being found in Bolton-le-Sands. Commuting by car is also important in areas close to the County's southern boundary with journeys to Merseyside and Greater Manchester. Lowest travel to work by car areas are in the more isolated rural areas and in the towns themselves (Lancashire County Council, 1984).

Heavy Goods Vehicles

12.34   Of the 1988 total vehicles licensed in Lancashire 109,000 are either heavy goods vehicles (HGVs) or vans (Department of Transport, 1989c). There is no precise estimate of HGV ownership in the County. The number of licensed HGVs in the UK increased by more than 6% between 1987 and 1988, and since 1982 HGV traffic has grown by 3–4% per year. Although there has been recent growth in HGV numbers, at the end of 1988 there were still less HGVs on Britain's roads than in the peak year of 1979 (Lancashire County Council, 1990a).

12.35   There has also been a change in composition of goods vehicle stock with a decrease in the number of medium sized vehicles (smallest HGVs from 7.5–16 tonnes gross vehicle weight) but an increase in the number of small vehicles between 3.5 and 7.5 tonnes gross vehicle weight (Lancashire County Council, 1990a).

12.36   In 1983, the Government raised the maximum weight of lorries and their loads from 32.5 tonnes on four axles to 38 tonnes on five axles. It was initially thought there would be a substantial increase in the numbers of the heaviest articulated lorries. However, this did not occur because by increasing the capacity of lorries without any increase in size, fewer lorries were able to do the same job (Lancashire County Council, 1990a). Heavier lorries will be allowed on Britain's roads from the beginning of 1999 following a European Community decision made in 1989 (Department of Transport, 1990).

Table 134   Car Ownership by District in Lancashire. 1981

District	Cars per Household	% of Households Owning Cars
Lancaster	0.74	59
Wyre	0.86	66
Ribble Valley	1.02	73
Blackpool	0.61	51
Fylde	0.90	68
Preston	0.65	52
South Ribble	0.92	72
West Lancashire	0.92	69
Chorley	0.90	68
Blackburn	0.61	50
Hyndburn	0.65	54
Burnley	0.61	50
Pendle	0.68	54
Rossendale	0.71	56
LANCASHIRE	0.75	59

Source: Lancashire County Council (1988a)

Note: England and Wales—0.78 and 60.5%

Taxis

12.37   There are a total of 3,437 Hackney Carriages and private hire vehicles licensed with District Councils in Lancashire and an analysis of their distribution amongst the 14 Districts is shown in Figure 174. Blackpool (736) has by far the highest number of licensed taxis in the County, and Ribble Valley the lowest (49).

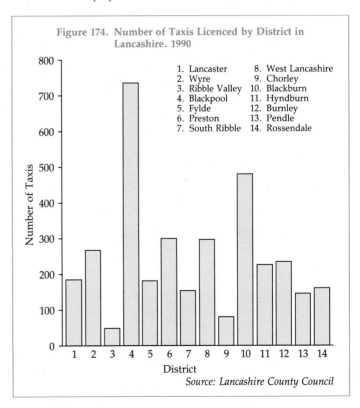

Figure 174. Number of Taxis Licenced by District in Lancashire. 1990

1. Lancaster
2. Wyre
3. Ribble Valley
4. Blackpool
5. Fylde
6. Preston
7. South Ribble
8. West Lancashire
9. Chorley
10. Blackburn
11. Hyndburn
12. Burnley
13. Pendle
14. Rossendale

Source: Lancashire County Council

Figure 175
Bus Network Map of Lancashire. 1990

1. Lancaster
2. Wyre
3. Ribble Valley
4. Blackpool
5. Fylde
6. Preston
7. South Ribble

8. West Lancashire
9. Chorley
10. Blackburn
11. Hyndburn
12. Burnley
13. Pendle
14. Rossendale

—— Bus roads

● Towns or villages served

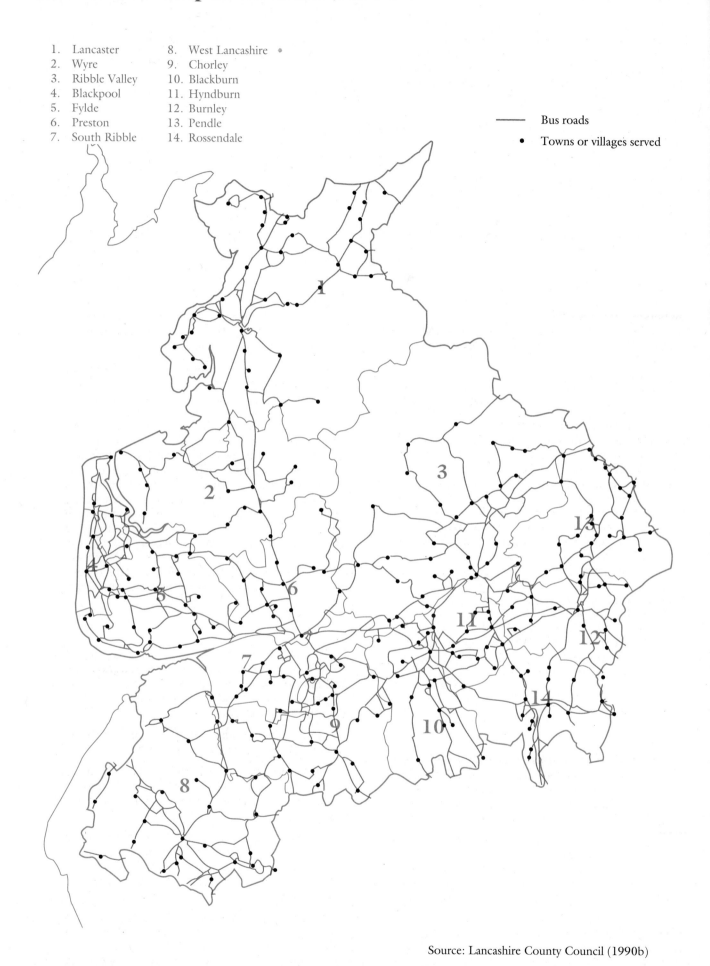

Source: Lancashire County Council (1990b)

Buses

12.38   Bus routes on the road network are shown in Figure 175. Not surprisingly, it shows a concentration of routes into urban areas, with a paucity in the countryside. East Lancashire is well served, and the north of the County far less so. In rural areas community transport schemes help to compensate for the lack of conventional bus services. Such schemes operate in Lancaster, West Lancashire and Pendle (Lancashire County Council, 1990a).

12.39   The 1981 Census revealed that 16% of people in Lancashire use public transport to get to work, 55% use car and 20% walk to work. More than nine in ten of those who use public transport travel to work by bus (Lancashire County Council, 1984). So bus is by far the most important means of public transport in Lancashire (Lancashire County Council, 1988a).

12.40   Wards with the highest proportion of users of public transport are in urban areas where car ownership rates are below average and bus networks well developed. This applies particularly in Preston, Blackburn, Darwen, Accrington, Burnley and the Rossendale Valley. Use of public transport also exceeds the national average in parts of Blackpool and Lancaster.

12.41   Until de-regulation in October 1986, services were primarily provided by two private companies and nine Local Authorities, but there are now 115 operators providing bus services in the County. Since the 1950s, there has been a downward trend in bus use. An analysis of the passengers carried by all the main stage carriage bus operators in Lancashire prior to de-regulation between 1976/7 and 1984/5, showed that passenger numbers fell by 29% during this period (Lancashire County Council, 1988a). The downward trend in bus and coach patronage began to level out in the early 1980s, but since then it has again begun to fall (Lancashire County Council, 1990a). No bus patronage figures are available for 1986/89. Since de-regulation bus operators are not obliged to publish such information. However, the County Council supports 291 services operating 5.4 million vehicle miles and carrying 4.5 million passengers a year.

Cycleways and Cycling

*   Segregated cycle routes – these involve physical separation of cyclists from motor vehicles either by means of cycle tracks (exclusive or shared with pedestrians), cycle crossings within junctions, old railway lines and so on;

*   Signed routes along quiet streets – involving no physical separation from motor vehicles but including cycle lanes, signing along quiet streets, or suggested routes along lightly trafficed roads in rural areas for recreational use.

12.43   The length of cycleways by District is shown in Table 135. Not included in these totals is the Lancashire Cycleway, a scenic route totalling 420 km (260 miles) in length, whose route is shown in Figure 168. There are a total of 118 km of dedicated

Table 135 Cycleways in Lancashire. 1990			
District	Segregated Cycle Routes	Routes along Quiet Streets	Total
	(km)	(km)	(km)
Lancaster	20.02	1.64	21.66
Wyre	4.26	6.16	10.42
Fylde	1.40	—	1.40
Preston	4.30	25.70	30.00
South Ribble	11.65	21.35	33.00
West Lancashire	21.80	—	21.80
Pendle	3.50	2.00	5.50
LANCASHIRE	66.93	56.85	123.78

Source: Lancashire County Council.

cycleways in the County. A 3.5 km cycleway linking Preston with Bamber Bridge along a disused railway line is to be implemented soon.

12.44   There are no statistics available relating to the use of the County road network by cyclists. Figures do exist for journey to work use from the 1981 Census; at this time 1.2% of people in Lancashire cycled to work. The majority lived in the western half of the County. Most use occurred in the suburbs of the Fylde and Central Lancashire and the villages of West Lancashire. Noticeable concentrations occurred in Fleetwood, Lytham St. Annes and Leyland. Outside these areas, Garstang, Clitheroe and parts of Morecambe also had above average numbers of cyclists. The determining factors were thought to be availability of employment fairly close to home and flat terrain. Numbers were very low in the Calder and Rossendale Valleys where walking to work was more significant (Lancashire County Council, 1984).

Footpaths and Pedestrians

12.45   Lancashire has a network of 6,466 km of footpaths, bridleways and byways throughout the rural areas of the County. These are defined by the legislation as 'highways' just like roads, but their functions are different:

*   A Public Footpath is a highway over which the public have a right of way on foot only;

*   A Public Bridleway is a highway over which the public have a right of way on foot, cycle and on horseback, possibly with a right to drive animals;

*   A Byway is a highway over which the public have a right of way for vehicular and all other kinds of traffic, but which is used by the public mainly for the purpose for which footpaths and bridleways are used.

Rights of Way are now used primarily for leisure purposes, rather than for commuting between home and work and so on. A breakdown of the Footpath, Bridleway and Byway network by District is given in Table 127 of Chapter 11.

Table 136 Traffic Growth in Parts of Lancashire. 1985/86 to 1988/89	
Screenlines	**Annual Growth (%)**
a) Between Towns	
Blackburn/Preston North–South	5.6
North Rossendale East–West	8.3
Burnley/Pendle East–West	6.6
Fylde North–South	5.6
Preston/Lancaster East–West	6.0
b) Around Towns	
Blackburn	2.3
Burnley	2.3
Lancaster	2.0
Blackpool Urban	0.5

Source: Lancashire County Council (1990a).

12.46 In 1981, 20% of people in Lancashire walked to work, compared with 16% nationally, suggesting a greater physical proximity of workplace and residence. In many urban wards upwards of a quarter, and often more than a third, of residents walked to work. It appears therefore that the closeness of dwellings to factories (a characteristic of Lancashire settlements dating back to the Industrial Revolution) still influences transport mode. However, for the vast majority of people employment is divorced from place of residence and in most areas only a very small proportion of the workforce can walk to work.

Origin and Destination of Road Users

12.47 Analysis of journey to work patterns from 1951–81 shows a pattern of increasing net outward commuting from Lancashire. In 1981, 43,600 people travelled to work to destinations outside the County, whilst 27,400 people came from locations outside the County to work; a net outward workflow balance of more than 16,000. Small net workflow gains to Lancashire were made from Cumbria and Yorkshire but by far the most dominating influences were the conurbations of Greater Manchester and Merseyside.

12.48 In 1981 the majority of residents in employment within the County continued to live and work

Table 137 Motorway Traffic Growth in Lancashire. 1985–89	
County Site	**Annual Growth rate (%)**
M6 Ellel/M55 Woodplumpton	4.9 (1985–1988)
M55 Woodplumpton	5.9 (1986–1988)
M65 South of Brierfield Link	12.8 (1986–1989)

Source: Lancashire County Council (1990a).

in the same District. Overall, more than 70% of Lancashire's work trips ended within the District of origin, although there were some sizeable variations between Districts. At one extreme was Lancaster, a very self-contained District, with well over 90% of residents in employment working within the District itself. On the other hand, less than half the employed residents of South Ribble actually worked within the District (Lancashire County Council, 1988a).

12.49 Results of more up-to-date roadside surveys carried out by the County Council suggest that the majority of trips (55%) by road involve journeys which start and finish within the boundaries of Lancashire. Some 30% of trips start in Lancashire and terminate elsewhere or come into the County from origins outside whilst an estimated 15% of journeys, mostly on motorways, both start and finish outside Lancashire.

Road Traffic

12.50 The use of the road network by all vehicles generates traffic which is monitored in the County by use of screenline and cordon counts at specific sites (see 'Monitoring'). Existing traffic flows on the County road network are shown in Figure 173. In terms of the volume of traffic, the most heavily used road in Lancashire is the M6 Preston By-pass which carried 89,000 vehicles on an average day in 1989 (Lancashire County Council, 1990d). In 1974, 46,000 vehicles a day and in 1986 74,000 vehicles a day used this road (Lancashire County Council, 1988a). The growth in traffic over the 12 year period between 1974 and 1986 totalled 61% and for the three year period between 1986 and 1989 traffic growth totalled 20%.

12.51 Traffic growth at Lancashire's screenlines from 1985/86 to 1988/89 is summarised in Table 136. Indications are that traffic between Lancashire towns has grown faster than the national average and has been particularly high in North East Lancashire. The figures from screenlines around towns suggest that traffic growth within main urban areas is less than between towns. It is likely that this is partly a reflection of the growth of major out of town developments, which cater exclusively for car-borne trade, and partly an increasing mobility of the workforce (Lancashire County Council, 1990a).

12.52 Table 137 shows traffic growth rates on Lancashire's motorways. Annual counts are made at these sites. The high growth rate on the M65 reflects the re-direction of motor vehicle trips on the major road network of North East Lancashire following the opening of the eastern extension of the M65 to Colne early in 1989 (Lancashire County Council, 1990a).

12.53 The actual volume of traffic, however, is not the best indicator of the performance of the road network. This can best be illustrated by relating the volume of traffic using the road to the maximum volume of traffic that the road is able to carry without congestion arising. The maximum uncongested traffic flow level, known as the design capacity of the road, is defined in criteria laid down by the DTp. Overloading of the road network leads to road safety and environmental problems.

Congestion

12.54 Recent traffic growth in the County has resulted in the exacerbation of existing traffic problems and the emergence of new problems. Demographic and economic changes in the County have created problems which were not apparent 20 years ago.

12.55 Although car ownership levels are lower in North East Lancashire than other parts of the County, traffic has grown faster here since 1979 than elsewhere. This has worsened existing problems and created new ones on roads in the area. Roadspace in North East Lancashire is restricted by topography, in contrast to the flatter areas of Central and North Lancashire where new road building solutions to traffic problems have been easier to carry out.

12.56 In North East Lancashire, there are many important roads which pass through built-up areas for much of their lengths. Through-traffic is forced to compete with local traffic, average speeds are lower, and congestion and accidents are likely to occur. The most serious traffic problems in North East Lancashire have always been associated with east-west movement of traffic. The opening of the M65 from Blackburn to Nelson has eased the situation, but localised problems still exist.

12.57 Within North East Lancashire towns the most serious congestion occurs in Blackburn together with peak hour problems in other smaller towns. However, work has started on the Blackburn Inner Relief Road and the M65 to M6 link has been given the go-ahead by the Secretaries of State. Both will help relieve problems in Blackburn.

12.58 Recent economic development in Lancashire has been predominantly in the Central and North Lancashire areas and it is here that population levels have stayed constant or grown (see Chapter 2), whereas there has been a decline in North East Lancashire. Population growth is centred on the Districts of Chorley, Fylde, Lancaster, Preston, South Ribble and West Lancashire. Car ownership is generally higher here than North East Lancashire and these factors create adverse conditions on some parts of the road network.

12.59 In the last ten years, road traffic associated with the Ports of Fleetwood and Heysham has grown substantially and this has led to increasing pressure on the road links serving the Ports. Environmental problems have been exacerbated by the high proportion of HGV traffic involved. Traffic problems in Lancaster result from a combination of its rôle as the main service centre for North Lancashire, the lack of a suitable link from Morecambe and Heysham to the M6 and the problems of constructing new links in the centre of an historic town.

12.60 Serious traffic congestion also occurs at times within Blackpool. Problems are particularly acute during the summer holiday period and during the Illuminations.

12.61 In Central Lancashire, Preston is the largest town and heavy commuter movements along its main radial routes cause serious congestion at peak times. There is still peak period congestion in Leyland primarily associated with major employers near the town centre. Although the A6 through Chorley has been partly by-passed, and parts of the town centre pedestrianised, there are still unsatisfactory conditions for pedestrians and traffic on the major shopping street along the A6.

12.62 A considerable amount of road building has been carried out by the Central Lancashire New Town Development Corporation to cater for the growth in population and industry since the New Town was designated in 1970. Commuting flows within the New Town areas, in particular the area between Preston and Leyland, are very heavy.

12.63 The two main urban areas in West Lancashire are Ormskirk and Skelmersdale New Town. The Skelmersale Road Network as approved in the Town's Development Plan is now virtually complete. Ormskirk lies at the intersection of two primary routes and on market days and at holiday times there is much delay, congestion and pedestrian/vehicular conflict. However, a scheme to by-pass Ormskirk is included in the DTp's road programme.

Rail

12.64 The rail network in Lancashire is shown in Figure 176 and a statistical breakdown in Table 138. The rail network totals 326.4 km within the County boundary.

12.65 The electrified West Coast Main Line from London-Glasgow is the central axis from which local lines provide east-west communications. Lines run from Preston to Blackpool North and Blackpool South, Ormskirk, Manchester and Colne; from Blackburn to Manchester and Hellifield; from Carnforth to Skipton and Barrow-in-Furness and from Lancaster to Morecambe. There are 57 stations in the passenger network and 17 private sidings for freight (Figure 176) (Railfreight, pers. comm).

12.66 British Rail has a major investment programme for the West Coast Main Line amounting to nearly £100 million up to 1992 for new locomotives, coaches and travel centres and has recently announced a £750 million 10-year plan for new trains, better signalling and track upgrading. (British Rail, 1990b).

12.67 Two new rail stations have been opened in the County since 1986, at Blackpool Pleasure Beach and Manchester Road, Burnley. In conjunction with BR the County Council has carried out an initial review of potential new stations in Lancashire. About 29 sites have been identified where there may be the potential for new stations (Lancashire County Council, 1990a).

12.68 A three year, £3 million programme of improvements to stations under the title 'Lancashire Lines' is also being carried out, jointly funded by British Rail and the County Council. Environmental improvements along rail corridors

Table 138	The Rail Network in Lancashire. 1990	
Route		Length (km)
London–Glasgow West Coast Mainline		68.5
Preston–Blackpool N		26.53
Preston–Blackpool S (Branch)		19.71
Preston–Ormskirk		27.76
Preston–Manchester		18.51
Preston–Colne		41.44
Blackburn–Clitheroe–Hellifield		33.00
Blackburn–Manchester		13.28
Burnley–Todmorden		10.00
Southport–Manchester		13.68
Liverpool–Ormskirk		5.23
Lancaster–Morecambe–Heysham		14.08
Carnforth–Skipton		15.69
Carnforth–Barrow-in-Furness		6.03
Goods only lines		13.00
LANCASHIRE		326.44

Source: British Rail (1990a).

are also planned under the title of 'East Lancashire Line Railside Revival'. Park and ride facilities have been established at seven stations between 1986 and 1989 (Lancashire County Council, 1990a). These are: Adlington, Ormskirk, Wennington, Bare Lane, Leyland, Lostock Hall and Bamber Bridge.

12.69   A new passenger service has started to operate on Saturdays only on the Blackburn-Hellifield line between Clitheroe, Blackburn and Preston. Services on the Blackpool-Preston-Manchester line have been improved with the introduction of Sprinter Units allocated in 1987. Transport links to West Yorkshire have been improved by the introduction of a direct service between Blackpool, Preston and Leeds via the East Lancashire towns in 1986. Following concerted action by local government, including the County Council and local pressure groups, the closure of the Settle-Carlisle line for regular services, proposed by British Rail in 1986, was averted and now continues to run profitably.

Table 139	Rail Freight Transport Through Lancashire Sidings. 1989/90		
Direction	No. of Trains	No. of Wagons	Freight in Tonnes
Inward	1,334	18,875	816,368
Outward	170	7,572	344,766
TOTAL	1,504	26,447	1,161,134

Source: Railfreight (pers. Comm)

12.70   The County Council is undertaking a comprehensive study into the potential for restoring a regular passenger service on the Blackburn–Hellifield line. The Government has also given the go-ahead for a Manchester Airport Rail Link which will result in one direct service per hour to and from Preston and Blackpool North. A stop has also been introduced at Lancaster for the Stockport–Heysham boat service in 1989 (Lancashire County Council, 1990a).

12.71   Data are not available from British Rail to show the passenger use of the County rail network, due to commercial confidentiality. However, it is known that around 3.5 million people a year use the West Coast Main Line running through the County, and this forms more than one third of Inter City's total customers (British Rail, 1990b). It can be said, also, that British Rail passenger traffic is enjoying a boom period if one compares the results of the last four years with the deteriorating situation in the early 1980s when passenger numbers slumped (Lancashire County Council, 1990a).

12.72   This growth is in spite of fare increases which have recently been above the rate of inflation. Whilst recent passenger growth has increased fare receipts, British Rail still find it difficult to maintain the investment necessary to provide a modern, efficient service. British Rail have to operate within financial guidelines set by Government, which provides a subsidy for the whole of the passenger system. This was reduced by 25% between 1986/87 and 1989/90 (Lancashire County Council, 1990a). Inter City services ceased to qualify for grant after 1987/88 and this sector now shows an operating profit. Confidence in Inter City services is shown by the investment plans for the West Coast Main Line announced by British Rail.

12.73   It is possible to say more about rail freight use of the County network. In 1954, 54% of freight in the UK (millions of tonnes) was carried by rail and only 38% by road (Department of Transport, 1986). In 1974, 18% was carried by rail and 65% by road. In 1985 only 9% of goods were moved by rail and 60% were moved by road (Lancashire County Council, 1988a). The general trend has, therefore, been for freight to be transferred from rail to road. The growth in pipeline and coastal shipping transport pushed road freight down from 65% to 60% comparing 1974 with 1985.

12.74   There are 17 private sidings in Lancashire where freight is imported to, or exported from, by rail. Three of these (at Carnforth, Blackburn and Bamber Bridge) are publicly available although privately owned (Railfreight, pers. comm.). The movements in and out of these sidings in 1989/90 are summarised in Table 139.

12.75   There is a greater import of freight to private rail sidings in the County than there is out. A large proportion of this tonnage is domestic, and other waste, which arrives at Appley Bridge by train from the Greater Manchester area and is then landfilled into quarries.

Figure 176

Railways, Tramways, Canals, Sea Ports and Airports in Lancashire. 1990

1. Lancaster
2. Wyre
3. Ribble Valley
4. Blackpool
5. Fylde
6. Preston
7. South Ribble
8. West Lancashire
9. Chorley
10. Blackburn
11. Hyndburn
12. Burnley
13. Pendle
14. Rossendale

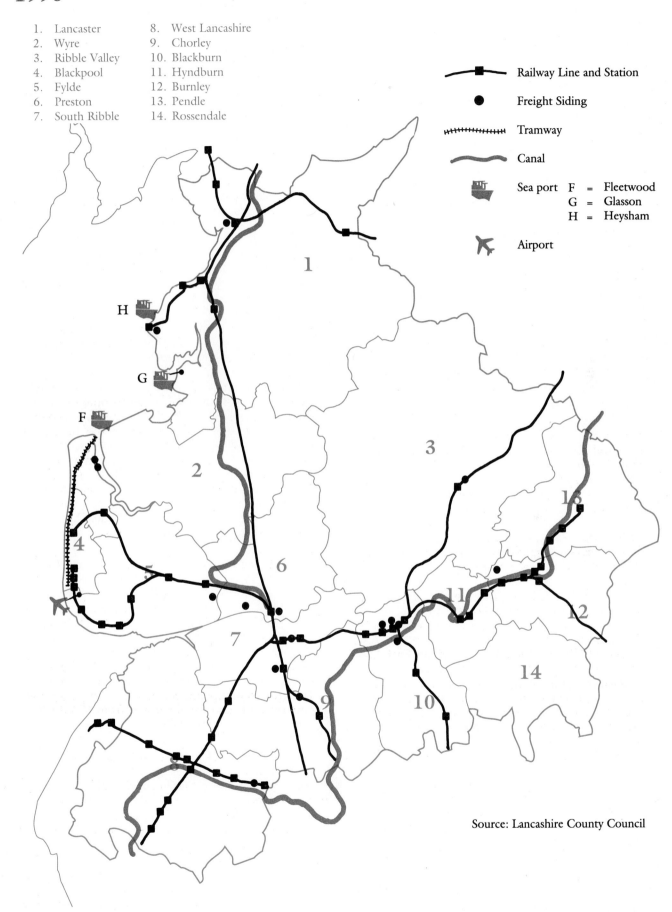

Railway Line and Station

Freight Siding

Tramway

Canal

Sea port   F = Fleetwood
             G = Glasson
             H = Heysham

Airport

Source: Lancashire County Council

Table 140	Traffic Through Lancashire Sea Ports. 1989				
Port	Vessel Movements		Freight Traffic (Tonnes)		Passengers
	Inwards	Outwards	Imports	Exports	
Fleetwood	3,593	3,593	513,625	575,767	52,046
Glasson	388	387	170,111	88,910	0
Heysham	2,315	2,315	824,501	759,389	321,495
LANCASHIRE	6,296	6,295	1,508,237	1,424,066	373,541

Source: Lancaster Port Commission, Sealink Harbours Ltd., Associated British Ports, Isle of Man Steam Packet Company, Pandoro Ltd. (pers. comm.)

Trams

12.76 The Blackpool Tramway is an on-street line running for 18 km from Starr Gate to Fleetwood along Blackpool Promenade. It operates throughout the year but with changes in frequency from trams every 12 minutes during the summer to every 30 minutes during the winter. There are 80 operational cars on the tramway and passenger use during 1988/89 is estimated at 5.4 million people. The Tramway forms an important part of the local transport system in Blackpool but it also has an important economic function as a tourist attraction which, with the Illuminations, helps extend the tourist season well into the autumn.

Canals

12.77 Two canals pass through Lancashire – the Lancaster and the Leeds and Liverpool (Figure 176), giving a total length of 164.8 km. The Lancaster Canal covers 72.3 km from Tewitfield, in the north of the County, to Preston, and has a short branch from Galgate to Glasson Dock. It is land-locked and cannot be reached from the surrounding canal network. Boats can, however, enter from Glasson

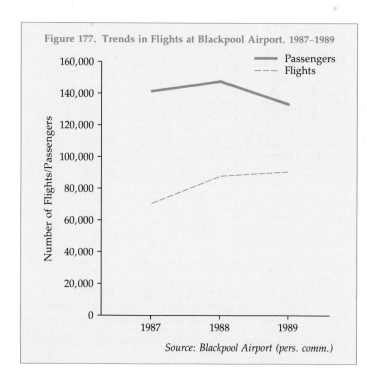

Figure 177. Trends in Flights at Blackpool Airport. 1987–1989

Source: Blackpool Airport (pers. comm.)

Dock where the three mile branch to Galgate provides a link with the sea via the Lune Estuary. There were 800 registered boats on the canal in 1990 (BWB, pers. comm.) A feasibility study is being carried out by the Ribble Link Group to see if the canal can be connected into the river Ribble, and thence to the national system by the river Douglas and Rufford Branch.

12.78 The Leeds and Liverpool Canal runs for 92.5 km from Barnoldswick in Pendle to Downholland Cross in West Lancashire. A branch from Rufford to Tarleton gives access to the Douglas and the open sea. The canal is linked to the rest of the canal network, so that the 929 boats registered on the canal in 1990 (BWB, pers. comm.) are likely to be swelled greatly by holiday traffic. Neither of Lancashire's canals currently carries any freight.

Sea Ports

12.79 Lancashire is served by three commercial ports (Figure 176) – Heysham, Fleetwood and Glasson Dock. Preston closed in 1988 and is now used only by leisure craft. Lancaster's port was important historically but is now used only by small fishing boats.

12.80 Heysham provides a passenger ferry service to the Isle of Man and freight services to the Isle of Man and Ireland. It is also the marine supply base for the Morecambe Gas Field. Fleetwood has a summer-only Isle of Man passenger service and all year freight links to Ireland. Glasson Dock imports and exports freight from the UK and Europe on a smaller scale.

12.81 Traffic through Lancashire's ports is shown in Table 140.

12.82 Fleetwood has a deep-water roll-on/roll-off terminal for freight, but carries less tonnage than Heysham. In recent years, Fleetwood has suffered as a result of changes affecting the ports industry nationally. More efficient methods of handling cargoes have been developed with many goods now being transported in containers. Ships have become much larger and there has been a shift in traffic to the east coast ports which are closer to Europe and the main trade routes.

12.83 Glasson Dock is the smallest port dealing in bulk cargoes, mainly animal feedstuffs. It also imports and exports general cargo, coal, sand and chippings to Europe. The cargoes, after import, are transferred to lorries for road transport throughout the UK.

12.84 Heysham is the largest port in Lancashire and is the principal port in the UK for sailings to the Isle of Man. A year round passenger service is operated whilst freight is taken to the Isle of Man, Belfast and Warrenpoint by three freight companies. All types of general cargo and containers are handled. Trade cars are also exported.

Airports

12.85 The only commercial airport in Lancashire is at Squires Gate, Blackpool. It has regular flights to the Isle of Man, Belfast, Londonderry, Dublin and Jersey and business and holiday flights to Holland,

Majorca and Yugoslavia. A helicopter service operates to the Morecambe Gas Field and there are also various freight charter flights.

12.86   Trends in passenger and freight flights from Blackpool Airport (1987–1989) are shown in Figures 177 and 178. A total of 91,476 transport movements were recorded in 1989, showing a slight increase on the previous two years. A total of 133,902 passengers and 1,424 tonnes of freight passed through the airport in 1989 using both scheduled and charter flights (Blackpool Airport, pers. comm.).

Pipelines and Powerlines

12.87   Oil, gas and ethylene are transported by underground pipeline through the County and electricity is transported via overhead and underground powerlines. The lengths of each are given in Table 141. The total length of pipeline and powerlines is 780 km. Shell UK are anticipating constructing a new ethylene pipeline from north to south through the County roughly along the line of the M6 in 1991, subject to a public inquiry decision. There are also water supply pipelines that run across the County.

Comparison of Transport Infrastructure

12.88   A comparison between the major components of the land and water-based transport network is shown in Figure 179. This is a comparison of infrastructure in terms of lengths of each component and takes no account of traffic. It shows the massive road infrastructure in comparison with rail, cycleways, canals and pipelines. For example, 118 km of dedicated cycleway represents just 1.6% of the 7,408 km of roads in the County. The dominance of roads is explained by the fact that historically the County was criss-crossed by roads long before the canals of the eighteenth century, the railways of the nineteenth century and the airports of the twentieth century set up in competition with road transport.

12.89   In addition, roads have the advantage of being able to cross almost any terrain and have been driven to remote settlements where canals could not have been constructed and where a railway would have been an uneconomic proposition. However, the development of the road network has clearly taken precedence over any other component of the transport network in Lancashire.

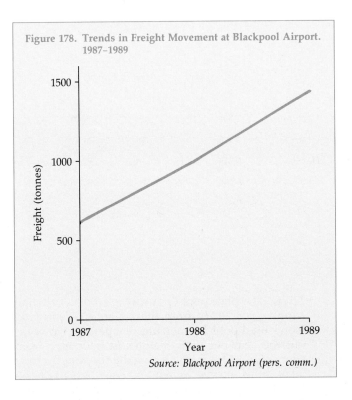

Figure 178. Trends in Freight Movement at Blackpool Airport. 1987–1989

Year

Source: Blackpool Airport (pers. comm.)

Environmental Effects

General

12.90   Transport has major effects on the environment. It accounts for just over a quarter of the nation's energy consumption (Department of

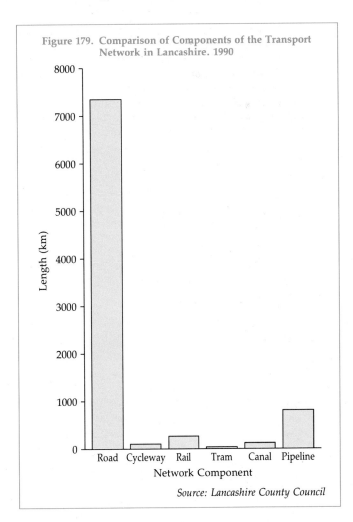

Figure 179. Comparison of Components of the Transport Network in Lancashire. 1990

Source: Lancashire County Council

Table 141	Pipelines and Powerlines in Lancashire. 1990
Item	**Length (km)**
Gas pipeline	399
High Voltage O/H Electricity pylon	229
Ethylene pipeline	89
Oil pipeline	63
LANCASHIRE	780

Source: Lancashire County Council.

Transport, 1989b) and is one of the greatest contributors of gases which add to air pollution and the greenhouse effect (see Chapter 3). There are other effects too. Aircraft noise is a serious problem especially for those that live close to airports (see Chapter 6) and sea transport can cause pollution incidents which damage marine and shore life.

12.91   However, it is roads and cars that are the main cause for concern. Since 1960, our vehicle population has trebled to about 24 million, and car use – in terms of passenger kilometres travelled – has increased too. Over the same period, the use of rail has hardly increased at all, the use of buses and coaches has decreased by 40% and the use of bicycles has halved. (The Observer, 15/4/90).

12.92   Accommodating the growth in demand for road transport, which the Government forecasts will grow by between 83% and 142% by 2025, and alleviating the congestion that is already bringing the road network to a halt, is a major challenge. The choice would seem to lie between building more and more new roads to keep pace with the increase in demand, or putting a stop to all new road building, because new roads facilitate the growth of traffic. Given that society shows no signs of wishing to surrender the mobility provided by motoring, but also wishes to see the environment improved, the solution must be somewhere between these two extremes. The major issue is where the roads will go. The Government has announced its intentions to spend £12 billion over the next ten years on widening many existing motorways and trunk roads and building new ones (Department of Transport, 1989a).

12.93   This road programme, and other roads planned to be built or improved within the County, will have major environmental effects. Some will be beneficial. New by-passes and roads relieve communities of heavy traffic and improve the quality of life of those affected. They can relieve congestion and, by doing so, reduce vehicle emissions. They also provide miles of road and motorway verges that become linear nature reserves; along with new roads come much new landscaping and tree planting, which can develop into wildlife habitat. One of the most important beneficial effect of new roads is the overall reduction in accidents that they produce. This is clearly demonstrated by a long term study of accidents on the A6 between Preston and Lancaster before the construction of the M6, compared with accidents on both roads together after the opening of the motorway. The number of accidents on both roads, combined, in 1989 is significantly lower than on the A6 alone prior to the opening of the M6. Furthermore, non-motorised road users, such as pedestrians and cyclists, have benefited greatly.

12.94   However, the adverse environmental effects of roads; damage to countryside and towns, pollution and accidents caused by road traffic, the diversion of development away from towns, are of great concern. Studies of the environmental effects of new schemes have to be carried out by Government and highway authorities in order to ascertain what the environmental impacts will be and whether these are of sufficient magnitude to stop or

ameliorate the scheme. Such studies are called environmental assessments and are standard practice now on all major transport projects (Department of the Environment, 1989). Adverse impacts are not restricted to new road construction. Many similar problems arise from the construction and widening of railways (with the exception of pollution). Indeed, the degree of adverse affect is often greater with railways due to the requirement for flatter gradients and easier curves.

12.95   Motorways and trunk roads are not subject to planning control but are approved under procedures set out in the Highways Act 1980. The DTp may consult the public about alternative routes before selecting a preferred route for a new road. The Highways (Assessment of Environmental Effects) Regulations 1988 require an environmental statement (the document resulting from an environmental assessment) to be published at the same time as the draft orders for the preferred route.

12.96   Roads developed by local authorities and private developers require planning permission and are subject to the Town and Country Planning (Assessment of Environmental Effects) Regulations 1988 which apply to two separate lists of projects. Most roads belong to the Schedule 2 list of projects where an environmental assessment is only required if the project is likely to give rise to "significant environmental effects" (Department of the Environment, 1989). Schedule 2 also includes other transport infrastructure projects like oil and gas pipelines, tramways and aqueducts.

12.97   To date in Lancashire, environmental statements have only been prepared for the Shell ethylene pipeline, the M65–M6 Blackburn Southern By-pass and the widening of the M6 from Junction 30 to 32 (the latter being part of the £12 billion package announced by the Government). The assessment of environmental effects can be conveniently addressed under the following categories, which are based on the above Regulations:

* Effects on Human Beings, Buildings and Manmade Features;
* Effects on Flora, Fauna and Geology;
* Effects on Land;
* Effects on Water;
* Effects on Air and Climate;
* Other Indirect and Secondary Effects.

Effects on Human Beings, Buildings and Manmade Features

12.98   This includes the effects during construction and when the road is in operation. It includes the visual impact on the surrounding area and landscape, the levels and effects of noise, the effects on buildings through pollutants, visual intrusion or vibration, accidents and severance. These will be considered in turn.

12.99   Wherever possible, a new road should merge unobtrusively into the countryside it crosses. This may involve using natural features, such as rises or woodlands to conceal the road. Or it may be a matter of choosing a sensitive alignment that flows with the landscape, rather than being imposed upon it (Department of Transport, 1988). There is very little information available to allow an assessment of the success of this strategy in Lancashire.

12.100   The noise impact of road traffic has been discussed in Chapter 6. The police report that in 1989, 90 vehicle owners were prosecuted for noise offences under the Road Traffic Acts. This compares with 101 in 1988 and 79 in 1987 (Lancashire Constabulary, pers. comm.).

12.101   The County Council as Highway Authority has duties to deal with any problems of noise that might be caused by the use of new highways. The Noise Insulation Regulations 1975 enable residents subjected to additional noise at, or above, a specified level because of new or improved roads, to benefit from grants for double glazing, supplementary ventilation and, where appropriate, double or insulated doors.

12.102   Within six months of the opening of a new highway the Highway Authority publishes a notice detailing rights under the Regulations, and a map on which are shown all properties qualifying for insulation. Any householder has a right to appeal against non-inclusion for insulation. In addition, there are discretionary powers available under the Regulations to provide insulation against noise caused by the construction of new highways.

12.103   It is difficult to predict, with accuracy, the levels of construction noise at particular sites but, if it is shown that properties are reasonably certain to qualify for insulation against construction plant noise, then these can be made at an early stage. An alternative to providing insulation is to offer residents, who would be seriously disturbed by construction operations, short term temporary accommodation elsewhere. This has recently been offered to residents in Preston affected by the construction of the Penwortham By-Pass.

12.104   In the past five years, the County Council has carried out Noise Insulation connected with the following twelve schemes:

* Burnley Inner Relief Road Phase I, Burnley;
* Hyndburn Link Road, Hyndburn;
* Bamber Bridge By-Pass Phase III, South Ribble;
* Chorley Town Centre By-Pass Phase I, Chorley;
* Link to North Valley Road, Colne, Pendle;
* Chorley Town Centre By-Pass Phase II, Chorley;
* Western Primary Route, Moss Lane to Pope Lane, South Ribble;
* Western Primary Route, Cop Lane to Pope Lane, South Ribble;
* Penwortham By-Pass, Strand Road to Cop Lane, South Ribble/Preston;
* A671 Padiham Road Improvement, Burnley;
* Ingol District Distributor, Preston;
* Eden Street, William Street Improvement, South Ribble.

12.105   Many towns and cities have already suffered from road construction, with some historic buildings demolished. Historic towns and cities, like Lancaster, were not built to cope with the amount of traffic that now passes through their centres. Such traffic causes vibration, especially if road surfaces are uneven, possibly leading to minor damage like cracking of plaster and brittle material. However, extensive research on a range of different building types has not shown a direct link between exposure to traffic vibration and structural defects (Department of Transport, 1990). One solution to the problem is to build by-passes to remove heavy traffic from town centres.

12.106   The atmospheric pollutants resulting from vehicle emissions, and their effect on health, are discussed in Chapter 3. Their effects on human beings has been little documented in the County, although the Lancaster University Epidemological Unit is to report on some aspects in due course. Briefly, evidence suggests lead from petrol can impair brain functions, especially in children (see Chapter 3). Carbon monoxide is a poisonous gas, whilst nitrogen oxides and hydrocarbons (under conditions of bright sunlight) combine to form ozone and photochemical smogs. These can aggravate heart disease, bronchitis and emphysema in humans. Lancaster recorded high levels of low-level ozone in 1986.

12.107   Community severance is the separation of residents from places of work and facilities and services they use within the community as a result of changes in road patterns and traffic levels. There are no data on the number of people that have been affected by such severance in the County. On the other hand, the removal of 'through-traffic' from urban areas can improve communication across road corridors and improve safety and the state of local air.

12.108   During most of the last decade, road traffic accidents in Lancashire have declined slowly. However, the figures for 1988 and 1989 show a disturbing reversal of this with the total for 1989 rising to 7,969 casualties. This is an increase of 6.8% of all casualties over the base point (defined as the average of the years 1981–85).

12.109   Figure 180 shows the number of casualties for each District for 1989. Preston records the highest number of casualties (992) and Ribble Valley the lowest (301). All Districts showed an increase in numbers of casualties in 1989 over 1988 except Rossendale, Hyndburn and Blackpool. Blackburn showed the largest rise of 23.4% over the previous year (Lancashire County Council, 1990c).

12.110   The number of casualties by road user group is shown in Figure 181. Car users formed 51.8% of the 1989 total, pedestrians 20.6%, motorcyclists 12.4% and pedal cyclists 8.1%. Others, (a group including goods vehicles, PSV and miscellaneous road users), formed 7.1% of the total. The number of pedestrian, cyclist and motorcyclist casualties decreased up until 1987, followed by a slight increase in 1988 and 1989. Car user casualties, however, have shown a rising trend since 1985 and add up to a total of 29.5% since 1981 (Lancashire County Council, 1990c).

12.111   A year round analysis of casualty figures shows that casualties are at a minimum in February and maximum in May. By day, casualties are at a maximum on Fridays and a minimum on Tuesdays. During the day there is a marked peak for casualties

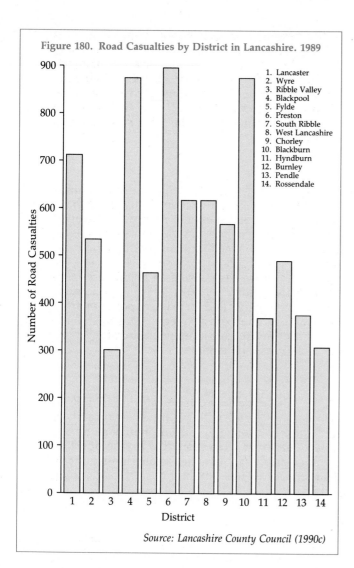

Figure 180. Road Casualties by District in Lancashire. 1989

1. Lancaster
2. Wyre
3. Ribble Valley
4. Blackpool
5. Fylde
6. Preston
7. South Ribble
8. West Lancashire
9. Chorley
10. Blackburn
11. Hyndburn
12. Burnley
13. Pendle
14. Rossendale

Source: Lancashire County Council (1990c)

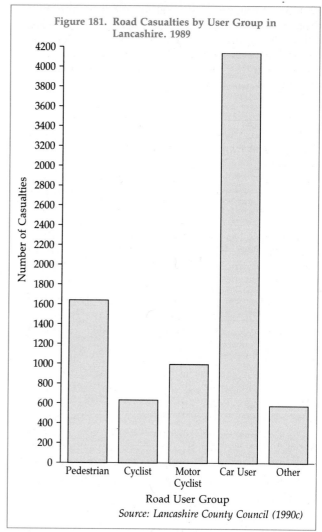

Figure 181. Road Casualties by User Group in Lancashire. 1989

Source: Lancashire County Council (1990c)

Table 142	Nature Conservation Sites Affected by Road Proposals in Lancashire. 1990

Site name	District	Status	Road Proposal	Extent of damage	Agent
Boilton Wood	Preston	SSSI	M6 widening, Junctions 30–32	Loss of small part of SSSI	DTP
Cuerden Valley Park and Walton Banks Wood	Chorley	Country Park	M65–M6 Blackburn Southern By-pass	Passes through N. end of Park	DTp
Stanworth Wood	Blackburn	Ancient woodland	M65–M6 Blackburn Southern By-pass	Cuts through wood	DTp
Mammon Wood	Ribble Valley	Ancient woodland	A59 Mellor Brook By-pass	Cuts through wood	DTp
Wallett's Wood	Chorley	Ancient woodland	Chorley Western By-pass	Will have to cut through wood	LCC

Source: Lancashire County Council.

between 8.00–9.00 am, a slight decrease in casualties in the early/mid afternoon and a sharp decrease after midnight. Some 72% of all casualties occur in urban areas, 45% occur on 'A' roads, 30% on unclassified roads, 14% on 'B' roads, 6% on 'C' roads and 5% on motorways (Lancashire County Council, 1990c).

Effects on Flora, Fauna and Geology

12.112 Every 1.6 km of motorway takes 10 ha of land. Roads have already been built over much valuable countryside and open space. In a response to the Government White Paper, 'Roads to Prosperity', nine leading environmental groups identified threats to AONB, SSSI, ancient monuments and historic buildings posed by the £12 billion road building programme (Council for the Protection of Rural England *et al.* 1989). The Royal Society for Nature Conservation estimate that over 1,500 wildlife sites nationally, will be damaged or destroyed by this programme. One of these sites is Boilton Wood SSSI near Preston, threatened by the widening of the M6. Boilton Wood is affected by this scheme in order to protect an area of herb-rich grassland on the opposite (west) side of the M6 at this point. Four other sites of nature conservation value in Lancashire are also currently under threat from road scheme proposals contained in the Lancashire Structure Plan (1987) or TPP. They are listed in Table 142.

12.113 There can be positive wildlife benefits, though. Many highway verges now provide habitats for species which were once common in our countryside. Clearly in all cases roads have to be planned carefully in order to protect the flora and fauna of the County.

Effects on Land

12.114 The physical effects of road building can change local topography by creating cuttings and embankments. They also have more fundamental effects on land use and land resources; sometimes positively, sometimes negatively. For example, new roads may open up land for new development. Alternatively, they can take agricultural land, sterilise mineral resources or have effects on surrounding land uses. These factors are taken into account on an individual road scheme basis but County-wide data for effects on land has not been collated.

12.115 The Land Compensation Act 1973 confers a right of compensation for depreciation of the value of certain interests in land or premises resulting from physical factors caused by the use of new highways. The factors involved are noise, vibration, smell, fumes, smoke, artificial lighting or the discharge on to land of any solid or liquid substances. On completion of all new schemes, a notice is published advising members of the public of their right to claim compensation under the provisions of this Act. During the last five years, claims have been considered for the following schemes in Lancashire:

* Blackpool Central Railway Route, Blackpool/ Fylde (69);
* Calder Valley Motorway M65, Nelson to Colne, Pendle (9);
* Link to North Valley Road, Colne, Pendle (12);
* Western Primary Route (Pope Lane to Moss Lane), South Ribble (3);
* Bamber Bridge By-Pass Phases I and II, South Ribble (120);
* Ingol District Distributor, Preston (1);
* Fulwood District Distributor, Preston (16).

The number of claims (230 in all) are given in brackets.

Effects on Water

12.116 Road building can have effects on the drainage pattern in an area, affecting water-courses and groundwater levels. This can also affect wetland wildlife habitats whose plants may be dependent upon a high water table. Once built, roads can also affect water quality in an area because of pollutants entering streams from run-off from the road surface. Rock salt and urea (occasionally) are used for de-icing the road surface. A total of between 30,000–50,000 tonnes of road salt is used on highways in the County in an average year. Use varies according to winter conditions. Some of this rock salt ends up in storm water sewers which lead to sewage treatment works, before being discharged into the County's rivers. A large proportion, however, filters through the ground, or discharges directly to watercourses.

12.117 None of the sea transport vessels operating out of Lancashire's three sea ports carry oil products, so the risks of marine pollution from oil spills is reduced. However, vessels from other ports using the Irish Sea could cause a pollution accident affecting the Lancashire coast. The incident involving the MV Ardlough in 1988 demonstrated vividly how cargo lost from shipping in the Irish Sea can be brought long distances by the tide to Lancashire's shoreline.

Effects on Air and Climate

12.118 The burning of fuels in road vehicles creates pollution of various kinds, and these have been elaborated in Chapter 3. A study is currently being undertaken into vehicle emissions arising from the newly-opened Kirkham-Wesham By-Pass. Aircraft also produce pollutants. However, the combusion processes inside a jet engine are more efficient than those in most land-based internal combustion engines and there is less pollution from unburnt fuel. There are also regulations to limit the emission of smoke from jet engined aircraft (Department of Transport, 1988).

Other Indirect and Secondary Effects

12.119 These can arise due to traffic (road, rail, air or water) associated with the transport project, or from the extraction, and consumption of materials, water, energy or other resources by the development. Quarrying for road aggregates, and its attendant environmental implications, is a common secondary effect of road or rail building.

Monitoring

12.120 The County Council, as highway authority, carries out a wide variety of monitoring operations to ensure that the existing highway network is functioning satisfactorily and to assess the need for, and the environmental impact of, new or improved roads.

12.121 At the planning application stage for a new or improved road there is firstly an evaluation of whether a formal Environmental Assessment is needed to accompany the application. Environmental Assessment is now mandatory for a number of (Schedule 1) developments and discretionary on a larger list of (Schedule 2) developments. Most developments for transport in the County fall into the second category and the County Council takes a 'common sense' view treating each case on its merits. Secondly, if a full Environmental Assessment is not required, the County Council will still carry out a study of the effect of the new road route on landscape, ecology, heritage, etc. Thirdly, the County Council will produce a landscape plan to accompany the planning application and help mitigate environmental effects of the road.

12.122 Other monitoring data gathered by the County Council includes traffic data, where both the volume of traffic using a length of road and (when assessing the need for new roads), its origins and destinations are recorded. The County Council undertakes, on behalf of the DTp, regular classified counts for three days each month at five sites in Lancashire. At approximately 350 other sites, (selected as part of a six-yearly rolling programme), the

County Council conducts annually classified counts for one day. This information is used to calculate trends in traffic growth at both regional and national levels. Information on origins and destinations is obtained by directly questioning a representative sample of motorists using the road. Approximately 20 roadside interview surveys are carried out each year.

12.123 The Lancashire Constabulary supplies details of all personal injury and reported damage-only accidents each month. Analysis of this accident data is used to identify sites where remedial measures are required to improve road safety. The County Council produces an annual Road Safety Plan (Lancashire County Council, 1990c).

12.124 The County Council carries out regular surveys of the surface condition of its existing roads. An ice-warning/weather prediction system was installed in 1987/88 to provide more reliable data to aid responses to emergency conditions in winter and reduce the unnecessary use of road de-icing salt.

12.125 The County Council operates a Highways Laboratory which carries out soil surveys in connection with road and bridge design and testing during construction. The Highways Laboratory will also carry out surveys of traffic noise levels before and after the construction of a new highway. The results help to assess whether any adjacent properties qualify for sound insulation measures. The laboratory also records ground vibration arising from construction works.

12.126 There are 1,350 bridges in Lancashire which carry public roads. In order to ensure that all bridges comply with DTp standards, it has been established that 1,147 of these bridges will need to be assessed. In addition, there are approximately 382 private bridges carrying public roads, most of which are owned by British Rail or the British Waterways Board. It is estimated that at least 344 of these private bridges will need to be assessed. The County Council, as agents for the DTp, is also responsible for the maintenance of 478 bridges on trunk roads.

Traffic Management

12.127 In addition to the construction, or improvement, of roads to relieve the effects of traffic, traffic management measures are an important means of limiting conflict between different classes of vehicles and pedestrians. The use of Traffic Regulation Orders to control waiting, to impose speed limits or one-way orders, to prevent particular turning movements or to prohibit certain vehicles by virtue of their weight or width are numerous in the County. However, the following measures are of particular interest. Their locations are shown by number on Figure 182.

12.128 Measures to prevent the passage of heavy goods vehicles (apart from those requiring access to premises), known as 'lorry controls', have been introduced in the following areas:

1. Lancaster;
2. Gregson Lane (Walton-le-Dale) Zone;
3. Bolton-by-Bowland Zone;
4. Pendle Hill Zone;
5. Bashall Zone;
6. Kellet Lane (Carnforth) Zone;
7. Heysham.

12.129 Measures to prohibit vehicles from parts of town centres, either permanently or for certain hours of the day, to enable pedestrians to enjoy the benefits of traffic-free shopping, have been introduced in:

8. Accrington;
9. Blackburn;
10. Blackpool;
11. Burnley;
12. Chorley;
13. Lancaster;
14. Leyland;
15. Lostock Hall;
16. Morecambe;
17. Nelson;
18. Ormskirk;
19. Preston.

12.130 Traffic signals are an effective way of controlling conflicting traffic movements at busy junctions. In urban areas, where there are many sets of traffic signals in close proximity, greater efficiency can be obtained by linking them to a central computer. This has been done in the following towns:

20. Blackpool;
21. Lancaster;
22. Preston.

12.131 In order to reduce the impact of fast-moving traffic in residential areas, various traffic calming measures can be introduced. Road humps, mini-roundabouts, reduction in the width of the carriageway and use of contrasting surfacing material, (rumble strips) have been used in various locations, including:

23. Blackburn (Brookhouse);
24. Blackpool (Layton);
25. Cleveleys;
26. Clitheroe;
27. Freckleton;
28. Mellor;
29. Nelson;
30. Preston (Broughton).

12.132 The integration of land use and transportation planning is an essential step in minimising the environmental impact of traffic generating proposals. Many major developments generate high volumes of traffic, especially commercial vehicles. Their impact on existing road systems and local communities can be reduced by locating such developments in strategic positions in relation to the road network.

12.133 This process is carried out through the forward planning proposals drawn up by the County and District Councils in Structure and Local Plans and in consultations between planning authorities on individual applications. When the County Council is consulted by District Councils on 'strategic' planning applications, it assesses the

Figure 182
Traffic Management Measures in Lancashire. 1990

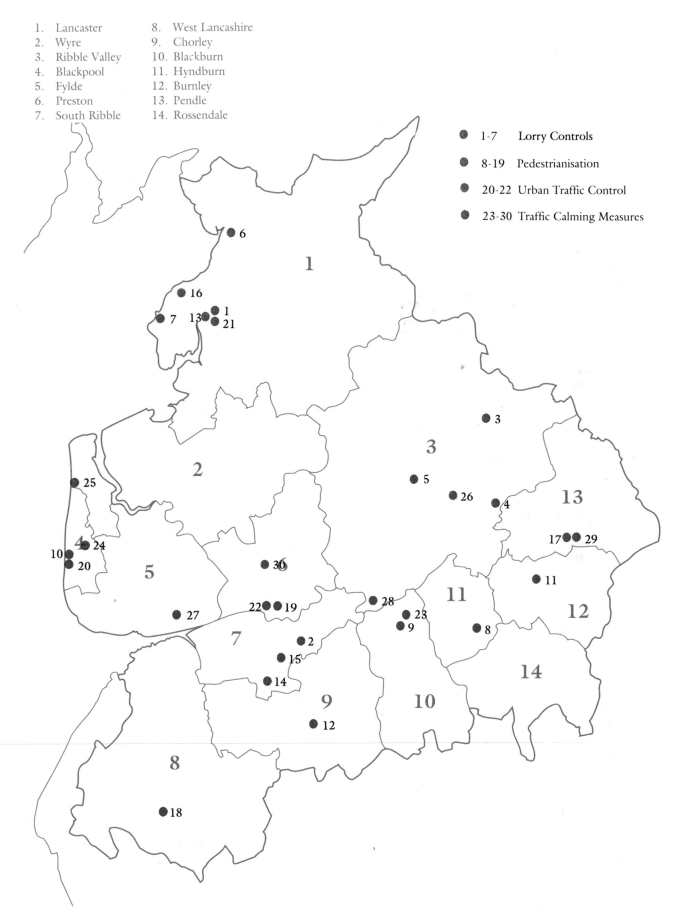

1. Lancaster
2. Wyre
3. Ribble Valley
4. Blackpool
5. Fylde
6. Preston
7. South Ribble
8. West Lancashire
9. Chorley
10. Blackburn
11. Hyndburn
12. Burnley
13. Pendle
14. Rossendale

- 1-7   Lorry Controls
- 8-19   Pedestrianisation
- 20-22   Urban Traffic Control
- 23-30   Traffic Calming Measures

Source: Lancashire County Council

proposed site in relation to the existing and planned road network. It takes into account the County Road Hierarchy mentioned above and Structure Plan policies which aim to locate major new developments where they can be conveniently served by public transport (Lancashire County Council, 1987).

12.134 An analysis of all major planning applications for retail, industrial, minerals, storage and wholesale, waste disposal and hotels between 1986–1989 revealed that the vast majority of major developments are located close to the strategic road network, and that most proposals at some distance from the network were refused. There are some locations not close to the main road network, where new development has been permitted; for instance, Longridge, Glasson Dock, West Chorley and Blackpool (South Shore).

12.135 There is a growing problem caused by the generation of HGV traffic movements from local depots with sub-standard access routes, located in environmentally inappropriate areas (Lancashire County Council, 1987). Attempts are being made to deal with this at the planning application stage, but it has proved difficult and many objections are over-ruled by the DTp (Lancashire County Council, 1990a).

Promotion of Public Transport

12.136 Apart from the activities of British Rail and the private bus companies, the County Council plays a part in promoting public transport in Lancashire. The County Council provides bus timetables and allied information and publishes leaflets showing the services of all operators on commerical and tendered routes. Information Centres and telephone enquiry line services have been established which have been successful (Lancashire County Council, 1990a). The provision of an adequate public transport service requires not only the maintenance of good bus services but also improvements to facilities for both operators and the public. The County Council can provide 50% of the costs of bus station improvements, subject to the availability of resources. The bus stations in Burnley, Whalley, Ormskirk, Nelson, Colne, Earby, Morecambe, Accrington, Rawtenstall and Waterfoot have been improved in this way over the last three years.

12.137 A recent innovation has been the establishment of a Park and Ride car park off Strand Road, Preston providing a frequent mini-bus service for motorists into the town centre. However, although bus lanes have been established in the County, no new schemes have been implemented since 1986 (Lancashire County Council, 1990a).

12.138 In addition to the Inter-City rail route through the County, local rail services are of considerable importance to the communities they serve, to the environment and to the economy. They provide mass transit and an alternative to road travel. They link the County to the Inter-City network and to the adjacent centres of Liverpool and Manchester. They also bring visitors to our coastal resorts.

12.139 The County Council seeks to retain and improve the existing rail passenger network and services, including the electrification of the Blackpool-Preston-Manchester line. Although the County Council plays a positive rôle in promotion and has instigated developments of the rail network, implementation of this policy is dependent on British Rail (Lancashire County Council, 1990a).

References

British Rail (1990a). British Rail Passenger Timetable. BR.

British Rail (1990b). Railnews, No. 329. BR.

Council for the Protection of Rural England et al. (1989). Roads to Ruin. CPRE.

Department of the Environment, (1989). Environmental Assessment. HMSO.

Department of Transport (1986). Transport Statistics in Great Britain. HMSO.

Department of Transport (1988). Transport and the Environment. HMSO.

Department of Transport (1989a). Roads for Prosperity. HMSO.

Department of Transport (1989b). Transport – A Guide to the Department. HMSO.

Department of Transport (1989c). Transport Statistics in Great Britain. HMSO.

Department of Transport (1990). Lorries in the Community. HMSO.

House of Commons Transport Committee (1989). Fourth Report on the Government's expenditure plans for transport 1989–90 to 1991–92. HMSO.

Lancashire County Council (1984). Census Atlas of Lancashire. LCC.

Lancashire County Council (1987). The Lancashire Structure Plan. LCC.

Lancashire County Council (1988a). Technical Report 6 Transport: Trends. LCC.

Lancashire County Council (1988b). Technical Report 7 Transport: Traffic Forecasts and Road Needs. LCC.

Lancashire County Council (1990a). Moving into the 21st Century. A Discussion Document. LCC.

Lancashire County Council (1990b). Bus Map and Guide to Lancashire. LCC.

Lancashire County Council (1990c). Road Safety Plan. LCC.

Lancashire County Council (1990d). Transport Policies and Programme 1991–92. LCC.

Nature Conservancy Council (1988). Lancashire Inventory of Ancient Woodlands (Provisional). NCC.

Chapter Thirteen

Issues for the Future of Lancashire's Environment

Introduction

13.1 This first-ever Green Audit of Lancashire has two main purposes. Initially, it seeks to help people gain a better understanding of the overall health of their local environment. But it also reveals the environmental problems and opportunities that need to be tackled in the County and by doing so, provides a bridge to the next stage. This will be the preparation of an Action on the Environment strategy and programme, on which work will now commence. The County Council is committed to developing this action plan in partnership with the public and its colleagues on the Lancashire Environment Forum. To help focus attention on the important matters that now need to be considered, this last Chapter presents the main issues which arise from the Audit's findings. There are 150 issues in all, organised under the Chapter headings that have gone before. They appear, generally, in the order in which they are raised in the text and have been numbered consecutively, for ease of reference.

The Issues

13.2 General Issues

1. How best to harness the commitment, expertise and involvement of members of the Lancashire Environment Forum in developing and implementing the Action on the Environment strategy and programme.

2. How best to involve and inform the public in developing and implementing the Action on the Environment strategy and programme.

3. The most effective way of ensuring maximum access to, and use of, the Green Audit environmental database for information and educational purposes.

4. How best to use the Green Audit to help the County Council, and its partners, to reduce any adverse environmental impact arising from their operations and practices.

5. The need for wider assistance and co-operation from the region, the government and the EC in ensuring that continued efforts are made, and are resourced, to deal with Lancashire's environmental problems.

6. How best to prioritise and resource the steps that need to be taken.

13.3 Air Quality Issues

7. The need to make air quality information available to the public.

8. The adequacy of existing monitoring arrangements for smoke and sulphur dioxide, lead in air and nitrogen dioxide which are the subject of EC Directives.

9. The reasons for the rise in sulphur dioxide levels in Accrington and how to remedy this.

10. The need to reduce Lancashire's emissions of smoke, sulphur dioxide, lead, nitrogen dioxide, ozone and other air pollutants to the atmosphere.

11. The problem of comparatively high nitrogen dioxide levels in the County, especially in urban areas and near busy roads, and how to remedy them.

12. The lack of ozone and acid rain monitoring in the County.

13. Various problems associated with air pollution from industry including; the provision of better public information on emissions, examining any hazards to local populations near to industrial plants, tackling the problem of odours from industry and ensuring that HMIP and District Councils are adequately resourced to administer Integrated Pollution Control.

14. The lack of data on the nature of emissions from hospital waste incinerators and crematoria and the adequacy of arrangements for controlling emissions.

15. The need for greater public awareness of vehicle emissions and measures that could be taken to reduce them.

16. The need to examine the effect of acid rain on soils, water and vegetation in the County.

17. The need to examine the consequences of global warming on the environment in Lancashire with particular regard to sea level rise.

18. The need to reduce Lancashire's contribution to greenhouse gases as part of support for wider action on global warming.

19. The need for continued monitoring of radioactivity in the environment of the County including radon monitoring in homes.

20. The need to keep under scrutiny atmospheric emissions from the County's two nuclear installations – Springfields and Heysham – and identify action to reduce emissions further.

13.4 Water Quality Issues

21. The need to maintain or improve the level of biological and chemical water quality monitoring of rivers and streams in the County and the need to carry out bacteriological monitoring.

22. The limited monitoring of offshore water quality and the limited monitoring of designated bathing waters in terms of number of monitoring points and number of parameters measured.

23. The limited monitoring of groundwater quality and the limited access to data regarding the quality of water at supply reservoirs.

24. The need to maintain the quality of 1a/1b waters and to upgrade Class 2, 3 and 4 waters – many of which are in the south and east of the County.

25. The degree of pollution of the East Lancashire Calder, Hyndburn Brook, River Hyndburn, River Darwen, River Douglas, River Tawd and River Irwell and how to tackle the problem.

26. The need to tackle problems of organic pollution and nutrient enrichment in the County's watercourses both at specific point sources (consented and unconsented discharges) and over a diffuse area (agricultural run off).

27. The need to maintain and improve the water quality of canals and estuaries.

28. The failure of Lancashire's designated bathing beaches to meet the EC Directive bacteriological standards.

29. The need to reduce Lancashire's contribution to pollution levels in the Irish Sea by cleaning up rivers and estuaries and ending sewage discharges both from outfalls and sludge dumping.

30. The need to improve the quality of discharges from Sewage Treatment Works, particularly the four works that failed to comply with their consents in 1989/90 and the 13 works that were granted relaxed consents in 1989.

31. The number of water pollution incidents from farm, trade and sewage sources and the comparatively low rate of prosecutions that result.

32. The need to tackle high coliform contamination in those parts of the River Ribble used for bathing or recreation, and to identify and deal with similar problems on other inland waters.

33. The need to further investigate and tackle the problems of acidification and hypereutrophication of water bodies.

34. The radioactive •contamination of Lancashire's intertidal areas, fish and shellfish by Sellafield discharges and the dose received by houseboat dwellers in the Ribble, Lune and Wyre estuaries and by people that eat fish and shellfish from the Irish Sea.

35. The difficulty in interpreting drinking water quality data for members of the public and the adequacy of monitoring of private supplies.

36. The large number of relaxations for iron and manganese and undertakings for lead, aluminium, coliforms, colour and turbidity which apply to Lancashire treatment works and water supply zones.

37. The failure of 51% of Lancashire's water supply zones to meet the PCV for lead, 24% of supply zones that fail to meet the PCV for aluminium and 7% that fail to meet the standard for coliforms and how to tackle these deficiencies.

38. The poor bacteriological quality of many private water supplies.

39. The effects of water abstractions on river water quality.

40. The need to update information on Lancashire's sea defences and their adequacy for flood prevention now and in the future given the likelihood of sea level rise.

13.5 Waste Issues

41. The need to reduce the quantity of waste arising in the County.

42. The disposal of agricultural and mining wastes arising in the County which are not governed by the Control of Pollution Act 1974 or the Environmental Protection Act 1990.

43. The validity and safety of importing special wastes into the County particularly through the sea ports.

44. The best method of disposing of sewage sludge whether to the sea, on land or by incineration and its environmental effects.

45. The production, transport and disposal of radioactive waste in the County.

46. The production and disposal of clinical waste by incineration.

47. The reliance on landfill for waste disposal in the County and the viability and environmental impacts of alternatives.

48. The location and impact of existing and completed landfill sites in the County in relation to geology, groundwater, surface water, areas at risk from flooding, areas of landscape and wildlife importance.

49. The importation of special wastes to Chemical Recovery Plants and the incineration of special waste at one Chemical Recovery Plant and the emissions produced.

50. The need to promote waste recycling in all sectors of the community.

51. The scope for increased waste recycling at Waste Transfer Stations and Household Waste Disposal Centres.

52. The need to increase numbers of collection points in some Districts, particularly of glass and paper.

53. The need to identify all former landfill sites where landfill gas may be produced and to ensure that it is prevented from causing a hazard, or is used for energy production.

54. The need to identify and treat all contaminated land arising from waste disposal and other operations in the County.

55. Ameliorating nuisance from waste disposal operations.

56. Providing the best restoration and aftercare for waste disposal and waste management sites.

57. The need for continued monitoring of all waste disposal sites.

58. The need for more information on, and better solutions to, the litter problem.

59. The need for tougher action on those who cause litter.

13.6 Noise Pollution Issues

60. The need for systematic and comprehensive monitoring of noise in the environment in Lancashire.

61. The reason for the high number of noise complaints recorded in some Districts.

62. The need to tackle the problem of domestic noise.

63. Shortcomings in sound insulation grant arrangements for people affected by road traffic noise.

64. The need to investigate further noise caused by low flying military jets that pass over the County.

65. The absence of legislation allowing the public to take action over aircraft noise and the adequacy of sound insulation grant arrangements.

66. The absence of legislation and sound insulation grants to deal with railway noise.

67. The adequacy of arrangements to prevent noise from premises licensed for public entertainment.

68. The need for continued monitoring and action by the Health and Safety Executive on occupational noise.

69. Whether Noise Abatement Zones could be beneficially established in the County.

70. Whether the issuing of noise abatement notices is an effective way of controlling noise nuisance.

13.7 Energy Issues

71. The need to examine in a more comprehensive way the sources of energy in the County, their production, supply and use.

72. The environmental effects and risks associated with energy production from Heysham and Padiham Power Stations.

73. The environmental effects of gas extraction and supply from Morecambe Bay.

74. The environmental effects of coal burning by domestic consumers particularly in East Lancashire.

75. The possible impact of further gas and oil exploration in the County.

76. The lack of Lancashire specific data on energy consumption.

77. The growing consumption of gas and electricity and how to ameliorate this.

78. The need to investigate further the use of renewable energy sources in Lancashire particularly water power, solar power, wind power and biofuels.

79. The need to reduce greenhouse gases and emissions which contribute to acid rain produced by the burning of fossil fuels in the County.

80. The need to investigate the location of contaminated land arising from old gaswork sites in the County and how to deal with them.

81. The transport and disposal of radioactive waste from Heysham Power Stations and from Springfields.

82. The need to improve energy efficiency in all user sectors in order to economise and reduce emissions of greenhouse gases.

83. The need to promote energy efficiency in homes in Lancashire in particular.

84. The need for better energy efficiency in transport through improved driver habits, improved public transport and use of rail, rather than road, for freight haulage.

13.8 Land and Agriculture Issues

85. The lack of a comprehensive land-use inventory of the County.

86. The need to examine whether the land resource in Lancashire is being put to its best and most productive use, particularly with regard to agricultural land.

87. The location and practice of livestock farming, dairying, arable cropping, pig and poultry rearing and horticulture in the County and their environmental effects.

88. The reliance of the farming industry in the County on livestock rearing and dairying and the impact on the environment of possible changes in EC subsidies.

89. The lack of data on commercial forestry and game management and productivity in the County.

90. The reason for the large number of water pollution incidents that arise from farm waste and how to prevent them.

91. The possible long-term effect on groundwater of the use of nitrogen based fertilisers on arable land and improved grassland.

92. The effect on surface waters of nutrient enrichment from fertilisers.

93. The impact of Hill Livestock Compensatory Allowance payments within the Less Favoured Area and whether this is leading to ecological damage.

94. The poor take-up of Set-Aside and Farm Woodland Scheme grants in the County.

95. The need to further the case for Environmentally Sensitive Area status for the County's AONB and West and South Pennine areas.

13.9 Wildlife Issues

96. The need to complete the Phase 1 habitat survey of Lancashire to give a comprehensive wildlife habitat inventory and how best to use this to conserve and enhance wildlife.

97. The need to protect the woodland resource in the County, particularly ancient woodlands.

98. The need to increase broadleaved woodland cover in the County.

99. The need to protect old species-rich grasslands, particularly limestone and neutral grasslands which have rich flora and fauna.

100. The need to protect limestone pavements, of which Lancashire has some of the best examples in the UK.

101. The need to protect moorland, particularly for their breeding bird species.

102. The need to protect lowland peat mosses which have been reduced to a fragment of their original extent.

103. The need to protect swamp and fen habitat which is particularly important for birds.

104. The lack of data on the County's freshwater habitats.

105. The need to protect Lancashire's coastal habitats which are of international significance for birds and form one of the County's paramount environmental assets.

106. The lack of data on the County's marine, urban and industrial and linear habitats.

107. The need to designate Morecambe Bay and the Lune and Ribble Estuaries as Ramsar Sites and to complete the designation of Bowland Fells and the Ribble Estuary as Special Protection Areas.

108. The need to extend Statutory Nature Reserve protection (particularly LNR) to other sites in the County.

109. The need to serve Limestone Pavement Orders in the County.

110. The need for more data on habitat change in the County in order to understand how best to safeguard sites.

13.10 Landscape and Townscape Issues

111. The need for an up-to-date Scenic Quality Survey of Lancashire.

112. The adequacy and effectiveness of landscape policy designations and measures in protecting and maintaining landscape character.

113. The extent of Green Belt that still remains to be identified and approved in District Local Plans.

114. The small number of archaeological sites given statutory protection as Scheduled Ancient Monuments.

115. The lack of a mechanism to monitor landscape change in the County.

116. The justification in some situations for allowing the need for mineral workings to override landscape protection designations.

117. The adequacy of restoration of mineral workings given that they constitute most of Lancashire's derelict land.

118. The need to examine whether Green Belt policy is working adequately throughout the County with respect to housing development.

119. The lack of data on landscape enhancement.

120. The lack of any objective evaluation of townscape quality in the County.

121. The lack of a mechanism to monitor townscape change.

122. The extent and effectiveness of grant schemes for improving the physical fabric of towns in enhancing townscape quality.

123. The degree to which HRA will replace GIA and HAA.

13.11 Openspace Issues

124. The low provision of formally designated urban openspace in some parts of the County.

125. Ensuring wider and continuing community use of educational openspace.

126. Protecting all openspace, but particularly urban space, from loss to development.

127. The need to examine the availability of openspace to people with limited mobility.

128. The need to ensure that NWW recreational land remains available for use by the public.

129. The lack of rural openspace on the Fylde.

130. Reducing the damaging effects of vandalism and litter on openspace.

131. The management of competing recreational activities using openspace.

132. Reducing the impact of recreational activities that generate excessive noise and other environmental problems.

13.12 Transport Issues

133. The dominance of roads and cars in the transport system and transport planning in the County.

134. The higher than national average use of cars for commuting to work in the County.

135. The increase in HGV traffic nationally and in the County.

136. The lack of bus services in some of the rural areas of the County.

137. The lack of data regarding passenger use of bus services following de-regulation.

138. The problems of creating an integrated transport system with de-regulated bus services.

139. The lack of data on cycling in the County.

140. The opportunity to promote cycling to work and cycling generally.

141. The opportunity to promote walking to work and walking generally.

142. The lack of data regarding use of the footpath and bridleway network.

143. The lack of up to date figures on transport mode and journey purpose of the population.

144. Whether road building in Lancashire should be geared to meet the Government's predicted traffic growth rates of 83–142% by 2025.

145. The need to deal with congestion in Blackburn, Blackpool, Preston, Leyland, Chorley, Ormskirk and Lancaster and other locations.

146. The lack of data on passenger use of the rail network in Lancashire.

147. The extent, and environmental impact, of exhaust emissions from Lancashire's vehicles.

148. The small number of Environmental Impact Assessments that have so far been carried out on transport projects in the County.

149. The impact of current road proposals and transport use generally on nature conservation sites in the County.

150. The effectiveness of traffic management measures in the County.

Appendices

Appendix A

Terms of Reference and Members of the Lancashire Environment Forum. 1990

Terms of Reference

* To provide a Forum for the discussion and dissemination of all matters concerning the condition of Lancashire's environment;

* To secure co-operation, co-ordination and action between appropriate agencies and organisations on initiatives aimed at protecting and improving the County's environment;

* To give assistance and guidance to the preparation by Lancashire County Council of a State of the Environment Report for Lancashire, and to ensure the widest possible support for, and the input by member organisations of all relevant information and data to, the production of the report and to subsequent implementation and monitoring;

* To establish links with, and the co-operation of, other agencies, organisations and authorities on issues which affect the overall quality of Lancashire's environment in a regional and national context;

* To increase the awareness of Government, EEC, industry, commerce, and the public and private sector agencies and the general public of Lancashire, to the environment of the County and of the need for its protection and improvement.

Organisations in Membership

Central Government and Regional Agencies

Department of the Environment
Ministry of Agriculture, Fisheries and Food
Department of Energy
Nature Conservancy Council
Countryside Commission
National Rivers Authority
Health and Safety Executive
Department of Transport
British Waterways Board

Industry

Confederation of British Industry
National Chamber of Trade
Central and West Lancashire Chamber of Commerce and Industry
Lancaster and District Chamber of Commerce, Trade and Industry
Burnley and District Chamber of Commerce and Industry
North West Water
National Power
Nuclear Electric

British Nuclear Fuels
British Coal
British Railways Board
British Gas
North Western Electricity Board
Lancashire Enterprises Ltd
Lancashire Association of Trade Councils
TUC (North West)
National Farmers Union

Local Government in Lancashire

Lancashire County Council
Blackburn Borough Council
Blackpool Borough Council
Burnley Borough Council
Chorley Borough Council
Fylde Borough Council
Hyndburn Borough Council
Lancaster City Council
Pendle Borough Council
Preston Borough Council
Ribble Valley Borough Council
Rossendale Borough Council
South Ribble Borough Council
West Lancashire District Council
Wyre Borough Council
Association of Parish and Town Councils
Community Council of Lancashire
Lancashire Constabulary
North West Regional Health Authority
RADMIL

Interest Groups

Country Landowners Association
Friends of the Earth
Lancashire Trust for Nature Conservation
Council for the Protection of Rural England
Federation of Lancashire Civic Societies
Royal Society for the Protection of Birds
The Civic Trust in the North West
The Tidy Britain Group
Soil Association
Transport 2000
NW Federation of Sport Recreation and Conservation
Clean Air Society
Pendle Heritage Centre
Town and Country Planning Association
British Trust for Conservation Volunteers

Academic Establishments

Lancaster University
Lancashire Polytechnic
Edge Hill College of Higher Education
Lancashire College of Agriculture and Horticulture

Appendix B

HMIP Registered Works in Lancashire by District. 1990

Lancaster

1.	Nuclear Electric	Heysham
2.	Coolag Purlboard Ltd	Heysham
3.	ECC Construction Materials Ltd	Carnforth
4.	Great Lakes Chemical (Europe) Ltd	Lancaster
5.	J.A. Jackson Contractors (Preston) Ltd	Lancaster
6.	Nelsons Acetate Ltd	Lancaster
7.	Tarmac Roadstone Ltd	Nether Kellet
8.	Wimpey Asphalt Ltd	Carnforth

Wyre

9.	ICI Chemicals and Polymers Ltd	Thornton Cleveleys
10.	Vulnax International Ltd	Thornton Cleveleys
11.	Westbond Chemicals Ltd	Oakenclough, Garstang

Ribble Valley

12.	Castle Cement (Ribblesdale) Ltd	Clitheroe
13.	ICI Chemicals and Polymers Ltd	Clitheroe
14.	Philips Components Ltd	Simonstone
15.	Waddington Fell Quarries Ltd	Waddington

Blackpool

None

Fylde

16.	Albion Cylinder Ltd	St. Annes
17.	British Nuclear Fuels plc	Salwick
18.	NRL Springfields	Salwick

Preston

19.	Lanfina Bitumen Ltd	Riversway, Preston
20.	Liquid Plastics Ltd	Brockholes View, Preston
21.	Preston Coated Stone	Preston

South Ribble

22.	BTR Hose Ltd	Farington
23.	Compounding Ingredients Ltd	Bamber Bridge

West Lancashire

24.	ARC Western	Appley Bridge
25.	CBS Batteries Ltd	Skelmersdale
26.	CRP Marine Ltd	Skelmersdale
27.	Daryl Industries Ltd	Skelmersdale
28.	Electropac (UK) Ltd	Skelmersdale
29.	North West Water	Hoscar
30.	Permanite Ltd	Appley Bridge
31.	Permanite Ltd	Appley Bridge
32.	RODCO Ltd	Skelmersdale

Chorley

33.	Ashcroft J. and J. Ltd	Whittle-le-Woods
34.	Canadian Technical Tape (UK) Ltd	Chorley
35.	Golden Eagle Asphalt Co. Ltd	Chorley
36.	Royal Ordnance plc	Euxton
37.	Williams Thomas Euxton Ltd	Whittle-le-Woods
38.	Zebraflex Sealants and Surfacing Ltd	Chorley

Blackburn

39. ICI Chemicals and Polymers Ltd	Darwen
40. ICI Chemicals and Polymers Ltd	Darwen
41. TAC Construction Materials Ltd	Blackburn

Hyndburn

42. BTP Cocker Chemicals Ltd	Oswaldtwistle
43. Caligen Foam Ltd	Accrington
44. William Blythe and Co. Ltd	Accrington

Burnley

45. National Power	Padiham
46. Chemiblend Ltd	Burnley
47. Specialist Anodising Co. Ltd	Burnley
48. William Blythe and Co. Ltd	Hapton, Burnley

Pendle

49. Colne Anodising Co. Ltd	Laneshaw Bridge, Colne
50. Colne Laminates and Engineers Ltd	Colne
51. Decorpart Ltd	Nelson

Rossendale

52. Baxenden Chemical Co. Ltd	Baxenden
53. Eskett Quarries Ltd	Haslingden
54. Rossendale Combining Co. Ltd	Rawtenstall
55. Whitworth Quarries Ltd	Whitworth

Appendix C

Scheduled Processes at Registered Works in Lancashire by District. 1990

Type of Process and District	Noxious Substances

Lancaster

4 × Minerals	Smoke, dust, grit, fumes
Anhydride	Acetic, maleic, phthalic, anhydrides and their acids
Bi-sulphate	Sulphur dioxide
Bromine	Bromine and its compounds
Chemical incineration	Smoke, dust, grit, fumes
Chlorine	Chlorine and its compounds
Di-isocyanate	Di-isocyanate

Wyre

2 × Chemical incineration	Smoke, dust, grit, fumes
3 × Chlorine	Chlorine and its compounds
Carbon di-sulphide	Carbon di-sulphide
2 × Di-isocyanate	Di-isocyanate
Electricity	Smoke, dust, grit, fumes
Fluorine	Fluorine and its compounds
Gas and coke	Smoke, dust, grit, fumes
Hydrochloric acid	Hydrogen chloride, smoke, dust, gas
Lead	Lead, smoke, dust, grit
Nitrate and iron chloride	Nitric acid, oxides of nitrogen chlorine and its compounds
Nitric acid	Nitric acid and oxides of nitrogen
Vinyl chloride	Vinyl chloride, smoke, dust, grit
Sulphide	Hydrogen sulphide

Ribble Valley

Cement	Smoke, dust, grit, fumes
Chlorine	Chlorine and its compounds
Hydrochloric acid	Hydrogen, chlorine, smoke, dust, gas
Iron and Steel	Smoke, dust, grit, fumes
Large glass	Smoke, dust, grit, fumes
Mineral	Smoke, dust, grit, fumes
2 × Nitric acid	Nitric acid and oxides of nitrogen

Blackpool

None

Fylde

2 × Uranium	Uranium and its compounds
Di-isocyanate	Di-isocyanate
Fluorine	Fluorine and its compounds
Hydrofluoric acid	Fluoride gas, smoke, grit, dust
Nitric acid	Nitric acid, oxides of nitrogen
Petrochemical	Sulphurous compounds, smoke, grit, dust, fumes

Preston

Di-isocyanate	Di-isocyanate
Mineral	Smoke, dust, grit, fumes
Petroleum	Sulphurous compounds, smoke, dust, grit, fumes
Tar and Bitumen	Sulphurous compounds

South Ribble

Lead	Lead, smoke, dust, grit
Di-isocyanate	Di-isocyanate

Type of Process and District	Noxious Substances
West Lancashire	
Chemical incineration	Smoke, dust, grit, fumes
Chlorine	Chlorine and its compounds
Copper	Smoke, dust, grit, fumes, copper, zinc, cadmium, lead
Di-isocyanate	Di-isocyanate
Lead	Lead, smoke, dust, grit
Mineral	Smoke, dust, grit, fumes
Nitric acid	Nitric acid and oxides of nitrogen
Tar and Bitumen	Smoke, dust, grit, fumes
Chorley	
2×Di-isocyanate	Di-isocyanate
2×Mineral	Smoke, dust, grit, fumes
2×Tar and Bitumen	Smoke, dust, grit, fumes
Chemical incineration	Smoke, dust, grit, fumes
Lead	Lead, smoke, grit, dust
Nitric acid	Nitric acid, oxides of nitrogen
Blackburn	
2×Acrylates	Acrylate
Mineral	Smoke, dust, grit, fumes
Hyndburn	
2×Chlorine	Chlorine and its compounds
Arsenic	Arsenic and its compounds
Bisulphite	Sulphur dioxide
Di-isocyanate	Di-isocyanate
Hydrochloric acid	Hydrogen chloride, smoke, dust, gas
Nitric acid	Nitric acid, oxides of nitrogen
Zinc	Dust and fumes
Burnley	
Ammonia	Ammonia
Bisulphite	Sulphur dioxide
Chlorine	Chlorine and its compounds
Electricity	Smoke, dust, grit
Lead	Lead, smoke, grit, dust
Nitric acid	Nitric acid, oxides of nitrogen
Sulphide	Hydrogen sulphide
Pendle	
2×Nitric acid	Nitric acid, oxides of nitrogen
Di-isocyanate	Di-isocyanate
Rossendale	
2×Di-isocyanate	Di-isocyanate
2×Mineral	Smoke, dust, grit, fumes
Acrylates	Acrylate
Chemical incineration	Smoke, dust, grit, fumes

Source: HMIP (pers. comm.)

Lancashire's Green Audit – Your Views

Now you've read the State of the Environment Report, the County Council is interested to hear your views on Lancashire's environment. These will help us to decide on priorities for action.

Please complete the questions and return in an envelope (no stamp required) to:

The County Planning Officer,
Lancashire County Council,
FREEPOST,
East Cliff County Offices,
Preston, PR1 3BR

* I/We have/have not found the State of the Environment Report useful (delete as applicable).

* For each of the topics listed below please indicate how important you think they are to the state of the environment in Lancashire (please use one tick for each topic).

TOPIC	VERY IMPORTANT	IMPORTANT	NOT IMPORTANT
Air Quality	☐	☐	☐
Water Quality	☐	☐	☐
Waste and Litter	☐	☐	☐
Noise	☐	☐	☐
Energy	☐	☐	☐
Land and Agriculture	☐	☐	☐
Wildlife	☐	☐	☐
Landscape and Townscape	☐	☐	☐
Openspace	☐	☐	☐
Transport	☐	☐	☐

* Of the 150 issues listed in the Report, are there any you would particularly like to see action on. Please list the relevant numbers:

....

* Have we omitted any issues that you would like to see addressed?

Please list them:...

....

* Other comments (continue on separate sheet(s) if you wish)..

....

* Name...

Address...

....

Thank you for your help.

Appendix D

Drinking Water Supply Zones in Lancashire. 1990

Supply Zone Number	Supply Zone Name	Supply Zone Number	Supply Zone Name
56	Silverdale/Yealand	98	Waddington
57	Regional/Caton Filter House	99	Newton
58	Haweswater/Lune Valley	100	Cliffe
59	Morecambe/Carnforth	101	Accrington West
60	Lancaster Central/Galgate	102	Mitchells
61	Langthwaite Filter House	103	Burnley Road
62	Dolphinholme/Welby Crag	104	Sabden
63	Cockerham	105	Lanehead
64	Lowgill	106	Swinden Direct
65	Barnacre	107	Cant Clough, Hurstwood
66	Fleetwood	108	Burnley South West
67	Cleveleys and Thornton	109	Burnley Mixed
68	Warbreck Tower	110	Simonstone and Altham
69	Stocks Direct	111	Padiham
70	Blackpool South	112	Thursden
71	Lytham St. Annes	113	Wigan North West
72	Warton	198	Ainsdale
73	Chipping Springs		
74	Dilworth	201	Southport North
75	Haighton	202	Halsall
76	Preston South	203	Ormskirk East
77	Preston, Ribbleton, Fulwood	204	Tarleton
78	Preston West		
79	Samlesbury	206	Skelmersdale Lower
80	Bamber Bridge	207	Skelmersdale Higher
81	Leyland	208	Upholland
82	Chorley	209	Aughton
83	Heapey		
84	Dunsop	213	Springs
85	Tosside		
86	Fishmoor Boosted	215	Wayoh North
87	Fishmoor Sunnyhurst		
88	Laneshaw	219	Haslingden
89	Barrowford		
90	Coldwell	221	Loveclough
91	Trawden	222	Clough Bottom Direct
92	Blackburn South I	223	Clough Bottom Bacup
93	Blackburn South II	224	Cowpe
94	Blackburn West	225	New Hall Direct
95	Blackburn North		
96	Ribble Valley	231	Cowm
97	Lowcocks		

Source: NWW (pers. comm.)

Notes: WSZ boundaries are shown on Figure 70. 4 WSZ lying mostly in Merseyside have very small areas falling in Lancashire. Their numbers are 196, 197, 199 and 205. No data for these zones has been incorporated into the text.

Appendix E

'Special Wastes' – Listed Substances as Defined by the Control of Pollution (Special Waste) Regulations. 1980 SI 1980 No. 1709 – (Schedule 1, Part 1)

Acid and alkalis.
Antimony and antimony compounds.
Arsenic compounds.
Asbestos (all chemical forms).
Barium compounds.
Beryllium and beryllium compounds.
Biocides and phytopharmaceutical substances.
Boron compounds.
Cadmium and cadmium compounds.
Copper compounds.
Heterocyclic organic compounds containing oxygen, nitrogen or sulphur.
Hexavalent chromium compounds.
Hydrocarbons and their oxygen, nitrogen and sulphur compounds.
Inorganic cyanides.
Inorganic halogen-containing compounds.
Inorganic sulphur-containing compounds.
Laboratory chemicals.
Lead compounds.
Mercury compounds.
Nickel and nickel compounds.
Organic halogen compounds, excluding inert polymeric materials.
Peroxides, chlorates, perchlorates and azides.
Pharmaceutical and veterinary compounds.
Phosphorous and its compounds.
Selenium and selenium compounds.
Silver compounds.
Tarry material from refining and tar residues from distilling.
Tellurium and tellurium compounds.
Vanadium compounds.
Zinc compounds.

Source: Department of the Environment (1986)